the Comprehensive Guide to VBScript

The Encyclopedic Reference for VBScript, HTML & ActiveX

the Comprehensive Guide to VBScript

The Encyclopedic Reference for VBScript, HTML & ActiveX

Richard Mansfield

VENTANA

The Comprehensive Guide to VBScript

Library of Congress Cataloging-in-Publication Data

Mansfield, Richard.
The comprehensive guide to VBScript : the encyclopedic reference for VBScript, HTML & ActiveX / Richard Mansfield.
p. cm.
Includes index.
ISBN 1-56604-470-7
1. VBScript (Computer program language) 2. HTML (Document markup language) 3. World Wide Web (Information retrieval system) I. Title.
QA76.73.V27M36 1996
005.2—dc20 96-9750
CIP

First Edition 9 8 7 6 5 4 3 2 1
Printed in the United States of America

Ventana Communications Group, Inc.
P.O. Box 13964
Research Triangle Park, NC 27709-3964
919.544.9404
FAX 919.544.9472
http://www.vmedia.com

Chief Executive Officer
Josef Woodman

Vice President of Content Development
Karen A. Bluestein

Managing Editor
Lois J. Principe

Production Manager
John Cotterman

Technology Operations Manager
Kerry L. B. Foster

Product Marketing Manager
Jamie Jaeger Fiocco

Creative Services Manager
Diane Lennox

Art Director
Marcia Webb

Acquisitions Editor
Neweleen A. Trebnik

Project Editor
Jennifer R. Huntley

Copy Editor
Marion Laird

Assistant Editor
Patrick Bragg

Technical Director
Dan Brown

Technical Reviewer
Evangelos Petroutsos

Desktop Publisher
Jaimie Livingston

Proofreader
Christopher Riffer

Cover Designer
Alice Whicker

About the Author

Richard Mansfield's books on computer programming have sold more than 400,000 copies worldwide. He was editor of *Compute* magazine for seven years. His published work includes magazine articles, columns on computer topics, and several short stories. He is co-author of *Visual Basic Power Toolkit* (Ventana) and author of *Machine Language for Beginners* (Compute Press), *The Visual Guide to Visual Basic for Windows* (Ventana), *Microsoft Windows NT 4 Workstation Desktop Companion* (Ventana), and 14 other computer books.

Acknowledgments

Considerable gratitude goes to Jennifer Huntley and Marion Laird for their careful and thoughtful editing. Thanks also to Evangelos Petroutsos, who provided a helpful technical edit. Special thanks to Neweleen Trebnik for shepherding this project.

Dedication

For Tracy.

Contents

Note: The following is an alphabetical list of entries, categorized by subject.

ActiveX

ActiveX Control

ActiveX Event

ActiveX Property

Function

HTML

Internet Explorer 3.0

Netscape Navigator

Properties

VBScript

VBScript Event

VBScript Function

VBScript Method

VBScript Object

VBScript Operator

VBScript Property

VBScript Statement

Miscellaneous

Introduction

The purpose of this book is to provide a clear and thorough reference to the three major Internet programming tools: Visual Basic Script, HTML, and ActiveX Controls. In other words, everything you need to know to create effective, attractive, and rich Internet Web sites.

The book is divided into two primary sections. In this Introduction, you'll find a comprehensive tutorial on creating and maintaining Internet Web sites. We'll explore, step-by-step, how to use Microsoft's ActiveX Control Pad to integrate Visual Basic Script (henceforth in this book referred to as VBScript or VBS), HTML, and ActiveX Controls to build exciting, state-of-the-art Web pages.

The second section, the bulk of the book, is designed like an encyclopedia. You'll find in-depth explanations of every element of VBScript, HTML, and Microsoft's ActiveX Controls. The entries are structured for easy reference; they include the following headings:

- **Description**—a general overview of the utility of the entry and its place in the overall scheme of Internet programming.
- **Used with**—the other elements of Visual Basic or HTML with which the entry interacts. (This entry is included where appropriate but appears less frequently than the other entries.)
- **Variables**—the syntax and punctuation required by the entry, and any exceptions, alternatives, or variations. This section shows you how to write a line of programming that will invoke the entry and make it work in a program.

- **Uses**—sensible, real-world answers to the question: "What is this good for?" Most elements of the language have one or more uses. In some cases, however, the only comment under Uses is "None." (See "Let," for instance.)
- **Cautions**—things to watch out for. Why it might not work as expected. Exceptions to the rule, conflicts, and workarounds.
- **Example**—in many computer books the examples are all-too-often unreal. They just show the syntax and punctuation, but nothing really happens. This book tries to avoid that by providing tested, practical examples that do something meaningful and demonstrate the real utility and behavior of the command or feature. For most entries, you can just cut the example and paste it directly into the Microsoft ActiveX Control Pad to test it and see precisely how the example works.
- **See also**—related entries, alternatives, or suggested further reading.

Online Updates

As we all know, the Internet is constantly changing. We've tried hard to make our information current; nevertheless, new ActiveX Controls and modifications to VBScript and HTML are ongoing. Ventana provides an excellent way to tackle this problem and to keep the information in the book up-to-date: *The Comprehensive Guide to VBScript* Online Updates. You can access this valuable resource via Ventana's World Wide Web site at http://www.vmedia.com/updates.html. Once there, you'll find updated material relevant to *The Comprehensive Guide to VBScript*.

Who Needs This Book?

Who's the intended audience for this book? Anyone interested in creating or working on Internet sites, whether they've been programming for 15 years or only one day. Just as a dictionary is useful to both a sixth grader and John Updike, this book can assist anyone from the beginner to the accomplished professional programmer.

Although helpful to beginners, *six pages* on the uses of the For...Next command may be considered by veterans an unnecessary amount of detail. However, Internet programming is rapidly evolving, and even old pros will likely be interested in knowing the details about all the new Controls, Properties, Objects, and Methods. And most of us, even if we work with VBScript, ActiveX Controls, and HTML every day for years, will sometimes need a clear, quick refresher on things like the subtleties of randomizing in VBScript or the best way to use style sheets, frames, client-side mapping, and all the other tools now available for creating dynamic Internet sites. I hope this is one book you'll want to keep close to your computer whenever you're programming for the Internet.

So go ahead—follow the step-by-step overview of Internet programming in this Introduction, or jump around, trying out examples throughout the book. Whatever approach you take and whatever your level of programming expertise, VBScript and ActiveX Controls will likely seduce you.

There's an alternative to VBScript for those looking for an effective Internet programming language. The alternative, JavaScript, *is* effective—it does many of the same things that VBScript can do. It's effective but not as *efficient* as VBScript. JavaScript is not as easy to use as VBScript because Java and JavaScript are descendants of the C programming language and have inherited the complex and confusing syntax of that language. Many people find C and JavaScript difficult to learn, hard to remember, and easy languages in which to make mistakes.

VBScript, by contrast, is a descendant of Visual Basic. The major goals of Basic are that its programs should read like ordinary English, that they be easily understood, and that the commands, syntax, and punctuation should be as simple and straightforward as possible.

In the past few years, Visual Basic has become the language of choice for Windows programming. In the competition between JavaScript and VBScript, many observers predict that VBScript will emerge the popular favorite.

Internet Fundamentals

There are several terms and conventions you should understand before working on Internet documents. The early and still fundamental Internet programming language is HTML—HyperText Markup Language. It is essentially a *page description language*, meaning that many of its commands describe how text and graphics should be formatted—how large they are, where they appear on the screen "page," their colors, borders, and other visual elements.

Links

Hypertext means providing the user (a person who goes to your Web site) with *links*. A link is usually a piece of text that's in a different color from ordinary text. Links are also often underlined. When users click on a link, they are taken to a different location within your Web site, or to an entirely different Web site. This way, users can bounce around the Internet, freely following a chain of links that interest them. This is called *surfing* the Internet.

Links need not be text. Sometimes icons, graphic images, or parts of graphic images provide jump-off points. A set of links might underlie, for example, a picture of several buildings in New York. Clicking on any building will take you to a page that describes the building's location, size, and other information (see "Image").

Tip

In this book, we provide frequent cross-references. When you come upon a phrase like "see Image," it means to turn to the "I" section of the book and look for the entry on Image. If you come across the phrase "which see," this means that the subject being discussed has its own entry, which you should turn to. When we're merely referring you to a location further down in the entry you're currently reading, we'll say "see the example " or "see Cautions."

In addition to their usual job as hypertext jump-off points, links are sometimes merely definitions rather than new locations. Sometimes when a user clicks on a link, a window pops up defining a term or expanding on an idea. In those cases, the user doesn't *go anywhere*. He or she is still in the same page (one screen's worth of information) of your document (all the pages in your Web site).

URLs

In general, the target of a link (the location or address it provides) is called a *URL*, or Uniform Resource Locator. The most familiar URLs are addresses of Web sites on the Internet, and they begin with *http://www*, followed by the specifics of the address, such as msn.com for Microsoft. However, a URL can also point to a location on your hard drive, and in this book that's our most common use of URLs.

Where to Store Graphics

Most Internet documents contain graphics. Frequently throughout this book we mention that you should put a graphic file into the same subdirectory (folder) as your .HTM document's file. The reason for this is that it helps avoid mysterious errors such as blank Image Controls. When you create a document that you want to test, the easiest way is to merely test it within your own computer. You don't publish it on the Internet, then have your Internet browser start the modem to dial that site. Instead, you create an .HTM file and simply store it on your hard drive. Then, with your browser, you simply load in that .HTM file and it behaves as if it were on the Internet. You can test all your HTML, VBScript, and ActiveX Controls in this way much more easily than if you had to "publish" the .HTM file during each testing cycle. Likewise, if your document contains a graphic image—wallpaper, icons, or a high-resolution photo—you'll simplify things if you put the image in the same subdirectory that contains the .HTM document. This way, you can just provide the filename of the graphic rather than a full disk path:

```
<BODY BACKGROUND="ROUGH.GIF">
```

instead of

```
<BODY BACKGROUND="C:\GRAPHICS\INTER\ROUGH.GIF">
```

When the browser sees a simple filename like *ROUGH.GIF*, it looks for that graphic in the same directory as the original .HTM file. If it doesn't find the graphic, no error messages are displayed, but the graphic isn't displayed either. So, to simplify things, we suggest you put your .GIF or .JPG files (or .BMP for some ActiveX Controls) into the same folder where you store your .HTM file.

Language Conventions

HTML, though primarily devoted to describing how a document should look, *is* a computer language. It has some facilities for taking action, beyond merely controlling the color or size of text. However, VBScript adds considerable power to HTML. With VBScript you can accomplish many things that are difficult or impossible with HTML. For example, VBScript has facilities for advanced math calculations, a random number generator, date and time manipulation commands, and many other features.

There is a problem, though, when describing the components of computer languages. Computer language elements—the words, syntax, and punctuation—are categorized in various ways. Sometimes the categories are meaningless or capricious (terms that won't fit anywhere else are called *statements*). Sometimes the categories are redundant. What in HTML is called a *tag* is called a *structure* or *function* in other languages. What is called a *parameter* in Visual Basic is called an *attribute* in HTML. And so it goes.

Fortunately, this problem doesn't bedevil human languages. Everyone agrees that *eat* is a verb and *green* is an adjective. Why, then, didn't the developers of computer languages simply adopt the excellent grammatical categories that already exist? Why not divide computer language terms into the tried and true classifications: noun, verb, adjective, adverb, conjunction, and so on?

Perhaps eventually this will happen as computer languages evolve from their current mix of cryptomathematical and semi-natural-language components. For example, in VBScript, you can define the color white in two ways: "#FFFFFF" or "White." We expect "#FFFFFF" and all other terms like it to eventually disappear from computer languages. When that happens, don't you think it will be easier to stop referring to "White" as an *intrinsic constant* and more descriptively and sensibly refer to it as an *adjective*?

What do we do in the meantime? In this book, we've opted to use the computer language categories that are expressive and useful: Function, Subroutine (or Sub), Variable, Constant, Event, Method, Property, Control, and Object. Each of these categories is described in depth in separate entries in this book, with two exceptions: the *Constant* is defined in the "Variables" entry; the *Control* is defined in the "Objects" entry.

All the other terms currently used to categorize computer language elements are not used in this book because they can be more confusing than helpful. For *any* computer term, we use the generic word *command*. Throughout this book, *command* refers to tags, attributes, statements, structures, functions, properties, or keywords.

Internet Programming: A Tutorial

To explore, test, and work with the examples in this book, you need two free tools. First, you must have Microsoft Internet Explorer 3.0. You don't have to use this browser to contact the Internet, but you do have to use it to view many of the examples you'll find in these pages. You can download this free browser from http://www.microsoft.com/ie/.

Shortly, we'll go through the process of creating an .HTM file, then loading it from your hard drive into Internet Explorer to observe the document's behavior in a real Internet browser. There is almost never a difference in the behavior of a Web page—whether it's loaded into Internet Explorer "locally" from your hard drive or loaded from an active server on the Internet. In fact, the only feature described in this book that doesn't work locally is "Cookies." You can't deposit, then pick up, a Cookie locally. See the entry on "Cookies."

Second, you need a tool to create your *source code*, the various commands that describe the color, text, objects, behaviors, and all other elements of a Web page. The examples in this book were created using the Microsoft ActiveX Control Pad. You can get this free tool (along with the built-in HTML Layout Control and 13 other Controls) from http://www.microsoft.com/workshop/author/cpad/.

There are, of course, other ways to build Web pages, including Microsoft's own FrontPage. However, at this time the only editor that handles VBScript, HTML, *and* the HTML Layout Control is the ActiveX Control Pad.

When you go on the Internet, you provide an address, and a Web page (some source code) is presented to your browser. Internet browsers recognize source code and do things in response to what the source code says. Source code can be extremely simple. Let's try an example. Start the ActiveX Control Pad running. You should see a blank source code page, as shown in Figure I-1.

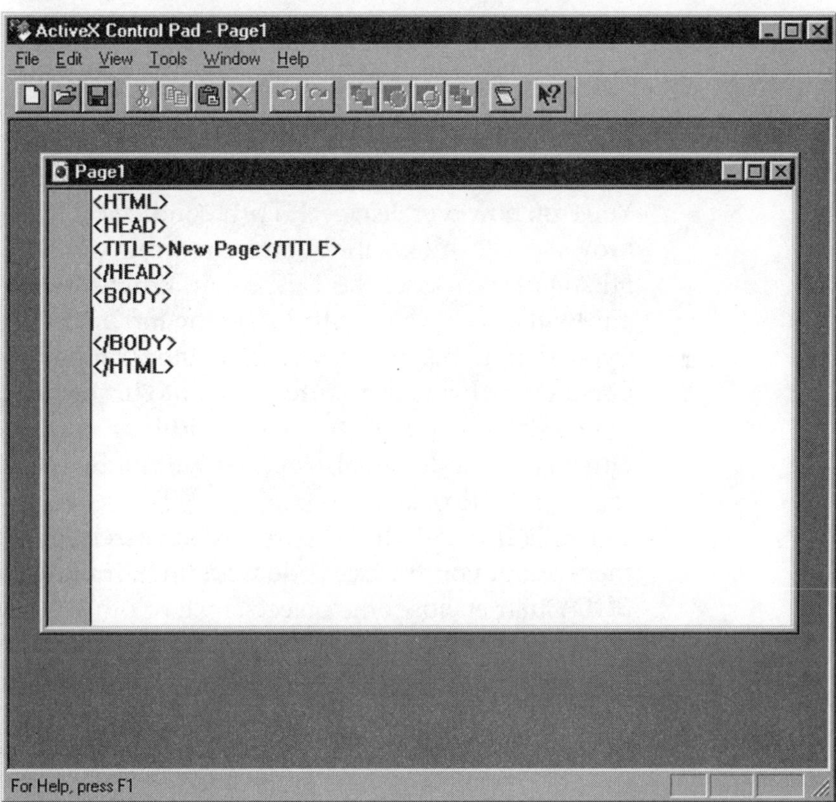

Figure I-1: When you start the ActiveX Control Pad, you're given this empty template.

Notice that you've been provided with a template, a bare-bones HTML document. HTML commands often come in pairs, indicating when something starts and ends. For example, you make a word italic by surrounding it with <I> and </I>:

```
This word will be <I>italic</I>.
```

The ending of the command pair is indicated by a slash /. Now let's take a look at the template you're provided with:

```
<HTML>
<HEAD>
<TITLE>New Page</TITLE>
</HEAD>
<BODY>

</BODY>
</HTML>
```

The HTML pair encloses the entire source code; it tells the browser that this is a HyperText Markup Language document. You can, however, leave <HTML> and </HTML> out and the browser will still go ahead and interpret your source code. The HEAD pair encloses the TITLE pair. Whatever's with the TITLE pair will appear in the title bar at the top of the user's browser. (Note that in this book we employ the term *user* to mean the person who loads our source code into his or her browser). The TITLE will not, however, appear within the browser window. Other commands can also appear within the HEAD pair. See the entry for "HEAD."

The TITLE and HEAD pairs are not essential. You can leave them out of your source code with no harm done. Finally, the BODY pair encloses the objects, text, or other elements that you want to present to the user within the browser window. Not surprisingly, you can leave out the BODY pair if you want.

The Simplest Page

Try this. Erase *everything* from the PAGE1.HTM source code window, then type in only these words:

```
A Simple Page
```

Now, click on Save As in the File menu. Save the .HTM file named Page1.HTM onto your hard drive. Start Internet Explorer 3.0 running, click on File | Open | Browse and load in the PAGE1.HTM file you just saved. You should see what's illustrated in Figure I-2:

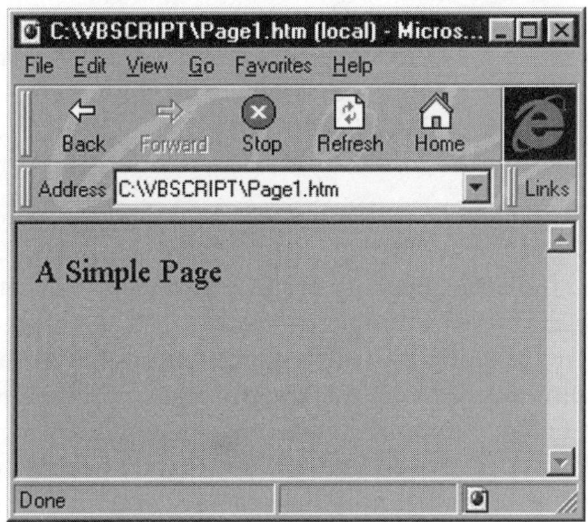

Figure I-2: The Internet Explorer browser will display these words, even if you've included nothing else in your source code.

Back to our Simple Page source code. No other computer programming language comes close to HTML's forgiveness. Try submitting *A Simple Page* to Basic, Pascal, C, or any other language. None of them will simply display the words. All of them will choke and throw out an error message.

Tip

There's a cycle to writing a computer program. (Writing Web pages for the Internet is computer programming, like any other.) First you write some source code. Then you save it to disk. Then you load it into Internet Explorer. Sometimes it doesn't do what you expected. Things are in the wrong place; they're the wrong color; they're missing; an error message pops up. Lots of things can go wrong. So you start the cycle over by fiddling with your source code in the ActiveX Control Pad, saving it again, and clicking on Refresh in Internet Explorer to reload it. And back and forth, until you get it where you want it. You can save yourself time if you click on Internet Explorer's menu Favorites | Add To Favorites. This way, the next time you want to work on some source code, you'll be able to click on Favorites and rapidly load in PAGE1.HTM to test it.

The good news is that the user will rarely be baffled by an error message from an Internet browser and will almost never experience a browser freeze-up or crash as a result of your programming. HTML was designed this way. It was supposed to be robust, to avoid crashing the user's computer or otherwise doing anything untoward. After all, when you go out into the Web, you're opening your computer and, in particular, your hard drive, to the world. And, as we all know, there are bad people out there who would like nothing more than to have you visit an Internet site with this source code:

```
Format C:
```

But what if you write a script that seems innocent enough but still causes a problem? One of the classic errors in computer programming is the endless loop. By accident, you set up some condition that can never be fulfilled. Once the VBScript interpreter gets to this loop, it can never get past it. In the following code, we're saying to do this loop (to keep repeating the instructions between Do and Loop) as long as X is less than 3. And our instructions make sure that X always remains 2. All previous operating systems would "hang," on this, just freeze up, and the user would have to turn the computer off, then back on.

```
<HTML>
<SCRIPT LANGUAGE=VBS>

Do While X < 3
  X = 2
Loop

</SCRIPT>
</HTML>
```

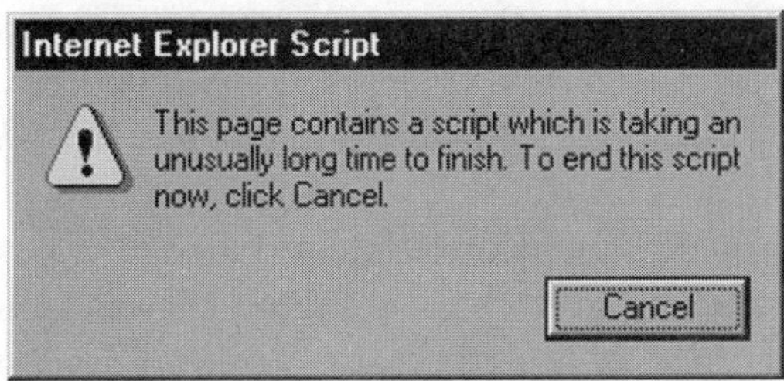

Figure I-3: Endless loops don't freeze Internet Explorer.

Internet Explorer, however, refuses to be frozen by an endless loop. Instead, it interrupts the loop to display the message to the user shown in Figure I-3.

Naturally, people want an Internet browser to be robust and safe to use. As a result, a number of commands found in Visual Basic have been stripped from VBScript. There are no provisions for exploring or otherwise directly contacting the user's hard drive (with one exception, see "Cookies"). You can't adjust the user's clock with the Time Statement, though you can *read* their clock with the Time Function. There are no Link commands for dynamic data exchange, nor can you access the user's printer or clipboard. No access is permitted to the user's Windows API (low-level Windows functions).

In other words, VBScript is limited to working within—well within—the operating environment of the browser. No contact with the user's peripherals or operating system is permitted.

A More Complex Page

Now that we've seen how well-protected the user is from any blunders on our part, and also how stripped-down an HTML page can be, let's try building a real-world Web page. We'll construct a home page for a fictional restaurant. We'll want to display the day's menu, in an ActiveX TextBox Control. That will be easy to change each day. Beyond that, we also want to provide an attractive background featuring our restaurant's logo, its name, hours of operation, and phone number.

For the static information, we could take several approaches: ordinary text written directly in the HTML source code, a Label Control, or a TextBox Control. Let's try them all. We'll also demonstrate how to add an ActiveX Control directly into HTML source code (a couple of Label Controls), and also how to add another ActiveX Control indirectly, by using an HTML Layout Control on which we'll place an Image Control and our TextBox.

Start the ActiveX Control Pad running and, in the template that it provides for the new PAGE1.HTM file, change the title to the name of our restaurant:

```
<TITLE>Poisson d'avril</TITLE>
```

This will now appear in the title bar of the Internet Explorer browser when our document is loaded in.

Also, adjust the BODY definition to specify a white background (not the default gray):

```
<BODY BGCOLOR="WHITE" BACKGROUND="PDA.JPG">
```

The BACKGROUND command also specifies a graphics file, PDA.JPG, that we've put into the same hard drive directory where we're storing this HTML source code file (PAGE1.HTM). Storing graphics files in the same directory simplifies things because the browser will first look there for the graphics file (see "Where to Store Graphics" earlier in the Introduction).

In any case, we used Micrografx's PicturePublisher, a photo-retouching program, to create a small, light-gray .JPG graphic of the initials of our restaurant.

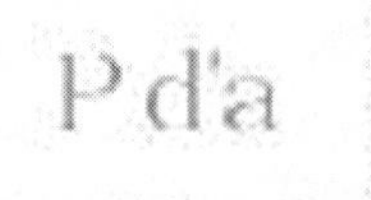

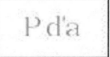

Figure I-4: This graphic will be tiled across the document, thanks to the BACKGROUND command.

Finally, we want to move down a line and also have all the objects and text elements in our page centered. These three HTML commands do it:

```
<BR>
<CENTER>

</CENTER>
```

At this point, your HTML source code should look like this:

```
<HTML>
<HEAD>
<TITLE>Poisson d'avril</TITLE>
</HEAD>
<BODY BGCOLOR="WHITE" BACKGROUND="PDA.JPG">
<BR>
<CENTER>
</CENTER>

</BODY>
</HTML>
```

Save this file as PAGE1.HTM into a directory on your hard drive where you've also saved the graphics file you want to use for the wallpaper. It can be a .GIF or .JPG file type. But whatever file you've specified with the BACKGROUND command should go in this same directory.

Now let's add an ActiveX Control directly into our HTML source code. We want to put the name of our restaurant into an ActiveX Label Control. Move your insertion cursor in the HTML source code between the <CENTER> and </CENTER> commands. This is where our Label will go. Click on the Control Pad's Edit menu and choose Insert ActiveX Control. You'll see a ListBox pop up. Choose Microsoft Forms 2.0 Label, as shown in Figure I-5.

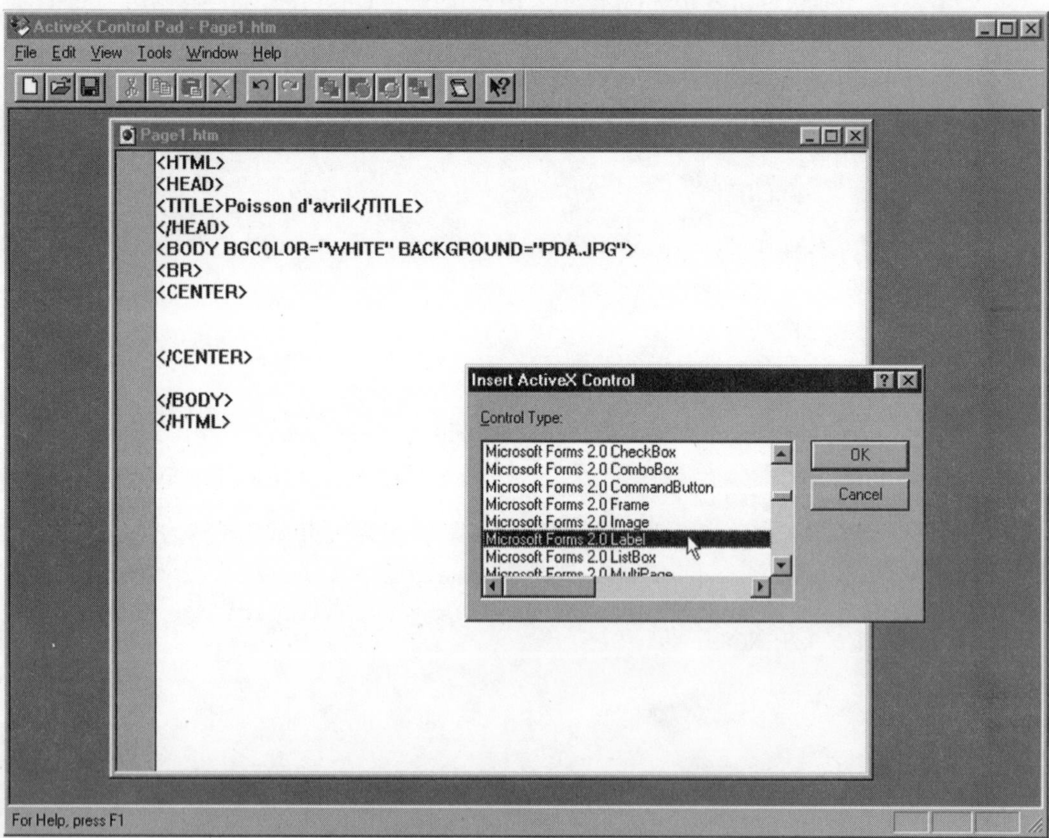

Figure I-5: Double-click on this Label Control to insert it into your source code.

As soon as you select the Control, two new windows appear. The Label itself appears within a window where you can drag it to resize it (but not reposition it—the CENTER command controls that). Also, you'll see the Label's Properties Window, as shown in Figure I-6.

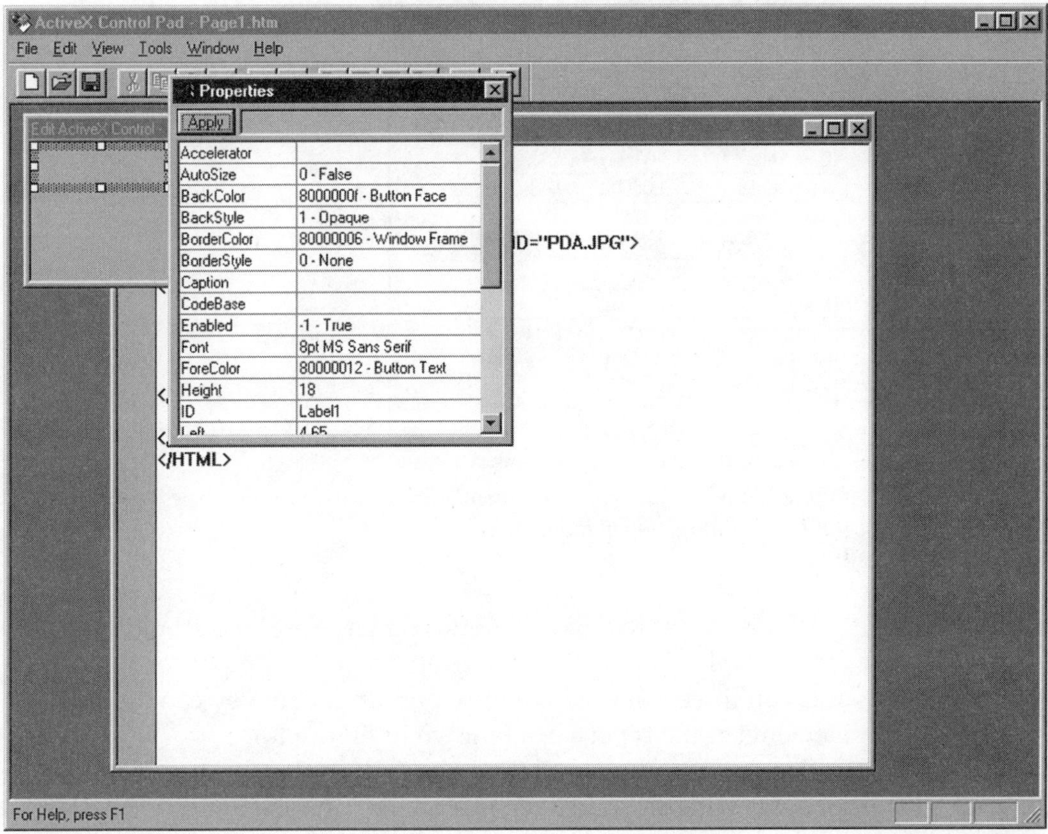

Figure I-6: You can make changes to a Control's Properties (parameters or qualities) directly in the Properties Window.

We want this Label to say Poisson d'Avril, the name of our restaurant. So click on the Caption Property in the Properties Window to highlight it. Then, in the TextBox at the top of the Properties Window, type in Poisson d'Avril, as shown in Figure I-7:

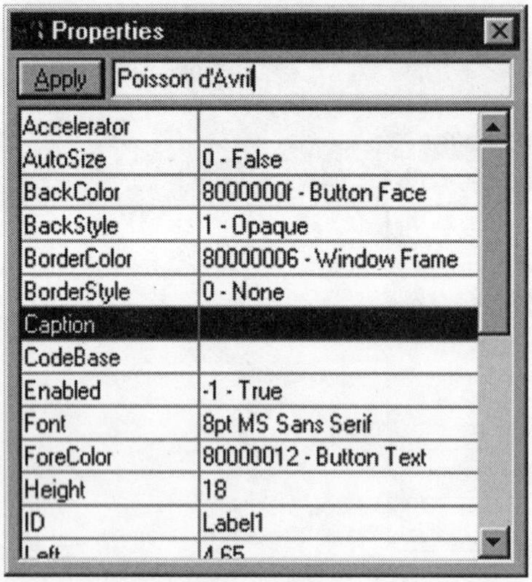

Properties

Apply | Poisson d'Avril

Accelerator	
AutoSize	0 - False
BackColor	8000000f - Button Face
BackStyle	1 - Opaque
BorderColor	80000006 - Window Frame
BorderStyle	0 - None
Caption	
CodeBase	
Enabled	-1 - True
Font	8pt MS Sans Serif
ForeColor	80000012 - Button Text
Height	18
ID	Label1
Left	4.65

Figure I-7: Make changes to a Control's Properties by typing a new value into the TextBox at the top of this window.

We also want to make the lettering large and use a bold typeface. Double-click on the Font Property in the Properties Window and you'll see a special window pop up where you can define elements of the typeface, as shown in Figure I-8.

Drag the window with the Label in it so the window is fairly large (as wide as your screen and about an inch high). Now drag the Label itself until it's big enough to comfortably display the name of the restaurant.

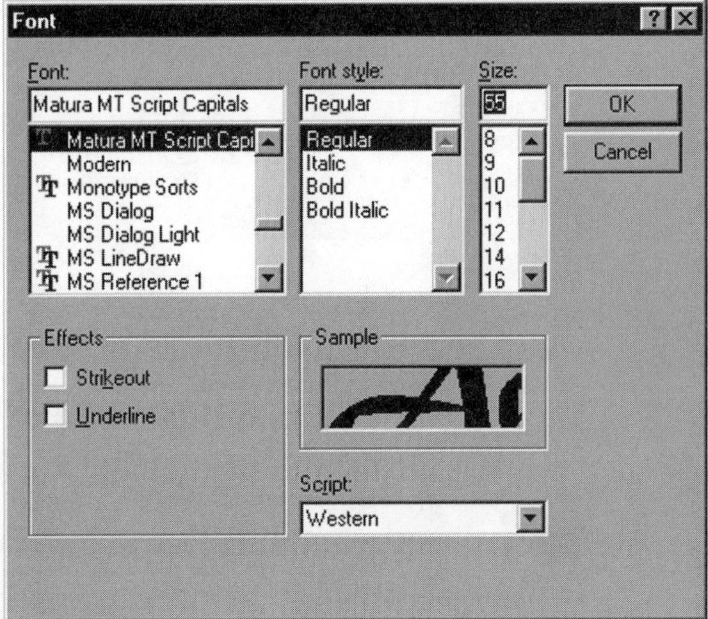

Figure I-8: In this special Font Window you can adjust various elements of a typeface.

To insert the HTML definition of our new Control (Object) into the HTML source code, click on the small x in the upper right corner of the window holding the Label. Your source code should now look something like this:

```
<HTML>
<HEAD>
<TITLE>Poisson d'avril</TITLE>
</HEAD>
<BODY BGCOLOR="WHITE" BACKGROUND="PDA.JPG">
<BR>
<CENTER>

<OBJECT ID="Label1" WIDTH=583 HEIGHT=88
 CLASSID="CLSID:978C9E23-D4B0-11CE-BF2D-00AA003F40D0">
  <PARAM NAME="BackColor" VALUE="16777215">
  <PARAM NAME="Caption" VALUE="Poisson d'Avril">
  <PARAM NAME="Size" VALUE="15416;2328">
```

```
    <PARAM NAME="FontName" VALUE="Matura MT Script Capitals">
    <PARAM NAME="FontEffects" VALUE="1073741825">
    <PARAM NAME="FontHeight" VALUE="1100">
    <PARAM NAME="FontCharSet" VALUE="0">
    <PARAM NAME="FontPitchAndFamily" VALUE="2">
    <PARAM NAME="FontWeight" VALUE="700">
</OBJECT>
</CENTER>

</BODY>
</HTML>
```

Notice that there's a small icon to the left of the Object definition, as shown in Figure I-9.

Figure I-9: Click on this icon to bring up the Properties Window and the resizing Window for an Object.

If you want to go back and again access the Properties Window for this Label, just click on the icon to its left in the source code. Alternatively, you can type changes to the PARAMs directly. For instance, if you want to change the Caption Property, edit this line:

```
<PARAM NAME="Caption" VALUE="Poisson d'Avril">
```

and make the change:

```
<PARAM NAME="Caption" VALUE="Poisson Bleu">
```

In any case, directly below the Label we want to display our hours of operation. We can do that by inserting a few lines of ordinary HTML source code:

```
<BR>
<FONT FACE="ARIAL" SIZE=2>
Open every day 6 pm to 1 am.
</FONT>
<BR><BR><BR>
```

We move down a line with <BR> so we're on a separate line from the Label, then change the typeface to Arial and make it fairly small with SIZE=2. Then we insert three more line breaks.

Let's see how we're doing. The process of creating a Web page involves cycling between the source code and then viewing the real-world results by loading the .HTM file into your browser. So start Internet Explorer running and in its File menu click on Open, then Browse. Locate PAGE1.HTM, our source code file. You should see something like Figure I-10.

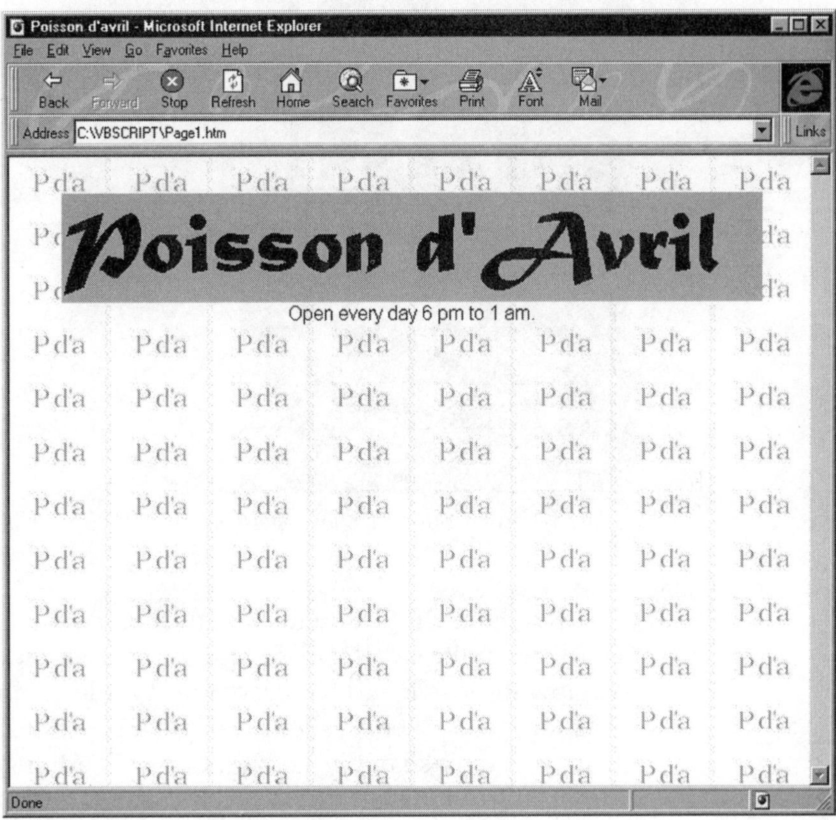

Figure I-10: So far, so good. But it would look better if we got rid of that gray background in the Label Control.

We can see things are going well enough, but that gray background in the Label isn't attractive. Click on the icon next to the <OBJECT ID> command in your HTML source code. When the Label's Properties Window pops up, double-click on the word BackColor. You'll see the special color selection window pop out. Choose white, as shown in Figure I-11.

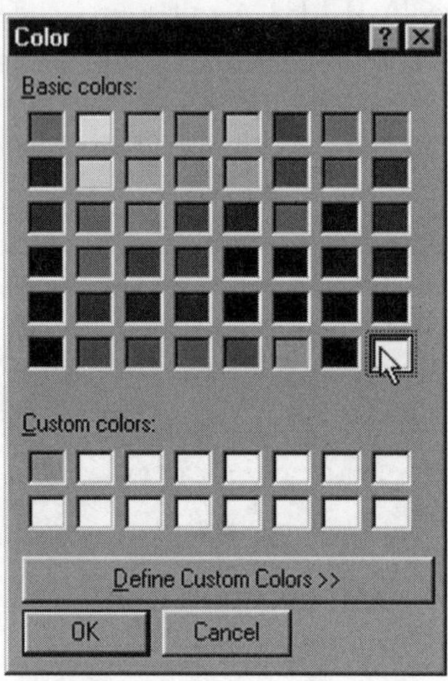

Figure I-11: This color selection palette makes adjusting colors easy.

Click on the OK button to close the color selection Window, then click on the small x in the upper right corner of the Label's Window to close it and the Properties Window. Now we're back to our source code. Let's test our change; it's mercifully easy to test changes you make in the ActiveX Control Pad. Just click on the third icon from the left (the disk symbol) in the Toolbar at the top of the ActiveX Control Pad. This will save your PAGE1.HTM file, complete with the change we just made to the BackColor Property. (If you don't see the Toolbar, click on the Control Pad's View menu, and choose Toolbar.)

Now, to load the latest version into Internet Explorer, just press Alt+Tab until you see Internet Explorer, then click on its Refresh button in the IE Toolbar. (If you don't see the IE Toolbar, click on the View menu, and choose Toolbar.)

This rocking back and forth between editing source code, and testing the effects of that editing, is simple and swift. It's painless to fiddle with the source code and view the results—which gives you the freedom to experiment and perfect your Web documents. Just click on the disk icon, press Alt+Tab, and click on the Refresh icon. There you are: no more gray BackColor behind the Label.

The HTML Layout Control: Easy Positioning

Now it's time to put an Image Control and a TextBox Control onto our page. We'll want to fiddle around with their sizes and positions, so this is a good job for the flexible *HTML Layout Control.* This Control is rather badly named because it's an ActiveX Control (one thinks of an HTML Control as being one of those objects created with the HTML INPUT command: <INPUT TYPE = Button VALUE = "Click Here to See More...">).

In any case, the Layout Control is unlike other ActiveX Controls in one important way: it acts as a container for all other ActiveX Controls. You place TextBoxes and Labels and any other ActiveX Control you want onto the Layout. This gives you precise control over the *positions* of the Controls. You can click on a Control then move your mouse pointer until you're on the gray frame that appears around it. When the mouse pointer turns into a pair of crossed arrows, you can drag the Control to position it wherever you wish within the container Layout Control.

So let's add an HTML Layout Control to our existing source code. Position your input cursor right below our last addition to the HTML source code:

```
</FONT>
<BR><BR><BR>
```

Click on the Edit menu. Choose Insert HTML Layout. You'll be asked for a name for your Layout. We named ours *pois*, but give it any name you want. Click on the Open button and you'll be told that POIS.ALX doesn't exist. Answer Yes, that you want to create it. Then you'll see a new OBJECT definition appear within your HTML source code:

```
<OBJECT CLASSID="CLSID:812AE312-8B8E-11CF-93C8-00AA00C08FDF"
ID="pois_alx" STYLE="LEFT:0;TOP:0">
<PARAM NAME="ALXPATH" REF VALUE="pois.alx">
 </OBJECT>
```

Note that when you put Controls, *or VBScript source code*, into a Layout Control, these Controls' OBJECT definitions and the VBScript programming are kept *in a separate file* on the hard drive from the .HTM file. This filename is the same as the name you gave the Layout Control, plus an .ALX suffix. So, the source code for our Layout Control will be in a file named POIS.ALX.

Click on the small icon to the left of the OBJECT CLASSID definition of our new Layout Control. You'll see the Layout Window pop up, including a Toolbox containing 13 icons representing a default set of 13 Controls, as shown in Figure I-12.

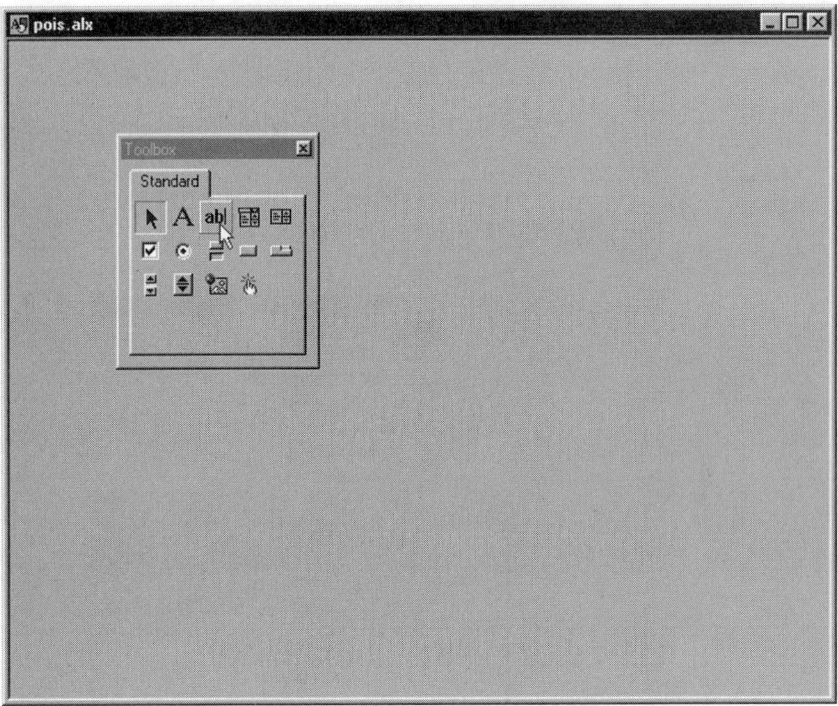

Figure I-12: This Toolbox contains 13 commonly used ActiveX Controls. Just drag them onto the Layout Control.

Tip

You can put any *ActiveX Control onto a Layout Control, not just the 13 that are on the Toolbox by default. To add a new Control to the Toolbox, right-click on the Toolbox, and choose Additional Controls, as shown in Figure I-13.*

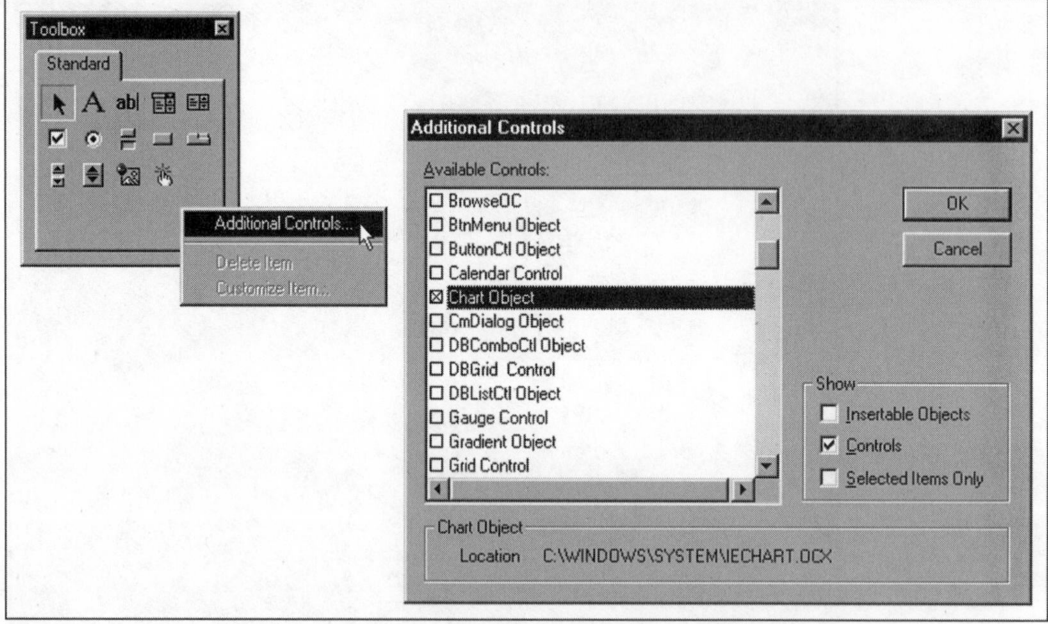

Figure I-13: If you want to add other Controls, in addition to the default 13, onto a Layout, just right-click on the Toolbox.

But the two Controls we're interested in are already on the Toolbox. So let's do it. Click on the Image (ISImage) icon in the Toolbox, then drag your mouse across the Layout until you've sized it roughly as shown in Figure I-14. Do the same with a TextBox.

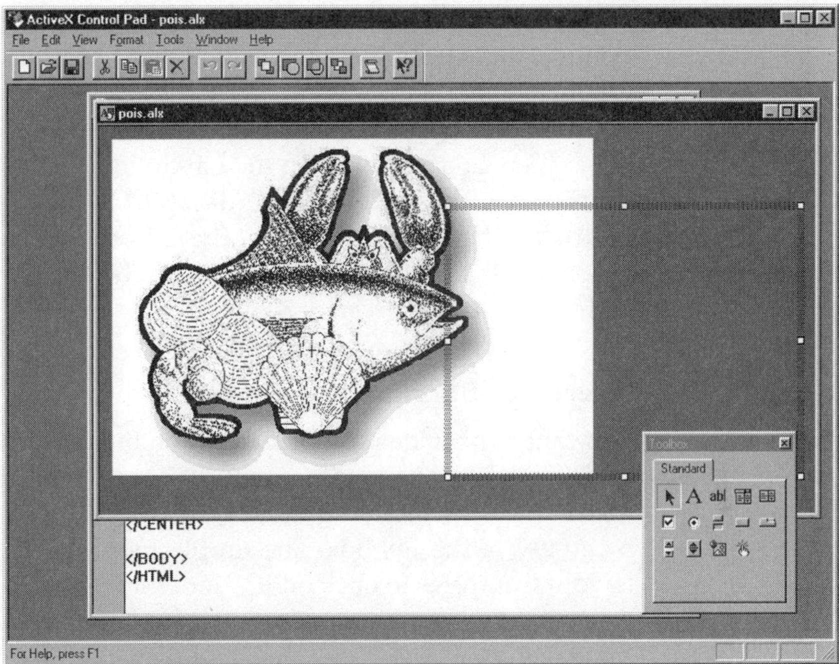

Figure I-14: Now we've positioned our Image and TextBox Controls on the Layout Control.

Double-click on the TextBox. Then, in its Properties Window, change MultiLine to True, SpecialEffect to Flat, and BackStyle to Transparent. We want it transparent so that our graphic image will show through under the text. Also, change the TextBox's Locked Property to True. This way, the user will be able to copy and paste the text (today's menu) but not edit it.

Double-click on the Image Control and type in, for its PicturePath Property, the name of a .GIF or .JPG graphic file. Just provide the name of the file (FISH.JPG) if you've put that file in the same directory on your hard drive where the .HTM file is located. Otherwise, provide a full path (C:\VBSCRIPT\FISH.JPG).

As soon as you click on the Apply button in the Properties Window, or simply press the Enter key, you should see your graphic appear within the Image Control.

One more thing. We want the Layout Control itself to appear light green. So right-click on the Layout itself and select Properties. You should see four Properties: BackColor, Height, ID, and Width. (In the future, we expect the Layout will have many more Properties than these.) Double-click on the BackColor Property and choose a light green.

Inserting VBScript

We want to provide today's date when the user loads in our document. We'll have to use the VBScript Date command (there's no comparable command in HTML). And we'll also assign the menu text to the TextBox. The simplest way to add VBScript to a Layout Control is to click on the Tools | Script Wizard menu. (If you want to add VBScript to plain HTML source code, click on the same menu.)

The Script Wizard itself is rather limited—there are many options and VBScript commands that it doesn't handle. We don't recommend using it, except as a shortcut way to insert the template for a piece of VBScript.

As shown in Figure I-15, just choose an event in the left pane, then choose an "action" in the right pane. It doesn't matter which events or actions you choose. All we're after is the template. When you've got an event/action chosen, click on the OK button to close the wizard.

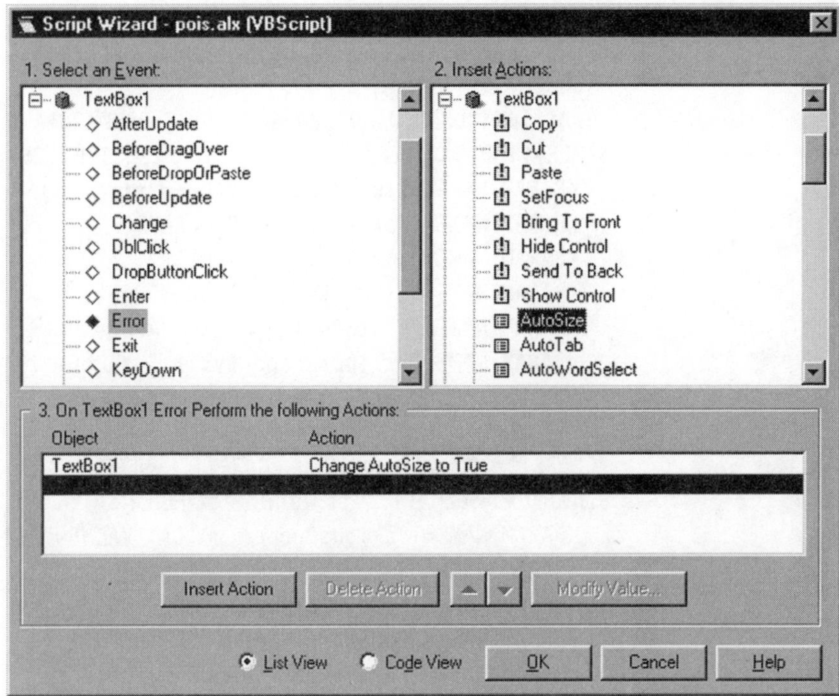

Figure I-15: The VBScript wizard isn't that useful.

What we've done is to insert some VBScript into the Layout Control's source code. Let's take a look. Right-click on the Layout Control and choose "View Source Code." Say Yes when asked if you want to save and close the Layout. You should then see a Notepad window open up with something like the following source code:

```
<SCRIPT LANGUAGE="VBScript">
<!--
Sub TextBox1_Error(Number, Description, SCode, Source,
HelpFile, HelpContext, CancelDisplay)
TextBox1.AutoSize = True
end sub
-->
</SCRIPT>
```

```
<DIV BACKGROUND="#408080" ID="pois"
STYLE="LAYOUT:FIXED;WIDTH:547pt;HEIGHT:270pt;">
 <OBJECT ID="Image1"
 CLASSID="CLSID:D4A97620-8E8F-11CF-93CD-00AA00C08FDF"
STYLE="TOP:9pt;LEFT:9pt;WIDTH:377pt;HEIGHT:257pt;ZINDEX:0;">
   <PARAM NAME="PicturePath" VALUE="fish.jpg">
   <PARAM NAME="BorderStyle" VALUE="0">
   <PARAM NAME="SizeMode" VALUE="3">
   <PARAM NAME="Size" VALUE="13300;9066">
   <PARAM NAME="PictureAlignment" VALUE="0">
   <PARAM NAME="VariousPropertyBits" VALUE="19">
 </OBJECT>
 <OBJECT ID="TextBox1"
 CLASSID="CLSID:8BD21D10-EC42-11CE-9E0D-00AA006002F3"
STYLE="TOP:65pt;LEFT:272pt;WIDTH:266pt;HEIGHT:183pt;TABINDEX:0;ZINDEX:1;">
   <PARAM NAME="VariousPropertyBits" VALUE="2894088215">
   <PARAM NAME="Size" VALUE="9384;6456">
   <PARAM NAME="SpecialEffect" VALUE="0">
   <PARAM NAME="FontName" VALUE="Arial">
   <PARAM NAME="FontHeight" VALUE="320">
   <PARAM NAME="FontCharSet" VALUE="0">
   <PARAM NAME="FontPitchAndFamily" VALUE="2">
   <PARAM NAME="FontWeight" VALUE="0">
 </OBJECT>
</DIV>
```

We're not interested in the nonsense code between the <SCRIPT> and </SCRIPT> commands, so delete that, leaving the template we do want to use. After we used, then closed, the Script Wizard as described above, the wizard left this code behind. But we're just saving ourselves the trouble of typing in the <SCRIPT> and other commands.

```
<SCRIPT LANGUAGE="VBScript">
<!--

-->
</SCRIPT>
```

Tip

Notice those HTML commands <!-- and --> that have been inserted into our script. When you use the Script Wizard to put some VBScript programming into the Microsoft ActiveX Control Pad, comment symbols are always inserted right after the <SCRIPT> and right before the </SCRIPT> tags. The reason for doing this is that if the user loads your document into a browser that's incapable of working with VBScript, the comment symbols prevent that browser from displaying the VBScript programming as text. (But if the browser does contain a VBScript interpreter, as does Internet Explorer, it will ignore these HTML comment symbols and go ahead and act on the VBScript commands.)

Into this VBScript template, type the following:

```
<SCRIPT LANGUAGE="VBScript">
<!--
Sub pois_OnLoad()
N = Date
cr = chr(13) & chr(10)

TextBox1.Text = "Menu for " & N & cr & cr & cr
TextBox1.Text = TextBox1.Text & "     Grilled Salmon →
Comfort" & cr & cr
TextBox1.Text = TextBox1.Text & "     Baby corn en →
brochette" & cr & cr
TextBox1.Text = TextBox1.Text & "     Flambe of Apricots →
Noches" & cr & cr

end sub
-->
</SCRIPT>
```

This OnLoad Event will be triggered whenever the user first loads (or Refreshes) our document. We define the Variable *N* as containing the current date. Then we define the carriage return (new line) characters that must be used with a TextBox. Whenever we insert a *cr*, we'll go down to the next line in our TextBox. Finally, we define the TextBox text by adding the Text Property to itself repeatedly, until at the bottom we've got the whole menu.

Back to HTML

All we've got to do now is display the phone number. We can do that by adding a Label Control directly onto the HTML source code. Close the Notepad window containing the Layout source code we just typed in (save the .ALX file).

Now you should be back in the ActiveX Control Pad's HTML source code window. Add a couple of

 (new lines) just below the Layout Control's </OBJECT> command, and click on the Edit | Insert ActiveX Control menu. Follow the instructions given earlier to add a Label Control. You'll see a ListBox pop up. Choose Microsoft Forms 2.0 Label, as shown in Figure I-5. Resize it and adjust its Properties so the caption reads "Call 245-6788 for reservations," the Font is Arial, and the FontSize is about 11. Click on the small x in the top right of the Label's window to close it.

You should see an object definition in your HTML source code that looks something like this:

```
<OBJECT ID="Label1" WIDTH=255 HEIGHT=39
 CLASSID="CLSID:978C9E23-D4B0-11CE-BF2D-00AA003F40D0">
   <PARAM NAME="BackColor" VALUE="16777215">
   <PARAM NAME="Caption" VALUE="    Call 245-6788 for reserva-
tions">
   <PARAM NAME="PicturePosition" VALUE="262148">
   <PARAM NAME="Size" VALUE="6738;1032">
   <PARAM NAME="FontName" VALUE="Arial">
   <PARAM NAME="FontHeight" VALUE="220">
   <PARAM NAME="FontCharSet" VALUE="0">
   <PARAM NAME="FontPitchAndFamily" VALUE="2">
   <PARAM NAME="FontWeight" VALUE="0">
</OBJECT>
```

We've finished our Web page now, so click on the disk icon on the Control Pad's Toolbar to save our source code. Then, in Internet Explorer, open PAGE1.HTM and you should see results like those shown in Figure I-16.

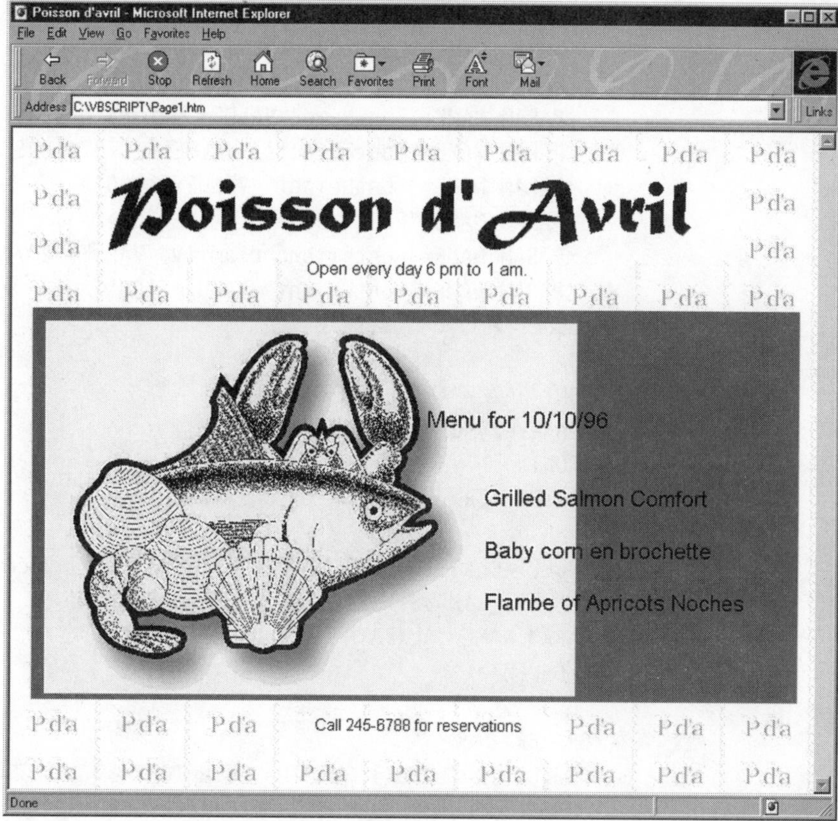

Figure I-16: The finished home page for our restaurant.

The complete HTML source code for Figure I-16 (saved in the file PAGE1.HTM) looks like this:

```
<HTML>
<HEAD>
<TITLE>Poisson d'avril</TITLE>
</HEAD>
<BODY BGCOLOR="WHITE" BACKGROUND="PDA.JPG">
<BR>
<CENTER>

<OBJECT ID="Label1" WIDTH=591 HEIGHT=89
 CLASSID="CLSID:978C9E23-D4B0-11CE-BF2D-00AA003F40D0">
```

```
  <PARAM NAME="BackColor" VALUE="16777215">
  <PARAM NAME="Caption" VALUE="Poisson d'Avril">
  <PARAM NAME="Size" VALUE="15628;2364">
  <PARAM NAME="FontName" VALUE="Matura MT Script Capitals">
  <PARAM NAME="FontEffects" VALUE="1073741825">
  <PARAM NAME="FontHeight" VALUE="1100">
  <PARAM NAME="FontCharSet" VALUE="0">
  <PARAM NAME="FontPitchAndFamily" VALUE="2">
  <PARAM NAME="FontWeight" VALUE="700">
</OBJECT>
<BR>
<FONT FACE="ARIAL" SIZE=2>
Open every day 6 pm to 1 am.
</FONT>
<BR><BR><BR>

<OBJECT CLASSID="CLSID:812AE312-8B8E-11CF-93C8-00AA00C08FDF"
ID="pois_alx" STYLE="LEFT:0;TOP:0">
<PARAM NAME="ALXPATH" REF VALUE="pois.alx">
 </OBJECT>

<BR><BR>
<OBJECT ID="Label1" WIDTH=255 HEIGHT=39
 CLASSID="CLSID:978C9E23-D4B0-11CE-BF2D-00AA003F40D0">
  <PARAM NAME="BackColor" VALUE="16777215">
  <PARAM NAME="Caption" VALUE="    Call 245-6788 for →
reservations">
  <PARAM NAME="PicturePosition" VALUE="262148">
  <PARAM NAME="Size" VALUE="6738;1032">
  <PARAM NAME="FontName" VALUE="Arial">
  <PARAM NAME="FontHeight" VALUE="220">
  <PARAM NAME="FontCharSet" VALUE="0">
  <PARAM NAME="FontPitchAndFamily" VALUE="2">
  <PARAM NAME="FontWeight" VALUE="0">
</OBJECT>

</CENTER>

</BODY>
</HTML>
```

And the Layout Control source code for Figure I-16 (saved in the text file “POIS.ALX”), looks like this:

```
<SCRIPT LANGUAGE="VBScript">
<!--
Sub pois_OnLoad()
N = Date
cr = chr(13) & chr(10)

TextBox1.Text = "Menu for " & N & cr & cr & cr
TextBox1.Text = TextBox1.Text & "     Grilled Salmon →
Comfort" & cr & cr
TextBox1.Text = TextBox1.Text & "     Baby corn en →
brochette" & cr & cr
TextBox1.Text = TextBox1.Text & "     Flambe of Apricots →
Noches" & cr & cr

end sub
-->
</SCRIPT>

<DIV BACKGROUND="#408080" ID="pois"
STYLE="LAYOUT:FIXED;WIDTH:547pt;HEIGHT:270pt;">
  <OBJECT ID="Image1"
  CLASSID="CLSID:D4A97620-8E8F-11CF-93CD-00AA00C08FDF"
STYLE="TOP:9pt;LEFT:9pt;WIDTH:377pt;HEIGHT:257pt;ZINDEX:0;">
   <PARAM NAME="PicturePath" VALUE="fish.jpg">
   <PARAM NAME="BorderStyle" VALUE="0">
   <PARAM NAME="SizeMode" VALUE="3">
   <PARAM NAME="Size" VALUE="13300;9066">
   <PARAM NAME="PictureAlignment" VALUE="0">
   <PARAM NAME="VariousPropertyBits" VALUE="19">
 </OBJECT>
 <OBJECT ID="TextBox1"
  CLASSID="CLSID:8BD21D10-EC42-11CE-9E0D-00AA006002F3"
STYLE="TOP:65pt;LEFT:272pt;WIDTH:266pt;HEIGHT:183pt;TABINDEX:0;ZINDEX:1;">
   <PARAM NAME="VariousPropertyBits" VALUE="2894088215">
   <PARAM NAME="Size" VALUE="9384;6456">
   <PARAM NAME="SpecialEffect" VALUE="0">
   <PARAM NAME="FontName" VALUE="Arial">
```

```
    <PARAM NAME="FontHeight" VALUE="320">
    <PARAM NAME="FontCharSet" VALUE="0">
    <PARAM NAME="FontPitchAndFamily" VALUE="2">
    <PARAM NAME="FontWeight" VALUE="0">
  </OBJECT>
</DIV>
```

Now that we've constructed a document, let's conclude this Introduction by turning our attention to a couple of additional issues: security and debugging.

Security & ActiveX Objects

At the time of this writing, Microsoft is officially supporting only 25 ActiveX Controls. These Controls are from Microsoft itself (they aren't necessarily developed by Microsoft, but they are "published" by Microsoft). Other Controls published or written by other companies are currently being reworked to include security. If you click on the ActiveX Control Pad's Edit | Insert ActiveX Control menu, you'll see this set of Controls: their names begin with Microsoft Forms 2.0 or Microsoft IE 3.0.

Why security? If a user is browsing the Web with Internet Explorer and comes upon a page that includes an ActiveX Control that isn't already on the user's hard drive (or is a newer version of a Control the user has), Internet Explorer will attempt to download that Control to the user's hard drive. However, before this alien (and potentially virus-ridden) object is permitted to reside and run rampant through the user's computer, the user is given an opportunity to refuse permission, to refuse to allow the object to be installed.

Microsoft has asked developers of ActiveX Controls to "digitally sign" their Controls. A secure signature is said to authenticate a Control and provide you with assurance that it originates from the company that claims to have written it. In other words, the Control hasn't been tampered with and won't inject a rampaging virus into

your computer system. All these security schemes are still being developed, though. Another scheme has Controls tested for viruses by an independent organization, then cleared for use on the Web.

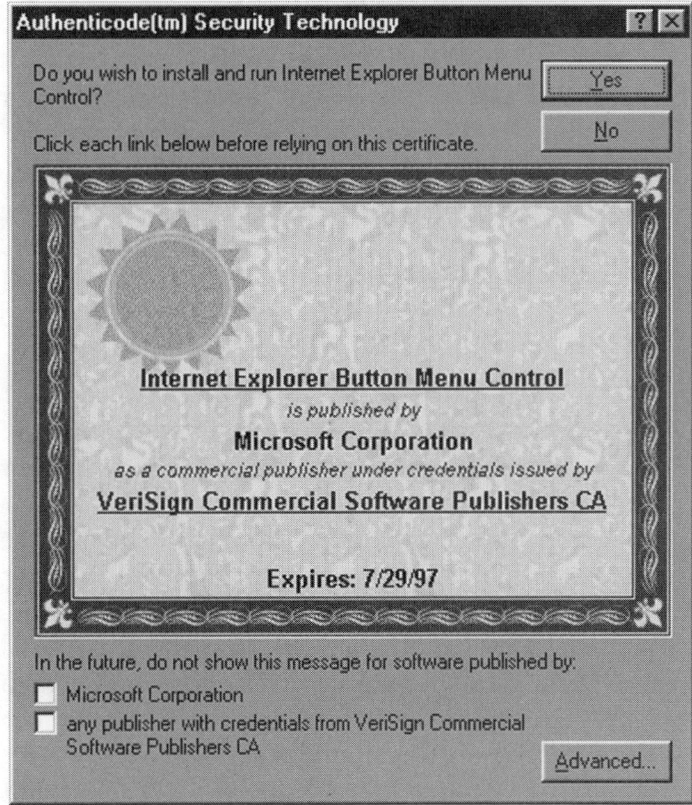

Figure I-17: This "Authenticode" window pops up, verifying the integrity of a downloaded Control.

At this time (in addition to the 13 on the Microsoft HTML Layout Control's Toolbox, described above), the Controls certified by and available from Microsoft are: Animated Button, Chart, Gradient, Label, Marquee, Menu, Popup Menu, Popup Window, Preloader, Stock Ticker, Timer, and View Tracker. These Controls are all covered in this book, with the exception of the Stock Ticker. And all 13 Layout Control objects are covered as well.

Debugging: Fixing Errors

Errors in HTML source code are generally just ignored by browsers. If you feed this impossible HTML source code (there's no such command as OFF WHITE) to the Internet Explorer browser, the background will, inexplicably, turn bright red:

```
<HTML>
<HEAD>
<TITLE>HTML Bugs</TITLE>
</HEAD>

<BODY BGCOLOR="OFF WHITE">

</BODY>
</HTML>
```

Bright red isn't quite what you intended, but at least the browser didn't freeze up or crash or otherwise do some damage and frighten the user.

Errors made in VBScript, though, can be more serious. Typos and other kinds of bugs can interrupt your VBScript by displaying an error message to the user—a message that's unlikely to be understood by most users and that makes it less likely that they will visit your site again. Logic errors won't generate an error message, but they can result in ridiculous information. For example, your document might announce to the user that the gas for a trip from Atlanta to Orlando costs $.28. This kind of thing isn't reassuring to users either.

At this time, the ActiveX Control Pad (and the VBScript engine in browsers like Internet Explorer) have very few facilities to assist you in debugging your programs. Let's take a look at the kinds of errors that crop up when writing computer programs, and what you can do about them in VBScript.

"Bugs" (errors in scripts or programs) are almost inevitable. You can be enormously careful, tidy, and thoughtful, but if your script is more than 50 lines long, errors are likely. If it's longer than 100 lines, errors are virtually certain.

There are three types of errors in computer programming:

- Typos
- Runtime errors
- Logic errors

Typos

Typos are the easiest errors to deal with. VBScript knows at once that you've mistakenly typed *MgsBox* instead of *MsgBox*: if it doesn't recognize a command, it can detect the error. If you insert this into your HTML source code, then load this document into Internet Explorer, you'll see the error message shown in Figure I-18.

```
<HTML>
<HEAD>
<TITLE>Debugging</TITLE>
</HEAD>
<BODY BGCOLOR="WHITE">

<SCRIPT LANGUAGE="VBScript">
<!--
MgsBox "What gives?"
-->
</SCRIPT>

</BODY>
</HTML>
```

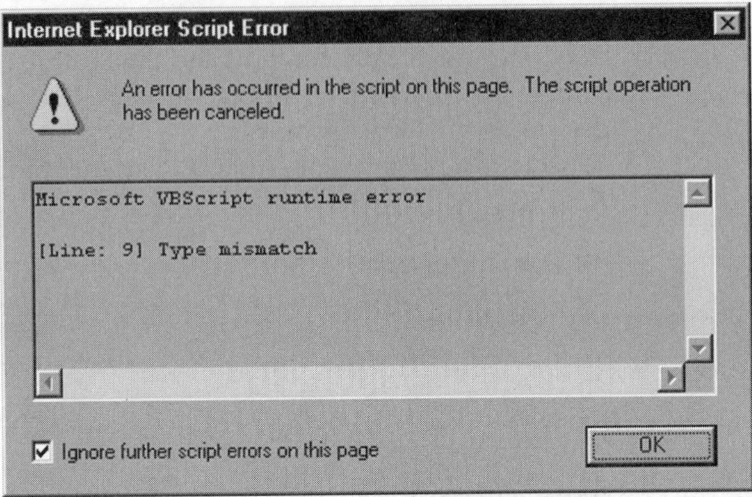

Figure I-18: A misspelling of a VBScript command generates this error message.

You're also told that the error is located in line 9, so take a look at your source code in the ActiveX Control Pad and count down from the top to line 9. Then look for a typo and fix it.

Also, another kind of typo—impossible commands—are easily noticed and reported; for example, *Erase the blackboard.* VBScript cannot digest this command, so it reports the problem. It does understand and recognize the command *Erase*, but it expects the Erase command to be followed by the name of an Array. That's how Erase is supposed to work. Not finding that, it reacts with an error message. But this error message is even more helpful than the previous one. Now VBScript shows you the offending line of source code and even displays an arrow pointing out the location *within this line of source code* where it found a problem, as shown in Figure I-19.

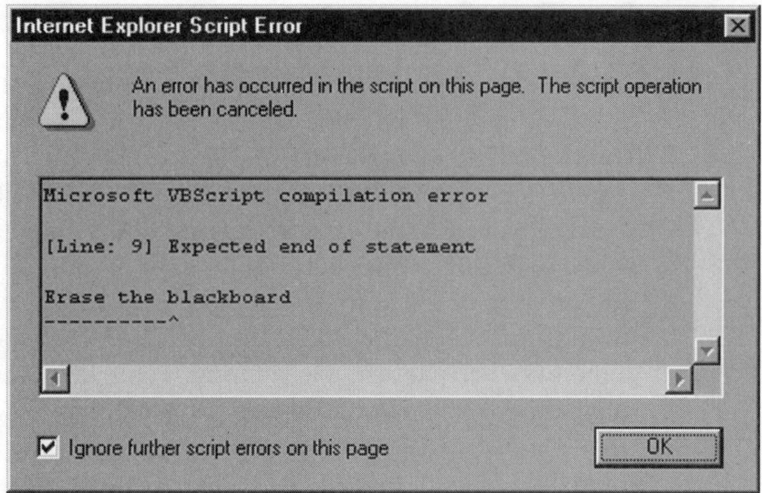

Figure I-19: If you misuse a recognized VBScript command, you'll get an even more detailed report.

Related to typos are errors in providing the amount or type of information necessary for VBScript to carry out a command:

```
X = Sqr("five")
```

You can't square a piece of text. This function wants a real number, 5. In response to this kind of error, you get the same error message you get for a classic typo ("Type Mismatch"). This response indicates that something is mistyped or is missing.

A third variety of easily detected, easily fixed error is an inconsistency of some kind between parts of your script. Let's say you have a Subroutine that expects three Variables:

```
Sub Numbers (a, b, c)
End Sub
```

and you try to call it but provide only two numbers:

```
Numbers a, b
```

When you load the above into the browser, you'll get the error message "Wrong number of arguments or invalid property assignment."

Run-Time Errors

Strictly speaking, run-time errors are not bugs, but they are failures on a programmer's part nonetheless. These errors are difficulties your script encounters while a user is running it. However, you can largely forget about this category of error when writing VBScript. Classically, a run-time error is caused because your program tries to read a disk, but crashes because the user has forgotten to put a disk into drive A: or failed to close the drive door.

Run-time errors include all those unexpected situations that can come up when the script is running. There are a number of things you cannot know about the user's system. How large is the disk drive? Is it already so full that when your script tries to save a file, there won't be enough room? Are you creating an Array so large that it exceeds the computer's available memory?

With the exception of the huge Array problem, most run-time errors are impossible in VBScript because you, the programmer, are explicitly prevented from accessing any of the users' peripherals, including their disk drives. All file access commands (and other peripheral access commands, such as those for the printer) have been stripped from the VBScript language.

Logic Errors

The third major category of scripting bugs, logic errors, is the most puzzling of all. Some logic errors can be so subtle, so well concealed, that you might think you will be driven mad trying to locate the source of the problem.

A logic error means that you have followed all the rules of syntax, made no typos, and otherwise satisfied VBScript that your commands can be carried out. You, and VBScript, think everything is shipshape. However, when you run the script the entire browser window turns black; or if the user types in the number 10, your script changes it into 1,000.

What To Do: The key to fixing logic errors is finding out *where* in your script the problem is located.

Some computer languages have an elaborate debugging apparatus, sometimes even including the use of two computer monitors—one shows the results of the script as it runs, the other shows the lines of programming as they are executed. That is a good approach because when you are debugging logic errors you want to see beneath the surface of a running script. You want to locate the command or commands in your script that are causing the problem. *You want to know where, in the script, you are located at any given time in the process of running the script.*

You can see the symptoms of a logic bug: every time the user enters a number, the results are way, way off. You know that somewhere your script is mangling the numbers—but until you X-ray the script, you can't find out where the problem is located.

Another kind of logic error is unique to Event-driven languages like VBScript—the repeated triggering of an Event. (Try putting a MsgBox command within an Image Control's MouseMove Event.) These kinds of machine gun repeating errors can occur if, for example, you intend to do something only once while the script is running but you've put that command within an Event like MouseMove that triggers quite often.

Most computer languages have a suite of debugging tools: a watch window (to see when Variables change); a tracer (a single-step feature that allows you to move, line by highlighted line, through your source code while watching the effects); and breakpoints (you can set up conditions like: stop running and alert me as soon as X becomes greater than 50, for example).

VBScript doesn't yet have any of these features. Your best bet, if you're seeing mysterious behavior—but don't know where in your source code it's happening—is to insert MsgBoxes. Sure, they'll slow things up, but they can tell you the status of your Variables and the current location in the source code. This is the equivalent of the Variable Watch window available in many computer languages.

Let's try an example. Assume that you write a Function that calculates the cost of gas for a car trip:

```
Function TripCost (GasCost, Miles, MPG)
  TripCost = GasCost/Miles * MPG
End Function
```

Then you provide the three Variables to this Function and display the results:

```
<HTML>
<HEAD>
<TITLE>Logic Bugs</TITLE>
</HEAD>
<BODY BGCOLOR="WHITE">

<SCRIPT LANGUAGE="VBScript">
<!--

GasCost = 1.3
Miles = 100
MPG = 22
MsgBox "Your total cost for this trip is: $" & →
TripCost(GasCost, Miles, MPG)

Function TripCost (GasCost, Miles, MPG)
  TripCost = GasCost/Miles * MPG
End Function

-->
</SCRIPT>

</BODY>
</HTML>
```

When you run the above program by loading it into the Internet Explorer browser, you're told that the cost of your trip is 28 cents. That's not logical. This one is easy enough to track down because we've only got that one Function in the entire script. But in a more complex script, you'll find it useful to sprinkle MsgBoxes all around in various locations. To find out what's happening, you can add MsgBoxes here and there in your various Subroutines and Functions, reporting both the location and the status of the Variables. Then you can see when a Variable swings way out of range and things go wrong:

```
Function TripCost (GasCost, Miles, MPG)
MsgBox "Function TripCost:" & " GasCost = " & GasCost & " →
Miles = " & Miles & " MPG = " & MPG
   TripCost = GasCost/Miles * MPG
End Function
```

When this message box shows up onscreen, we know that VBScript is currently located within the TripCost Function and that the Variables are as expected. So, at this point (at the location of this message box), nothing has yet gone wrong. The next line of source code, though, reveals that we should adjust our formula. Our math is wrong. The gas cost should be divided by the MPG, and then that result should be multiplied by the miles traveled:

```
totalcost = gascost / mpg * miles
```

Another approach to this same technique would be to use a TextBox to display location and Variables. Instead of inserting message boxes all over your source code, you call on a special Subroutine that fills the TextBox with the location and Variable values. Unlike the message box approach, the script won't be halted each time there is a report of location/Variables. However, like the classic "Trace" debugging feature in other languages, this technique provides you with a "printout" that you can read at a glance to see the pathways taken by your script, and the effect on Variables. Here's how to do it:

1. Put a TextBox Control into your HTML source code and set the TextBox's Multiline Property to True. Change its ScrollBars Property to Vertical.

2. Create this Subroutine to display a given location/Variable report:

```
Sub Report (data)
cr = chr(13) & chr(10)
TextBox1.Text = TextBox1.Text & cr & data
End Sub
```

3. Then insert a call to this report in all suspected locations within your VBScript source code. Here's how the whole thing looks as source code:

```
<HTML>
<HEAD>
<TITLE>Logic Bugs</TITLE>
</HEAD>
<BODY BGCOLOR="WHITE">

<OBJECT ID="TextBox1" WIDTH=563 HEIGHT=295
 CLASSID="CLSID:8BD21D10-EC42-11CE-9E0D-00AA006002F3">
   <PARAM NAME="VariousPropertyBits" VALUE="2894088219">
   <PARAM NAME="ScrollBars" VALUE="2">
   <PARAM NAME="Size" VALUE="14906;7796">
   <PARAM NAME="FontName" VALUE="Arial">
   <PARAM NAME="FontHeight" VALUE="220">
   <PARAM NAME="FontCharSet" VALUE="0">
   <PARAM NAME="FontPitchAndFamily" VALUE="2">
   <PARAM NAME="FontWeight" VALUE="0">
</OBJECT>

<SCRIPT LANGUAGE="VBScript">
<!--

GasCost = 1.3
Miles = 100
MPG = 22
Report "Before CallingTripCost. GasCost = " & GasCost →
& " Miles = " & Miles & " MPG = " & MPG

MsgBox "Your total cost for this trip is: $" & →
TripCost(GasCost, Miles, MPG)

Function TripCost (GasCost, Miles, MPG)
Report "In Function TripCost. GasCost = " & GasCost & →
" Miles = " & Miles & " MPG = " & MPG
   TripCost = GasCost/Miles * MPG
```

```
Report "After calculations in Function TripCost. →
GasCost = " & GasCost & " Miles = " & Miles & " MPG →
= " & MPG
End Function

Sub Report (data)
cr = chr(13) & chr(10)
TextBox1.Text = TextBox1.Text & cr & data & cr & cr
End Sub

-->
</SCRIPT>
</BODY>
</HTML>
```

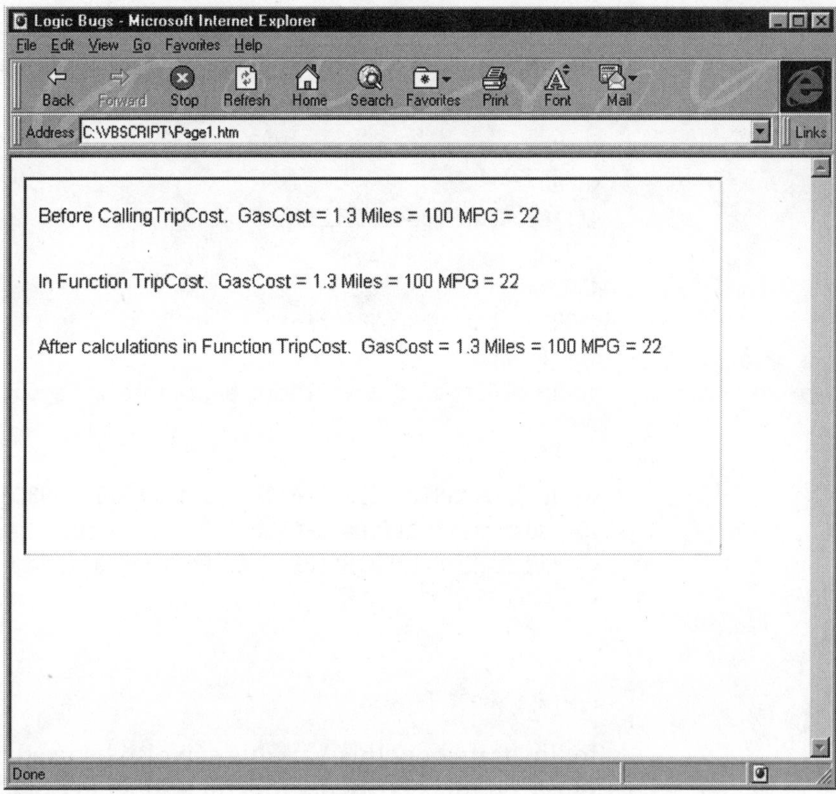

Figure I-20: Filling a TextBox with debugging reports is similar to a trace facility.

Err and On Error

Two important additional facilities related to debugging—the Err object and the On Error command—are fully covered in the "Err" entry in the body of this book.

Global Variables

Before concluding this overview of programming VBScript, we should briefly explore the issue of *scope.* (For additional information about scope, see the entry for the "Dim" command.)

There will be times when you want a Variable to be usable by an HTML document and also usable by a Layout Control. How do you create a Variable that can be seen in both places? Declare it with the Dim command in the HTML source code. Be sure that it's not within a procedure (with a Sub...End Sub or Function...End Function structure). Here we'll create a Variable named *myvar*. We'll also assign a piece of text to that Variable:

```
<HTML>
<HEAD>
<TITLE>New Page</TITLE>
</HEAD>
<BODY>
<SCRIPT LANGUAGE=VBScript>
dim myvar
myvar = "This is a variable passed to a Layout Control"
</SCRIPT>

<OBJECT CLASSID="CLSID:812AE312-8B8E-11CF-93C8-00AA00C08FDF"
ID="test_alx" STYLE="LEFT:0;TOP:0">
<PARAM NAME="ALXPATH" REF VALUE="test.alx">
 </OBJECT>

</BODY>
</HTML>
```

To illustrate how this Variable can also be used by any Layout Controls on this HTML document, add a Layout Control. Position your cursor within the HTML document, just after the </SCRIPT>

command. Then, in the ActiveX Control Pad, click on Insert HTML Layout. Depending on what name you choose to give it, you'll see something like this object inserted into your HTML document:

```
<OBJECT CLASSID="CLSID:812AE312-8B8E-11CF-93C8-00AA00C08FDF"
ID="test_alx" STYLE="LEFT:0;TOP:0">
<PARAM NAME="ALXPATH" REF VALUE="test.alx">
 </OBJECT>
```

Now, to use the Variable, click on the small button in the left margin next to <OBJECT CLASSID=. You'll be taken into the Layout Control editing window. Add a CommandButton to the Layout. Right-click on the Layout, then choose View Source Code. You should see the definition of your CommandButton. It should look something like this:

```
<DIV ID="test"
STYLE="LAYOUT:FIXED;WIDTH:400pt;HEIGHT:300pt;">
 <OBJECT ID="CommandButton1"
 CLASSID="CLSID:D7053240-CE69-11CD-A777-00DD01143C57"
STYLE="TOP:58pt;LEFT:41pt;WIDTH:107pt;HEIGHT:41pt;TABINDEX:0;ZINDEX:0;">
   <PARAM NAME="Caption" VALUE="CommandButton1">
   <PARAM NAME="Size" VALUE="3775;1446">
   <PARAM NAME="FontCharSet" VALUE="0">
   <PARAM NAME="FontPitchAndFamily" VALUE="2">
   <PARAM NAME="ParagraphAlign" VALUE="3">
   <PARAM NAME="FontWeight" VALUE="0">
 </OBJECT>
</DIV>
```

Outside of this definition (outside the <DIV> and </DIV> commands), type this in:

```
<SCRIPT LANGUAGE="VBScript">
<!--
Sub CommandButton1_Click()
MsgBox window.myvar
end sub
-->
</SCRIPT>
```

Then save this .ALX file. Now, when you test this document by clicking on the CommandButton in Internet Explorer, you'll see that our Variable *myvar* works within the Layout Control. When the button is clicked, the message box displays "This is a Variable passed to a Layout Control." By using the *window* Object (window.myvar), we can access the Variable anywhere within this window (in any Layout, or in the HTML document itself).

Continuing On...

Now that we've finished our overview of Internet programming with VBScript, ActiveX Controls, and the Microsoft ActiveX Control Pad, you're ready to plunge in and explore the intriguing world of Web site programming. Fortunately, thanks to VBScript and ActiveX Controls, you have the tools to create truly efficient and dynamic documents—Web sites of a functional and visual sophistication unimagined by earlier Internet programmers. We hope that this book will provide a helpful reference, refreshing your memory about the usage, and uses, of the many HTML, VBScript, and ActiveX commands.

æ ç © Ñ Æ ® ° and other symbols

See Special Characters

<!—

See Comment

+

See Operators

&

See Operators

/

See Operators

^

See Operators

A

\

See Operators

*

See Operators

-

See Operators

!DOCTYPE

HTML

Description To comply with specifications for HTML 3.2, you are asked to identify the version of HTML that you're using in your document. The !DOCTYPE command is supposed to be the first item in any HTML document. !DOCTYPE declares the HTML version being used. However, at this time HTML 3.2 is the only version of HTML that can recognize the !DOCTYPE tag. Therefore the situation is circular and, for now at least, there's no point to using this command.

Cautions Almost nobody is using this tag at this time. But it causes no problems. As with most any unrecognized command, a browser that doesn't understand !DOCTYPE will just ignore it.

Example This identifies the current document as HTML version 3.2:

```
<!DOCTYPE HTML PUBLIC "-//W3C//DTD HTML 3.2//EN">
```

A

HTML

A

Description This command specifies a hypertext link. It creates one of those areas in a page where the text is a different color (or underlined, or both) that the user can click on and jump to another location.

The link can be to one of three destinations: elsewhere on the Internet (a home page site, for example), into another .HTM file (which should be located on the same directory as the original .HTM file that created the current page), or elsewhere within the currently displayed document (for example, to another page). Note that technically the target of a link need not be in the same subdirectory. You could provide a complete disk *path* to the target. However, for simplicity in testing and exploring the examples in this book, we urge you to store graphic files and link targets in the same folder (subdirectory) as your document's .HTM file.

To see how to create all three types of links, see the example below.

In addition to links created with <A>, you can use the MAP and AREA commands to specify links ("hot spots") *within* a single graphic image. This way you could show a picture of the alphabet—and each letter of the alphabet, when clicked, would activate a different link. This more sophisticated way to create links (a set of buttons, a map of the world, whatever) can be particularly attractive and effective. To find out how to do this, see the entry for "MAP."

Variables To link to another site, provide its complete address:

```
<A HREF="http://altavista.digital.com"> Search Engine </A>
```

To link to another file, provide the filename or path:

```
<A HREF="mypict.htm">
```

To link elsewhere in the same document, first establish the location by using the NAME command to create a label (also see Cautions below):

```
<A Name="Hereitis"></A>
```

A

Then, to create a link to that label, use the # symbol. The following link, when clicked by the user, will cause the screen to jump to the location in the document of <A Name="Hereitis">:

```
<A HREF="#Hereitis"></A>
```

Uses

- This is *hypertext*: the user can click on these links or places within a document to jump to other documents, or to other locations within the same document.
- Many Internet pages provide links to other, related sites on the Internet, as a convenience to the user.
- You can also make a graphic image a link, by including it between the <A /A> symbols:

```
<A HREF="keypress.htm"><IMG SRC="ball.JPG"> Click here to go
to an alternative page.</A>
```

Compare the above to this one with no linked image:

```
<A HREF = "#First">First Things</A><BR>
```

Note that a linked image has a frame around it (the BALL.JPG file itself has no frame; a frame is created by the browser to show that it is a link).

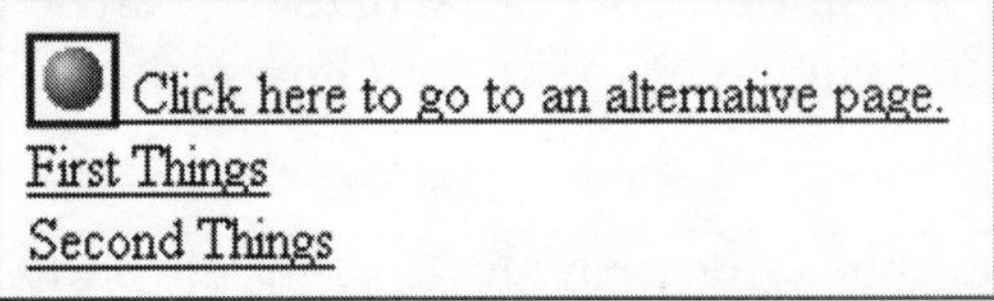

Figure A-1: You can also create links out of graphics. This ball, when clicked, sends the user to another page.

Cautions When you create a label (also called an *anchor*), such as the *Hereitis* in <A HREF="#Hereitis"> </A> (see Variables above), be sure that you use a letter of the alphabet as the first character (not a number): A1 is fine; 1A is not. Also note that these labels are case-sensitive: A1 and a1 are different labels.

A

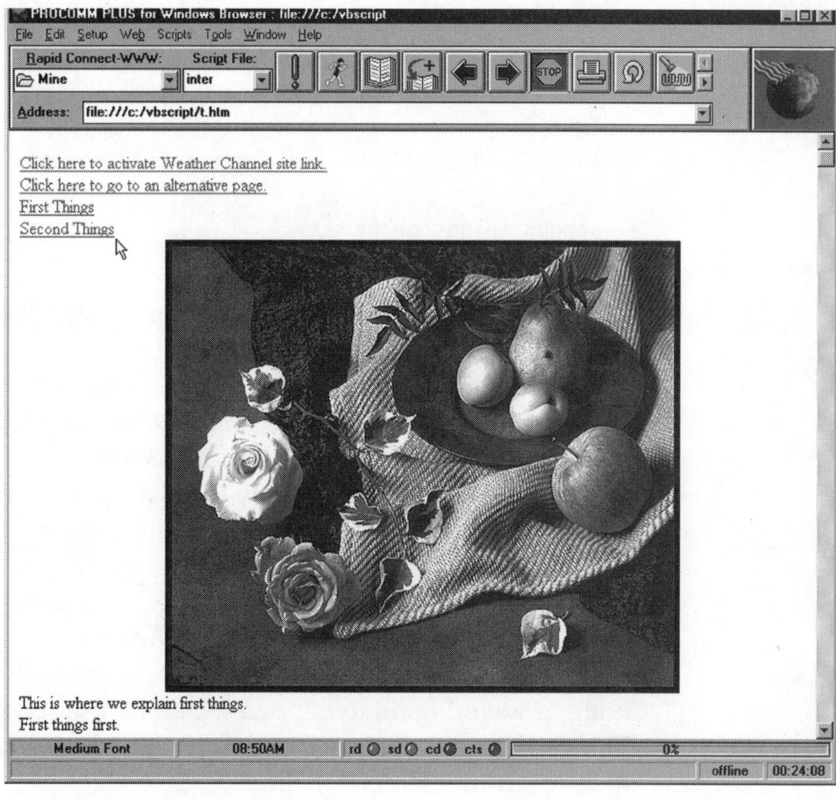

Figure A-2: This page contains all three varieties of text hyperlinks.

Example Here's how to create all three kinds of text hyperlinks.

```
<HTML>
<A HREF="http://www.weather.com/indexwx2.html"> Click here to
activate Weather Channel site link.</A>
<BR>
<A HREF="keypress.htm"> Click here to go to an alternative
page.</A>
<BR>
<A HREF = "#First">First Things</A><BR>
<A HREF = "#Second">Second Things</A><BR>
<BR>
<CENTER><IMG SRC="FRUIT.JPG"></CENTER>
<BR>
```

A

```
<A NAME="First">This is where we explain first things.</A>
<BR>
First things first.
<BR>
<A NAME="Second">This is about second things.</A>
<BR>
Second things go here.
</HTML>
```

The first hyperlink here is created in the first line, and we specify a specific URL (Uniform Resource Locator—a particular address on the World Wide Web of the Internet). When the user clicks on the phrase *Click here to activate Weather Channel site link,* their browser attempts to contact that Web site.

The second hyperlink merely loads another .HTM file (keypress.htm)—and it must be located in the same directory as the original .HTM file.

The third hyperlink causes the browser to jump down to the label (anchor) called "First" at the bottom of the page. We included a large .JPG graphic to show the jump. Without that FRUIT.JPG, nothing would seem to happen when the user clicks on "First Things" because the browser wouldn't have to repaint the screen to move from reference to target.

See also HotSpot, MAP, INPUT

Abs

VBSCRIPT FUNCTION

Description Abs is a rarely used function that gives you back a Variable of the same type. If the Variable was negative (such as –51), Abs changes it to positive (51). If it was positive, it stays positive. In effect, Abs removes a minus sign (–) from any number, if the number has one. You can use any numeric Variable of any type with Abs. (See Variables for more on numeric Variable types.)

Variables

```
x = -12
msgbox Abs (x)
```

OR

```
msgbox Abs(-12)
```

Results in

```
12
```

Uses The only time you'll need to use Abs is when you want to find out the difference between two numbers, but don't know which is the smaller number (in other words, which to subtract from the other). For example, your program is running and you don't know the current numbers in the Variables Payment and Cost. To find out the difference between them, you would program the following:

```
Difference = Abs(Payment - Cost)
```

If Payment = 17 and Cost = 14, then Difference = Abs(Payment – Cost) would result in Difference having a value of 3. (Without the Abs, the results wouldn't be the same in both versions because subtracting the larger from the smaller number would give you a negative number.)

Abs is used when trying to find days-between-dates (see "Date").

Example

```
<HTML>
<HEAD>
<TITLE>Abs Command</TITLE>
</HEAD>
<BODY BGCOLOR=#FFFFFF>
<INPUT TYPE=BUTTON VALUE="Click on me" NAME="Btn">
<CENTER><I><FONT SIZE=12 COLOR=#0000f0>The ABS Command<BR>
</FONT></I></CENTER>
<LEFT>
<INPUT NAME=AA VALUE="0" SIZE=8>
<INPUT NAME=BB VALUE="0" SIZE=8>
<INPUT NAME=CC VALUE="0" SIZE=8>

<SCRIPT LANGUAGE=VBS>
```

A

```
Sub Btn_OnClick
on error resume next

n X = 12:nY = 16: Z = abs(nX - nY)

if AA.VALUE = 0 and BB.VALUE = 0 then
msgbox "Please type in some numbers for X and Y before click-
ing..."
endif

CC.VALUE = ABS(AA.VALUE - BB.VALUE)

End Sub

</SCRIPT>
</FONT>
</BODY>
</HTML>
```

Accelerator

ACTIVEX

See Properties

Action

HTML

See Form

ActiveControl

ACTIVEX

See Properties

ActiveX Control

Description An ActiveX Control can save you a lot of time because considerable functionality is already programmed into it. You can pretty much use it "out of the box." For example, a Chart Control allows you to display many styles of charts with very little work on your part. Without the Chart Control, it would be extremely difficult to graph data and display it to the user in a chart format.

In this book we've included detailed descriptions of the 22 Controls that are currently provided by Microsoft and are stable enough to use in your Internet programming. There are 13 that come with the HTML Layout Control that's available in the Microsoft ActiveX Control Pad: CheckBox, Label, TextBox, ComboBox, ListBox, OptionButton, ScrollBar, SpinButton, Image, HotSpot, ToggleButton, CommandButton, and TabStrip. There are nine that are currently built into Microsoft Internet Explorer 3.0: Animation Button, Chart, Gradient, Marquee, PopUpMenu, PopUpWindow, PreLoader, Timer, and ViewTracker.

Each of these Controls has Properties, Events, and Methods. The Properties, Events, and Methods they have in common, such as Height or BackColor, are described in the entries on "Properties," "Events," and "Methods." Unique Properties, Events, or Methods are discussed in the entry on the Control with which they are associated, as well as in the common Properties, Events, and Methods entries.

Where do you get these Controls? Microsoft is expecting to include them with the Windows 95 upgrade package scheduled for release in late 1996. However, if you download the Microsoft ActiveX Control Pad, it will include the HTML Layout Control and the 13 Controls that come with it. You can download it from http://www.microsoft.com/activex/controls. To get Microsoft's Internet Explorer 3.0 (required for VBS programming), which includes its own set of nine Controls, download it from http://www.microsoft.com/ie.

For more details on the elements of ActiveX Controls, see each Control's entry. For an overview of the idea of *objects* in Internet programming, see "Objects." For a step-by-step tutorial on using the HTML Layout Control and the Microsoft ActiveX Control Pad, see the Introduction.

See Objects, the Introduction, or by specific name such as Label or TextBox

Add

ACTIVEX

See Methods

AddControl

ACTIVEX

See Events

AddItem

ACTIVEX

See Methods

ADDRESS

HTML

Description Causes text to be displayed as italics.

Uses

- Whenever you want to *stress* a word or phrase.
- To provide variety to the look of your pages.

Cautions As shown in the example below, using <ADDRESS> within a phrase forces a line break (a <BR>), pushing the following text down onto the next line on the page. <ADDRESS> was intended to provide the address of the creator of the HTML document, and was supposed to be placed at the bottom of the document so people could contact the creator with any questions or suggestions. For this reason, and because of the internal line break problem, you should use the <I> command when you want italics, rather than <ADDRESS>.

Examples

```
This is <ADDRESS>italic</ADDRESS>
```

Results in

```
This is
italic
```

```
<ADDRESS>This is italic</ADDRESS>
```

Results in

```
This is italic
```

See also I, Cite, Dfn, Em (each of these commands also renders text in italics); see B for boldface

AfterUpdate

ACTIVEX

See Events

Alert

VBSCRIPT FUNCTION

Description Alert works the same way as the MsgBox Function. It pops up a window and displays a message to the user.

See MsgBox

Alignment

ACTIVEX

See Properties

Anchor

HTML

See A

And

See Operators

Animation Button

ACTIVEX CONTROL

Description This button Control offers an alternative to the frequently used Command Button. A Command Button can have a picture on it, but the Animated Button can have a *moving* picture on it.

What's more, you can specify various start and end frames for different conditions like "mouse move," "mouse click," or "got focus" (the user pressed the Tab key until the button became the object on the document with the "focus"). This would permit you to display various different visuals based on what the user is doing in relation to the button.

Variables To specify in VBScript the name of the animation file, assuming this .AVI file resides in the same subdirectory as your document's .HTM file:

```
anbtn1.URL = "win95.avi"
```

To specify which sections (frames) within an .AVI movie should be looped (continuously played) when the user clicks on the animated button, in this example, start with frame 25 and play all frames up to frame 35, then repeat:

```
DownFrStart = 25
DownFrEnd = 35
```

The DefaultFrStart/End Properties describe the frames that should be played if the button does not have the focus (recall that being clicked, the "Down" activity, automatically gives it the focus), and the mouse is not moving over it. It's an attractive effect to display only the first frame (Frame 0) until the user moves the mouse onto the button. At that point, the movie starts. To do that, set the DefaultFrStart and End to Frame 0 (or some other frame, as long as they're both set to the same frame number):

```
Defaultfrstart = 0
Defaultfrend = 0
```

To specify that the entire .AVI should be shown, that all frames be shown, use -1 for the FrEnd:

```
Defaultfrstart = 0
Defaultfrend = -1
```

Properties

DefaultFrStart, DefaultFrEnd, DownFrStart, DownFrEnd, FocusFrStart, FocusFrEnd, MouseoverFrStart, MouseoverFrEnd, URL

Events

Click, DblClick, Enter, Focus, Leave

Methods

AboutBox

Note that Enter and Leave Events are triggered when the user moves the mouse into the button or off the button, respectively.

A

Uses Attract the user's eye with an animated icon or a high-resolution image—all in full motion. An attractive alternative to static elements, such as text links created with the A HTML command. If you offered a weather site, for example, the link to that site could be a picture of a lightning strike in progress.

Cautions

- Unlike the classic Command Button, the animated button Control has no visible elements of its own (such as a frame, a forecolor, or backcolor). The .AVI file is expected to provide whatever visual qualities you'd like displayed on the button.
- If you search your hard drive for .AVI files, you should find a variety of them—ranging from simple cartoon-like animated icons to high-resolution mini-films. You can test your animated button by pointing its URL Property to the full path of one of these .AVI files, or by copying the .AVI file into the same directory where your document's .HTM file resides.
- The .AVI file that you use must be RLE or 8-bit compressed. Also, any starting frame (for any of the various frame segments you can specify with the several FRStart Properties) must be a keyframe.
- The four possible conditions that the animation can be defined for—Down, MouseOver, Focus, and Default—can sometimes overlap. For example, when you left-click the button, you've also thereby given it the focus. Which of the segments within the .AVI file that you've attached to these four conditions (with the FRStart Properties) should be displayed when more than one condition pertains? The rules of precedence are: Down has precedence over all others, Default only pertains when nothing else is happening. Mouseover has precedence over Focus.

Example Within the ActiveX Control Pad, click on the Edit menu, then choose "Insert ActiveX Control." Look for the MicrosoftIE30 Animation Button Control. (For details on ActiveX Controls and how to use the ActiveX Control Pad, see the Introduction to this book.)

You should now see something like the following:

```
<OBJECT ID="anbtn1" WIDTH=127 HEIGHT=71
    CLASSID="CLSID:0482B100-739C-11CF-A3A9-00A0C9034920">
    <PARAM NAME="_ExtentX" VALUE="3360">
    <PARAM NAME="_ExtentY" VALUE="1879">
    <PARAM NAME="defaultfrstart" VALUE="0">
    <PARAM NAME="defaultfrend" VALUE="-1">
    <PARAM NAME="mouseoverfrstart" VALUE="0">
    <PARAM NAME="mouseoverfrend" VALUE="-1">
    <PARAM NAME="focusfrstart" VALUE="0">
    <PARAM NAME="focusfrend" VALUE="-1">
    <PARAM NAME="downfrstart" VALUE="0">
    <PARAM NAME="downfrend" VALUE="-1">
</OBJECT>
```

Note that by default, all the frame Properties are set to display the entire .AVI animation (from frame zero to frame -1).

Drag the button Control until you've made it large enough to display your .AVI file. In the Properties window, find the URL Property and type in the path to an .AVI file on your hard drive. At this point, you should see the animation begin.

Alternatively, you could assign the .AVI file dynamically when your document is loaded or refreshed:

```
<SCRIPT LANGUAGE="VBScript">
<!--
Sub window_onLoad()
anbtn1.URL = "win95.avi"
end sub
-->
</SCRIPT>
```

See also Command Button; A

AREA

Internet Explorer

Description So far, this command only works within Microsoft's Internet Explorer. It is a way of mapping a graphic image so the user can click in one or more zones within the image, and each zone can trigger a separate hypertext link. The coordinates that are used to create the mapping are expressed in pixels.

See the entry for "MAP" or "HotSpot" for a complete description of how to create links using areas within a graphic image. To find out how to make an *entire* graphic image act as a *single* link, see the entry for "A."

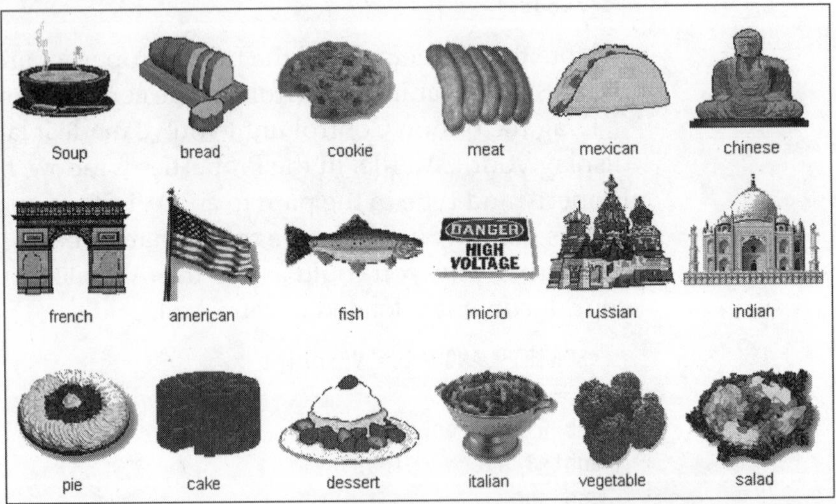

Figure A-3: You can display this single image, but create different links for each zone, each type of food, within the image.

See Map

Arrays

VBScript

A

Description Arrays are Variables that have been clustered together. Once inside an Array structure, the Variables share the same text name and are identified by an *index number*. Since numbers can be manipulated mathematically (and text names cannot), putting a group of Variables into an Array allows you to easily and efficiently work with the entire group. You can manipulate the elements (the items) in the Array by using Loops such as For...Next and Do...Loop structures.

Arrays are used in computer programming for the same reason ZIP Codes are used by the U.S. Postal Service. Picture hundreds of postal boxes with only unalphabetized, unorganized text labels. Imagine the nightmare of sorting thousands of letters each day into boxes that are not in some way indexed or numerically ordered.

Numbers vs. Names: Arrays are extremely useful. For example, if we want to manipulate the names of people coming to dinner this weekend, we can create an Array of their names: Dim Guest (5). This creates six (there is a zeroth item) "empty boxes" in the computer's memory, which serve as spaces for Variables. However, instead of five unique individual labels for the five Variables (like the words "GuestOne," "GuestTwo," and so on), the Variables in this cluster all share the single label Guest, with the individual boxes (Variables) identified by a unique index number from 1 to 5.

To fill this Array with the names of the guests, we assign the names just as we would to normal Variables, but use the index numbers. (You can tell an Array from a regular Variable because Arrays always have parentheses following the Array name.) So here we'll put the names into the Array:

```
Guest(1) = "Lois"
Guest(2) = "Sandy"
Guest(3) = "Rick"
Guest(4) = "Jim"
Guest(5) = "Mom"
```

A

Now these "boxes" somewhere in the computer's memory have been filled with information.

The process of filling an Array can be accomplished a couple of ways: by having the user type in the Array items, or, as we did above, by directly filling the Array with pieces of information.

Now that we have the Array filled, we can manipulate it in many ways, much more efficiently than if we were using ordinary Variables. What if we wanted to know if a particular name existed in the Array?

```
For I = 1 To 5
   If Guest(I) = "Rick" Then Msgbox "Rick has been invited."
Next
```

The key to the utility of Arrays is that you can search them, sort them, or delete from or add to them *using numbers* instead of text labels (unique Variable names) to identify each item in the group. Index numbers are much easier to access and manipulate than text labels.

Why Arrays Are Efficient: As an example, how would you figure your average electric bill for the year? You could go the cumbersome route, using an individual Variable name for each month:

```
JanElect = 90
FebElect = 122
MarElect = 125
AprElect = 78
MayElect = 144
JneElect = 89
JulyElect = 90
AugElect = 140
SeptElect = 167
OctElect = 123
NovElect = 133
DecElect = 125
YearElectBill     =
JanElect+FebElect+MarElect+AprElect+MayElect+
JneElect+JulyElect+AugElect+SeptElect+OctElect+
NovElect+DecElect
```

OR you could use an Array to simplify the process:

```
<HTML>

<HEAD>
<TITLE>Arrays</TITLE>
</HEAD>

<BODY BGCOLOR=#FFFFFF>
<FONT FACE=ARIAL>

<SCRIPT LANGUAGE=VBS>

Sub Btn_OnClick

dim i
dim a
Dim MonthElectBill(13)

on error resume next
cr = chr(13) + chr(10)

MonthElectBill(1) = 90
MonthElectBill(2) = 122
MonthElectBill(3) = 125
MonthElectBill(4) = 78
MonthElectBill(5) = 144
MonthElectBill(6) = 89
MonthElectBill(7) = 90
MonthElectBill(8) = 140
MonthElectBill(9) = 167
MonthElectBill(10) = 123
MonthElectBill(11) = 133
MonthElectBill(12) = 125


for i = 1 to 12
a = a + cstr(i) + ".  " + cstr(MonthElectBill(i)) + cr
next
```

A

```
MsgBox a

End Sub

</SCRIPT>

Click to see your monthly electric bills...
<BR>
<INPUT TYPE=BUTTON VALUE="Click me" NAME="Btn">

</FONT>
</BODY>
</HTML>
```

By grouping all the Variables under the same name, you can manipulate the Variables by individual index number. This might look like a small saving of effort, but remember that your program will probably have to use these Variables in several different situations. Assume that you want to display the entire list. If they're in an Array, you can display them as we did in the example above. But if they're not in an Array, you need to do this to display them:

```
Msgbox cstr(MonthElectBill1)
Msgbox cstr(MonthElectBill2)
Msgbox cstr(MonthElectBill3)
Msgbox cstr(MonthElectBill4)
Msgbox cstr(MonthElectBill5)
Msgbox cstr(MonthElectBill6)
Msgbox cstr(MonthElectBill7)
Msgbox cstr(MonthElectBill8)
Msgbox cstr(MonthElectBill9)
Msgbox cstr(MonthElectBill10)
Msgbox cstr(MonthElectBill11)
Msgbox cstr(MonthElectBill12)
```

Unless you have put these Variables into an Array, you'll have to access each by an individual text name.

Variables Arrays can be created by using either of the two Array-making commands: Dim or ReDim. (See Uses and Cautions for more about using these commands.) Each command defines a *range of influence* or *scope* (which sections of your program can access the Array).

However, both of these commands create Arrays in the same way: by "dimensioning" the new Array. This means that the computer is told how much space to set aside for the new Array. We'll use the Dim command in the examples below, but the ReDim command follows the same rules.

To create space for 51 text Variables that share the label, *Name,* and are uniquely identified by an index number ranging from 0–50, type the following:

```
Dim Names(50)
```

Multidimensional Arrays: The following example will be an Array with twelve "rows" and three "columns." This is a way to associate related information, such as names—each with an address and phone number Variable associated with it. VBScript allows you to create as many as 60 dimensions for a single Array! But few people can visualize, or effectively work with, more than two or three dimensions. That makes sense. We live in a four-dimensional world, but even the fourth dimension, time, is hard to integrate mentally with the other three.

A two-dimensional Array is like a graph, a crossword puzzle, or a spreadsheet—cells of information related in an X,Y coordinate system. A three-dimensional Array is like a honeycomb—it has not only height and width; it also has *depth*.

Most of us check out at this point. A four-dimensional Array cannot be physically constructed, so there is no example of one to study (unless you want to cheat a bit and think of it as a set of several honeycombs). Go beyond four dimensions and you've gone past physics into an abstract domain that would challenge Leonardo.

To make a two-dimensional Array:

```
Dim Names (1 To 12, 1 To 3)
```

You would read a two-dimensional Array like this: X = Names (6,2) to, for example, find out the address of the sixth person, whose *name* would be in Names (6,1) and whose address, you decided, would be in Names (6,2).

Dynamic Arrays: These can be handy because they conserve memory. Dynamic Arrays come into existence in your program when they're needed but then go away as soon as you leave the Event, Sub, or Function in which they reside. The ReDim Statement is used within a Sub or Function to bring a dynamic Array to life:

```
Sub Btn_Click
ReDim Ages (100)
End Sub
```

OR (combine several declarations on one line following a Dim or ReDim command by separating the different Arrays or Variables with commas):

```
Dim A, B( ), Counter(22), X
```

Array Default: Arrays, like all VBS Variables, are of the Variant type (which see). You can therefore mix text, numbers, and date/time data within the same Array.

Uses When you have a collection of related information—such as the names, telephone numbers, addresses, and birthdays of all your friends and relatives—use an Array.

Arrays group Variables under a common name so that they can be identified within a loop or other structure by accessing their index numbers.

Cautions

- When you first dimension an Array, all the elements of a numeric Array are set to 0, and all elements of a text Array (string Array) are set to empty strings (""). If you want to return an Array to this virgin state (after having used it to hold Variables you no longer need), use the Erase command (see the Erase command entry).

- When you dimension an Array, you must pay attention to the scope (the range of influence) you want the Array to have. If you want an Array to be accessible to the entire script—so it can be looked at or changed from any location in your script—you must use Dim instead of ReDim. And the Dim command must be outside of a Sub or Function. If you want the Array to be accessible only from within an individual Sub or Function, use the Dim or ReDim commands within a Sub or Function. If you need to store information that you'll provide to more than a single script, consider using a Cookie (see "Cookies").
- The important difference between the ReDim and Dim commands is that ReDim must be used within a procedure (a Sub or Function), whereas Dim can be used either outside or within a procedure. If Dim is used outside a procedure, the Array will be available for use by all other programming in the script. If Dim is used within a procedure, then, like ReDim, the declared Array is available only to programming that's also within that same procedure. This "range of influence" is known as the scope of a Variable or an Array.
- Use the ReDim command to declare an Array when you want the Array to lose its Variables and be accessible only within the Subroutine or Function within which the Array is declared. (Such an Array is called *local* as opposed to *public*.) This tactic saves space in the computer's memory because the Array is created but then extinguished after the program moves out of that procedure.
- You can't *imply* an Array. Some earlier versions of Basic allow you to imply an Array by just using it, like this:

```
Sub Tri
For I = 1 to 8
  A(I) = I
Next I
End Sub
```

This "implicit" use of Arrays is not permitted in VBS. VBS requires that you formally declare all Arrays. However, VBS *does* allow implicit individual Variables.

- An Array's index numbers start from zero rather than 1.

  The Zeroth Oddity: To a computer, the lowest item in a group is the *zeroth* item. Most humans prefer to think of the floors of a building starting at floor one and going up. Except in England, the first floor is the ground floor. But computers have at least this much in common with the British—the first element of a group is the zeroth.

  This Array will have 26 elements (26 index numbers) ranging from 0 to 25: That's just the way computers operate: Dim X (25).

- The ReDim command is somewhat different from Dim (the other command that creates Arrays). ReDim sets aside space in the computer's memory to *temporarily* hold an Array that will have a brief life and then go away. Arrays created with ReDim expand and then collapse, like a mud bubble in the hot pits at Yosemite Park.

  ReDim works only within an individual Subroutine or Function. A ReDimmed Array comes into existence between the Sub…End Sub or the Function…End Function. It cordons off some of the computer's memory to hold an Array, but when that particular Subroutine or Function is finished doing its work, the set-aside memory is released back to the computer for general use.

  Arrays that bloom and fade like this within a single procedure are called *dynamic* rather than *static*. Static Arrays, created by using the Dim command, offer more persistent storage.

  ReDim can create Arrays with a maximum of 60 dimensions. ReDim can be employed to redeclare an Array that has previously been declared using Dim with empty parentheses (). Such a public Dim command alerts VBScript that this will be an Array but doesn't declare the size of the Array (how many elements it should be sized to hold). When you use this approach, *you can ReDim no more than eight dimensions*.

A

If there is no previous Dim referring to this same Variable (by using the same name to declare it), you can use ReDim to create an Array with as many as 60 dimensions—but who would?

- How often can you ReDim a temporary (dynamic) Array? The number of elements in a ReDimmed Array can be changed at any time:

```
ReDim This(4)
This(3) = "Nadia C."
Msgbox This(3)
ReDim This(5)
This(4) = "Thomas R."
```

  This is perfectly legal. However, while you can change the number of elements, you *cannot* change the number of *dimensions* in the Array.

Wrong:

```
ReDim This(4)
This(3) = "Nadia C."
Msgbox This(3)
ReDim This(5, 2)
This(3,1) = "Thomas R."
```

That second ReDim attempted to create a two-dimensional Array. The Array had already been declared one-dimensional.

See also Dim, Erase, LBound, ReDim, UBound, Variables

Asc

VBSCRIPT FUNCTION

Description In computers, the letters of the alphabet are coded into numbers ranging from 0 to 255. Universal standards—the Unicode, ASCII, ANSI codes—have been adopted. (See the "Chr" entry, and Cautions, below.) The Asc function tells you which numeric value has been assigned to a particular letter, according to the Unicode character code. There is also an AscB function that returns a single-byte value. Asc returns a two-byte Unicode value.

Asc is no longer of much use to the programmer. It used to be more important before Visual Basic came along to handle the input and output for you.

Used with Text characters

Variables To find out the code of a literal text letter:

```
x = Asc("F")
```

OR (lowercase):

```
x = Asc("f")
```

OR (to use a text Variable. If the text contained within the Variable b is longer than a single letter, you get the code of the first letter):

```
b = "Tom"
x = Asc(b)
```

Uses One use for the Asc command is in simple encryption. The user could save text files that are unreadable unless the password is known. (This isn't a very tough code to crack, but it's more trouble than many people would go to.)

First you decide on the code value; here we used 22, but you could allow the user to enter a password and, for example, use the Asc value of the third letter in the password as your "secret code" Variable.

The first loop in this example picks off each character in a, the text Variable we're going to encode. Each character is put into x. Then, we build a new text Variable called "encrypt" by adding each new character after we've distorted it by subtracting our secret code from the Asc value of the original character.

The second loop just reverses the process to decode the encrypted text—in this case we *add* the secret code value to each character and build a text Variable called final.

```
<HTML>

<SCRIPT LANGUAGE=VBS>
dim b
dim ox
secretcode = 22
a = "This is the message."
For i = 1 To Len(a)

b = Mid(a, i, 1)
    ox = Asc(b)
    encrypt = encrypt & chr(ox - secretcode)
Next
For i = 1 To Len(encrypt)
  x = Mid(encrypt, i, 1)
  final = final + Chr(Asc(x) + secretcode)
Next
Msgbox a
Msgbox encrypt
Msgbox final

</SCRIPT>

</HTML>
```

Results in

```
This is the message.
>RS]
  S]
^RO
WO]]KQo|
This is the message.
```

Cautions

```
x = Asc(b)
```

- If the text contained within the Variable b here is longer than a single letter, you get the numeric value of the first letter only.

```
c = ""
```

- This creates a text Variable called a "string-type variant Variable" (*string* means a character or series of characters, as opposed to a true number). In this example, we are providing an empty set of quotation marks and the result is called a "null string." That means it has no characters in it. If you feed a null string to Asc, you'll generate an error when the program is run:

```
x = Asc(c)
```

This entry, Asc, describes character codes used since programming began. But with the 32-bit versions of operating systems now becoming common, things have changed. It was long assumed that since a single byte of memory can express 256 different numbers, a single byte was plenty big enough to hold the alphabet (26 lowercase, 26 uppercase), 10 digits, and miscellaneous punctuation, with room left over for other things like the dingbat of the smiley face.

But what about other alphabets, non-English alphabets? Some of them are rather large, too. OLE, Windows 95, and the NT operating system have abandoned the familiar single-byte ASCII and ANSI codes in favor of a new 2-byte code, UniCode. Two-byte units can express over 65,000 numbers, so UniCode has lots of room to provide code numbers for many alphabets of the world, including Chinese.

In the past, some programmers have relied on text Variables being 1-byte large. They could store, retrieve, and manipulate information efficiently in strings or string Arrays. For example, there is a whole set of string manipulation commands—like Left, Mid, Right, InStr, Chr, Space, and others which were heavily relied on by some for low-level database management programming. In other words, these programmers stored any kind of data, not just text, in string Variables and Arrays. Programs written using these techniques will no longer work correctly in a 32-bit world.

- String manipulation commands, such as Asc in VBScript, work as they always did with text, but in 2-byte chunks. The byte data type does have a few commands dedicated to it: ChrB, RightB, MidB, and LeftB, which work the same way as their namesakes but on the older single-byte characters (instead of the new 2-byte units).

Example

```
Msgbox Asc("x")
```

Results in

```
120
```

See also Chr (this is the opposite of Asc; Chr returns the printable character equivalent of a code number). Unlike Asc, Chr has several uses, particularly to allow you to access and display characters that are not available from a standard keyboard. Chr can also be used to send special configuration codes to the screen or printer.

Atn

VBSCRIPT FUNCTION

Description Atn gives you the arctangent (the inverse tangent) of a number, a numeric Variable, or a numeric Constant. The result is an angle, expressed in radians, of the numeric expression you provided to the Atn command.

Used with Numeric expressions (see Variables)

Variables

```
MsgBox Atn(x)
F = Atn(.5)
```

Uses Advanced mathematics.

If you're working with trigonometry, you'll sometimes need to use the value of pi stored in a Constant or Variable. Here's how to stuff pi into a Variable:

```
p = 4 * Atn(1)
```

Example

```
z = Atn(3.3)
msgbox z
```

Results in

```
1.27656176168371
```

See also Cos, Sin, Tan (other trigonometric functions)

AutoSize

ACTIVEX

See Properties

AutoTab

ACTIVEX

See Properties

AutoWordSelect

ACTIVEX

See Properties

B

B

HTML

Description Causes text to be displayed in **boldface**.

Used with ***Can be enclosed by***

<A>, <ABBREV>, <ABOVE>, <ACRONYM>, <ADDRESS>, <AU>, <B>, <BANNER>, <BAR>, <BELOW>, <BIG>, <BODY>, <BODYTEXT>, <BOX>, <BT>, <CAPTION>, <CITE>, <CODE>, <CREDIT>, <DD>, <DDOT>, <DEL>, <DFN>, <DIV>, <DOT>, <DT>, <EM>, <FIGTEXT>, <FN>, <FORM>, <H1>, <H2>, <H3>, <H4>, <H5>, <H6>, <HAT>, <I>, <INS>, <ITEM>, <KBD>, <LANG>, <LH>, <LI>, <MATH>, <NOTE>, <OF>, <P>, <PERSON>, <PRE>, <Q>, <ROOT>, <S>, <SAMP>, <SMALL>, <SQRT>, <STRONG>, <SUB>, <SUP>, <T>, <TD>, <TH>, <TILDE>, <TT>, <U>, <VAR>, <VEC>

Can enclose

<A>, <ABBREV>, <ACRONYM>, <AU>, <B>, <BIG>, <BR>, <CITE>, <CODE>, <DEL>, <DFN>, <EM>, <I>, <IMG>, <INS>, <KBD>, <LANG>, <MATH>, <PERSON>, <Q>, <S>, <SAMP>, <SMALL>, <STRONG>, <SUB>, <SUP>, <TAB>, <TT>, <U>, <V>

Variables

```
This word is now made <B>bold</B>.
```

Uses

- Whenever you want to make a word or phrase **stand out**.
- Provide variety to the look of your pages.

Cautions There is another command, <STRONG>, that does the same thing.

Example

```
This is <B>bold</B>
```

Results in

This is **bold**

See also STRONG, I

BackColor

ACTIVEX

See Properties

BACKGROUND

HTML

Description You provide the path or URL to a .GIF or .JPG picture, then that picture is put in the background of the body of a document, or the background of a table. If the image is smaller than the size of the document or table, the image will be tiled so that no blank areas are left visible.

Used with BODY, TABLE, TD, TH, TR

Variables

```
<BODY BACKGROUND="keys.jpg">
```

Uses Provide background textures—paper, marble, views of Paris—that underlie the text and other elements of a document or table. Pages look nicer and more professional with backgrounds. And since they are automatically tiled, you can provide relatively small texture files so there need be no serious download penalty. Large, high-resolution graphics can make a user wait quite a while. Small-texture files come in quickly, then tile across the entire browser.

Cautions In the example above we provided only the name of this .JPG file because it is located in the same subdirectory as our document's .HTM file. If it were in another location, we'd have to provide a complete path to the .JPG file.

B

Example This will tile the graphic image BACK1.GIF across the background of the table:

```
<TABLE BACKGROUND="BACK1.GIF" BORDER>
 <TR><TH>Item<TH>Weight<TH>Size<TH>Style<TH>Use
 <TR><TH>Pumiz<TD> 77kg <TD> lg<TD> double <TD ALIGN=CENTER>
With potatoes
 <TR><TH>Dalor<TD> 83kg <TD> exlg<TD> speckled <TD
ALIGN=CENTER> Soups
</TABLE>
```

See also IMG, BODY, TABLE, TD, TH, TR

BackStyle

ACTIVEX

See Properties

BASE

HTML

Description Specifies the document's URL (Internet address). The primary purpose of BASE is to permit the LINK command to refer, by a shortcut, to other pages in the document (see "Link"). Another purpose of including this tag (it's not visible to the user) is that it allows someone who might be reading source code (the HTML programming) to locate the real, original document.

Rather than providing the entire URL (Internet address) to your document each time you refer to it (when using the LINK or A commands), you can merely refer to the BASE address.

Normally, when you're reading source code, you've loaded it into a text viewer (like Notepad) or chosen "Source View" from within a browser (like Netscape or Internet Explorer). Therefore, you already know the .HTM filename—you've got it loaded into your viewer. Nevertheless, it's possible that the source might have been saved as plain text into a text file, or otherwise divorced from the .HTM file. With a BASE tag in the text, you can then track down the .HTM file.

Variables `<BASE>HREF=...</BASE>`

Cautions The BASE command is normally used in the head (see <HEAD>).

Uses Helps you track down an original .HTM file.

Example

```
<BASE HREF="http://www.spydr.com/myhome.htm">
```

BASEFONT

NETSCAPE

Description Changes the basic (default) font size for the document. Note that headlines are *relative* to this base font size. In other words, if you specify a larger BASEFONT, when you then create headlines with the H1, H3, or other headline commands, those headlines will themselves be larger.

Used with ***Can be enclosed by***

<A>, <ADDRESS>, <B>, <BLINK>, <BLOCKQUOTE>, <BODY>, <CENTER>, <CITE>, <CODE>, <DD>, <DT>, <EM>, <FONT>, <FORM>, <H>, <I>, <KBD>, <LI>, <NOBR>, <P>, <SAMP>, <STRONG>, <TT>, <VAR>

Can enclose

Nothing—it has no end command.

Variables The range of SIZE is between 1 and 7, and if you don't use the BASEFONT command, the SIZE defaults to 3. Note that these numbers are merely relative—they don't refer to points, inches, pixels, or any other measurement system.

```
<BASEFONT SIZE=4>
```

Then, if you want to use math to adjust the font size later in your document, you can use the <FONT> command in this way:

```
<BASEFONT SIZE=4>
<FONT SIZE=-2>
```

Results in a font size of 2.

```
<FONT SIZE=+3>
```

Results in a font size of 7.

Uses Set the default font size for all the text in your document.

Cautions The BASEFONT command is currently ignored by all browsers except Internet Explorer and Netscape.

Example

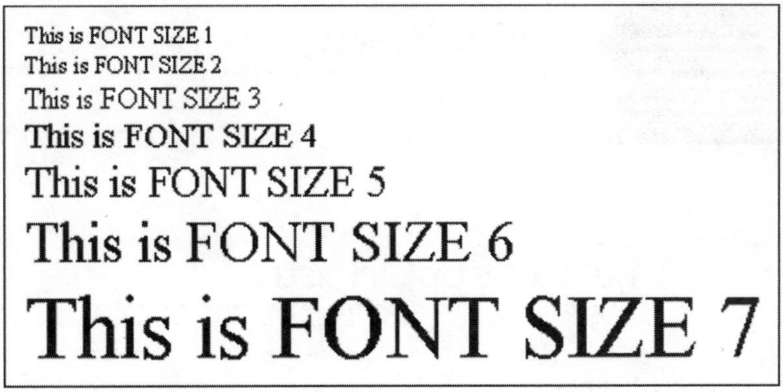

This is FONT SIZE 1
This is FONT SIZE 2
This is FONT SIZE 3
This is FONT SIZE 4
This is FONT SIZE 5
This is FONT SIZE 6
This is FONT SIZE 7

Figure B-1: Adjusting font sizes is easy.

```
<BASEFONT SIZE=2>
<FONT SIZE=-1>
This is FONT SIZE 1
</FONT><BR>
<FONT SIZE=2>
```

B

```
This is FONT SIZE 2
</FONT><BR>
<FONT SIZE=3>
This is FONT SIZE 3
</FONT><BR>
<FONT SIZE=4>
This is FONT SIZE 4
</FONT><BR>
<FONT SIZE=5>
This is FONT SIZE 5
</FONT><BR>
<FONT SIZE=6>
This is FONT SIZE 6
</FONT><BR>
<FONT SIZE=7>
This is FONT SIZE 7
</FONT>
```

See also FONT, H1

BeforeDragOver

ACTIVEX

See Events

BeforeDropOrPaste

ACTIVEX

See Events

BeforeUpdate

ACTIVEX

See Events

BEHAVIOR

HTML

Description Used with the Marquee command, BEHAVIOR=SCROLL, SLIDE, or ALTERNATE. The default is SCROLL, which starts the text entirely off to either the left or right side, then scrolls the text all the way off the opposite side before repeating. SLIDE starts like SCROLL, but the text stops once it reaches the opposite side. ALTERNATE moves text back and forth between each side of the marquee.

See Marquee

BGCOLOR

HTML

Description This command specifies the background color of a document, table, or marquee.

Used with BODY, TABLE (plus TD, TH, and TR), and MARQUEE

Variables This produces the standard Windows gray:

```
<BODY BGCOLOR=COCOCO>
```

You can provide a hexadecimal number that describes the color you're after. (See "Hex Numbers for the COLOR command" in the entry for "BODY.") Alternatively, you can use a common English word for the color.

Uses As an alternative to a plain gray or white background, a background color can be attractive. Consider also the BACKGROUND command, which displays a tiled background graphic (usually a texture) across a document BODY or TABLE.

Many New Colors

```
<BODY BGCOLOR=BLUE>
```

Here are the 16 common color names that work in Netscape as well as Internet Explorer 2.0 and earlier browsers: aqua, black, blue, fuchsia, gray, green, lime, maroon, navy, olive, purple, red, silver, teal, white, and yellow.

To the original 16 color names, Internet Explorer 3.0 adds 124 additional names that you can use: aliceblue, antiquewhite, aqua, aquamarine, azure, beige, bisque, black, blanchedalmond, blue, blueviolet, brown, burlywood, cadetblue, chartreuse, chocolate, coral, cornflowerblue, cornsilk, crimson, cyan, darkblue, darkcyan, darkgoldenrod, darkgray, darkgreen, darkkhaki, darkmagenta, darkolivegreen, darkorange, darkorchid, darkred, darksalmon, darkseagreen, darkslateblue, darkslategray, darkturquoise, darkviolet, deeppink, deepskyblue, dimgray, dodgerblue, floralwhite, forestgreen, fuchsia, gainsboro, ghostwhite, gold, goldenrod, gray, green, greenyellow, honeydew, hotpink, indianred, indigo, ivory, khaki, lavender, lavenderblush, lawngreen, lemonchiffon, lightblue, lightcoral, lightcyan, lightgoldenrodyellow, lightgreen, lightgrey, lightpink, lightsalmon, lightseagreen, lightskyblue, lightslategray, lightsteelblue, lightyellow, lime, limegreen, linen, magenta, maroon, mediumaquamarine, mediumblue, mediumorchid, mediumpurple, mediumseagreen, mediumslateblue, mediumspringgreen, mediumturquoise, mediumvioletred, midnightblue, mintcream, mistyrose, moccasin, navajowhite, navy, oldlace, olive, olivedrab, orange, orangered, orchid, palegoldenrod, palegreen, paleturquoise, palevioletred, papayawhip, peachpuff, peru, pink, plum, powderblue, purple, red, rosybrown, royalblue, saddlebrown, salmon, sandybrown, seagreen, seashell, sienna, silver, skyblue, slateblue, slategray, snow, springgreen, steelblue, tan, teal, thistle, tomato, turquoise, violet, wheat, white, whitesmoke, yellow, and yellowgreen.

Anomaly alert: Note that there are various shades of gray in the above list, including lightslategray, slategray, gray, darkslategray, darkgray, and lightgrey. *Lightgrey?* How did that gray-with-an-e slip in there? That's right, if you spell it *Lightgray* it won't be recognized, so you have to get the misspelling right with Lightgr*e*y. And all the others must be gr*a*y.

Example The background of this table is the color of medium tan wood.

```
<HTML>
<HEAD>
<TITLE>BackgroundColors</TITLE>
</HEAD>
<BODY>

<TABLE BGCOLOR=burlywood BORDER>

 <TR><TH>Item<TH>Weight<TH>Size<TH>Style<TH>Use
 <TR><TH>Pumiz<TD> 77kg <TD> lg<TD> double <TD ALIGN=CENTER>
With potatoes
 <TR><TH>Dalor<TD> 83kg <TD> exlg<TD> speckled <TD
ALIGN=CENTER> Soups
</TABLE>
</BODY>
</HTML>
```

See also BODY, TABLE, TD, TH, TR, MARQUEE

BGPROPERTIES

HTML

Description In the future there may be more, but right now there is only one property of the background—whether or not a background graphic is scrolled (by default it is).

If, however, you want to create a "watermark" that will not be scrolled, use BGPROPERTIES=FIXED.

Used with The BODY command and the BACKGROUND command.

Variables

```
<BODY BACKGROUND="BALL.JPG" BGPROPERTIES=FIXED>
```

Uses Cause a graphic to appear static (if the document is scrolled, the graphic doesn't move). Also note that your graphic will be displayed *tiled*: if it's not as large as the window, the browser will fill the background with as many repetitions of the graphic as necessary to fill the window.

B

Example Start the Microsoft ActiveX Control Pad running and put enough text or other elements onto the document so that it will have enough content to be scrolled. Then, in the BODY definition, type this:

```
<BODY BACKGROUND="FIN.JPG" BGPROPERTIES=FIXED>
```

In place of "FIN.JPG," put the name of a .GIF or .JPG graphic file that's located in the same directory as your .HTM file for this document. When you load this .HTM file into Internet Explorer 3.0, you'll see that you can scroll the text, but the graphic remains stable and does not scroll.

See also BODY

BGSOUND

INTERNET EXPLORER

Description Plays a .WAV (or .AU) sound file, or a MIDI music file. When your page is loaded, the music or sound effects begin. You can cause the sound to play continuously by using the LOOP=INFINITE command.

Variables

```
<BGSOUND SRC="radiogag.mid">
```

OR

```
<BGSOUND SRC="gong.wav">
```

OR, to cause the sound to play four times:

```
<BGSOUND SRC="boing.wav"LOOP=4>
```

OR, to cause the sound to play continuously:

```
<BGSOUND SRC="boing.wav"LOOP=INFINITE>
```

Uses Add some excitement to your Web page.

Cautions The sound will begin playing as soon as the user loads your page. The user can replay the sound by choosing the Refresh (or Reload) option in their browser. The user can stop the sound by choosing the browser's Stop option.

Example
```
<BGSOUND SRC="moria.mid" LOOP=INFINITE>
```


BIG

HTML

Description Causes the text to go one size higher than its default size within the browser.

Variables
```
<BIG>Make this larger</BIG>
```

Example
```
<HTML>
<BODY>
NORMAL SIZE
<BIG>HELLO ONE SIZE BIGGER</BIG>
BACK TO NORMAL
</BODY>
</HTML>
```

See also FONT

BLOCKQUOTE (or BQ)

HTML

Description Indents a paragraph from both the left side and the right side. This punctuation is typically used when you're quoting a long passage. For short quotes, use quotation marks and keep the sentences within the body of your text. For long quotes, use BLOCKQUOTE.

Used with ***Can be enclosed by***

<BANNER>, <BODY>, <BODYTEXT>, <DD>, <DIV>, <FIGTEXT>, <FN>, <FORM>, <LI>, <NOTE>, <TD>, <TH>

Can enclose

<BODY>, <BODYTEXT>, <CREDIT>

Variables <BLOCKQUOTE>...</BLOCKQUOTE>
<BQ>...</BQ>

Uses To indicate that a passage within your document is quoted, not your own writing.

Cautions This same punctuation—quotation marks used for short excerpts and double-indenting for longer passages—is used in books and magazines.

Example

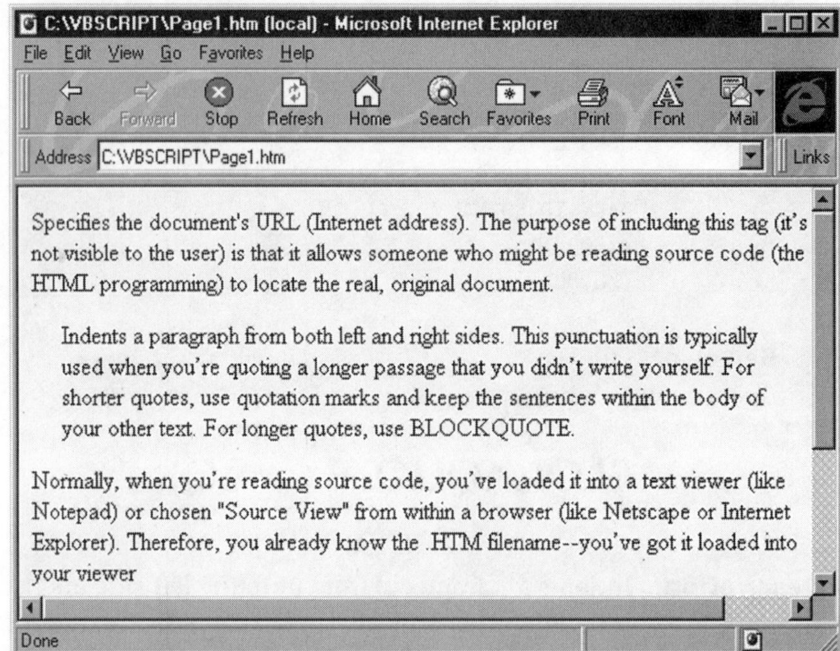

Figure B-2: Set off long excerpts with a block quote.

```
<HTML>
  Specifies the document's URL (Internet address). The pur-
pose of including this tag (it's not visible to the user) is
that it allows someone who might be reading source code (the
HTML programming) to locate the real, original document.
<BLOCKQUOTE>
  Indents a paragraph from both left and right sides. This
punctuation is typically used when you're quoting a longer
passage that you didn't write yourself. For shorter quotes,
```

```
use quotation marks and keep the sentences within the body of
your other text. For longer quotes, use BLOCKQUOTE.
</BLOCKQUOTE>
  Normally, when you're reading source code, you've loaded it
into a text viewer (like Notepad) or chosen "Source View"
from within a browser (like Netscape or Internet Explorer).
Therefore, you already know the .HTM filename--you've got it
loaded into your viewer.
</HTML>
```


BODY

HTML

Description This is an optional command—most browsers will work fine if you don't use it. However, there are a number of Variables you can use with it, such as setting a wallpaper background or setting the background color. BODY is intended to let browsers know that between <BODY> and </BODY> are the elements of the page that the user should see (as opposed to the nonvisual elements contained within the <HEAD></HEAD> section of a document).

Used with ***Can be enclosed by***

<HTML>

Can enclose

<A>, <ABBREV>, <ACRONYM>, <ADDRESS>, <AU>, <B>, <BANNER>, <BIG>, <BLOCKQUOTE>, <BODY>, <BODYTEXT>, <BQ>, <BR>, <CITE>, <CODE>, <DEL>, <DFN>, <DIR>, <DIV>, <DL>, <EM>, <FIG>, <FN>, <FORM>, <H1>, <H2>, <H3>, <H4>, <H5>, <H6>, <HR>, <I>, <IMG>, <INS>, <ISINDEX>, <KBD>, <LANG>, <MATH>, <MENU>, <NOTE>, <OL>, <P>, <PERSON>, <PRE>, <Q>, <S>, <SAMP>, <SMALL>, <STRONG>, <SUB>, <SUP>, <TAB>, <TABLE>, <TT>, <U>, <UL>, <VAR>

B

Variables There are several optional commands you can use with the BODY command.

You can use it by itself:

```
<HTML><BODY>This is a complete Web Page!</BODY></HTML>
```

Wallpaper

Use with the BACKGROUND command, to create tiled wallpaper. Note that for simplicity's sake, when testing put the .GIF or .JPG image file in the same directory as your original .HTM file.

```
<BODY>BACKGROUND="ROUGH.GIF">
Your page goes here.
</BODY>
```

Color

This is a Netscape command. You can specify the background color using hexadecimal numbers (see "Hex Numbers for the COLOR command" below). Essentially, the paired numbers specify the red, green, and blue content of the color. For example, if you wanted pure red, you would use FF0000; green is 00FF00; blue is 0000FF.

You can also use a set of ordinary English words, like *red*, instead of the hex number. The following words are recognized: black, white, green, maroon, olive, navy, purple, gray, red, yellow, blue, teal, lime, aqua, fuchsia, silver. These words also work with the following commands: TEXT, LINK, VLINK, COLOR, BORDERCOLOR, BORDERCOLORLIGHT, BORDERCOLORDARK.

This produces the standard Windows gray:

```
<BODY BGCOLOR=COCOCO>
```

OR, to use a common English word for the color

```
<BODY BGCOLOR=BLUE>
```

Watermark

A "watermark" is a graphic image, but it remains in the same position on the screen if the user scrolls your page. It also doesn't tile (repeating itself all over the background to fill the space). Note that if you only provide its filename, the .GIF or .JPG image file must reside in the same directory as your original .HTM file, or you must provide a complete path. To freeze the background, you set the BGPROPERTIES command to FIXED:

```
<BODY BACKGROUND="water.gif" BGPROPERTIES=FIXED>
```

Margins

These are Internet Explorer commands. You can set the margins of your page, in pixels. It varies, but you can roughly estimate 100 pixels to the inch. You can define the top or left margin:

```
<BODY LEFTMARGIN=100 TOPMARGIN=120>
```

Link Colors

These are Netscape (and IE3.0) commands. You can specify the color of hypertext links (see "A"):

```
<BODY LINK=GREEN>
```

and the color a link changes to after the user has visited that site:

```
<BODY VLINK=YELLOW>
```

Text Color

This is a Netscape command. You can specify the color of text:

```
<BODY TEXT=BLACK>
```

Hex Numbers for the COLOR Command

The computer doesn't count the way we do. You can visualize computer memory as tiny "light bulbs," and light bulbs can only be on or off. The computer bases its counting on a two-state, or *binary*, method.

We, on the other hand, use a *decimal*, or 10-state, counting method. We do this because we started counting by using our fingers. The number 3 always represents the same *idea* in any counting system, but how you *group* numbers determines how you'll manipulate them when dividing, counting change, and so on.

There are implications that arise from this distinction between us humans and computers. For one thing, we naturally divide numbers into groups that are multiples of 10: 100, 1,000, and so on. Computers, by contrast, naturally create divisions based on the powers of 2 (a *power* is a number multiplied by itself): 2, 4, 8...1,024, and so on. For example, computer memory is measured in kilobytes which should, by definition, mean 1,000 bytes, since *kilo* means 1,000. But to the computer, a kilo of something is 1,024 because that's a natural boundary when you count by twos. And 1,000 isn't.

Binary means two states, like a light bulb. A single *bit* is one of these binary objects—capable of either being on or off, true or false. However, for convenience, bits are often expressed as a group of eight bits called a *byte.* Another common counting unit in computer math is—*hexadecimal* or *hex*, and unlike our familiar 10-base decimal counting method, hex is based on 16 different digits.

Decimal	Hex	Binary
0	00	00000000
1	01	00000001
2	02	00000010
3	03	00000011 (1 plus 2)
4	04	00000100
5	05	00000101 (4 plus 1)
6	06	00000110
7	07	00000111
8	08	00001000
9	09	00001001
10	0A Note digit "A"	00001010
11	0B	00001011
12	0C	00001100
13	0D	00001101
14	0E	00001110
15	0F	00001111
16	10 Note new column	00010000
17	11	00010001

Table B-1: Decimal, hexadecimal, and binary numbers.

As you can see in the preceding table, column position matters when writing hex or binary numbers. A 2 in the "singles" column in decimal means 2. But in the 10's column, it means 20. Similarly, in the list of hexadecimal numbers, 2 in the rightmost column means 2, but in the next column over it means 32. Hex numbers are represented by a column of 1's, then the next column represents 16's. That's why hex numbers sometimes have A through F in them—you run out of the familiar 10 digits 0-9, and so A, B, C, D, E, and F are used to represent 10, 11, 12, 13, 14, and 15. Note that it's easiest to read hex numbers from right to left, starting with the least significant digits.

Notice also that hex and binary are quite similar. If you divide the eight digits of a binary number into two zones, they directly relate to the two columns of the hex equivalent: hex 10 (which represents decimal 16) is quite clearly the same as binary 0001 0000.

The first thing to remember about hex is that instead of the familiar decimal symbol 10, hex uses the letter *A* because 10 is where decimal numbers run out of digits (we only count with the symbols 0-9) and start over again with a 1 and a 0. The difference is that, in hex, the 1 in the "10's" column is really a decimal 16. *The second column in a hex number is a "16's" column.* Eleven, in hex, means 17 in decimal. To figure out the real meaning of a hex number, just multiply the left column by 16, and add the right column to it. Thus, 1A would be 1 * 16 plus 10, or 26. And, by extension, when you have additional columns in a hex number, you should use the powers of 16 for each column.

For example, the hex number 1011 would be translated by remembering that the rightmost column is the 1's, the next column from the right is the 16's. Therefore, 11 is 17. However, the next two digits from the right, 10, are also translated first (into 16), then multiplied by 256 (16 times 16, or 16^2), resulting in 4113.

Uses

- Set elements of the background, left and top margins, and the color of links and text.
- Distinguish the HEAD from the BODY of the source code for a document.

Cautions You should avoid setting the default colors for links—let the user specify the default in the Preferences section of their browser.

Example

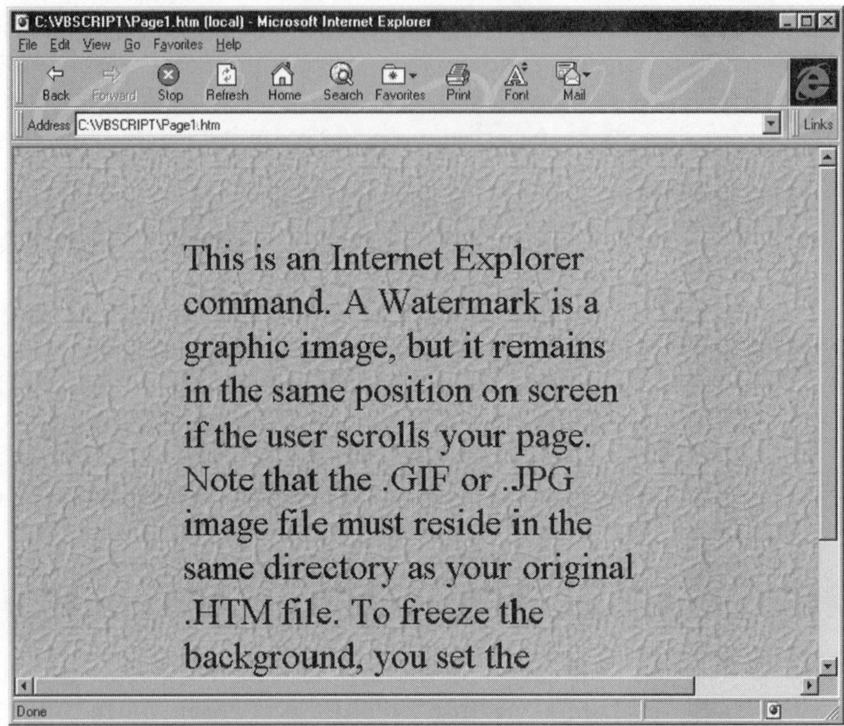

Figure B-3: We're using margins and a wallpaper background on this page.

```
<HTML><BODY BACKGROUND="rough.gif" LEFTMARGIN=150
TOPMARGIN=75>
<FONT SIZE=+3>
  This is an Internet Explorer command. A Watermark is a
graphic image, but it remains in the same position onscreen
if the user scrolls your page. Note that the .GIF or .JPG
image file should reside in the same directory as your
original .HTM file.
</BODY></HTML>
```

See also HEAD

Bold

ACTIVEX

See Properties

B

BORDER

HTML

Description Adds a border around an image or table. The thickness of the border is determined by the number you provide. When used with a graphic (the IMG command), the border will not be visible unless the image is being used as a hyperlink (with the A command). When invisible, the border around a graphic merely serves to set it off from surrounding text or the browser edges.

When the BORDER command is used with a table, BORDER specifies whether or not there is a set of lines around the table and each cell. BORDER, used by itself, defaults to a thickness of 1 but can be made larger: BORDER=5, for example, displays very thick frames. If you leave out the BORDER command, the table will have no lines around it, or around the individual cells within it.

The color of a border around a table is determined by the BORDERCOLOR (or BORDERCOLORLIGHT and BORDERCOLORDARK) commands. You can get very particular about the border, specifying different colors for the highlight and shadow elements of the border (see BORDERCOLOR).

Used with The IMG and TABLE commands.

Variables

```
<IMG SRC="rough.gif" BORDER=14>
```

OR

```
<TABLE BORDER=3 BGCOLOR=BLUE BORDERCOLOR=BLACK width=70%>
<TR><TD>Our table is blue</TD></TR>
</TABLE>
```

Uses If you decide you want a frame around an image or a table, use the BORDER command. It's also used to specify the size of the border.

Example

```
<TABLE BACKGROUND="BACK1.GIF" BORDER>
 <TR><TH>Car<TH>MPG<TH>Color<TH>Style<TH>Doors
 <TR><TH>Dorice<TD> 28 Highway <TD> Blue<TD> Sedan <TD
ALIGN=CENTER> 4
 <TR><TH>Caprix<TD> 26 Highway <TD> Black<TD> Wagon <TD
ALIGN=CENTER> 6
</TABLE>
```

See also IMG, TABLE, BORDERCOLOR

BorderColor

ACTIVEX

See Properties

BORDERCOLOR, BORDERCOLORLIGHT, BORDERCOLORDARK

HTML

Description When you use a border with a TABLE, you can specify its color with the BORDERCOLOR command. What's more, you can define a highlight (BORDERCOLORLIGHT=LIME) and a shadow (BORDERCOLORDARK=GREEN) element for the border. A highlight is created by using lighter-colored lines along the top or left of the entire table, and also along the top or left of the cells within it. The shadow is created by using darker lines for the bottom and right sides of the table and the cells within it.

Used with The TABLE and BORDER commands.

Variables For the BORDERCOLOR commands to have any effect, the TABLE must first have a border (you must use the BORDER command), then you can also specify a BORDERCOLOR:

```
<TABLE WIDTH=40% HEIGHT=75% BORDER=3 BORDERCOLOR=RED>
```

B

To specify the shadow portion of a 3-D border, use BORDERCOLORDARK; to specify the highlight portion of a 3-D border, use BORDERCOLORLIGHT:

```
<TABLE WIDTH=40% HEIGHT=75% BORDER=3 BORDERCOLORDARK=GREEN
BORDERCOLORLIGHT=LIME>
```

You can define colors with either hexadecimal numbers or, as we've done in these examples, ordinary English words like *Green* or *Lime*. For a complete list of all 140 English word colors you can use, see "Many New Colors" in the entry on "BGCOLOR." For an explanation of hexadecimal, see "Hex Numbers for the Color Command" in the entry on "BODY."

Uses Create more attractive tables.

Example

```
<TABLE WIDTH=40% HEIGHT=75% BORDER=3 BORDERCOLOR=peachpuff>
<TR><TH><TH>Hamburg<TH NOWRAP>Berlin Main Station
<TR><TH>9:00AM<TD> On Time <TD> 10 Minute Delay
<TR><TH>10:00AM<TD> On Time <TD> On Time
<TR><TH>11:00AM<TD> 4 Minute Delay <TD> On Time
<TR><TH>12:00 Noon<TD> On Time <TD> On Time
</TABLE>
```

See also BORDER, TABLE, COLOR, BGCOLOR

BorderStyle

ACTIVEX

See Properties

BoundColumn

ACTIVEX

See Properties

BR

HTML

B

Description Inserts a line break (moves the text down one line). To insert a blank line between two lines of text, use

.

Used with ***Can be enclosed by***

<A>, <ABBREV>, <ACRONYM>, <ADDRESS>, <AU>, <B>, <BANNER>, <BIG>, <BODY>, <BODYTEXT>, <CAPTION>, <CITE>, <CODE>, <CREDIT>, <DD>, <DEL>, <DFN>, <DIV>, <DT>, <EM>, <FIGTEXT>, <FN>, <FORM>, <H1>, <H2>, <H3>, <H4>, <H5>, <H6>, <I>, <INS>, <KBD>, <LANG>, <LH>, <LI>, <NOTE>, <P>, <PERSON>, <PRE>, <Q>, <S>, <SAMP>, <SMALL>, <STRONG>, <SUB>, <SUP>, <TD>, <TH>, <TT>, <U>, <VAR>

Can enclose

Nothing. It's a stand-alone command.

Variables To insert a simple line break:

```
<BR>
```

To insert multiple blank lines:

```
<BR><BR><BR><BR><BR>
```

To insert a *vertical* blank space to prevent text from "flowing" around a graphic image, use the CLEAR command with LEFT, RIGHT, or ALL. See the example.

Uses

- Separate paragraphs.
- Format your pages.

Example

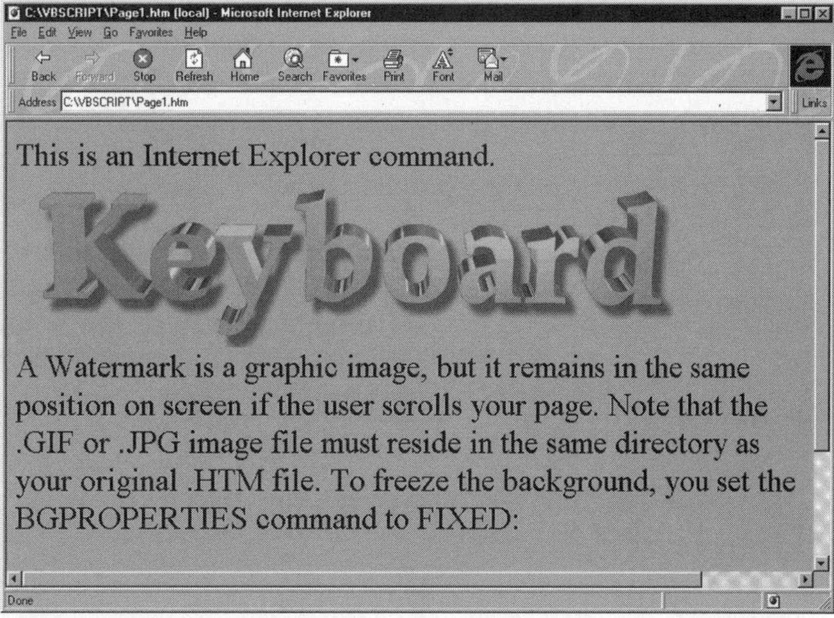

Figure B-4: When you use the CLEAR command, you can prevent text from "wrapping" or "flowing" around a graphic image.

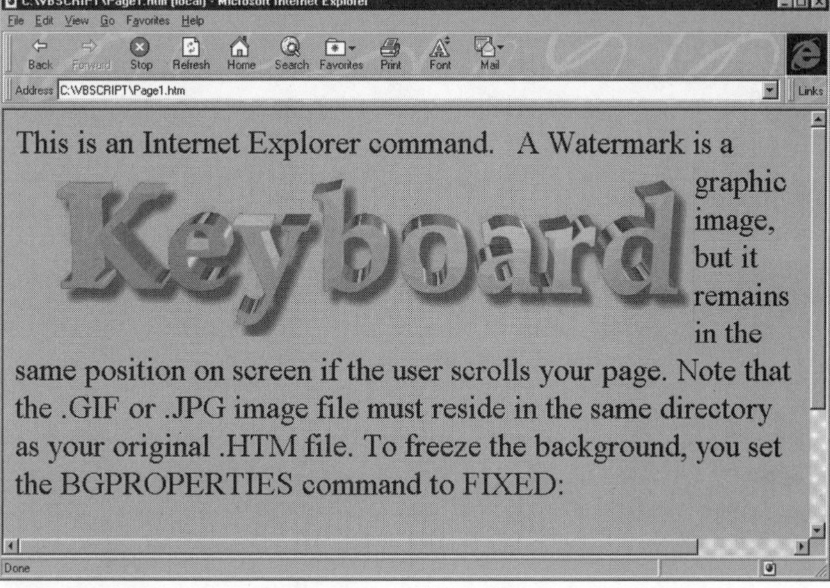

Figure B-5: Without the CLEAR command, text will wrap around a graphic—that's the default in HTML.

B

Figure B-4 was produced with the following programming:

```
<HTML>
<FONT SIZE=+3>
This is an Internet Explorer command.
<IMG SRC="keys.jpg" ALIGN=LEFT>
<BR CLEAR=LEFT>

  A Watermark is a graphic image, but it remains in the same
position onscreen if the user scrolls your page. Note that
the .GIF or .JPG image file must reside in the same directory
as your original .HTM file. To freeze the background, you set
the BGPROPERTIES command to FIXED:

</HTML>
```

See also P, PRE

C

Caching

See PreLoader

Call

VBSCRIPT STATEMENT

Description This Statement is somewhat unusual in that it's never really needed. As far as VBS is concerned, the following two lines will accomplish exactly the same thing:

```
BEEPER
CALL BEEPER
```

Like other holdovers from early versions of the Basic computer language (such as the Let command), Call is included to permit compatibility with programs written some time ago, or to allow people to use it for personal reasons. It *can* make your programs more readable because it immediately identifies a line of programming as a *Subroutine call,* not some other command within VBScript itself.

Subroutines are quite important in programming. They allow you to write little self-contained "black boxes" that can be plugged into any section of your script to perform a specific function. They're plugged in by simply using the name of the Subroutine. It's as if you're adding a new command to VBScript.

C

"Calling" a Subroutine: If you write a Subroutine, you can activate it merely by using its name, in this example *Show1*:

```
Show1
Sub Show1
  Msgbox "One"
End Sub
```

In this script, a message box will appear as soon as the page is loaded into a browser. However, without the Show1 line, nothing will happen. A Sub, by itself, will do nothing until it's explicitly *called* by using its name. This will do nothing:

```
Sub Show1
  Msgbox "One"
End Sub
```

The Call command can, optionally, be used in addition to merely using the name of a Subroutine:

```
Call Show1
```

Note that if you write some useful Subroutines, you can save them as a text file and then use them in other scripts by simply pasting them into your new scripts.

Used with Subroutines (see "Sub")

Variables

```
Call Sort
```

OR (to provide Variables to the called Subroutine, list them after the name of the Sub, enclosed in parentheses):

```
Call Sort (WhatToSort).
```

Uses Subroutines (and their close relatives, Functions) are valuable when you are going to need to do something repeatedly in different parts of your program. See the example below or see "Sub."

Cautions If you *do* use Call, you must put any *arguments* in parentheses. Arguments are Variables you want to send to the Subroutine you are calling (see the example). If you don't use Call (merely name the Subroutine when you want to use it), you must *not* use parentheses.

Example Let's say that you want to use different titles on your Message Boxes, depending on the current situation or on what buttons the user clicks. You could, of course, simply type in the titles, but sometimes it's easier to create a single Subroutine and accept a Variable (the title in this case). This can make your scripts easier to read, easier to update, and, if the Subroutine is lengthy, it makes your scripts shorter by avoiding repeating the (nearly) identical programming over and over.

Make a Subroutine and name it whatever you want:

```
Sub ShowMsg (Msg, Title)
Msgbox Msg, 0, Title
End Sub
```

Now any time you want a message, from anywhere in your script, you can simply do this:

```
ShowMsg "Hello", "Greeting"
```

OR

```
A = "Hi": B = "Howareya?"
ShowMsg A, B
```

OR

```
Call ShowMsg ("Good Luck", "Happy")
```

See also Function, Sub

Cancel

ACTIVEX

See Properties

CanPaste, CanRedo, CanUndo

ACTIVEX

See Properties

CAPTION

HTML

C

Description Adds a brief description to a table.

Used with The TABLE command

Variables

```
<CAPTION>
This caption will be below the table.
</CAPTION>
```

By default, all captions are centered and located at the bottom of a table. However, you can use the ALIGN=TOP command to position the caption at the top (the caption will be centered at the top). If you use ALIGN=RIGHT or ALIGN=LEFT, the caption will be at the top but will be left-aligned like most books and magazines, or right-aligned, which looks pretty strange.

```
<CAPTION ALIGN=LEFT>
This caption will be on top and left-aligned.
</CAPTION>

<CAPTION ALIGN=RIGHT>
This caption will be on top and right-aligned.
</CAPTION>

<CAPTION ALIGN=TOP>
This caption will be above the table.
</CAPTION>
```

Use Describes for the user the purpose or contents of a table.

Example

```
<HTML>
<HEAD>
<TITLE>Caption</TITLE>
</HEAD>
<BODY BGCOLOR=WHITE>
<HTML>
<TABLE WIDTH=40% HEIGHT=75% BORDER=4 BORDERCOLORDARK=GREEN
BORDERCOLORLIGHT=peachpuff>
<TR><TH><TH>Hamburg<TH NOWRAP>Berlin Main Station
```

```
<TR><TH>9:00AM<TD> On Time <TD> 10 Minute Delay
<TR><TH>10:00AM<TD> On Time <TD> On Time
<TR><TH>11:00AM<TD> 4 Minute Delay <TD> On Time
<TR><TH>12:00 Noon<TD> On Time <TD> On Time
<CAPTION ALIGN=LEFT>
This caption will be left aligned at the top of the table.
</CAPTION>
</TABLE>
</HTML>
</BODY>
</HTML>
```

See also TABLE

Caption

ACTIVEX

See Properties

cBool

VBSCRIPT FUNCTION

Description There are nine functions that do pretty much the same thing: cBool, cByte, cDate, cDbl, cInt, cLng, cSng, cStr, and cVerr. Each of these commands can transform a Variant Variable from its current "subtype" into a different subtype. Although all Variables in VBS are, technically speaking, of the Variant *type*, a Variant has different *subtypes*.

What all this means in practical terms is that when a Variable is holding text, the Variable is of the "text" subtype. When it's holding a small number with no decimal points, it's of the "integer" subtype. All this happens automatically—you generally don't have to worry about it—because when some data is loaded into ("assigned") to a Variable, the correct subtype is created by VBS. However, there are times when you'll want to change the subtype. Sometimes you'll want to be explicit about which subtype you want it to be. For example, if you've been working with non-fractional integers, and decide you want to start seeing fractions in the results, you would use cSng (or cDbl) to *coerce* the Variable into a new, fraction-capable subtype. For more on the meaning and qualities of the various subtypes, see "Variables." For more on Variants, see "Variant."

Numeric Variable Types: Beyond the text (or, as it's called, "string") subtype, there are several subtypes of numbers in Visual Basic Script, each having different strengths and weaknesses. Some, such as the Integer type, can hold only a limited range of numbers and are less precise than others. Other types are more precise (featuring many decimal places) or have larger ranges; but these take up more room in the computer's memory and take longer to compute.

A Variant data type looks at what you are doing at a particular place in your script and *knows* that you need some precision (some numbers beyond the decimal point):

```
X = 15/40
```

will result in .375 as the answer. The result of any math will be correct up to five digits to the right of the decimal point. In other words, the Variant will have transformed X into what's called the "single" subtype, because a single can hold fractions. However, if you did this:

```
X = 1 + 2
```

X would be transformed into the Integer subtype, which doesn't handle fractions. Why all these subtypes? Because the computer, like us humans, can calculate faster if it is allowed to ignore decimal places. So it's useful to have a plain vanilla Integer subtype—it's fast. But when fractions are necessary to do the job you want to do, you want a different subtype.

The *Boolean* subtype is the simplest numeric Variable. It can contain only two numbers: 0 and -1. Zero represents "false" or "off" and -1 represents "true" or "on." It's used for things like toggling—each time the user does something, you toggle the Variable:

```
Dim toggle
Toggle = Not Toggle
```

Here's an example that displays a message box every other time you click on the button.

```
<HTML>
<HEAD>
<TITLE>Array Command</TITLE>
</HEAD>
<BODY>
<INPUT TYPE=BUTTON VALUE="Click here to see Array"
NAME="Btn">
<SCRIPT LANGUAGE=VBS>
Dim toggle
Sub Btn_OnClick
Toggle = Not Toggle
if toggle then msgbox "YES, toggled!"
End Sub
</SCRIPT>
</BODY>
</HTML>
```

Used with Variables, to change a Variable into a Boolean subtype.

Variables To change a Variable into a Boolean subtype:

```
money = cBool (12)
```

(this would reduce 12 to -1, telling you only that there was some money, but the actual amount, 12, would be lost)

OR to change a "literal number" into a Boolean type:

```
dollarscents = cBool (15.88888)
```

OR to change a numeric expression (see "Variables") into a Boolean type:

```
money = cBool (somenumber + 15)
```

OR to change a numeric expression (see "Variables") into a Date type:

```
ourday = cDate (somenumber + 5)
```

C

Uses There aren't many practical uses for cBool. Use it if you ever need to force a result to a simple, binary value. One can't really imagine when you ever would. However, there are uses for some of the other "coercion" commands.

Use cInt (for simple integers) or cDbl (for large numbers with fractions) if you want to change a text variable type into a numeric (computable) variable. For more on this, see "Variables." Use cStr to force real numbers to become text digits. Note that the older Basic commands Str and Val are now abandoned in favor of cStr and cInt (or some other numeric coercion command).

The cDate command might seem to duplicate the behavior of the DateValue or TimeValue commands. There is a difference, though. DateValue converts to the date format, whereas TimeValue converts to the time format. cDate converts *both* date and time.

Cautions

- If you ever need to find out what subtype a Variable currently is, use the VarType command (which see).
- Some numbers, such as 1 divided by 3, can generate endless digits to the right of the decimal point. There must be a limit to the physical size of numbers that the computer can work with, or you could fill the computer's memory with infinite digits by this simple instruction:

```
X = 1/3
```

The computer would go on generating a series of .33333333s until it filled up with them or burned down, whichever came first. But try this:

```
X = 1/3
Msgbox X
```

Results in

```
.3333333
```

But if you use one of the "coercion" functions, cLng for example, you can force X to become a different "flavor" of Variable, thereby getting more digits—15 instead of 7. The cLng command makes a Variable into a double-precision floating-point number, and it can carry a fraction out further than a single-precision floating-point numeric Variable type. (See "Variables" for descriptions of the various subtypes.) In other words, different subtypes of Variables have different ranges and different degrees of precision. *Range* used here means the span of numbers that a Variable can contain (the Integer type has a small range, from –32,768 to 32,767). *Precision* means how many digits can be used to express the fractional portion to the right of the decimal. The greater the range or precision, the longer it takes the computer to calculate the result. And the more memory the Variables take up. That's why you're allowed the option of coercing a great range or precision by using one of the commands beginning with C that transforms a variant Variable into a different subtype.

Here's the effect of giving the Variable X a double-precision specificity:

```
X = 1/3
Y = CDbl(1/3)
Msgbox Y
```

Results in

```
3333333333333333
```

Unless you're involved in scientific work—astronomy or atomic physics, for example—where you're dealing with extremely large or small numbers, you can usually ignore these issues surrounding numeric Variable subtypes. You need to know that they exist as a resource and how to use them if necessary, but most of your everyday applications would never need such precision or range. Most computing involves real-world number ranges. Therefore, you normally won't need to use the C-functions. Just use *X* or *Y* or *BowlingScores*. And the new Variant default number type will make intelligent adjustments to the "type" for you.

Example To see the effect of cBool, try this:

```
x = 123
MsgBox cBool(x)
MsgBox cBool(x) + 3
```

After you use cBool, x becomes "true" when displayed in a message box. When you add 3 to it, it becomes 2 because the actual arithmetic is -1 + 3.

See also Variables; Variant; VarType; Int

C

cByte, cDate, cDbl

VBSCRIPT FUNCTION

See cBool

CENTER

NETSCAPE & INTERNET EXPLORER 3.0

Description Centers any text or graphics between <CENTER> and </CENTER>

Used with ***Can be enclosed by***
<BLOCKQUOTE>, <BODY>, <DD>, <FORM>, <LI>

Can enclose
<A>, <ADDRESS>, <B>, <BASEFONT>, <BLINK>, <BLOCKQUOTE>, <BR>, <CENTER>, <CITE>, <CODE>, <DIR>, <DL>, <EM>, <FONT>, <FORM>, <H>, <I>, <IMG>, <ISINDEX>, <KBD>, <LI>, <MENU>, <NOBR>, <OL>, <P>, <PRE>, <SAMP>, <STRONG>, <TT>, <UL>, <VAR>, <WBR>

Uses Make your pages look more symmetrical. This command is typically most useful with headlines or graphics because centered body text can often look strange. Exceptions include company information, addresses, or other such non-narrative body text.

Example

```
<CENTER> This is centered. </CENTER>
This is not.
```

Change

ACTIVEX

See Events

Chart

ACTIVEX CONTROL

Description With this Control you can display chart data. There are seven chart styles you can use: Pie Chart, Point Chart, Line Chart, Area Chart, Column Chart, Bar Chart, and Stock Chart. What's more, there is more than one flavor of each of these styles (for example, there is a "Simple" stock chart and a Wall Street Journal stock chart). Here are pictures of each of the 21 different ChartTypes:

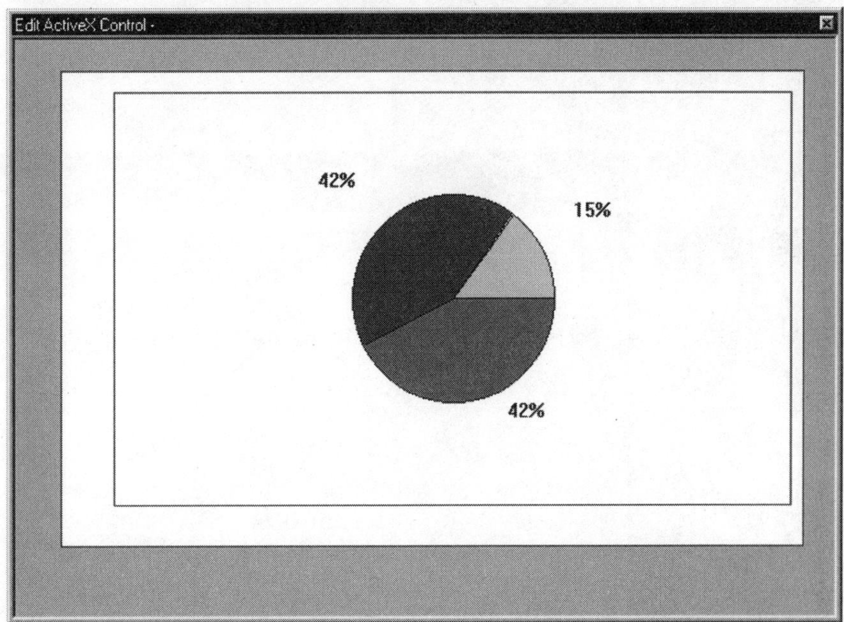

Figure C-1: ChartType = 0: The Simple Pie Chart.

C

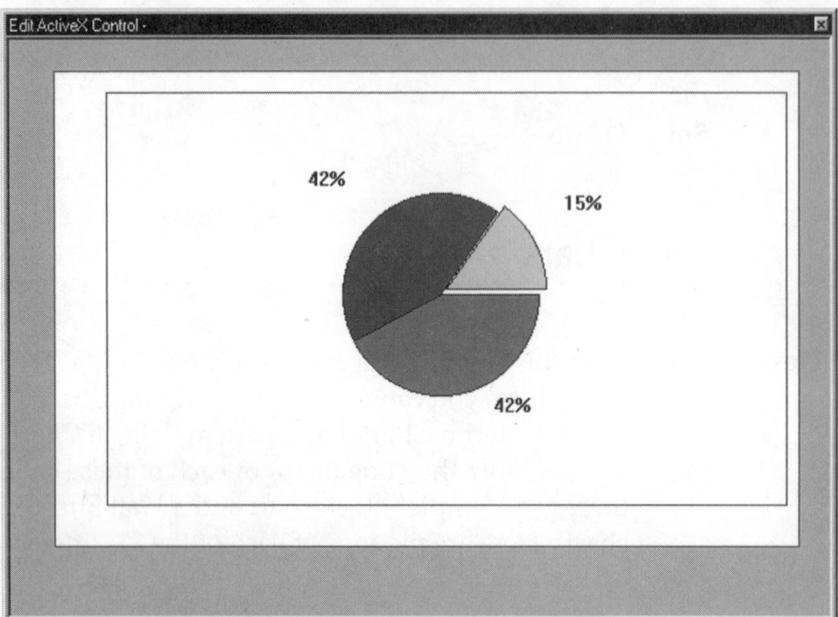

Figure C-2: ChartType = 1: The Special Pie Chart.

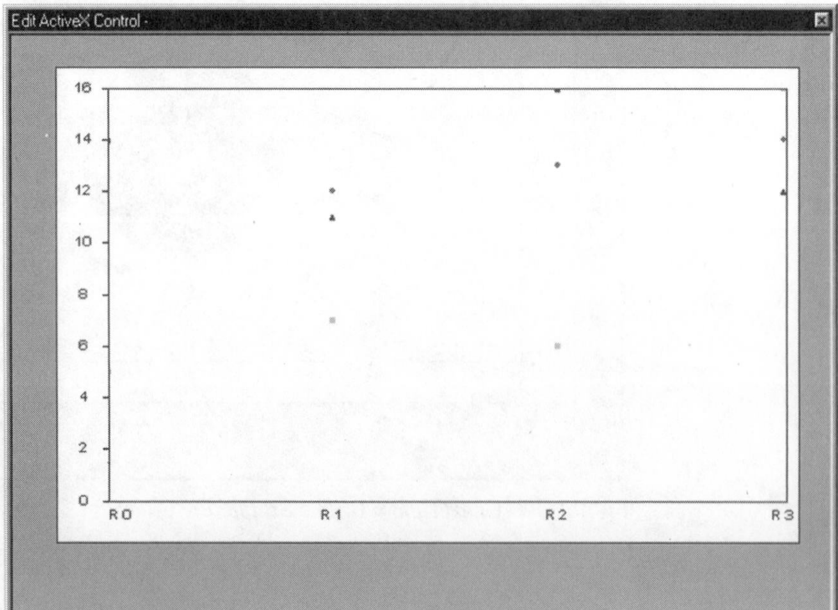

Figure C-3: ChartType = 2: The Simple Point Chart.

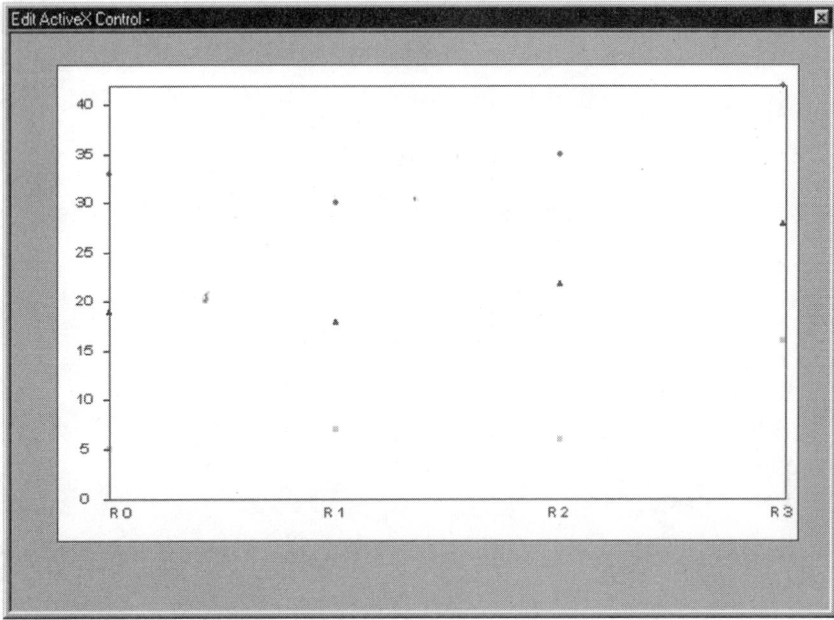

Figure C-4: ChartType = 3: The Stacked Point Chart.

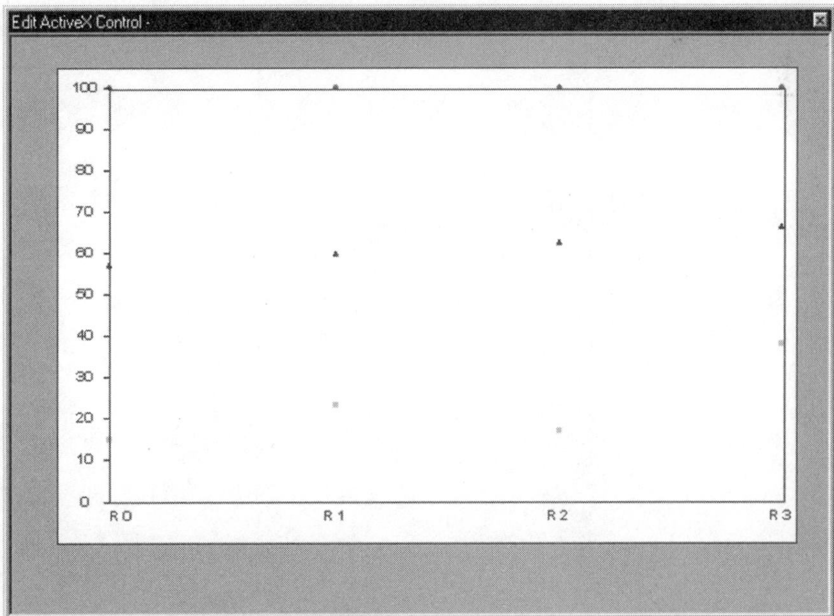

Figure C-5: ChartType = 4: The Full Point Chart.

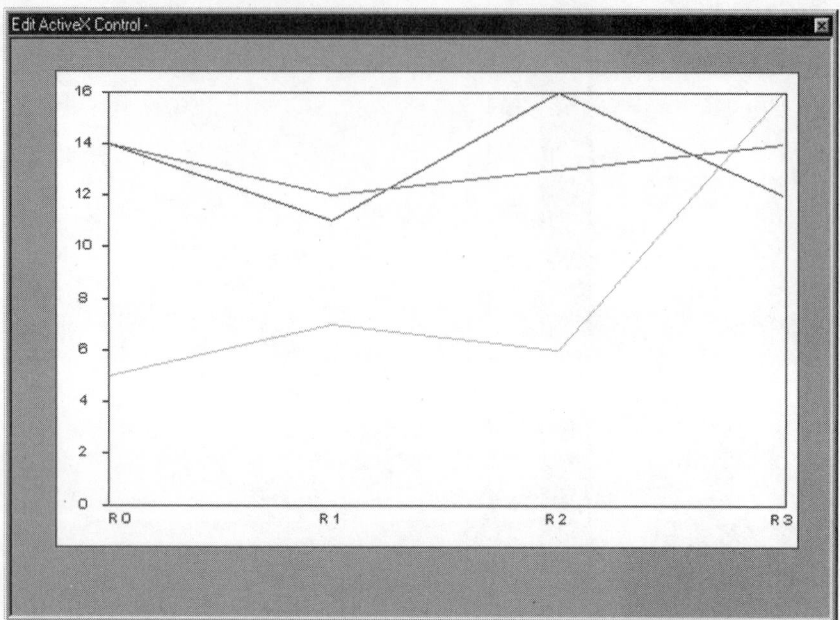

Figure C-6: ChartType = 5: The Simple Line Chart.

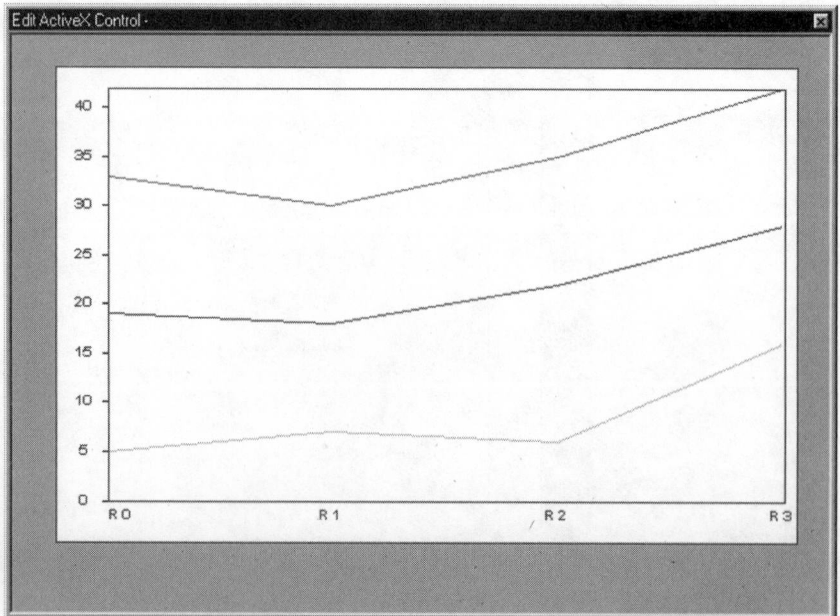

Figure C-7: ChartType = 6: The Stacked Line Chart.

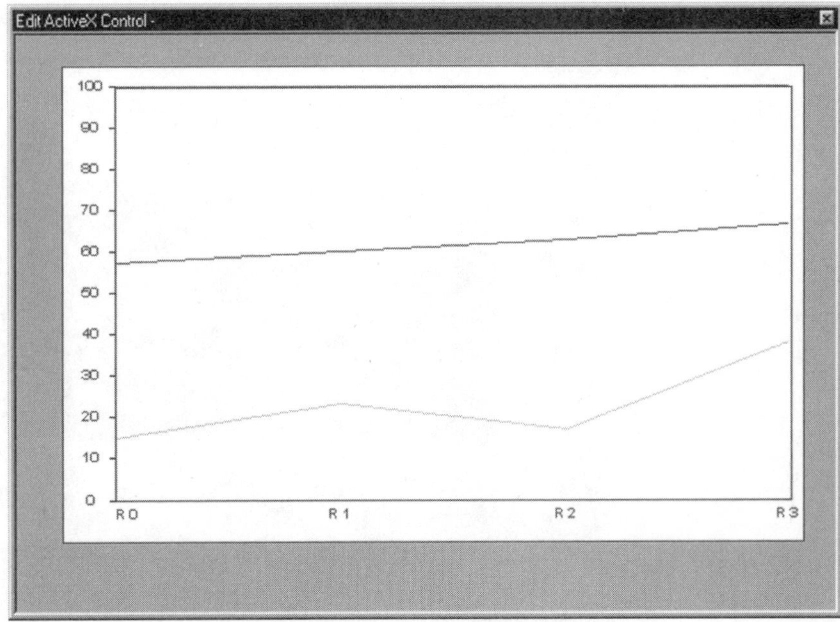

Figure C-8: ChartType = 7: The Full Line Chart.

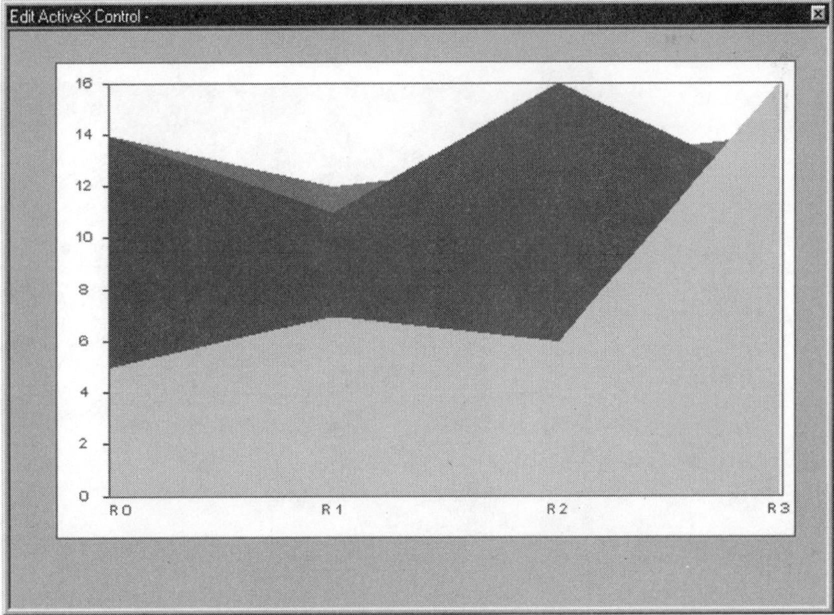

Figure C-9: ChartType = 8: The Simple Area Chart.

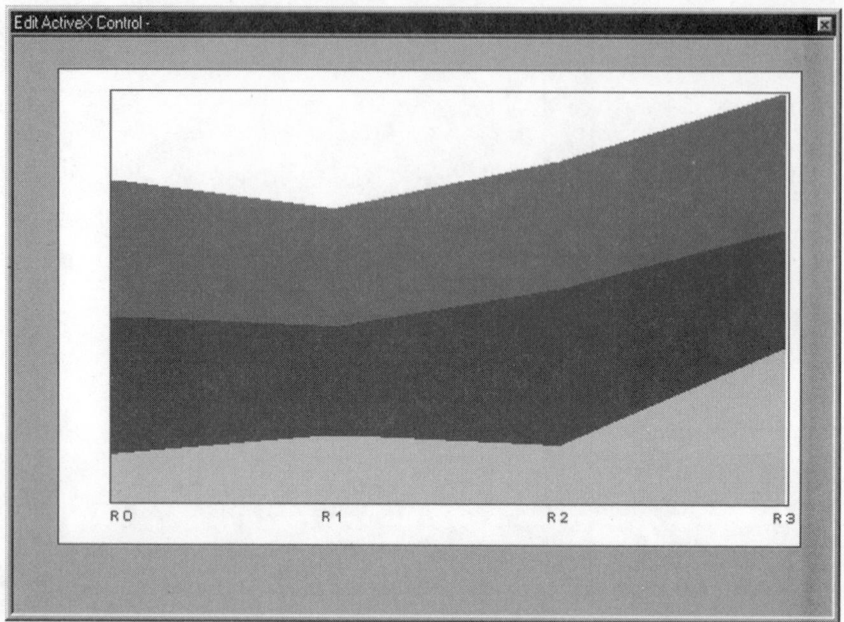

Figure C-10: ChartType = 9: The Stacked Area Chart.

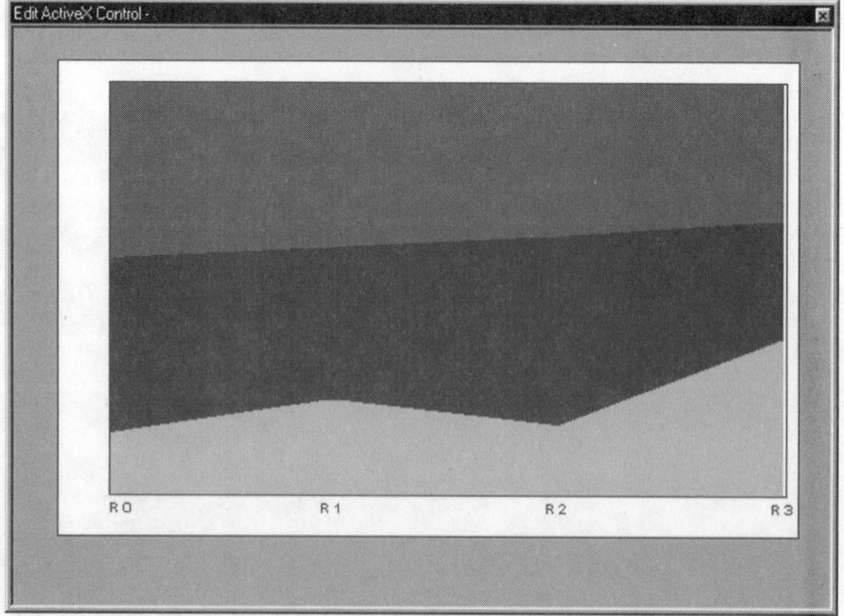

Figure C-11: ChartType = 10: The Full Area Chart.

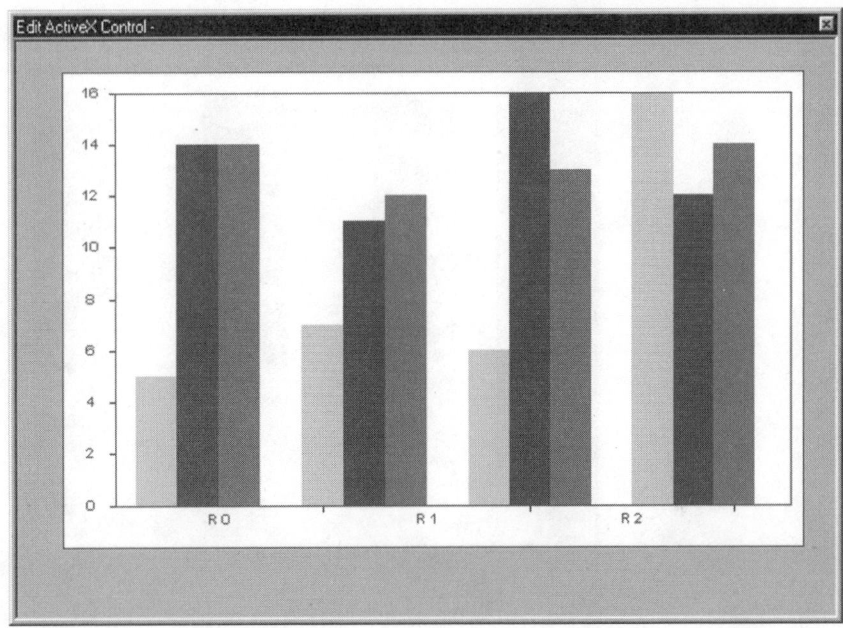

Figure C-12: ChartType = 11: The Simple Column Chart.

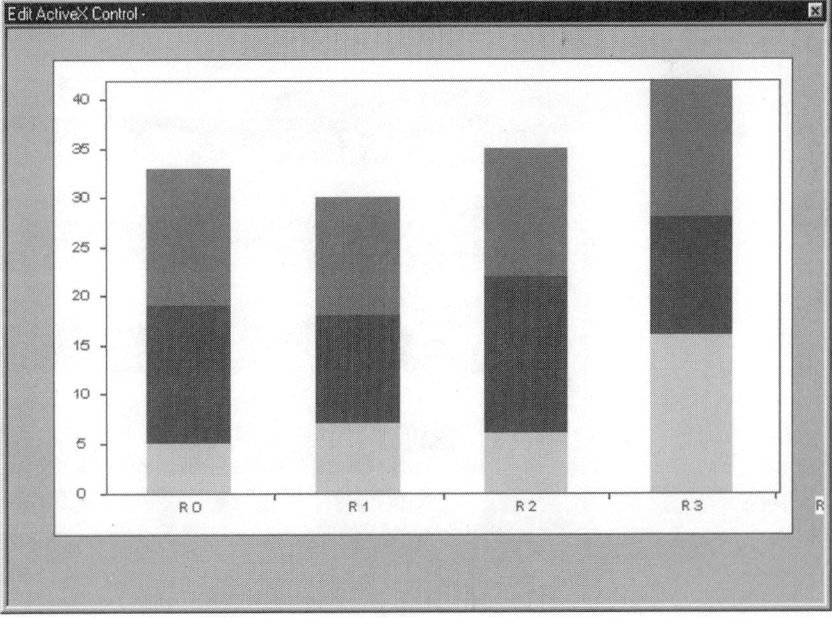

Figure C-13: ChartType = 12: The Stacked Column Chart.

C

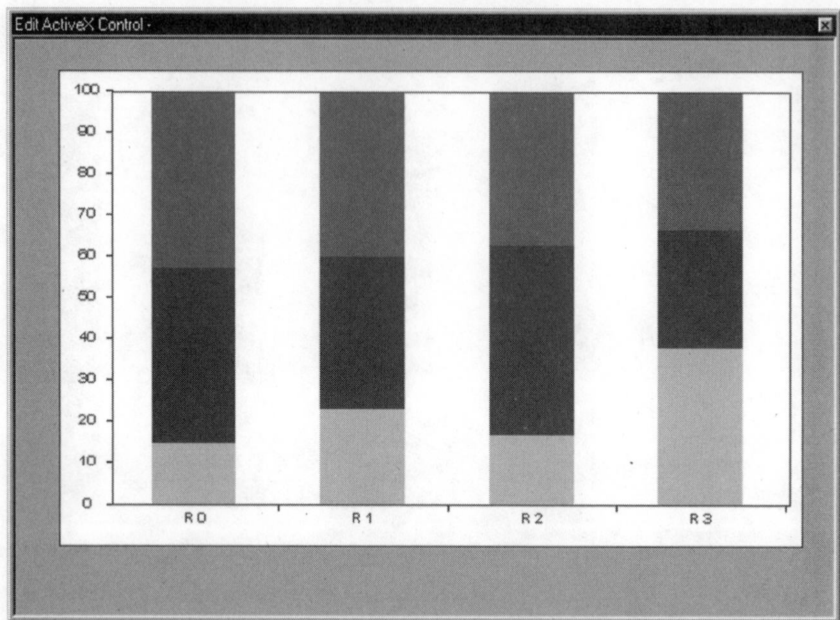

Figure C-14: ChartType = 13: The Full Column Chart.

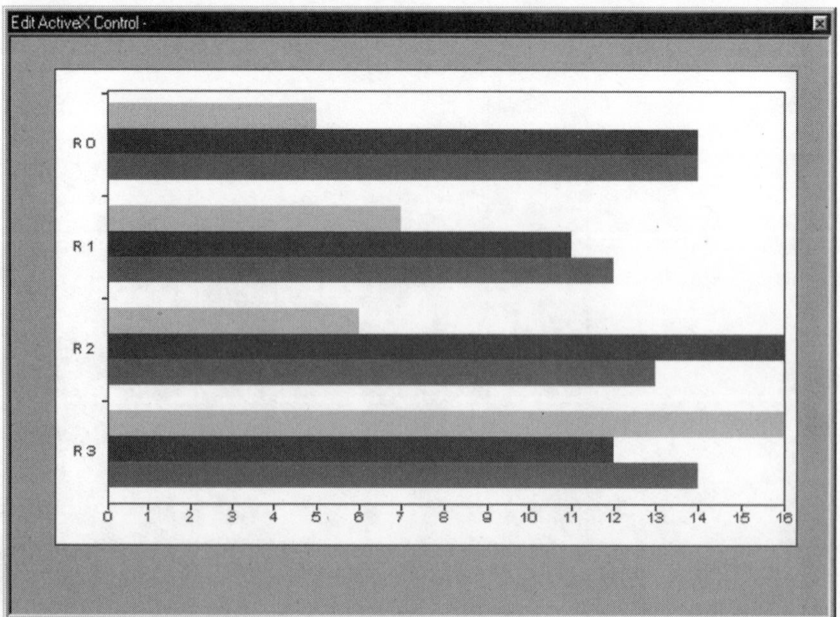

Figure C-15: ChartType = 14: The Simple Bar Chart.

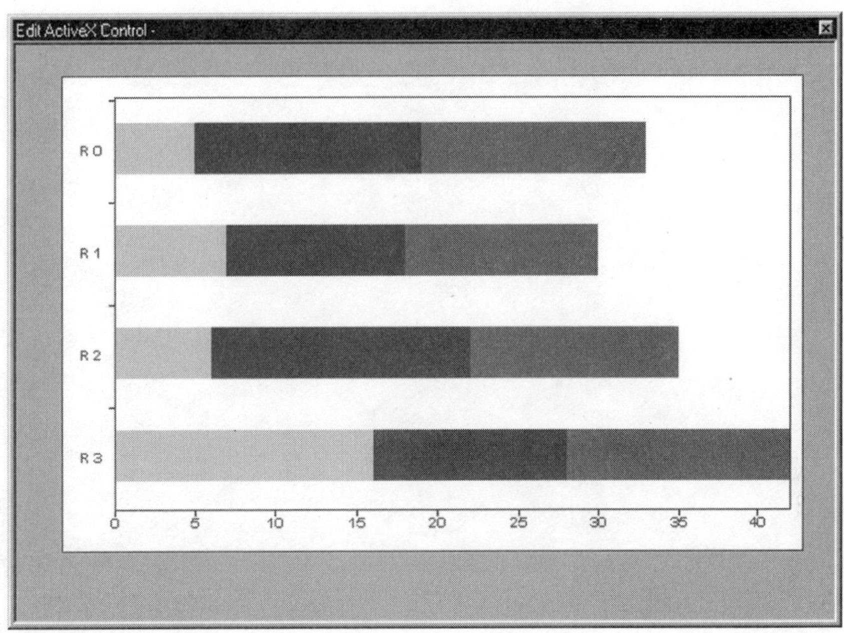

Figure C-16: ChartType = 15: The Stacked Bar Chart.

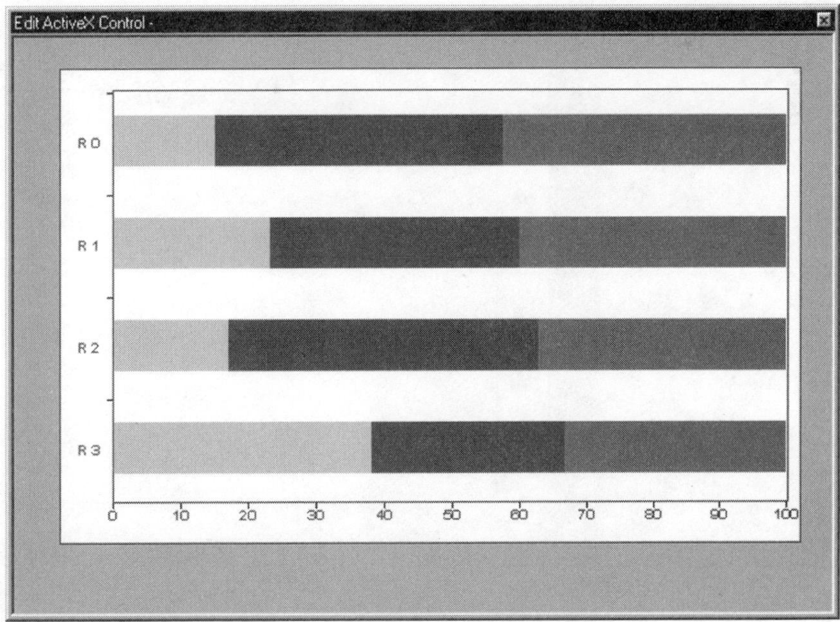

Figure C-17: ChartType = 16: The Full Bar Chart.

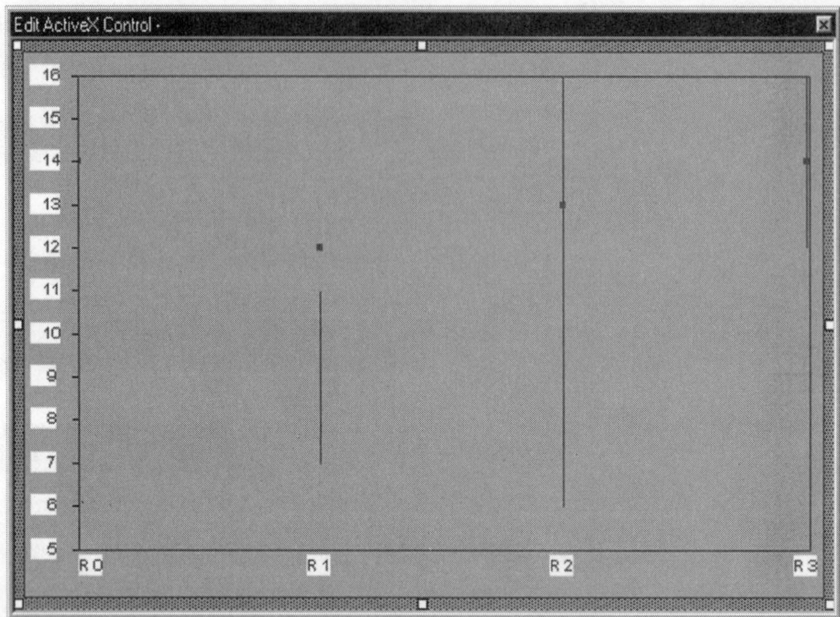

Figure C-18: ChartType = 17: The HLC Simple Stock Chart.

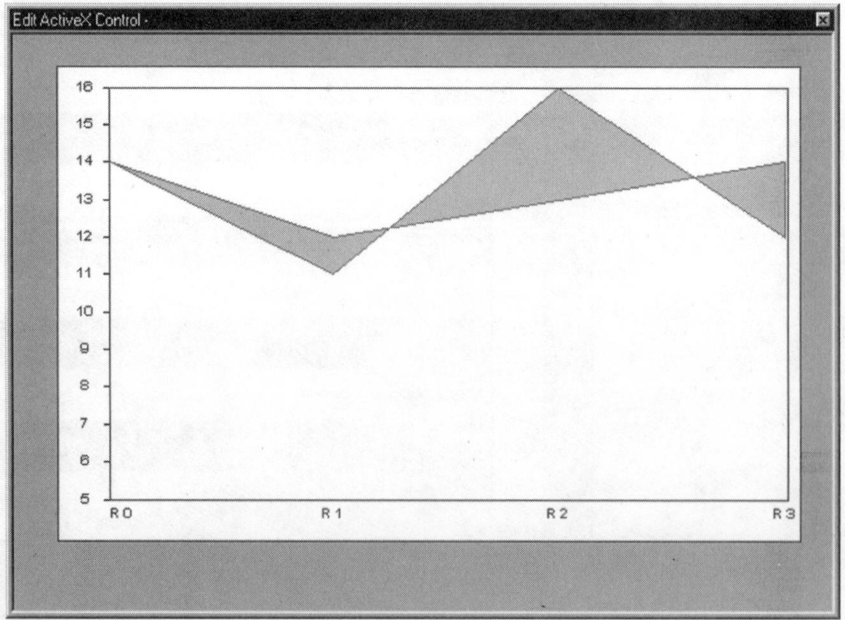

Figure C-19: ChartType = 18: The HLC WSJ Stock Chart.

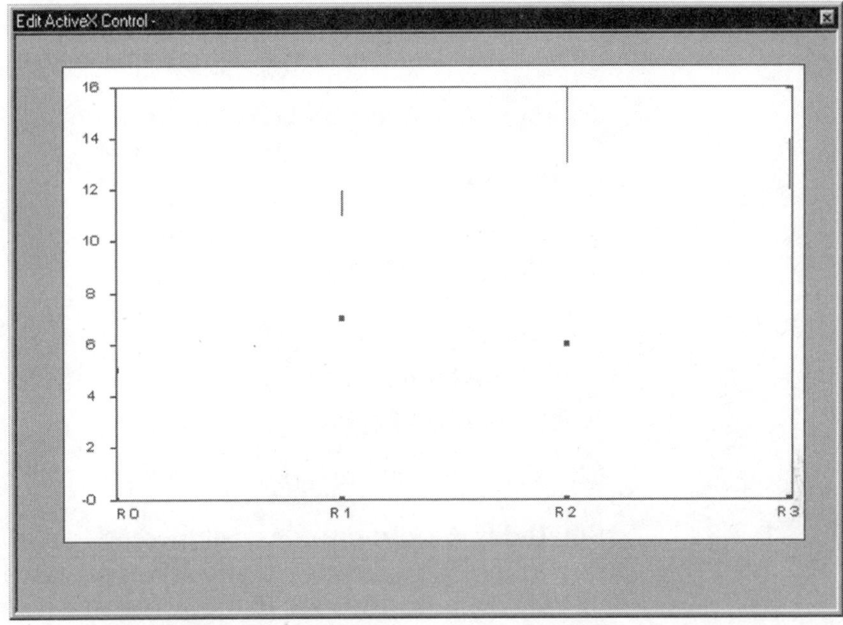

Figure C-20: ChartType = 19: The OHLC Simple Stock Chart.

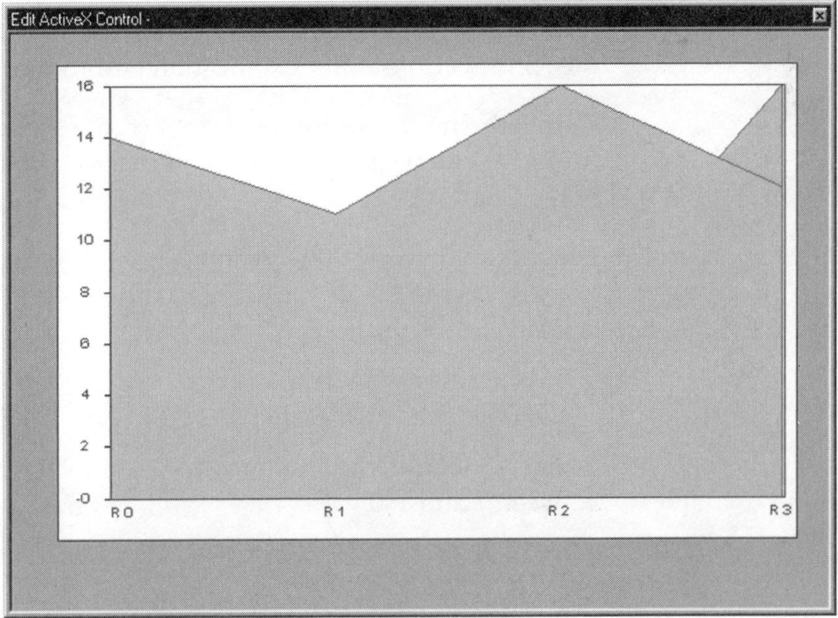

Figure C-21: ChartType = 20: The OHLC WSJ Stock Chart.

Variables ***Properties***

Rows: The number of rows in your data array.

Columns: The number of columns in your data array.

HGridStyle: Draws horizontal grid lines.

VGridStyle: Draws vertical grid lines.
0 No Grid
1 Solid Grid
2 Bold Grid
3 Dotted Grid
4 Bold Dotted Grid

ChartType: See figures above.

RowIndex & ColumnIndex: Set these in the Properties Window, then you can change the DataItem Property (the quantity that's in this row/column) or the ColumnName or RowName (the label that appears on the chart to identify that column or row). ColumnName and RowName can be highlighted at the top of the Properties Window, then press the Del key if you want no labels.

DataItem: The value, the number in a particular coordinate (RowIndex/ColumnIndex) location within the chart's data.

ColorScheme: There are five preset color schemes (ColorScheme=0 to 4). These colors are used to fill in areas in some of the ChartTypes.

BackStyle: If you set this to Transparent (0), the background color or wallpaper in the document will show through (except for the labels).

```
0 Transparent
1 Opaque (default)
```

Scale: By default, the scaling is 100%, but you can set it anywhere between 1 and 100.

C

URL: You can specify a data file that contains the ChartType, Number of Rows & Columns, names of Columns & Rows, and all the DataItems. The Chart Control will flow this data into itself.

The format of this data file is as follows:

- The first line describes the ChartType Property.
- The second line describes the number of rows.
- The third line describes the number of columns, followed by the optional column names (separated by tab characters).
- The fourth line and any additional lines beyond the fourth begin with an optional row name, followed by data items separated by tab characters. The total number of data items should be the same as the number of columns.

For example, this data file specifies ChartType 9 (a stacked area chart style), with 4 rows and 3 columns. The column names are FC, SC, and TC. The first row's name is TORBIN, the second row's name is SALKAR, and so on:

```
9
4
3       FC  SC  TC
TORBIN  1   5   3
SALKAR  23  3   82
ARISSD  84  95  53
NAIRS   22  32  12
```

Methods

AboutBox: Displays the About dialog box.

Events

None

Uses Display data graphically. You can reference a URL, a file that contains the data and that keeps your charts up to date.

C

Example

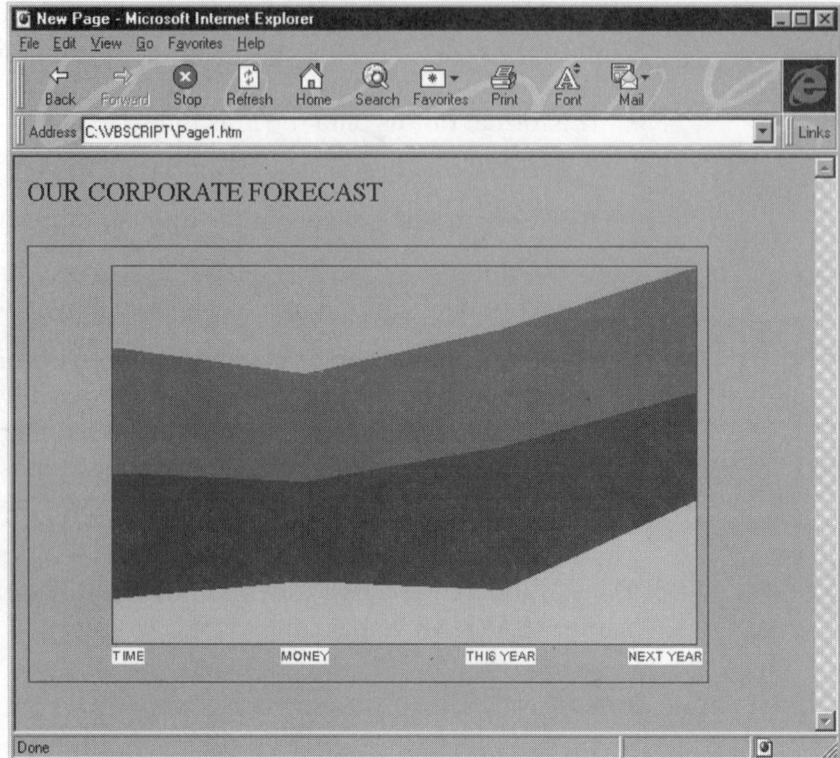

Figure C-22: This chart is drawn automatically by the Chart Control.

In this example we wanted to dynamically assign the various row names, so we used VBScript and, in the Window_OnLoad Event, specified each row, followed by the name we wanted it to have. Notice that each time we change the RowIndex, the RowName can be assigned to the new row. Similarly, if you want to use the Properties Window to assign names, you must first change the RowIndex Property and specify each row (starting with the 0th row). Only then can you adjust that particular row's RowName Property.

Run the ActiveX Control Pad (see the Introduction to this book) and, from its Edit menu, choose Insert ActiveX Control and choose Microsoft IE30 Chart Control. Then type in the script as shown below, or copy this example from the book's CD and paste it into your Microsoft ActiveX Control Pad.

C

```
<HTML>
<HEAD>
<TITLE>New Page</TITLE>
</HEAD>
<BODY>
<BIG>OUR CORPORATE FORECAST</BIG>
<BR><BR><BR>
  <SCRIPT LANGUAGE="VBScript">
<!--
Sub window_onLoad()
iechart1.RowIndex = 0
iechart1.RowName = "TIME"
iechart1.RowIndex = 1
iechart1.RowName = "MONEY"
iechart1.RowIndex = 2
iechart1.RowName = "THIS YEAR"
iechart1.RowIndex = 3
iechart1.RowName = "NEXT YEAR"
end sub
-->
    </SCRIPT>
  <OBJECT ID="iechart1" WIDTH=539 HEIGHT=335
CLASSID="CLSID:FC25B780-75BE-11CF-8B01-444553540000">
  <PARAM NAME="_ExtentX" VALUE="14261">
  <PARAM NAME="_ExtentY" VALUE="8864">
  <PARAM NAME="Rows" VALUE="4">
  <PARAM NAME="Columns" VALUE="3">
  <PARAM NAME="ChartType" VALUE="9">
  <PARAM NAME="Data[0][0]" VALUE="5">
  <PARAM NAME="Data[0][1]" VALUE="14">
  <PARAM NAME="Data[0][2]" VALUE="14">
  <PARAM NAME="Data[1][0]" VALUE="7">
  <PARAM NAME="Data[1][1]" VALUE="11">
  <PARAM NAME="Data[1][2]" VALUE="12">
  <PARAM NAME="Data[2][0]" VALUE="6">
  <PARAM NAME="Data[2][1]" VALUE="16">
  <PARAM NAME="Data[2][2]" VALUE="13">
  <PARAM NAME="Data[3][0]" VALUE="16">
  <PARAM NAME="Data[3][1]" VALUE="12">
  <PARAM NAME="Data[3][2]" VALUE="14">
```

```
    <PARAM NAME="HorizontalAxis" VALUE="0">
    <PARAM NAME="VerticalAxis" VALUE="0">
    <PARAM NAME="hgridStyle" VALUE="0">
    <PARAM NAME="vgridStyle" VALUE="0">
    <PARAM NAME="ColorScheme" VALUE="2">
    <PARAM NAME="BackStyle" VALUE="0">
    <PARAM NAME="Scale" VALUE="100">
    <PARAM NAME="DisplayLegend" VALUE="0">
    <PARAM NAME="BackColor" VALUE="16777215">
    <PARAM NAME="ForeColor" VALUE="32768">
</OBJECT>
</BODY>
</HTML>
```

CheckBox

ACTIVEX CONTROL

Description CheckBoxes allow the user to select from among options and also see the status of the CheckBoxes on the screen. A similar Control, the Option Button, differs in that it is mutually exclusive—click on any Option Button and all the other Buttons in its group are deselected (like the buttons on a car radio).

Therefore, you use Option Buttons when the user can select only a *single* option among several (boldface vs. normal text). Use CheckBoxes when the user can select more than one option (boldface and italic text; the user could choose boldface, italic, or both boldface and italic).

A third possibility is the new ToggleButton ActiveX Control. ToggleButtons act like CheckBoxes (individual discrete choices). See the entry for "ToggleButton." A fourth technique when offering the user a set of choices is the ListBox. It's valuable when you offer more than a few choices.

The user can trigger a CheckBox by clicking anywhere within the frame of a CheckBox (on the box image, on the caption, or even outside the caption if the frame is larger than the caption). The box that has the focus is indicated visually, while the program runs, by a dotted-line box around the caption. In other words, if a particular CheckBox—among all the Controls on a document—has the focus, it will have that faint gray line around it.

Variables

```
VALUE
```

The Value Property of CheckBoxes determines whether a given box is unchecked, checked, or contains a grayed check (meaning neither checked nor unchecked). The Value Property can be read:

```
X = CheckBox1.VALUE
```

or changed:

```
CheckBox1.VALUE = 0
VALUE = NULL
```

The item is neither selected nor cleared (a gray check appears within it). (For this NULL value to be possible, the TripleState Property must also be set to True. TripleState defaults to False.)

```
-1   True. The item is checked.
0   False. The item is blank, unselected.
```

OR (to change a CheckBox's caption while the program is running):

```
CheckBox1.Caption = "Disk Directory"
```

OR (to change the type size of a CheckBox's caption):

```
CheckBox1.FontSize = 12
```

OR (to make one box the same size vertically as another):

```
CheckBox1.Height = CheckBox2.Height
```

Properties

Accelerator, Alignment, AutoSize, BackColor, BackStyle, Caption, CodeBase, ControlTipText, Enabled, Font, ForeColor, Height, LayoutEffect, Left, Locked, MouseIcon, MousePointer, Name, Object, OldHeight (Width, Left & Top), Parent, Picture, PicturePosition, SpecialEffect, TabIndex, TabStop, Top, TripleState, Value, Visible, Width, WordWrap

C

Events
AfterUpdate, BeforeDragOver, BeforeDropOrPaste, BeforeUpdate, Change, Click, DblClick, Enter, Error, Exit, KeyDown, KeyPress, KeyUp, MouseDown, MouseMove, MouseUp

Methods
Move, SetFocus, ZOrder

For details about these Properties, Events, and Methods, see their corresponding entries—"Properties," "Events," and "Methods."

Uses

- Use CheckBoxes when you want the user to be able to customize or otherwise control the way your document looks or behaves—but among the choices the user can select more than one option. If the user should select only a single choice from among a group of choices, use an Option Button Control instead.
- CheckBoxes are not the most visually attractive Controls. If you need them, you might want to make them visible in a special frame of their own (selected, say, when the user clicks on a Command Button with the caption "OPTIONS"). Then hide that frame when it's no longer needed.

  Alternatively, you can fiddle with the way Option Buttons appear: make their borders overlap to bring the text lines closer together; offset the lines, staggering them; put them on a frame or an Image Control; or use icons in the Picture Property of the CheckBoxes themselves to provide more dramatic visual symbols.

Cautions

- CheckBoxes should not be confused with Option Buttons.
- CheckBoxes allow the user to select all, any, or none of the available boxes. On the other hand, Option Buttons are mutually exclusive. When you press an Option Button, the other Option Buttons pop out and are deselected, just like the buttons on a car radio (provided the Option Buttons have been *grouped*. See "Option Button.")

Use CheckBoxes when you want the user to be able to simultaneously activate more than one option in a group or set of options. Use Option Buttons where only one option at a time can be operative.

- At the current time, CheckBoxes have a GroupName Property in the Properties window, just like OptionButtons. This appears to be an error because it would defeat the purpose of CheckBoxes. See OptionButton for more on the uses for GroupName.

Example

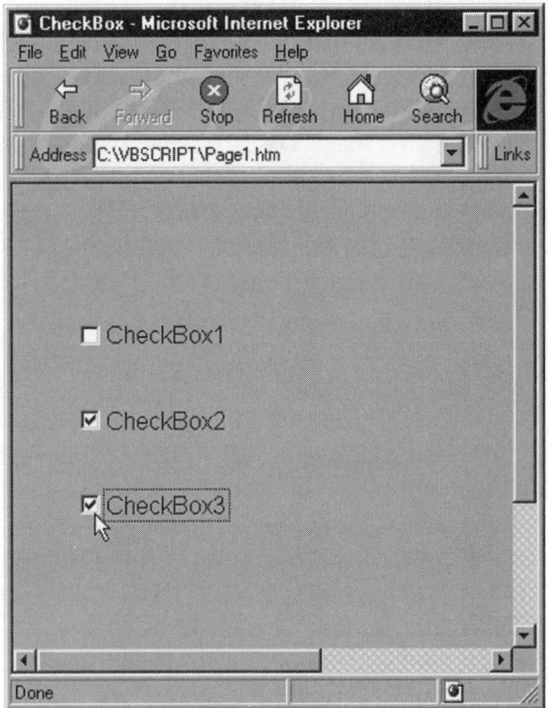

Figure C-23: CheckBoxes (unlike Option Buttons) are not mutually exclusive choices—you can select more than one at a time.

To create this example, start the Microsoft ActiveX Control Pad (see the Introduction) and click on Edit | Insert HTML Layout. Give the layout a new name and then click on the icon next to the <OBJECT> definition. Now from the toolbox, put three CheckBox

Controls on the layout. Using the Properties window (right-click on a CheckBox), change the font size of each box to 12 and change the font name to Arial. Then right-click on the layout and choose View Source Code. You should see the following source code:

```
<DIV ID="era" STYLE="LAYOUT:FIXED;WIDTH:400pt;HEIGHT:300pt;">
  <OBJECT ID="CheckBox1"
  CLASSID="CLSID:8BD21D40-EC42-11CE-9E0D-00AA006002F3"
STYLE="TOP:49pt;LEFT:26pt;WIDTH:118pt;HEIGHT:29pt;TABINDEX:→
0;ZINDEX:0;">
     <PARAM NAME="BackColor" VALUE="2147483663">
     <PARAM NAME="ForeColor" VALUE="2147483666">
     <PARAM NAME="DisplayStyle" VALUE="4">
     <PARAM NAME="Size" VALUE="4163;1023">
     <PARAM NAME="Caption" VALUE="CheckBox1">
     <PARAM NAME="GroupName" VALUE="are">
     <PARAM NAME="FontName" VALUE="Arial">
     <PARAM NAME="FontHeight" VALUE="240">
     <PARAM NAME="FontCharSet" VALUE="0">
     <PARAM NAME="FontPitchAndFamily" VALUE="2">
     <PARAM NAME="FontWeight" VALUE="0">
  </OBJECT>
  <OBJECT ID="CheckBox2"
  CLASSID="CLSID:8BD21D40-EC42-11CE-9E0D-00AA006002F3"
STYLE="TOP:88pt;LEFT:26pt;WIDTH:126pt;HEIGHT:36pt;TABINDEX:→
1;ZINDEX:1;">
     <PARAM NAME="BackColor" VALUE="2147483663">
     <PARAM NAME="ForeColor" VALUE="2147483666">
     <PARAM NAME="DisplayStyle" VALUE="4">
     <PARAM NAME="Size" VALUE="4445;1270">
     <PARAM NAME="Caption" VALUE="CheckBox2">
     <PARAM NAME="GroupName" VALUE="are">
     <PARAM NAME="FontName" VALUE="Arial">
     <PARAM NAME="FontHeight" VALUE="240">
     <PARAM NAME="FontCharSet" VALUE="0">
     <PARAM NAME="FontPitchAndFamily" VALUE="2">
     <PARAM NAME="FontWeight" VALUE="0">
  </OBJECT>
  <OBJECT ID="CheckBox3"
```

```
   CLASSID="CLSID:8BD21D40-EC42-11CE-9E0D-00AA006002F3"
STYLE="TOP:133pt;LEFT:26pt;WIDTH:119pt;HEIGHT:30pt;TABINDEX:→
2;ZINDEX:2;">
     <PARAM NAME="BackColor" VALUE="2147483663">
     <PARAM NAME="ForeColor" VALUE="2147483666">
     <PARAM NAME="DisplayStyle" VALUE="4">
     <PARAM NAME="Size" VALUE="4198;1058">
     <PARAM NAME="Caption" VALUE="CheckBox3">
     <PARAM NAME="GroupName" VALUE="are">
     <PARAM NAME="FontName" VALUE="Arial">
     <PARAM NAME="FontHeight" VALUE="240">
     <PARAM NAME="FontCharSet" VALUE="0">
     <PARAM NAME="FontPitchAndFamily" VALUE="2">
     <PARAM NAME="FontWeight" VALUE="0">
  </OBJECT>
</DIV>
```

See also Option Button, ToggleButton, ListBox

Chr

VBSCRIPT FUNCTION

Description In computer language, all *characters* (which include the uppercase and lowercase letters of the alphabet, punctuation marks, numbers, and special symbols) have a numeric code—from 0 to 255. (This is changing—a new code is now being used in 32-bit environments like Windows 95, called Unicode, which ranges from 0 to 65535. See "New in 32 Bits" later in this section.)

A computer works exclusively with numbers. The only purpose of text, from the computer's point of view, is to facilitate communication with humans.

When you type in the letter *a*, the computer "remembers" it as the number 97. When that character is to be printed on the screen or on paper, the computer translates 97 back into what it sees as a *graphic*, an *image:* a. Although we think of text in terms of information, to the computer the text characters are merely pictures that, when strung together, can have meaning to humans. It will be an important step toward artificial intelligence when text has as much meaning to the computer as mathematical and numeric data already does. Don't hold your breath.

Some code numbers used with text are not actual characters or graphics—for example, a Carriage Return code (code 13) merely moves the text down one line. There are times when you'll want to create a text (string) Variable that can be printed directly to the screen or a printer. If you're working with an object that has no provision for Carriage Returns built into it (such as a MsgBox), you can trigger a Carriage Return by creating a Carriage Return text Variable:

```
CR = Chr(13)
```

The following example shows how to insert a blank line between the text "Our retail cost" and the numeric Variable "retail." Notice that we defined the Variable *cr* as a "Carriage Return" by assigning it the character coded 13. (Also, the cStr command transforms the numeric Variable subtype into a text Variable subtype. For more on this, see "cBool.")

```
<HTML>
<HEAD>
<TITLE>VBScript</TITLE>
</HEAD>
<BODY BGCOLOR=#FFFFFF>
<FONT FACE=ARIAL>
<INPUT TYPE=BUTTON VALUE="Click me" NAME="Btn">
<SCRIPT LANGUAGE=VBS>
Sub Btn_OnClick
cr = chr(13)
retail = 54
msgbox "Our retail cost" + cr + cr + cstr(retail)
End Sub
</SCRIPT>
</FONT>
</BODY>
</HTML>
```

Used with Text Variables

Variables `CR = Chr(13)`

Uses

- Create special string Variables that can accomplish what can't be displayed directly. (You'll see how to simulate a double quote for MsgBoxes in the example.)
- One of the most common uses for Chr is to force a carriage return (new line) in a MsgBox or a TextBox. When you want text to move down one or more lines in a MsgBox, define CR = CHR(13), then use it within your message as illustrated in the example on the previous page.
- To force a new line in a TextBox, you must add another character to the CR (carriage return, code 13). You must also have an LF (line feed, code 10) character, like this:

```
cr = chr(13) & chr(10)
```


Cautions

New in 32 Bits: This entry, Chr, describes character codes used since programming began. But with the new 32-bit operating systems like Windows 95 and NT 4, things are changing. It was long assumed that since a single byte can express 256 different numbers, a single byte was plenty big enough to hold the alphabet (26 lowercase, 26 uppercase), 10 digits, and miscellaneous punctuation, with room left over for some dingbats like the smiley face and codes for carriage returns and a beep.

But what about other alphabets, non-English alphabets? Some of them are rather large. OLE and the 32-bit operating systems have abandoned the familiar single-byte ASCII and ANSI codes in favor of a new 2-byte code, UniCode. Two-byte units can express over 65,000 numbers, so UniCode has lots of room to provide code numbers for many alphabets of the world, including Chinese.

In the past, some programmers have relied on the fact that text (string) Variables were 1-byte large. They used this code for purposes that it wasn't designed for. They could store, retrieve, and manipulate information efficiently in strings or string Arrays. For example, there is a whole set of string manipulation commands—like Left, Mid, Right, InStr, Chr, Space, and others that were heavily relied on by some programmers for low-level database management programming. In other words, they stored any kind of data, not just text, in string Variables and

Arrays. Programs written using these techniques will no longer work correctly in the 32-bit world.

There is a *byte* Variable data subtype (a single byte) in VBS which can be used instead of the text string Variable data type. However, existing programs relying on the single-byte text data type will have to be rewritten to use the byte type. What's more, all the string manipulation commands commonly used in this kind of programming don't work with the byte data type. String manipulation commands in VBS/32-bit work as they always did with text, but in 2-byte chunks. The byte data type does have a few commands dedicated to it: InputB, RightB, MidB, and LeftB, which work the same way as their namesakes but on single bytes (instead of the new 2-byte units).

Example You cannot put quotes around words in MsgBoxes because the " (the quote mark) represents the end of the message. However, there is a way:

```
<HTML>
<INPUT TYPE=BUTTON VALUE="Click me" NAME="Btn">
<SCRIPT LANGUAGE=VBS>
Sub Btn_OnClick
quot = Chr(34)
MsgBox "We're trying to be " + quot + "polished." + quot
End Sub
</SCRIPT>
</HTML>
```

This is the result:

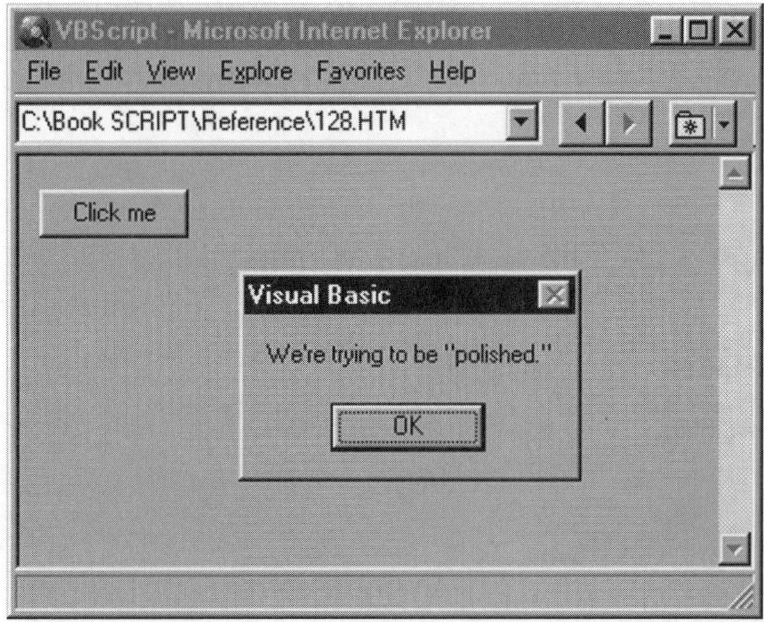

Figure C-24: Displaying quotation marks requires a little extra programming.

This accomplishes the same thing:

```
MsgBox "We're trying to be " + chr(34) + "happy." + chr(34)
```

However, if you're going to need the special character often, it's more efficient and your programming is more easily read and understood if you create a Variable, such as *quot*.

See also Asc

C

cInt

VBSCRIPT FUNCTION

Description cInt forces a Variable to become an Integer subtype. See "Variants" for definitions of the several subtypes.

See also cBool

CITE

NETSCAPE & INTERNET EXPLORER 3.0

Description Turns on italics.

See also I

Clear

VBSCRIPT METHOD

Description This resets the Err object to 0. The Err object (see "Err") in VBS allows you to trap (or ignore) errors that occur while your program is running. VBS automatically detects various kinds of errors, and then puts their error number into the Err object. This allows you to react to various errors in your programming.

However, there may be cases when you want to ignore an error. For example, you may have already dealt with it.

Used with The Err object

Variables Err.Clear

Uses If you're in a loop, for example, you won't want the Err object to trigger a response from your program more than once. Thus, reset the Err object to 0 to avoid repetitive, redundant error messages.

Cautions

- VBS automatically executes an Err.Clear whenever it encounters a Resume Statement, Exit Sub, or Exit Function, and also when it comes upon any On Error Statement. So you don't have to worry about resetting it, except in some rare situations when you want to clear it *within* a particular procedure (Sub or Function).
- You can accomplish the same thing as Err.Clear by this programming:

```
Err = 0.
```

Example

```
If Err Then Err.Clear
```

(You might program in VBS for 50 years and never use the Clear Method.)

See also Err, On Error

Clear

ACTIVEX

See Methods

Click

ACTIVEX

See Events

ClientHeight, -Left, -Top, -Width

ACTIVEX

See Properties

cLng

FUNCTION

See cBool

CODE

HTML

Description Used to display programming ("code") such as HTML source code. If you click on the View menu in Internet Explorer, then select Source, you'll be shown the "source code" that causes the currently loaded document to look and behave the way it does. Historically, computer programming was called *code* or *source code* and, in fact, it was so cryptic that code was the right term for it. However, as high-level languages like VBScript become increasingly popular, programming is increasingly less like code and more like English.

The font employed when you use the CODE command is small and fixed-width. Fixed-width means a font such as courier, a typewriter-style typeface where each character is the same width (the letter *i* is given the same amount of space as *w*). The opposite variety—variable-width type—is typified by the Times Roman font. Characters vary in width. Variable-width is the default HTML font for body text; fixed-width is the default for headlines and "code." However, most browsers permit the user to define his or her preferences in these matters.

Used with ***Can be enclosed by***

<A>, <ABBREV>, <ACRONYM>, <ADDRESS>, <AU>, <B>, <BANNER>, <BIG>, <BODY>, <BODYTEXT>, <CAPTION>, <CITE>, <CODE>, <CREDIT>, <DD>, <DEL>, <DFN>, <DIV>, <DT>, <EM>, <FIGTEXT>, <FN>, <FORM>, <H1>, <H2>, <H3>, <H4>, <H5>, <H6>, <I>, <INS>, <KBD>, <LANG>, <LH>, <LI>, <NOTE>, <P>, <PERSON>, <PRE>, <Q>, <S>, <SAMP>, <SMALL>, <STRONG>, <SUB>, <SUP>, <TD>, <TH>, <TT>, <U>, <VAR>

Can enclose

<A>, <ABBREV>, <ACRONYM>, <AU>, <B>, <BIG>, <BR>, <CITE>, <CODE>, <DEL>, <DFN>, <EM>, <I>, <IMG>, <INS>, <KBD>, <LANG>, <MATH>, <PERSON>, <Q>, <S>, <SAMP>, <SMALL>, <STRONG>, <SUB>, <SUP>, <TAB>, <TT>, <U>, <VAR>

C

Variables

```
<CODE> SOME HTML PROGRAMMING </CODE>
```

Uses Indicates that you are displaying nonstandard text (something that should be set off from ordinary body text). Many computer books, this one included, switch to a different font to indicate computer programming—lines that the user can type in to cause something to happen in a computer language such as HTML.

Example

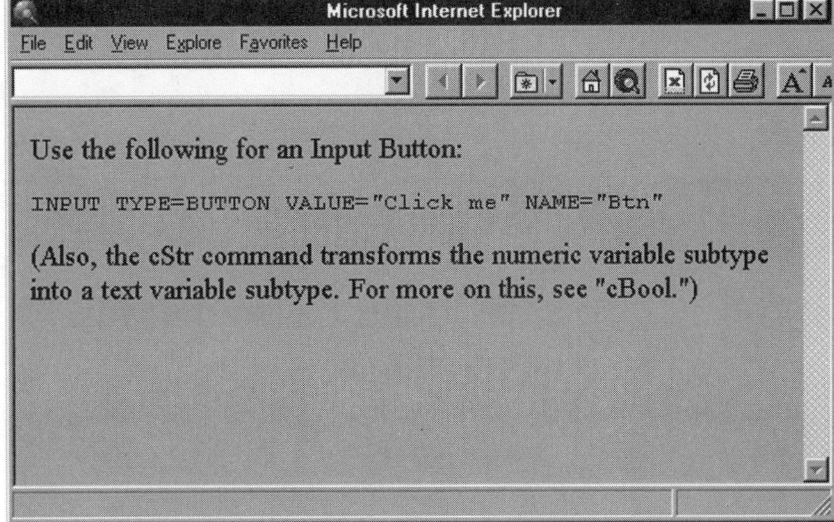

Figure C-25: The CODE command displays a typeface that indicates computer programming.

```
<HTML>
<FONT SIZE=+1>
Use the following for an Input Button:
<BR><BR>
<CODE>
```

```
INPUT TYPE=BUTTON VALUE="Click me" NAME="Btn"
</CODE>
 <BR><BR>
```

(Also, the cStr command transforms the numeric Variable subtype into a text Variable subtype. For more on this, see "cBool.")

```
</HTML>
```

CodeBase

ACTIVEX

See Properties

Column

ACTIVEX

See Properties

ColumnCount, ColumnHeads, ColumnWidths

ACTIVEX

See Properties

ComboBox

ACTIVEX CONTROL

Description ComboBoxes are similar to ListBoxes. A ListBox, however, displays a series of items, whereas a ComboBox must be clicked on and thus made to drop down before its contents can be seen. Also, a ListBox simply provides a list of options the user can choose from, but a ComboBox offers its list and also allows the user to type in additional items. (In one style of ComboBox, the user is not allowed to type in additional items. See Cautions.)

Your script can detect the user's selections—they trigger the box's Click Event. Your script can also know when the user starts typing—that act triggers the box's Change Event.

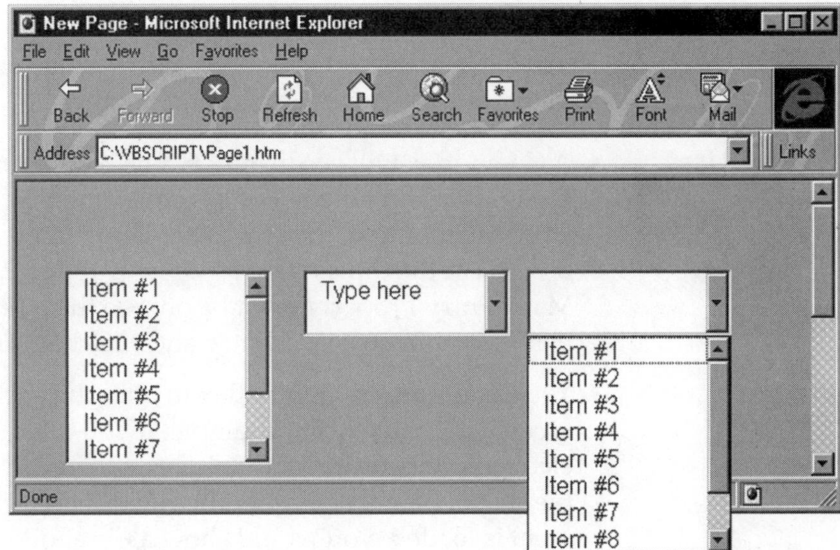

Figure C-26: A ListBox (left), a ComboBox (middle), a ComboBox with its list dropped (right).

Used with Lists that you want the user to be able not only to view but also type into. A ComboBox is like a ListBox, but with a mini-TextBox attached.

Variables The Value Property is the default Property. This means that when querying the Value, you need not use the word *Value*:

```
X = ComboBox1
```

OR

```
X = ComboBox1.Value
```

Your script can add or remove items from a ComboBox:

```
Combo1.AddItem "New York"
```

OR (to add a Variable):

```
Combo1.AddItem N
```

OR (to remove the fourth item from a ComboBox):

```
Combo1.RemoveItem 3
```

The items in a List or ComboBox start with a zeroth item, so the fourth item is removed by requesting number 3.

Uses

- A ComboBox will go directly to one of its elements if the user types in certain letters. For example, if the list contains a word beginning with *v*, then that item would appear in the text box at the top as soon as the user types the letter v. (The MatchEntry Property must be on. See the entry on "Properties" for more on MatchEntry and MatchRequired.)
- You can also use a ComboBox to offer the user choices but accept alternatives. For example, if you offered the user an electronic substitute for a Rolodex, you could keep track of the six people most frequently called. Then when the document is loaded, you would show a ComboBox with the names of these people listed so that the user could just click on one of them.

  Pressing ENTER would select the one that's highlighted. Pressing arrow keys moves the user up and down the list. The items in the list are alphabetized. And—the main feature—there's a place for the user to simply type in the name of a person not listed in the top six.

Cautions There are two styles of ComboBoxes, depending on how you set the Style Property:

```
DropDownCombo    (Style=0)
```

This is the default. The user can type into the TextBox portion or click on a value from the drop-down list.

```
DropDownList     (Style=2)
```

The ComboBox behaves as a list box. The user must choose a value from the list. Typing, unless it matches what's in the list, is ignored.

To see the items within a ComboBox, the user must click on the arrow (or other symbol, defined by the DropButtonStyle Property). An advantage of a List Box is that it shows the whole list (or as many items as will fit in its window) right from the start. However, if you're short on space in a document, concealing the items can make for a clean, uncluttered layout, and therefore a more attractive page. Note that a ComboBox's list can drop below the host window (see Figure C-26).

The Zeroth Problem: Because computer language designers still cling to the confusing habit of starting a count from zero, the first style of ComboBox is 0, the second is missing (it would be Style=1), and the third is 2. This can be a source of error; it also makes memorizing things difficult. Likewise, the items within a Combo or ListBox begin with the zeroth item, as you'll see in the example below.

Properties

AutoSize, AutoTab, AutoWordSelect, BackColor, BackStyle, BorderColor, BorderStyle, BoundColumn, CodeBase, Column, ColumnCount, ColumnHeads, ColumnWidths, Enabled, EnterFieldBehavior, Font, ForeColor, Height, HideSelection, ID, IMEMode, Left, List, ListCount, ListRows, ListStyle, ListWidth, Locked, MatchEntry, MatchRequired, MaxLength, MouseIcon, MousePointer, SelectionMargin, SelLength, SelStart, SelText, ShowDropButtonWhen, SpecialEffect, Style, TabIndex, TabStop, Text, TextAlign, TextColumn, Top, TopIndex, Value, Visible, Width

Events

AfterUpdate, BeforeDragOver, BeforeDropOrPaste, BeforeUpdate, Change, Click, DblClick, DropButtonClick, Enter, Error, Exit, KeyDown, KeyPress, KeyUp, MouseDown, MouseMove, MouseUp

C

Methods

AddItem, Clear, Copy, Cut, DropDown, Paste, RemoveItem, SetFocus, ZOrder

For details about these Properties, Events, and Methods, see their corresponding entries—"Properties," "Events," and "Methods."

Example Run the ActiveX Control Pad and click on the Edit menu. Choose Insert HTML Layout (see the Introduction to the book for more on using the ActiveX Control Pad). Then put a ListBox, a Command Button, and two ComboBoxes on the layout. Right-click on one of the ComboBoxes and select Properties. Set its Style Property to DropDown List, so you can see how that differs from the default style. Now, right-click on the background and choose View Source Code. Type this into the source code. We'll use the Layout OnLoad Event to fill each of our boxes with some items, by using the AddItem Method:

```
<SCRIPT LANGUAGE="VBScript">
<!--
Sub al_OnLoad()
for i = 1 to 10
ListBox1.AddItem "Item #" & cstr(i)
ComboBox1.AddItem "Item #" & cstr(i)
ComboBox2.AddItem "Item #" & cstr(i)
next
end sub
Sub CommandButton1_Click()
ComboBox2.RemoveItem 4
end sub
-->
</SCRIPT>
```

Save this to disk and load it into Internet Explorer. When you click on the CommandButton, you'll see that the *fifth* item (Item # 5) is removed, even though we've specified RemoveItem 4. That's because the first item would be removed by RemoveItem 0. For more on this, see "The Zeroth Problem" above.

See also ListBox

Command Button

ACTIVEX CONTROL

Description The Command Button is perhaps the most popular ActiveX Control in all of Visual Basic Script (aside from the "Layout Control" which, properly speaking, is a container of other Controls).

A Command Button provides visually intuitive, direct access—the user sees the caption and simply clicks the mouse on it to get something done. The button-down animation offers good, strong feedback; there's a real sense that something has happened, unlike some other VBScript selection methods. Put a group of buttons into a document and the user really feels in control of the situation.

Used with Many applications for user-input. This is Visual Basic Script's "make something happen" button.

Variables You can adjust a Command Button's various Properties from the Properties Window while designing your script (see Figure C-27)

OR (to adjust the FontSize of the Command Button's caption while the script is running):

```
CommandButton1.Left = CommandButton1.Left + 12
```

OR (to find out the Command Button's Height while the script is running):

```
X = CommandButton1.Height
```

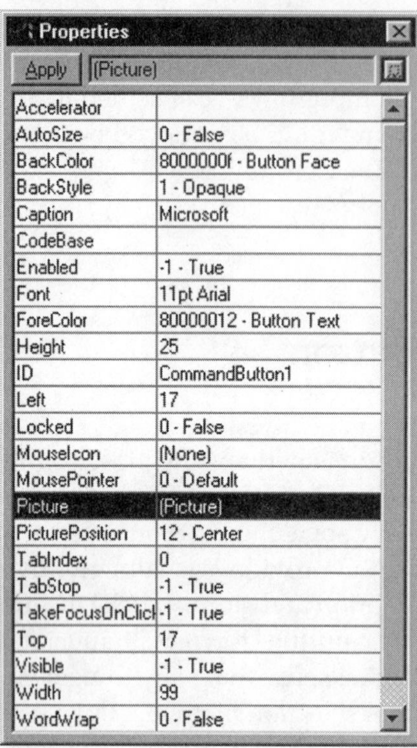

Figure C-27: Using the ActiveX Control Panel's Properties Window to change the picture in a Command Button.

Uses Use Command Buttons in many situations when the user needs to make something happen in your pages. Put something into their Picture Property, or associate them with Labels and other Controls and you'll be tapping into the real power of Visual Basic Script as a significant visual improvement over standard HTML.

Example A set of Command Buttons looks far nicer and more professional than a group of text hyperlinks. We've got a document that has three links. We could use the HTML A command to display the three links:

```
<A HREF="http://www.microsoft.com"> Microsoft </A>
<A HREF="http://altavista.digital.com"> Search </A>
<A HREF="http://www.sunday-times.co.uk/news"> London Times
</A>
```

But that results in a plain text listing. A better alternative is to provide Command Buttons with their built-in animation.

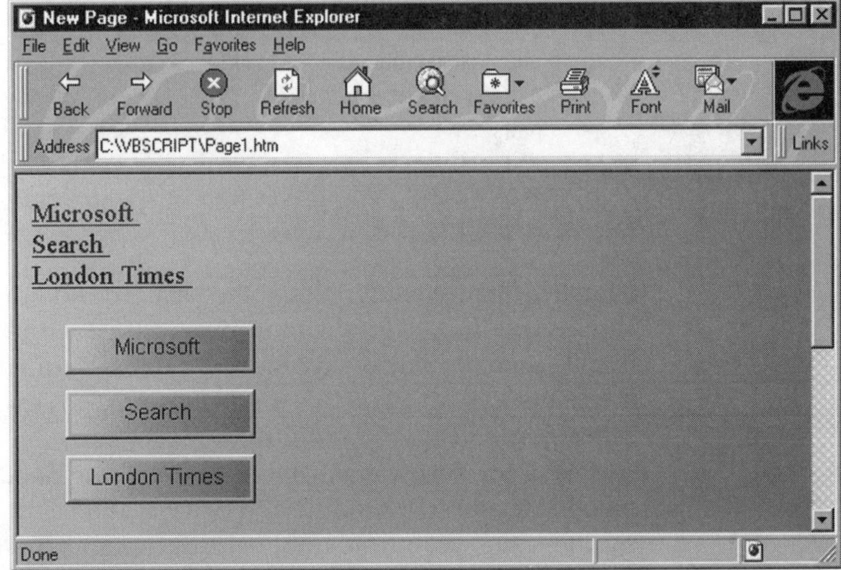

Figure C-28: Which links look more professional, the text or the buttons?

To create this example, follow these steps:

1. Start ActiveX Control Pad and select Edit | Insert HTML Layout.
2. Put three Command Buttons on the layout.
3. Using the Properties Sheet for each Command Button, type in a caption that matches whatever URL you're going to put into that button's Click_Event.
4. Right-click on the layout (not on one of the buttons) and choose View Source Code from the popout menu.
5. Then type in the following to make these buttons link to Web sites:

```
<SCRIPT LANGUAGE="VBScript">
<!--
Sub CommandButton1_Click()
```

C

```
window.location.href = "http://www.microsoft.com"
end sub
Sub CommandButton2_Click()
window.location.href = "http://altavista.digital.com"
end sub
Sub CommandButton3_Click()
window.location.href = "http://www.sunday-times.co.uk/
news"
end sub
-->
</SCRIPT>
```

Metallic Gradients: Note that the background graphic (<BODY BACKGROUND="gradient.gif">) and the Picture Property of each Command Button in Figure C-28 is a gradient. These metallic gradients look so attractive that we wanted to describe the technique here so you can add it to your pages.

One of the best ways to avoid dull-looking documents is to use metallic shading. It's subtle and conservative enough for any business site, yet considerably more attractive than plain gray. You can even switch from gray to golden or other shades. Whatever color you choose, gradients are among the finest backgrounds you can employ.

You can make your own gradients with Corel PhotoPaint, Picture Publisher, or most any photo-retouching application. It's easy to create gradients. Here's how to do it.

The best metallic gradient is a gradual shift between two shades: light gray (or white) and the typical Windows gray (the light 25% gray often used as BackColor, the same gray that's used on the VBScript Command Button and many other Controls). Another, somewhat more powerful effect can be achieved by using the darker 50% gray used to shadow Command Buttons and other Controls. (If you want a golden gradient, use very light yellow and a deep chocolate-brown yellow. If you're using gray, save the file as a "Grayscale" .GIF file. If you're using any color, save it as an "RGB" or "Truecolor" .JPG file. With color gradients, you'll get an ugly banding effect if you try to reduce them to 256-color .GIF files.)

So to capture a gray that will fit in with VBScript's (and Windows') color scheme, put a Command Button on a Layout Control (see the Introduction to this book), and then press ALT+PrintScrn to capture the layout to the clipboard. Then open a photo-retouching program like Photoshop or Corel's PhotoPaint. From the Edit menu, select Paste to bring in the picture.

All retouching scripts have a "color picker" tool. It sometimes looks like an eyedropper. Use it to select the color of the Command Button's shadow, thereby placing it into the main color selection. Change the alternate color (sometimes called "backcolor" or "secondary color") to white or light gray. (If you don't want to use the picker, adjust the main color directly to shadow gray by setting RGB to 75% each, or to white, by setting RGB to 100% each. If you're specifying colors in CMYK rather than RGB, the percentages for gray are 25% for the first three and 0% for K.)

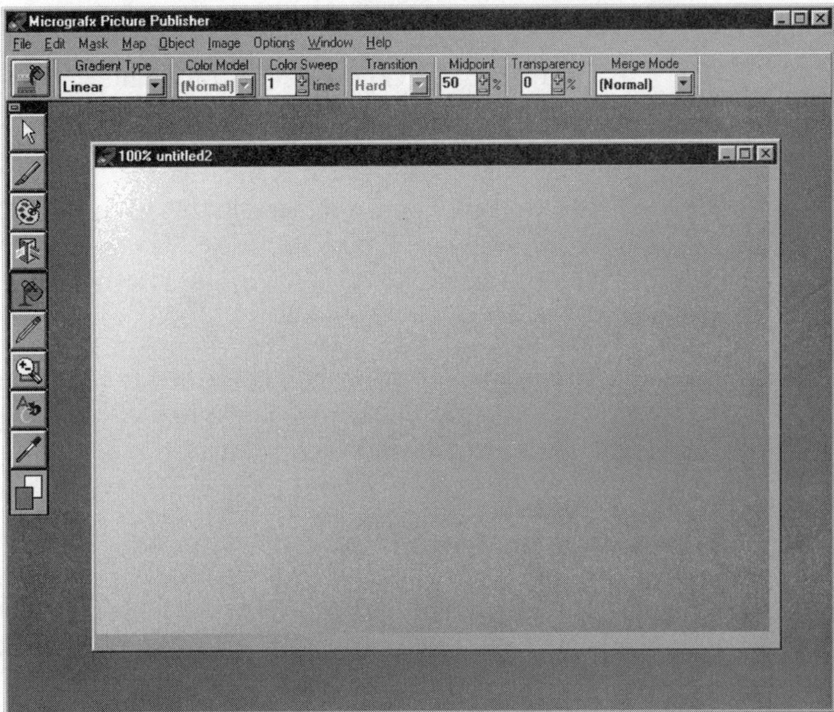

Figure C-29: Creating a metallic gradient for a layout's background.

Now create a new graphic (click on the File | New menu) and drag your gradient so that the gray shadow is in the lower right corner and lighter gray or white is in the upper left corner. Use the linear gradient option (not circular, radial, or some other type). Save the results to disk as a .BMP file for later use. You might also make several differing sizes of small gradients as .BMP files to load into the Picture Property of various size Command Buttons.

To put a gradient across the background, create a huge one (big enough to fill a 1024x768 screen, anyway) and save it as, for example, bigrad.bmp (in the same directory where your .HTM file is located). Then make it the background by typing this into your .HTM file in the ActiveX Control Pad:

```
<BODY BACKGROUND="bigrad.gif">
```

To add gradients to a layout (which has no Picture Property), just put an Image Control inside the layout and drag it until it's as big as the layout. Load your big gradient .BMP file into the Image. Then use the Move Backward or Move Forward options on the ActiveX Control Pad's Format menu to get the Image Control behind any other Controls like Command Buttons.

Properties

Accelerator, AutoSize, BackColor, BackStyle, Caption, CodeBase, Enabled, Font, ForeColor, Height, ID, hWnd, Left, Locked, MouseIcon, MousePointer, Picture, PicturePosition, TabIndex, TabStop, Top, Value, Visible, Width, WordWrap

Events

AfterUpdate, BeforeDragOver, BeforeDropOrPaste, BeforeUpdate, Click/DblClick, Enter, Exit, Error, KeyDown, KeyPress, KeyUp, MouseDown, MouseMove, MouseUp

Methods

Move, SetFocus, ZOrder

For details about these Properties, Events, and Methods, see their corresponding entries—"Properties," "Events," and "Methods."

Comment

HTML

Description Allows you to insert notes to yourself (or others who might read your HTML source code) about the behavior of your HTML document, with explanations of potentially confusing or obscure commands or structures. Comments aren't required. They will have no visible effect on the pages when seen by the user; they will be ignored by browsers.

When you use the Script Wizard to put some VBScript programming into the Microsoft ActiveX Control Pad, comment symbols are always inserted right after the <SCRIPT> and right before the </SCRIPT> tags. The reason for doing this is that if the user loads your document into a browser that's incapable of working with VBScript, the comment symbols prevent it from displaying the VBScript programming as text. (But if the browser does contain a VBScript interpreter, as does the Internet Explorer, it will ignore these HTML comment symbols and go ahead and act on the VBScript commands):

```
<SCRIPT LANGUAGE="VBScript">
<!--
MsgBox "You have VBScript!"
-->
</SCRIPT>
```

Variables

```
<COMMENT> put your remarks here </COMMENT>
```

OR

```
<!-- put your remarks here -->
```

Uses

- Many people like to heavily comment their programming—they feel it makes the purpose of the program lines (the HTML codes) easier to read and thereby you can more quickly fix errors. They use comments to indicate unusual situations or commands, or just to show the design of their work. Other programmers rarely include comments—they find it's easier just to read the program lines. This kind of programmer is rather like an experienced conductor who can look at, and understand, a Mozart symphony by reading the raw sheet music. How many, if any, comments you include is up to you.

C

- Prevent users from seeing your VBScript source code (as simple text), if the user doesn't have a VBScript-capable browser. See Description above.

Example

```
<!-- This reacts when the user clicks on the button -->
<SCRIPT LANGUAGE=VBS>
Sub Btn_OnClick
cr = chr(13)
retail = 54
msgbox "Our retail cost" + cr + cr + cstr(retail)
End Sub
</SCRIPT>
```

Concatenation

VBSCRIPT

Description To attach two pieces of text, use the & command:

```
N = "This " & "and that."
Msgbox N
```

Results In

```
This and that.
```

See Operators, the & operator

Constants

See Variables

ControlTipText

ACTIVEX

See Properties

Cookies

Description Cookies allow you to save Variables between pages or sessions. A Cookie is a piece of data, such as the date that the user last visited a particular Web site. This piece of data is stored client-side. That is, it's stored on the user's hard drive. The next time the user visits that Web site, the Cookie can appear and startle the user with something like, "Hi. We haven't seen you for 23 days. Welcome back!"

To understand the value and utility of Cookies, let's briefly consider how information can be stored in VBScript. The issue of how widely available a Variable (and its data) are is called *scope*.

When you create a Variable within a Sub or Function, that Variable's contents are only available *within* that same Sub or Function. So the scope is said to be only procedure-wide. In this next example, the Variable N's contents, the word RONE, will be displayed by the message box in the CommandButton1 Sub but not in the CommandButton2 Sub. The Variable N is simply not available outside of the CommandButton1 Sub:

```
<SCRIPT LANGUAGE="VBScript">
<!--
Sub CommandButton1_Click()
  N = "RONE"
  msgbox N
end sub
Sub CommandButton2_Click()
  msgbox N
end sub
-->
</SCRIPT>
```

C

Going further out, when you create a Variable within a script (but *outside* of any Sub or Function), that Variable is available to any Sub or Function within the same script. In this next example, both message boxes will display the contents of N. Of course you have to click on CommandButton1 at least once before CommandButton2 will display RONE. That's because RONE is put into N within the CommandButton1 sub:

```
<SCRIPT LANGUAGE="VBScript">
<!--
Dim N
Sub CommandButton1_Click()
  N = "RONE"
  msgbox N
end sub
Sub CommandButton2_Click()
  msgbox N
end sub
</SCRIPT>
```

For more on this, see "Dim."

But how can you pass information (or set ActiveX Control Properties) from one Control on a page to another Control on another page or frame elsewhere in your document? In other words, where can you store information *outside of scripts*? Cookies are one way. Just store the information on the user's hard drive.

Variables You save a Cookie this way:

```
Document.Cookie = "The Information"
```

and you read a Cookie like this:

```
X = Document.Cookie
```

If you want to save more than one item, concatenate them:

```
N = InputBox "Tell us your name"
A = InputBox "Tell us your age"

Document.Cookie = "TheName =" & N & "; TheAge =" & A & ";ex-
pires=03-Dec-96 GMT"
```

Then, when you retrieve the Cookie and want to separate out the various information contained within the Cookie, you get a text Variable that contains something like this:

```
TheName = Sam Johnson; TheAge = 32;expires=03-Dec-96 GMT
```

To extract the various pieces of data, use the InStr command (see "InStr").

Uses

- Password Security.
- User site customization. Some Web sites allow you to customize various elements of the document—which links are displayed, colors, fonts, and so on. Where do they keep that information? In Cookies.
- Accessing Variables from different scripts, in different pages, in a document.

Cautions Note that at this time, Cookies work on the Web *but not locally*. In other words, set the following example into a document that you then put onto a real Internet Web server. When your computer then contacts that site on the Internet, the Cookie will be saved and retrieved. However, if you merely open this .HTM file on your own hard drive, then—without going onto the Internet—just load in this document into the browser *locally*, the Cookie will not work. Most of the examples in this book can be tested locally, but the following one cannot.

A user can refuse to permit Cookies. In Internet Explorer 3.0, click on the View menu, then choose Options. Click on the Advanced tab. You'll see that one of your choices is to "Warn before accepting cookies."

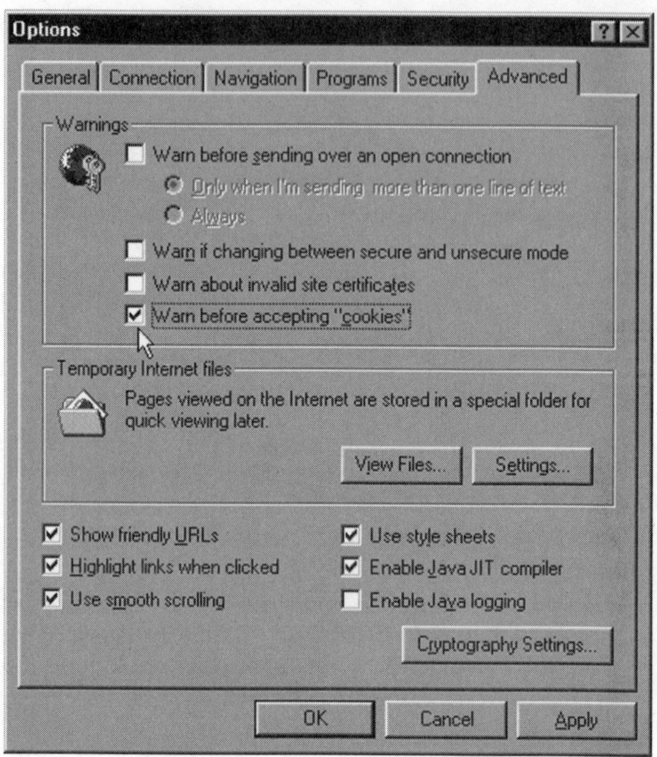

Figure C-30: Not all users will permit Cookies. This is where they can require that they be alerted whenever a Cookie is attempting to get onto their hard drive.

Cookies are harmless enough—just Variable names and the data associated with those names. They're not executable programs so it would be impossible for a virus to invade someone's hard drive from a Cookie. Nonetheless, you're given the option of permitting or refusing Cookies. So be aware that some users will likely decline your efforts to provide them with a Cookie.

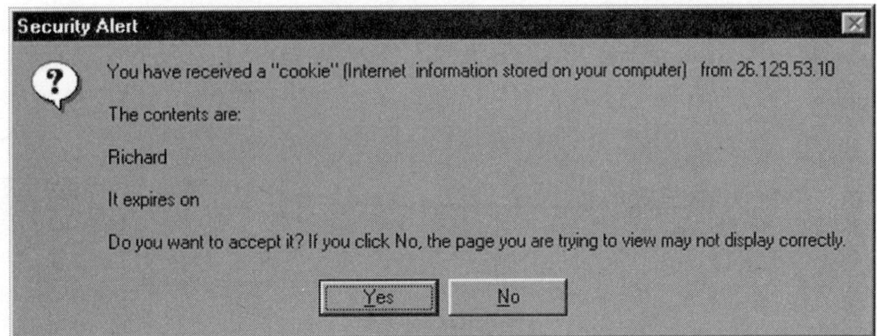

Figure C-31: If you want to know when a Cookie is being saved to your hard drive, Internet Explorer's View | Options | Advanced allows you to cause this dialog box to pop up whenever a Cookie attempts entrance into your system.

When you write a Cookie:

```
Document.Cookie = "The Information"
```

any existing Cookie for this page will be obliterated.

Example If you want to see your Cookies, look in the Windows\Cookies folder. You're likely to find some .TXT and .DAT files in there—things that have been stored during visits to various Web sites. A typical Cookie, viewed in Notepad, might look like this:

```
RMID 06810207738f77cf nomedia.com/ 0 617916800 29316075
876579296 29068624 *
```

Here's an example of how to store a Cookie. Note that unlike the rest of the examples in this book, this one cannot be tested *locally*. In other words, to test Cookies, you must put your .HTM file up onto a real Internet Web server. See Cautions above.

```
<INPUT TYPE=BUTTON NAME=COMMANDBUTTON1 VALUE="Cookie">
<SCRIPT LANGUAGE="VBScript">
<!--
Sub CommandButton1_OnClick()
Document.Cookie = "Myvar" & "=" & "Johnny Rohm" & ";ex-
pires=01-Oct-96 GMT"
MsgBox Document.Cookie
end sub
-->
</SCRIPT>
```

Unless you specify an expiration date, a Cookie will be destroyed after the user leaves the current session. If you specify a date as shown in the example above, the Cookie will remain on the user's hard drive until the specified date.

See also Variables

Copy

ACTIVEX

See Methods

Cos

VBSCRIPT FUNCTION

Description Cos gives you the cosine of an angle, expressed in radians. You provide a *numeric expression*: a literal number, a numeric Variable, a numeric Constant, or a combination of these. You can get the cosine of any subtype of Variable (Integer, Floating-Point, and so on). (See "Variables" for a definition of *expression* and numeric Variable *types*.)

Variables

```
MsgBox Cos(x)
```

OR

```
F = Cos(.3)
```

Uses Advanced mathematics; Trigonometry

Example

```
z = Cos(.3)
MsgBox z
```

Results in

```
.9553365
```

See also Atn, Sin, Tan

C

Count

ACTIVEX

See Properties

cSng

FUNCTION

See cBool

cStr

FUNCTION

See cBool

CurLine

ACTIVEX

See Properties

Cut

ACTIVEX

See Methods

cVerr

VBSCRIPT FUNCTION

See Err

D

DD

HTML

See DL

Data Types

Description In VBScript, you cannot specifically declare variable types. This is not permitted:

```
Dim T As Integer
```

All you can do is declare the Variant type (see "Variants"):

```
Dim T
```

The Variant is the default type in VBScript. Then, if you want to be sure that the contents of a variable are being interpreted by VBScript accurately, you use one of the *coercion* commands to force the Variant into the proper subtype for your purposes (see "cBool").

Examples Let's assume that you are adding two numbers, one of which contains a fraction, but you *don't want to see the result as a fraction.* In earlier versions of Visual Basic, you would be explicit that A was a single-precision floating point (can hold fractions) Variable type, but C, the Variable that holds the result, was an Integer type (cannot hold fractions):

```
Dim A As Single
Dim C As Integer
A = 144.2
B = 35
C = A + B
MsgBox C
```

D

Results In

```
179
```

The fractional part of the result has been stripped off because we defined C as an Integer type. If we try the same math in VBScript, we must rely merely on Variants (no need to Dim them):

```
A = 144.2
B = 35
C = A + B
MsgBox C
```

Results In

```
179.2
```

Therefore, if your VBScript work involves math calculations, you should consider using the "coercion" commands (see "cBool") to force Variants into what are now called Variable "subtypes."

To force our result to be an Integer in the above example using VBScript:

```
A = 144.2
B = 35
C = cInt(A + B)
MsgBox C
```

Results In

```
179
```

See Variables

Date

VBSCRIPT FUNCTION

Description Tells you the date (from the user's computer clock). When your programming is running on a user's machine, you can't know the date. To find out, use the Date Function.

Variables

```
D = Date
```

Uses

- Use the other VBS Date Functions to calculate elapsed days or weeks since you posted the message.
- Display the current date.

Example

```
<HTML>
<SCRIPT LANGUAGE=VBS>

msgbox date

</SCRIPT>
</HTML>
```

See also Now, Time

D

DateSerial

VBSCRIPT FUNCTION

Description DateSerial transforms dates into numbers in a series so you can manipulate the dates mathematically.

Here's how it works. Suppose you arbitrarily decide that January 1, 100 A.D., will be day 1 of a huge list that includes every day thereafter through the year 9999. Then you give a date such as November 14, 1992, to your assistant, and ask him or her to find a serial number for that date. Your assistant discovers that November 14, 1992, is day 33922 on the list, so the serial number for that date is 33922. Now give your assistant another date. Once you've got a serial number for each of the two dates, you can perform *math* on the dates. For example, you can get the number of days between the two dates.

VBScript can work with a much longer list of numbers in series as you might imagine, because it considers *each second* between 1/1/100 and 12/31/9999 a different number in its series. Astonishing as it seems, Visual Basic Script can provide and manipulate individual serial numbers for every *second* of every day between January 1, 100, and December 31, 9999. These serial numbers are coded representations of all the hours, days, months, and years between 100 and 9999.

Variable subtype: double-precision floating-point (Variant)

Variables

```
X = DateSerial(1992, 6, 2)
```

OR (to use Variables or even calculations as arguments):

```
X = DateSerial(yr,mnth - 2,dy)
```

Uses

- Create calendars and other applications involving manipulation of dates as if they were numbers in a series.
- Using Date, automatically generate a "registration number" or unique number that combines the user's name (translated via the ASC command) with the date or time serial number.

Cautions

- Dates prior to Dec. 30, 1899, give negative serial numbers.

```
X = DateSerial(1822, 6, 2)
y = cdbl(x)
msgbox y
```

Results in

```
28335
```

- Use the Abs function to find days-between-dates.
- You must supply DateSerial with the date in this peculiar order: year, month, day.
- You can include arithmetic when you provide the date to be serialized:

```
x = DateSerial(1993, 12 - 2, 8)
```

- The number of seconds in a span of 9,899 years is obviously quite large. There are 31,536,000 seconds in a single year. That is why the Variable that will hold the serial number returned by DateSerial is of a "Double" subtype (see "Variables"), a double-precision floating-point Variable. This subtype of Variable is capable of holding an extremely large range of numbers. VBS date/time serial numbers contain the day, month, and year to the left of the decimal point, and the hour, minute, and second numbers to the right of the decimal point. However, the meaning of the serial number is encoded. There is no direct way to examine the serial number and extract the various information contained therein. That is why VBS provides various functions—Second, Minute, Hour, Day, Month, Year—to decode that information for you, turning the serial number back into English. Those functions are, in that sense, doing the opposite of what DateSerial does.

Example Here we'll show the number of days in the first six months of 1992. This reveals, via month #2, that it is a leap year.

```
<HTML>
<HEAD>
<TITLE>DateSerial Command</TITLE>
</HEAD>
<BODY>

<OBJECT ID="TextBox1" WIDTH=237 HEIGHT=295
CLASSID="CLSID:8BD21D10-EC42-11CE-9E0D-00AA006002F3">
  <PARAM NAME="VariousPropertyBits" VALUE="2894088219">
  <PARAM NAME="Size" VALUE="6279;7779">
  <PARAM NAME="FontCharSet" VALUE="0">
  <PARAM NAME="FontPitchAndFamily" VALUE="2">
  <PARAM NAME="FontWeight" VALUE="0">
</OBJECT>

<SCRIPT LANGUAGE="VBSCRIPT">
cr = chr(13) + chr(10)

A = "In 1992..." + cr + cr

x = DateSerial(1992, 1, 1) 'Get January 1st serial number

For I = 2 to 13

n = DateSerial(1992, I, 1)

z = cstr(I - 1)

textbox1.value = textbox1.value + z + ". " + →
cstr(abs(x - n)) + "days." + cr
x = n
Next
```

```
</SCRIPT>

</BODY>
</HTML>
```

See also Date, DateValue, Day, Month, Now, TimeValue, Weekday, Year

D

DateValue

VBSCRIPT STATEMENT

Description DateValue translates a *text* representation of a date (such as Jan 1, 1992) into a VBS date/time serial number that can be computed with, and manipulated, mathematically. DateValue's job is similar to DateSerial's job, but DateSerial translates a *numeric* expression into a date/time serial number. See "DateSerial" for more.

Variables Variable subtype: Text ("string")

```
DateValue (Date)
```

OR

```
DateValue (dat)
```

where you can create the date in any of the following formats:

```
Dat = "1-1-1992"
OR 1-1-92
OR Jan 1, 1992
OR January 1, 1992
OR 1-Jan-1992
OR 1 January 92
```

Uses

- The uses for DateValue are the same as DateSerial (which see); however, DateValue is more flexible in the variety of Variables it can translate. While DateSerial gives you the same results, DateValue accepts *text* as a Variable rather than numbers. Therefore, for situations where the user is typing in a date, DateValue is somewhat easier to work with.

- DateValue can translate a wide variety of text representations of dates (review Variables above).
- If you know the date—June 24, 1982, for instance—you know the month and year, but not the day of the week. DateValue offers a way to find that out (although there is also a Weekday command for that purpose built into VBS).

D

Cautions

- DateValue can handle dates between 1–1–100 and 12–31–9999.
- Dates prior to Dec. 30, 1899, give negative serial numbers.
- If you leave out the year, DateValue will assume you mean the current year.

```
X = DateValue("Mar 23")
Msgbox X
```

Results in

```
3-23-1996
```

Example

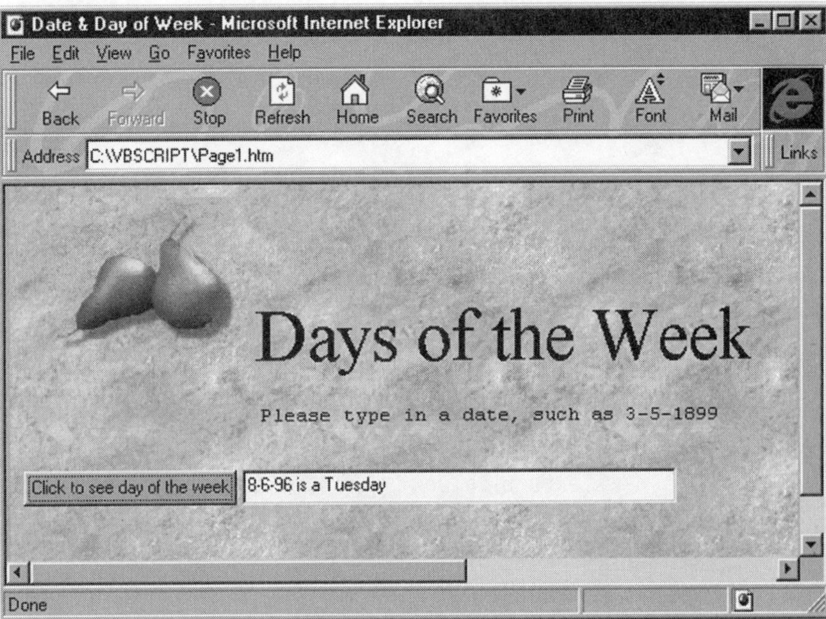

Figure D-1: This page will calculate the day of the week for any date.

D

```
<html>
<head>
<title>Date & DayOfWeek</title>
</head>
<BODY BACKGROUND="back2.gif">

<CENTER>
<IMG src="file:///C|/CSERVE/HPWIZ/Image/pears4.gif"
height=108 width=135>
<FONT SIZE=18>Days of the Week
</CENTER>

<pre>     Please type in a date, such as 3-5-1899</pre>

<br>
<INPUT TYPE=BUTTON VALUE="Click to see day of the week"
NAME="Btn">
<INPUT TYPE=TEXT VALUE="" NAME="Textbox" SIZE = 55>

<SCRIPT LANGUAGE=VBS>
Sub Btn_OnClick

Dim Daynames(8)
Daynames(1) = "Sunday"
Daynames(2) = "Monday"
Daynames(3) = "Tuesday"
Daynames(4) = "Wednesday"
Daynames(5) = "Thursday"
Daynames(6) = "Friday"
Daynames(7) = "Saturday"
n = Textbox.VALUE
x = DateValue(n)
p = Weekday(x)
result = Daynames(p)
Textbox.Value = n + " is a " + result

End Sub
</SCRIPT>

</BODY>
</HTML>
```

Using DateValue along with the Weekday Function, we can easily provide the day of the week for any date between Roman times and 9999. Note that we use the Textbox Control as both an input device (where the user enters a date) and an output device:

```
Textbox.Value = n + " is a " + result.
```

<BODY BACKGROUND="back2.gif"> is HTML that tiles the .GIF file across the screen to provide background texture. Superimposed on that is the PEARS4.GIF image, which is also centered. The <PRE> command is HTML that permits internal formatting. For example, we wanted the "Please type in..." text to line up with the headline above it, so we inserted spaces. Without <PRE>, those spaces would be ignored when the page was displayed.

For more about the DIM command, and the list of days, see "Arrays."

See also Date, DateSerial, Day, Month, Now, TimeSerial, TimeValue, Weekday, Year

D

Day

VBSCRIPT FUNCTION

Description Day extracts the day of the month from the serial number created by the DateValue, DateSerial, or Now Function.

(See "DateSerial" for more on VBScript's date/time serial numbers.)

Variables

```
Msgbox Day(Now)
```

Results in

```
5
```

(if it's the fifth of the month)

Uses Calendar applications and calculations involving dates.

Cautions

- Day can handle dates between 1–1–100 and 12–31–9999.
- Dates prior to Dec. 30, 1899, use negative serial numbers.

Example

```
X = DateValue("December 22, 1914")
D = Day(X)
Msgbox D
```

Results in

```
22
```

See also DateSerial, DateValue, Day, Hour, Minute, Month, Second, TimeSerial, TimeValue, Weekday, Year

Description

PROPERTY

Description Allows you to set (create) or read (find out) a brief piece of text associated with a particular error. It is used in this fashion:

```
Err.Description = "There was no response"
```

or, to read it:

```
Z = Err.Description
```

See Err

DblClick

ACTIVEX

See Events

Default

ACTIVEX

See Properties

Delay

ACTIVEX

See Properties

DFN

HTML

Description Changes text to italics.

See I

Dim

VBSCRIPT STATEMENT

Description The Dim command can accomplish three things:

- Create a fixed Array.
- Create a dynamic Array.
- Explicitly declare a Variable.

Dim is one of two VBS commands used to create an Array or to declare a Variable. The other is ReDim. The important difference between the ReDim and Dim commands is that ReDim must be used within a procedure (a Sub or Function), whereas Dim can be used either outside or within a procedure. If Dim is used outside a procedure, the Array will be available for use by all other programming in the script. If Dim is used within a procedure then, like ReDim, the declared Array is available only to programming that's also within that same procedure. This "range of influence" is known as the scope of a Variable or an Array. (See "Arrays" and "Variables.")

Used with Variables and Arrays

D

Variables To create space in the computer's memory for numbers, each with an index (the number in parentheses) so you can use loops to conveniently access them. This creates, in other words, an *Array*:

```
Dim Accounts(6)
```

which you can then use in a loop:

```
For i = 0 to 6: Accounts(i) = i: Next
```

Here is a sample that creates an Array with the Dim command, then fills the Array with numbers, then displays the Array's contents in a text box:

```
<HTML>
<HEAD>
<TITLE>New Page</TITLE>
</HEAD>
<BODY>
<OBJECT ID="TextBox1" WIDTH=137 HEIGHT=243
CLASSID="CLSID:8BD21D10-EC42-11CE-9E0D-00AA006002F3">
  <PARAM NAME="VariousPropertyBits" VALUE="-1400879077">
  <PARAM NAME="Size" VALUE="3620;6403">
  <PARAM NAME="FontCharSet" VALUE="0">
  <PARAM NAME="FontPitchAndFamily" VALUE="2">
  <PARAM NAME="FontWeight" VALUE="0">
</OBJECT>

<SCRIPT LANGUAGE="VBSCRIPT">
cr = chr(13) + chr(10)
Dim Accounts(6)
For i = 0 to 5: Accounts(i) = i: Next
For i = 0 to 5
n = accounts(i)
textbox1.value = textbox1.value + cr + "Item #" + cstr(n)
Next
</SCRIPT>

</BODY>
</HTML>
```

OR (to create space for two Arrays, each with *double* indexes):

```
Dim X (50, 400), Y (50, 500)
```

Each of these Arrays—X( ) and Y( )—has been defined (dimensioned) as a two-dimensional Array. A two-dimensional Array can be accessed in this fashion:

```
For I = 1 to 50
  For J = 1 to 500
    MsgBox X(I,J)
    MsgBox Y(I,J)
--  Next
Next
```

OR (used with ReDim, to create a *dynamic* Array, one that appears when a Subroutine or Function is triggered, does its thing, and ceases to exist when the procedure is finished with End Sub or End Function):

```
Dim Tempwords ( )
```

The important thing to notice is the empty parentheses that indicate the creation of a dynamic Array. However, using Dim in this fashion is optional. ReDim can be used by itself with no preceding Dim.

Then, after the optional Dim with empty parentheses:

```
Sub Box_Click()
ReDim Tempwords (30)
End Sub
```

An alternative use of Dim is to explicitly announce the existence of Variables. Some programmers feel that you should always declare every Variable you use in a program. Languages like Pascal require these declarations, but in Basic, explicit declaration is optional. For more on this, see "Variables."

Uses

- To set aside some space in the computer's memory to hold a collection of related pieces of information (called an *Array*).
- Dim with empty parentheses ( ) announces a dynamic Array. A dynamic Array saves space because the Array, later redimensioned (ReDim) within an Event Procedure (a Sub or Function procedure), can be freely resized to use up only the amount of space needed. A dynamic Array can be resized more than once, to reflect current needs as the program runs.

And dynamic Arrays can create a big temporary Array, then let go of the memory when it is no longer needed. However, you can use ReDim by itself; the original Dim isn't required by VBS. (See "Arrays.")

D

Cautions When you first use Dim, all the elements of a numeric Array are set to 0, and all elements of a text Array (string Array) are set to empty strings ("").

Example (See "Arrays" for further information about how to use this essential programming tool.)

```
<HTML>
<HEAD>
<TITLE>New Page</TITLE>
</HEAD>
<BODY>
  <OBJECT ID="TextBox1" WIDTH=192 HEIGHT=333
CLASSID="CLSID:8BD21D10-EC42-11CE-9E0D-00AA006002F3">
  <PARAM NAME="VariousPropertyBits" VALUE="-1400879077">
  <PARAM NAME="Size" VALUE="5075;8811">
  <PARAM NAME="FontCharSet" VALUE="0">
  <PARAM NAME="FontPitchAndFamily" VALUE="2">
  <PARAM NAME="FontWeight" VALUE="0">
</OBJECT>

<SCRIPT LANGUAGE="VBSCRIPT">
cr = chr(13) + chr(10)
Dim Fractions (3, 3)
For I = 0 to 2
For J = 0 to 2
Fractions (I, J) = I + J / 9
textbox1.value = cr + textbox1.value + cstr(Fractions(I,J)) +
cr
Next
Next
</SCRIPT>
</BODY>
</HTML>
```

We created an Array called *Fractions*. The Array has two dimensions, each capable of storing data indexed by 0 to 3 (in other words, each dimension can hold four data items). Then we stored data in the Array, and displayed it in a TextBox. Notice that you specify items in a multi-dimensional Array by using more than one index—(I, J) in our example above.

See also Arrays, DefType, Erase, LBound, ReDim, UBound, Variables, Variant

DIR

HTML

Description Creates a list (with no bullets) featuring words of less than 20 characters. It's called a "directory list" because it's similar to the file directory lists (short filenames were used) in older operating systems.

Used with ***Can be enclosed by***

<BANNER>, <BODY>, <BODYTEXT>, <DD>, <DIV>, <FIGTEXT>, <FN>, <FORM>, <LI>, <NOTE>, <TD>, <TH>

Can enclose

<LI>

Variables

```
<DIR>
<LI>Cars
<LI>Buses
<LI>Trucks
</DIR>
```

Uses Not many (see Cautions).

Cautions Some browsers put the list of terms in a vertical column, others don't. For this reason, DIR isn't of much use—you can't tell how it will look to various users.

DL

HTML

Description Creates a list that resembles a "definition list"—something like the way a glossary is formatted. It's a two-column list, with terms against the left margin and their definitions indented, moved down one line, or both (browsers interpret this command differently.)

Used with ***Can be enclosed by***

<BANNER>, <BODY>, <BODYTEXT>, <DD>, <DIV>, <FIGTEXT>, <FN>, <FORM>, <LI>, <NOTE>, <TD>, <TH>

Can enclose

<DD>, <DT>, <LH>

Variables This command features two subcommands, tags that describe the two elements within a glossary list:

- DT—the *term* being defined
- DD—the *definition* of that term

Uses When you want to create something that looks like a glossary of terms.

Cautions Browsers currently interpret this formatting structure in various ways.

Example

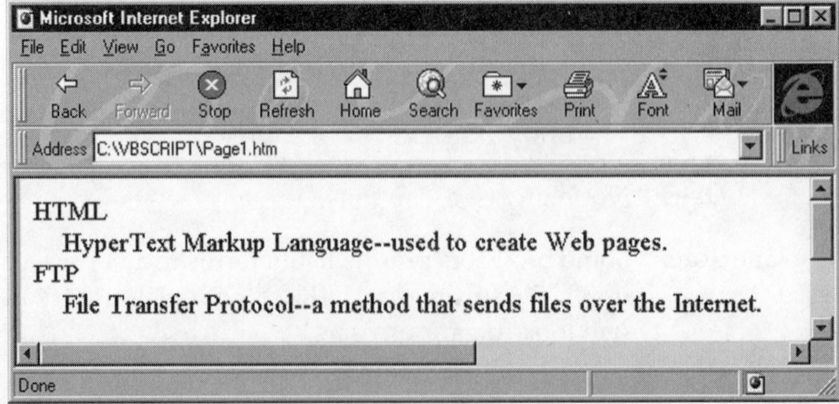

Figure D-2: The DL command formats text like a typical glossary.

```
<DL>
<DT>HTML
<DD>HyperText Markup Language--used to create Web pages.
<DT>FTP
<DD>File Transfer Protocol--a method that sends files over
the Internet.
</DL>
```

D

Document

VBSCRIPT OBJECT

Description VBScript sees an HTML document as an *object*. This means that you can do things with it from within VBScript. One common use of the Document Object is to reference HTML Controls that have been used within the Form command. In this example, we have a Form that we've named *MyForm*. To refer to it (and the Controls on MyForm) within VBScript, we use Document.MyForm. In this example, we used the Set command to create an Object Variable (see "Form" and "Set").

```
<HTML>
</HEAD>
<BODY>
<FORM NAME="MyForm">
Please type in your name:
<INPUT NAME="Text1" TYPE="TEXT" SIZE="42">
<INPUT NAME="Submit" TYPE="BUTTON" VALUE="Submit">
</FORM>
</BODY>
<SCRIPT LANGUAGE="VBScript">

Sub Submit_OnClick
 Dim F
 Set F = Document.MyForm
   If IsNumeric(F.Text1.Value) Then
      MsgBox "Please type in your name, not your address or
phone number."
   Else
MsgBox "We'll send it in."
```

```
F.Submit
 End If
End Sub

</SCRIPT>
</HTML>
```

D

Another use for the Document Object is to put some text directly onto an HTML page *from within VBScript*. As you know, you can put text onto an HTML document by merely typing it in between <HTML> and </HTML> in the body of your HTML source code. However, if you want to put some text onto a page from within VBScript, use the Document.Write command:

```
Document.Write "Put this directly on the page."
```

In HTML there's no way to calculate and display the results as plain text on the document. With VBScript, you can, for example, tell users the date when, 30 days from now, their subscription expires. And you can put this right on the page with ordinary text:

```
<HTML>
<HEAD>
<TITLE>Document</TITLE>
</HEAD>
<BODY>

<BIG>Important Notice...<BIG>
<P><P>

<SCRIPT LANGUAGE="VBScript">
<!--

N = DateValue(now)
N = N + 30 'add 30 days

Document.Write "<BIG>OUR SUBSCRIPTION SERVICE</BIG>"
Document.Write "<P>Your sub expires on " & N

-->
</SCRIPT>
</BODY>
</HTML>
```

Notice in the above example that when you use Document.Write, you're not simply printing text. In fact, you're feeding HTML source code to the browser. Therefore, you can include any HTML commands, as we've done above with <BIG> and <P>.

Variables

```
<script language="VBScript">
  document.bgColor = "Cyan"
</script>
```

D

Properties

Anchors: A list (an "Array") of the hypertext links within the document. See Links below.

bgColor, fgColor: The background and foreground (text) colors of the document. In Internet Explorer 2.0 this change could only take effect when the document was loaded (parsed)—for example, within the Window_OnLoad Event. It would not change these colors in response, for example, to a user clicking on a button. However, it does work now in any situation with Internet Explorer 3.0:

```
<HTML>
<HEAD>
<TITLE>Document</TITLE>
</HEAD>
<BODY>

<BIG>OUR CORPORATE FORECAST</BIG>
<BR><BR><BR>

<OBJECT ID="CommandButton1" WIDTH=96 HEIGHT=32
CLASSID="CLSID:D7053240-CE69-11CD-A777-00DD01143C57">
  <PARAM NAME="Caption" VALUE="Click for Red">
  <PARAM NAME="Size" VALUE="2540;846">
  <PARAM NAME="FontCharSet" VALUE="0">
  <PARAM NAME="FontPitchAndFamily" VALUE="2">
  <PARAM NAME="ParagraphAlign" VALUE="3">
  <PARAM NAME="FontWeight" VALUE="0">
</OBJECT>
```

```
<SCRIPT LANGUAGE="VBScript">
<!--
Sub CommandButton1_Click
  document.bgColor = "Red"
End Sub


-->
  </SCRIPT>

</BODY>
</HTML>
```

D

Cookie: Reports or changes the "Cookie" of a document. A Cookie is a piece of data that is left on the user's hard drive. It can provide information to your script about the user's previous visit to your site (so you can customize it for him or her). Cookies are also a way to store truly global Variables. In fact, there are numerous situations where you might want to leave some information on the client side, then later retrieve it. For more detail, see the entry on "Cookies."

```
<script language="VBScript">
C = document.cookie
msgbox C
</script>
```

OR, to change the Cookie:

```
<script language="VBScript">
document.cookie = "We made this in five hours."
</script>
```

Forms: A list (an "Array") of any Forms within the document. See Links below.

LastModified: Reports the date of the last modification of the document.

```
<script language="VBScript">
D = document.lastmodified
msgbox D
</script>
```

LinkColor: The color of hypertext links (see "A") created by:

```
<A HREF="keypress.htm"> Click here to go to an alternative
page.</A>
<script language="VBScript">
     document.LinkColor = "White"
</script>
```


Tip

You can define colors with either hexadecimal numbers or, as we've done in these examples, ordinary English words like White. *For a complete list of all 140 English word colors you can use, see "Many New Colors" in the entry on "BGCOLOR." For an explanation of hexadecimal, see "Hex Numbers for the Color Command" in the entry on "BODY."*

You can also *read* (find out) the current LinkColor:

```
document.LinkColor = "White"
X = document.LinkColor
MsgBox X
```

Results in

```
#FFFFFF
```

There is a related Property, **vLinkColor**, that sets (changes) or provides (reads) the color of the "visited" links—sites on the Internet that the user has already gone to.

Links: A list (an "Array") of the hypertext links within the document. These Links are themselves *objects,* illustrating that objects can be contained within other objects (Document.Links). You can't "Write" an object onto an HTML page. However, you can Write the Links' HREF, as illustrated in this example:

```
<HTML>
<HEAD>
<TITLE>Document Links</TITLE>
</HEAD>
```

```
<BODY>

<A HREF="keypress.htm"> Click here to go to an alternative
page.</A>
<A HREF="http://www.microsoft.com"> Click here to go to
Microsoft.</A>
<A HREF="http://altavista.digital.com"> Search Engine </A>
<br>

<script language="VBScript">
x = document.links.length
document.write x & "<BR>"

for i=0 to x - 1
document.writeln document.links(i).href
document.write "<BR>"
next

</script>
</BODY>
```

Notice that the Links.Length provides the actual number of links (in this example, three). However, the Links "array" begins counting from zero, so you need to use X - 1 as the upper limit of your loop when querying this "array." At the start of this example, we create three links. Then, in our script, we find out how many links there are (X), and, within the For...Next loop, use document.links(i).href to directly write their names onto the document itself.

```
<script language="VBScript">
S = document.location
msgbox S
</script>
```

Referrer: The URL location of the document (if any) that provided the link to the current document. For example, if you were in Microsoft's home page and clicked on a link to bring up the current document, the Referrer would be http://www.microsoft.com. In effect, the Referrer is the equivalent of the contents of the Back button found on most browsers.

```
<script language="VBScript">
R = document.referrer
msgbox R
</script>

<HTML>
<HEAD>
<TITLE>Document Properties</TITLE>
</HEAD>
<BODY>
<br>

<script language="VBScript">
T = document.Title
msgbox T
</script>

</BODY>
</HTML>
```

Methods

```
<HTML>
<HEAD>
<TITLE>Document Properties</TITLE>
</HEAD>
<BODY>

<PRE>
<SCRIPT LANGUAGE="VBScript">
document.writeLn "This line ends in a carriage return (new
line)."
document.write "These lines go "
document.write "together."
</SCRIPT>

</BODY>
</HTML>
```

D

Uses

```
<HTML>
<HEAD>
<TITLE>New Page</TITLE>
</HEAD>
<BODY>
Welcome to our home page.
<BR>
<SCRIPT LANGUAGE="VBScript">
Document.Write "Welcome to our home page. Today is " & →
Date() & "."
</SCRIPT>
</BODY>
</HTML>
```

Example Here both the ordinary HTML method of displaying text and the VBScript method are illustrated. Notice that with VBScript, information can be displayed that is dynamic and depends on conditions.

```
<HTML>
<HEAD>
<TITLE>Document Object</TITLE>
</HEAD>
<BODY>
<BR>
<INPUT NAME="Button1" TYPE="Button" VALUE=" Click me for a →
Thrill! ">
<BR>
This is ordinary HTML text.

<BR><BR>
<PRE>
<SCRIPT LANGUAGE="VBScript">
Document.WriteLn "This is VBScript text, put upon the page →
dynamically"
Document.WriteLn document.referrer

Sub Button1_OnClick ()
Msgbox Document.Title
End Sub
```

```
</SCRIPT>
</BODY>
</HTML>
```

Do...Loop

VBSCRIPT STATEMENT

Description This is the most powerful of the commands generally called *Loops*. A Loop structure halts the program's forward progress until something happens to fulfill the requirements of the Loop. It's as if some repetitive task interrupts your stroll in the woods—remove burrs before continuing on.

An alternative to the Do...Loop structure is For...Next, which is the most commonly used Loop structure. If you *know* how many times a Loop should repeat the commands within it, use For...Next. For...Next uses a *counter* to determine how long to continue repeating. The counter is the I Variable in For I = 1 to 300. "I" will keep increasing by 1 each time the Loop repeats. When the Loop has repeated 300 times, the program will continue on past the For...Next Loop.

The reason that For...Next is used so often is that when you're writing your program, you often know how many times you want something done: print the total number of names in an Array; put 12 Picture Boxes on the screen; and so forth. For I = 1 to 100 makes the program repeat a Loop 100 times, doing whatever is within the Loop 100 times:

```
For I = 1 to 100
  Msgbox I,
Next
```

This produces a list of the digits from 1 to 100, each one triggering a message box.

Another alternative is the new For Each...Next structure for use with Collection "Arrays." See "For Each."

Do...Loop: You use a Do...Loop structure when you can't know while you're writing your program how often the Loop should repeat. Perhaps your program asks the user to specify the number of times something should appear onscreen; or perhaps you're displaying the number of days until the end of the month. The number of times a Loop should execute these things will be different for each user of your program or each time a particular user runs the program.

D

The Do...Loop structure keeps going through its Loop until some condition happens, rather than counting up to a number like For...Next. (Exactly what condition triggers the end of the Loop will vary depending on the purposes of your program.) In any event, you don't know, when creating the program, the literal number of times the Loop should execute.

As an aside, sometimes you use For...Next even if you don't know how many times it will Loop until the program actually runs. For that, you'd Loop a variable number of times. For example, you'd use For I=1 to *Items* to start a Loop that reads in a number of items in a file, where the count was stored as the first line in the file itself. Sometimes the essential difference between For and Do Loops is not how many times the Loop runs, but that For runs a Loop a certain number of times and Do runs it while a certain condition remains true.

Nevertheless, Do...Loop is used when you can't know while designing your program the number of Loop repetitions you'll need: "Get enough bags of potato chips for the number of people coming over for the party." Another way to state the difference is that you use a Do...Loop based on current conditions while the program is running.

Do...Loop is also quite flexible in that you can set up interior tests and quit the Loop with the Exit Do command. And you can place a quit condition at the beginning or end of the Loop. Putting the quit condition test at the end ensures that the Loop *will always happen at least once.* If you put the test at the start of the Loop and the test fails, the Loop will never happen. VBS will skip over the commands within the Loop. If you want the Loop to always execute at least once, put the condition test at the bottom of the Loop:

```
<HTML>

<INPUT TYPE=BUTTON VALUE="Click to see day of the week"
NAME="Btn">
<INPUT TYPE=TEXT VALUE="" NAME="Textbox" SIZE = 65>

<SCRIPT LANGUAGE=VBS>
Sub Btn_OnClick

A = Textbox.Value

Do
  x = x + 1
  n = Mid(A, x, 1)
Loop Until n = Empty

Textbox.Value = "There are " + cStr(x) + " characters in " →
+ A

End Sub
</SCRIPT>

</HTML>
```

In the example above, you don't know the number of characters in the text box until you've gone through them. The number of characters will vary depending on what the user types in before clicking the button.

Do...Loop also permits two kinds of conditional tests: *While* and *Until*. This distinction is only a matter of how you want to express things, like the difference between "Sweep *until* the porch is clean" versus "Sweep *while* the porch is dirty." The computer doesn't care about such things. However, expressing the condition in a particular way can sometimes make your meaning clearer to you and other humans who read your program.

The third available Loop structure is While...Wend, a less powerful version of Do...Loop that merely continues Looping while a condition remains true. To Loop as long as X is less than 100:

```
While X < 5: X = X + 1: Msgbox X: Wend
```

While...Wend has no exit command, and it is also limited to testing the condition at the start of its Loop. You may want to use the Do...Loop structure, and forget that While...Wend exists at all—it's limited and unnecessarily crude in a language that includes Do...Loop.

Accomplish the above with:

```
Do While X < 5
   X = X + 1
   Msgbox X
Loop
```

Variables To test the exit condition within the Loop:

```
Do
   Msgbox Y
   Y = Y + 1
   If Y > 11 Then Exit Do
Loop
```

OR (to test the exit condition at the start of the Loop using Until):

```
Do Until Y > 10
   Msgbox Y
   Y = Y + 1
Loop
```

OR (to test the exit condition at the start of the Loop using While):

```
Do While Y < 11
   Y = Y + 1
Loop
```

OR (to test the exit condition at the end of the Loop using Until):

```
Do
   y = y + 1
Loop Until Y = 10
```

OR (to test the exit condition at the end of the Loop using While):

```
Do
   y = y + 1
Loop While Y < 10
```

There are times when you need to put the exit condition test at the end. See the example below.

Uses As a generalization, when you want something done repeatedly but don't know the number of times you want it repeated, use a Do...Loop instead of a For...Next Loop. For...Next is for when you do know the number of times something should be done.

Use Do...Loop when you know a condition that must be satisfied rather than the precise number of times a task should be performed.

- For...Next is: "Brush my hair 150 times."
- Do...Loop is: "Brush my hair until it shines."

Cautions You can inadvertently create the dreaded *infinite Loop* when using a Do...Loop in one of your programs. When your program gets into an infinite Loop, it will keep going round and round with no way out. The computer is attempting to finish an unfinishable job. You've accidentally given the Loop an exit condition that will never be satisfied, and therefore the Loop will never be exited. Unlike For...Next, which at least has been given an upper limit—a specified number of times it will Loop—a clumsily constructed Do...Loop could go on forever. Here's one:

```
<HTML>
<INPUT TYPE=BUTTON VALUE="Click to see how high we can
count!" NAME="Btn">
<INPUT TYPE=TEXT VALUE="" NAME="Textbox" SIZE = 65>

<SCRIPT LANGUAGE=VBS>
Sub Btn_OnClick

Do Until X < 0
X = X + 1
Textbox.Value = cStr(X)
Loop

End Sub
</SCRIPT>
</HTML>
```

However, Internet Explorer permits only about 30 seconds of this nonsense, then puts up the message shown in Figure D-3:

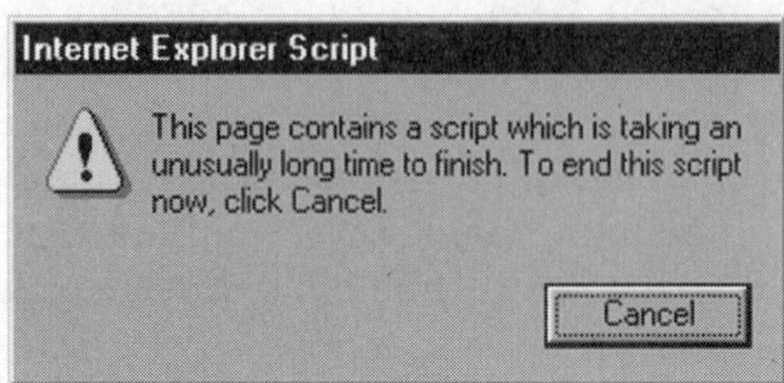

Figure D-3: If your program goes into an endless loop, Internet Explorer waits 30 seconds, then displays this message.

The exit condition we've given this Loop—that the Variable X becomes less than zero—could never come true. There is no command within the Loop that could cause X to go below zero.

You might want to avoid putting one Do...Loop inside another because things can get too complex quickly. Be aware that nested Do...Loops are strange, counterintuitive things. Nesting For...Next Loops can also be fairly confusing, but at least they're usually understandable—ultimately.

Example Say the user types in a sentence. You cannot know while you're writing your program what kind of sentence the user will type; but your script has to count the number of words in that sentence for some reason.

The InStr command can count the spaces in the sentence, thereby telling you the number of words. The InStr command will give back a 0 when it cannot find any more spaces. In this situation you want to place the "exit condition" at the end of the Loop. This way, the Loop happens at least one time, no matter what the user types. In other words, we want to do the following:

```
Do "find the next space"
Until we get a 0
```

(We get a 0 when InStr returns 0 to us, saying that it cannot find any more spaces inside the user's message.)

```
<HTML>
<HEAD>
<TITLE>New Page</TITLE>
</HEAD>

<BODY>

<HTML>
<INPUT TYPE=TEXT VALUE="I cannot be at the office tomorrow."
NAME="Textbox" SIZE = 65>
<INPUT TYPE=BUTTON VALUE="Word Count" NAME="Btn">

<SCRIPT LANGUAGE="VBSCRIPT">
Sub Btn_OnClick

A = Textbox.Value

Lastposition = 1 'start off with the first letter in the
sentence.

Do
  Pointer = InStr(Lastposition, A, " ")
  X = X + 1
  Lastposition = Pointer + 1
Loop Until Pointer = 0


Textbox.Value = "The number of words in the sentence is: " →
+ cStr(X)

End Sub

</SCRIPT>

</BODY>

</HTML>
```

Results in

```
The number of words in the sentence is: 7
```

(We put the conditional test at the *end* of the Loop this time because our pointer, when we enter the Loop, is zero and that would have bounced us right off the Loop before we had even gotten started if the test were at the start of the Loop.)

See also For...Next, For Each, While...Wend

DragBehavior

ACTIVEX

See Properties

DropButtonClick

ACTIVEX

See Events

DropButtonStyle

ACTIVEX

See Properties

DropDown

ACTIVEX

See Methods

E

EM

HTML

Description Changes text to italics, for *em*phasis. (In some browsers, though, this command underlines instead.)

See I

Enable

ACTIVEX

Description The PreLoader, unique among Controls, has an *Enable* Property. For all other Controls with this same feature, it's called the *Enabled* Property (Timer1.Enabled = True, for example). Alas, this sort of slip-up results in confusion and errors. Just remember that Enable means the same as Enabled.

See PreLoader

Enabled

ACTIVEX

See Properties

Enter

ACTIVEX

See Events

EnterFieldBehavior

ACTIVEX

See Properties

EnterKeyBehavior

ACTIVEX

See Properties

Eqv

VBSCRIPT OPERATOR

See Operators

Erase

VBSCRIPT STATEMENT

Description The Erase command works two ways, depending on whether it's applied to a *Static* or a *Dynamic* Array. (See "Arrays.")

- With Static Arrays, Erase resets all the Array elements to "Zero" (if they're numeric Variable subtypes), to "Nothing" (if they're Objects), to "" (blank text Variable subtypes), or to "Empty" (if they're pure Variants).
- With Dynamic Arrays, Erase collapses the entire Array structure and gives the computer back the use of the memory that the Array had occupied.
- Even after Erase, a Static Array still exists like an empty honeycomb. A Dynamic Array after Erase, however, no longer exists at all.
- In an Array of Variants (which see), each element is reset to "Empty." In an Array of Objects (which see), each item is reset to "Nothing." In a programmer-defined Array (see "Type"), each element is reset according to its Variable subtype.

Used with Arrays (which see)

Variables Erase MyArrayName

```
<HTML>
<HEAD>
<TITLE>Erase Command</TITLE>
</HEAD>
<BODY>

<INPUT TYPE=BUTTON VALUE="Click this..." NAME="Btn">

<SCRIPT LANGUAGE="VBSCRIPT">

Sub Btn_OnClick

Dim N(5)

N(1) = 123

msgbox cStr(n(1))

Erase n

msgbox cStr(n(1))

End Sub

</SCRIPT>
</BODY>
</HTML>
```

In the above example, the message box that is displayed first reveals contents in the Array N at Index 1. The contents are the number 123, because we just put that data into N(1). However, after the Erase command, the message box displays nothing. The entire Array has been emptied.

Uses

- Frees up computer memory for other uses when a Dynamic Array is no longer needed by your program.
- Makes sure that a Static Array is completely clean, completely free of data.

E

Cautions Note that all the Variables (including Arrays) declared within a procedure (a Sub or Function) are temporary—dynamic and usable when the procedure is being run, but discarded when the program moves on to another procedure. (The exception would be Arrays or Variables declared *outside* the procedure with the Dim command.)

With Dim (used outside a procedure but within the <SCRIPT> commands), however, all the Variables within it are permanent, persistent, and stable as long as the script is running. That is, there can be variations in the numbers (or text) they hold, but the Variable names, the memory space they reserve, *and the data they hold* will not be automatically destroyed when the script moves on to other procedures.

The important difference between the ReDim and Dim commands is that ReDim must be used within a procedure (a Sub or Function), whereas Dim can be used either outside or within a procedure. If Dim is used outside a procedure, the Array will be available for use by all other programming in the script. If Dim is used within a procedure, then, like ReDim, the declared Array is available only to programming that's within that same procedure. This "range of influence" is known as the scope of a Variable or an Array.

Example

```
<HTML>
<HEAD>
<TITLE>DateSerial Command</TITLE>
</HEAD>
<BODY>
   <OBJECT ID="TextBox1" WIDTH=324 HEIGHT=567
   CLASSID="CLSID:8BD21D10-EC42-11CE-9E0D-00AA006002F3">
   <PARAM NAME="VariousPropertyBits" VALUE="-1400879077">
   <PARAM NAME="Size" VALUE="8567;15002">
   <PARAM NAME="FontCharSet" VALUE="0">
   <PARAM NAME="FontPitchAndFamily" VALUE="2">
   <PARAM NAME="FontWeight" VALUE="0">
</OBJECT>

<SCRIPT LANGUAGE="VBSCRIPT">
cr = chr(13) + chr(10)
```

```
Dim Test(21)

For i = 1 To 20
  Test(i) = i
  textbox1. value = textbox1.value + cstr(Test(i)) + cr
Next

Erase Test

textbox1. value = textbox1.value + "Erase Test" + cr

textbox1. value = textbox1.value + "Now the Test Array is
empty..." + cr

For i = 1 To 20

textbox1. value = textbox1.value + cstr(Test(i)) + cr

Next

</SCRIPT>
</BODY>
</HTML>
```

See also Arrays, Dim, ReDim

Err

VBSCRIPT OBJECT

Description Let's be honest, browsers are remarkably forgiving little operating systems. You can write pretty bad HTML and the browser won't crash, choke, or even tell the user that there's been a problem. The browser just displays whatever it can, as best it can.

When you're writing VBScript, the Err object can tell you what error occurred, if any, while your script was running. Err uses VBScript's error code system (to look up an error number and an error message describing the problem). Err can also report an outside OLE entity as the source of an error and accomplish other tasks.

If a problem occurs while your script is running, the Err object will not contain a zero. Therefore, you can query Err to check for a problem and, perhaps, respond to it within your script. For a tutorial discussion of debugging techniques that work with VBScript and ActiveX Controls, see the Introduction to this book.

When an error occurs, VBScript displays a message to the user, as shown in Figure E-1.

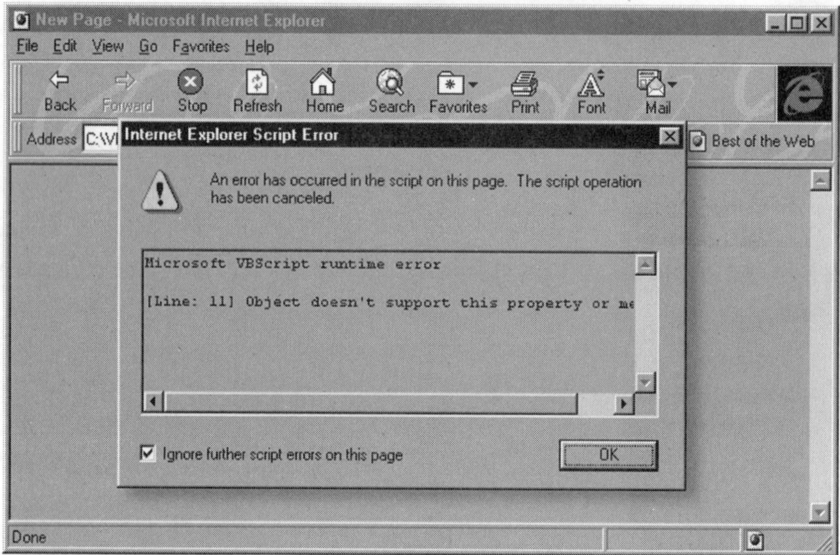

Figure E-1: Don't frighten visitors to your Web site with messages like this.

This is the VBScript that caused the error reported in Figure E-1:

```
<SCRIPT LANGUAGE="VBScript">
Sub window_onLoad()
msgbox top.nort
end sub
</SCRIPT>
```

VBScript saw that you wanted to display an object named "top.nort," and it didn't know how to handle that situation. So it reported the problem. When you test your documents, you'll see this error report and, presumably, fix the problem.

However, as everyone knows, you can't anticipate all problems when writing a computer program. For example, what if you asked the user to enter her age and she responded by typing in the word Texas? If your VBScript program then attempts to compare her age to the average visitor to your site, an error will occur. You can't do math with Texas. Wrong user input and dozens of other situations can lead to run-time errors (errors that occur while a script is running).

Instead of frightening users with cryptic error message windows, use the On Error Resume Next command. It tells VBScript to just go on executing the next commands, even if an error occurs. Don't stop and display any message to the user. Behave like HTML and do your best, given the circumstances.

Some computer languages offer special error-trapping and error-handling features. VBScript is rather restrictive. It only allows you to handle problems *within the same procedure in which the error occurred*. You can't refer all errors to some general-purpose Sub or Function. No, if you're going to do anything at all about an error, you must provide the programming within the same Sub or Function where the error occurred. One thing you might do is provide a more user-friendly error message than the default VBS messages. You could also give the user a second chance to, say, answer a question. Without error handling, a user typing in Texas when asked for her age would get the message "Line 4 Type Mismatch," which would mean less than nothing to most users:

```
<SCRIPT LANGUAGE="VBScript">
Sub window_onLoad()
Z = InputBox ("Please enter your age")
Z = cInt(Z)
end sub
</SCRIPT>
```

To us, the programmers, that message is useful. It says that the Z = cInt(Z) command failed because we were asking VBS to transform the word Texas into a numeric Variable subtype, clearly an impossible task (see "cBool"). To the user, though, it merely seems you have constructed a foolish Web page.

E

E

Adding On Error Resume Next is an improvement. The user gets no error message:

```
<SCRIPT LANGUAGE="VBScript">
Sub window_onLoad()
On Error Resume Next
Z = InputBox ("Please enter your age")
Z = cInt(Z)
end sub
</SCRIPT>
```

To the user, all seems normal, thanks to the inclusion of On Error Resume Next. Of course, you've got bad data and you might later display some puzzling messages to the user: "You're the third person today to visit this site who is 0 years old" or something like that.

The best solution is to anticipate problems with user entry. Out of the 200,000 people to visit your site, it's likely *some* of them will type in something like Texas as their age, no? Combine On Error Resume Next with error-trapping, like this:

```
<SCRIPT LANGUAGE="VBScript">
Sub window_onLoad()
On Error Resume Next
Z = InputBox ("Please enter your age")
Z = cInt(Z)
If Err then
Z = InputBox ("It seems you've made a small mistake. You
typed in " & Z & " as your age, an impossibility. Please re-
enter your age")
End If
end sub
</SCRIPT>
```

For a detailed discussion of debugging your scripts, see the Introduction to this book.

Used with The On Error Statement and the Error Statement

Variables In VBS, Err is an object—an object built into the language, with its own Properties and Methods.

The complete syntax for the Err object is:

```
Err.Number
```

Number is the default Property of the Err object, so you can just leave it off:

```
MsgBox Err
```

The number is an error code assigned to the particular error that occurred. See "Visual Basic Error Codes" below.

```
Err.Description
```

The Description Property is a brief text message describing the error.

```
Err.Source
```

This Property tells you what language or object caused the error. It is primarily designed to report when errors occur outside of the current language—in an OLE Automation object. However, since you cannot write OLE Automation objects with VBScript, Err. Source will always report: "Microsoft VBScript Runtime Error."

```
Err. Helpfile
```

This is the path and filename of any help file associated with this error. It provides the user with more detailed information on the nature of the error and its possible cure.

```
Err.HelpContext
```

This is the specific location within an associated helpfile, relevant to the current error.

The following is the most frequent use of Err. If an error has occurred while the program is running, this example provides the error code, which is held in Err, to the VBS Error command. Error then translates that code into a brief text explanation of the code. This explanation is then presented to the user in a message box:

```
Sub window_onLoad()
on error resume next
msgbox top.nort
```

```
if err then
  msgbox err.description
end if
end sub
```

OR (to find out what error code exists, if any):

```
X = Err
```

E

If you want to simulate errors to test your program's response to them, you can use the Raise command to pretend that a particular error occurred. This allows you to simulate errors while testing your program. In this way, you can see how your program responds, and write code that will handle errors effectively and gracefully. However, at this time, no lists of error codes for VBScript are available (though they seem to be the same as the codes for Visual Basic 4.0). If you suspect that a particular error might occur and you want to see how your script responds, you might want to deliberately induce that error rather than using Raise. The original purpose of the Raise Method was to allow programmers to define their error codes and descriptions for OLE Automation objects that the programmers wrote. However, VBScript does not permit you to create OLE Automation objects; Raise exists in VBS solely as a debugging technique. And it is a technique of dubious utility.

```
Err.Raise(number, source, description, helpfile, helpcontext)
```

The five arguments for the Raise Method are identical to the five Properties of the Err Object, described above.

If you want to pretend that the user entered the word Texas, rather than an expected number and your script generated an error because you tried to divide the word by 2, then you could use error number 13 (type mismatch):

```
<SCRIPT LANGUAGE="VBScript">
<!--
Sub window_onLoad()
on error resume next
err.raise 13
if err then
  msgbox err.description
end if
```

```
end sub
-->
</SCRIPT>
```

OR (to reset Err so that it no longer reports or triggers an error, use the Clear Method):

```
Err.Clear
```

You can also *coerce* a Variable into an error subtype, using the cVerr command. This allows you, the programmer, to define a new error code. However, the current version of VBScript does not support the cVerr command.

E

Visual Basic Error Codes

Table E-1 provides a list of Visual Basic 4.0 error codes and the associated Err.Description. Some of these errors are, of course, impossible in VBScript. For example, no commands exist in VBScript that permit contacting the user's hard drive. We don't want some innocent Web surfer wandering into the site of a poisonous person—a person who has written the following VBScript disk-destroying code:

```
<SCRIPT LANGUAGE="VBScript">
<!--
Sub window_onLoad()
Format C:
end sub
-->
</SCRIPT>
```

Therefore, file- and disk-handling error messages like "file not found" or "disk not ready" will never occur in VBScript.

Error Code	Description
3	Return without GoSub
5	Invalid procedure call
6	Overflow
7	Out of memory
9	Subscript out of range
10	This Array is fixed or temporarily locked

Error Code	Description
11	Division by zero
13	Type mismatch
14	Out of string space
16	Expression too complex
17	Can't perform requested operation
18	User interrupt occurred
20	Resume without error
28	Out of stack space
35	Sub, Function, or Property not defined
47	Too many DLL application clients
48	Error in loading DLL
49	Bad DLL calling convention
51	Internal error
52	Bad file name or number
53	File not found
54	Bad file mode
55	File already open
57	Device I/O error
58	File already exists
59	Bad record length
61	Disk full
62	Input past end of file
63	Bad record number
67	Too many files
68	Device unavailable
70	Permission denied
71	Disk not ready
74	Can't rename with different drive
75	Path/File access error
76	Path not found

Error Code	Description
91	Object Variable or With block Variable not set
92	For loop not initialized
93	Invalid pattern string
94	Invalid use of Null
325	Invalid format in resource file
380	Invalid property value
423	Property or method not found
424	Object required
429	OLE Automation server can't create object
430	Class doesn't support OLE Automation
432	File name or class name not found during OLE Automation operation
438	Object doesn't support this property or method
440	OLE Automation error
443	OLE Automation object does not have a default value
445	Object doesn't support this action
446	Object doesn't support named arguments
447	Object doesn't support current locale setting
448	Named argument not found
449	Argument not optional
450	Wrong number of arguments
451	Object not a collection
452	Invalid ordinal
453	Specified DLL function not found
454	Code resource not found
455	Code resource lock error
457	This key is already associated with an element of this collection
481	Invalid picture

Table E-1: Visual Basic 4.0 error codes.

Uses Error handling, or *trapping*, means making provisions in your program in case something untoward happens that could cause problems while the program is running. The primary source of run-time (when the program is run by a user, as opposed to when you are designing the program) errors in traditional (non-Internet) programming was a failed attempt to use or contact a peripheral, such as the disk drive. Expecting to find a file, but failing (because the user had moved or renamed it) was a typical error. In VBS Internet programming, however, the most common source of errors is attempting to use an OCX or some other object—and failing. Probably the second most common source of run-time errors is bad user input (typing in Texas when the program asks for age).

What you want to avoid is generating an error that displays a mystifying error message that the user neither comprehends nor knows what to do about. To a programmer, that is a catastrophic collapse of craft.

Cautions Err starts out with a zero in it when the program starts running. And Err is *reset to zero* if your program moves on to a different procedure (a Subroutine or Function), or if it runs past the following Statements: *Resume Next* or *On Error Resume Next*. Any error handling that you attempt to do must be located within the same procedure (Sub or Function) where the error occurred.

If an error occurs, Err is given the error code, source, and description appropriate to that error; if a second error occurs, the first code, source, and description are replaced by the features of the second error.

Example This procedure attempts to divide 134 by zero, but you can't divide numbers by zero. The attempt cannot work, so an error will be generated.

```
<SCRIPT LANGUAGE="VBScript">
Sub window_onLoad()
On Error Resume Next
N = 134/ 0
If Err then
Msgbox Err.Description & "...Error Number: " & Err
End If
end sub
</SCRIPT>
```

Results in

```
Division by zero…Error Number: 11
```

Error

ACTIVEX

See Events

Events

ACTIVEX

Description Events are things that can *happen to* a Control (an ActiveX Object), like the user clicking on a TextBox and thereby triggering the TextBox's Click Event. (*Methods*, on the other hand, are things a Control can *do*, such as removing all the items within a List Box with the Clear Method.)

When a Control is clicked with the mouse, the Control's Click Event is triggered. If you've put any programming into a Sub for that Click Event, that programming will be immediately carried out:

Put a Label and a CheckBox onto an ActiveX Layout, then type in the following VBScript programming. To learn how to do this, see the Introduction to this book.

```
<SCRIPT LANGUAGE="VBScript">

Label1.Move 100,100

Sub CheckBox1_Click
Label1.Caption = "It's Clicked"
End Sub

</SCRIPT>
```

When the document containing the above example is loaded into a browser, VBScript will *parse* (interpret) the script. The *Move* command will be carried out immediately because it is not contained within a procedure (a Sub or Function). However, the adjustment to the caption of this Label may or may not ever take place. To carry out commands contained within a procedure, that procedure must be run. This CheckBox1_Click procedure will be triggered and subsequently parsed whenever the user clicks on the CheckBox.

You can see a list of all the Events associated with a given Control by putting that Control in a script in the ActiveX Control Pad, then choosing Script Wizard from the Tools menu. In the left pane, click on the + next to a Control. Alternatively, you could look up the Control in Help.

What follows are descriptions of all the Events available in VBScript. Remember that not all Controls react to all Events. Also see the entries in this book for each ActiveX Control.

AddControl & RemoveControl Events

These are Events of the Layout Control; they apply to no other Controls. At the time of this writing, these Events were not yet working. For more on the Layout Control, see the discussion of the Layout Event later in this section.

AfterUpdate Event

The AfterUpdate Event is triggered when the user makes a change to a Control—edits text in a TextBox or clicks a List Box. There is also a BeforeUpdate Event, and *that* Event can be used to reverse (undo) the user's change to a Control. Just set its Cancel argument to True. The BeforeUpdate Event means "before the computer has digested this change." AfterUpdate means "it's too late to change this programmatically; it's already been recognized and acted upon." AfterUpdate is not triggered if you, the programmer, change the value or contents in a Control via a script. It must be the user. AfterUpdate occurs prior to the Exit Event of a Control but after the BeforeUpdate Event. AfterUpdate also occurs prior to the Enter Event for the next Control in the tab order (see TabIndex above for more on tab order). Note that BeforeUpdate and AfterUpdate are not working at the time of this writing.

```
Sub TextBox4_AfterUpdate
MsgBox "You made a change."
End Sub
```

BeforeDragOver Event

The BeforeDragOver Event occurs when the user is dragging something. You can make the color of a Control change, for example, when something is dragged over it. The BeforeDragOver Event can tell you when the mouse pointer enters, pauses, or leaves the location of your Control. The full syntax for BeforeDragOver is:

```
Sub TextBox1_BeforeDragOver(ByVal Cancel, ByVal Data, ByVal →
X, ByVal Y, ByVal DragState, ByVal Effect, ByVal Shift)
```

Note that the *ByVal* command is not yet working at the time of this writing.

If the Cancel Variable is False (the default), then the Control should contain programming to deal with this Event; if True, the browser handles it. If you, within this Event, set Cancel to True (Cancel=True), the drop will be aborted. The Data Variable is the object being dragged. X and Y contain the coordinates of the object within the Control that is being dragged over. The DragState Variable can be 0, 1, or 2. 0 means that the mouse pointer is inside the Control; 1 means outside; 2 means the pointer has moved but is still inside.

Effect describes the activities supported by the object being dragged: 0 means the object won't copy itself or move to the target Control; 1 means it will copy itself; 2 means it will move; 3 means it will copy itself or move. Shift describes which special keys have been pressed during the drag operation: 1 means the Shift key; 2 means Ctrl; 4 means Alt. These can be combined: 3 means that both Shift and Ctrl are being pressed.

Note that the TabStrip Control has an additional Variable, Index, which comes first in the list, before Cancel. Index tells you which tab or button on the TabStrip is the current target of the drop.

BeforeDropOrPaste Event

The BeforeDropOrPaste Event is identical to the BeforeDragOver Event described above, with three exceptions. It has a Ctrl Variable (the Control that is the target of the drag and drop operation). It has an Action Variable that describes the result of the operation. And it has no dragstate or X or Y Variables.

```
Sub object_BeforeDropOrPaste(ByVal Cancel, ByVal Action, →
ByVal Data, ByVal Effect, ByVal Shift)
End Sub
```

The Action Variable will be 2 if the dragged object is going to be pasted into the target (such as inserting a piece of text into a TextBox's current text). If Action=3 then the dragged object will be dropped into the target (such as dropping an entire .DOC file object into a TextBox).

You, the programmer, can optionally change the Action Variable to specify that something other than the default behavior happens when the object is released onto your Control (the user releases the mouse button). If the Effect Variable is set to 3, you can set Action to 0 (Do nothing), 1 (Copy), or 2 (Move). If Effect is set to 1 or 2, you can change Action to 0 (Do Nothing). If Effect is set to 0, you can't change Action.

The TabStrip Control has an additional Index Variable, as described above for BeforeDragOver.

BeforeUpdate Event

The BeforeUpdate Event is triggered before VBScript reacts to a change the user has made to the contents or value of a Control (see AfterUpdate above). It occurs before data in a control is changed.

```
Sub TextBox6_BeforeUpdate(Cancel)
MsgBox "You've made a change, but it's not yet registered."
End Sub
```

If Cancel is False (the default), the Control deals with this Event. True means that the application is supposed to deal with the Event, and the update (by the Control) is aborted.

Should you set Cancel to True, the AfterUpdate and Exit Events are not triggered, and the focus remains on this Control. BeforeUpdate is not triggered if you, the programmer, change the value or contents in a Control via a script. It must be triggered by the user.

Change Event

The Change Event is similar to the BeforeUpdate and AfterUpdate Events; however, unlike them, it reacts to *any* changes made to the contents or value of a Control. In other words, the Change Event is triggered by user actions as well as by any programmatic changes; when you, the programmer, for example, change the contents of a TextBox using VBScript:

```
TextBox2.Value=""
```

This would clear the text within the TextBox, trigger the Change Event, and cause any commands you'd inserted into this Event to be carried out:

```
Sub TextBox2_Change
MsgBox "We just cleared out the Text Box"
End Sub
```

The Change Event is useful if you want to synchronize more than one Control. For instance, if you want to use a set of three ScrollBars to adjust the color of a TextBox, you could make the adjustments to the color whenever one of the Change Events within one of the ScrollBars was triggered.

The Change Event detects when the user (or, in some cases, your program) does something to a Control. Precisely what triggers its Change Event varies from Control to Control:

- Combo, List, and TextBoxes—when the user types something in (or when your script changes a Property while running).
- ScrollBars—when the tab is adjusted by the user (or when your program changes the Value Property while running).
- CheckBox, Option Button, or ToggleButton—when the Value Property is changed or when the user clicks on one of these Controls.

- Label—when your program changes the Caption Property while running.
- TabStrip—when a different tab is made active.
- SpinButton—when clicked.

Caution

Change can cause a feedback loop effect if you create a self-changing Control. For example, you can't have your program insert new text into a TextBox by using that box's *Change Event.* The new text you printed would itself represent a change. *Therefore, it would trigger Change continually. Avoid writing commands within a Control's Change Event Procedure that cause changes to* that *Control.*

Click Event

The Click Event triggers when the left mouse button is pressed. Click is, as you might expect, one of the most important events in a mouse milieu. It's always happening in browsers—it's often the primary way that a user communicates. The *left* button always means that something on the screen has been selected or activated. The *right* (and *middle*, in some cases) button can mean various things to various programs. But the left button nearly always means: do this thing that I've moved to and am now choosing by clicking it.

```
Sub CommandButton1_Click
End Sub
```

In many scripts, you'll put a considerable percentage of the script's instructions between the Sub Click and End Sub commands of various Controls. The Click Event is the area where you'll locate many of the things you want to happen while a VBScript runs.

The Click Event can also be triggered when the Value in a Control changes (such as when the user presses the spacebar if an OptionButton Control has the focus). It is also triggered if the user presses an accelerator key to give a Control focus.

Before the Click Event triggers, the MouseDown and MouseUp Events trigger.

For the TabStrip Control, the Click Event has an Index Variable, telling you which tab was clicked:


```
Sub TabStrip1_Click (Index)
```

DblClick Event

The DblClick Event is triggered when the user clicks the left mouse button twice, in rapid succession. There is something of a convention in Windows applications whereby a Click Event simply selects something for highlighting, yet a DblClick Event both selects and executes. For instance, from within a ListBox that allows the user to go to a different URL, a single click would only highlight the selected target (or perhaps move the URL's name into a box at the top of the list). This allows the user to type in additional information, or ponder his or her choice. A double-click on a URL, however, could cause several things to happen: the ListBox closes and the URL double-clicked upon is summarily loaded into the browser.

There is a Cancel Variable used with DblClick:

```
Sub Label2_DblClick (Cancel)
```

Cancel defaults to False, meaning that the Control's DblClick Event will respond. However, if you set Cancel=True, any programming within the DblClick Event will not be carried out. Also, setting Cancel to True has the effect of making VBScript trigger a Click Event rather than a DblClick. Before the DblClick Event triggers, the MouseDown, MouseUp, and Click Events trigger.

For the TabStrip Control, the Click Event has an additional Variable, Index, telling you which tab was clicked.

E

DropButtonClick Event

This Event—only available for the ComboBox Control—takes place when the drop-down list becomes visible or disappears. Here we'll change the backcolor of a ComboBox to blue every time the user drops it down, then restore it to white when the user closes the box:

```
<SCRIPT LANGUAGE="VBScript">
Dim Toggle

Sub ComboBox1_DropButtonClick()
Toggle = Not Toggle

If Toggle then
  ComboBox1.BackColor = 16744448
Else
  ComboBox1.BackColor = 16777215
End If

End sub
</SCRIPT>
```

Current documentation for the ActiveX Control says that pressing the F4 key will also trigger the DropButtonClick Event, and that the TextBox has a DropButtonClick Event. Neither of these features are currently working, nor can we think of a reason to provide this Button or Event to a TextBox. For additional techniques involving this Event for the ComboBox, see the DropButtonStyle item within the "Properties" entry later in this book.

Enter & Exit Events

The Enter and Exit Events react to a change in focus. When the user presses the Tab key, the *focus* moves from Control to Control in an ActiveX layout. This provides an alternative to using the mouse: the user can cycle through the tab order to give the focus to a particular Control (just as if the user had clicked on that Control with the mouse). Then, when it has the focus, other keys can be used to trigger or manipulate that Control (the Enter key triggers a Command Button, arrow keys move within a ListBox, the spacebar toggles a CheckBox, and so on).

Therefore, the Enter and Exit Events are triggered when a Control gets the focus because it was clicked on or tabbed to. In fact, Enter is triggered just before a Control gets the focus, and Exit is triggered just before a Control loses the focus.

Exit has a Cancel Variable that, if set to True, will prevent the focus from moving.

You can use Enter to provide the user with information about a Control that's about to get the focus; use Exit to save information that's been modified.

Error Event

The Error Event is triggered when something goes wrong but the Control is unable to send the error information to whatever "called" (initiated) the Control. Generally, errors are handled by the browser: the browser provides error messages and otherwise deals with mishaps. The user sees, for example, the message "Server Not Found" when a link to a URL fails. However, it's possible that the browser won't or can't deal with some errors that are Control-specific.

```
Sub CheckBox1_Error(ByVal Number, ByVal Description, ByVal
SCode, ByVal Source, ByVal HelpFile, ByVal HelpContext, ByVal
CancelDisplay)
```

Note that the ByVal command is not working at the time of this writing.

The Number Variable is the error code, a number (Integer) taken from a list of possible errors. It is supplied by the Control. The description is a text description of the meaning or source of the error. The SCode is also a number, but this one specifies an OLE error code. The Source Variable is a text identifier, specifying which Control triggered the Error Event. The HelpFile is a path (location) to the Help file that explains the error. The HelpContext is a number (Long Integer) that provides the location of the error description within the HelpFile. CancelDisplay is a Boolean Variable (True or False) that specifies whether to show a message box to the user containing the error description text.

You can specify, within the Error Event, how you want the Control to react when there's an error. For instance, you might provide a more understandable error message than those typically offered by the Control itself with its Description Variable. Note that the Visual Basic commands On Error…Resume Next are not available in VBScript.

KeyDown & KeyUp Events

The KeyDown and KeyUp Events are triggered when the user presses, or releases, a key on the keyboard.

When you press a key, the KeyDown Event in the Control that has the focus is triggered. (The focus is on only one Control at a time or on the ActiveX Layout Control itself if there are no other Controls Enabled or Visible on the layout.) *Focus* means that this Control will receive anything that is typed on the keyboard. For example, if there are two TextBoxes, the one with the focus will display typed characters.

KeyDown and KeyUp tell you the full status of *every key on the keyboard*. That means Alt, Shift, Ctrl, function keys, arrow keys, or any other key *or combination of keys*.

By contrast, the KeyPress Event only detects the ordinary letter and number keys and a few other keys, and is insensitive to key combinations. An advantage of KeyPress is that it is simpler to work with and uses the standard ANSI character code. KeyPress is most often used with TextBoxes and the like for checking that the user is not entering things you don't want, or for changing intercepted characters such as forcing uppercase.

The KeyDown, KeyPress, and KeyUp Events are triggered in that order.

Far Finer Control

The advantage of KeyDown and KeyUp is precise control over the keys, or combinations of keys, that are being typed by the user. KeyDown or KeyUp are used for such global activities as acting on function keys, macro keys (such as Ctrl+S), or other combinations; for example, Ctrl+Shift+F2. Many computer applications offer key combinations as shortcuts to menus or other actions. Most programs, for example, interpret the F1 key as a request for Help. If you want to provide such features in your scripts, you'll need to use KeyDown to detect the pressing of nontext keys and combinations.

KeyUp is normally used to cause something to happen repeatedly as long as the KeyUp has not occurred. For instance, as an alternative to dragging, the user could hold down the Left arrow key to move an Image Control left across the screen. When the user released the key, the KeyUp Event would be triggered, and you would put programming in the KeyUp Event to stop the Picture Box at that point.

The KeyDown/KeyUp Variables

The KeyDown and KeyUp Events provide you with two Variables: *KeyCode* and *Shift*.

The KeyCode Variable provides a unique number for *every* key on the keyboard—even distinguishing between the 3 on the numeric keypad and the 3 in the row above the alphabetic keys. In this way, you can have your program react to *anything*—the arrow keys, the NUM LOCK key, and so on.

Table E-2 shows the KeyCodes provided by the KeyUp and KeyDown Events.

(Note that the KeyCodes for uppercase and lowercase letters, A and a, for example, are the same. Also, the normal and shifted digits, such as 3 and #, are the same. To detect a shifted key, use the Shift Variable, also provided by the KeyUp and KeyDown Events.)

KeyCode	Description
8	BACKSPACE
9	TAB
12	5 (keypad)
13	ENTER (keyboard and keypad)
16	SHIFT
17	CTRL

➥

KeyCode	Description
18	ALT
19	PAUSE (Break)
20	CAPS LOCK
27	ESC
32	SPACE
33	PgUp and 9 (keypad)
34	PgDn and 3 (keypad)
35	END and 1 (keypad)
36	HOME and 7 (keypad)
37	LEFT ARROW and 4 (keypad)
38	UP ARROW and 8 (keypad)
39	RIGHT ARROW and 6 (keypad)
40	DOWN ARROW and 2 (keypad)
45	INS and 0 (keypad)
46	DEL and decimal point
48	0 and)
49	1 and !
50	2 and @
51	3 and #
52	4 and $
53	5 and %
54	6 and ^
55	7 and &
56	8 and * (not keypad *)
57	9 and (
65	A
66	B
67	C
68	D
69	E
70	F

KeyCode	Description
71	G
72	H
73	I
74	J
75	K
76	L
77	M
78	N
79	O
80	P
81	Q
82	R
83	S
84	T
85	U
86	V
87	W
88	X
89	Y
90	Z
96	INSERT and 0 (with NUM LOCK on)
97	END and 1 (keypad) (with NUM LOCK on)
98	DOWN ARROW and 2 (keypad) (with NUM LOCK on)
99	PgDn and 3 (keypad) (with NUM LOCK on)
100	LEFT ARROW and 4 (keypad) (with NUM LOCK on)
101	5 (keypad) (with NUM LOCK on)
102	RIGHT ARROW and 6 (keypad) (with NUM LOCK on)
103	HOME and 7 (keypad) (with NUM LOCK on)
104	UP ARROW and 8 (keypad) (with NUM LOCK on)
105	PgUp and 9 (keypad) (with NUM LOCK on)
106	* (keypad)

➡

E

KeyCode	Description
107	+ (keypad)
109	– (keypad)
110	DEL and decimal point (with NUM LOCK on)
111	/ (keypad)
112	F1
113	F2
114	F3
115	F4
116	F5
117	F6
118	F7
119	F8
120	F9
121	F10
122	F11
123	F12
144	NUM LOCK
145	SCROLL LOCK
186	; and :
187	= and + (same as keypad =)
187	= (keypad)
188	, and <
189	- and _ (not keypad –)
190	. and >
191	/ and ? (not keypad /)
192	‘ and ~
219	[and {
220	\ and |
221	] and }
222	‘ and “

Table E-2: KeyCodes provided by the KeyUp and KeyDown Events.

There are other codes; keyboards do vary, and you may have keys that are not represented by this list. But these are the ones most users are likely to have. Going much beyond the above list is risky. Most keyboards don't have such keys as MENU and EXECUTE, for instance.

If you want to discover other codes, see the example below.

Detecting Shift, Alt, Ctrl

KeyDown/KeyUp also lets you determine if a key is being pressed at the same time as the Shift, Alt, or Ctrl key, thus allowing you to create macros or other shortcuts within your program. A typical macro might allow the user to press Ctrl+S, for example, to save his or her work as an alternative to accessing a menu or pressing a Command Button.

The Variable called Shift, available to you by a KeyDown or KeyUp Event, tells you the status of the Shift, Alt, and Ctrl keys as follows:

SHIFT = 1
SHIFT + CTRL = 3
SHIFT + ALT = 5
SHIFT + CTRL + ALT = 7
CTRL = 2
CTRL + ALT = 6
ALT = 4

So, to tell if the user is pressing Alt+Shift+F3:

```
If Shift = 5 and Keycode = 114 Then
```

KeyDown Example

Here's how you can detect and act upon the KeyCode or Shift Variables:

```
<SCRIPT LANGUAGE="VBScript">
<!--
Sub CommandButton1_KeyDown(KeyCode, Shift)
MsgBox "KeyCode is " & Keycode & " Shift is " & Shift
end sub
```

```
-->
</SCRIPT>
```

If the user presses the A key, the message box will say: KeyCode is 65 Shift is 0.

KeyPress Event

A KeyPress Event is triggered when a key is pressed on the keyboard. If a key is held down, a KeyPress Event is repeatedly triggered. The KeyPress Event is triggered in the Control that has the *focus*. The focus is on only one Control at a time (or on an ActiveX Layout itself if it has no Controls Enabled or Visible on it). *Focus* means that this Control will receive anything that is typed on the keyboard. For example, if there are two TextBoxes, the one with the focus will display typed characters.

The alternative to KeyPress is the KeyDown and KeyUp Events. KeyPress, however, works primarily with the normal characters A–Z, 1–0, %, and so on—that is, characters that can appear in a message box. It also detects a few others, such as the Enter key (code 13), and so forth. But KeyPress Events are insensitive to Ctrl, Shift, Alt, function keys, etc.

KeyPress Variables

The KeyPress Event provides you with a Variable called KeyAscii—a code number for the key that was pressed. Here is the first half of the KeyAscii code (the codes from 128–255 are graphics, special text, and so on):

ASCII	Key	ASCII	Key	ASCII	Key	ASCII	Key
0	NUL	32	Space	64	@	96	‘
1	SOH	33	!	65	A	97	a
2	STX	34	“	66	B	98	b
3	ETX	35		67	C	99	c
4	EOT	36		68	D	100	d
5	ENQ	37	%	69	E	101	e

ASCII	Key	ASCII	Key	ASCII	Key	ASCII	Key
6	ACK	38	&	70	F	102	f
7	BEL	39	‘	71	G	103	g
8	BS	40	(	72	H	104	h
9	Tab	41	)	73	I	105	i
10	LineFeed	42	*	74	J	106	j
11	VT	43	+	75	K	107	k
12	FF	44	,	76	L	108	l
13	Enter	45	-	77	M	109	m
14	SO	46	.	78	N	110	n
15	SI	47	/	79	O	111	o
16	DLE	48	0	80	P	112	p
17	DC1	49	1	81	Q	113	q
18	DC2	50	2	82	R	114	r
19	DC3	51	3	83	S	115	s
20	DC4	52	4	84	T	116	t
21	NAK	53	5	85	U	117	u
22	SYN	54	6	86	V	118	v
23	ETB	55	7	87	W	119	w
24	CAN	56	8	88	X	120	x
25	EM	57	9	89	Y	121	y
26	SUB	58	:	90	Z	122	z
27	ESC	59	;	91	[	123	{
28	FS	60	<	92	\	124	|
29	GS	61	=	93	]	125	}
30	RS	62	>	94	^	126	~
31	US	63	?	95	_	127	

Table E-3: The KeyAscii codes.

The real value of KeyAscii is that you can change the KeyAscii code before the character is sent to the screen or elsewhere—you are intercepting the keystrokes and can examine and adjust them.

For example, you could force them into a mathematical contortion for a password; or you could ignore errors (such as a text character typed into a phone number field that wants only digits). (For passwords, also see the PasswordChar Property of the TextBox.)

KeyPress Example

Here's a way to ignore any alphabetic characters that the user tries to insert when asked for a telephone number:


```
<SCRIPT LANGUAGE="VBScript">
Sub TextBox1_KeyPress(KeyAscii)
If KeyAscii > 57 Then Msgbox "Wrong Key"
End sub
</SCRIPT>
```

The user can still enter such symbols as parentheses and the minus sign, but cannot, for instance, type in one of those "memorable" half-text numbers like this one for a veterinarian: 454–MEOW.

Layout Event

Layout is an Event that's only found in the Layout Control—the form on which you can place other ActiveX Controls. When you run the ActiveX Control Pad (see the Introduction to this book) then select "Insert HTML Layout" from the Edit menu, a new Layout Control is created.

This Layout object is a kind of blank canvas on which you can place other Controls. It is the rough equivalent of a Form in Visual Basic.

The Layout Event is triggered when, for one reason or another, a Control or Controls on the Layout Control are resized and, therefore, the screen must be repainted. (It's similar to the Visual Basic Refresh Event.)

If, for example, you change the size of a Label Control:

```
Label1.Width = 210
```

the Layout Control's Layout Event is triggered. Likewise, if the Font Size within a Label is changed (and the Label's AutoSize Property is set to True), the Label will resize itself, thereby triggering the Layout Event.

At the time of this writing, the Layout Control has only one working Event, OnLoad, that's triggered when the browser first loads your document (or refreshes it). Obviously, we'll want it to react to, for example, mouse-clicks. What's more, the Layout Control isn't yet automatically given an ID by the ActiveX Control Pad. You can add an ID to the source code. We added ID="lay" like this:

```
<DIV BACKGROUND="#8080ff" ID="lay"
STYLE="LAYOUT:FIXED;WIDTH:464pt;HEIGHT:299pt;">
```

While in the layout view of the Control Pad, right-click on the layout and choose "View Source Code" from the pop-up menu. Then type in the ID="lay" or whatever name you want to give it. Then you can create an Event for the Layout Control:

```
<SCRIPT LANGUAGE="VBScript">
Sub lay_OnLoad()
MsgBox "HI"
end sub
</SCRIPT>
```

However, the Layout, Click, AddControl, RemoveControl, and any additional Events provided for the Layout Control are not yet working at the time of this writing.

MouseDown & MouseUp Events

The MouseDown and MouseUp Events are triggered when the user clicks the mouse (or releases a pressed mouse button) on one of the Controls that is sensitive to this Event in an ActiveX Layout.

A Click Event occurs when the user *presses and releases* the mouse button. MouseDown reacts to the press; MouseUp reacts to the release—thereby giving you finer control over position and duration as the user maneuvers the mouse in a window.

MouseDown and MouseUp also provide more information than does a Click Event. MouseDown and MouseUp provide three kinds of information:

- which button was pressed.

- whether or not the user simultaneously pressed the Shift, Ctrl, or Alt key (or any combination of them) when the mouse button was pressed.
- the current X, Y location within the Form or Control where the MouseDown or MouseUp Event occurred.

This distinction between Click and MouseDown/Up is similar to the one between KeyPress (which merely provides the code for a text-type single character that the user pressed) and the KeyDown and KeyUp Events (which tell you much more: the status of the Shift, Ctrl, and Alt keys, plus Function keys, arrow keys, and other special, non-printable keys like Esc).

The mouse-related Events are triggered in this order: MouseDown, MouseUp, Click, DblClick, MouseUp.

To detect which button has been pressed, look at the Button Variable:

- 1—the left button was pressed.
- 2—the right button was pressed.
- 4—the middle button was pressed.

```
<SCRIPT LANGUAGE="VBScript">
Sub Label1_MouseDown(ByVal Button, ByVal Shift, ByVal X,
ByVal Y)
Select Case Button
 Case 1
  MsgBox "Left Button Just Pressed"
 Case 2
  MsgBox "Right Button Just Pressed"
 Case 4
  MsgBox "Middle Button Just Pressed"
End Select

end sub
</SCRIPT>
```

Shift, Ctrl, Alt

The Shift Variable provides codes that tell you all possible combinations of the Shift, Ctrl, and Alt keypresses, when they are being held down at the same time that the user presses a mouse button:

No key pressed	0
SHIFT	1
SHIFT + CTRL	3
SHIFT + ALT	5
ALT	4
ALT + CTRL	6
CTRL	2
SHIFT+CTRL+ALT	7

X, Y

These coordinates provide the current location within the Control or Layout, the horizontal and vertical positions where the MouseDown or MouseUp Event was triggered. Like all other coordinates in VBScript, X and Y are expressed in pixels.

Note that, as usual, a TabStrip Control has an additional parameter, *Index* (a Long Integer), that comes before the Button parameter. It tells you which tab was clicked or, if -1, that the user clicked within the TabStrip, but outside of any tab.

Cautions

Once the mouse button is pressed, VBScript assumes that any MouseMoves, the MouseDown and any associated Shift, Ctrl, or Alt keypresses, and the final MouseUp Event *all take place within the Control (or Layout) in which the MouseDown Event first took place*. That is, if you press the mouse while its pointer is over the Layout, the Layout's mouse-related Events all register mouse activity until the mouse button is released.

If, for instance, you click on an Image Box, hold the button down, and drag the mouse *outside the Image Box onto the Layout*, the Image Box's Event nevertheless continues to report the X, Y coordinates. If you release the mouse button while on the Layout, the *Image Box's* MouseUp Event will be the one triggered, not the Layout's.

It is important to remember that the object first getting the MouseDown Event trigger is the one that will provide all additional information about the mouse until the MouseUp Event takes place. This doesn't restrict your programming but it can cause confusion if you forget about it. To detect when the mouse has moved beyond

E

the borders of the Image Box and onto the Layout, check the coordinates inside the MouseMove Event of the Image Box. *The X or Y coordinate to the left or above the Image Box border will become negative.* A negative coordinate is clearly impossible; normally, (0,0) is the upper left point within any Control's coordinates. To test for moves beyond the right or bottom borders, check the X or Y value against the Width or Height Properties of the Image Box.

Also, if the user presses more than one mouse button (without releasing the first button pressed), the rules outlined above apply until *all buttons are released.*

Finally, for MouseDown and MouseUp, the Button Variable provides information about only one of the buttons on the mouse—whichever button initially triggered the Event. The MouseMove Event provides information on the state of *all* the buttons. In other words, MouseMove tells you if the left, right, and middle buttons are being depressed and in what combination.

Example of MouseDown

To see all the Variables provided by MouseDown, put a Label and two TextBoxes on an ActiveX Layout. Then, in the Label's MouseDown Event, type this:

```
<SCRIPT LANGUAGE="VBScript">

Sub Label1_MouseDown(ByVal Button, ByVal Shift, ByVal X,
ByVal Y)

TextBox1 = "MOUSEDOWN EVENT X: " & cStr(x) & " Y: " & cStr(y)
TextBox2 = "Button: " & button & " Shift: " & shift

End Sub

</SCRIPT>
```

MouseEnter & MouseExit Events

These two Events trigger when the mouse pointer moves into (and out of) a particular control (but no mouse buttons need to be pressed, the mouse is merely hovering). According to current specifications for VBScript, this is quite similar to the MouseMove Event, which you can also use to detect that the mouse pointer has entered, or left, a Control's space. The only difference is that MouseMove is repeatedly triggered while the pointer is moving within a Control's space, whereas MouseEnter and MouseExit are triggered only once—at the entrance and exit respectively.

The buttons at the top of Microsoft's Internet Explorer become colored as you move the mouse pointer over them. You might want to duplicate that effect in your document, or you might want to play some music when the mouse hovers over a Command Button. To accomplish these and other tricks, the single triggering of MouseEnter is better than the multiple triggering of MouseMove. Likewise, MouseExit is by far the easiest way to know that the pointer has moved off a given Control (and the color or music should therefore stop).

MouseMove Event

Whenever the user moves the mouse, the MouseMove Event reports that—along with whether the mouse buttons are being pressed; whether any of the Ctrl, Alt, or Shift keys are being pressed; and the current position on the Control or Layout of the mouse pointer.

The four Variables (or *arguments* as they're sometimes called) provided by MouseMove are available to your program from within the MouseMove Event:

```
Sub Label4_MouseMove(ByVal Button, ByVal Shift, ByVal X,
ByVal Y)
```

E

Button

To detect which button has been pressed, look at the Button Variable for one of these values:

Left button is pressed	1
Left + right	3
Left + middle	5
Middle	4
Middle + Right	6
Right	2
Left + Right + Middle	7

Note that, as usual, a TabStrip Control has an additional parameter, Index (a Long Integer), that comes before the Button parameter. It tells you which tab was clicked or, if the Index is -1, that the user clicked within the TabStrip but outside of any tab.

Shift, Ctrl, Alt

The Shift Variable provides codes that tell you all possible combinations of the Shift, Ctrl, and Alt keypresses when they are being held down at the same time that the user is holding down a mouse key:

No key pressed	0
SHIFT	1
SHIFT + CTRL	3
SHIFT + ALT	5
ALT	4
ALT + CTRL	6
CTRL	2
SHIFT + CTRL + ALT	7

X, Y

These coordinates provide the current location within the Control or Layout, the horizontal and vertical positions where the MouseMove Event is being triggered. These Variables will change rapidly as the user moves the mouse around. Even a small mouse movement triggers the MouseMove Event repeatedly and often. Depending on how quickly the user moves the mouse, moving across one inch of space could generate as many as 100 MouseMove Events. The average range is probably between 40 and 100 triggered MouseMove Events per inch. The Events are triggered by the user's computer's clock, not by the distance moved—that's why the number of Events triggered will vary depending on the speed of the movement.

Like all other coordinates in VBScript, X and Y are expressed in pixels.

Cautions

For MouseMove, the status of *all* the mouse buttons is available from the Button Variable via a code. In other words, MouseMove tells you if the left, right, and middle buttons are being depressed and in what combination. (See the "Button" subsection above.)

Once the mouse button is pressed, VBScript assumes that any MouseMoves, the MouseDown, any associated Shift, Ctrl, or Alt keypresses, and the final MouseUp Event *all take place within the Control (or Layout) in which the MouseDown Event first took place.* That is, if you press the mouse while its pointer is over the Layout, the Layout's mouse-related Events all register mouse activity until the mouse button is released.

If, for instance, you click on an Image Box, hold the button down, and drag the mouse *outside the Image Box onto the Layout,* the Image Box's Event nevertheless continues to report the X, Y coordinates. If you release the mouse button while on the Layout, the Image Box's MouseUp Event will be the one triggered, not the Layout's.

It is important to remember that the object first getting the MouseDown Event trigger is the one that will provide all additional information about the mouse until the MouseUp Event takes place. This doesn't restrict your programming but it can cause confusion if you forget about it. To detect when the mouse has moved beyond the borders of the Image Box and onto the Layout, check the coordinates inside the MouseMove Event of the Image Box. *The X or Y coordinate to the left or above the Image Box border will become negative.* A negative coordinate is clearly impossible; normally, (0,0) is the upper left point within any Control's coordinates. To test for moves beyond the right or bottom borders, check the X or Y value against the Width or Height Properties of the Image Box.

Also, if the user presses more than one mouse button (without releasing the first button pressed), the rules outlined above apply until *all buttons are released.*

Scroll Event

This Event works with the ScrollBar Control and the Layout Control. It is triggered when the tab within the ScrollBar is moved. Add a TextBox and a ScrollBar to a Layout Control (see the Introduction to this book). Then type this into the Scroll Event:

```
<SCRIPT LANGUAGE="VBScript">
Sub ScrollBar1_Scroll()
TextBox1 = ScrollBar1.Value
end sub
</SCRIPT>
```

When you move the tab up and down within the ScrollBar, you'll see the ScrollBar's current Value (a number between its Min and Max Properties), indicating the position of the tab within the ScrollBar.

The ScrollBar has a Change Event which provides the same functionality as the Scroll Event—but with an important difference. The Change Event is only triggered when the user releases the mouse button—thereby stopping the tab from moving within the ScrollBar. The Scroll Event is triggered *continuously* while the tab is being moved (it's similar to the MouseMove Event in this respect). Therefore, use the Scroll Event when you want a continuously changing effect, as illustrated in the example above where we display the current numeric position of the tab by putting it into the TextBox.

How the Scroll Event will apply to a Layout Control remains to be seen; it's not working at this time.

SpinDown & SpinUp Events

These Events are available only for the SpinButton Control. They are functionally identical to the Scroll Event for the ScrollBar Control—they are triggered continuously if the user holds down the left mouse button while positioned on one of the SpinButton arrows. Therefore, the SpinDown and SpinUp Events are useful when you want to display some continuously changing data or quality in response to pressing the SpinButton.

The SpinButton has a Change Event that provides the same functionality as the SpinDown and SpinUp Events—but with an important difference. The Change Event is only triggered when the user releases the mouse button, so you can react only once per mouse click. However, the SpinDown and SpinUp Events are triggered *continuously* while the user depresses the mouse button (similar to the MouseMove Event in this respect). Here's a continuous updating of a TextBox, based on the user's holding down the mouse button while the mouse pointer is on the up button of a SpinButton:

```
<SCRIPT LANGUAGE="VBScript">
Sub SpinButton1_SpinUp()
TextBox1 = SpinButton1.Value
end sub
</SCRIPT>
```

E

Zoom Event

This is an Event of the Layout Control; it is used with no other Controls. At the time of this writing, the Zoom Event is not yet working. Eventually, the Zoom Event will trigger when the Layout's Zoom Property is changed. The Zoom Property can be set to anything between 10 and 400—with 100 being the original size of the Layout Control. If the Zoom Property goes below 100, the Layout Control and all Controls on it are resized smaller. If it goes above 100, everything is expanded. Presumably, the Zoom Event will alert you when the user (or your VBScript programming) has resized a Frame or the Browser itself—thereby causing everything to expand or contract when repainted on the user's screen.

```
Sub Layo_Zoom (Percent)
   If Percent < 51 then Label1.Font = "Arial"
End Sub
```

This example illustrates one use for the Zoom Event. If there are some formatting issues you want to deal with, you could accomplish them within the Zoom Event. For example, if the Layout Control goes below 50%—there is a Percent Variable provided to you—you might want to change to a typeface that's more readable in small point sizes.

For more on the Layout Control, see the discussion of the "Layout Event" described earlier in this section.

Exit

VBSCRIPT STATEMENT

Description Exit forces the program to leave early from a Function, Subroutine, Do...Loop, or For...Next loop.

Used with Loops and Procedures

Variables

```
Exit Do
```

OR

```
Exit For
```

OR

```
Exit Function
```

OR

```
Exit Sub
```

Uses Abort a running Loop or Procedure.

Example The Exit command is most commonly used to provide alternative ways to get out of a Loop. Here's an example of searching through a piece of text. You want to quit if you come upon a special Control code (see "Chr") or one of those Greek symbols (anything that's not a normal alphabetic character) embedded within the text.

```
<HTML>

<HEAD>
<TITLE>Array Command</TITLE>
</HEAD>
<BODY>

<INPUT TYPE=BUTTON VALUE="Click here to see Array"
NAME="Btn">

<SCRIPT LANGUAGE=VBS>

Sub Btn_OnClick ()
cr = chr(13)
a = "This is the message."
a = a + cr + "THIS FOLLOWS."
L = Len(a)
P = 1
```

```
Do
   x = Mid(a, P, 1)
      If Asc(x) < 32 Then Exit Do
      If Asc(x) > 126 Then Exit Do
      P = P + 1
Loop Until P > L

Msgbox cstr(p)
end sub

</SCRIPT>
</BODY>
</HTML>
```

First we create a Variable that includes an interior Control code: Chr(13). While searching through each character in the Do...Loop, we check to see whether its ASC code value is less than 32 (which means it's a Control code) or above 126 (which makes it a symbol). In either case, we exit this Loop and display the location where we exited.

Exit

ACTIVEX

See Events

Exp

FUNCTION

Description Calculates e, the base of a natural log, to the power of x.

Used with Scientific and advanced mathematical calculations

Variables You can provide Exp with any numeric expression. (See "Variables" for a definition of "expression.")

To calculate using a Variable:

```
E = Exp(X)
```

OR (to use a literal number):

```
E = Exp(2.5)
```

E

Uses

- Scientific calculations.
- Calculating log values. This is used to calculate decibels, log charts, and for many other scientific applications.

Cautions

- The exponent [the number inside the parentheses in Exp (X)] cannot be larger than 88.02969 if you're using single-precision Variables, or 709.782712893 with double-precision numbers.
- If you give Exp a single-precision or Integer Variable subtype, it will calculate e with single-precision arithmetic. In all other cases, Exp is double-precision. See "Variables" for more information on precision.

Example

```
<HTML>
<SCRIPT LANGUAGE=VBS>

cLng(E)
E = Exp(1)
msgbox cstr(E)

</SCRIPT>

</HTML>
```

Results in

```
2.71828182845905
```

See also Log, Sqr

Exponentiation

VBSCRIPT OPERATOR

See Operators

F

Focus

Description *Focus* means the Control that will react to keypresses. For example, if there are three TextBoxes on a document, only one of them can have the focus at a given time. If the user presses K on the keyboard, that letter will appear in whatever TextBox currently has the focus. The focus can be changed by Script commands (TextBox1.SetFocus), by the user clicking the mouse pointer on a Control, or by the user pressing the Tab key, which cycles the focus among the Controls on a document. Often something visual happens to indicate which Control has the focus. A CommandButton with the Focus will have a dotted line surrounding its caption; a TextBox with the focus has a blinking insertion cursor showing where the next character will appear within the text.

FONT

NETSCAPE & INTERNET EXPLORER

Description FONT allows you to adjust the color, typeface, and size of the text characters in your document.

Used with ***Can be enclosed by***

<A>, <ADDRESS>, <B>, <BLINK>, <BLOCKQUOTE>, <BODY>, <CAPTION>, <CENTER>, <CITE>, <CODE>, <DD>, <DT>, <EM>, <FONT>, <FORM>, <H1>, <H2>, <H3>, <H4>, <H5>, <H6>, <I>, <KBD>, <LI>, <NOBR>, <P>, <PRE>, <SAMP>, <STRONG>, <TD>, <TH>, <TT>, <VAR>

Can enclose

<A>, <B>, <BASEFONT>, <BLINK>, <BR>, <CITE>, <CODE>, <EM>, <FONT>, <I>, <IMG>, <KBD>, <NOBR>, <SAMP>, <STRONG>, <TT>, <VAR>, <WBR>

Variables To change the color:

```
<FONT COLOR=0000FF>This is blue.</FONT> This isn't
```

OR to use English:

```
<FONT COLOR=Blue> </FONT> This isn't
```

F

You can use a set of ordinary English words, like blue, instead of hex numbers, to define the color. The following words are recognized: black, white, green, maroon, olive, navy, purple, gray, red, yellow, blue, teal, lime, aqua, fuchsia, and silver. These words also work with the following commands: TEXT, LINK, VLINK, BODY, BORDERCOLOR, BORDERCOLORLIGHT, BORDERCOLORDARK. However, Internet Explorer 3.0 recognizes a total of 140 color words, including Forestgreen and Papayawhip.

Tip

You can define colors with either hexadecimal numbers or, as we've done in these examples, with ordinary English words like blue. *For a complete list of all 140 English word colors you can use, see "Many New Colors" in the entry on "BGCOLOR." For an explanation of hexadecimal, see "Hex Numbers for the Color Command" in the entry on "BODY."*

To change the typeface:

```
<FONT FACE="Arial, Times Roman, Courier"></FONT>
```

If the user's operating system has Arial, it will be used. If not, then Times Roman. If that's not available, then Courier. If none are available, the default is used (no change occurs).

To change the size, relative to the current size:

```
<FONT SIZE=+2> Now the font size is 5.</FONT>
```

The range of SIZE is between 1 and 7, and if you don't use the BASEFONT command (which see), the SIZE defaults to 3. Note that this command adjusts the relative size of the text characters, from a default of 3 to anything between 1 and 7.

OR to specify the size:

```
<FONT SIZE=4> Now the font size is 4.</FONT>
```


Uses

- Add variety to your pages.
- Format your screens so that they are divided, visually, into logical sections.

Cautions Most of these options are available, as of now, within Internet Explorer. In the Netscape flavor of the FONT command, SIZE is the only option.

Example

This is the default SIZE 3, default black, default Times Roman.

This is now SIZE 6, blue and Arial.

Figure F-1: We change the size, face, and color.

```
<HTML>
This is the default SIZE 3, default black, default Times
Roman.

<FONT COLOR=Blue SIZE=6 FACE="Arial">

<BR>

This is now SIZE 6, blue and Arial.

</HTML>
```

See also BASEFONT

Font

ACTIVEX

See Properties

For...Next

VBSCRIPT STATEMENT

F

Description One of the most useful commands in any computer language, For creates a *loop* that repeatedly carries out the instructions between it and its companion command, Next. The number of times the computer will loop is defined by the two numbers listed right after the For:

```
Z = 12

For I = 1 To 100
  Z = Z + Z
Next I
```

In this example, the value of the Loop counter Variable (in this case we used the Variable I) is incremented each time the program gets to the Next Statement. The Next Statement does three things: it adds one to the Variable I; it checks to see if I has reached the limit we set in the For Statement (100 in this example); and, if the limit has not been reached, Next sends the program back up to the For Statement to continue the repetitions. Any commands within the loop are carried out each time the loop cycles.

Variables The For Statement comes in three varieties:

- You can specify the number of loops (see the example).
- You can use other Variables to specify the number of loops. Say that you want to allow the user to specify how many copies of a document should be mailed. You could use an InputBox to get the number from the user. Then use that number to specify the number of loops.
- There is an optional command that works with For...Next called *Step*. Step can be attached at the end of the For...Next

structure to allow you to skip numbers, to *step* past them. When the Step command is used with For...Next, Step alters the way the loop counts.

Normally, a loop counts by one:

```
<HTML>
<HEAD>
<TITLE>ForNext</TITLE>
</HEAD>
<BODY>

<TEXTAREA NAME=RESULT VALUE = "TIRE" ROWS=12 COLS = 45>
</TEXTAREA>
<INPUT TYPE=Button VALUE="Show Numbers" NAME="Btn">

<SCRIPT LANGUAGE="VBSCRIPT">

cr = chr(13) + chr(10)

For I = 1 to 5
RESULT.VALUE = RESULT.VALUE + cstr(I) + cr
Next

</SCRIPT>
</BODY>
</HTML>
```

Results in

```
1
2
3
4
5
```

However, when you use the Step command, you change the way a For...Next loop counts.

It could count every other number (Step 2):

```
For I = 1 to 5 Step 2
RESULT.VALUE = RESULT.VALUE + cstr(I) + cr
Next
```

F

Results in

```
1
3
5
```

Or you could Step every seventy-third number (Step 73) or count down backward (For I = 10 to 1 Step –1), and even count by fractions such as four steps for each number (Step .25).

```
For I = 15 to 90 Step 15
  RESULT.VALUE = RESULT.VALUE + cstr(I) + " "
Next
```

Results in

```
15 30 45 60 75 90
```

Additional Notes: For...Next loops can be *nested*, one inside the other. At first, this sort of structure seems confusing, and it often is; but trying out various numbers for the counter Variables and moving commands around in the "inner" or "outer" loop will eventually produce the results you're after.

Nested loops can be confusing because you've added a new dimension when you use an interior loop. The inner loop interacts with the exterior loop in ways that are clear only to the mathematically gifted. Essentially, the inner loop does its thing the number of times specified by its own counter Variable—multiplied by the counter Variable of the outer loop.

Simply *hack* away, substituting counter numbers (and maybe moving commands from one loop to the other) until things work the way they should. *Hacking* to a programmer means precisely the same thing as carving to a sculptor—chipping away until the desired result emerges.

```
<HTML>
<HEAD>
<TITLE>ForNext</TITLE>
</HEAD>
<BODY>
```

```
<OBJECT ID="TextBox1" WIDTH=192 HEIGHT=333
CLASSID="CLSID:8BD21D10-EC42-11CE-9E0D-00AA006002F3">
  <PARAM NAME="VariousPropertyBits" VALUE="-1400879077">
  <PARAM NAME="Size" VALUE="5075;8811">
  <PARAM NAME="FontCharSet" VALUE="0">
  <PARAM NAME="FontPitchAndFamily" VALUE="2">
  <PARAM NAME="FontWeight" VALUE="0">
</OBJECT>

<SCRIPT LANGUAGE="VBSCRIPT">
cr = chr(13) + chr(10)

For I = 0 to 2
For J = 0 to 2
textbox1.value = textbox1.value + cstr(I) + ", " + ➞
cstr(j) + cr
Next
Next
</SCRIPT>

</BODY>
</HTML>
```

Notice that you can start counting anywhere; you need not start the counter with 1. And the Step size can be whatever you wish, including negative numbers if you want to count *down* instead of up.

```
For I = 10 To 1 Step - 2
textbox1.value = textbox1.value + cstr(I) + ", " + ➞
cstr(j) + cr
Next
```

Results in

```
10 8 6 4 2
```

The counter numbers and the Step number can be fractional (you could also use .2 for this Step):

```
For I = 12 To 13 Step 1/5
```

Results in

```
12 12.2 12.4 12.6 12.8 13
```

You can even mix and match:

```
For I = 1 / 2 To 5.5 Step .7
```

Results in

```
.5 1.2 1.9 2.6 3.3 4 4.7 5.4
```

Any *numeric expression* can be used with For...Next. (See "Variables" for a definition of "expression.") However, the range you're counting must be *possible*. The following is not possible:


```
For i = -10 To -20 Step 2
```

This loop does nothing—it cannot. You're asking it to count downward, but your Step command is positive. As any intelligent entity would when confronted with a senseless request, VBScript does nothing with these instructions. You have to make the Step negative with –2:

```
For i = -10 To -20 Step -2
```

Additional Notes: It's common practice to indent the commands between For...Next, If...Then, and other structures (Do...Loop, Select Case, and so on), which indicates that the indented items are subordinate, that they are controlled by a surrounding structure in some fashion.

Uses For...Next is useful when you want to repeat something a certain number of times, such as printing a particular number of copies of a letter, or drawing 75 circles, or reporting the electric bill for each of 12 months. The Do...Loop structure performs the same job as For...Next, but with For...Next you know when writing your program how many iterations, how many repetitions, you'll want. With Do...Loop, you keep cycling through the loop until some condition is satisfied (for example, until the user presses a key to stop the looping).

Also, you can vary events within the For...Next Loop by using the *counter* (the *I* in For I = 12 to 33) to generate the variations. To calculate 5 $^{1}/4$ percent interest on savings for amounts between 1,000 and 10,000, in increments of 1,000:

```
<HTML>
<HEAD>
<TITLE>ForNext</TITLE>
</HEAD>
<BODY>
  <OBJECT ID="TextBox1" WIDTH=192 HEIGHT=333
  CLASSID="CLSID:8BD21D10-EC42-11CE-9E0D-00AA006002F3">
  <PARAM NAME="VariousPropertyBits" VALUE="-1400879077">
    <PARAM NAME="Size" VALUE="5075;8811">
    <PARAM NAME="FontCharSet" VALUE="0">
    <PARAM NAME="FontPitchAndFamily" VALUE="2">
    <PARAM NAME="FontWeight" VALUE="0">
  </OBJECT>
  <SCRIPT LANGUAGE="VBSCRIPT">
cr = chr(13) + chr(10)

For I = 1000 To 10000 Step 1000
textbox1.value = textbox1.value + "The interest on " +
cstr(I) + " is " + cstr(I * .0525) + cr
Next
  </SCRIPT>
</BODY>
</HTML>
```

The alternative structure to For…Next is the Do...Loop structure (and its less flexible cousin, While...Wend). You use a Do...Loop structure when you do not know how many times you want the instructions repeated—you therefore cannot supply the counter numbers you would give to a For...Next Loop. For...Next is used far more often, however. You usually *do* know the number of times you want something done.

Even if you can't know the precise number while creating your program, your program itself will usually know while running the number that should be used as the counter. If you allow the user to select the number of copies of the text in a Text Box that will be sent to the printer, you won't know his or her choice when you design the program; but you can put the user's choice into a Variable that you give as the counter for a For...Next Loop:

```
Numberofcopies = InputBox("How many copies do you want?")
For I = 1 to Numberofcopies
```

One advantage of Do…Loop is that it can often result in highly readable programming. Do...Loop utilizes its associated commands—Until and While—to produce those readable lines of programming for which Basic is famous. Do Until Character = "M" is practically regular English.

Cautions

- If you set up an impossible situation for the For...Next counter (such as For I = 5 To 2), nothing will happen. Such a loop won't execute even once. (This is as opposed to ANSI standard Basic, where every For...Next loop executes its contents at least once, even when your stated conditions are impossible.)

  VBScript, by contrast, will understand that you can't count up from 5 to 2, since you didn't put a negative *Step* command in your For...Next structure, thereby forcing the counting to go downward. VBScript will ignore such a loop and just continue on past it.

- For...Next loops can be as large as you wish, containing as many instructions between the For and the Next as you want. And you can put a small For...Next structure all on one line, too:

  ```
  For J = 1 To 5: Msgbox J: Next
  ```

- Avoid changing the counter Variable within the loop:

  ```
  For J = 1 To 5
     J = 3
  Next J
  ```

- If you use Step 0, you will create a loop that never ends. This is called an *infinite loop* or an *endless loop*, and such a structure has few uses. In effect, it causes the computer to go into a state of suspended animation. Step 0 is not advised.

Example

```
For I = 1 To 50000
   If I = 34786 Then Msgbox "Found It"
Next
```

See also Do...Loop, For Each...Next, While...Wend

ForeColor

ACTIVEX

See Properties

FORM

HTML

Description FORMS are important elements when creating certain kinds of Internet pages. The primary job of the FORM is to provide methods for user input, a way for the user to communicate with you (by sending data back to the server). Now, though, with the advent of sophisticated ActiveX Controls for user input, the utility of the HTML Form is dwindling.

For the most part, writing Internet pages is a matter of presenting visuals and text to the user—the person out there on the World Wide Web who will be viewing your efforts. The FORM, on the other hand, has a variety of facilities that allow the user to send information back to you, to respond.

There are two basic jobs you must do to permit a user to contact you: 1) Put an input box (or other input contrivance such as a TextBox) on your page, and include a text description (a label or something) of what input the user can provide. 2) Furnish a way for the data in the input box (or other input gadget) to get back to you over the Internet. These "contrivances" or "gadgets" are generally referred to as *Controls* or *Objects*.

Note that you *can* put these Controls outside of the <FORM> </FORM> tags, but when you do, you lose the ability to submit information back to your server.

The following Controls are available for user input within a FORM:

Buttons: Buttons ("Command Buttons") that the user can click on to trigger something, to make something happen.

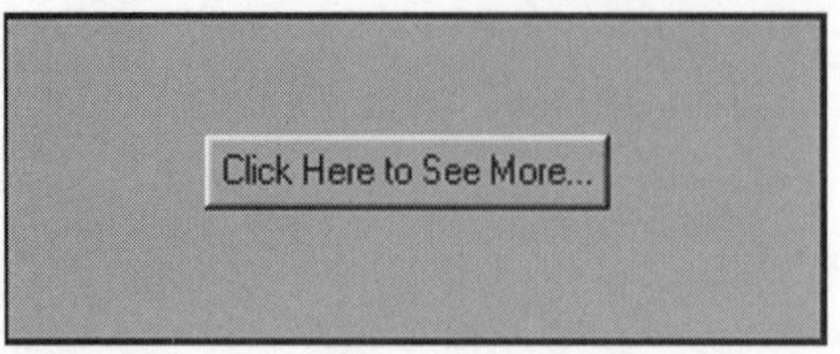

Figure F-2: A button can be clicked on to trigger some action (some Subroutine).

```
<FORM><INPUT TYPE = Button VALUE = "Click Here to See
More...">></FORM>button
```


CheckBoxes:

Figure F-3: Any number of CheckBoxes can be selected by the user (as opposed to radio buttons—they permit only a single selection).

```
<FORM><INPUT TYPE = CheckBox VALUE = "QUIT?"></FORM> checkbox
```

File Controls: To attach files to forms.

Hidden Controls: Controls that the user doesn't see but that you can use for your own purposes.

Images: Images that can be clicked on by the user.

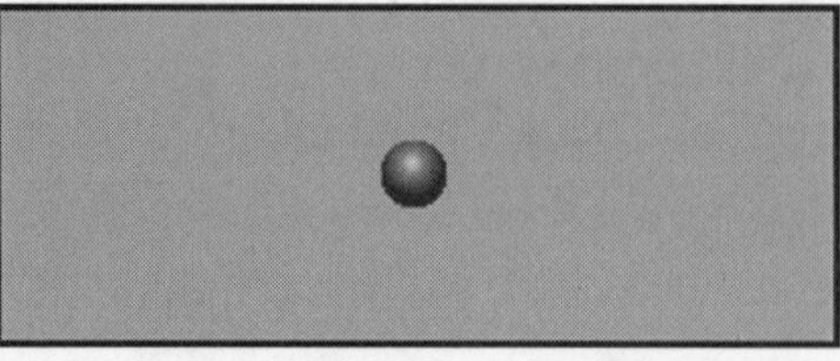

Figure F-4: The user can click on this graphic image, and your page can respond (see ABS for an example).

```
<FORM><INPUT TYPE = Image SRC="ball.gif"></FORM>image
```

ListBoxes: (See SELECT.)

Radio buttons:

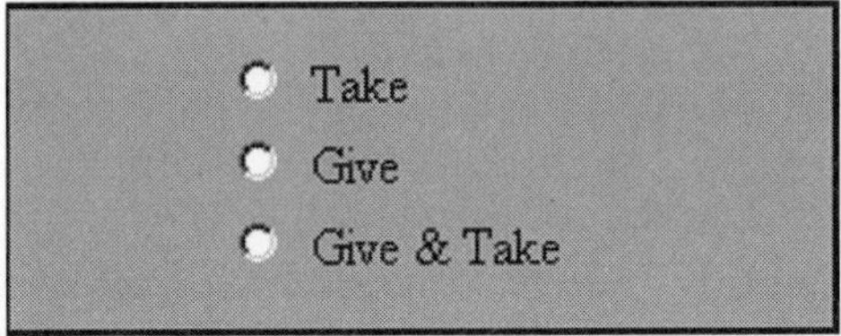

Figure F-5: The user can only choose one from among a set of radio-style buttons.

```
<FORM>
<INPUT TYPE = radio VALUE = "Take">Take
<BR><BR>
<INPUT TYPE = radio VALUE = "Give">Give
<BR><BR>
<INPUT TYPE = radio VALUE = "Give & Take">Give & Take
</FORM>
```

Reset buttons: To restore the original contents to a Control.

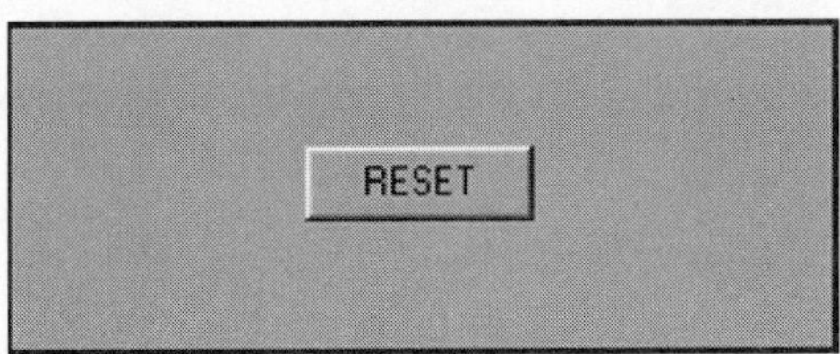

Figure F-6: If the user clicks on this type of button, all other input Controls in the document are restored to their original values. It acts as a kind of "undo" or "clear" feature.

```
<FORM><INPUT TYPE = reset VALUE = "RESET"></FORM>reset
```

Submit buttons: Buttons to send a FORM's contents to the server.

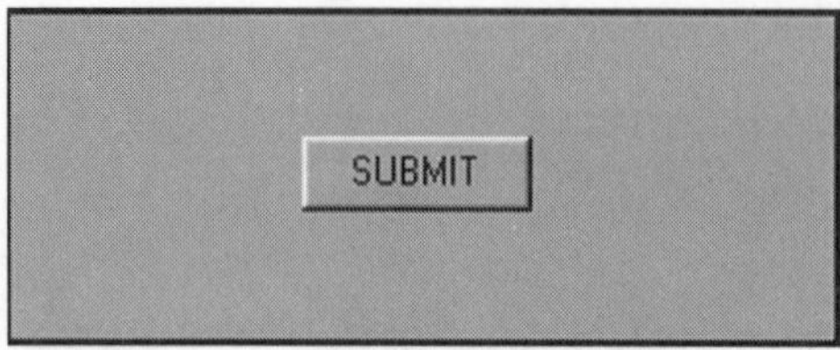

Figure F-7: If the user clicks on this type of button, the contents (VALUE) of all other input Controls in the document are sent to the server. (See ACTION.)

```
<FORM><INPUT TYPE = submit VALUE = "SUBMIT"></FORM>submit
```

TextBoxes: Single (TEXT) or multi-line (TEXTAREA).

Figure F-8: This is a single-line text box. If you require multiple lines, see TEXTAREA, discussed later in this section.

```
<FORM><INPUT TYPE=text VALUE="QUIT?"></FORM>text
```

Tip

If you want to specify precisely where HTML Controls appear on your document, try placing them inside HTML tables. For the ultimate in ease of positioning and sizing, however, try using the ActiveX "HTML Layout Control." With it, you can drag to reposition or resize Controls with great precision. See the Introduction of this book for more details.

VBScript & Validation

VBScript allows you to check the user's input locally on the client-side (within the user's computer), *before* sending that input data back to the server. To do that, you must work with the Value

Property of the text box. It's necessary to use some programming that, to some people, will be unfamiliar. It's necessary to create an "object Variable" out of the form. Once you've got a Form Variable pointing to this particular form, you can then reference the objects on the form and their Properties. To do this, you first create a Variable (Dim F), then you use the special Set command. Set assigns an object to a Variable (as opposed to assigning data like text or a number to an ordinary Variable). Thereafter, we can use the Variable name to represent this form and, by separating them with periods, the objects on that form and some of their Properties: F.Text1.Value. Finally, when we're satisfied with the user's input, we return the data to the server with the Submit command.


```
<HTML>
</HEAD>
<BODY>
<FORM NAME="MyForm">
Please type in your name:
<INPUT NAME="Text1" TYPE="TEXT" SIZE="42">
<INPUT NAME="Submit" TYPE="BUTTON" VALUE="Submit">
</FORM>
</BODY>

<SCRIPT LANGUAGE="VBScript">

Sub Submit_OnClick
 Dim F
 Set F = Document.MyForm
   If IsNumeric(F.Text1.Value) Then
     MsgBox "Please type in your name, not your address or
phone number."
   Else
MsgBox "We'll send it in."
F.Submit
   End If
End Sub

</SCRIPT>
</HTML>
```

Used with ***Can be enclosed by***

<BANNER>, <BODY>, <BODYTEXT>, <DD>, <DIV>, <FIGTEXT>, <FN>, <LI>, <NOTE>, <TD>, <TH>

Can enclose

<A>, <ABBREV>, <ACRONYM>, <ADDRESS>, <AU>, <B>, <BIG>, <BLOCKQUOTE>, <BQ>, <BR>, <CITE>, <CODE>, <DEL>, <DFN>, <DIR>, <DIV>, <DL>, <EM>, <FIG>, <FN>, <FORM>, <H>, <HR>, <I>, <IMG>, <INPUT>, <INS>, <ISINDEX>, <KBD>, <LANG>, <MATH>, <MENU>, <NOTE>, <OL>, <P>, <PERSON>, <PRE>, <Q>, <S>, <SAMP>, <SELECT>, <SMALL>, <STRONG>, <SUB>, <SUP>, <TAB>, <TABLE>, <TEXTAREA>, <TT>, <U>, <UL>, <VAR>

F

Variables A variety of commands are used with the Form command. We've divided them below into various groups, according to the purpose they serve.

Commands That Take Action on the Contents of the FORM:

- ACTION is a URL (an Internet address, such as http://www.myplace.com) where the information entered by the user should be sent to be processed by an application. If you leave out the ACTION command, the URL of the document itself is used. Just *how* the data is sent back depends on the settings you give to the ENCTYPE and METHOD commands below.
- METHOD describes the protocol (method) that is to be used to send back the data the user has entered. The two possible methods are POST or GET. GET is the default, unfortunately. GET's great weakness is that it slams all the data together into a single, potentially long, piece of text ("string"). This is lamentable because many operating systems limit the length of single pieces of text to 255 characters. Therefore, some data can be lopped off when the GET method is used.
- ENCTYPE determines which protocol will be used to encode the data. It defaults to: "application/x-www-form-urlencoded."

Commands That Display Input Controls to the User:

- INPUT: The INPUT command is a way to display most of the kinds of Controls with which the user can communicate back to you. With INPUT you use the TYPE command to specify which of the following input devices you want displayed or used on your document: CHECKBOX, HIDDEN, IMAGE, PASSWORD, RADIO, RESET, SUBMIT, and TEXT (the default is TEXT). There are also two input Controls *that are not used with INPUT*, SELECT (a List Box), and TEXTAREA (a multiline Text Box).
- TYPE: The TYPE command specifies which of the various Controls that can be used with INPUT is the desired one. See the examples below.

Commands That Modify Controls or Behavior:

- ACCEPT: ACCEPT is used with the FILE command and allows you to provide a list of MIME file types that will be permitted to be attached.
- ALIGN: ALIGN is used with the Controls that include graphics—IMAGE, SCRIBBLE, and SUBMIT. You use it to position the Control relative to the text line by specifying TOP, MIDDLE, or BOTTOM. ALIGN=LEFT, for example, forces the Control to the left margin, and causes any text (that follows the ALIGN command) to wrap around to the right of the Control.
- CHECKED: CHECKED works with either a CheckBox or Radio Button Control, and specifies that, by default, the Control is "on"—has a check mark or dot in it. It's as if the user had clicked on the Control to select it. Use this if you want the Control to be, by default, selected.
- DISABLED: DISABLED displays a Control that can't be used. For example, you might have a CheckBox labeled "Send a catalog to my friend, too!" along with some text boxes where the user can type in his friend's address. However, until the user clicks on the CheckBox, you make the text boxes

disabled—they won't accept any typing the user might attempt. Likewise, a disabled Control, in the Windows operating system among others, *looks different* from an enabled Control. It is generally darker or grayer than an active Control.

- ERROR: ERROR provides an error message if the user incorrectly enters something into an input Control (the date 3/44/96, for instance).
- MAXLENGTH: MAXLENGTH specifies the maximum number of characters permitted in a password or text Control. (Also see "Size" below.)
- NAME: NAME is a text Variable associated with a particular Control. It doesn't matter whether or not any capitalization is used; NAME is not case-sensitive. You use NAME to later refer to the data within a Control. For example, here we use NAME to identify a Button Control. When the user clicks this button, a Subroutine takes action. The Subroutine identifies its association with the button because it uses the NAME of that button, *btn* in this example:

```
<INPUT TYPE=BUTTON VALUE="Click on me" NAME="Btn">

<SCRIPT LANGUAGE=VBScript>

Sub Btn_OnClick
  MsgBox "You Clicked it!"
End Sub

</SCRIPT>
```

  NAME is also used with the A (linking) command.

- SIZE: SIZE specifies the *visible* width of a password or text Control. This way you can create text input boxes that will accept longer input than would be visible within the actual width of the box itself. The user can just keep on typing. For typefaces like Times Roman (where the width of characters varies), SIZE refers to "en spaces" (one-half the point size or roughly the width of the letter *n*); for fixed-width typefaces (such as Courier), SIZE refers to the number of characters.

- VALUE: VALUE works with knobs, sliders, and text Controls. It can be a number that specifies the initial status of a Control that handles a range (knobs or sliders). If the range of a slider is 10 and you specify VALUE=5, the pointer in the slider will be at the midpoint when the document is first displayed. Similarly, VALUE can be text that initially appears within a text box: VALUE="United States." Value, then is a way of providing defaults. The user wouldn't have to type in "United States," but, if he didn't live in America, he could change the contents as appropriate.

- SELECT: The SELECT command creates a list box Control, a scrollable list that the user can click on to choose from among a group of options. (For some reason, this Control isn't categorized along with those explained above, Controls that are triggered by the INPUT command. SELECT is used by itself, without the INPUT command.)

  Note that the SELECT list box will automatically size itself to be wide enough to display the widest text item you provide for its list (see OPTION below). The following programming produces the results shown in Figure F-9.

```
<HTML>

<H2>CHOOSE YOUR FREE VIDEO!</H2>
<BODY BGCOLOR=WHITE>
<FONT SIZE=+4>
<FORM METHOD="POST" ACTION="/cgi/videos">

<SELECT NAME="video" SIZE="5" MULTIPLE>
<OPTION>Vanities
<OPTION>New Orleans Fishfry
<OPTION>Sand, Our Friend
<OPTION>Ancient Mornings
<OPTION>Recipe for Disaster
<OPTION>Jane
<OPTION>Marlboro: Duke of Kent or Scrabbie?
<OPTION>Glassmaking in Ancient Ur
</SELECT>
```

F

```
</FORM>
</FONT>
</HTML>
```

Figure F-9: List Boxes are efficient and user-friendly input devices.

Options Used With SELECT:

- ALIGN (See ALIGN above.)
- DISABLED, in theory, prevents the user from clicking on the list to make a selection. However, in practice, most browsers ignore this command.
- ERROR (See ERROR above.)
- MULTIPLE means the user can make more than one selection.
- NAME is the list box's Variable name. In other words, whichever item in the list the user clicks on is identified by the NAME Variable. This allows you to send the information—the user's selection—back to your home site or wherever you're going to process the information. (You can also use NAME.VALUE to create a default selection—to highlight one of the items in the list. In programming terminology, you can *set* or *read* this Variable.)
- OPTION is the command you use to create each item within the list:

```
<OPTION>Ancient Mornings
<OPTION>Recipe for Disaster
<OPTION>Sand, Our Friend
```

- SIZE specifies the *visible* number of items within the list. You must use quotes: <SELECT SIZE="12">. You can still add as many items as you want, but only SIZE number will be visible at one time to the user. This is a way of conserving screen space—you can have a long list, but it only takes up a little room.

- TEXTAREA is the final input device. It's similar to the Text Box, but instead of being limited to a single line, TEXTAREA permits multiple lines of text to be entered. Horizontal and Vertical scrollbars are available on the TEXTAREA text box, so the user can scroll in either direction if the text overflows the visible area of the box.

Options Used With TEXTAREA:

- NAME is the TEXTAREA's Variable name. In other words, the contents of the TEXTAREA are identified by the NAME Variable. This allows you to send the information—the user's selection—back to your home site or wherever you're going to process the information. (You can also use NAME.VALUE to *assign* the text that will be displayed in the TEXTAREA. This is a way of displaying information to the user dynamically—while the page is being viewed. You can also use it to provide default text. In programming terminology, you can *set* or *read* this Variable.)

- ROWS is the number of rows (lines of text) that will appear within the TEXTAREA. This determines the height of the TEXTAREA.

- COLS is the number of columns (how many characters in a single line)—this determines the width of the TEXTAREA.

  You can provide contents for TEXTAREA by just typing things in, when designing your page, between the <TEXTAREA> and </TEXTAREA> commands.

  To learn how to use a TEXTAREA Control, see the example below.

Cautions FORMs are fairly well supported by Netscape, Mosaic, and Internet Explorer. However, other browsers—mercifully in the minority—can react unpredictably to FORMs and the elements within FORMs. If this concerns you (for example, you are selling something and want to get orders from as many customers as possible), consider providing a way for users to respond via e-mail as an alternative to your FORM.

Example

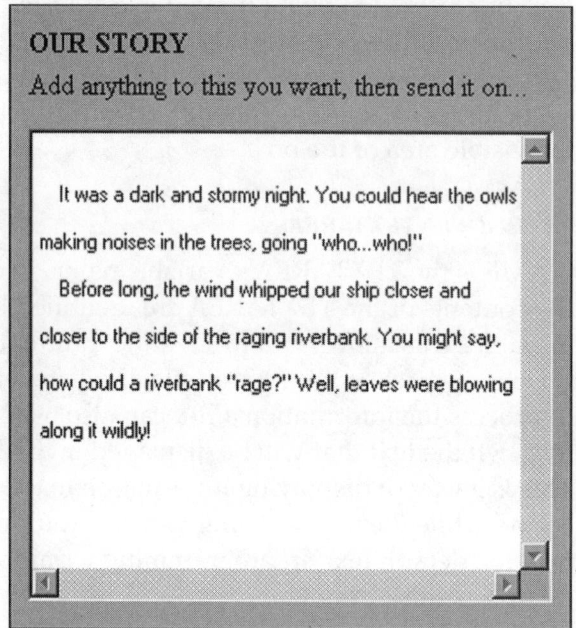

Figure F-10: Use TEXTAREA for multiline user input (or multiline displays to the user that can't be part of the body of your document because the data changes).

```
<HTML>

<H4>OUR STORY</H4>

Add anything to this you want, then send it on...

<FORM METHOD="POST" ACTION="/cgi/story">

<TEXTAREA NAME="thestory" ROWS="18" COLS="60">
 It was a dark and stormy night. You could hear the owls
```

```
 making noises in the trees, going "who...who!"
 Before long, the wind whipped our ship closer and
 closer to the side of the raging riverbank. You might say,
 how could a riverbank "rage?" Well, leaves were blowing
 along it wildly!
</TEXTAREA>

</FORM>

</HTML>
```

See also INPUT, ISINDEX, INPUTBOX

F

FRAME

NETSCAPE

Description If you want to display several windows within a single document, use the FRAME command. In the Windows environment, this technique has been called a *Multiple Document Interface*, or *Child Windows*. It is used by word processors, for example, to permit the user to view and independently scroll through more than one document at a time.

You create a frame by making multiple documents, each a separate .HTM file, with one (invisible) host document that governs their size and position. At the simplest level, you can create two frames, plus the host "frameset." First, create and save the host frameset. We'll save it with the name frame.htm:

```
<HTML>
<FRAMESET ROWS="10%, *">
  <FRAME SRC="upper.htm">
  <FRAME SRC="lower.htm">
</FRAMESET>
</HTML>
```

The ROWS command above specifies that the upper frame should take up 10% of the vertical dimension of this document, and the * means use the rest of the document to display the lower frame. Using the ROWS command causes the browser to be divided horizontally (the long way, as you can see in Figure F-11). If we used the COLS command, the browser would be divided into frames vertically. For additional ways to specify size, see ROWS below.

Then make the two documents, the frames that will actually be displayed, saving them with the names upper.htm and lower.htm:

```
<HTML>
This Is The Upper Frame
</HTML>

<HTML>
This Is The Bottom Frame
</HTML>
```

And here's the result when the browser loads the host document that we saved as frame.htm:

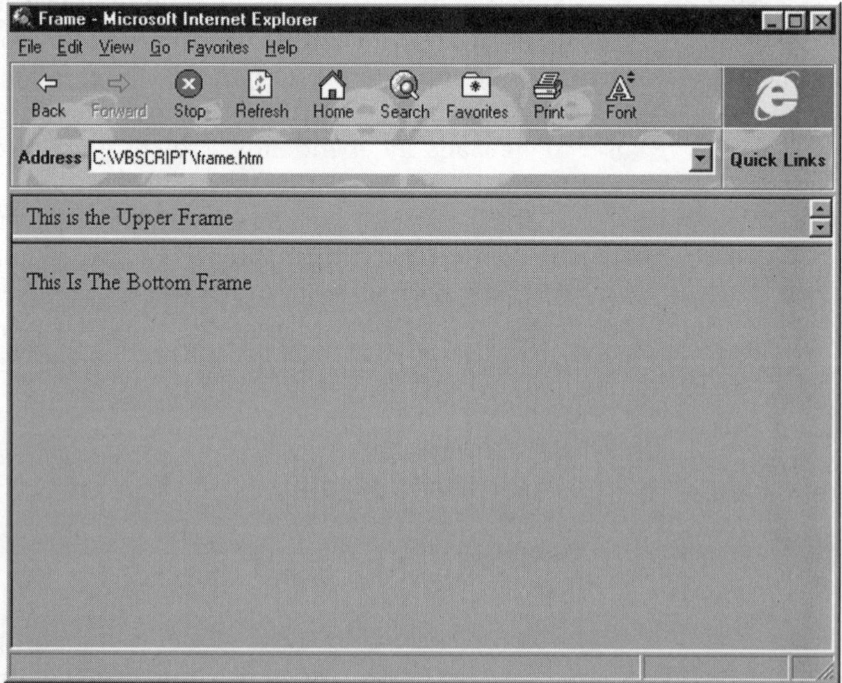

Figure F-11: Our example above results in the simplest possible set of frames.

Note that the user can resize the frames by dragging the divider; however, you can disable this feature if you wish, with the NORESIZE command (see below). Also notice that, because there is more to display in the upper frame than our 10% space allocation permits, a scroll bar is automatically added to that upper frame.

Variables ***COLS & ROWS: Size, Position & Number of Frames***

As usual when programming Internet Pages, you can specify size either relatively (with percentages or fractions) or absolutely (in pixels). However, it's always risky to use absolute specifications because there is such variation among users' screen resolution and browser window size. But you should also consider the fact that the browser will make its own decisions about sizing your frames if you provide instructions that are either incomplete or impossible.

Vertical Frames

COLS (and ROWS) specify the number, size, and position of the frames. If you use COLS, the screen will be divided vertically into columns; if you use ROWS, the screen will divide horizontally into rows. However, both COLS and ROWS share the same parameter specifications to indicate the size of the frames. There are several ways you can specify the size. <FRAMESET COLS="40%,*"> means divide the screen into two frames; the first one should take up 40 percent of the screen and the other the remaining 60 percent. Here's how to set up these two columnar frames:

1. Create the "host" or "parent" document that describes the two "child" documents (the frames). Save this document as PARENT.HTM

```
<HTML>
<HEAD>
<TITLE>Frame</TITLE>
</HEAD>
<BODY>
  <FRAMESET COLS="40%, *">
  <FRAME SRC="frame1.htm">
```

F

```
    <FRAME SRC="frame2.htm">
    </FRAMESET>
  </BODY>
  </HTML>
```

2. Notice that we've described our two child documents as FRAME1.HTM and FRAME2.HTM, so let's create those documents and save them (in the same directory) under those two names:

F

```
<HTML>
<HEAD>
  <TITLE>Frame1</TITLE>
  </HEAD>
  <BODY>
  This is FRAME 1
  </BODY>
  </HTML>
```

and

```
  <HTML>
  <HEAD>
  <TITLE>Frame2</TITLE>
  </HEAD>
  <BODY BACKGROUND="ROUGH1.GIF">
  THIS IS FRAME 2
  </BODY>
  </HTML>
```

3. With these three HTM files in the same directory, you can now load the parent (we saved the parent file as PARENT.HTM) into a browser and see the result in Figure F-12.

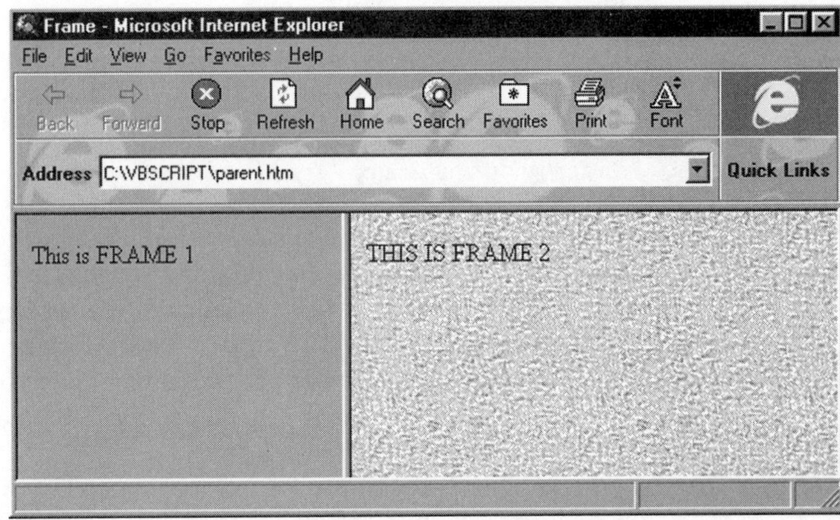

*Figure F-12: COLS="40%, *" causes frames divided vertically between 40 percent and 60 percent of the browser window.*

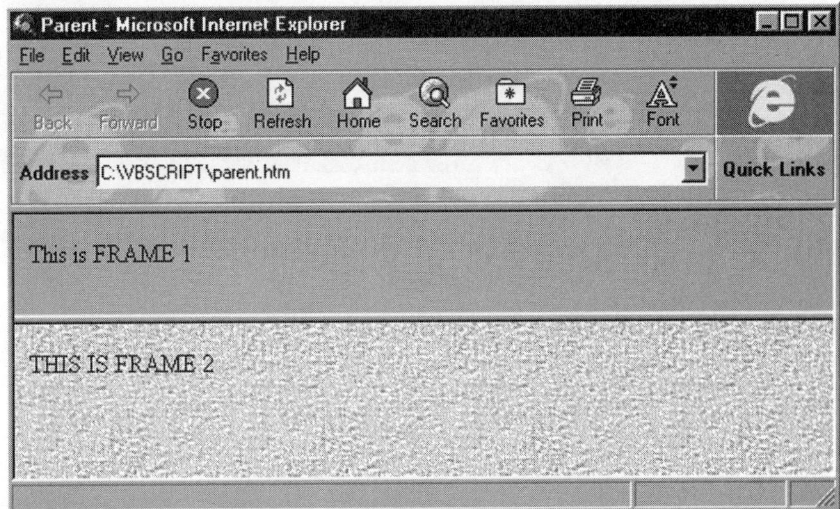

*Figure F-13: ROWS="40%, *" causes frames divided horizontally between 40 percent and 60 percent of the browser window.*

Horizontal Frames

To create frames divided horizontally, use the ROWS command. This is the only change you need to make to all the HTML programming above to turn Figure F-12 into Figure F-13:

```
<FRAMESET ROWS="40%, *">
```

Alternative Size Specifications

In addition to the "60%, *" approach to specifying the size of your frames, you can specify the precise number of pixels high or wide the frame should be: ROWS="240, *" would make the top frame 240 pixels high, and the bottom frame whatever space is left over. COLS="240, *" would make the left frame 240 pixels wide, and the right frame whatever's left over.

Yet another way of specifying involves a kind of "fractional" specification. COLS="*,3*" would divide the window into two frames: the left one would be 1/4 of the total width and the right frame would be 3/4 of the total.

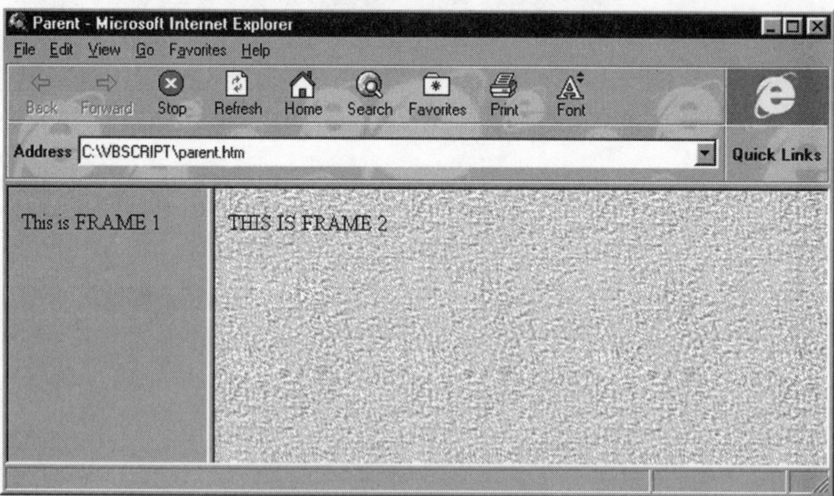

Figure F-14: The fractional size specification uses 3 to mean 3/4 of the total width in the specification COLS="*,3*".*

You can also mix and match the size specifications. The following example says: Make the leftmost frame 95 pixels wide, the middle frame 2/3 of the remaining space, and the rightmost frame whatever's left over (one-third of the total width of the browser window, minus 95 pixels):

```
<FRAMESET COLS="95, 2*, *">
```

Frame Borders & Margins

You can modify the appearance of your frames using the following commands.

MARGINWIDTH defines how far from the frame's sides the contents of the frame should be placed. For example, if you've got some text in the frame, the MARGINWIDTH describes the left and right margins where that text will wrap around.

MARGINHEIGHT does the same thing, but describes the top and bottom margins. As you can see in Figure F-15, the left frame's contents are positioned within the default frame margins, but the text in the right frame is lowered and squeezed because we've specified both a MARGINWIDTH and a MARGINHEIGHT:

```
<FRAME SRC="frame1.htm">
<FRAME SRC="frame2.htm" MARGINWIDTH=55 MARGINHEIGHT=55>
```

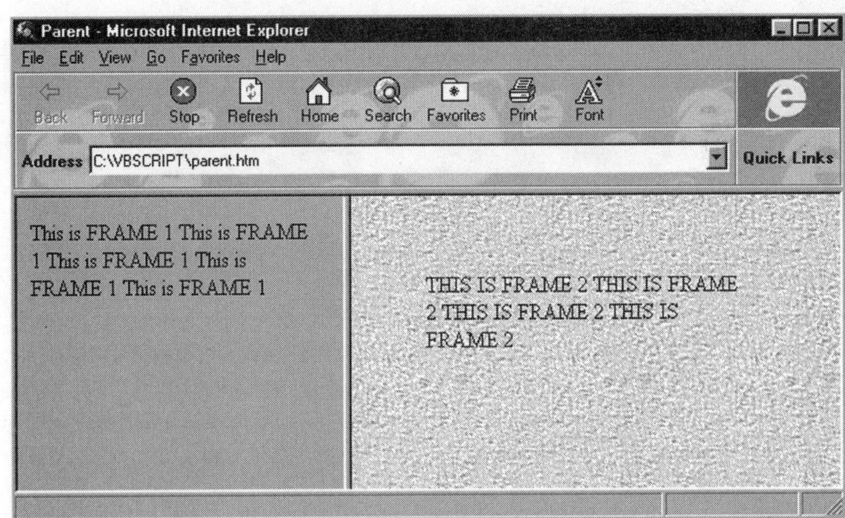

Figure F-15: When you include MARGINWIDTH or MARGINHEIGHT specifications, you can control how much space surrounds the contents in a frame—how far the contents are from the borders of the frame.

FRAMEBORDER allows you to turn off frame borders or to specify how thick the borders are. If you are using frames to create a fixed, static element of your page (like a button bar), you might not want any visible borders around the frames. You want the button bar to persist on the screen and always be visible to the user, but the remaining section of the document (the other frame) should permit the user to scroll or page. In such cases, you can eliminate the visible framing with this set of commands:

```
<HTML>
<HEAD>
<TITLE>Parent</TITLE>
</HEAD>
<BODY>
   <FRAMESET ROWS="15%, *" FRAMEBORDER=0 FRAMESPACING=0>
   <FRAME SRC="frame1.htm">
   <FRAME SRC="frame2.htm">
</FRAMESET>
</BODY>
</HTML>
```

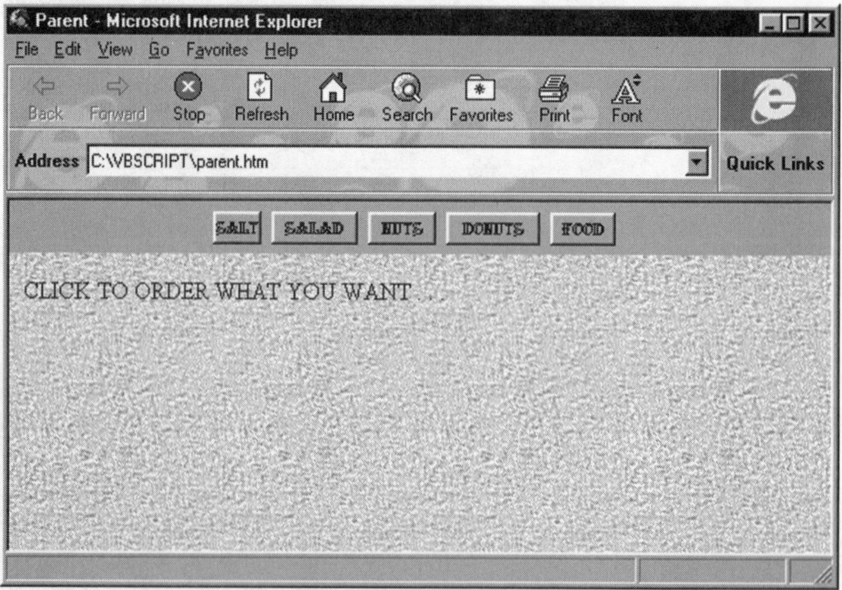

Figure F-16: The fixed button bar above is separated from the scrollable content of this page (below). We used the FRAMEBORDER and FRAMESPACING commands to create borderless frames.

Here's an example of a borderless set of frames, that allows the (usually invisible) parent document to show through. In the parent, give it a texture with the BACKGROUND option inside the BODY command, or use, as we've done, a different color with the BGCOLOR command. This way, you'll actually see the underlying page since it won't blend in with the frame pages. By setting FRAMESPACING to 30, we reveal the underlying Parent page:

```
<HTML>
<HEAD>
<TITLE>Frame</TITLE>
</HEAD>
<BODY BGCOLOR=WHITE>
  <FRAMESET COLS="40%, *" FRAMEBORDER=0 FRAMESPACING=30>
  <FRAME SRC="frame1.htm">
  <FRAME SRC="frame2.htm">
  </FRAMESET>
</BODY>
</HTML>
```

Tip

When you're using borderless frames, you often want to position the contents smack against the sides or top of the user's browser window. Browsers generally add a bit of default spacing between their frames and the contents in the window. To get flush against the window border, use these commands within the BODY specification:

```
<BODY TOPMARGIN=0 LEFTMARGIN=0>
```

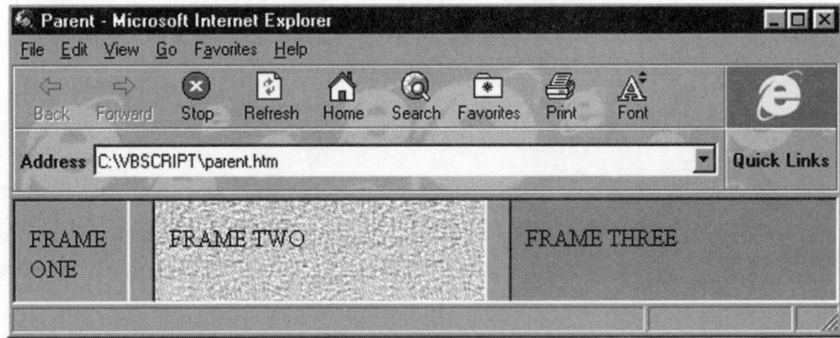

Figure F-17: You can adjust the width of the borders by changing the FRAMESPACING command.

The thicker borders shown in Figure F-17 were created by setting FRAMESPACING to 15 pixels wide:

```
<FRAMESET COLS="15%, *,*" FRAMESPACING=15>
```

The FRAMEBORDER and FRAMESPACING commands only work in the Internet Explorer browser at this time.
SCROLLING, when set to "YES," adds a scroll bar to a frame. However, most browsers will automatically add scroll bars if the contents are not completely displayed within the frame:


```
<FRAME SRC="frame1.htm" SCROLLING="Yes">
```

If you set SCROLLING to "NO," scroll bars will never appear on the frame. The default is "AUTO" and permits the browser to add a scroll bar at its discretion.

NORESIZE prevents the user from dragging the corners of your frame to adjust its size. By default, users are permitted to resize frames.

```
<FRAME SRC="frame1.htm" NORESIZE>
```

Floaters: Frames Anywhere

If you want a frame or frames to float within the browser (instead of butting up against each other in one of the patterns we've been illustrating in the examples above), try this:

```
<HTML>
<HEAD>
<TITLE>Frame</TITLE>
</HEAD>
<BODY>
<FRAME WIDTH=75% HEIGHT=75%
HSPACE=25 VSPACE=25
SRC="http://www.microsoft.com/">
</BODY>
</HTML>
```

By simply inserting the FRAME command within a document, describing its height and width, and pointing to the contents (the

URL), you'll get a frame that butts up against the left top of the browser window. You can, of course, substitute exact pixel dimensions for the percentages above:

```
WIDTH=150 HEIGHT=130
```

If you want to position it elsewhere within the browser, use the HSPACE and VSPACE commands as illustrated above. Likewise, you can use the ALIGN command to position your floating frame.

For Those Who Can't See Frames

If you want to provide for users with browsers that cannot handle frames, put your messages and content for them between:

```
<NOFRAMES>

This is for those who cannot see frames in their browsers.

</NOFRAMES>
```

For example, the .HTM file that contains the description of your frameset (the one we've been calling PARENT.HTM in the examples above) normally doesn't display anything in the user's browser. It's just a container that describes the FRAMESET and lists the .HTM files that will be visible frames. However, if the user's browser can't show frames, you can still provide information to him or her. Just put it into the PARENT.HTM file (or whatever you've named this parent file containing the FRAMESET command):

```
<FRAMESET COLS="20%, *">
  <FRAME SRC="row1.htm">
  <FRAME SRC="row2.htm">
  </FRAMESET>

  <NOFRAMES>
  Welcome to my home page! Click below to see my vacation
photos...
  etc.
  </NOFRAMES>

  </HTML>
```

F

```
<HTML>
<HEAD>
<TITLE>Frame</TITLE>
</HEAD>
<BODY>
  <FRAMESET COLS="40%, *">
  <FRAME SRC="frame1.htm">
  <FRAME SRC="frame2.htm">
  </FRAMESET>

<NOFRAMES>
This is our favorite list of sites. Just click on one:
</NOFRAMES>

</BODY>
</HTML>
```

Users who don't see your frames will see "This is our favorite list of sites. Just click on one:" and anything else you put between the <NOFRAMES>...</NOFRAMES> pair. Therefore, you'd want to duplicate the content in your frames files (in this example, the content in FRAME1.HTM and FRAME2.HTM).

TARGET: Linking Within & Without

NAME is an optional identifier:

```
<FRAME NAME="Buttons">
```

You can use the NAME to point to the frame when using the TARGET command. In this way, a link in one frame can, for example, update the contents of another frame.

Every frame is a separate document—just as if it were filling the entire browser all by itself, just as if *each frame were a complete browser*. Therefore, if you put a link or links within a frame, and the user clicks on one of those links, the frame will fill with the new document pointed to by that link. The other frames, however, will remain unaffected.

You might, though, want a link in one frame to fill a *different* frame with a new document. Use the NAME command to give each frame a NAME, an identifier tag.

Here's how to create a link in one frame that causes a different frame to be loaded with a new document:

1. Give each frame a NAME:

```
<HTML>
<HEAD>
<TITLE>Parent</TITLE>
</HEAD>
<BODY>
<FRAMESET COLS="45%, *">
  <FRAME SRC="frame1.htm" NAME="left">
<FRAME SRC="frame2.htm" NAME="right">
</FRAMESET>
</BODY>
</HTML>
```

(Save this document as PARENT.HTM.)

2. Put a link in the FRAME1.HTM document that points to the FRAME2.HTM document:

```
<HTML>
<HEAD>
<TITLE>Frame1</TITLE>
</HEAD>
<BODY>
<BR>
<A HREF="http://www.microsoft.com" TARGET="right">
Click here to see the Microsoft home page in the right
pane</A>

</BODY>
</HTML>
```

Note that the link (A) points to the TARGET frame, using the NAME we gave to that frame in step 1 above.

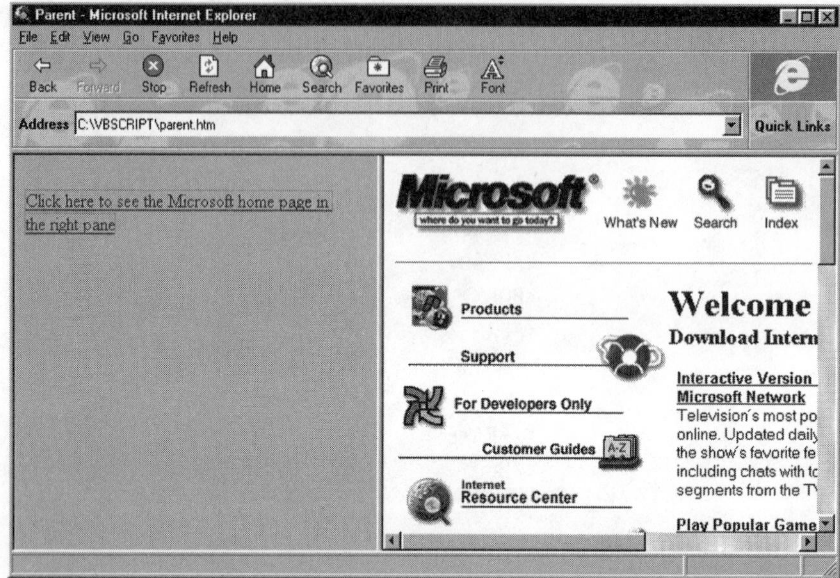

Figure F-18: When the user clicks on the link in the left frame, the right *frame will be filled with Microsoft's home page.*

SPECIAL LINKS: Single Window & Blank Window

If you want to create a link that restores the browser to a single window with no frames, use the special word "_TOP" for your TARGET:

```
<A HREF="http://www.microsoft.com" TARGET="_TOP"> Click here
to see the Microsoft home page fill your browser</A>
```

If you want a new, blank browser window, use the special word "_BLANK":

```
<A HREF="http://www.microsoft.com" TARGET="_BLANK"> Click
here for a blank window. </A>
```

SRC is a URL, describing the location of the frame's contents:

```
<FRAME SRC="frame1.htm">
```

Multiple Frames

To create more complicated frame arrangements, you can embed a FRAMESET within another FRAMESET. See the example below.

Uses

- Zone your page into smaller logical "virtual pages." Notice that frames can be, to the user, essentially identical to full-size Web pages: a frame can have its own URL address (so it can be loaded and reloaded with data, without affecting other frames on the page); it can have a NAME (so it can be the target of a hypertext link); and it can be optionally scrolled and resized independently of other frames.
- Create indexes or tables of contents in one frame that when clicked display their results in another frame or frames.
- Button bars and toolbars can be placed in a frame—thereby remaining fixed even if the user scrolls or pages through a separate frame displaying information. Because a frame can be frozen on a page, it's also a good way to create information that you always want displayed, such as copyright information or the title of your site.

Cautions

- Frame sizing and positioning will be decided by the user's browser if you provide specifications that are either impossible or incomplete. For example, COLS="90%,70%" is impossible; it's asking the browser to create two frames that are wider than 100% of the window.
- The NAME identifier must begin with a letter of the alphabet.

Example

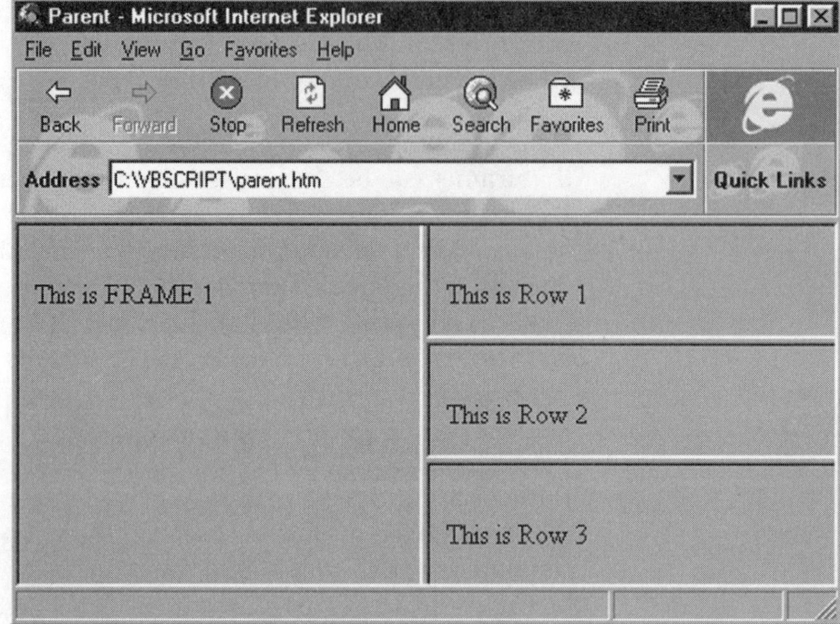

Figure F-19: Make your document as complex as you dare by embedding additional FRAMESETS.

Let's say that you wanted to divide the screen into two vertical frames (COLS), but you also wanted to divide the right frame into three separate horizontal (ROWS) frames. First set up the main controlling FRAMESET in an .HTM file we'll call PARENT.HTM. This file describes the screen divided into two vertical frames. But notice that *instead of a second FRAME SRC= reference,* it contains a second FRAMESET structure instead. Thus, you can use a frameset within another frameset, subdividing the screen real estate in this fashion as much as you want (save this document as PARENT.HTM):

```
<TITLE>Parent</TITLE>
</HEAD>
<BODY>
<FRAMESET COLS="50%, *">
  <FRAME SRC="frame1.htm">
```

```
<FRAMESET ROWS="33%, 33%, *">
  <FRAME SRC="row1.htm">
  <FRAME SRC="row2.htm">
  <FRAME SRC="row3.htm">
</FRAMESET>

</FRAMESET>
</BODY>
</HTML>
```

Then create the frame files (we'll call them FRAME1.HTM and ROW1.HTM, ROW2.HTM, and ROW3.HTM):

```
<HTML>
<HEAD>
<TITLE>Frame1</TITLE>
</HEAD>
<BODY>
<BR>
This is FRAME 1
</BODY>
</HTML>
```

(Save this document as FRAME1.HTM.)

```
<HTML>
<HEAD>
<TITLE>Row1</TITLE>
</HEAD>
<BODY>
<BR>
This is Row 1
</BODY>
</HTML>
```

(Save this document as ROW1.HTM.)

```
<HTML>
<HEAD>
<TITLE>Row2</TITLE>
</HEAD>
<BODY>
```

```
<BR>
This is Row 2
</BODY>
</HTML>
```

(Save this document as ROW2.HTM.)

```
<HTML>
<HEAD>
<TITLE>Row3</TITLE>
</HEAD>
<BODY>
<BR>
This is Row 3
</BODY>
</HTML>
```

(Save this document as ROW3.HTM.)

See also Table

Function

VBSCRIPT STATEMENT

Description Functions are rather like super Variables. They act like Variables within other statements (within "expressions"), but they can also perform some action on the information they contain. Normal Variables cannot adjust the piece of text or number they hold. Normal Variables merely "contain" a piece of information—some outside agent must be used to change or process the contained data.

A key distinction between a Function and a Subroutine is that a Function *can return* something to the location in the program that "called" the Function: X = Funct( ). The Variable X would be *given* something from the actions taken by the Function. Many times, though, you don't care what the Function returns and just ignore it.

```
X = "Hide the Secret."
```

X “holds” the phrase in this ordinary Variable, but X cannot, by itself, have any effect on the phrase it holds. A Function is like an intelligent Variable: a Function can analyze, modify, and report information, or take action based on the thing it holds.

Many Functions are built into VBScript, and you can create your own Functions too. InStr is an important built-in Function:

```
<HTML>

<INPUT TYPE=Button Name="Btn">

<SCRIPT LANGUAGE=VBS>

Sub Btn_OnClick()

X = "WARNING!! The Martians Have Landed."

If InStr(X, "Martians") <> 0 Then
  Msgbox "Head for the ocean!"
Else
  Msgbox "No Problem"
End If

End Sub
</SCRIPT>

</HTML>
```

The InStr Function returns (will be equal to) 0 if it doesn’t find the word *Martians* inside X. Otherwise, it returns the character position in X where the word *Martians* begins. Imagine how difficult getting this information would be using the Mid command or some other approach.

Notice that we used the Function as if it were a Variable. It’s as if we said, If X <> 0 Then...; but instead the Function *did something*. It analyzed the X within the If...Then expression.

Functions are very similar to Subroutines. Both act as “containers” for an instruction or a series of instructions that you give to the computer so it can accomplish some task when the program runs.

Automatic activation: Functions and Subroutines are the two basic units of organization when you're programming in VBScript. Each Subroutine and Function has a name, so you can "call" (refer to) it to activate it. Subroutines and Functions, as a category, are often referred to as *procedures.* Some procedures are activated automatically by VBScript itself. For example, Sub Btn_OnClick means that if the user clicks on the Command Button named *Btn*, then trigger this Subroutine (carry out the instructions contained between the Sub and End Sub).

Subroutines and Functions can accept Variables "passed" to them when you "call" them by name and put any Variable you want to pass following their names. Subroutines and Functions can also change the passed Variables.

Passing Variables: Here's an example of how to pass Variables. Create a Subroutine and tell it that it will be getting a Variable passed to it. You do this by putting a Variable name—any name you want to use—inside the parentheses following the sub's name: Sub Dosomething (X). (Procedures that don't expect to be passed a Variable have empty parentheses.) Then, you pass a Variable when you *call* the Sub. You need not use the same Variable name:

```
B = 5
Dosomething B
```

If Dosomething adds 5 to whatever number gets passed to it:

```
Sub Dosomething (X)
   X = X + 5
End Sub
```

But notice that outside this sub the value of x remains the same *unless* x is declared (see "Dim") outside the sub.

When you create them, you give Functions and Subroutines unique names. We called the example Sub above "Dosomething." This way, other places within your program can simply use the word Dosomething to trigger this Sub.

There is a distinction between Subs and Functions. One way to think of this is that although both Subs and Functions can manipulate Variables, only a Function directly passes back a Variable to the command that called the Function.

```
   Function ( )
X = Dosomething (Z)
```

Subroutine

```
DoSomething Z
```

VBScript has many built-in Functions:

```
X = UCase("bombs away")
```

The UCase Function changes the characters involved to all uppercase:

```
MsgBox X
```

Results in

```
BOMBS AWAY
```

Variables No matter how many Variables you *pass* to a Function, it always returns only one Variable:

```
Function AddStrings (A, B)
   AddString = A + B
End Function
X = AddStrings ("Hit", " The Deck")
MsgBox X
```

Results in

```
Hit The Deck
```

Here we passed two Variables; but, as always with a Function, we get only one back. In this case, X.

Notice that the Variable you pass back is the name *of the Function*, AddStrings. X equals AddString, and AddStrings contains the result of the Function's actions. This is why we can think of Functions as super Variables. You can use them as if they were Variables, within all the kinds of "expressions" where Variables are used:

```
Print AddStrings ("Hit", " The Deck")
```

Though you can only get one Variable back from a Function, you can still send more than one Variable to a Sub or Function. Variables that are passed to the Function, no matter how many you pass, cannot, however, be permanently changed by the Function. In VBScript, variables are passed "by value," which means that only a copy of a Variable is passed, not the real variable. The Sub or Function can use these copies of variables for information (and can make any changes they want *to the copies*), but can make no changes to the real variables. When you return, you'll find that any Variables "changed" by the Function have not changed at all outside the Function. (VBScript doesn't support argument passing "by reference" using the ByRef command, which *would* allow passed variables to be changed. The actual variable would be passed, not a copy.)

- You can either pass Variables, or pass the literal thing you want changed. Above, we passed the literal "Hit" and "The Deck." Here we pass Variables:

```
d = "Hit"
y = " the Deck"
x = AddStrings(d, y)
```

- Using the Dim command (outside a Sub or Function) preserves the contents of a Variable. In other words, Dim outside of a procedure prevents the values of the Variables from being destroyed (though they can be changed). Normally, Variables local to a procedure exist only while a Sub or Function is active. The important difference between the ReDim and Dim commands is that ReDim must be used within a procedure (a Sub or Function), whereas Dim can be used either outside or within a procedure. If Dim is used outside a procedure, the Array will be available for use by all other programming in the script. If Dim is used within a procedure then, like ReDim, the declared Array is available only to programming that's also within that same procedure. This "range of influence" is known as the scope of a Variable or an array.

- A Function must follow the same rules that apply to any Variable. (You can't use words already used by VBScript itself, such as MsgBox, you can't use words you used previously for Variables in the same Form, and so forth.)
- All Variables within a Function or Sub (except those passed to it) are *local* to that Function. They come into being when the Function runs; they die when the Function is finished with its job (You can preserve them by using the DIM command, outside the Function or Sub).
- You must always call a Function by its name followed by parentheses ( ), even if the parentheses are empty because this particular Function does not receive Variables.

F

Uses Use Functions when you need to accomplish the same task in several different places in one of your programs, and you also want to use the Function as part of an "expression."

A Function is exactly like a Subroutine, except that a Function can directly return a result to the place in your program that called the Function. In versions prior to VBScript 4, a Function must be used within a larger structure (an expression) such as an If...Then Structure. For a definition of "expression," see "Variables."

Why Subroutines and Functions Are Useful: Many programs, even some large ones, are written without creating any Functions. However, Subs and Functions are convenient when you want to accomplish a task several times but you want to write the instructions for this task only one time. Also, you'll want to use procedures that are automatically triggered by VBScript when the user does something (see "OnClick" above). VBScript can recognize many built-in "Event" triggers. Most ActiveX Controls have a list of Events—things that can happen to them such as the MouseOver Event. If you want your VBScript to react when the user's mouse pointer passes over the Control, create a Sub that will be triggered by the MouseOver Event. Use the Control's name (you'll see it in your HTML code as OBJECT ID=) to do this:

```
Sub Image1_OnMouseOver ()
MsgBox "They moved their mouse over this image!"
End Sub
```

OR

```
Sub Button1_OnClick ()
```

or whatever Control's Event you want to react to.

But when should you use a Function instead of a Subroutine? Functions are less commonly used than Subroutines. A Function lends itself to cases where you want to use the Function within larger expressions such as:

```
If X = MyFunction (Z) Then...
```

You can always use a Subroutine instead of a Function, but this usually requires an extra step in programming:

```
MySubroutine Z
If X = Z Then...
```

However, this presumes that this Variable Z can be recognized in both locations in your programming. Variables declared (DIM) within a procedure *are only recognized within that procedure.* A Function, however, doesn't limit you this way: a Variable is *passed* back to whatever location in the program called that Function.

Functions are also useful when you want to *return an error code*:

```
If SaveAllMyData("ThisFile.Dat") = FatalError Then End
```

Cautions You can use the Exit Function command to abruptly quit a Function prior to its normal conclusion (at the End Function command). Sometimes, based on things that happen while your Function does its tasks, you may want to quit early and not do everything that's listed to do within the Function.

You can use as many Exit Functions as you wish:

```
Function NewValue (X)
X = X + 4
If X > 12 Then
  Exit Function
Else
  X = 7
End If
End Function
```

Example

```
Function Findcat (X As String)
  Findcat = InStr(X, "cat")
End Function
```

Here we created a specialized version of the built-in VBScript Function InStr. Let's say we often need to check string Variables for the word *cat*. So, instead of writing InStr(X, "cat") every time we need to check, we wrote a Function that does the job and reports the results. We could as easily have made this a Subroutine, but making it a Function gives us the added flexibility of being able to use it in expressions like: *If Findcat (M) Then*

```
<HTML>

<SCRIPT LANGUAGE="VBSCRIPT">
N = "Hide the cat"
M = "Feed the dog"
If Findcat (N) Then
  MsgBox "It was in N"
End If
If Findcat (M) Then
  MsgBox "It was also in M"
End If

Function Findcat (X)
  Findcat = InStr(X, "cat")
End Function
</SCRIPT>
</HTML>
```

See also Sub

G

GetFormat

ACTIVEX

See Methods

Global Scope

Description VBScript has no Global or Public command. The only provision for extending the scope of a Variable beyond an individual procedure is to define it with the Dim command *outside of any procedure*, but still within the <SCRIPT> </SCRIPT> tags. Doing so makes the Variable available script-wide: all procedures in that script—*and any other scripts in your document*—will have access to the Variable. They can all modify or read the contents of that Variable. For a detailed discussion of scope in VBScript, see "Dim."

If you need more than script-wide scope, try a Cookie. For information on how to save data between sessions (between a user's visits to your sites, so you can say "Welcome back, Jerry! You last visited us three weeks ago!"), see "Cookies."

See Dim

Gradient

ACTIVEX CONTROL

Description At first sight, you might wonder what you're going to do with a Control that merely looks pretty. Gradients have no Events—they won't react to anything, not even a mouse-click. They're purely decorative.

Nevertheless, it's dangerous to dismiss beauty. Among other things, you want your visitors to be impressed with the appearance of your Web pages. A gradient is an essential element of real-world visuals. True three-dimensional objects often display gradients: a gradient is a smooth transition between two different colors or two shades of the same color.

Unfortunately, at this time if you attempt to add a Gradient Control to your Web page, you'll have to settle for a small one. Increasing the width or height to 400 x 350, for example, will freeze Internet Explorer 3.0. Also, if you attempt to use the Microsoft ActiveX Control Pad's Edit | Insert ActiveX Control menu option, that, too, will crash Internet Explorer. The only way we've found to insert a Gradient Control is illustrated below in the example. And it's too small to be of much use. To see how to add true, large gradients to your Web pages, take a look at the section titled "Metallic Gradients" in the example under the entry for "Command Button." As you'll discover with that example, it's far better to create your own gradients and put them into the background of a document as wallpaper, or into the Picture Property of various Controls. It's better because your own gradients load and repaint faster, allow more creativity (circular gradients, for example), and, at this time, your own gradients won't crash Internet Explorer.

Variables The Gradient has only the RePaint and AboutBox Methods, and no Events. Its Properties define the colors and the shape of the gradient (horizontal, radiating from the center of the rectangle, and so on).

G

Properties

StartColor: If you're using a horizontal gradient (Direction=0), the StartColor is the color on the left side. For a vertical gradient (Direction=1), the StartColor is the color on the top.

EndColor: The opposite of StartColor. If you're using a horizontal gradient, the EndColor is the color on the right side.

Tip

Using colors when creating Internet documents can be confusing if you're not used to the hexadecimal numbering system. There are, after all, over 16 million possible colors. For details about handling color when creating Web documents, see the section titled "Many New Colors" under the entry on BGCOLOR, and also see "Hex Numbers for the COLOR command" in the entry on BODY.

Direction: There are eight possible directions (shapes) for a gradient. In the following figures, we're using white as a StartColor and black as an EndColor.

Figure G-1: Direction=0 creates a horizontal gradient.

Figure G-2: Direction=1 creates a vertical gradient.

Figure G-3: Direction=2 radiates from the center of the rectangle.

Figure G-4: Direction=3 radiates from the corner of the rectangle.

Figure G-5: Direction=4 radiates out from the center diagonally top left to bottom right.

Figure G-6: Direction=5 radiates out from the center diagonally bottom left to top right.

Direction=6 radiates out from the point specified in the **StartPoint** Property.

Direction=7 radiates out from a line described by the **StartPoint** and **EndPoint** Properties.

We can't provide figures illustrating the final two options for the Direction Property (Direction=6 or =7) because adding them to the PARAM list in the HTML source code, then loading the result into Internet Explorer currently crashes IE. Likewise, attempting to change them in the ActiveX Control Pad using the Properties Window crashes the Control Pad.

Methods

RePaint: Refreshes the Control after you've changed its Direction or color Property. See the example below.

```
iegrad1.Repaint
```

AboutBox: Shows information to the user about the Gradient Control.

Events

None

Uses Provide attractive backgrounds, buttons, and frames around other Controls. However, there's a simpler, better way to add gradients to your Web pages. See the description above.

Cautions

- The Gradient Control is an excellent idea, but it's not yet functional. See the final paragraph under description above.
- Unlike the Events of other Controls (which do their job automatically), you have to use a *RePaint* command.

Example

Figure G-7: This gradient will change colors every two seconds.

This example will work *if* you merely cut and paste it from this book's CD into the Microsoft ActiveX Control Pad. Then from the Pad's File menu, save the .HTM file. Finally, load that .HTM file into Internet Explorer 3.0 (using IE 3.0's File menu's File | Open | Browse feature).

```
<HTML>
<BODY>

<OBJECT
  ID="iegrad1"
     CLASSID="clsid:017C99A0-8637-11CF-A3A9-00A0C9034920"
 CODEBASE="http://activex.microsoft.com/controls/iexplorer/
iegrad.ocx#Version=4,70,0,1161"
```

```
    TYPE="application/x-oleobject"
    WIDTH=100
    HEIGHT=50
>
    <PARAM NAME="StartColor" VALUE="#0000ff">
    <PARAM NAME="EndColor" VALUE="#000000">
    <PARAM NAME="Direction" VALUE="2">
</OBJECT>

  <SCRIPT LANGUAGE="VBScript">
<!--
Sub IeTimer1_Timer()
N = Int(Rnd * 16000000)
P = Int(Rnd * 16000000)
iegrad1.EndColor = N
iegrad1.StartColor = P
iegrad1.Repaint
end sub
-->
</SCRIPT>

  <OBJECT ID="IeTimer1" WIDTH=39 HEIGHT=39
  CLASSID="CLSID:59CCB4A0-727D-11CF-AC36-00AA00A47DD2">
    <PARAM NAME="_ExtentX" VALUE="1005">
    <PARAM NAME="_ExtentY" VALUE="1005">
    <PARAM NAME="Interval" VALUE="2000">
  </OBJECT>

</BODY>
</HTML>
```

See also Command Button

G

H

HTML

Description <H1> Creates a headline. Headlines are ordinarily rendered in a sans-serif typeface—clean, no variations in line width, no curlicues (see the example below):

THIS IS SANS
This is Serif

Figure H-1: The typeface style above (sans) is used for headlines; the one below (serif) is used for body text.

When you use the H command, the browser will automatically format your page around it—inserting any necessary blank lines, changing the font to sans, and creating white space around the headline.

You can specify headlines in six sizes: H1, H2, H3, H4, H5, and H6. Note that H1 is the largest, H6 the smallest.

Used with ***Can be enclosed by***

<A>, <BANNER>, <BODY>, <BODYTEXT>, <DIV>, <FIGTEXT>, <FN>, <FORM>, <NOTE>, <TD>, <TH>

Can enclose

<A>, <ABBREV>, <ACRONYM>, <AU>, <B>, <BIG>, <BR>, <CITE>, <CODE>, <DEL>, <DFN>, <EM>, <I>, <IMG>, <INS>, <KBD>, <LANG>, <MATH>, <PERSON>, <Q>, <S>, <SAMP>, <SMALL>, <STRONG>, <SUB>, <SUP>, <TAB>, <TT>, <U>, <VAR>

Variables ALIGN: By default, headlines are placed against the left margin of your page. However, you can use the ALIGN command to specify otherwise:

- ALIGN=CENTER: Centers the headline.

```
<H1 ALIGN=CENTER>CENTERED HEADLINE</H1>
```

- ALIGN=JUSTIFY: Causes a multi-line headline to be rendered in a solid block (the characters line up vertically on the right side, as well as the left). This happens only if the browser and the headline's length permit it.
- ALIGN=LEFT: Restores the default flush left.
- ALIGN=RIGHT: Makes the headline move to the right margin.
- NOWRAP: This command will cause some browsers to avoid "wrapping" the headline (moving it down to the next line with an automatic line break, if a line will not fit on the user's screen). You, then, would use the BR command to specify where you want the headline's lines to break.

Uses Use headlines in your Web pages in the same way, and for the same purposes, that they are used in magazines. Headlines serve to separate a document into logical sections, allowing the reader to skip around, reading the body text if they're interested.

Cautions Headline and body-text sizing is somewhat confusing. H1 is the largest; H6 is the smallest.

Body text, by contrast, is specified by FONT SIZE=1 through FONT SIZE=7, with 7 being the largest size. In other words, the scheme for defining head size *is the opposite* of the scheme for defining body text size. This is just one of those kinks that creep into computer languages that everybody has to live with after the initial mistake is made by the language designers.

Example This illustrates how you can render a headline in the traditional sans-serif style. First we set the FONT FACE to ARIAL, then print the headline. After that, we restore the traditional serif body text style by specifying TIMES ROMAN. Note that if the user's operating system cannot supply one of these typefaces, the browser will resort to the default typeface and no harm will be done.

```
<HTML>
<BODY BGCOLOR=WHITE>
<FONT FACE=ARIAL>
<H1 ALIGN=CENTER>CENTERED HEADLINE</H1>
<FONT FACE=TIMES ROMAN>

  Use headlines in your Web pages in the same way, and for
the same purposes, that they are used in magazines. Headlines
serve to separate a document into logical sections, allowing
the reader to skip around, reading the body text if they're
interested.

</BODY>
</HTML>
```

CENTERED HEADLINE

Use headlines in your Web pages in the same way, and for the same purposes, that they are used in magazines. Headlines serve to separate a document into logical sections, allowing the reader to skip around, reading the body text if they're interested.

Figure H-2: Headlines serve the same purpose in a Web page as they do in a magazine or newspaper.

See also SIZE, FONT

HEAD

HTML

Description This is a section of a document, at the top. The other main section is the BODY. The HEAD is used primarily to enclose information about the document, information that is not directly displayed to the user (except for the TITLE, which usually appears in the title bar of the browser).

Used with ***Can be enclosed by***

<HTML>

Can enclose

<BASE>, <ISINDEX>, <LINK>, <META>, <NEXTID>, <TITLE>

Variables None

Uses The HEAD provides an area where you can identify your document (with a brief description) and provide its URL (so other elements of your document such as graphics or other pages can use a shorthand to refer to the "Base URL").

Cautions A HEAD isn't strictly required; most browsers will have no problems displaying your page if it lacks a head. However, it looks better if the browser can display a brief title (because you include a TITLE), rather than the default URL (which will appear in the title bar of the browser if you omit the TITLE). Also, if you are constructing a complicated, multipage document, having a BASE identification makes things simpler (see BASE).

Example

```
<HTML>
<HEAD>
<TITLE>Our Special Site</TITLE>
<BASE HREF="http://www.randor.com/thispg.htm"
</HEAD>
<BODY BGCOLOR=WHITE>
<P>Use titles to identify the page; use BASE HREF to provide
an anchor URL.
</BODY>
</HTML>
```

H

See also BASE, BODY

Height

ACTIVEX

See Properties

HelpContext, HelpFile

PROPERTIES

Description Together, HelpContext and HelpFile provide your VBScript program with the same kind of "Help" feature that comes with VBScript's design environment and other Windows applications. Both of these Properties are always used with the Err object.

The HelpFile is the name of a file you've created with the Windows Help compiler. This compiler is available with Microsoft language products. The HelpFile would contain whatever information you wanted to give the user about your program's behaviors.

The HelpContext is a number that identifies a specific location within your HelpFile. You can have as many screens of Help as you want, and each can be identified by different HelpContext Property settings for the various Controls and zones in your document. If the user presses the F1 key, VBScript looks for a HelpContext number in the currently active (with focus) Control. If no number is found in the Control's Property, then VBScript looks for a HelpContext number in the Property of the Control's container document. If none is found, then VBScript displays the main, first screen of the HelpFile, which is generally the "Contents" screen.

Used with HelpFile and HelpContext are used with the Err object (which see) to give the name of the Help file associated with your VBScript application.

Variables **Variable types:** HelpFile (text "string" Variable); Helpcontext (long integer)

The word Err refers to any error that has been generated.

Assuming that your HelpFile is named MyProgs.Hlp and is located in the C:\WINDOWS directory:

```
Err.HelpFile = "C:\Windows\MyProgs.Hlp"
Err.Helpcontext = 12440
```

Note that if a path to a help (.HLP) file is not specified, the VBScript HLP file will be displayed.

Uses Provide the user of your documents with context-sensitive help.

H

Example We'll use the Internet Explorer HelpFile to illustrate this:

```
Err.HelpFile = "C:\WINDOWS\Iexplore.hlp"
```

Generating an error should bring up whatever help file is specified.

See also Properties, Err, Description

Hex

VBSCRIPT FUNCTION

Description Hex translates a normal decimal number into a computer-friendly hexadecimal number. Hex gives you a *text* Variable that contains the hex version of a decimal number. Now you can display this hex number. However, you cannot use this "text-subtype" Variable in any calculations. If you want to use a hex number in calculations, you can signify that the number is to be read as hex by using the &H symbols. For example, 10 would be ten; &H10 would be sixteen, because &H means that the 10 is to be interpreted as a hex number.

Hexadecimal arithmetic is one of those weird compromises people have been making to facilitate talking to computers. It won't be around forever, but for now we must occasionally bend to the way the computer thinks rather than the other way around. For an example of the use of hex in HTML programming, see "Hex Numbers for the Color Command" in the entry on "BODY."

We're used to thinking of numbers in groups of 10, our decimal system. There's nothing magic about 10. Long ago it seemed like a natural grouping because that's the number of fingers we have to count with. There is nothing, though, in nature to suggest that ten is somehow special. We're just very, very used to it.

The computer bases its number system on 2—a *binary* system—because computers store and manipulate things in an on-off fashion, like a light switch. Consequently, numbers naturally cluster for the computer around the powers (multiples) of 2: 2 4 8 16 32 64 128 256 512 1,024. This is why computer memory is measured in kilobytes (1024 bytes), and why so many computer-based appliances offer, for example, 128 different sounds on a synthesizer or 256 storage places on a calculator. VBScript allows you 16 named Colors. These are all powers of two.

Decimal Arithmetic Is Awkward for the Computer

An important byproduct of the number of digits you use is the way you count: we have 10 digits, 0–9, then we start over again with 10 and go forward. No matter how big the number, we express it with only 10 symbols, the 10 digits.

The arithmetic for this kind of counting is clumsy for the computer—it's not natural. The computer wants to work with things in groups of 8 or 16, but decidedly *not* 10. The number 10 has an awkward mathematical relationship to 2, and the computer wants things to work in relation to 2.

There arose two kinds of computer arithmetic: octal (based on groups of 8 digits) and hexadecimal (based on 16 digits). Hex, for short, is the more commonly used for communicating with computers. Hex has 16 digits 0 1 2 3 4 5 6 7 8 9 A B C D E F. (We run out of traditional digits and have to start borrowing letters of the alphabet.)

Fortunately, VBScript has eliminated the need to use hex very often, although RGB colors are specified with hex. To indicate a hex number, you use the # symbol before the number. By itself, 16 is 16 as we understand it—16 in hex (#16) is 22 to us, in decimal.

Used with Decimal numbers to translate them into hex numbers.

Variables

```
Hex(15)
```

OR (to use a Variable instead of a literal number):

```
X = 15
Hex(X)
```

Uses Use Hex if you ever need to display a number in the hexadecimal format. This is purely to allow the user to see what the hex equivalent (of a decimal number) would be. The resulting number is not a *numeric* Variable subtype and so cannot be used in calculations. It is for display purposes only. If you want to do any mathematical things with it, just use the original number you gave to the Hex Function.

Today, hex numbers are most often used when communicating with something outside your computer. Some modem communications protocols use hex values encoded into text (string) Variables as their way of sending information over the phone lines.

Cautions

- Hex does not involve fractions, so it will round off any fractions.
- Hex does not turn a decimal number into some different number; it merely gives you a text Variable that is not usable in mathematical calculations or a Variable you could use for, say, an RGB color.

Example

```
<HTML>
<HEAD>
<TITLE>Hex</TITLE>
</HEAD>
<BODY>
<SCRIPT LANGUAGE="VBSCRIPT">

n = hex(23)
msgbox n
```

H

```
</SCRIPT>

</BODY>
</HTML>
```

HideSelection

ACTIVEX

See Properties

H

HotSpot

ACTIVEX CONTROL

Description With the HotSpot Control you can define an area that will react to clicks, double-clicks, or even the mouse merely entering, exiting, or moving over the area defined by the HotSpot.

In other words, when the user moves his or her mouse pointer into the zone described by your HotSpot, its MouseEnter Event is triggered. Any VBScript commands that you've placed within that zone will be carried out.

Maybe you'll show a map of Italy to your Web page visitors. Then, if they click on Sicily you'll play appropriate music and bring up a recipe for pizza. But if they click on Rome, they hear something different and see a recipe for fettuccine alfredo.

Of course, you can also use the HotSpot Control to add sensitivity to other Controls (or the background HTML Layout Control). For instance, an Image Control has no double-click Event. If you want to be able to do something in response to a user's double-click, just stretch a HotSpot on top of the Image Control and you can then trap double-clicks that take place within the Image Control.

Uses Trap and react to user input (mouse moves, clicks) in zones *within* a Control, such as areas within an Image Control's picture (see Figure H-4). In other words, HotSpots provide a more efficient way to accomplish what the HTML MAP and AREA commands endeavor to achieve (see the example below).

Trap and react to user input with Controls that are insensitive to it. For example, the background of a Layout Control isn't able to detect mouse clicks (so far, anyway). You could, therefore, put HotSpots on the background to permit something to happen (to trigger one of your VBScripts) when the user clicked or double-clicked on the background.

Used with The Image Control (to create mapped hot zones) or any Control that needs additional Events (the Image Control has no double-click Event).

Variables It's interesting that you can provide for keyboard access to hot spots. Put your programming in the HotSpot's MouseEnter Event (which will be triggered by pressing Enter if the HotSpot has the focus). When the user cycles through all the enabled Controls in the browser by repeatedly pressing Tab, the user is giving the focus to each Control in turn. If the HotSpot's Enabled property is set to True, the user can use this tabbing technique to move to the HotSpot, giving it the focus. When that happens, the user can press Enter and trigger the Enter Event.

See Cautions below for an explanation of the enigmatic Visible Property.

Properties

CodeBase, Enabled, Height, ID, Left, MouseIcon, MousePointer, TabIndex, TabStop, Visible, Width

Events

Click, DblClick, Enter, Exit, MouseDown, MouseMove, MouseUp, MouseEnter, MouseExit

Methods

Move, ZOrder

For details about these Properties, Events, and Methods, see the entries for "Properties," "Events," and "Methods."

Cautions Mysteriously, there is a Visible Property for the HotSpot Control, and it defaults to True. However, under no current circumstances does the HotSpot become visible to the user.

Evidently, Microsoft intends to add BorderStyle and BackStyle Properties to the HotSpot Control. These Properties are mentioned in the Help file for the ActiveX Control Pad. It is stated that if you set the BackStyle Property to other than its default (Transparent), or the BorderStyle to other than its default (none), the user will see the hot spots if you leave Visible set to True. More typically, though, a hot spot is indicated by a change in the mouse cursor—by convention it changes to a hand with a pointing finger (indicating a link of some sort).

Unhappily, of the 16 possible MousePointers you can change the mouse cursor to, that hand symbol is not among them. So, unless you have access to the hand symbol (and can therefore supply it to the MouseIcon Property), your best bet is probably to use the arrow+question mark symbol to indicate a hot spot, like this:

```
Sub HotSpot1_MouseMove(Button, Shift, X, Y)
HotSpot1.MousePointer = 14
end sub
```

In this way, when users move the mouse pointer onto a hot spot, at least they have a visual clue that clicking here will do something.

H

Example

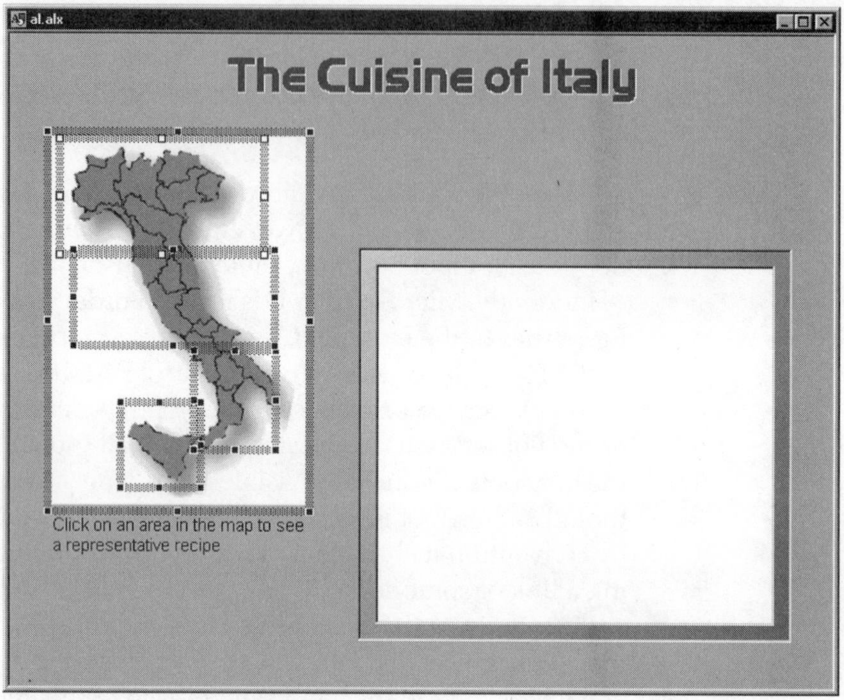

Figure H-3: *Hold down the Shift key and click on each HotSpot to see the coverage.*

Start ActiveX Control Pad and select Edit | Insert HTML Layout. (See the Introduction for details about using the Control Pad.) Put an Image Control on the Layout and put a picture into it that has areas, like our map of Italy in this example.

We're going to let the user click on any of four areas in Italy, each of which displays a recipe indigenous to that area. So put four HotSpot Controls onto the map, dragging them until they divide the country into logical areas, as shown in Figure H-3. Then put a TextBox onto the Layout (for details on how we created the gradient frame behind the TextBox, see "Image").

The ActiveX .HTM file programming looks like this:

```
<HTML>
<HEAD>
</HEAD>
<BODY>
```

```
<OBJECT CLASSID="CLSID:812AE312-8B8E-11CF-93C8-00AA00C08FDF"
ID="al_alx" STYLE="LEFT:0;TOP:0">
<PARAM NAME="ALXPATH" REF VALUE="file:C:\Program
Files\ActiveX Control Pad\al.alx">
 </OBJECT>

</BODY>
</HTML>
```

And the Layout Control .ALX file programming looks like the following. Notice that we first created four Variables—a, b, c, and d—outside of any Sub. Therefore, these Variables will be available for use anywhere within this script (see "Variables" for more on this *scope* issue). Then, when the Layout Control is first loaded into the user's browser (the OnLoad Event), we define the first recipe and assign it to the Variable *a*. You can go on and follow this same technique to create recipes for hot spots 2, 3, and 4 as well, assigning them to Variables b, c, and d, respectively. Our recipe in *a* will be for hot spot #1, northern Italy.

Then each HotSpot is provided with a Click Event that displays the appropriate recipe in the TextBox.

```
<SCRIPT LANGUAGE="VBScript">
<!--

Dim a, b, c, d

Sub al_OnLoad()
cr = chr(13) & chr(10)
a = "Northern Cioppino" & cr & cr & "1 lb firm white fish,
1/2 lb shrimp, clams or oysters, "
a = a & "other fish as desired, 1 28 oz. can Italian toma-
toes, 1 8 oz. can tomato sauce, "
a = a & "2 c. chicken or clam broth, 2 cloves minced garlic,
1/4 c olive oil, "
a = a & "1/4 c chopped parsley, 1 tsp basil, 1/2 tsp oregano,
1/2 tsp pepper."
a = a & cr & cr & "Cut fish into small pieces. Cook onion and
garlic in oil until tender. "
a = a & "Add everything else except seafood. Cover and simmer
```

```
about 30 minutes. Add fish and simmer 10-20 minutes. "
a = a & " Add clams and shrimp. Cover and simmer 5 minutes
more."

end sub

Sub HotSpot1_Click()
TextBox1 = a
end sub

Sub HotSpot2_Click()
TextBox1 = b
end sub

Sub HotSpot3_Click()
TextBox1 = c
end sub

Sub HotSpot4_Click()
TextBox1 = d
end sub

->
</SCRIPT>
<DIV ID="a1" STYLE="LAYOUT:FIXED;WIDTH:539pt;HEIGHT:413pt;">
  <OBJECT ID="Image1"
  CLASSID="CLSID:D4A97620-8E8F-11CF-93CD-00AA00C08FDF"
STYLE="TOP:65pt;LEFT:29pt;WIDTH:167pt;HEIGHT:236pt;ZINDEX:0;">
    <PARAM NAME="PicturePath" VALUE="c:\vbscript\italy.bmp">
    <PARAM NAME="BorderStyle" VALUE="0">
    <PARAM NAME="SizeMode" VALUE="3">
    <PARAM NAME="Size" VALUE="5891;8326">
    <PARAM NAME="PictureAlignment" VALUE="0">
    <PARAM NAME="VariousPropertyBits" VALUE="19">
  </OBJECT>
  <OBJECT ID="HotSpot1"
```

```
  CLASSID="CLSID:2B32FBC2-A8F1-11CF-93EE-00AA00C08FDF"
STYLE="TOP:69pt;LEFT:37pt;WIDTH:130pt;HEIGHT:68pt;ZINDEX:1;">
    <PARAM NAME="VariousPropertyBits" VALUE="8388627">
    <PARAM NAME="Size" VALUE="4586;2399">
  </OBJECT>
  <OBJECT ID="HotSpot2"
  CLASSID="CLSID:2B32FBC2-A8F1-11CF-93EE-00AA00C08FDF"
STYLE="TOP:140pt;LEFT:46pt;WIDTH:128pt;HEIGHT:56pt;ZINDEX:2;">
    <PARAM NAME="VariousPropertyBits" VALUE="8388627">
    <PARAM NAME="Size" VALUE="4516;1976">
  </OBJECT>
  <OBJECT ID="HotSpot3"
  CLASSID="CLSID:2B32FBC2-A8F1-11CF-93EE-00AA00C08FDF"
STYLE="TOP:203pt;LEFT:125pt;WIDTH:49pt;HEIGHT:58pt;ZINDEX:3;">
    <PARAM NAME="VariousPropertyBits" VALUE="8388627">
    <PARAM NAME="Size" VALUE="1729;2046">
  </OBJECT>
  <OBJECT ID="Image2"
  CLASSID="CLSID:D4A97620-8E8F-11CF-93CD-00AA00C08FDF"
STYLE="TOP:236pt;LEFT:77pt;WIDTH:48pt;HEIGHT:49pt;ZINDEX:4;">
    <PARAM NAME="BorderStyle" VALUE="0">
    <PARAM NAME="SizeMode" VALUE="3">
    <PARAM NAME="Size" VALUE="1693;1729">
    <PARAM NAME="PictureAlignment" VALUE="0">
    <PARAM NAME="VariousPropertyBits" VALUE="19">
  </OBJECT>
  <OBJECT ID="Image3"
  CLASSID="CLSID:D4A97620-8E8F-11CF-93CD-00AA00C08FDF"
STYLE="TOP:135pt;LEFT:230pt;WIDTH:282pt;HEIGHT:249pt;ZINDEX:5;">
    <PARAM NAME="PicturePath" VALUE="c:\grad.gif">
    <PARAM NAME="BorderStyle" VALUE="0">
    <PARAM NAME="SizeMode" VALUE="1">
    <PARAM NAME="SpecialEffect" VALUE="2">
    <PARAM NAME="Size" VALUE="9948;8784">
    <PARAM NAME="PictureAlignment" VALUE="0">
    <PARAM NAME="VariousPropertyBits" VALUE="19">
  </OBJECT>
```

```
    <OBJECT ID="TextBox1"
    CLASSID="CLSID:8BD21D10-EC42-11CE-9E0D-00AA006002F3"
STYLE="TOP:146pt;LEFT:242pt;WIDTH:260pt;HEIGHT:228pt;TABINDEX:3;ZINDEX:6;">
      <PARAM NAME="VariousPropertyBits" VALUE="2894088219">
      <PARAM NAME="ScrollBars" VALUE="2">
      <PARAM NAME="Size" VALUE="9172;8043">
      <PARAM NAME="FontName" VALUE="Arial">
      <PARAM NAME="FontHeight" VALUE="240">
      <PARAM NAME="FontCharSet" VALUE="0">
      <PARAM NAME="FontPitchAndFamily" VALUE="2">
      <PARAM NAME="FontWeight" VALUE="0">
    </OBJECT>
    <OBJECT ID="Image4"
    CLASSID="CLSID:D4A97620-8E8F-11CF-93CD-00AA00C08FDF"
STYLE="TOP:13pt;LEFT:133pt;WIDTH:279pt;HEIGHT:48pt;ZINDEX:7;">
      <PARAM NAME="PicturePath" VALUE="c:\cuisine.gif">
      <PARAM NAME="BorderStyle" VALUE="0">
      <PARAM NAME="SizeMode" VALUE="3">
      <PARAM NAME="Size" VALUE="9834;1702">
      <PARAM NAME="PictureAlignment" VALUE="0">
      <PARAM NAME="VariousPropertyBits" VALUE="19">
    </OBJECT>
    <OBJECT ID="Label1"
    CLASSID="CLSID:978C9E23-D4B0-11CE-BF2D-00AA003F40D0"
STYLE="TOP:305pt;LEFT:29pt;WIDTH:168pt;HEIGHT:32pt;ZINDEX:8;">
      <PARAM NAME="Caption" VALUE="Click on an area in the map
to see a representative recipe">
      <PARAM NAME="Size" VALUE="5927;1129">
      <PARAM NAME="FontName" VALUE="Arial">
      <PARAM NAME="FontHeight" VALUE="220">
      <PARAM NAME="FontCharSet" VALUE="0">
      <PARAM NAME="FontPitchAndFamily" VALUE="2">
      <PARAM NAME="FontWeight" VALUE="0">
    </OBJECT>
</DIV>
```

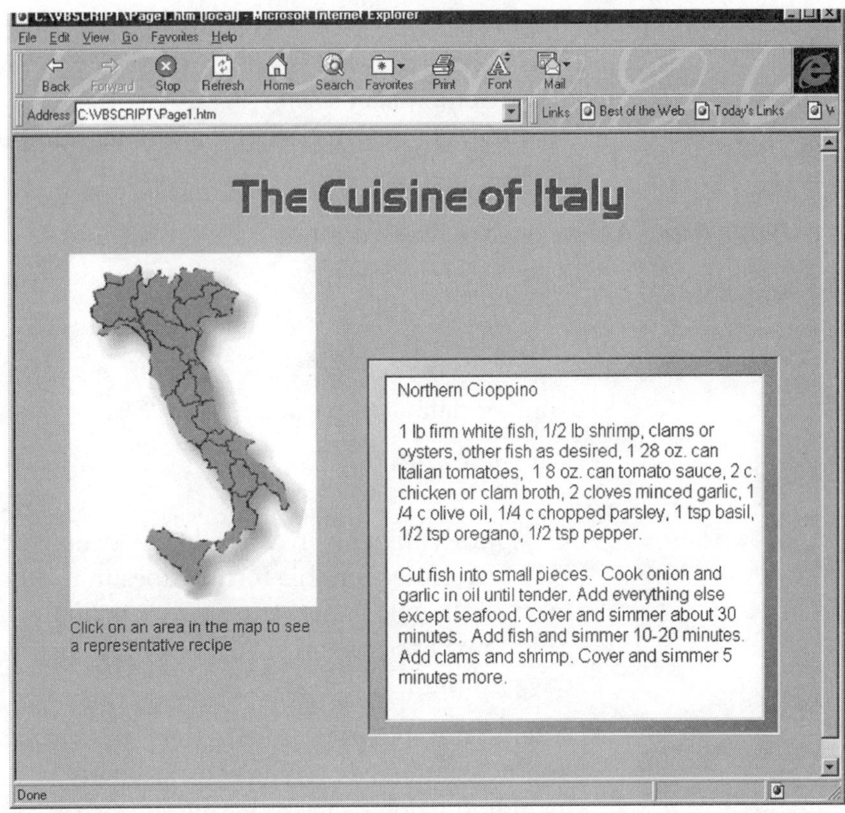

Figure H-4: Our map of Italy was easily divided into clickable areas with the HotSpot Control.

See also Image, Map

Hour

VBSCRIPT FUNCTION

Description Hour tells you the hour of the day, based on a special *serial number* that VBScript generates in response to such Functions as Now. VBScript has an especially rich set of commands that deal with time and dates: you can manipulate time and dates *mathematically* based on this serial number to find out such things as whether or not 17 March 1784 was a Thursday; the number of days between 1 Feb. 1900 and 5 Jan. 2050; or how many Friday the 13ths occurred in 1950. VBScript gives you the powers of a calendar-oriented *idiot savant*.

For a complete description of these *serial* numbers, see "DateSerial."

Used with A time or date *serial* number.

Variables

```
X = Hour(Now)
```

Uses

- Create "digital" clocks.
- Time or data-stamp data.
- Calculate with time.

Cautions

- The Hour you get is in the military format: 0 is 12 AM, and 23 is 11 PM. However, this format does make it easier to perform arithmetic than having two sets of hours from 0 to 12, plus a text appendage of AM or PM to distinguish between day and night.
- A serial number you provide to Hour is a *double-precision floating-point number* (it has an extremely large range and can include fractions and decimal points). See "Variables" for more information on the different available numeric "types" and their symbols.
- Serial numbers can range between 1 January 100 and 31 December 9999.
- The whole number portion of the serial number holds the date; the fractional part (to the right of the decimal point) holds the time.

Example

```
<HTML>
<HEAD>
<TITLE>Hour</TITLE>
</HEAD>
<BODY>
```

```
<TEXTAREA NAME=RESULT ROWS=12 COLS = 45>

<BR>
<BR>
<INPUT TYPE=Button VALUE="Show Results" NAME="Btn">

<SCRIPT LANGUAGE="VBSCRIPT">

Sub Btn_OnClick
cr = chr(13) & chr(10)
x = cdbl(Now)
RESULT.VALUE = RESULT.VALUE & "The serial number for Now is:
" & cstr(x) & cr
RESULT.VALUE = RESULT.VALUE & "Which translates into..." & cr
& cr
Hr = Hour(x): Mn = Minute(x): Sec = Second(x)
D = Day(x): Wkdy = Weekday(x): Mnth = Month(x): Yr = Year(x)
A = "Second: " & cstr(sec) & cr
A = A & "Minute: " & cstr(Mn) & cr
A = A & "Hour: " & cstr(Hr) & cr

Select Case Wkdy
  Case 1
    dy = "Sunday"
  Case 2
    dy = "Monday"
  Case 3
    dy = "Tuesday"
  Case 4
    dy = "Wednesday"
  Case 5
    dy = "Thursday"
  Case 6
    dy = "Friday"
  Case 7
    dy = "Saturday"
 End Select
A = A & "Name: " & cstr(dy) & cr
A = A & "Day: " & cstr(D) & cr
```

```
A = A & "Month: " & cstr(Mnth) & cr
A = A & "Year: " & cstr(Yr) & cr
RESULT.VALUE = RESULT.VALUE & A
End Sub

</SCRIPT>
</BODY>
</HTML>
```

Results in

```
The serial number for Now is: 35236.4359375
Which translates into...
Second: 45
Minute: 27
Hour: 10
Name: Thursday
Day: 20
Month: 6
Year: 1996
```

Notice that there are a couple of oddities here. First of all, we had to *coerce* many of the numeric subtype Variables into text subtype Variables (using the cStr command) before they would be accepted and displayed by TEXTAREA. This same problem also occurs when you try to provide numeric Variables to such text-only items as the MsgBox command. We assume that, as VBScript matures, it will properly display any kind of Variable subtype in a text or message box, rarely requiring this coercion.

Note: In situations like this, the Select Case structure is somewhat cumbersome. Older versions of Basic had Data and Read Statements. This paired set of commands was worthwhile in some circumstances. They made things like naming the weekday a little simpler to deal with. But Data and Read have been eliminated in VBScript. (VBScript's elimination of the Data and Read commands is mystifying, given that some of the widely discredited and thoroughly dubious dinosaur commands, such as Let, have been retained.)

See also Date, DateSerial, DateValue, Day, Minute, Month, Now, Second, Weekday, Year

HR

HTML

Description Displays a horizontal rule (line).

Used with ***Can be enclosed by***

<BANNER>, <BODY>, <BODYTEXT>, <DIV>, <FIGTEXT>, <FN>, <FORM>, <NOTE>, <TD>, <TH>

Can enclose

Nothing

Variables (The following are Netscape commands, with the exception of COLOR, which is Internet Explorer.)

- ALIGN=LEFT (RIGHT or CENTER)
- COLOR=RED

See BODY for a description of the hex numbers you can use with the COLOR command. You can specify the rule's color, using hexadecimal numbers. Essentially, the paired numbers specify the red, green, and blue content of the color. For example, if you wanted pure red, you would use FF0000; green is 00FF00; blue is 0000FF.

H

You can also use a set of ordinary English words, like red, instead of the hex number. The following words are recognized by most browsers: black, white, green, maroon, olive, navy, purple, gray, red, yellow, blue, teal, lime, aqua, fuchsia, silver.

Tip

You can define colors with either hexadecimal numbers or, as we've done in this example, ordinary English words like red. *For a complete list of all 140 English word colors you can use, see "Many New Colors" in the entry on "BGCOLOR." For an explanation of hexadecimal, see "Hex Numbers for the Color Command" in the entry on "BODY."*

- NOSHADE: Draws a single line (no shading).
- SIZE: Thickens the rule vertically; makes it fatter. SIZE is measured in pixels. SIZE=5 would make the line five pixels thick.
- WIDTH=75%: Makes the rule 75% of the page width. WIDTH=150 makes the rule 150 pixels wide.

Uses Divide your documents into logical sections. Separate, for example, the description of your product from the order form.

Cautions You could also use a .GIF or .JPG image as a way of dividing your pages. Some of these include rainbow rules or embossed shapes. The default rule created with <HR> is an engraved rule, as shown in Figure H-5.

Example

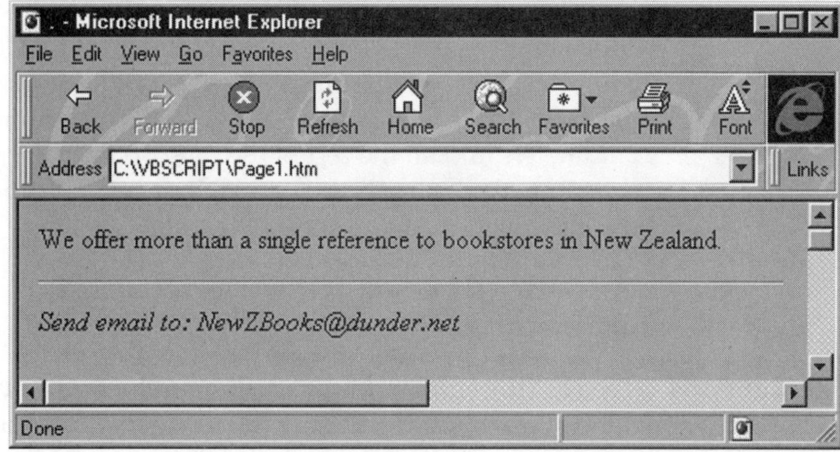

Figure H-5: The standard <HR> engraved rule. If the background isn't gray, the rule looks awkward. If the background is white, you get only a single black line.

```
<HTML>
We offer more than a single reference to bookstores in New
Zealand. <BR>
<HR>
<ADDRESS>
Send email to: NewZBooks@dunder.net
</ADDRESS>

</HTML>
```

See also VR

HTML

HTML

Description HTML provides the shell for the rest of the document; it is the outermost command, enclosing all other commands within it:

```
<HTML>
everything else goes here
</HTML>
```

H

HTML stands for HyperText Markup Language and an HTML "document" is made up of all the commands between <HTML> and </HTML> (all the "tags" such as <BIG>; "attributes" such as the *WHITE* in BGCOLOR=WHITE; VBScript commands; Object parameters and all the rest of the *source code* that, collectively, constitute the instructions for a Web page). For more on this, see the Introduction of this book.

Uses Identify the document as HyperText Markup Language source code (programming).

Cautions The HTML command isn't strictly required; most browsers will not be thrown off if you omit it. However, this could change in the future.

Example

```
<HTML>

This is my Internet document.
</HTML>
```

See also BODY

HTML Layout

ACTIVEX CONTROL

See The Introduction to this book.

I

I

HTML

Description Causes text to be displayed as italics.

Used with ***Can be enclosed by***

<A>, <ABBREV>, <ABOVE>, <ACRONYM>, <ADDRESS>, <AU>, <B>, <BANNER>, <BAR>, <BELOW>, <BIG>, <BODY>, <BODYTEXT>, <BOX>, <BT>, <CAPTION>, <CITE>, <CODE>, <CREDIT>, <DD>, <DDOT>, <DEL>, <DFN>, <DIV>, <DOT>, <DT>, <EM>, <FIGTEXT>, <FN>, <FORM>, <H1>, <H2>, <H3>, <H4>, <H5>, <H6>, <HAT>, <I>, <INS>, <ITEM>, <KBD>, <LANG>, <LH>, <LI>, <MATH>, <NOTE>, <OF>, <P>, <PERSON>, <PRE>, <Q>, <ROOT>, <S>, <SAMP>, <SMALL>, <SQRT>, <STRONG>, <SUB>, <SUP>, <T>, <TD>, <TH>, <TILDE>, <TT>, <U>, <VAR>

Can enclose

<A>, <ABBREV>, <ACRONYM>, <AU>, <B>, <BIG>, <BR>, <CITE>, <CODE>, <DEL>, <DFN>, <EM>, <I>, <IMG>, <INS>, <KBD>, <LANG>, <MATH>, <PERSON>, <Q>, <S>, <SAMP>, <SMALL>, <STRONG>, <SUB>, <SUP>, <TAB>, <TT>, <U>, <V>

Uses

- Whenever you want to *stress* a word or phrase.
- Provide variety to the look of your pages.

Example

```
This is <I>italic<I>
```

See also ADDRESS, Cite, Dfn, Em (each of these commands also renders text in italics); see B for boldface

ID

ACTIVEX

See Properties

ID

HTML

Description Although you'll find it easier to handle mapping and linking with the ActiveX Image and HotSpot Controls (see "Image") you *can* cause VBScript to react to the HTML A (anchor) graphic or text. You do this by providing an ID to the anchor, then trapping user mouse-clicks (or mousemoves, for that matter). See the example for this entry.

Used with The A command.

Variables

```
<A ID="ClickPic" HREF="MyImage.Gif">
```

Now that we've given this image a name, an *ID*, we can refer to it in a Sub:

```
<SCRIPT LANGUAGE="VBSCRIPT">

Sub ClickPic_OnClick
Location.HREF="http://www.netscape.com"
End Sub

</SCRIPT>
```

Uses Display graphics that send the user to different places in your document or elsewhere on the Internet (links), when the user clicks on the graphic.

Cautions

- Notice that there are two kinds of Control objects in Internet programming. There's a set of ActiveX Controls (see the entry for "Objects"). Then, there's a separate set of HTML objects like this anchor (or an HTML TextBox or CheckBox—see the entry for "INPUT").

- When you're creating a Sub that is supposed to react to a user mouse-click on an HTML object, you use the word *OnClick*. When creating a Sub that is supposed to react to a user mouse-click on an ActiveX object, you use the word *Click,* like this:

```
Sub TextBox1_Click
```

Example Put a .GIF graphic file named Bork.GIF into the same subdirectory as the .HTM file that we're going to create. That way, you can type in the following example exactly as printed here. Then start the Microsoft ActiveX Control Pad running (see the Introduction to this book) and type this in:

```
<HTML>
<HEAD>
<TITLE>ID</TITLE>
</HEAD>
<BODY>

<A ID="ClickPic" HREF="http://www.netscape.com"><IMG
SRC="bork.gif">

<SCRIPT LANGUAGE="VBSCRIPT">

Sub ClickPic_OnClick

Msgbox "Thank you for visiting our site. You're now going to
Netscape..."

End Sub

</SCRIPT>
</BODY>
</HTML>
```

In this example, we've decided that if the user clicks on our link to Netscape, we want to intercept that click and display a message box first. This gives you an opportunity to bid the visitor good-bye. Our VBScript traps the user's click first. Then, when the VBScript has finished with whatever it wants to do, the browser takes over and sends the user off to the link target.

You could use this same technique to display additional information about a set of links *before* the user clicked on one of them. Put a Label onto your document, then provide an ID for each image/link as described above in this example. Then, instead of the OnClick event, use the MouseMove Event, like this:

```
Sub ClickPic_MouseMove(shift, button, x, y)

Label1.Caption = "Click here to go to Netscape, the →
alternative-reality browser."

End Sub
```

You can, of course, also use all the facilities of the MouseMove Event. For examples, see MouseMove in the "Events" entry.

See also A, Image, IMG, HotSpot

If...Then...Else

VBSCRIPT STATEMENT

Description If...Then is one of the most important structures in any computer language, indeed in any kind of language.

If...Then is how decisions are made. Then, after the decision is made, actions are taken appropriate to the decision. A program is said to *branch* at this point, as if the path split into more than one trail. The path the program follows is decided here at the If...Then junction.

Many times a day we do our own personal branching using a similar structure: *If* it's cold outside, *then* we get the heavier jacket. *If* the car is locked, *then* we insert the key in the door. *If* we're too close to the edge of the driveway, *then* we adjust the steering wheel. This constant cycle of testing conditions and making decisions based on them is what makes our behavior intelligent, or at least adaptive.

Used with

- Else. The Else command precedes any instructions that you want carried out if the original If...Then is not carried out.

```
X = InputBox("How many calories did you take in today?")
If X > 3000 Then
     M = "Keep that up and you'll get huge."
```

```
  Else
    M = "Good self-control, on your part."
End If
Msgbox M
```

- ElseIf. This allows you to test more than one condition. In a way, it's like using two If...Thens in a row. However, an ElseIf doesn't get triggered unless a preceding If or ElseIf fails to trigger.

```
If X = "Bob" Then
  MsgBox "Hello Bob"
ElseIf X = "Billy" Then
  MsgBox "Hello Billy"
End If
```

Variables If...Then tests to see if something is *true*. If it is true, then the instructions within the If...Then structure are carried out. If it is not true, then your program ignores the instructions within the structure and goes on to the first instruction following the If...Then—the line following End If. (If you've included an Else or ElseIf, these are also checked to see if they are true.)

```
X = InputBox ("Please Enter The Password...")
If X <> Pass Then
  MsgBox ("Access Denied")
  End
End If
MsgBox "Password verified. Thank you."
```

The <> symbol means "not equal." So the meaning of our If...Then test above is: If it is true that X doesn't equal the password (Pass), then print a denied message and End the program. If the user *does* enter the word that matches Pass, then the program bypasses the structure and prints the thank-you message.

There are some optional variations to If...Then structures:

- You can insert an *Else* between the If and the End If. Else means: If the test to see if something was true fails, do the following instructions, which in our example above would allow us to put the "Password Verified" message within the

If...Then structure. This can make it easier to read and understand the intent of the structure. (It also creates a compact either/or structure. You can put a series of Else statements in an If...Then structure.)

```
If X <> Pass Then
  MsgBox ("Access Denied")
  End
Else
  MsgBox "Password verified. Thank you."
End If
```

- You can nest several If...Thens within the same structure by using ElseIf. However, the Select Case structure is usually preferable in situations where you want to do multiple tests.

```
If X = 0
  MsgBox "Zero"
ElseIf X = 1
  MsgBox "One"
ElseIf X = 2
  MsgBox "Two"
End If
```

See also Select Case

Image

ACTIVEX CONTROL

Description The Image Control displays a picture. How is this superior to the HTML IMG command, or the other ways of displaying graphics in Web pages?

For one thing, using an Image Control in conjunction with the HotSpot Control makes it quite a bit easier to create clickable image maps (allowing the user to click within a graphic to play some music, go to a link, or otherwise take action). You can display, for example, a picture of the solar system. When the user clicks on a particular planet within the image, a page comes up describing the body's size, weather, and so on.

HTML has the Map and Area commands (see their entries) for this purpose, but these commands are relatively difficult to work with: you have to describe coordinates within the image. With the ActiveX Image Control and the HotSpot Control, you can drag and stretch clickable areas within a graphic. For detailed examples of this technique see "HotSpot."

Also, when compared to other ways of displaying graphics in HTML, the Image Control is more flexible: it offers you various ways of aligning, sizing, tiling, or cropping a graphic within the Control. It also offers five frame styles (flat, raised, etched, sunken, and bump); a single-line border in any color; and finally, like most ActiveX Controls, it allows you to react, in a script, to various actions that the user might take: dragging, moving into or out of the Image, or mouse-clicking.

Variables You can adjust the Properties of an Image Control within the Properties window, as shown in Figure I-1, or within a script.

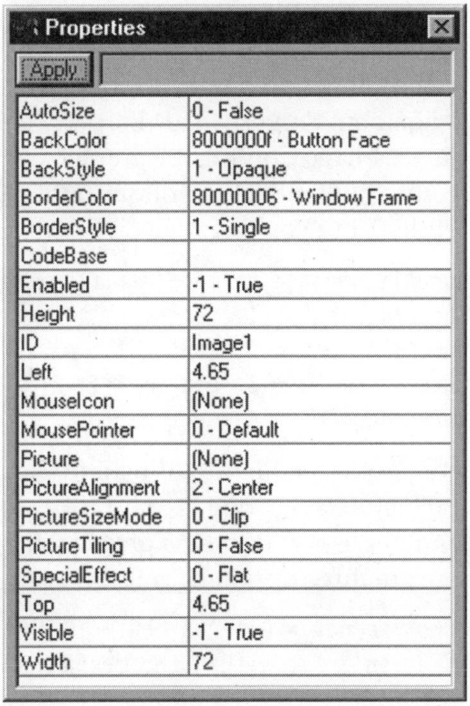

Properties

Apply

AutoSize	0 - False
BackColor	8000000f - Button Face
BackStyle	1 - Opaque
BorderColor	80000006 - Window Frame
BorderStyle	1 - Single
CodeBase	
Enabled	-1 - True
Height	72
ID	Image1
Left	4.65
MouseIcon	(None)
MousePointer	0 - Default
Picture	(None)
PictureAlignment	2 - Center
PictureSizeMode	0 - Clip
PictureTiling	0 - False
SpecialEffect	0 - Flat
Top	4.65
Visible	-1 - True
Width	72

Figure I-1: Change the Image Control's Properties here, or within a script.

To change the picture inside the Image Control:

```
Image1.PicturePath = "c:\gallery\egypt.bmp"
```

Or, to find out the Width:

```
X = Image1.Width
```

Or you can adjust it directly in the Image's HTML Object definition:

```
<PARAM NAME="SpecialEffect" VALUE="1">
```

The PictureTiling, PictureAlignment & PictureSizeMode Properties

The Image Control will display a graphic in a variety of ways, based on how you set the three Picture Properties. If you set PictureTiling to True (it defaults to False), then any graphic smaller than the dimensions of the Image Control will be repeated (tiled) within the Image frame until the entire Image Control is filled. This is the equivalent of selecting Tile for Windows wallpaper.

Precisely *how* the tiling is accomplished depends on how you've set the PictureAlignment Property. This Property determines where, within the container Image Control, the graphic will be placed: top-left, top-right, center, bottom-left, or bottom-right. PictureAlignment defaults to 0 (top-left), but you can adjust it like this:

```
Image1.PictureAlignment = 0 'top-left (the default)
Image1.PictureAlignment = 1 'top-right
Image1.PictureAlignment = 2 'center
Image1.PictureAlignment = 3 'bottom-left
Image1.PictureAlignment = 4 'bottom-right
```

Also interacting with the PictureTiling and PictureAlignment Properties is the PictureSizeMode Property. This Property describes yet another aspect of how a graphic image will be displayed. There are three options:

```
Image1.PictureSizeMode = 0 'crop, cut-off any portion of the
graphic that doesn't fit within the container.
```

```
Image1.PictureSizeMode = 1 'stretch, make the image the same
size as the container. Unless the container is the same
aspect ratio as the original graphic, the graphic will appear
distorted, stretched.

Image1.PictureSizeMode = 3 'enlarge, make the image the same
size as the container, but don't permit any distortion. If
the aspect ratios of the container and graphic aren't identi-
cal, there will be blank strips along the sides (or the top
and bottom) to preserve the aspect ratio of the original
graphic and prevent distortion. This is the default setting.
```

Note: At the time of this writing, the default settings for PictureAlignment and PictureSizeMode *differ* depending on whether you directly insert an Image into an HTML page (ActiveX Control Pad's Edit | Insert ActiveX Control menu) or drag the Image onto an HTML Layout Control (ActiveX Control Pad's Edit | Insert HTML Layout menu). Above we've described the defaults as PictureAlignment defaulting to top-left and PictureSizeMode defaulting to 3, enlarge. These are the defaults for the Layout Control approach and they seem to be the most logical defaults, the settings you'd most commonly want to use for these Properties. Nonetheless, if you take the Insert ActiveX Control approach, PictureAlignment defaults to 2 Center and PictureSizeMode defaults to 0 Crop.

The SpecialEffect Property

The SpecialEffect Property determines what kind of frame or outline will be placed around an Image. You have a choice of five options: 0 Flat (no framing, the default), 1 Raised (good for some images), 2 Sunken (also good for some images), 3 Etched (looks as if it were impressed or stamped into the background—a more subtle version of Sunken), and 6 Bump (a rather odd one that looks as if the graphic were framed by a very thin noodle).

Properties

AutoSize, BackColor, BackStyle, BorderColor, BorderStyle, CodeBase, Enabled Height, ID, Left, MouseIcon, MousePointer, Picture, PictureAlignment, PictureSizeMode, PictureTiling, SpecialEffect, Visible, Width

Events

BeforeDragOver, BeforeDropOrPaste, Enter, Exit, MouseDown, MouseMove, MouseUp

Methods

Move, ZOrder

For details about these Properties, Events, and Methods, see the entries for "Properties," "Events," and "Methods."

Uses

- Display graphics, but also allow the user to have control over what image is displayed, how it is zoomed and tiled.
- Create "maps"—graphics that send the user to different places in your document or elsewhere on the Internet, depending on where in the graphic the user clicks. (See "HotSpot" for examples of this technique.)
- You can also use the Image's SpecialEffect Property to create various attractive frames around the image.
- Fill an entire HTML Layout Control with a background or wallpaper (the Layout Control has no Picture Property of its own). Just stretch the Image Control to the size of the Layout Control while designing your page.

- Or use the OnLoad Event of the Layout Control to set the Width and Height Properties of the Image to the values of the Width and Height Properties of the Layout Control:

```
Sub al_OnLoad()
Image1.Width = al.Width
Image1.Height = al.Height
end sub
```

- Allow the user to view an image at various levels of zoom:

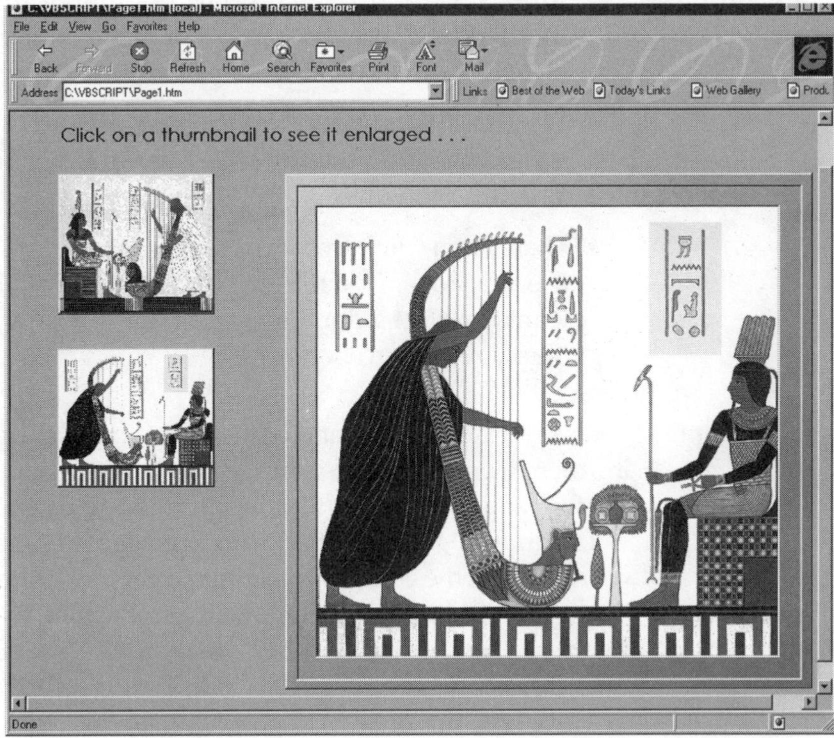

Figure I-2: When the user clicks on one of the smaller Images, the picture is blown up to the large Image.

Assuming that the user clicks on Image1, the small Image on top in Figure I-2, the path (location) of Image1's graphic file is provided to the large Image Control on the right (Image3). This places that same image in the big Image Control.

```
<SCRIPT LANGUAGE="VBScript">
Sub Image1_MouseDown(Button, Shift, X, Y)
Image3.PicturePath = Image1.PicturePath
end sub
</SCRIPT>
```

Cautions

- An Image Control can display four graphic file types: .BMP, .WMF (Windows MetaFile), and the two file types used by HTML, .GIF, and .JPG.
- Note that if you select BorderStyle=Single, any SpecialEffect is cancelled. So you probably want to leave BorderStyle to its default, "None."
- There is no Click Event for the Image Control, but you can use the MouseDown Event to detect user clicking. Or, if you want to detect a double-click, superimpose a HotSpot Control onto your Image Control.

Example You can create complex and highly attractive frames by superimposing more than one Image Control. Use the one on top to display a graphic, and use those in the background to create a frame.

To create the framing effect shown in Figure I-3, see "Metallic Gradients" in the entry on "Command Button." After you've created a couple of .BMP grayscale gradient graphic files, load them into the two background Image Controls (using their PicturePath Property). Then right-click on each Image Control and use the Move Backward or Move Forward options to position them into a proper stack.

Figure I-3: Use stacked Images to create attractive frames around graphics or any other ActiveX Control.

See also IMG, HotSpot

IMG

INTERNET EXPLORER

Description Many browsers will display a static single image when you use the IMG command. However, Internet Explorer 2.0 and 3.0 can show a movie in addition to the static image. Just provide the URL address of an .AVI (Audio Video Interleave) movie for the DYNSRC command.

Variables **ALIGN=TOP, MIDDLE, or BOTTOM:** Describes how to handle the positioning of any text or other element of your document that's near the IMG.

```
<IMG SRC="rough.gif" ALIGN=MIDDLE>
```

This text will be placed so it begins at (aligns with) the middle of our picture, the middle horizontally.

ALT="This text will display if the user's browser is set to display text only."

```
<IMG SRC="rough.gif" ALT="This is a picture of stucco">
```

BORDER: If you don't want surrounding text (or other elements) on your page to butt up directly against the image (or movie), add a border, specified in pixels:

```
<IMG SRC="rough.gif" BORDER=14>
```

Also see HSPACE, VSPACE below.

CONTROLS: Displays two controls beneath the video, so the user can start, stop, fast forward, and rewind the movie (with a slider).

```
<IMG DYNSRC="doggie.avi" CONTROLS>
```

Figure I-4: The CONTROLS command places a button and a slider beneath the video—the user can get to any frame in the movie with this Control.

DYNSRC: This is the address of an .AVI file. It can be a URL or just the name of an .AVI, if that .AVI is in the same directory as the URL of your document.

```
<IMG DYNSRC="doggie.avi">
```

HEIGHT, WIDTH: You can use these commands to specify a particular size, in pixels, that the image (or movie) will take in the user's browser. The image or movie will be stretched as necessary to meet your specifications. By default, though, if you leave these specifications out, the size will be determined dynamically based on the original size of the image or .AVI file. Generally, let the default determine size (surrounding text and other elements will make room for it). If you set the HEIGHT and WIDTH, you can cause annoying distortions of the original image.

```
<IMG SRC="rough.gif" WIDTH=220 HEIGHT=130>
```

HSPACE, VSPACE: These commands (along with the BORDER command) specify margins, in pixels, that will surround the image. The difference between these two commands and BORDER is slight: if the image is being used as a link, the BORDER command will cause the border to be rendered in the user's link color.

```
<IMG SRC="rough.gif" HSPACE=14 VSPACE=14> We've given this
graphic a border of 14 pixels on all sides.
```

LOOP: Tells the browser how many times to play the video. You can specify a particular number, or use the INFINITE command to make it repeat until the user changes to a different document, or presses the STOP button in the browser.

```
<IMG DYNSRC="doggie.avi" LOOP=INFINITE> This will play
continuously.
<IMG DYNSRC="doggie.avi" LOOP=4> This will play four times.
```

LOOPDELAY: How long the browser should pause between "showings" of the movie. If you've set LOOP to display the video more than once, LOOPDELAY=1500 would cause a 1.5 second delay after the movie ends and before it restarts. LOOPDELAY is specified in milliseconds, so 3000 means 3 seconds.

SRC: If you provide an SRC, a static image (a .GIF or .JPG file) will appear. The user's browser permits movies to be displayed, then the SRC will first display, followed by the .AVI specified by DYNSRC. Use the START command (see below) to control whether the movie automatically starts (as soon as the file has been loaded) or whether the user must move his or her mouse cursor over the image to start the show.

```
<IMG SRC="rough1.gif" DYNSRC="scroll.avi">
```

Or you can provide a URL:

```
<IMG SRC="http://www.myplace.com/bizzat.gif">
```

START: Determines what triggers the movie, what makes it start (or, if you're displaying a static image too, when the movie replaces that image). You can use FILEOPEN (the default) to start the movie as soon as it's loaded, or MOUSEOVER to hold the movie until the user moves the mouse cursor over the image (this mouse movement is called the MouseMove Event in VBScript and works with the Image, TextBox, and other ActiveX Controls).

```
<IMG SRC="rough.gif" DYNSRC="doggie.avi" START=MOUSEOVER>
```

This "doggie" movie will play once (we've not used the Loop command to increase the number of plays). Thereafter it will restart if the user moves the mouse over the graphic.

Uses

- Display a graphic image.
- Give the user a real treat—show a movie with sound (Internet Explorer).

Example

Figure I-5: We've given the user control over this movie with the Controls command.

```
<HTML>
<HEAD>
<TITLE>Img</TITLE>
</HEAD>
<BODY BACKGROUND="ROUGH1.GIF">

<IMG DYNSRC="doggie.avi" CONTROLS>

</BODY>
</HTML>
```

See also Image Control (ActiveX)

Imp

VBSCRIPT OPERATOR

See Operators

Index

ACTIVEX

See Properties

INPUT

HTML

Description This is the object with which users can *respond* to your Internet pages. There are several input types—TEXT, BUTTON, and CHECKBOX among them—and when the user types or clicks on one of these types, your page can react. A BUTTON can trigger a VBScript Subroutine; information the user has typed into a TEXT box can be sent to a file or to your server for further action. Ordinarily, an INPUT Control is put within the FORM command (see the example).

Variables See "FORM" for visual examples of each of the following Controls.

The Controls Available for Use With INPUT

- **Buttons** ("Command Buttons")—The user can click on these to trigger something, to make something happen.

```
<INPUT TYPE = Button VALUE = "Click Here to See
More...">
```

- **Checkboxes**—Make sure that the Checkbox, when first viewed by the user, is checked by default.

```
<INPUT TYPE = Checkbox CHECKED=TRUE>
```

- **Hidden Controls**—The user doesn't see these, but you can use them for your own purposes.
- **Images**—These can be clicked on by the user.

```
<INPUT TYPE = Image SRC="ball.gif"></FORM>
```

- **Radio button/s**

```
<INPUT TYPE = radio VALUE = "Take">Take
<BR><BR>
<INPUT TYPE = radio VALUE = "Give">Give
<BR><BR>
<INPUT TYPE = radio VALUE = "Give & Take">Give & Take
```

- **Reset buttons**—These restore the original contents to a Control.

```
<INPUT TYPE = reset VALUE = "RESET">
```

- **Submit buttons**—These send a FORM's contents (to a disk file or across the Internet).

```
<INPUT TYPE = submit VALUE = "SUBMIT">
```

- **Text Boxes**—For single (TEXT) or, for multi-line text input, see TEXTAREA.

```
<INPUT TYPE = text>
```

Commands Associated With INPUT

- **NAME**—Identifies a Control object. It "holds" any data that was entered by the user (it is the same as a *Variable name* in traditional computer programming). For example, you use the NAME of a BUTTON to trigger a VBScript Subroutine:

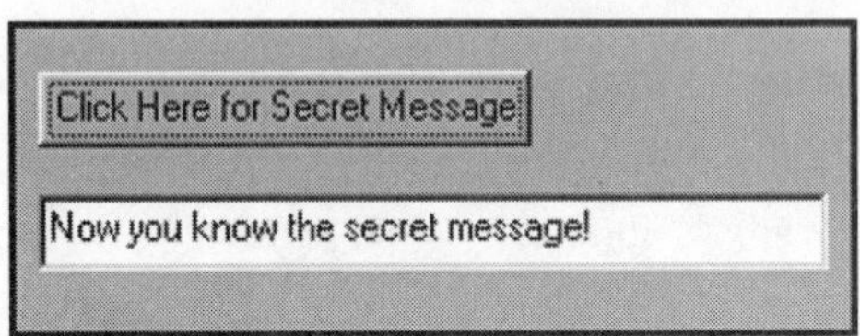

Figure I-6: Use NAME to identify Controls.

In this example, we establish two Controls: a Button and a Text Box (a Text Box is the default INPUT type, if you don't specify any type). Notice how the NAME "Btn" is used as a way of triggering the Subroutine. Also, note how the NAME "Box" is used, along with the box's VALUE (contents), to change the contents of the Text Box.

```
<HTML>
<INPUT TYPE=BUTTON VALUE="Click Here for Secret Message"
NAME="Btn">
<BR><BR>
<INPUT NAME="Box" SIZE=45>

<SCRIPT LANGUAGE=VBS>
Sub Btn_OnClick
Box.Value = "Now you know the secret message!"
End Sub
</SCRIPT>

</HTML>
```

- **TYPE**—Specifies which of the various INPUT Controls will be displayed. See "The Controls available for use with INPUT" above. TYPE defaults to Text Box, if you don't mention the TYPE.

- **VALUE**—Is, sometimes, the "contents" of an INPUT Control. You can usually either "read" (find out) or "write" (change) the VALUE within VBScript. The VALUE of a Text Box, for instance, is the text inside the box (see the example above under "NAME"). However, the "contents" might be given another name. For example, the "contents" or status of a Checkbox is the CHECKED command. The content of a graphic image input type is the SRC command.

Uses Get input back from the people who view your documents.

Cautions Although they are not used with the INPUT command, there are two additional user-input Controls you should be aware of. The SELECT command displays a list of items within a scrolling List Box. The user can click on the item of interest. The TEXTAREA command displays a scrollable Text Box that accepts multiple lines of text.

Example

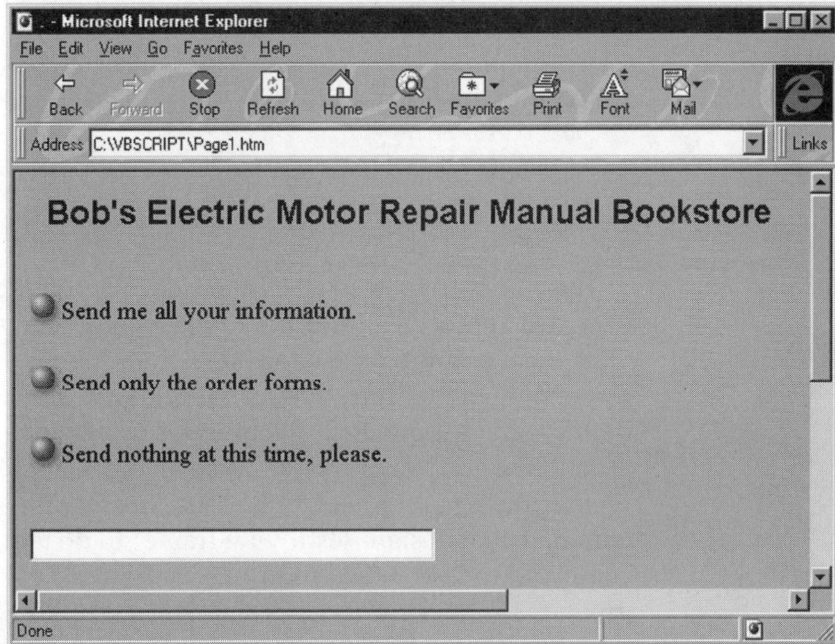

Figure I-7: Each of the golden balls on the left can be clicked; they are user-input devices. But we have to resort to a workaround to get this to function.

Alas, we have to play a couple of tricks (a.k.a. "workarounds") to get this example to work. First, the IMAGE type does not seem to react to mouse clicks. For example, the straightforward way of allowing the user to click on a graphic doesn't work at all:

```
<INPUT TYPE=IMAGE SRC="ball.jpg" NAME="Btn1"> Send me all
your information.

<SCRIPT LANGUAGE="VBSCRIPT">
Sub Btn1_OnClick
Box.VALUE = "They clicked on Button #1"
End Sub
</SCRIPT>
```

Forget it. The Btn1_OnClick Event is never triggered when the user clicks on the graphic. Instead, we have to define a Subroutine via JavaScript (shudder), then point to it like this:

```
<A HREF="javascript:firstball()"><IMG SRC ="ball.jpg"></A> →
Send me all your information.

<SCRIPT LANGUAGE="VBSCRIPT">
Sub firstball
Box.VALUE = "They clicked on Button #1"
End Sub
</SCRIPT>
```

This Sub is triggered when the user clicks on the image. However, this approach—resorting to the A command to create a "link" that points to one of our own Subroutines—tortured and clever though it is, introduces an unpleasant side effect. When you define a graphic as a link, the browser draws an ugly frame around the graphic (purportedly to alert users that they can click on the graphic and travel to the link). In any case, we want to eliminate that design-destroying frame. To do that, use the LINK command to define the link-frame as the same color as the background. The background is that omnipresent Windows gun metal gray. So, to hide the link-frame:

```
<BODY LINK=#COCOCO>
```

Here's the whole HTML and VBScript for what you see in Figure I-7:

```
<HTML>
<BODY LINK=#C0C0C0>

<FONT FACE=ARIAL>
<H2 ALIGN=CENTER>Bob's Electric Motor Repair Manual →
Bookstore</H2>
<FONT FACE=TIMES ROMAN>
<FONT SIZE=+1>
<BR><BR>
<A HREF="javascript:firstball()"><IMG SRC ="ball.jpg"></A> →
Send me all your information.
<BR><BR><BR>
<A HREF="javascript:secondball()"><IMG SRC ="ball.jpg"></A> →
Send only the order forms.
<BR><BR><BR>
<A HREF="javascript:thirdball()"><IMG SRC ="ball.jpg"></A> →
Send nothing at this time, please.
<BR><BR><BR><BR>

<INPUT NAME="Box" SIZE=55>

<SCRIPT LANGUAGE="VBSCRIPT">
Sub firstball
Box.VALUE = "They clicked on Button #1"
End Sub

Sub secondball
Box.VALUE = "They clicked on Button #2"
End Sub

Sub thirdball
Box.VALUE = "They clicked on Button #3"
End Sub
</SCRIPT>
</FONT>
</BODY>
</HTML>
```

In this example, we placed three high-resolution (.JPG) golden balls on a document. This is an attractive way of providing the user with clickable buttons—a nice alternative to the rather drab gray BUTTON Control. When the user clicks on one of these balls, VBScript programming reacts by reporting this Event in the Text Box.

See also FORM, SELECT, A, TEXTAREA

InputBox

VBSCRIPT FUNCTION

Description You may be tempted to use InputBox when other Controls such as Option Buttons, TextArea, or Text Boxes would be easier for the user. InputBox has a most unpleasant effect: like MsgBox, InputBox halts the program until the user responds. It's rather like being arrested.

InputBox is sometimes necessary, perhaps, but the more you employ this command, the more you'll annoy the user. It's similar to MsgBox but requires the user to enter some text or at least click a button to close the box.

InputBox is commonly used when you need some specific information from the user, but the information is either too unpredictable or too infrequently needed to offer the user a list of choices via Command Buttons, Option Buttons, List Boxes, or other, less-intrusive approaches.

It's best to confine your use of InputBox to near-emergency situations where you feel you must demand that the user react. One example would be if the user attempts to go to another URL before having saved some changes he or she made to a Text Box. Another good use is to request that the user enter a password where you want access to be restricted. However, there is a superior ActiveX Password Control.

In general, you should try to use INPUT TYPE=TEXT or TEXTAREA for most text input from the user. Not only can you leave Text Boxes lying around on the screen for the user to work with when he or she chooses to, but Text Boxes also have a number of user-friendly features not available to InputBox.

Variables You can control five qualities of an InputBox, but only the first one, the *MessageToUser*, is required:

```
X = InputBox (MessageToUser, TitleBar, Default, XPosition, →
YPosition, HelpFile, Context)
```

MessageToUser

The text message you provide to the user when the box pops up, often called a *prompt*. An example would be: "Please type in your name..."

TitleBar

The text displayed in the Title Bar of the box (optional; if you put nothing in, the Title Bar will say VBSCRIPT).

Default

Any text you want provided by default within the user's "edit box" entry space in the InputBox, the place where the user is to type in text. If you think you know in advance how the user will respond, perhaps you shouldn't be interrupting the program in the first place. It might be better to use Preferences Menus or Buttons. (Default text is optional and sometimes annoying to users, since they frequently have to delete what you've so presumptuously entered for them.)

XPosition

The location of the box measured over from the left side of the screen. If you specify position, it's possible for the InputBox to appear outside of the user's browser if they've got the browser sized so it doesn't completely fill the screen. (Xposition and Yposition are expressed in pixels.)

YPosition

The location of the box as measured down from the top of the screen.

HelpFile

If you want a Help button to appear on your InputBox, add a text ("string") Variable or expression that names the help file. You must also include a Context, as described below.

Context
This is a numeric Variable or expression defining the "Help context number." It displays the appropriate topic within the larger Help file. See the entry on "HelpFile" for more.

Uses Other methods of getting user input are less restrictive and more pleasant for the user: Text Boxes, Option Buttons, dragging Icons, and so on. Since InputBox forces your program to halt until the user responds, it's an uncomfortable moment at best. MsgBox and InputBox are not really in the spirit of the open-ended, visually oriented, and freedom-loving environments of Windows, Visual Basic, and the Internet.

There will doubtless be times when you can think of no better alternative; but a document filled with MsgBox and InputBox roadblocks should be redesigned. The idea is to allow the *user* to guide your program's behavior. At least this has been true in the past few years, once computers became powerful enough to support rich, supple, graphical operating systems. This means that you can't keep slapping messages onto the screen, immobilizing the browser until the user acknowledges your message or provides the information you're demanding *now*.

VBScript is an event-driven language. Its programs should not be *linear*, not a series of experiences that must happen in a strict order, like the Mad Hatter ride at Disneyland or the dozens of forms you must fill out to get into North Korea. Older Basic programs were heavily linear; the programmer told the user what to do and in what order to do it. Contemporary GUI's and Internet browsers are unhappy hosts to InputBox.

The trend in computing now is for the programmer to create *opportunities* for the user, providing a well-designed vehicle and an appealing visual landscape. Control over the computer is passing from the programmer to the user. Option Menus and Preference Menus are proliferating. Few elements of an event-driven program are strictly cause-and-effect. The paradigm is a relaxing, generous self-serve buffet as opposed to a rigid, nerve-wracking formal dinner.

Windows, Visual Basic, and the Internet are important contributors to this altogether welcome development. There's even a symbolic difference between the *look* of the older two-dimensional, black-and-white programs and the colorful, three-dimensional

Windows programs. DOS and UNIX programs used to look like blackboards with white chalk text—a school metaphor. Programmers should now try to create visual contexts—color, motion, sound, and above all, freedom of choice—that behave in the spirit of the independence that users increasingly expect.

Cautions

- Your prompt text cannot be larger than 255 characters.
- To create a prompt with more than one line, you must add Carriage Return and Line Feed characters to any text Variable where you want to move down to the next line:

```
CR = Chr(13) + Chr(10)
MyPrompt1 = MyPrompt1 + CR
MyPrompt2 = MyPrompt2 + CR
```

- If you include the X position, you must also supply the Y position. If you leave these specifications out, the InputBox is placed one-third of the way down from the top of the user's screen and centered horizontally.
- If the user clicks on the Cancel Button or does not enter any text (and you have not provided any text in the Variables you supply to InputBox), an empty text Variable is the result (""). You can check for this with the following: If X = "".

Example

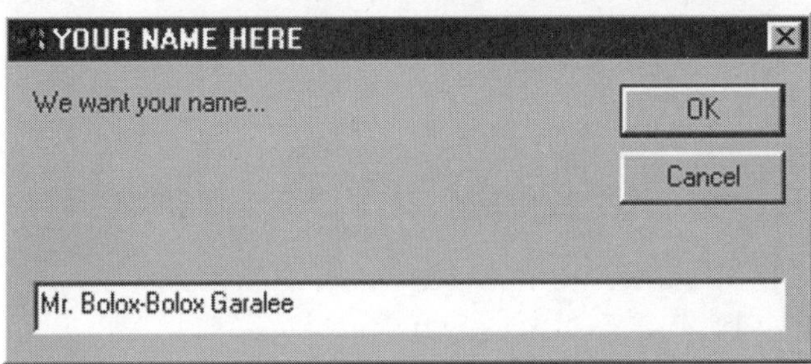

Figure I-8: An InputBox stops your program until the user responds.

The following code will put the first message "We want your name..." into the "Prompt" zone of the box, "YOUR NAME HERE" into the Title Bar, and "Mr." into the user's input box zone. It will then paste the box 5,000 twips down from the top of the screen and 5,000 twips over from the left—about 3½ inches. Then, after the user enters a name and clicks on the OK button, a message box displays the results.

```
<HTML>
<HEAD>
<TITLE>InputBox</TITLE>
</HEAD>
<BODY>

<SCRIPT LANGUAGE="VBSCRIPT">
x = InputBox("We want your name...", "YOUR NAME HERE", "Mr.",
5000, 5000)
msgbox x
</SCRIPT>

</BODY>
</HTML>
```

See also Text Box; MsgBox; the various other Controls that accept user responses more smoothly, and far less coercively, than InputBox.

InsideHeight, InsideWidth

ACTIVEX

See Properties

InStr

VBSCRIPT FUNCTION

Description This function helps you to isolate some characters within a larger piece of text (often called *parsing*). It's useful for verifying user input and also for adding some artificial intelligence to your programs. For example, if you're selling books and have an input box asking them to type in a brief description of their interests, you could use InStr to identify various categories by searching for "mechanics," "mechanic," "automotive," "automobile," "auto repair," and so on.

InStr looks through a text-type Variable, searching for a character, word, or phrase. It tells you whether it found the target and, if so, the character position within the larger text where the target was located.

Used with Variables (text subtype)

Variables

```
L = InStr(1, BigText, Target)
```

OR (if you want to search for Target starting from the first character in BigText, you can optionally leave out the first Variable or Literal, the 1 above, that tells InStr at which character position within BigText to start searching):

```
L = InStr(BigText, Target)
```

OR *BigText* and *Target* can also be literal text enclosed between quotation marks:

```
L = InStr("ABCDEFGHIJ", "A")
```

Uses

- Search for a particular piece of text within a larger Variable.
- Locate a piece of text, then remove unwanted surrounding text.
- Search text for various alternative spellings or key words.

Cautions

- InStr stops at the first match it finds.
- InStr is case-sensitive; it makes a distinction between *Upper* and *upper*.
- Characters *used to be* represented in single-byte units within the computer. The ASCII code, for example, represented the letter *A* by the number 65. A single byte can contain numbers from 0 to 255, so all the letters of the alphabet, both lowercase and uppercase, plus the ten digits and lots of symbols like @#$%, could easily fit within that 0-255 range. Now, though, characters are represented within 2-byte units, to permit manipulation of character sets of greater complexity, such as those of some languages. The InStr command works with these 2-byte character codes.

- All this doesn't really matter unless you're dealing with languages other than English. However, if you are, you'll want to be aware of the alternative command, InstrB, that works with the older individual-byte character codes rather than the 2-byte units now in use. Likewise, there are single-byte versions of the Asc and Chr commands (AscB and ChrB).

Example What if you want to know whether there is more than one *Target* item within the *BigText*? You can easily find them by using the result of a previous InStr search. InStr, when it finds a match, reports the location, the character position within the *BigText* where the *Target* was found. (For this next example, we're going to use the UCase Function to make sure that capitalization won't affect the outcome. UCase converts everything into uppercase letters. Remember that InStr will not see a match if the letters are not all in the same "case.")

Here we use the Loop command to keep going through the text, looking for our target. Each time the target is found, we get a position (Y) within the text. We use that position to start our next search just after the previous hit (X = Y+1). We use Z to count the number of times we hit a target. The loop continues until InStr reports a failure to locate any more targets (Y = 0: finding no match, InStr puts a 0 into Y).

```
<SCRIPT LANGUAGE="VBSCRIPT">
Big = "Abracadabra"

Target = "bra"
Big = UCase(Big)
Target = UCase(Target)
Do
 X = Y + 1
 Z = Z + 1
 Y = InStr(X, Big, Target)
Loop Until Y = 0
Z = Z - 1
N = "We found " & Target & " " & Z & " times inside " & Big
MsgBox N
</SCRIPT>
```

Results in

We found BRA two times inside ABRACADABRA.

See also UCase

Int (& Fix)

VBSCRIPT FUNCTION

Description Int crudely "rounds off" a number that contains a fraction, making it a whole number with no fractional part. Int is crude because it just chops off the fraction and doesn't truly round the number off. As far as Int is concerned, 5.1 and 5.9 are both 5. (There is a way to compensate for this crudity. See "Rounding Numbers" later in this section.)

Int reduces the original number to the next lowest whole number. Positive numbers get their fractions chopped off, but negative numbers change to a different number.

Used with

- Numeric Variables

```
X
```

- Groups of numeric Variables in a mathematical relationship

```
X + Y
```

OR

- Literal numbers

```
12.5
```

- Variables

```
Y = Int(X)
```

OR

```
Y = Int (X + Z)
```

OR

```
Y = Int (Z * 22.75)
```

(You can use Int with any *numerical expression*. See "Variables" for an explanation of "expressions.")

Uses You'll probably find that you rarely if ever use the Int command. Fractions and rounding just don't matter that much in most applications, even if Int *could* intelligently round off numbers. Int's one main use is with the Rnd command.

Int does something similar to assigning a number to an Integer Variable type with cInt (see "cBool"). However, assigning a decimal number to an Integer Variable causes a true rounding effect:

```
Z = 4.7
Y = cInt(Z)
Msgbox Int(Z)
Msgbox Y
```

Results in

```
4
5
```

The only even reasonably frequent use of Int is to round off the results when creating a random number. The Rnd Function—used often in games to simulate unpredictable and varying behavior on the part of enemy aliens, dice, and so on—provides you with a fractional number, a "double-precision floating-point" number that has an extremely large range. This range, however, is between 0 and 1. Rnd gives a fraction. So to get, for example, random rolls of a die, you would multiply the random fraction, building it up beyond 1, then use Int to round off the result.

Int can also be useful for integer division: when you want to know how many 16s are in 243, you divide 243 by 16 to get 15. To get the remainder, use the MOD command, or this formula:

```
X-INT(X/Y)*Y
```

Rounding Numbers: There *is* a way to round numbers accurately:

```
X = Int(N + .5)
```

By adding that .5 to whatever number we want rounded by the Int command, we can be sure that we'll get true rounding.

If the fraction is less than one-half:

```
N = 4.226
X = Int(N + .5)
Msgbox X
```

Results in

```
4
```

And if the fraction is more than one-half:

```
N = 4.889
X = Int(N + .5)
MsgBox X
```

Results in

```
5
```

Cautions

- Int rounds down. It's as if you just chopped off the fraction and handed back the whole number. See the example below.
- Int also behaves badly with negative numbers, so VBScript includes another Function called Fix (see the entry for Fix, if any of this is of use to you).

Example

```
Int(5.2)
```

Results in

```
5
```

AND

```
Int(5.7)
```

Results in

```
5
```

What kind of "rounding" is *this*? To make Int round correctly when the fraction is higher than .5, you need to add .5 to the number you want rounded:

```
Int(5.7 + .5)
```

See also cInt, DefType, Fix, Rnd

I

IntegralHeight

ACTIVEX

See Properties

Is

VBSCRIPT OPERATOR

See Operators

I

ISINDEX

HTML

Description If you want to permit the user to search a list or database (located on your server), provide them with the ISINDEX input device. It prompts them for a response and provides them with a Text Box into which they can type their query.

When the user is finished, and clicks on an associated SUBMIT button (or presses the Enter key), the text the user typed in is sent to the document's URL as a query. At this point, software can search for the target text and respond by sending information back to the user.

Used with ***Can be enclosed by***

<BANNER>, <BODY>, <BODYTEXT>, <DD>, <DIV>, <FIGTEXT>, <FN>, <FORM>, <HEAD>, <LI>, <NOTE>, <TD>, <TH>

Variables By default, ISINDEX displays this prompt: "You can search this index. Type the keyword(s) you want to search for:"

However, you can substitute a customized prompt of your own:

```
<ISINDEX PROMPT="Type in any video title you're interested in
(punctuation and capitalization are ignored): ">
```

<ISINDEX>=*filename*: This syntax provides a gateway program that is designed to receive the user's input (the text typed into the Text Box).

Uses Allow users of your page to search database information that you've collected. For example, if you sell videotapes, you could permit the user to search your list of tapes and see if you offer a particular title and how much it costs.

Example

Figure I-9: Here are the two styles of Search Controls: the default (above) and customized prompt text (below).

```
<HTML>
<FONT FACE=ARIAL>
<H2 ALIGN=CENTER>Fauna of the Southeast</H2>
<FONT FACE=TIMES ROMAN>
<FONT SIZE=+1>
<ISINDEX>

<ISINDEX PROMPT="Please type in the name of an ancient beast">

</FONT>
</HTML>
```

IS Queries (IsArray, IsDate, IsEmpty, IsError, IsNull & IsNumeric, IsObject)

VBSCRIPT FUNCTIONS

Description As we move toward object-oriented programming, there will be times, believe it or not, when the *programmer* will not know the data subtype of a Variable. A Variant Variable (the VBScript default Variable type), like a shape-shifter, can morph into several different Variable types dynamically while a program is running. This can happen without the programmer's knowledge or consent. A Variant will accept *whatever* the user types into a Text Box, for example. It is then your responsibility, as the creator of a document, to figure out what type of data the user has entered. If you asked for the user's age and he typed in the words *sixty-three* instead of what you expected (63), you can't then start doing arithmetic on the text *sixty-three*.

In the brave new world of objects, a user can sometimes even be permitted to create new objects in some situations. What's more, with OLE Automation, one program can make use of another program's features. And what about the fact that a Variant Array can hold items of various different data types?

One side effect of all this freedom (and the possible resulting mutations of your original expectations about Variable types when you designed the program) is that you, as a programmer, might sometimes have to ask your running program to tell you the subtype of a Variable.

Used with Variables and Arrays

Variables To display any members of an Array that are not numeric:

```
<HTML>
<HEAD>
<TITLE>Array Command</TITLE>
</HEAD>
<BODY>
```

```
<SCRIPT LANGUAGE="VBSCRIPT">
Dim SomeFacts (3)

SomeFacts(0) = 1425.33
SomeFacts(1) = "Misty"
SomeFacts(2) = "Jeb said he would return late."
SomeFacts(3) = 77 * 33

For I = 0 to 3
  z = (SomeFacts(I))
  If Not IsNumeric (z) Then MsgBox z
Next
</SCRIPT>
</BODY>
</HTML>
```

Results in

```
Misty
Jeb said he would return late.
```

Uses To tell you the type or contents of a Variant Variable or Variant Array.

Cautions

- Empty and Null (see their entries) have special meanings. Null is what you typically think of as an "empty" Variable (A = "" makes A Null). Empty, by contrast, means that the Variable has *never even been used* in the program, has never been initialized at all.
- When testing for Null, you can't use something like If Var = Null. (If an expression includes the Null command, the whole expression automatically becomes Null itself.) You must use IsNull to test for nullness.

Example This example uses IsDate to check the user's input and, if it's correct, to tell the user how old he or she is. The user's response is put into a Variant Variable, *x*, which will adapt itself to *whatever* Variable subtype is appropriate for whatever the user types in. (All Variables in VBScript default to the Variant type. Variants will happily accept large numbers, fractions, text, or digits.) However, our program can avoid an error here if it can determine just what the Variant turned into. So we use the IsDate Function to let us know how to proceed:

```
<SCRIPT LANGUAGE="VBSCRIPT">

x = InputBox("Please type in the date of your birthday...")
If IsDate(x) Then
   z = (Now - DateValue(x)) / 365
   MsgBox "You are " & Int(z) & " years old."
Else
   MsgBox "We can't understand " & x & " as a date..."
End If

</SCRIPT>
```

See also VarType, Variant

Is TypeOf

VBSCRIPT

Description There is a special kind of If...Then peculiar to Visual Basic, which allows you to find out if a Name represents a certain kind of Control or object. Say we have an object on the Form to which we've given the Name *Showit:*

```
If TypeOf Showit Is TextBox Then
   Showit.Text = "Hi, Johnny!"
ElseIf TypeOf Showit Is CommandButton Then
   Showit.Caption = "Hi, Johnny!"
End If
```

You'll want to remember the "TypeOf Is" instruction. There's no substitute for it in some (admittedly rare) situations. In the above example, we wanted to print a message. However, since a Command Button has no Text Property and a Text Box has no caption Property, we had to find out which type of Control we were printing on. For more, see "Objects."

Your test condition for an If...Then need not be a single test; you can combine several tests using AND and OR:

(With AND, both of these conditions must be true for the instructions following Then to be carried out.)

```
If A = "Bob" AND B = "Ralph" Then
```

(With OR, if either one of these conditions is true, carry out the instructions following Then.)

```
If A = "Bob" OR B = "Ralph" Then
```

In short, If...Then can test "expressions," compound Variables, literals, and Constants related to one another by "operators." (See "Variables" for a definition of "expression" and "operator.")

I

Uses Test a condition (a Variable, for instance) and, depending on the result, perform one set of commands instead of another set.

Cautions Some programmers use this type of readable but dangerous abbreviation:

```
If X Then
```

OR

```
If NOT X Then
```

This kind of shortcut is possible, because just naming a Variable causes Basic to respond "True" if the Variable is –1 and "False" if it is 0. The NOT command reverses the test. NOT in the above example means: If X = 0.

Text Variables ("strings") respond "True" if they contain any text and "False" if they are empty "" strings.

The danger in using this approach is that you can get erroneous reactions in special situations if you intend that any number other than zero in a Variable should cause a response of True. However, in Visual Basic, only –1 causes the IF NOT X to respond True.

It's safer to spell it out:

```
If X <> 0 Then
```

AND

```
If X = 0 Then
```

Example

```
If X > 123 Then
   MsgBox "X is larger than 123"
Else
   MsgBox "X is smaller than 123"
EndIf
```

See also Select Case, If…Then…Else

Italic

ACTIVEX

See Properties

I

K

KBD

HTML

Description KBD adjusts the typeface, thereby setting a piece of text off from the surrounding text. KBD is intended to highlight characters that the user is supposed to type in (on their keyboard). The KBD typeface is non-proportional (all letters the same width, like Courier) and boldface.

It is essentially the same idea as the CODE command, which is intended for computer programming text (such as HTML source code).

Used with ***Can be enclosed by***

<A>, <ABBREV>, <ACRONYM>, <ADDRESS>, <AU>, <B>, <BANNER>, <BIG>, <BODY>, <BODYTEXT>, <CAPTION>, <CITE>, <CODE>, <CREDIT>, <DD>, <DEL>, <DFN>, <DIV>, <DT>, <EM>, <FIGTEXT>, <FN>, <FORM>, <H1>, <H2>, <H3>, <H4>, <H5>, <H6>, <I>, <INS>, <KBD>, <LANG>, <LH>, <LI>, <NOTE>, <P>, <PERSON>, <PRE>, <Q>, <S>, <SAMP>, <SMALL>, <STRONG>, <SUB>, <SUP>, <TD>, <TH>, <TT>, <U>, <VAR>

Can enclose

<A>, <ABBREV>, <ACRONYM>, <AU>, <B>, <BIG>, <BR>, <CITE>, <CODE>, <DEL>, <DFN>, <EM>, <I>, <IMG>, <INS>, <KBD>, <LANG>, <MATH>, <PERSON>, <Q>, <S>, <SAMP>, <SMALL>, <STRONG>, <SUB>, <SUP>, <TAB>, <TT>, <U>, <VAR>

Example

If you want to receive our mailing, type the following into the text box below:
SUBSCRIBE:UA@EMAIL@DAEMON
and we will send the letters to you.

Figure K-1: The text the user is to type in is highlighted by a special typeface.

```
<HTML>

<FONT SIZE=+2>
If you want to receive our mailing, type the following into
the text box below:
<BR>

<KBD>SUBSCRIBE:UA@EMAIL@DAEMON</KBD>

<BR>
and we will send the letters to you.

</FONT>
</HTML>
```

See also CODE, TT

KeepScrollBarsVisible

ACTIVEX

See Properties

KeyDown

ACTIVEX

See Events

KeyUp

ACTIVEX

See Events

KeyPress

ACTIVEX

See Events

L

Label

ACTIVEX CONTROL

Description The primary purpose of the Label Control is to add text to a document. HTML is replete with many text-description commands (FONT, BIG, LI, LISTING, and dozens of others). What does the Label Control do that you can't do in HTML?

Labels are more efficient. It's easy to drag the Label around with the mouse to position it. Positioning HTML text can be awkward.

Labels are more flexible. They can have backcolors and borders in your choice of colors. They can be made to auto-size (to automatically make themselves large enough to display whatever text or picture is placed into them). It's easy to adjust the text's color (with the ForeColor Property), typeface, and type size (with the Font Property). You can specify that when the user moves the mouse over the label, the mouse pointer changes to a different symbol. The background of the label can be either transparent or opaque. You can add a graphic to a label and position the graphic (with the PicturePosition Property) 13 different ways relative to the text. You can choose from five different SpecialEffects—various frames including sunken, raised, and etched. You can position the text within the Label three ways: left- or right-aligned, or centered. Text can be made to wrap to the next line, or not, with the WordWrap Property.

Obviously, you can do much more with text in a Label, and do it more easily, than you can in plain HTML.

Variables As with all Controls, you can adjust their Properties in three ways: the Properties Window, the source code, and dynamically while a script is running.

Properties

Apply | 80000006 - Window Frame

80000003 - Inactive Caption
80000004 - Menu
80000005 - Window
80000006 - Window Frame
80000007 - Menu Text
80000008 - Window Text
80000009 - Caption Text
8000000a - Active Border
8000000b - Inactive Border

Accelerat	
AutoSize	
BackColo	
BackStyl	
BorderCo	
BorderSty	
Caption	
CodeBase	
Enabled	-1 - True
Font	8pt MS Sans Serif
ForeColor	000080ff - Unknown
Height	47
ID	Label1
Left	29
MouseIcon	(None)
MousePointer	0 - Default
Picture	(None)
PicturePosition	7 - AboveCenter
SpecialEffect	0 - Flat
TabIndex	0
TabStop	0 - False
TextAlign	1 - Left
Top	32
Visible	-1 - True
Width	143
WordWrap	-1 - True

Figure L-1: You can adjust a Label's Properties in the Properties Window.

In Figure L-1, above, you can see how to adjust a Label's Properties in the Properties Window. You can also change the source code in the ActiveX Control Pad. If you've inserted your Label directly into the .HTM file, you're looking at the source code in the ActiveX Control Pad's main window. If you've put the Label on a Layout Control, right-click on the Layout Control and choose "View Source Code." You'll see something like this. If you want to change the caption, change the text inside the quotes following "'Caption' VALUE=."

```
<DIV ID="n" STYLE="LAYOUT:FIXED;WIDTH:400pt;HEIGHT:300pt;">
  <OBJECT ID="Label1"
  CLASSID="CLSID:978C9E23-D4B0-11CE-BF2D-00AA003F40D0"
STYLE="TOP:32pt;LEFT:29pt;WIDTH:143pt;HEIGHT:47pt;ZINDEX:0;">
  <PARAM NAME="ForeColor" VALUE="33023">
  <PARAM NAME="Caption" VALUE="Label1">
  <PARAM NAME="Size" VALUE="5045;1658">
  <PARAM NAME="FontCharSet" VALUE="0">
  <PARAM NAME="FontPitchAndFamily" VALUE="2">
  <PARAM NAME="FontWeight" VALUE="0">
  </OBJECT>
</DIV>
```

Finally, you can change a Property while a script is running:

```
<SCRIPT LANGUAGE="VBScript">
<!--
Sub Label1_Click()
Label1.backcolor = 12512412
end sub
-->
</SCRIPT>
```

Properties

Accelerator, AutoSize, BackColor, BackStyle, BorderColor, BorderStyle, Caption, CodeBase, Enabled, Font, ForeColor, Height, ID, Left, List, MouseIcon, MousePointer, Picture, PicturePosition, SpecialEffect, TabIndex, TextAlign, Top, Visible, WordWrap, Width

Events

AfterUpdate, BeforeDragOver, BeforeDropOrPaste, BeforeUpdate, Click DblClick, Enter, Error, Exit, MouseDown, MouseMove, MouseUp

Methods

ZOrder

For details about these Properties, Events, and Methods, see the entries for "Properties," "Events," and "Methods."

Uses

- Describe objects on a document.
- Use them like a Command Button. The user can click on a label to travel to a link, to start a calculation, whatever action you've provided for in the Label's Click or other Event. Labels have virtually all the features of a Command Button with the exception of the Command Button's animated depression when you click it.
- Tell users what to do.
- Any text that's read-only. If you want the user to be able to change some text, use the TextBox command.
- Display changing information (by changing the Label's Caption Property in a script), but with greater flexibility than by using the MsgBox command or HTML text.
- Make your pages more *dynamic*. It's easier to design the look of your document with Labels than with HTML text. If you move an Image Control, for example, you can likewise move any associated Labels, then position them the way that looks best.
- Add captions or other descriptive text to Controls that have no Caption Properties of their own—such as Scroll Bars.
- Use messages to apprise the user of changing conditions while your script runs: a frame is being loaded, something is being sorted, and so on.

Cautions The most important element of a Label is its Caption Property, which is where you put your descriptive text. The default Property of a Label is the caption. Therefore, you can leave off the word caption:

```
Label1 = "This is the text"
```

works the same as:

```
Label1.Caption = "This is the text"
```

A Label wraps its text at its right edge. (It breaks lines at a space character.) You can take advantage of this fact to format multiline labels. First, create a Label that is a couple of lines high, and type some words separated by spaces into its Caption Property. When you reach the edge of the Label, the words move to the next line. If you want to force a line down, keep typing space characters until it drops. A Label is limited to 1,024 characters. A Label's TextAlign, AutoSize, and WordWrap Properties determine how text is displayed within the Label. Note that if you have a picture in your Label, AutoSize will size the Label to fit the picture or the caption, whichever is larger.

There are currently two Label Controls from Microsoft floating around out there. There's one that's built into Internet Explorer 3.0 (it's the one you get when you use the Edit | Insert ActiveX Control option in the Microsoft ActiveX Control Pad). The Insert ActiveX Control version has this ID:

```
CLASSID="CLSID:99B42120-6EC7-11CF-A6C7-00AA00A47DD2">
```

The alternative label is the one you get when you use the Edit | Insert HTML Layout option in the Microsoft ActiveX Control Pad. Its ID is:

```
CLASSID="CLSID:978C9E23-D4B0-11CE-BF2D-00AA003F40D0"
```

Eventually these Controls will be reconciled into a single version. For this book, we've used the older, more conservative Label object, the one that's available to the HTML Layout Control. Notice that the alternative (Insert ActiveX Control version) includes an interesting Angle Property with which you can tilt or even rotate the Label.

Example This example illustrates how you can create a background for an HTML Layout Control that adds visual quality, effects that are otherwise impossible. Using the ActiveX Control Pad (see the Introduction to this book), start a new HTML Layout Control (from the Edit menu). Put an Image Control onto the Layout and stretch it so it's the same size as the Layout. Right-click on the Image and choose "Send to Back."

Put five labels and an Image on the Layout. Put a picture into the smaller Image—we used a high jumper from the past. Create a gradient as a .BMP file and load it into each Label's Picture Property (see "Metallic Gradients" under "Command Button"). Put another label on the top and for its caption type in **Camping & Hiking Gear**. At this point your page should look like Figure L-2.

L

Figure L-2: BEFORE: This is our document before we add drop shadows, texture to the headline, and screws.

Our goal is to create a background that will supplement the Labels and the headline. Here's the trick. Press the PrintScrn key to capture this document. Then paste the document into Picture Publisher, Photoshop, or some other photo-retouching application. First we used the selection wand to select the labels, the picture, and the headline. Then we deselected all but the labels and applied an 11 x 12-pixel drop shadow (at 28% gray). This was done with a plug-in for the graphic application (you can buy these plug-ins from various vendors, such as Alien Skin).

Next we selected the headline, added a 7 x 6-pixel drop shadow, and filled the headline with a texture called "rug." Finally we added four high-res screws, with drop-shadows, around the picture of the high jumper. We saved the results as a .BMP graphics file, then loaded it into the PicturePath Property of the background Image Control. The real Label Controls cover up the background graphic "Labels"—but the drop shadows are positioned right where they should be to make it look like the real Labels are shadowed. All that remains is to remove the headline Label Control so you can see its texture and drop shadow. We can remove the headline because it has no Events, no reaction if the user clicks on it. However, we want the real Labels to trap user clicks and to display pricing and other options in response.

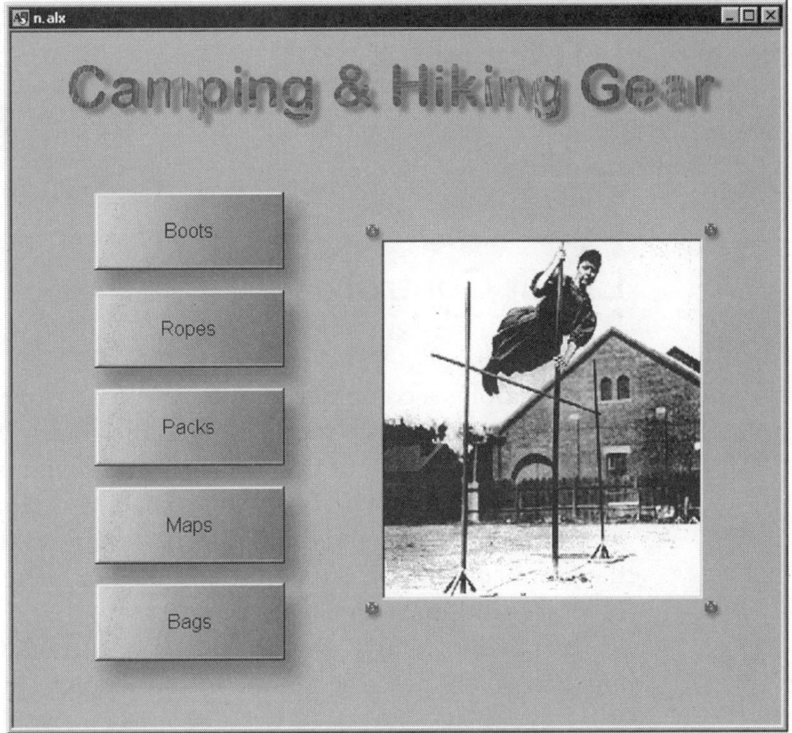

Figure L-3: AFTER: We've added drop shadows to our Labels and other elements that improved the quality of this document.

See also Command Button, A

LargeChange, SmallChange

ACTIVEX

See Properties

LayOut

ACTIVEX EVENT

See Events

HTML Layout

ACTIVEX CONTROL

See Introduction

Layout Control

ACTIVEX CONTROL

Description This Control is a container for other ActiveX Controls. Its primary virtue is that it offers various design efficiencies. You can drag Controls on a Layout to position and size them visually. You can group them (hold down Shift while clicking on them) to adjust—with only one change to the Properties Window—any Properties the grouped Controls have in common. The Layout Control offers several additional efficiencies as well.

The Layout Control—and its host, the ActiveX Control Pad—are extensively described in the Introduction to this book.

See Introduction

LBound

VBSCRIPT FUNCTION

Description LBound tells you the lower limit of an Array's index. You won't use this Function because you *know* when you are writing your program how big your Arrays are—you must define Arrays, including their range. What's more, in VBScript you're not allowed to create Arrays that begin with any index other than 0. Dim MyArray (3 To 100) is not permitted; Dim MyArray (100) is the format, so no adjustment of the lowest index is possible. (For more information, see "Arrays.")

However, if you are writing a Subroutine (called from more than one location in your program or used by more than one program because you import it as a part of your "toolkit of useful Routines"), you may very well need to know the dimensions of a passed or global Array. We're assuming that, in the future, VBScript will permit Arrays with lower limits other than 0.

```
<SCRIPT LANGUAGE="VBSCRIPT">
Dim A (50)
X = LBound(A)
Msgbox cstr(X)
</SCRIPT>
```

Results in

```
0
```

Used with Arrays

Uses LBound can be used if an Array is redimensioned based on a range defined by the program's user. However, this information could just as easily be retained in a Variable at the time the Array is redimensioned.

Cautions

- The related UBound Function tells you the upper limit of an Array's index while a program is running.
- You can omit the "dimension number" (the 2 in LBound(A,2)) if there is only one dimension. Dim A As String has only one dimension; Dim A (5, 7, 4) has three dimensions.

Example The important difference between the ReDim and Dim commands is that ReDim must be used within a procedure (a Sub or Function), whereas Dim can be used either outside or within a procedure. If Dim is used outside a procedure, the Array will be available for use by all other programming in the script. If Dim is used within a procedure then, like ReDim, the declared Array is available only to programming that's also within that same procedure. This "range of influence" is known as the *scope* of a Variable or an Array.

```
Sub OurDeal ()
ReDim A (44)
X = LBound (A)
MsgBox X
End Sub
```

Results in

```
0
```

See also Arrays, Dim, ReDim, UBound

LCase

VBSCRIPT FUNCTION

Description LCase forces all the characters of a text (string) Variable subtype to become lowercase letters. For example, it changes "VIRGIL" to "virgil."

Used with Text Variables, text Constants, text expressions, or literal text. See "Variables" for an explanation of these terms.

Variables

```
A = "Declaration of Independence"
B = LCase(A)
MsgBox B
```

Results in

```
declaration of independence
```

OR (because LCase is a Function, you can use it as part of an *expression*):

```
A = "Declaration of Independence"
Print LCase(A)
```

Results in

```
declaration of independence
```

Because the symbols (like %) are not text characters, they remain unaffected by LCase.

Uses

- Some VBScript commands are *case-sensitive*. One frequently used command, InStr, makes a distinction between *This* and *this*.

  You cannot always know how users might capitalize the input when typing something into your program. To avoid a problem, you can force the user's text to all-lowercase letters and not worry about unwanted mismatches. It's a good idea to build the LCase function into any general-purpose text-handling Subroutines and Functions you write. That way you don't have to worry about capitalization when providing Variables to the Subs or Functions. (See the example.) However, VBScript also provides a StrComp command that can compare pieces of text and includes case-insensitivity as an option.

- If you write a Subroutine that capitalizes the first letter of each word or the first letter of each word in a name, use LCase or UCase first to get all the words to a known state.

- You can also use LCase when storing a text Variable that will later need to be matched (such as a password).

- In searching through documents or databases for a match (using the InStr command), you could use LCase to make capitalization variations irrelevant to your search. (See the example.)

Cautions Only alphabetic letters are affected by LCase—not digits like 8 or symbols like &.

Example

```
A = "Hibernation"
MsgBox LCase(A)
```

Results in
hibernation

See also StrComp, UCase

Left

ACTIVEX

See Properties

Left

VBSCRIPT FUNCTION

Description Left allows you to extract a specified amount of text from the left side of a text Variable:

```
X = "We Employ A Maid From Planet X."
Y = Left(X,18)
MsgBox Y
```

Results in

```
We Employ A Maid
```

```
X = "We Employ A Maid From Planet X."
Y = Left(X,9)
MsgBox Y
```

Results in

```
We Employ
```

As usual, you can eliminate a step when using expressions (see "Expressions") if you wish:

```
X = "We Employ A Maid From Planet X."
MsgBox Left(X,9)
```

Results in

```
We Employ
```

A variation, the LeftB function, allows you to specify the length in *bytes* rather than *characters*. (Characters in VBScript are 2-byte units.)

Used with Text ("string") Variables

Variables To put the first 15 characters from the Variable *Large* into the Variable *Partial*:

```
Partial = Left(Large,15)
```

Uses *Parse* some text—pull out the various elements of the text.

Left is used along with several other Functions that manipulate text—Right, Mid, Instr, and Len—to isolate and extract a piece of text from within a larger group of characters.

Right pulls out a number of characters, counting backward from the right side:

```
X = "We Employ A Maid From Planet X."
Y = Right(X,9)
MsgBox Y
```

Results in

```
Planet X.
```

Mid pulls out a piece of text anywhere from within a larger text. It has the format Y Mid(LargerText, StartingCharacter, NumberOfCharacters). Use Mid when the target piece of text isn't flush against the left or right of the larger text:

```
X = "We Employ A Maid From Planet X."
Y = Mid(X,23,6)
MsgBox Y
```

Results in

```
Planet
```

Len tells you the length, in characters, of a text ("string") Variable.

```
X = "We employ a maid from Planet X."
MsgBox Len(X)
```

Results in

```
31
```

Instr finds the location of the first character of a piece of text within a larger group of characters:

```
L = Instr(X, "maid")
MsgBox L
```

Results in

```
13
```


Instr will give back a 0 if it cannot find the text. Instr is case-sensitive; looking for "Maid" would give back a 0, meaning "not found," because the searched text does not capitalize the *m*. This is why before using Instr it's useful to use the LCase or Ucase Functions to force all characters into the same case.

Cautions The group of characters from which Left extracts a smaller piece of text will usually be a text ("string") Variable. However, it can also be a *string expression*. (See "Variables" for a full explanation of *expression*.)

Briefly, an *expression* is a group of Variables, literals, or Functions connected together by operators such as + or >. An expression can be reduced to a single answer: True or False.

```
If Y = Left(X,3) = "We " Then
```

This is not an expression because Y = Left(X,3) = "We" cannot be evaluated into a single result by VBScript.

```
Left(X, 2) + Right(X, 3) = "We X."
```

This *is* an expression, because it can be evaluated as True or False (–1 or 0) and can therefore be used in a larger structure, such as If...Then.

```
X = "We employ a maid from Planet X."
If Left(X, 2) + Right(X, 3) = "We X." Then Msgbox "Yes."
End If
```

Results in

```
Yes.
```

- The number of characters you are requesting Left to extract—the 15 in Left(X, 15)—can be a literal number like 15 or a numeric Variable like N.
- The number of characters you are requesting Left to extract from a larger piece of text can be as many as 65,535, but if you ask for more characters than exist in the larger piece of text, you get back the entire larger text.

Example

```
X = "1234567890"
For I = 1 to Len(X)
  TextBox.Value = TextBox.Value + Left(X,I)
Next I
```

Results in

```
1
12
123
1234
12345
123456
1234567
12345678
123456789
1234567890
```

See also Instr, Len, Mid, Right, StrComp

Len

VBSCRIPT FUNCTION

Description Len tells you the length—the number of characters—in a text ("string") Variable.

Used with

- Text ("string") Variables, to determine their length.
- User-defined *Type* Variables, to determine the amount of memory or disk space they use.

Variables

```
X = Len(A)
```

Uses

- You use Len with text, when you don't know how long the piece of text is. This usually means that the user entered the text. You can make your programs more responsive to the user, more forgiving of variations in how the user might enter or request information—even more "artificially" intelligent. One way to do this is to use Len, along with other text-analysis commands such as Mid and Instr, to take a sentence apart. Once you have the individual words, your program can take a look at them and react with a degree of understanding.

  Let's say there is a general-purpose TextBox that the user can access any time, entering a question that your program is supposed to answer. If the user enters any one of the words *costs, cost, expense, expenses, payment*, etc., you would switch to a special budget window that would list the months and years for which budget data exist in the program (or load in a disk file with that information).

  Better yet, if the user has also entered the name of a month (Jan, January, Jan., etc.), your program notices that and provides the expense information for that month only. You can also check for other words that would further narrow the criteria and permit you to require the user to interact with fewer menus, submenus, or command buttons. Your program could analyze the user's English-language request intelligently and zoom right in on the data the user requests. You might check to see if a subset of the budget request includes text like Car, 1990, All, Lowest, and so on, making adjustments in how you present the data based on the meaning of these terms. See the example below.

- Len's other primary use is to tell you how much space a user-defined Variable type takes up in memory or on disk. (See "Variables" for a discussion about *Variable types*.)

Cautions If you want a *byte* count in 32-bit VBScript, use the LenB function. In 32-bit VBScript, Len doesn't return the number of *bytes* because characters are two bytes large. See "Chr" for more on this.

Example

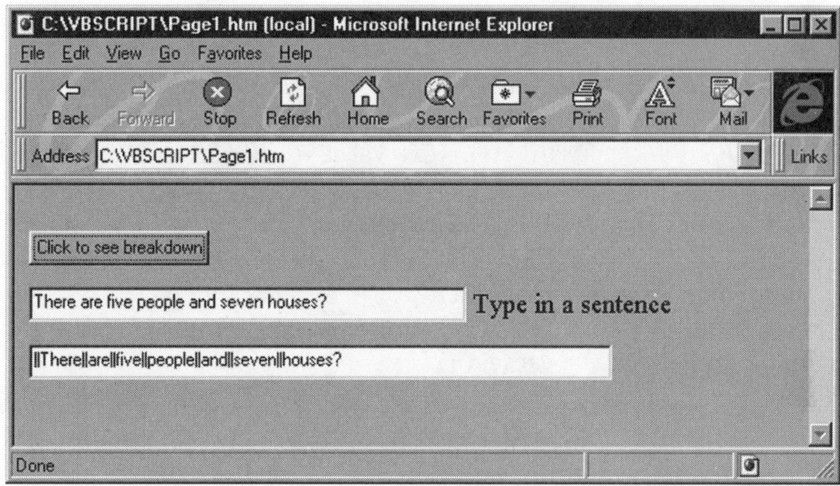

Figure L-4: Breaking a sentence into its components—the first step in analyzing the meaning of the user's request.

When the user types a question into the top box, our program prepares to analyze the question and respond intelligently. The first step is to break the sentence down into individual words. For purposes of illustration, we separate the individual words by a || symbol and display them in the second box.

As soon as we have the words, we can look them up in a little database list we've created, and have the program react intelligently to any trigger words. Using Select Case or If...Then, we can make the program switch to an expenses screen, get the data for the requested month and year, and even highlight the medical, insurance, auto, or whatever particular information the user might have requested.

Because our program will often need to break a text Variable into its component words, we write a Function called Parse. Parse accepts a single text Variable and pulls it apart. We "pass" that single Variable to the Parse Function when we use it: Parse "This piece of text" or Parse (n).

```
<HTML>
<BR>
<INPUT TYPE=BUTTON VALUE="Click to see breakdown" NAME="Btn">
<BR>
<BR>
<INPUT TYPE=TEXT VALUE="" NAME="Textbox1" SIZE = 55>Type →
in a sentence
<BR><BR>
<INPUT TYPE=TEXT VALUE="" NAME="Textbox2" SIZE = 75>
<BR>
<SCRIPT LANGUAGE=VBS>

Sub Btn_OnClick
n = Textbox1.VALUE
z = parse (n)

Textbox2.Value = z

End Sub

Function Parse (A)

L = Len(A)

For I = 1 To L
   P = InStr(I, A, Chr(32))
   If P = 0 Then Exit For
   T = Mid(A, I, P - I)
   R = R + "||" + T
   I = P
Next
```

L

```
T = Mid(A, I, L - P)

R = R + "||" + T
Parse = R

End Function

</SCRIPT>

</HTML>
```

First off in our Function, Len tells us the length of the passed Variable. Then we use a For...Next Loop to extract each character.

P holds the location of any space within A. (Chr(32) is the code for a space.) Instr looks for a space, but if P is 0, then it did not find a space (A has only one word), or we've been through the loop several times and have found all the spaces (and therefore all the words) already.

As soon as we *do* find a space, we assign the word to T. We know where within A the Mid Function should extract the new word. The Variable I holds the starting position of the new word, and P holds the position where we came across a space. So P–I is the *length* of the new word. Finally we add T to the box so we can see it. Then we move our place marker, the I Variable, up to where we found the space and look for the next space.

Notice that when we've found no more spaces, we still have to add that one last word in A to the box. In this final situation, we use L, the length of A, to provide the last character and subtract the most recent position (P), so we know how many characters to tell our final Mid to extract.

See also Chr, Instr, Left, Mid, Right, Variables (for Variable *types*)

Let

VBSCRIPT STATEMENT

Description Let is no longer used. It is retained in Visual Basic for compatibility with extremely ancient programs. Let has not been used in Basic for over ten years.

In the very early days, though, Basic required Let when you were *assigning* a number or piece of text to a Variable.

```
Let MonthlyBudget = 800
```

OR

```
Let PowerCoName = "Duke Power"
```

However, it was quickly realized that the equals (=) symbol is never used by itself like this (outside of a larger structure), *except* when assigning to a Variable. Basic could figure out that when you said X = 15 or Y = N you were assigning, so Let got dropped.

Let also served what the designers of Basic thought was an important purpose: it helped people understand that *assignment* did not mean precisely the same thing as *equality*. Everyone who takes algebra learns that = means that the items on either side of the equals sign are equal to each other. This had to be unlearned to program a computer.

An equals sign is used in two different ways in computer programming:

1. *Assignment*. By itself, when simply connecting a Variable with a literal (Y = "No") or connecting a Variable with another Variable (X = Y), an equals sign means "now let the item on the left be *assigned* (given) the value on the right." Prior to the assignment, X might have held anything—"MAYBE" or "Portland," or perhaps it had not been used yet and was an empty text Variable "". However, after assignment (X = Y), X contains a piece of text, a copy of what was in Y.

2. *Equality*. Used inside a larger structure, such as If...Then, an equals symbol *does* represent equality in the algebraic sense.

```
X = 12
Y = 12
If X = Y Then MsgBox "They are Equal."
```

L

X = Y is called an *expression*, which means that Basic can "evaluate the truth of it." An expression is a group of Variables, Constants, literals, and/or Functions connected to each other by operators (such as < or / or =). An expression can be reduced to True (–1) or False (0) after being evaluated by Basic.

```
X = 4: Y = 15
```

We can evaluate the expression X > Y (X is greater than Y), by putting it within an If...Then structure:

```
If X > Y Then
```

In this instance, the evaluation would result in a False (0), and whatever instructions followed the Then command would not be carried out. The expression Y > X would return a True (–1) result to the If...Then structure, and commands following Then in the structure would be carried out.

The differences between assignment and equality may seem rather trivial at first, but they represent two essentially different uses of the equals sign in programming. After some experience communicating with computers, people quickly grasp the difference. They come to recognize that used by itself = gives content or "value" to the Variable. It's like putting five dollars in an envelope, or three pencils in your pocket.

Used within a larger structure such as Select Case or If...Then, = comes closer to its algebraic meaning of equality. And thus the descriptive function of Let is not necessary.

Used with Not used.

Variables

```
Let X = 175
```

Uses None

Cautions None

Example

```
Let Z = "Nova Scotia"
```

is precisely the same as

```
Z = "Nova Scotia"
```

See also There is no referent for this dead command.

LI

HTML

Description The LI command tells a browser that the following text is to be displayed in a "list" format, like a shopping list. It is used alone (there is no </LI> command) and is intended to be enclosed with <DIR> (a "filename-like" style), <MENU> (a list made up of short phrases), <OL> (ordered list—numbers are automatically added at the start of each item), or <UL> (bulleted list—bullets, small dots, are automatically added at the start of each item).

There is also a set of additional formatting codes that can be used with any LI command. See the Variables section below.

See the example below for illustrations of each list format.

Used with ***Can be enclosed by***

<DIR>, <MENU>, <OL>, <UL>

Can enclose

<A>, <ABBREV>, <ACRONYM>, <AU>, <B>, <BIG>, <BLOCKQUOTE>, <BQ>, <BR>, <CITE>, <CODE>, <DEL>, <DFN>, <DIR>, <DL>, <EM>, <FIG>, <FN>, <FORM>, <I>, <IMG>, <INS>, <ISINDEX>, <KBD>, <LANG>, <MATH>, <MENU>, <NOTE>, <OL>, <P>, <PERSON>, <PRE>, <Q>, <S>, <SAMP>, <SMALL>, <STRONG>, <SUB>, <SUP>, <TAB>, <TABLE>, <TT>, <U>, <UL>, <VAR>

Variables Note that the following TYPE commands currently work only with Netscape browsers.

```
<LI TYPE=A>      Uses large characters
<LI TYPE=a>      Uses small characters
<LI TYPE=I>      Start with large Roman numerals
<LI TYPE=i>      Start with small Roman numerals
<LI TYPE=1>      Start with numbers
```

Uses

- Format a list of items.
- Create bulleted or numbered lists.

Example

This is a directory-style list.
Second item
Third item

This is a menu-style list.
Second item
Third item

1. This is an ordered list.
2. Second item
3. Third item

- This is an unordered list.
- Second item
- Third item

Figure L-5: Notice that all browsers will not format all LI items as expected. This is Internet Explorer's interpretation of the four LI styles.

```
<HTML>
<FONT SIZE=+1>
<BODY BGCOLOR=WHITE>
<DIR>
<LI>This is a directory-style list.
<LI>Second item
<LI>Third item
</DIR>
<BR>
<MENU>
<LI>This is a menu-style list.
<LI>Second item
<LI>Third item
```

```
</MENU>
<BR>
<OL>
<LI>This is an ordered list.
<LI>Second item
<LI>Third item
</OL>
<BR>
<UL>
<LI>This is an unordered list.
<LI>Second item
<LI>Third item
</UL>
</BODY>
</HTML>
```

See also DIR, MENU, OL, UL

LineCount

ACTIVEX

See Properties

List, ListCount, ListIndex

ACTIVEX

See Properties

ListBox

ACTIVEX CONTROL

Description A ListBox is the same as a ComboBox, except the user cannot type anything into a ListBox. He or she can only click on one or more of the listed items, thereby selecting that item or set of items. By contrast, with the default Style Property of a ComboBox

(DropDown), the user can type into the TextBox portion at the top of the ComboBox or click on a value from the drop-down list. If the Style Property of a ComboBox, however, is set to the DropDownList option, the ComboBox then behaves like a ListBox: the user must choose a value from the list. Typing, unless it matches what's in the list, is ignored.

A second major distinction between List and ComboBoxes is that the items in a ComboBox are not visible to the user until the user clicks on the box and drops it down. The contents of a ListBox, however, are visible to the user at all times (unless there are more items that can be displayed within the height of the box, in which case a ScrollBar is automatically added).

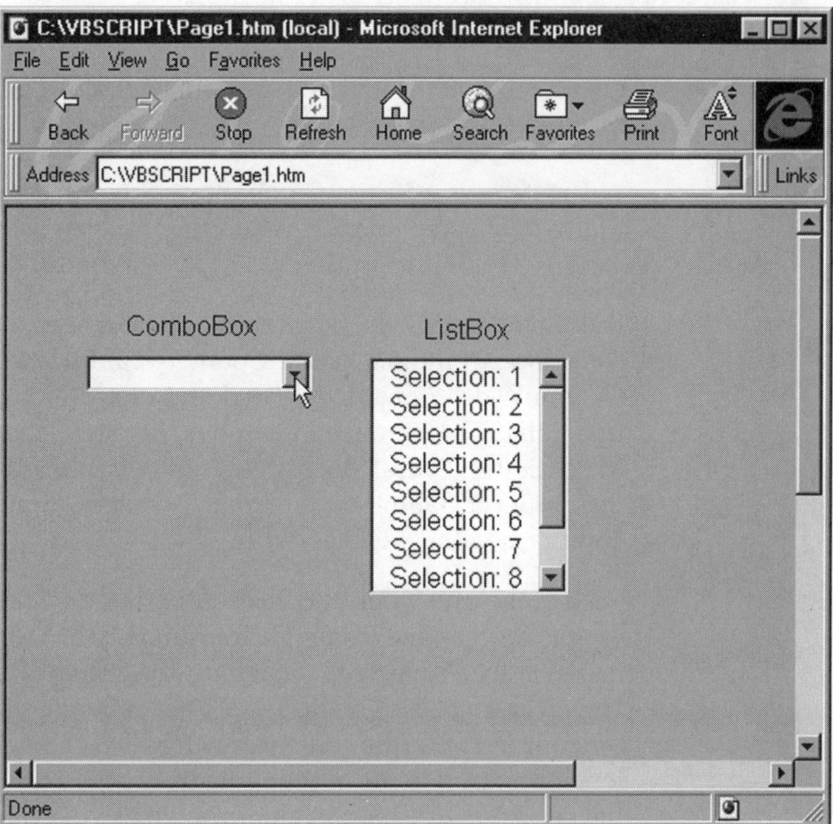

Figure L-6: The ListBox on the right doesn't require that the user click to see the options. The ComboBox on the left won't reveal its contents until the user clicks on it.

Used with Lists that you want the user to be able to see right away, without having to click or otherwise manipulate the Control.

Variables The Value Property is the default Property. This means that when querying the Value, you need not use the word Value:

```
X = ListBox1
```

OR

```
X = ListBox1.Value
```

Your script can add or remove items from a ListBox:

```
List1.AddItem "persimmons"
```

OR (to add a Variable):

```
List1.AddItem N
```

OR (to remove the fourth item from a ListBox):

```
List1.RemoveItem 3
```

L

The items in a List or ComboBox start with a zeroth item, so the fourth item is removed by requesting number 3.

Properties

BackColor, BackStyle, BorderColor, BorderStyle, BoundColumn, CodeBase, Column, ColumnCount, ColumnHeads, ColumnWidths, Enabled, Font, ForeColor, Height, ID, IMEMode, IntegralHeight, Left, List, ListIndex, ListStyle, Locked, MatchEntry, MouseIcon, MousePointer, MultiSelect, Selected, SpecialEffect, TabIndex, TabStop, Text, TextColumn, Top, TopIndex, Value, Visible, Width

Note that the Value and Text Properties are identical, just two words for the same Property. Traditionally in Visual Basic, Text has been the Property that contains the currently selected item. However, increasingly the word *Value* is coming into use to represent, for instance, the contents of an HTML Text Control. *Value* has long been used to mean the contents of a Variable. It seems that the designers of VBScript are trying to use the word *value* to represent "contents of something." Therefore Value and Text can now be used interchangeably and are synonyms—something quite rare in computer languages. (Note that a third term, *caption*, is the Property that represents the contents of a Label Control.)

Events

AfterUpdate, BeforeDragOver, BeforeDropOrPaste, BeforeUpdate, Change, Click, DblClick, Enter, Error, Exit, KeyDown, KeyPress, KeyUp, MouseDown, MouseMove, MouseUp

Methods

AddItem, Clear, RemoveItem, SetFocus, ZOrder

For details about these Properties, Events, and Methods, see the entries for "Properties," "Events," and "Methods."

Uses

- Provide the user with a list of "hard-wired" choices reflecting your judgment about appropriate options. If you want the user to select between light, medium, and dark blue for the BackColor of a Layout, put only those names in a ListBox. The user must follow your aesthetic rules; those are the only options you offered.
- Provide the user with the only *possible* choices. There are only two choices for FontBold: bold or not. So your ListBox would contain only those two options. If, however, there are only two choices, perhaps an Option Button or CheckBox might be more easily recognized as a True/False, On/Off Control.
- Make a ListBox more accommodating to the user. Add a TextBox or other Controls to the Layout, as adjuncts to a ListBox, offering the user more flexible Control than what a lone ListBox would normally offer. Let the user, for instance, select from CheckBoxes or Option Buttons to "Add-Items" to your ListBox, using the AddItem command described below.

You can make ListBoxes more efficient in some situations by adjusting their MultiSelect, ColumnCount, and TopIndex Properties (see "Properties"). MultiSelect permits the user to select more than a single item at a time; ColumnCount displays more than a single vertical list of items; and TopIndex allows you to *scroll* the list by commands from within a script, independent of the user.

Cautions A ComboBox with its Style Property set to 2 is called a "DropDownList" style ComboBox and is almost identical to a ListBox. The user cannot type anything into the box and is presented with a list of options. The one difference is that the DropDown Combo shows none of the items it contains unless the box has the focus and the user starts typing characters that appear in any of the items. The ComboBox (List style) merely displays a blank box the size of a single item, plus an arrow the user can click on to reveal the actual list. This blank box can confuse users, but if you have a particularly crowded screen, a ComboBox saves space.

Use a ComboBox (default Style "DropDownCombo") when the user should have the option of adding new items to the list by typing them in. Use a ListBox when the options are provided by your script.

You can allow the user to add or remove items from your list, with the AddItem and RemoveItem Methods (see the example below). One approach would be to have a single click highlight an item, then a keypress of the Delete key delete the item, and the Insert key replace the item (or the plus key could pop up another list from which the user could select items to add).

The Text (and Value) Properties of a ListBox always contain the currently selected item (available as a text ("string") Variable):

```
<SCRIPT LANGUAGE="VBScript">
<!--

Sub ListBox1_Click
X = ListBox1.Text
If x = "Selection: 4" then msgbox "You chose #4"
End sub

-->
</SCRIPT>
```

This would allow your script to examine and react to the selected item in the box. The Text Property of a ComboBox, however, can contain something the user may have typed in, some text that is not part of the box proper.

The user can select an item from a ListBox by clicking on it or by typing in its first letter. Typing a first letter triggers a Click Event, without using the mouse.

By convention, List and ComboBoxes are usually accompanied by Option Buttons, CheckBoxes, or Command Buttons. These extra Controls define how the script will respond to a user selecting from the ListBox—a click (to select) or a double-click (to take action).

Example The ListStyle Property of a ListBox allows you to display CheckBoxes or ComboBoxes within the box. Unfortunately, the circles and squares displayed are visually crude compared to the sleek 3D look that has been used with most Controls since the advent of the Windows 95 user interface design. Compare the OptionButton and CheckBox Controls above the ListBox's imitations in Figure L-7:

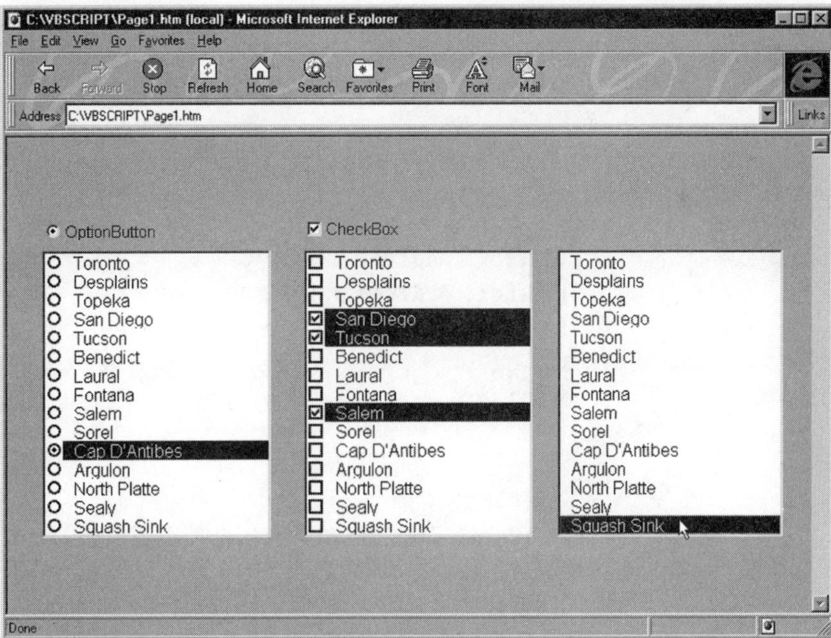

Figure L-7: If you wish, you can use two additional "ListStyles" for a ListBox: the faux option button and faux check box styles. Alas, the visual effect is crude compared to the real buttons and boxes. On the far right is the plain, default ListBox.

The HTML Layout Control source code for the example shown in Figure L-7 is:

```
<SCRIPT LANGUAGE="VBScript">
<!--
Sub n_OnLoad()
Dim N(14)
N(0) = "Toronto"
N(1) = "Desplains"
N(2) = "Topeka"
N(3) = "San Diego"
N(4) = "Tucson"
N(5) = "Benedict"
N(6) = "Laural"
N(7) = "Fontana"
N(8) = "Salem"
N(9) = "Sorel"
N(10) = "Cap D'Antibes"
N(11) = "Argulon"
N(12) = "North Platte"
N(13) = "Sealy"
N(14) = "Squash Sink"

for i = 0 to 14
  ListBox1.AddItem N(i)
  ListBox2.AddItem N(i)
  ListBox3.AddItem N(i)
next
end sub

-->
</SCRIPT>
<DIV ID="n" STYLE="LAYOUT:FIXED;WIDTH:559pt;HEIGHT:271pt;">
 <OBJECT ID="ListBox2"
  CLASSID="CLSID:8BD21D20-EC42-11CE-9E0D-00AA006002F3"
STYLE="TOP:44pt;LEFT:200pt;WIDTH:160pt;HEIGHT:200pt;TABINDEX:1;ZINDEX:0;">
  <PARAM NAME="ScrollBars" VALUE="3">
  <PARAM NAME="DisplayStyle" VALUE="2">
  <PARAM NAME="Size" VALUE="5644;7056">
  <PARAM NAME="MatchEntry" VALUE="0">
  <PARAM NAME="ListStyle" VALUE="1">
```

L

```
  <PARAM NAME="MultiSelect" VALUE="1">
  <PARAM NAME="FontName" VALUE="Arial">
  <PARAM NAME="FontHeight" VALUE="220">
  <PARAM NAME="FontCharSet" VALUE="0">
  <PARAM NAME="FontPitchAndFamily" VALUE="2">
  <PARAM NAME="FontWeight" VALUE="0">
 </OBJECT>
 <OBJECT ID="ListBox1"
  CLASSID="CLSID:8BD21D20-EC42-11CE-9E0D-00AA006002F3"
STYLE="TOP:44pt;LEFT:17pt;WIDTH:160pt;HEIGHT:200pt;TABINDEX:0;ZINDEX:1;">
  <PARAM NAME="ScrollBars" VALUE="3">
  <PARAM NAME="DisplayStyle" VALUE="2">
  <PARAM NAME="Size" VALUE="5644;7056">
  <PARAM NAME="MatchEntry" VALUE="0">
  <PARAM NAME="ListStyle" VALUE="1">
  <PARAM NAME="FontName" VALUE="Arial">
  <PARAM NAME="FontHeight" VALUE="220">
  <PARAM NAME="FontCharSet" VALUE="0">
  <PARAM NAME="FontPitchAndFamily" VALUE="2">
  <PARAM NAME="FontWeight" VALUE="0">
 </OBJECT>
 <OBJECT ID="ListBox3"
  CLASSID="CLSID:8BD21D20-EC42-11CE-9E0D-00AA006002F3"
STYLE="TOP:44pt;LEFT:378pt;WIDTH:160pt;HEIGHT:200pt;TABINDEX:2;ZINDEX:2;">
  <PARAM NAME="ScrollBars" VALUE="3">
  <PARAM NAME="DisplayStyle" VALUE="2">
  <PARAM NAME="Size" VALUE="5644;7056">
  <PARAM NAME="MatchEntry" VALUE="0">
  <PARAM NAME="FontName" VALUE="Arial">
  <PARAM NAME="FontHeight" VALUE="220">
  <PARAM NAME="FontCharSet" VALUE="0">
  <PARAM NAME="FontPitchAndFamily" VALUE="2">
  <PARAM NAME="FontWeight" VALUE="0">
 </OBJECT>
 <OBJECT ID="OptionButton1"
  CLASSID="CLSID:8BD21D50-EC42-11CE-9E0D-00AA006002F3"
STYLE="TOP:17pt;LEFT:19pt;WIDTH:104pt;HEIGHT:20pt;TABINDEX:3;ZINDEX:3;">
  <PARAM NAME="BackColor" VALUE="2147483663">
  <PARAM NAME="ForeColor" VALUE="2147483666">
  <PARAM NAME="DisplayStyle" VALUE="5">
```

L

```
    <PARAM NAME="Size" VALUE="3651;688">
    <PARAM NAME="Caption" VALUE="OptionButton">
    <PARAM NAME="FontName" VALUE="Arial">
    <PARAM NAME="FontHeight" VALUE="220">
    <PARAM NAME="FontCharSet" VALUE="0">
    <PARAM NAME="FontPitchAndFamily" VALUE="2">
    <PARAM NAME="FontWeight" VALUE="0">
  </OBJECT>
  <OBJECT ID="CheckBox1"
   CLASSID="CLSID:8BD21D40-EC42-11CE-9E0D-00AA006002F3"
STYLE="TOP:19pt;LEFT:203pt;WIDTH:116pt;HEIGHT:17pt;TABINDEX:4;ZINDEX:4;">
    <PARAM NAME="BackColor" VALUE="2147483663">
    <PARAM NAME="ForeColor" VALUE="2147483666">
    <PARAM NAME="DisplayStyle" VALUE="4">
    <PARAM NAME="Size" VALUE="4101;608">
    <PARAM NAME="Caption" VALUE="CheckBox">
    <PARAM NAME="FontName" VALUE="Arial">
    <PARAM NAME="FontHeight" VALUE="220">
    <PARAM NAME="FontCharSet" VALUE="0">
    <PARAM NAME="FontPitchAndFamily" VALUE="2">
    <PARAM NAME="FontWeight" VALUE="0">
  </OBJECT>
</DIV>
```

Notice that we created an Array of names (see "Array") and then used the AddItem Method to insert all the names into the three ListBoxes. Also notice that if you change a ListBox's ListStyle Property from the default "Plain" to "Option" (or change the VALUE from the default 0 to 1), you get the "Option Button Style" ListBox shown on the left in Figure L-7. If you go further and *also* set a ListBox's MultiSelect Property to Multi (VALUE = 1) from the default Single (0), you get the "CheckBox Style" ListBox shown in the middle in Figure L-7. The ListBox on the right in Figure L-7 is the traditional, plain ListBox. Perhaps as time goes on, a 3D effect will be added to these new variations on the ListBox.

If you're tempted to use these faux boxes or buttons, consider instead a group of real CheckBoxes or OptionButtons.

See also ComboBox

LISTING

HTML

Description Changes the typeface to a non-proportional style (such as Courier). Used to display programming ("code") such as HTML source code. The font used is fixed-width. Fixed-width (non-proportional) means a font such as Courier, a typewriter-style typeface where each character is the same width (*i* is as wide as *w*). (The opposite variety—variable-width type—is typified by Times Roman. Characters vary in width. Variable width is the default HTML font for body text. The CODE, PRE, and TT commands do essentially the same thing as LISTING.

Used with ***Can be enclosed by***

<A>, <ABBREV>, <ACRONYM>, <ADDRESS>, <AU>, <B>, <BANNER>, <BIG>, <BODY>, <BODYTEXT>, <CAPTION>, <CITE>, <CODE>, <CREDIT>, <DD>, <DEL>, <DFN>, <DIV>, <DT>, <EM>, <FIGTEXT>, <FN>, <FORM>, <H1>, <H2>, <H3>, <H4>, <H5>, <H6>, <I>, <INS>, <KBD>, <LANG>, <LH>, <LI>, <NOTE>, <P>, <PERSON>, <PRE>, <Q>, <S>, <SAMP>, <SMALL>, <STRONG>, <SUB>, <SUP>, <TD>, <TH>, <TT>, <U>, <VAR>

Can enclose

<A>, <ABBREV>, <ACRONYM>, <AU>, <B>, <BIG>, <BR>, <CITE>, <CODE>, <DEL>, <DFN>, <EM>, <I>, <IMG>, <INS>, <KBD>, <LANG>, <MATH>, <PERSON>, <Q>, <S>, <SAMP>, <SMALL>, <STRONG>, <SUB>, <SUP>, <TAB>, <TT>, <U>, <VAR>

Uses Indicate that you are displaying nonstandard text, something that should be set off from ordinary body text. Many computer books, this one included, switch to a different font to indicate computer programming—lines that the user can type in to cause something to happen in a computer language such as HTML.

Example

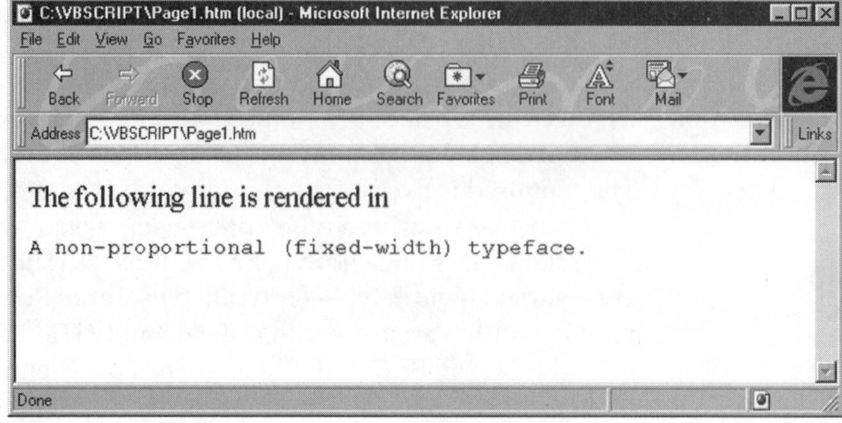

Figure L-8: The most common non-proportional font is Courier, a typical typewriter typeface.

```
<HTML>
<FONT SIZE=+1>
<BODY BGCOLOR=WHITE>

The following line is rendered in
<BR>
<LISTING>A non-proportional (fixed-width) typeface.</LISTING>

</HTML>
```

See also <PRE>, <CODE>, <TT>

ListRows, ListStyle, ListWidth

ACTIVEX

See Properties

Literals

Description A *literal* is a piece of data. The word *Brian* is a literal. The number 145 is a literal. You can use literals in computer programming:

```
MsgBox "Brian"
```

Literals are an alternative to *Variables*. Variables are not, themselves, data. They are names *pointing to* data. You can create a variable by merely assigning some literal data to it:

```
HisName = "Brian"
```

Then, after this assignment, you can use the Variable, in place of the literal:

```
MsgBox HisName
```

You can also combine Variables and literals:

```
MsgBox HisName & " Thornsen"
```

Results In

```
Brian Thornsen
```

See Variables

L

Local Scope

Description VBScript does not have a Local or Private command. The way that you make a Variable available only within a particular procedure is to define it with the Dim command (or just use it, without defining it) *within that procedure.* Doing so makes the Variable available to that procedure alone. *No other procedures in that script, nor any other scripts in your document* will have access to that Variable. They can't modify or read the contents of that Variable. For a detailed discussion of scope in VBScript, see "Dim." To create Variables that have "document-wide" scope, use the Dim command to define the Variable *outside* of any procedure.

And if you need more-than-script-wide scope, try a Cookie. For information on how to save data between sessions (between a user's visits to your sites, so you can say "Welcome back, Jerry! You last visited us three weeks ago!"), see "Cookies."

See Dim

Location.href

HTML

Description Use this command when you want the browser to load in a different document. Of course you can create links using the A command. But that requires a user-click to launch things. What if you, the programmer, want to launch things?

If you want to cause the browser to jump to another location from within your VBScript—in response to *whatever trigger you choose*—use the location.href command.

For example, let's say that instead of the traditional text or image (see "A" or "HotSpot") linking, you could provide a group of CommandButtons. When the user clicks on a Button, the browser takes off and brings in the new document:

```
<SCRIPT LANGUAGE="VBScript">

Sub CommandButton1_Click
  location.href = "http://www.yahoo.com"
End Sub

</SCRIPT>
```

Locked

ACTIVEX

See Properties

Log

VBSCRIPT FUNCTION

Description Log is an advanced math function, like Cos and Tan, that you would find on a scientific calculator.

Log tells you the "natural logarithm" of a number.

Variables

```
X = Log(3)
MsgBox X
```

OR

```
X = 3
Y = Log(X)
MsgBox Y
```

OR

```
MsgBox Log(3)
```

Result in

```
1.098612
```

Uses Advanced mathematical calculations

Cautions Log returns a single-precision number if you provide it with a single-precision value or an Integer Variable. Otherwise, it provides a double-precision value. (See "Variables" for an overview of the several types of numeric Variables.)

Example

```
X = Log(.5)
Print X
```

Results in

```
-.6931472
```

See also Exp, Sqr

Logical Operators

See Operators

LTrim

VBSCRIPT FUNCTION

Description LTrim removes any spaces from the left side of a text ("string") Variable:

    Andy Doodie

Changes to

Andy Doodie

Used with Text ("string") Variables

Variables

```
A = " Nobody home."
MsgBox LTrim(A)
```

Results in

```
Nobody home.
```

OR (To assign the results to a text Variable):

```
X = LTrim(A)
Print X
```

Results in

```
Nobody home.
```

Uses

- Clean up user input.

  You can never tell what the user might do. When typing in a lot of data, the user might accidentally hit the Tab key or enter some extra spaces. If your program is going to alphabetize a list and one of the items has a space as its first character, that item will appear before the *A*'s as the first item in the list. To prevent this, you want to clean up any items that you are about to alphabetize (or are going to compare, such as If A < B).

Use LTrim to make sure that you are comparing apples to apples and not dealing with some accidental leading spaces. And, while you're at it, you might as well eliminate random capitalization with the LCase Function, too. (For an alternative to LCase, see "StrComp.")

- Clean up numbers translated by Str. You can transform a number into a text ("string") Variable (into printable digits rather than a pure number) by using Str(X). However, Str inserts an extra space in front of a number to provide room for a minus sign. LTrim is a way of getting rid of this extra space. (See the example below.)
- When reading text files, you can remove paragraph indentations, centering, or other formatting that involves using space characters to achieve a visual effect.

Cautions LTrim works the same with either Variable-length or fixed-length text ("string") Variables. (See "Variables.")

Example When you transform a positive number into a text ("string") Variable, VBScript inserts an extra space to allow for a possible minus (–) sign. This has mystified programmers for a generation, but that's what happens. This space is inserted so that a column of numbers would line up when displayed on screen or printed. This vertical, columnar formatting only works if you add a space to positive numbers and leave negative numbers with their minus (–) sign intact.

Contemporary computers no longer format columns, though, by counting character spaces. The characters now most commonly used are *proportional* (the characters vary in width), so it is useless to use characters as a way of formatting displayed text. For vertical formatting, use Tables.

Nonetheless, Str still adds a space character to the left of a positive number. LTrim gets rid of the space. Here's an example:

```
x = 144
   MsgBox x
y = Str(x)
   MsgBox y
```

```
   MsgBox LTrim(y)
x = -144
   MsgBox x
y = Str(x)
   MsgBox y
   MsgBox LTrim(y)
```

Results in

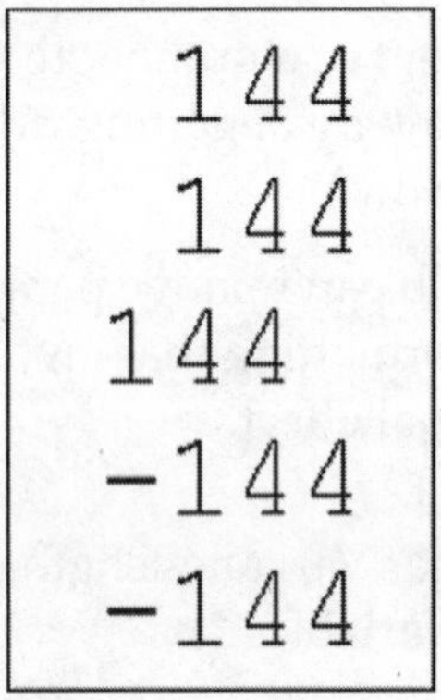

```
  144
  144
144
 -144
 -144
```

Figure L-9: Note that LTrim does not remove symbols like the minus sign.

See also LSet, RSet, RTrim

MAP

HTML

Description With the MAP command, you can assign links to areas within a graphic image (or use those areas as triggers to play sounds, run movies, and stage other events). The user sees these areas—perhaps pictures of various bestselling novels—displayed within a single graphic. The user can click on any of the books to get additional information about that particular novel.

If all your hypertext is simply unrelieved *text*, it's quite boring after a while. Give the user a more intuitive and more attractive alternative now and then—graphic links. However, there's an easier way than using this MAP command to achieve the worthwhile goal of providing visually engaging links. Instead of wrestling with the coordinates required by the MAP and AREA commands to describe the location of each link within the graphic image, consider instead using the new ActiveX HotSpot Control along with the ActiveX Image Control (see "HotSpot").

You've seen *text* links—you click on some words and you're sent to another location within the currently displayed document, or to another Web site altogether. Text links are usually displayed in a different color and also underlined. (See "A.") But a more advanced kind of link is graphic—a picture of a set of buttons, a photo of a group of magazines, a map of a city, whatever. The user clicks on an *area* within this graphic, on a particular magazine, for example, and is taken to the target of the link, the home page for that magazine. The effect is the same as clicking on a text link, but visual links look better on a page than plain text.

Variables **NAME:** Specifies the name of the map. After you give your map a name, you then refer back to it later when using the IMG command.

```
<MAP NAME="mymap">
```

AREA: Used within the <MAP> and </MAP> commands to specify the coordinates, shape, and target of a "hot zone" that can be clicked by the user within the image. This example says: Display the Web page called "100.HTM" if the user clicks within a rectangle that starts in the upper left of the graphic and extends 48 pixels over to the right and 32 pixels down from the top. The graphic is located in the same directory as the .HTM file that displays the original page. The graphic is named "BTNS.JPG" and has no border. You can use multiple AREA statements to define multiple hotspots within the image.

```
<MAP NAME="mymap">
<AREA SHAPE="RECT" COORDS="0, 0, 48, 32" HREF="100.htm">
</MAP>
<IMG BORDER=0 SRC="btns.jpg" USEMAP="#mymap">
```

M

COORDS: Define the coordinates of a shape within a graphic image, a shape that when clicked triggers the HREF action.

```
<AREA SHwAPE="RECT" COORDS="50, 25, 150, 125" HREF="http://
www.noa.com">
```

Figuring Out Coordinates

Coordinates are expressed in pixels, those small dots you can see if you get up close to a TV set. It depends on the resolution of the monitor, but 50 pixels might be about half an inch. In any case, when you want to describe the position of a rectangle, you provide the coordinate positions for the upper left and lower right of the rectangle. In other words, you give the upper left horizontal distance (from the left edge of the image), and vertical distance down (from the top of the image) and then you give the lower right horizontal and vertical locations. Therefore, in our example above, COORDS="50, 25, 150, 125" means that this hotspot (the area within the graphic that reacts to a user-click) is a rectangle that starts 50 pixels over from the left of the graphic and 25 pixels down from the top of the graphic. Furthermore, the rectangle is 100 twips wide and 100 twips high. So, using those four coordinates (X1,Y1,X2,Y2) we are able to provide both the location of the rectangle within the graphic and the size of the rectangle.

The COORDS command can have the following arguments: RECT or RECTANGLE; CIRC or CIRCLE; POLY or POLYGON. Note that when you want to define a circular hotspot with the CIRC or CIRCLE commands, you only have to provide three coordinates: the x (horizontal) and y (vertical) position of the circle's center (within the larger image) and the radius of the circle (the distance from the center of the circle to its outer edge). The POLY or POLYGON can have three or more pairs of coordinates, depending on how many sides your polygon shape has.

HREF: Specifies the URL (the address of the Web page file) that should be loaded if the user clicks on the defined hotspot. This example sends the user to http://www.noa.com, just as if the user had typed that address into the "Address:" text box in their browser and then pressed the Enter key.

```
HREF="http://www.noa.com"
```

If you define a hotspot region but use the NOHREF command instead of HREF, nothing will happen when the user clicks within that zone:

```
<AREA SHAPE="RECT" COORDS="0, 25, 150, 25" NOHREF>
```

Tip

You can do more with HREF than merely link to other documents or other locations on the Internet. For one thing, you can link to other locations within the current document (see the entry for "A"). What's more, you can even play a tune instead of traveling to another location:

```
<AREA SHAPE="RECT" COORDS="0, 0, 48, 32" →
HREF="radiogag.mid">
```

Here we've given a midi music file, radiogag, *as the target of our link. We just provided the name of this .MID file because it is located in the same subdirectory as our document's .HTM file. If it were in another location, we'd have to provide a path to the .MID file.*

M

TARGET: Allows you to specify where the link will be displayed. If you specify TARGET=_blank, then a new browser window will be spawned (you'll have two frames of Internet Explorer on your desktop—one displaying the image with the hotspot you clicked and the new browser displaying the HREF you specified):

```
<AREA TARGET=_blank SHAPE="RECT" COORDS="50, 25, 150, 125"
HREF="http://www.noa.com">
```

- *Parent* loads the HREF into the parent of the document that contains your link (your hotspot).
- *Self* loads the HREF into the same window that contains your link (your hotspot).
- *Top* forces the HREF to take up the entire space of the window.

You can also name a window by putting it in quotes:

```
TARGET="mywindow"
```

M

ALT: Provides a text description for people whose browsers don't display graphics:

```
<AREA SHAPE=CIRCLE COORDS="50,50,40" HREF="apple.html"
ALT="Granny Smith Apples">
```

Uses MAP provides the name for the list of "hotspots" that the user can click on in an image. This is a way of creating links to other locations on the Internet, other locations within the current document, or even just playing a music file (see HREF under Variables below).

Essentially, the MAP command can save you time, and also can look better than one alternative you might consider: a set of *framed* small images used as links. Instead of having to put 18 different graphics onto a page to create the links shown in Figure M-1, we can map each link by describing its boundaries within the one large graphic. But even if you did put 18 different link graphics onto the page, each would be surrounded by a frame (as shown in Figure M-2)—so you wouldn't end up with the continuous graphic shown in Figure M-1.

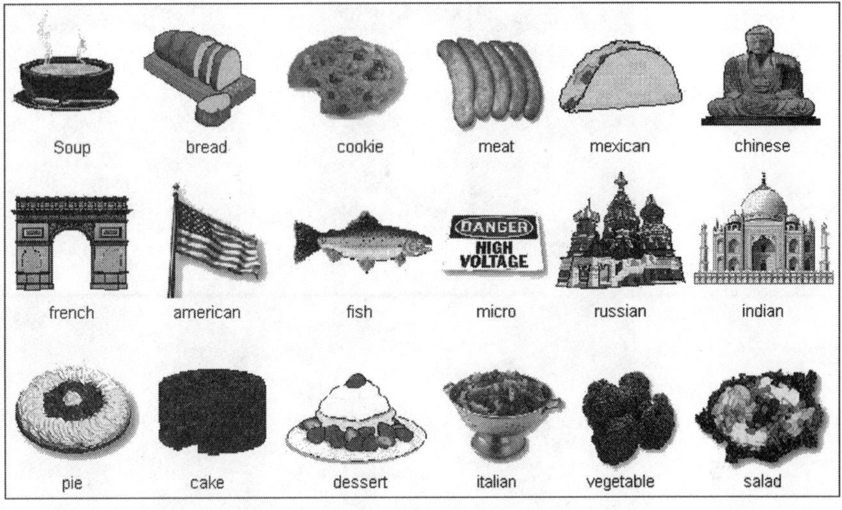

Figure M-1: It's easier to create this as a single graphic image (with 18 areas) than to design this page as 18 separate graphic images.

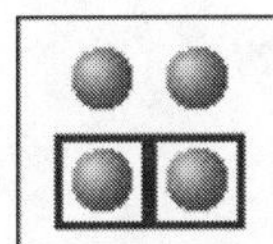

Figure M-2: When contiguous images are used as links, there are always those frames (bottom) separating the images visually.

Cautions You can use as many AREA commands as you want. If two areas overlap, the one that appears first in the map definition takes precedence. Likewise, you can provide the same HREF for more than one AREA command. If part of your graphic image isn't described by any coordinates in any of the AREA commands, when the user clicks on that dead area nothing happens.

Some images, because they are continuous, like the one shown in Figure M-3, cannot be separated into individual graphics, then butted together to simulate a single image with several links.

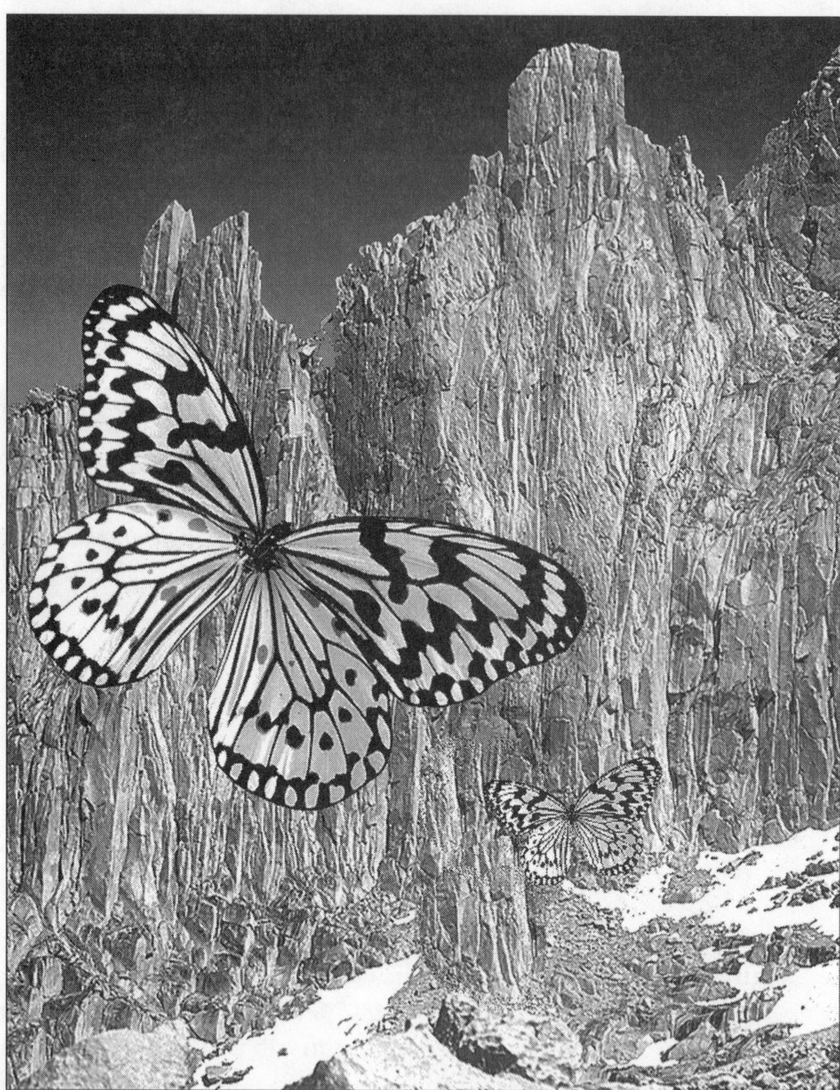

Figure M-3: It would be impossible to cut this image into pieces, then create links for each piece.

M

You *can* butt images up against each other on a page, by merely referencing them right after each other. The following programming creates the two balls shown on the top in Figure M-2.

```
<IMG SRC="ball.JPG"><IMG SRC="ball.JPG">
```

However, these aren't links. If the user clicks on them, nothing happens. To create links under an image, you must use the A command:

```
<A HREF="keypress.htm"><IMG SRC="ball.JPG"><IMG
SRC="ball.JPG"></A>
```

(For more on this, see the entry for "A.") Notice, however, that even though these two balls are butted up against each other, they will be *framed* instead of continuous (see the bottom of Figure M-2). HTML adds this border whenever an individual image is used as a link.

If you leave out the SHAPE Variable, RECT is assumed.

Example This is an example of a "client-side" map. The link is not resolved and handled by the server (the originating computer that stores the current document). The link is analyzed and acted on inside the user's computer when he or she views this page, then clicks on our image. First we created the set of four buttons shown in Figure M-4:

Figure M-4: Each button is 49x32 pixels; when the user clicks on a button, a page unique to that button is loaded into the browser.

Then we saved it as BTNS.JPG *in the same subdirectory that holds the .HTM file for the entire page*. Note that this image, and the .HTM files that we're going to link to portions within the image, all must either include their entire path or be located in the subdirectory where the original .HTM file is located.

We loaded this page into Internet Explorer and, moving the mouse pointer over the buttons on the image, we were able to figure out the coordinates (look at Figure M-5 and see how the .HTM file link is displayed in the status bar as you move the mouse pointer):

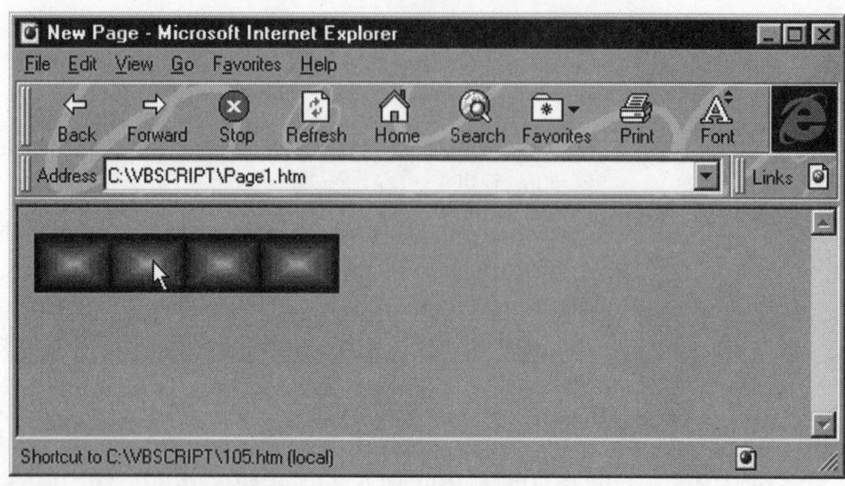

Figure M-5: As you move the mouse pointer, you can see in the status bar at the bottom which link will be activated if you click.

```
<HTML>
<HEAD>
<TITLE>ImageMapping</TITLE>
</HEAD>
<BODY>

<MAP NAME="mymap">
<AREA SHAPE="RECT" COORDS="0, 0, 48, 32" HREF="100.htm">
<AREA SHAPE="RECT" COORDS="49, 0, 99, 32" HREF=105.htm>
<AREA SHAPE="RECT" COORDS="100, 0, 149, 32" HREF="101.htm">
<AREA SHAPE="RECT" COORDS="150, 0, 199, 32" HREF="102.htm">
</MAP>

<IMG BORDER=0 SRC="btns.jpg" USEMAP="#mymap">
</BODY>
</HTML>
```

See also HotSpot, Area

M

Marquee

HTML

Description Currently Marquee is one of the few ways to add animation to an Internet document. It creates a horizontally scrolling message—like the famous news display at Times Square. For a far more flexible approach to this technique, see the entry for "Marquee ActiveX Control."

Variables **ALIGN=TOP, MIDDLE, or BOTTOM:** This describes how the text *outside* the marquee on your page should be formatted.

BEHAVIOR=SCROLL, SLIDE, or ALTERNATE: The default is SCROLL, which starts the text entirely off to the left or right side, then scrolls the text all the way off the opposite side before repeating. SLIDE starts like SCROLL, but the text stops once it reaches the opposite side. ALTERNATE moves the text back and forth between each side.

BGCOLOR=FF0000 (or RED): This specifies the background color of the marquee. You can specify the background color, using hexadecimal numbers (see "Hex"). Essentially, the paired numbers specify the red, green, and blue content of the color. For example, if you wanted pure red, you would use FF0000; green is 00FF00; blue is 0000FF. You can also use a set of ordinary English words, like RED, instead of the hex number. The following words are recognized by most browsers: black, white, green, maroon, olive, navy, purple, gray, red, yellow, blue, teal, lime, aqua, fuchsia, silver.

M

Tip

You can define colors with either hexadecimal numbers or ordinary English words like green *or* lime. *For a complete list of all 140 English word colors you can use—including many rare colors like powderblue, seashell, and indigo—see "Many New Colors" in the entry on "BGCOLOR." For an explanation of hexadecimal, see "Hex Numbers for the Color Command" in the entry on "BODY."*

DIRECTION=LEFT or RIGHT: Defaults to LEFT, but you can make the message come in from the right side if you wish.

HEIGHT=55 or HEIGHT= 20%: You can describe the vertical size of the marquee by either specifying pixels (dots on a TV screen, see "Area") or use the percent symbol to specify the height as a percentage of the total height of the screen.

HSPACE=15: How much "blank" space should be around the left and right sides of the marquee (outside it) as a margin. The measurement is in pixels. HSPACE=15 means that no outside text will be displayed on either side of the marquee inside a 15-pixel border. VSPACE specifies the margin around the top and bottom (vertical space).

LOOP=22 or LOOP=INFINITE: How many times the animation should complete a cycle. INFINITE is the default. If you provide a number, the animation will stop after that number of cycles.

SCROLLAMOUNT=14: This determines how far the text will "jump" within the marquee each time it is redrawn. A smaller number will produce smoother animation.

SCROLLDELAY= 4: This determines how much time (in milliseconds) elapses between each redraw of the marquee text.

VSPACE=12: See "HSPACE" above.

WIDTH=45 or WIDTH = 60%: See "HEIGHT" above.

Uses Make your pages come to life.

Example

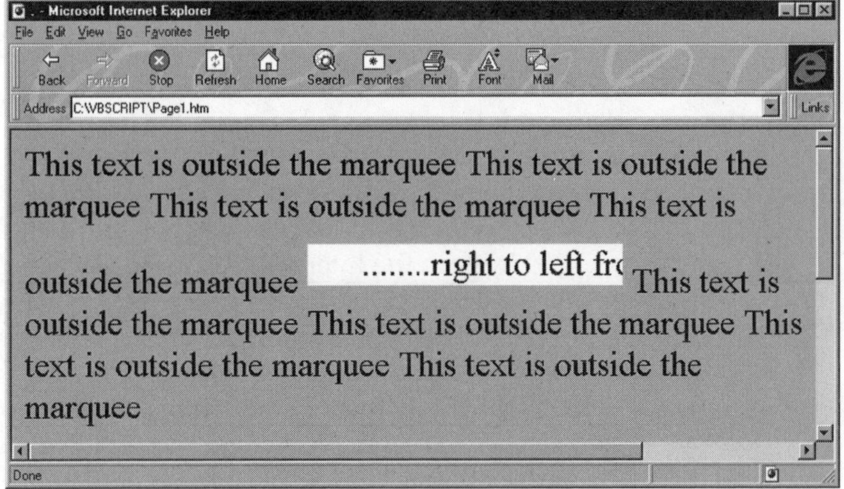

Figure M-6: The text in this marquee will continuously scroll from left to right.

```
<HTML>
<FONT SIZE=+3>
This text is outside the marquee This text is outside the →
marquee
This text is outside the marquee This text is outside the →
marquee
<MARQUEE BGCOLOR=BLUE DIRECTION=RIGHT WIDTH=40%
BEHAVIOR=SCROLL
SCROLLAMOUNT=20 SCROLLDELAY=300 ALIGN=BOTTOM HEIGHT=35
VSPACE=15>
........right to left from move this Watch.....</MARQUEE> →
This text is outside the marquee This text is outside the →
marquee
This text is outside the marquee This text is outside the →
marquee
</HTML>
```

We've used most of the optional Variables that you can use with the Marquee command in this example. Note, however, that the ALIGN command does the best it can. The alignment (of the text to the right and left of the marquee) should be at the bottom but is actually a bit high.

Marquee

ACTIVEX CONTROL

Description Within this Control, any .HTM file can be scrolled horizontally or vertically.

You can scroll a URL (a separate .HTM file located on the same subdirectory as the .HTM file that contains the Marquee Property or an address on the Internet). Also, you can scroll a graphic, or a .JPG or .GIF file. At this time, .BMP files will not work.

In addition, there is a whole set of Properties you can adjust to suit your needs. See Variables below.

Note that at the time of this writing, clicking on the icon next to the Marquee Object in the ActiveX Control Pad crashes the Control Pad. Until this is fixed, change Properties by adjusting them in the .HTM source code, as illustrated in the example below.

Variables At the time of this writing, clicking on the icon next to the Marquee Object in the ActiveX Control Pad crashes the Control Pad. So you can't adjust a Marquee's Properties with the Properties Window. Instead, we'll use the PARAM list to specify Properties, as illustrated in the example below.

The Marquee Control has a set of Properties, many of which are unique to it:

M

Properties

Note that for most ActiveX Control Properties, Methods, and Events, we refer you to the "Properties," "Methods," and "Events" entries in this book. However, the Marquee Control has so many elements unique to it, we're describing them here. For one thing, instead of the Click or OnClick Events, the Marquee, for some reason, calls this same Event OnLMouseClick.

The LoopsX and LoopsY Properties determine how many times the target URL (or .GIF or .JPG file) is completely scrolled, in both the X (horizontal) and Y (vertical) directions. If you set it to 5, the user will see the contents of the displayed URL or graphic five times. If you leave it set at -1, the default, scrolling, will be continuous.

The ScrollDelay Property (along with the ScrollPixelsX and ScrollPixelsY Properties) determines the speed of the scrolling. ScrollDelay specifies how long the browser will wait between each scroll movement (the distance of this movement is determined by the ScrollPixelsX and ScrollPixelsY Properties). The delay is expressed in milliseconds (1000ths of a second) and defaults to 100 (1/10th of a second).

ScrollPixelsX and ScrollPixelsY determine how many pixels the URL (or .GIF or .JPG file) will traverse within each move (the delay between moves specified by the ScrollDelay Property). The default is 75 pixels for X and zero for Y. Therefore, if you don't adjust these Properties, the scrolling will be horizontal only.

You provide the URL (or .GIF or .JPG file) that you want scrolled with the szURL Property. Note that this is called CurrentURL in the Properties Window, but we're not using that approach to adjusting Properties (see the example below). The URL you provide can be a path on a server's (or if you're just testing things, your local) hard drive:

```
<PARAM NAME="szURL" VALUE="c:\vbscript\page2.htm">
```


OR, you can provide a site address:

```
<PARAM NAME="szURL" VALUE="http://www.blighter.edu">
```

ScrollStyleX and ScrollStyleY can be set to Bounce or Circular (the default). *Circular* scrolls the target .HTM file (the URL or .GIF or .JPG file) until it reaches the end of the contents of that file, then starts over again from the beginning. *Bounce,* when it reaches the end, reverses direction. In other words, it shows the top, then middle, then end of the target .HTM page, then shows the end, middle, top, middle, end, middle, and so on. This example would cause the .HTM to reverse back and forth, on the Y axis (vertically):

```
<PARAM NAME="ScrollStyleY" VALUE="Bounce">
```

ScrollStyleX governs the movement horizontally (see ScrollPixelsX and ScrollPixelsY).

The WhiteSpace Property defines how much blank (white) space will appear between scrolling URLs (or .GIF or .JPG files). In other words, if you want some blank space to appear before the next appearance of your URL, change this Property from its default of 0. The space is measured in pixels.

You can display your .HTM or graphic file's contents larger or smaller than normal. The Zoom Property reduces or expands your target at larger- or smaller-than-life size. It's a percent. It defaults to 100, but if you set it to 50, things will appear half as big. And 300 will make them three times larger than usual.

The WidthOfPage Property should really be called *HorizontalWhiteSpace*. It does the same thing as the WhiteSpace Property but for the horizontal area of the Marquee's window. WidthOfPage defines how wide a blank white space will be between horizontally scrolling URL's or graphics files. If you're using only vertical scrolling (because you've set the ScrollPixelsX Property to zero and have provided some positive number, like 23, to the ScrollPixelsX Property), a blank white area will appear on the right side of the Marquee window. The WidthOfPage Property defaults to 640.

Methods

The AboutBox method shows the About dialog box to the user.

You can stop and start the scrolling with the Pause and Resume Methods:

```
<SCRIPT LANGUAGE="VBScript">
<!--
Sub CommandButton1_Click()
call Marquee1.Pause()
end sub
-->
</SCRIPT>
```

The Zoom Method allows you to shrink or blow up the data. See the example below.

There is a set of four Methods that manage a URL list. Presumably you'll be allowed to request a set of more than one URL to be scrolled in sequence; however, at the time of this writing, you can list only a single szURL. The InsertURL Method allows you to specify a location within the URL list to insert a new URL. DeleteURL allows you to remove a URL from the list. QueryURL provides you with a text Variable containing the URL at a particular index location within the URL list. QueryURLCount tells you how many URLs are in the list. Note that at the time of this writing, only QueryURLCount and DeleteURL are listed in the Microsoft ActiveX Control Pad Script Wizard when you try to program a Marquee Control. What's more, neither of those Methods work within the Wizard—you get an error message. There's also a DrawImmediately Property that can be used to determine whether or not you want the URLs in your list to be scrolled one after the other. This Property is not working at this time either.

Events

The OnStartOfImage Event is triggered immediately before the URL (or .GIF or .JPG file) starts scrolling (also see OnScroll below). The OnEndOfImage Event is triggered immediately after the URL has completely scrolled:

```
Sub Marquee1_OnEndOfImage(HorizontalOrVertical)

end sub
```

M

The *HorizontalOrVertical* Variable is supposed to return an "H" when any horizontal scrolling ends and a "V" when any vertical scrolling ends (they might not end at the same time). However, these Events aren't working at the time of this writing.

The OnBounce Event is triggered when the URL bounces (see ScrollStyleX above). It won't be triggered unless one of the ScrollStyle Properties is set to "bounce." There's a returned Variable, *SideBouncedOff*, that tells you which of four possible sides the URL has bounced off (an "L" means the bounce was off the left side; "R" means right; "T" means top; and "B" means bottom).

The OnStartOfImage Event is triggered just before a URL or graphic file is about to scroll *for the first time*. Thereafter, OnStartOfImage is not triggered, but the OnScroll Event is triggered. In other words, the OnScroll Event triggers each time the URL is about to repeat itself (it isn't triggered the first time the URL scrolls; nor is it triggered by any bounces—see the ScrollStyle Property).

```
Sub Marquee1_OnScroll(HorizontalOrVertical)
If HorizontalOrVertical = "H" then
  Label1.Caption = "Horizontal Scroll"
Else
  Label1.Caption = "Vertical Scroll"
end sub
```

The OnLMouseClick Event is identical to the Click or OnClick Events for other ActiveX Controls. In other words, OnLMouseClick is triggered when the user left-clicks the mouse.

Uses

- Provide animation on an otherwise static page.
- Draw attention to some information you want the reader to see.
- Offer updated information by changing the target .HTM file, without having to change the container .HTM file.

Cautions For reasons best left unimagined, the designers of the Marquee Control decided to muddy the VBScript waters by renaming the Click Event. For several years, most Visual Basic Controls have had a Click Event (the user clicks the left mouse button and that triggers the Click Event).

A few VBS and HTML objects have an OnClick Event (it's the same as the Click Event). Now, the Marquee Control adds the OnLMouseClick Event (with no corresponding OnRMouseClick Event).

At the time of this writing, several of the Events and Methods for the Marquee Control are not yet working. See the above descriptions.

Attempting to click on the icon next to the Marquee Object in the ActiveX Control Pad crashes the Control Pad. Until this is fixed, change Properties by adjusting them in the .HTM source code, as illustrated in the example below. Or you can use the Tools | Script Wizard option to create scripts that will change Properties dynamically while your document is being viewed by the user.

Example

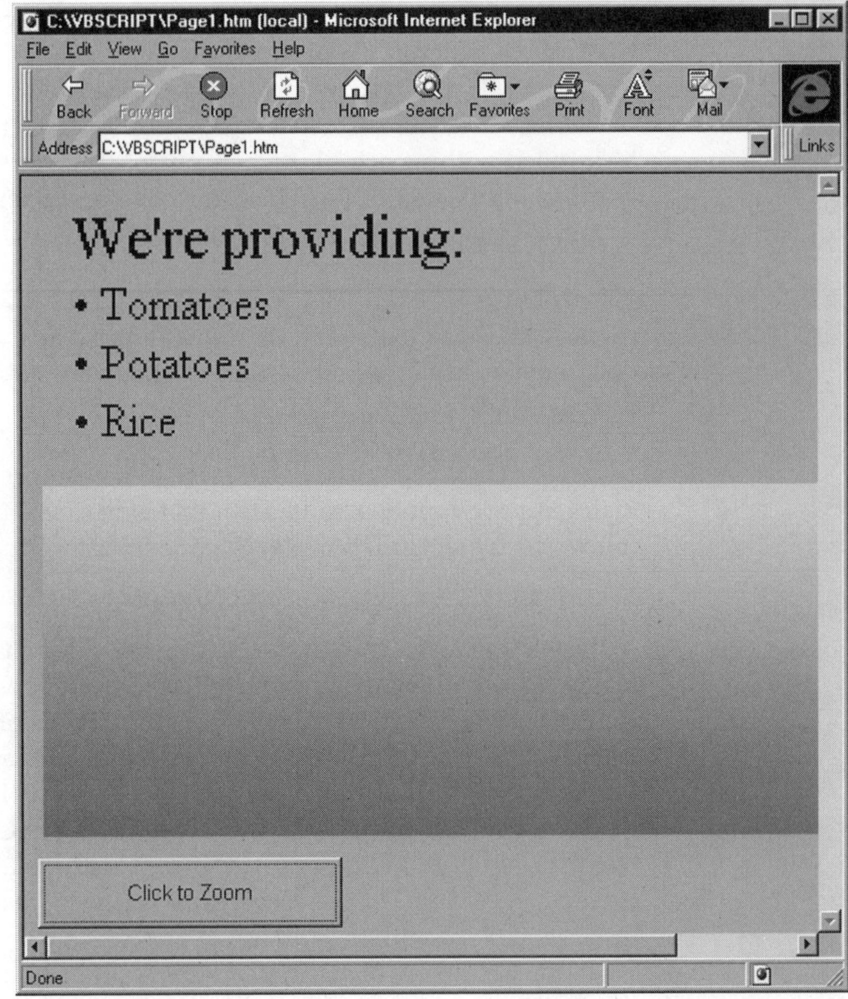

Figure M-7: When the user clicks on our Command Button, the upper Marquee freezes and also zooms by 200%, as you can see here. The lower Marquee displays a .JPG gradient graphic.

For this example, put two Marquee Controls on your document. Start the Microsoft ActiveX Control Pad and click on the Edit | Insert ActiveX Control menu option. Scroll the list of available Controls until you find "Microsoft IE3.0 Marquee Control." Click on it to insert it into your page. It will, by default, be named

Marquee1. Repeat the above steps to insert a second Marquee Control. Then, look in that same menu for a "Microsoft Forms 20 Command Button" and insert that, too, onto your page.

Define two URLs (or .GIF or .JPG graphic files) that you want to be scrolled within each Marquee Control. Type in the URL or graphic in this way, within the Control's parameter list:

```
<PARAM NAME="szURL" VALUE="myfile.htm">
```

Use the above example if you have an .HTM file named myfile.htm that's located in the same directory as your document's .HMM file. Otherwise, you have to provide the complete path on your hard drive, like this:

```
<PARAM NAME="szURL" VALUE="c:\vbscript\myfile.htm">
```

OR, if you want to scroll a URL that exists on the Internet, follow the usual HTTP://WWW convention:

```
<PARAM NAME="szURL" VALUE="http://www.microsoft.com">
```

M

We want to allow the user to click on the Command Button to toggle Marquee1. When first clicked, the scrolling will stop (we'll trigger Marquee1's pause Event) and the contents of Marquee1 will be blown up to twice normal size (by setting the Marquee's Zoom Property to 200). First we have to create a Variable that exists *outside* the Sub…End Sub structure (but still within the <SCRIPT>…</ SCRIPT> structure. This permits the Variable to retain its contents even when the Sub isn't actively running (for more on this, see the discussion of *scope* in the entry on "Variables.")

So, the first order of business in our script is to define a Variable that will switch back and forth between two states, like a light switch. We'll call it Toggle:

```
Dim toggle
```

That done, we write the Sub that reacts to user-clicks on the Command Button. When the Click Event is triggered, we change the contents of the Toggle Variable by using the Not command:

```
toggle = not toggle
```

The Not command has the effect of switching a Variable between -1 (or "True") and 0 ("False"). A Not (-1) becomes 0 and a Not (0) becomes a -1. Therefore, the effect is to go back and forth between these two values.

We can test the value currently in the toggle Variable by asking:

```
If toggle
```

That's shorthand for:

```
If toggle = -1
```

which has the same effect. If toggle is "True" then we pause and zoom Marquee1. If toggle is otherwise (Else) we *Resume* the Marquee's scrolling and restore it to the default, normal-size zoom (Marquee1.Zoom = 100).

```
<HTML>
<BODY>
<BR>
<OBJECT ID="Marqueel" WIDTH=650 HEIGHT=240 align=CENTER
BORDER=1 HSPACE=5
  CLASSID="CLSID:1A4DA620-6217-11CF-BE62-0080C72EDD2D">
   <PARAM NAME="WhiteSpace" VALUE="42">
   <PARAM NAME="szURL" VALUE="page2.htm">
   <PARAM NAME="_ExtentX" VALUE="124">
   <PARAM NAME="_ExtentY" VALUE="125">
   <PARAM NAME="Zoom" VALUE="100">
   <PARAM NAME="ScrollPixelsX" VALUE="0">
   <PARAM NAME="ScrollPixelsY" VALUE="14">
   <PARAM NAME="WidthOfPage" VALUE="300">
 </OBJECT>

<OBJECT ID="Marquee2" WIDTH=650 HEIGHT=240 align=CENTER
BORDER=1 HSPACE=5
  CLASSID="CLSID:1A4DA620-6217-11CF-BE62-0080C72EDD2D">
   <PARAM NAME="szURL" VALUE="gradi.jpg">
   <PARAM NAME="_ExtentX" VALUE="124">
   <PARAM NAME="_ExtentY" VALUE="125">
   <PARAM NAME="Zoom" VALUE="100">
```

```
    <PARAM NAME="ScrollPixelsX" VALUE="0">
    <PARAM NAME="ScrollPixelsY" VALUE="24">
   </OBJECT>

<SCRIPT LANGUAGE="VBScript">
<!--

dim toggle

Sub CommandButton1_Click()
toggle = not toggle
if toggle then
call Marquee1.Pause()
Marquee1.Zoom = 200
else
call Marquee1.Resume()
Marquee1.Zoom = 100
end if
end sub
-->

</SCRIPT>
<BR><BR>
<OBJECT ID="CommandButton1" WIDTH=215 HEIGHT=48
   CLASSID="CLSID:D7053240-CE69-11CD-A777-00DD01143C57">
    <PARAM NAME="Caption" VALUE="Click to Zoom">
    <PARAM NAME="Size" VALUE="5689;1270">
    <PARAM NAME="FontName" VALUE="Arial">
    <PARAM NAME="FontHeight" VALUE="220">
    <PARAM NAME="FontCharSet" VALUE="0">
    <PARAM NAME="FontPitchAndFamily" VALUE="2">
    <PARAM NAME="ParagraphAlign" VALUE="3">
    <PARAM NAME="FontWeight" VALUE="0">
   </OBJECT>

</BODY>
</HTML>
```

See also Marquee (HTML)

M

MatchEntry, MatchFound, MatchRequired

ACTIVEX

Description These Properties work with the ComboBox Control and determine what happens when the box has the focus and the user types in some characters. Does the list automatically scroll to the "S" section if the user types an *S*? Has the user typed in a word that precisely matches one of the items in the list? The MatchEntry Property also works with ListBoxes.

See Properties

Max

ACTIVEX

Description Max is the position at the far right of a Horizontal ScrollBar Control or the position at the bottom of a Vertical ScrollBar Control. For a SpinButton, Max is the highest possible value.

See Properties

MaxLength

ACTIVEX AND HTML

Description MaxLength is an attribute of the HTML INPUT command (with TYPE=TEXT or TYPE=PASSWORD). MaxLength is also a Property of the ActiveX TextBox and ComboBox Controls. In all cases, you can assign a number to MaxLength and thereby limit the number of characters that the user is permitted to type into the object.

See Properties

MENU

HTML

Description This is yet another HTML formatting style that displays a list. See LI for alternatives. The MENU style (as distinct from the DIR style) is intended for displaying short items (just brief phrases or individual words).

Used with ***Can be enclosed by***

<BANNER>, <BODY>, <BODYTEXT>, <DD>, <DIV>, <FIGTEXT>, <FN>, <FORM>, <LI>, <NOTE>, <TD>, <TH>

Can enclose

<LI>

Uses Display a list for the user.

Example

Which city do you want to visit?
Tucson
Boulder
Boston
New York

Figure M-8: Use the MENU style for a list of short items.

```
<HTML>
<BODY BGCOLOR=WHITE>
<MENU>
<LH>Which city do you want to visit?</LH>
<BR>
<LI><A HREF="tucson.htm">Tucson</A>
<LI><A HREF="boulder.htm">Boulder</A>
<LI><A HREF="boston.htm">Boston</A>
<LI><A HREF="newyork.htm">New York</A>
</MENU>
</HTML>
```

See also LI, DIR, OL, UL, DD, DL, DT

M

Message Box

VBSCRIPT FUNCTION

See MsgBox

Methods

ACTIVEX

Description Some ActiveX Controls have Methods—things that the Control can *do*. Examples include Clear and Add. If you Clear a ListBox, all the entries in the box are removed and it's empty. If you Add to a TabStrip Control, a new tab appears.

(There are three possible elements of a Control: Properties, Events, and Methods. Properties are *qualities* like width or color. Events are things that can happen *to* a Control, such as Click or DblClick. Elsewhere in this book you'll find extensive descriptions of all Properties and Events for all the common ActiveX Controls. See "Properties" and "Events.")

There are many more Events and Properties than there are Methods. For example, there are over 130 Properties, but only around 32 Methods. We can't be precise because at the time of this writing, Properties, Events, and Methods are being added and subtracted as VBScript stabilizes.

Methods are invoked by separating the Control (or object) and the Method with a (.) period. For example, put a ListBox and a Command Button on an HTML document, or on an ActiveX Layout Control. Then type in the following script:

```
<SCRIPT LANGUAGE="VBScript">
<!--
for i = 1 to 23
listbox1.additem " This Item is " & i
next

Sub CommandButton1_Click
  ListBox1.Clear
end sub
-->
</SCRIPT>
```

M

When you run this script, the ListBox fills with 23 entries. However, when you click on the Command Button, the Clear Method of the ListBox is triggered. It causes the ListBox to empty and, if there was a ScrollBar on the ListBox, it disappears as well. The Clear Method has taken effect.

Add

This Method is used in two ways. It can add new Controls dynamically (while a script is running) to a Layout, or it can add new tabs to a TabStrip Control.

The companion Method, Remove, gets rid of a member of a collection (like a tab from the Tabs collection) or Control added dynamically.

To add tabs, you must resort to using the rather strange command Set. Set is used to assign something to an object or a collection of objects. To adjust the number of tabs in a TabStrip, you must deal with the "Tabs collection"—the set of tab objects that, collectively, exist on a TabStrip. The proper syntax for adding tabs is:

```
for i = 1 to 5
Set TabStrip1.Tabs = TabStrip1.Add
next
```

TabStrip1.Tabs means: the Tabs collection of the TabStrip Control named TabStrip1. Taken *together* the entity TabStrip1.Tabs is an *object.* To that object, we are adding five new entities. Always remember that a collection of objects (like a stamp collection) can, itself, be viewed as an object (the stamp album, for instance, is an object—containing all the individual stamp objects). The reason you must remember this convoluted way of thinking is that "object-oriented-programming" is currently a major influence on computer programmers and the way they design computer languages like VBScript. In practical terms, most people just memorize the various syntaxes. The TabStrip1.Tabs = TabStrip1.Add syntax isn't very meaningful really—it's hard to parse, hard to translate into sensible English, and hard even to explain in terms of what's happening. What's more, the syntax for similar object manipulations differs from command to command in the language.

If you don't specify the additional optional parameters when using Add with a TabStrip, parameters will be generated automatically for you by VBScript. The Name and Caption Properties of each tab will be identical: Tab3, Tab4, and so on (Tab1 and Tab2 are automatically there by default on a TabStrip Control and don't need to be Added).

Here's the full syntax of the Add command for a TabStrip Control:

```
Set TabStrip1.Tabs = TabStrip1.Add (Name, Caption, Index)
```

The *Name* parameter is an additional optional way to reference an individual tab in the Tabs collection. Each tab has its index (its location within the tabs Array for that TabStrip). However, you can also reference a tab by a name if you wish:

```
TabStrip1.Tabs(2).Caption = "I'm Third"
TabStrip1.Tabs(Tab3).Caption = "I'm Third"
```

Recall that most Arrays (a collection is a kind of Array) in computer programming begin with a zeroth item. Therefore, the tab with an index of 0 will be given a caption of Tab1 (and a name of Tab1) unless you change the name or caption. Changing the Index Property changes the tab's position within the Tabs collection.

AddItem

Allows you to add a word or words (a text "string" Variable subtype) to a ListBox or ComboBox while your script is running.

Put a ListBox onto an ActiveX Layout. Then type in this script:

```
<SCRIPT LANGUAGE="VBScript">
<!--

For i = 1 to 3
ListBox1.AddItem "This is item " & i
Next

ListBox1.AddItem "Tracy", 2

-->
</SCRIPT>
```

Results in

```
This is item 1
This is item 2
Tracy
This is item 3
```

Note that by specifying 2 as the index, we insert "Tracy" into the third position. The items in a List or ComboBox are counted from 0 on up, so "This is item 1" has an index of 0. Also, if the index is greater than the box's ListCount Property, you'll generate an error. You'd be trying to insert a new item beyond the total number of existing items—an impossibility.

The formal syntax is:

```
ListBox1.AddItem Text, Index
```

The *Text* can be a text Variable or literal text (in quotes). Index is optional and if you leave it out, the item will be appended to whatever other items already exist within the Control. Surprisingly, the Text parameter, too, is optional. You can just create some blank, empty elements within the List or ComboBox if you want to:

M

```
for i = 1 to 3
ListBox1.AddItem "This is item " & i
next

for i = 1 to 8
ListBox1.AddItem
next
msgbox ListBox1.ListCount
```

Results in

```
11
```

However, the visible entries within the ListBox are merely as follows:

```
This is item 1
This is item 2
This is item 3
```

followed by a group of blanks. If the number of invisible items exceeds the height of the ListBox, a ScrollBar will automatically be added—even though it's not needed with these blank entries.

If you're working with a Multicolumn List or ComboBox, an entire new row is added when you use the Add Method. To add text to elements beyond the first column, you can use the List or Column Properties, specifying the row and column of the item. (See "Properties" elsewhere in this book.) Also, you can add many rows at a time by using the List Property of a List or ComboBox.

Also see RemoveItem below.

Clear

With a ListBox or ComboBox, the Clear Method removes all items, leaving the box blank and empty:

```
ListBox1.Clear
```

This ListBox's ListCount Property will also now be 0.

Copy

This is a Method of a TextBox or the user-input section of a ComboBox (the top section, where the user can type things in). It copies any *selected* contents to the clipboard. Once there, it can be put into other Controls, or otherwise made use of, with the Paste Method.

If you put two TextBoxes and a Command Button on a Layout then type something into TextBox1 and select a portion of that text by dragging the mouse over it to highlight it, this will move the selected text into TextBox2:

```
Sub CommandButton1_Click
TextBox1.Copy
TextBox2.Paste
End Sub
```

Of course, there's the more straightforward way to copy the entire contents of one TextBox to another:

```
TextBox2 = TextBox1
```

(We don't even have to use TextBox1.Text because .Text is the default Property of a TextBox.)

Cut

The Cut Method behaves like the Copy method described above, except the contents sent to the clipboard are deleted from the TextBox or ComboBox. The text to be cut must be selected:

```
TextBox1.Cut
```

DropDown

This Method displays the list in a ComboBox Control. Ordinarily the user clicks on the button at the top right of a ComboBox to drop the list. However, you can drop it within a script if you want to. This would allow you to provide a customized button for dropdown, or merely drop the list in response to something else that happened on the document making the list's visibility desirable.

```
ComboBox1.DropDown
```

GetFormat

This Method tells you if a particular format is being stored in the Data Object. However, at this time, the Data Object only permits text to be stored, so that's the only format.

The Data Object is similar to the clipboard—they're both way stations to allow you to move data between objects or Controls. Data on the clipboard, though, exists until the computer is turned off; data on the Data Object exists only while the current application is running. The clipboard can store pictures and text; at the present time, the Data Object can store only text. The clipboard can store a picture and a piece of text simultaneously, but as soon as a new picture or new piece of text are copied to the clipboard, the previous picture or text is replaced. The clipboard cannot handle drag-and-drop, but the Data Object can.

Move

The Move Method repositions or resizes a Control anywhere within an ActiveX Layout (see "Layout"). You can relocate objects by merely changing their Left and Top Properties. You can resize with the Height and Width Properties. Move merely combines any or all of these adjustments into a single command.

We'll put a Label 300 points (about 4 inches; there are 72 points to an inch) down from the top and over from the left of the layout:

```
<SCRIPT LANGUAGE="VBScript">
Label1.Move 300,300
</SCRIPT>
```

Move has five parameters: CommandButton1.Move Left, Top, Width, Height, Layout.

The Left and Top parameters are required; the rest are optional. The movement caused by the Move command is *absolute,* not *relative.* Move describes a particular location on the layout to which the Control will move. It does not describe how far to move from the current position of the Control.

The Layout parameter is either True or False (the default). If you make it true, the Layout Event is triggered in the Control's parent (the container of the Control).

Paste

See Copy

Remove

This Method is used in two ways. If you have added new Controls dynamically (while a script is running) to a Layout using the Add Method, you can get rid of any or all of these Controls with the Remove Method. The second use for Remove is to get rid of tabs on a TabStrip Control.

Note that the "Tabs Collection" object can be addressed two ways: by index number (starting with the zeroth index and working up), or by the *Name* Property, a text Variable. If you don't specify the additional optional parameters when using Add with a TabStrip, they'll be generated automatically for you by VBScript. The Name and Caption Properties of each tab will be identical: Tab3, Tab4, and so on (Tab1 and Tab2 are automatically there by default on a TabStrip Control and don't need to be Added).

Think of the Tabs Collection as an Array. You can reference it these two ways:

```
TabStrip1.Tabs.Remove(3)
```

M

OR

```
TabStrip1.Tabs.Remove(Tab2)
```

Notice that the positioning of items in a list of object names is often counter-intuitive. There are many situations where you put the parenthetic (index) number following the word *Tabs*:

```
TabStrip1.Tabs(2).Caption = "I'm Third"
```

However, you don't use that syntax with Remove. No, instead, you push the parenthetic index to the end of the phrase, following *Remove*:

```
TabStrip1.Tabs.Remove(2)
```

Confusing, right?

You also always have to remember that most Arrays in computer programming begin with a zeroth item. Therefore, the tab with an index of 0 will be given a caption of Tab1 (and a name of Tab1) unless you change the name or caption. Changing the Index Property changes the tab's position within the Tabs collection.

```
<SCRIPT LANGUAGE="VBScript">
<!--

Set TabStrip1.Tabs = TabStrip1.Add

Sub CommandButton1_Click()
  X = TabStrip1.Tabs.Count - 1
  TabStrip1.Tabs.Remove(X)
end sub

-->
</SCRIPT>
```

RemoveItem

This Method works with a ListBox or a ComboBox. It allows you to remove items from a box while a script is running. Put a ListBox and a Command Button on an HTML Layout. Then type in this script:

```
<SCRIPT LANGUAGE="VBScript">
For i = 1 to 8
  ListBox1.AddItem "This is item " & i
Next

Sub CommandButton1_Click
N = ListBox1.ListCount - 1
ListBox1.RemoveItem(N)
End Sub
</SCRIPT>
```

Each time the user clicks the CommandButton, the item at the bottom of the ListBox will be removed.

SetFocus

The SetFocus Method moves the focus onto a particular Control:

```
CheckBox1.SetFocus
```

M

See "TabIndex" in the entry on "Properties" for a detailed description of *focus*.

ZOrder

The ZOrder Method allows you to position a Control on the Z axis (depth). In other words, it determines which Controls appear on top of other Controls when those Controls overlap each other.

There are two possible arguments: 0 and 1. This moves the Control to the bottom of the ZOrder (underneath all other Controls on the layout):

```
CommandButton2.Zorder = 1
```

This moves the Control to the top of the ZOrder:

```
CommandButton2.Zorder = 0
```

The ZOrder Method cannot directly adjust a Control's order—putting it, say, third from the bottom of a pile. ZOrder can only put it on the top or the bottom of a pile of Controls. Adjust the ZOrder of several Controls several times, however, and you can arrange the pile in any fashion you want. For instance, in a pile of four objects, you could move the top object to the third position by first moving the third object, and then the second, to the top.

ZOrder is not like an index number or the Tab Property or other indices to groups of Controls. You cannot directly specify that a Control should assume the second position in a pile, though you can manipulate the ZOrders of the Controls in a pile until you get the arrangement you are after.

If you want to adjust the ZOrder while designing your document, click on the Format menu in the ActiveX Control Pad and choose Bring to Front, Send to Back, Move Forward, or Move Backward.

Mid

VBSCRIPT FUNCTION

Description Mid extracts a piece of text from a larger piece of text. For instance, Mid could pull *suite* out of *Meet me in the penthouse suite at seven.*

The *Left* command pulls out a piece of text from the left side of a larger body of text, but the extracted piece must start at the left side of the larger text. In the preceding example, Left could pull out *M, Meet, Meet me,* and so on, but the first letter of the extracted piece would have to be *M.* The Right command operates the same way as Left, but pulls pieces from the right side of the larger body of text.

Therefore, Mid is the most flexible of the three ways to extract words or phrases from larger bodies of text. The tradeoff is that you must supply Mid with two numbers: where within the larger text to start extracting and how many characters to extract. For Left and Right, you need only supply the number of characters, not the starting position.

A variation, the MidB Function, allows you to specify the Start and Length parameters in *bytes.* (Characters in VBScript are now expressed as 2-byte codes; see CHR.) Mid specifies Start and Length in *characters.*

Used with Text ("string") Variables

Variables

```
<HTML>

<SCRIPT LANGUAGE=VBS>

A = "This person, named Malia Borzini, was caught shoplift-
ing."
B = Mid(A, 19, 13)
msgbox B

</SCRIPT>

</HTML>
```

Results in

```
Malia Borzini
```

OR (to illustrate the various effects of putting Mid within a Loop structure):

```
<HTML>

<SCRIPT LANGUAGE="VBScript">

K = "1234567"
cr = CHR(13) & CHR(10)

For i = 1 To Len(K)
   A = A + cr + Mid(K, i, 1)
Next

For i = 1 To Len(K)
   A = A + cr + Mid(K, 1, i)
Next

For i = 1 To Len(K)
   A = A + cr + Mid(K, i, i)
Next

MsgBox A

</SCRIPT>

</HTML>
```

Results in

```
1
2
3
4
5
6
7
1
```

```
12
123
1234
12345
123456
1234567
1
23
345
4567
567
67
7
```

Uses

- Use Mid with the InStr command to find, then extract, a piece of text within a phrase, sentence, paragraph, or larger body of text. InStr searches for a matching letter, word, or phrase. If InStr finds what you've asked it to look for, InStr tells you the character *position*, within the larger text, where it found the match. You can feed this information to Mid as the starting position where it should begin extracting text. (See the example.)
- Mid is often used in combination with one or more of these other text-manipulation commands: Len, InStr, UCase, LCase, Left, Right.
- Left (pulls out a number of characters from the left side of a piece of text).
- Right (pulls out a number of characters from the right side of a piece of text).
- Len (tells how long a piece of text is, how many characters it contains).
- InStr (tells where a letter, word, or phrase is located within a piece of text).

By using these commands in various combinations, you can extract, search, replace, scramble, rearrange, edit, or otherwise manage text.

Cautions Normally, you provide two numbers to Mid—the starting character position and the number of characters to extract. However, if you leave out the number of characters, Mid will extract all the text from the starting position to the end of the larger body of text (behaving, then, like the Right command):

```
A = "ABCDEFGHI"
MsgBox Mid(A,4)
```

Results in

```
DEFGHI
```

This is the equivalent of:

```
X = Len(A)
MsgBox Right(A, X - 3)
```

Example One valuable use for Mid is to get rid of extraneous text. Assume we've got a police report, and we want the computer to locate a suspect's name (using InStr) and then provide an extraction (using Mid), just the immediate context, from a large report. It has been a busy night in Williamsport and we want only the brief facts about this one perp, Malia. Start an HTML Layout Control by clicking on the Edit | Insert HTML Layout in the ActiveX Control Pad (see the Introduction to this book for a tutorial on using the ActiveX Control Pad). Name this new Layout *n* when you're asked for a "filename." Then right-click on the Layout Control and choose "View Source Code." Type this into the source code:

```
Sub n_OnLoad()

A = "This person, named Malia Borzini, was caught shoplifting
Bess Myerson's autobiography."
Search = LCase(InputBox("Please enter the perp's name..."))
StartPos = InStr(LCase(A), Search)
If StartPos = 0 then MsgBox (Search & " didn't get into any
trouble yesterday."): Exit Sub
EndPos = InStr(StartPos, A, ".")
lngth = EndPos - StartPos + 1
MsgBox Mid(A, StartPos, lngth)

end sub
```

Note that we used LCase to make sure that we found a match, regardless of the capitalization in the police report or in the user's request (also see "StrComp" for an alternative to LCase).

By having the user enter the name into the Variable *Search*, we can then find the Search within the report (A). If StartPos is 0, we tell the user that the name wasn't found in the report and exit the Subroutine.

Otherwise, we look for a period (.) so we can extract all the information between the search name and the end of the sentence where the name was located. This search gives us the end position for our extraction.

Mid wants the *length* of the extraction, the number of characters. So we subtract StartPos from EndPos, adding 1 to make it come out right. Then we MsgBox the results to the screen:

```
Malia Borzini was caught shoplifting Bess Myerson's autobiog-
raphy.
```

See also InStr, Left, Len, Right, StrComp

M

Min

ACTIVEX

See Properties

Minute

VBSCRIPT FUNCTION

Description The Minute command tells you the minute of the hour, giving you a number between 1 and 59. By default, Minute is an Integer Variable subtype (see "Variables").

The Now command can give you any hour between January 1, 100, and December 31, 9999, using VBScript's built-in "serial number" representation of date+time. VBScript can provide or manipulate individual serial numbers *for every second* between

A.D. 100 and 9999. These serial numbers also include coded representations of all the hours, days, months, and years between 100 A.D. and 9999. (For more on the date/time serial number, see "DateSerial.")

Used with Often used with the Now Function to tell you the current minute as registered by your computer's clock:

```
MsgBox Minute(Now)
```

The Now Function provides the serial number for the current date and time. Minute extracts the minute portion of that serial number.

Variables

```
X = Minute(Now)
```

X will contain an Integer Variable subtype between 1 and 59.

Uses

- Create "to-do" scheduler programs, keeping track of appointments by comparing Year(Now), Month(Now), and Day(Now) against the information stored when the user first identified a particular appointment. You create a serial number for a date by using either the DateSerial or DateValue Function.
- Date-stamp data. Add the serial number to information stored by your program (data the user types in, a picture the user creates, whatever is being saved to the user's disk for future use). (See "Cookies.") You can get the current serial number by entering: X = cDbl(Now). Then, if you save X along with the other data, you'll always have a precise record of the exact second when that data was created and stored. Note that X = Now will return a *text* version of the date and time (like 9/30/96 5:40:39 PM), not the serial number. To get the serial number, you have to coerce the Variable into a "double" subtype. See "cBool" for an explanation of coercion.
- Create "digital" clocks.

Example

```
cr = chr(13) & chr(10)
X = cdbl(Now)
Y = cdbl(Minute(Now))
Z = cStr(X) & cr & cStr(Y)
MsgBox Z
```

Results in

```
33606.7413773148
47
```

Of course, the serial number, the X, will always differ, based on what your Now is when you're reading this. Every time you use Now, the serial number will be a higher number until January 1, 10000, at which date nobody knows what will happen.

In fact, Visual Basic Script's serial number is unique for every second between January 1, 100, and December 31, 9999—the range over which VBScript can calculate date and time. The number of seconds in this span of 9,899 years is obviously quite large. There are more than 30 million seconds in a single year, which is why you can assume that the Variable X's subtype (see "Variables") is a double-precision floating-point type. This kind of Variable subtype is capable of holding an extremely large range of numbers.

The VBScript date+time serial number contains the day, month, and year to the left of the decimal point, and the numbers to the right of the decimal point contain the hour, minute, and second. However, the meaning of the serial number is encoded. There is no direct way to examine the serial number and extract the information contained therein. VBScript, therefore, provides various Functions—Second, Minute, Hour, Day, Month, Year—to decode that information for you.

See also DateSerial, Day, Hour, Month, Now, Second, Weekday, Year

MOD

VBSCRIPT OPERATOR

Description MOD provides you with the *remainder* after a division. In other words, if you use MOD to divide 20 by 6, you get 2:

```
MsgBox 20 MOD 6
```

Uses

- If you want to know what's left over (the remainder) after division. For example, if you know how many months someone will be gone, you might want to translate that into years + months remaining:

```
Mnths = 78
Y = cInt(Mnths / 12)
R = Mnths MOD 12

MsgBox "They'll be gone " & Y & " years and " & R & " →
months."
```

Results In

```
They'll be gone 6 years and 6 months.
```

- The second common use for MOD is to do something at regular intervals. For instance, if you wanted to count to 500,000, and let the user view the progress, it wouldn't be practical to display something *500,000* times. No, you'd want to make something visible to the user perhaps every 50,000th iteration. MOD is useful for this kind of interval checking. To do this, you divide with MOD by the interval, then see if it's zero (no remainder). If so, you're at the interval, so take some action:

```
For I = 1 to 500000
If I MOD 50000 = 0 Then
MsgBox "We're at " & I
End If
Next
```

In VBScript, though, this tactic isn't too practical because repeated message boxes are hardly a pleasant way to inform the user of the progress of some job. And within a loop, if you try to, say, update a Label with the latest value of I, nothing will happen in the Label until the entire loop is finished. There is no equivalent to Visual Basic's DoEvents command in VBScript that would allow you to multitask in that fashion. DoEvents pauses the looping to update anything else that is waiting to be accomplished. In VBScript, however, a loop freezes things until the loop is completed.

See Operators

Month

VBSCRIPT FUNCTION

Description The Month command tells you the month of the year, giving you a number between 1 and 12.

Month can provide an accurate date and time for any day between January 1, 100, and December 31, 9999, using VBScript's built-in serial number representation of date+time. VBScript can provide or manipulate individual serial numbers *for every second* between those two dates. Each serial number includes a coded representation of a particular second of a minute of an hour of a day of a month of one of the years between 100 A.D. and 9999. Needless to say, there are many serial numbers available, and each is unique.

(For more on the serial number, see "DateSerial.")

Used with Often used with the Now Function to tell you the current month as registered by your computer's clock:

```
MsgBox Month(Now)
```

The Now Function provides the serial number for the current date and time. The Month Function extracts the month portion of the serial number.

M

Variables `X = Month(Now)`

Uses

- Create calendar programs.
- Create "to-do" scheduler programs, keeping track of appointments by comparing Year(Now), Month(Now), and Day(Now) against the information stored when the user first identified a particular appointment. You create a serial number for a date by using either the DateSerial or DateValue Function.
- Date-stamp data. Add the serial number to information stored by your program (data the user types in, a picture the user creates, whatever is being saved to disk for future use). You can get the current serial number by entering: X# = Now. Then, if you save X# to a disk file along with the other data, you'll always have a precise record of the exact second when that data was created and stored.

M

Example Here's how the serial number works:

```
X = cDbl(Now)
Y = (Month(Now))
MsgBox X
MsgBox Y
```

Results in

```
33608.132349537
1
```

Of course, the serial number, the X, will always differ, based on what your Now is when you're reading this. Every time you use Now, the serial number will be a higher number until January 1, 10000, at which date nobody knows what will happen.

In fact, VBScript's serial number is unique for every second between January 1, 100, and December 31, 9999—the range over which VBScript can calculate date and time. The number of seconds in this span of 9,899 years is obviously quite large. There are more than 30 million seconds in a single year, which is why you can assume that the Variable X's subtype (see "Variables") is a double-precision floating-point type. This kind of Variable subtype is capable of holding an extremely large range of numbers.

The VBScript date+time serial number contains the day, month, and year to the left of the decimal point, and the numbers to the right of the decimal point contain the hour, minute, and second. However, the meaning of the serial number is encoded. There is no direct way to examine the serial number and extract the information contained therein. VBScript, therefore, provides various Functions—Second, Minute, Hour, Day, Month, Year—to decode that information for you.

See also Day, Hour, Minute, Now, Second, Weekday, Year

MouseDown & MouseUp

ACTIVEX

See Events

MouseEnter & MouseExit

ACTIVEX

See Events

MouseIcon, MousePointer

ACTIVEX

See Properties

Move

ACTIVEX

See Methods

MsgBox

VBSCRIPT FUNCTION

Description A MsgBox appears onscreen and waits until the user clicks on it (or presses the Esc key). You can also display a simple message box by using the Alert command:

```
<HTML>
<HEAD>
  <SCRIPT LANGUAGE="VBScript">
<!--
Sub window_onLoad()
alert "Watch out!"
end sub
-->
  </SCRIPT>
</HEAD>
</BODY>
</HTML>
```

M

A message box won't go away and the user cannot access any other windows in your program until the message box is clicked. (MsgBoxes and InputBoxes are called *modal*, which means that they freeze the action, any additional behaviors in your program, until the user acknowledges them.)

As a Statement: You can use a MsgBox in its *Statement* mode (you can even omit the parentheses) if you merely want to tell the user something and don't care about the user's reaction:

```
MsgBox ("Please remember to enter your name before →
requesting budget information.")
```

As a Function: Functions always return some information to your program, so they are always in the form of an "equation":

```
X = MsgBox ("Are you sure you want to quit the program?",4)
```

Use the "Function" style of MsgBox when you want information back from the user. Here we added the ,4 to the MsgBox command, causing it to display Yes and No Buttons for the user to click. Without ,4 the message box would have displayed the single OK Button, which is the default.

If the user clicks on the Yes Button, X will contain 6, and clicking on the No Button returns 7 to X. Therefore, your program can use X to decide what to do based on the user's response:

```
If X = 6 Then End
```

Used with Use message boxes in places in your program *where you want to force the user to respond to the program.*

Whenever possible, you should avoid using the MsgBox or InputBox commands because they violate the spirit of user control that Windows brings to PC computing (as distinct from programmer-control).

Windows programs—unlike the rigidly designed programs of years past—provide the user with a set of objects and tools that he or she can manipulate. The user expects to be able to manipulate these objects to the extent, and at the time, that he or she chooses.

Objects like Text Boxes can be scrolled, typed into, or even ignored by the user. This means that you should try to write your programs in such a way that the user can participate in the design of the program and determine how the program behaves. You provide a set of tools, and the user selects the tools that are appropriate to his or her goals.

MsgBox and InputBox freeze up the program and demand a response before they release the program and the user from captivity. In emergency situations you will need to resort to MsgBox or InputBox—if the user is about to exit before saving important data, for instance. But you should probably check to see if there isn't a preferable alternative to freezing the program. Perhaps you could have your program automatically save that data and provide an Undo Button to retrieve it for the user.

Most users, most of the time, know what they are doing. And most users quickly grow tired of a program that carps, that repeatedly asks some variation of "Are you SURE?"

VBScript's (or Visual Basic Scripting Edition's) rich set of commands provides a variety of ways for your program to interact with the user—to accept or provide information. When you are tempted to use MsgBox or InputBox, you might want to see if there is a better approach. There often is.

Variables Used as a Statement: You *don't* need to use parentheses with the *Statement* version of MsgBox.

```
Msg = "Attention! Program is sorting data."
MsgBox Msg
```

However, you *do* need parentheses if you are including the text in the *MsgBox command proper* (not using a text Variable):

```
MsgBox ("Attention! Program is sorting data.")
```

Used as a Function: A Function-style MsgBox *always* requires parentheses around the text, whether it's literal text within quotation marks or a text Variable. That—and the fact that a Function gives back a Variable to tell your program how the user responded—are the only two differences between the Function and Statement approaches to MsgBoxes.

```
X = MsgBox ("Attention! Program is sorting data.")
```

Additional Variables You Can Provide: The fully armed MsgBox looks like the following:

```
X = MsgBox ("Please confirm that you intend to delete this →
item from the list.", 4, "ALERT!" Helpfile, Context)
```

The 4 puts a set of Yes and No buttons on the message box, and the "ALERT!" is put into the Title Bar of the box.

Your choices for which buttons should be displayed are as follows:

0	OK (the default)		
1	OK	Cancel	
2	Abort	Retry	Ignore
3	Yes	No	Cancel
4	Yes	No	
5	Retry	Cancel	

Table M-1: MsgBox button choices.

You also can include icons built into the message box that symbolize the meaning of the message. To include these, you *add* the icon's number to the button's number:

16	Critical Message (a red stop sign)
32	Warning, plus question mark (a question mark inside a green circle)
48	Warning alone (an exclamation point enclosed within a yellow circle)
64	Information (a lowercase *i* inside a small, blue circle)

Table M-2: MsgBox icons.

To display OK and Cancel Buttons plus a Warning icon, add 1 to 48:

```
MsgBox ("Are you sure?"),49
```

Finally, you have three possible ways to *focus* the buttons—focus means which button will respond if the user presses the Esc or Enter key (rather than clicking on a particular button):

0	First Button (the default)
256	Second Button
512	Third Button

Table M-3: Choices for deciding which button has focus.

The Meaning of the Variable Showing Which Button the User Clicked:

```
X = MsgBox ("Please Answer",2)
```

When the user clicks on a button, X holds one of the following values and thereby tells your program how to respond to the user's selection:

1	OK
2	Cancel
3	Abort
4	Retry
5	Ignore
6	Yes
7	No

Table M-4: Button values in a message box.

Note that if the message box contains a Cancel Button, pressing the Esc key *is the same* as clicking on the Cancel Button: X will contain a 2.

If you want a Help Button to appear on your message box, add a text ("string") Variable or expression that names the Help file. You must also include a Context, as described below. Context This is a numeric Variable or expression defining the "Help context number." This displays the appropriate topic within the larger Help file.

Uses

- When the user is about to do something dangerous, something that could irretrievably destroy data, for instance.
- When you're trying to track down a bug in your script, you can sprinkle message boxes all through your source code so you can watch the behavior of Variables and also see if particular procedures are ever being activated. VBScript doesn't have tracing, Variable watch, or other debugging facilities available in more mature languages. Sometimes the only way to find out what's going wrong (or, to be precise, *where* something is going wrong) is to douse your code with message boxes. For more on debugging VBScript, see the Introduction to this book.

- When the program is doing something that could generate an error. If you are using Err and On Error Resume Next, that part of your program might benefit from MsgBox. If the user is about to divide by zero, that will generate an error message in the program, and you may well want to respond by putting a message box in front of the user:

```
On Error Resume Next
N = 12
Z = N/D
If Err Then MsgBox err.description
```

- MsgBox is sometimes used when the program has to pause for some length of time to, for example, search through a large amount of information. Users become uneasy if the computer seems to be doing nothing—even for a few seconds. They may even start typing or mouse clicking, fearing that something has gone terribly wrong. To assuage this concern, when a program does something that will take time, a message box can be displayed, remarking that the user should be patient.

  Nevertheless, MsgBox is not the best or even the second best choice in this situation. Perhaps the nicest way to keep the user calm is to show the progress of the task with a gauge: by showing percentages, such as 10% and 20%, you can update the user as the program finishes its task. Your second best choice might be simply to display a window that says "Searching," for example, and then have your program remove that window when the job is done.

Cautions

- If you don't include the title Variable for a MsgBox, then the Title Bar of the MsgBox will say Visual Basic.
- You can put as many as 1,024 characters into a MsgBox, and the lines will automatically be wrapped within the box. If you want to end a line before it reaches the right side of the box (for formatting purposes), define a Variable to hold the code for a Carriage Return, then add it to your message like this:

```
cr = chr(13)
msg = "Break the line here" & cr & "and start the next →
line here."
msgbox (msg)
```

- The user can either click on one of the buttons on your message box, press the Esc key, or press the Enter key. Any of these approaches gets rid of the message box.
- Once your program has displayed a MsgBox or InputBox, the program itself cannot make it disappear. The user *must* respond.
- VBScript will decide where the MsgBox appears onscreen and how large it is. Neither you, the programmer, nor the user has any control over this.

Example

```
<HTML>
<SCRIPT LANGUAGE=VBS>
MsgBox ("We are experiencing some delays.")
</SCRIPT>
</HTML>
```


See also Error, InputBox

MultiLine, MultiRow, MultiSelect

ACTIVEX

See Properties

N

Name

ACTIVEX

See Properties

NOBR

NETSCAPE

Description NOBR blocks automatic line breaking.

Normally a browser automatically decides when to insert a carriage return within your text. Just like a word processor, a browser moves down one line and continues displaying your text whenever the text reaches the right margin. It looks for the closest space character to make the line break because the text should not be broken *within* a word. Note that this "automatic line wrapping" must usually be left up to the browser—it's not something you can predetermine when you are writing the text. There are two reasons for this: 1) User screen sizes will differ, and 2) The user might resize the window, requiring adjustments to the line breaks.

However, if for compelling formatting reasons you want to control where a line breaks, you can use NOBR and WBR (Word Break, which forces a line break where *you* determine the next line should start).

Used with ***Can be enclosed by***

<A>, <ADDRESS>, <B>, <BLINK>, <BLOCKQUOTE>, <BODY>, <CAPTION>, <CENTER>, <CITE>, <CODE>, <DD>, <DT>, <EM>, <FONT>, <FORM>, <H>, <I>, <KBD>, <LI>, <NOBR>, <P>, <SAMP>, <STRONG>, <TD>, <TH>, <TT>, <VAR>

Can enclose

<A>, <B>, <BASEFONT>, <BLINK>, <BR>, <CITE>, <CODE>, <EM>, <FONT>, <I>, <IMG>, <KBD>, <NOBR>, <SAMP>, <STRONG>, <TT>, <VAR>, <WBR>

Variables WBR (Word Break) is used to force a line break within a NOBR pair.

```
<NOBR>

No matter how wide the user's browser window<WBR>
we've forced a line break at this spot<WBR>
here.
</NOBR>
```

Uses

- If you have some text that you want to remain on a single line, even if it goes off the side of the user's screen, use NOBR.
- If you want to specify precisely where a line will break (move the remaining text down to the next line), regardless of the width of the browser, use WBR.
- The BR command inserts a blank line within your text.

N

Example

```
<HTML>
<BODY BGCOLOR=WHITE>
<NOBR>

Note that this "automatic line wrapping" must usually be →
left up to the browser--it's not something you can →
predetermine when you are writing the text. There are two →
reasons for this: 1) User screen sizes will differ, and 2) →
The user might resize the window, requiring adjustments to →
the line breaks.

</NOBR>
</HTML>
```

The line above is not supposed to break—forcing the user to move the horizontal scroll bar at the bottom of the browser to read the entire line. However, as you can see in Figure N-1, the browser does actually break the line after 200 characters.

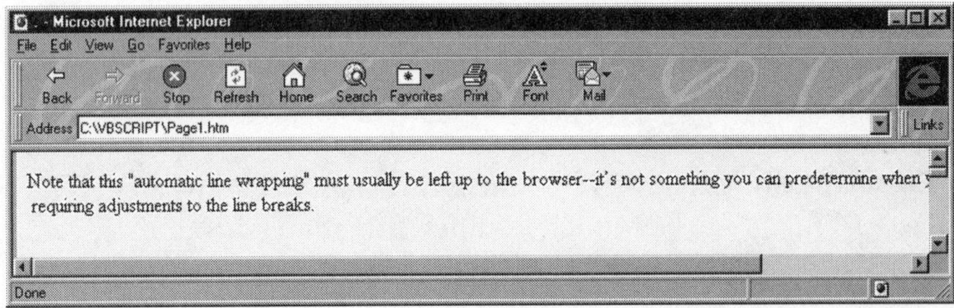

Figure N-1: The NOBR command isn't absolute. Even though we've specified no line breaks, Internet Explorer does finally break this line at the 200th character.

See also BR

NOFRAME

NETSCAPE

Description Not all browsers can display frames. Just in case the user's browser is unable to handle them, you can provide alternative information within the <NOFRAME> and </NOFRAME> commands so they won't be entirely in the dark.

If the browser can display frames, everything between <NOFRAME> and </NOFRAME> will be ignored.

Uses When you use a frame, you can provide information for users with browsers that can't handle frames.

Example

```
<NOFRAME>If you want to see this kind of information, you
should get a browser that can display it. Try Netscape or
Internet Explorer.</NOFRAME>
```

See also FRAME

NOT

VBSCRIPT OPERATOR

See Operators

NOTE

HTML

Description The NOTE command causes text between <NOTE> and </NOTE> to be formatted differently than surrounding text. However, as the example below illustrates, in Internet Explorer, this merely means that the text is set to the default FONT SIZE (3). The effect will vary from browser to browser.

Used with ***Can be enclosed by***

<BANNER>, <BODY>, <BODYTEXT>, <DD>, <DIV>, <FIGTEXT>, <FN>, <FORM>, <LI>, <NOTE>, <TD>, <TH>

N

Can enclose

<A>, <ABBREV>, <ACRONYM>, <ADDRESS>, <AU>, <B>, <BIG>, <BLOCKQUOTE>, <BQ>, <BR>, <CITE>, <CODE>, <DEL>, <DFN>, <DIR>, <DIV>, <DL>, <EM>, <FIG>, <FN>, <FORM>, <H1>, <H2>, <H3>, <H4>, <H5>, <H6>, <HR>, <I>, <IMG>, <INS>, <ISINDEX>, <KBD>, <LANG>, <MATH>, <MENU>, <NOTE>, <OL>, <P>, <PERSON>, <PRE>, <Q>, <S>, <SAMP>, <SMALL>, <STRONG>, <SUB>, <SUP>, <TAB>, <TABLE>, <TT>, <U>, <UL>, <VAR>

Uses Text format for footnotes or warnings to the user.

Example

This is normal body text.
Please resize your window to display all our text.

Figure N-2: In Internet Explorer, the NOTE command merely changes the font size to the default value (3). It's the equivalent of using this command: <FONT SIZE=3>.

```
<HTML>
<BODY BGCOLOR=WHITE>
<FONT SIZE=+1>
This is normal body text.<br>
</FONT>
<NOTE>
Please resize your window to display all our text.
</NOTE>
</HTML>
```

See also FONT

Now

VBSCRIPT FUNCTION

Description The Now command checks the computer's clock and provides a text representation of the date and time. In fact, Now is essentially a combination of what you would get if you combined the Date Function with the Time Function.

Now accesses a VBScript "serial number" that represents the current date and time.

The serial number accessed by the Now command is one of a large list of unique numbers calculated by VBScript. There is a different serial number for every *second* between January 1, 100 A.D., and December 31, 9999. One implication of this splendid profligacy is that whenever you request a serial number by using the Now command (which tells you the current moment), the serial number will be a higher number.

The serial number encodes the second, minute, hour, day, month, and year.

After being translated into a serial number, the current time can be *manipulated mathematically* with the serial numbers of other times and dates. (See "DateSerial" for more information.)

Used with Various VBScript commands can extract specific information from Now. For example, to find out the current month:

```
X = Month(Now)
```

Results in

(if the current month is February, X will be 2)

The Functions that can extract information from the Now serial number are as follows: Second, Minute, Hour, Day, Month, and Year.

Variables To find out the current year:

```
X = Year(Now)
```

OR (to use a Variable):

```
X = Now
MsgBox Minute(X)
```

Uses

- Create calendar programs or timer programs that pop up with reminders at the appropriate times.
- Create "to-do" scheduler programs, keeping track of appointments by comparing Year(Now), Month(Now), and Day(Now) against the information stored when the user first identified a particular appointment. You create a serial number for a date by using either the DateSerial or DateValue Function.
- Date-stamp data. Add the serial number to information stored by your program (data the user types in, a picture the user creates, whatever is being saved for future use). You can get the current serial number by forcing Now to be read as a double-precision floating point Variable rather than a text Variable:

```
x = cdbl(Now)
```

Then, if you save X to a disk file along with the other data, you'll always have a precise record of the exact second when that data was created and stored.

Cautions

- The mathematics that translate a serial number into meaningful date and time information is complex. VBScript therefore automatically coerces the results of the Now Function into a text-style Variable. VBScript also provides Functions, such as Day, Month, Year, Hour, and Second to translate the serial information for you.
- You can *directly* manipulate the serial number that Now provides, but perhaps it's not worth the trouble because VBScript does it so well for you.

Technical Note: If you *do* want to get into direct date serial number manipulation, the whole-number portion of a date+time serial number represents the date portion, and it is calculated by this formula:

```
TheYear*365 + fix(TheYear/4) + 2 + DayOfYear.
```

For example, March 28, 1992, would give us 33691. (Use the 92 in 1992 for TheYear.)

About 0.000011574 Each Second: The decimal portion of the serial number contains the time since midnight of the date. The value increases by about 0.000011574 each second, so you could divide the fractional portion of the serial number by this number to get the number of seconds that have elapsed since midnight. (This is the same as using the Second function, only more accurate.) The serial number is only updated each second, as can be seen by repeatedly getting the value.

- The date/time serial numbers cover an enormous range of numbers, as if you had a roll of theater tickets, each stamped with a unique serial number, that stretched to the moon and back.

Example

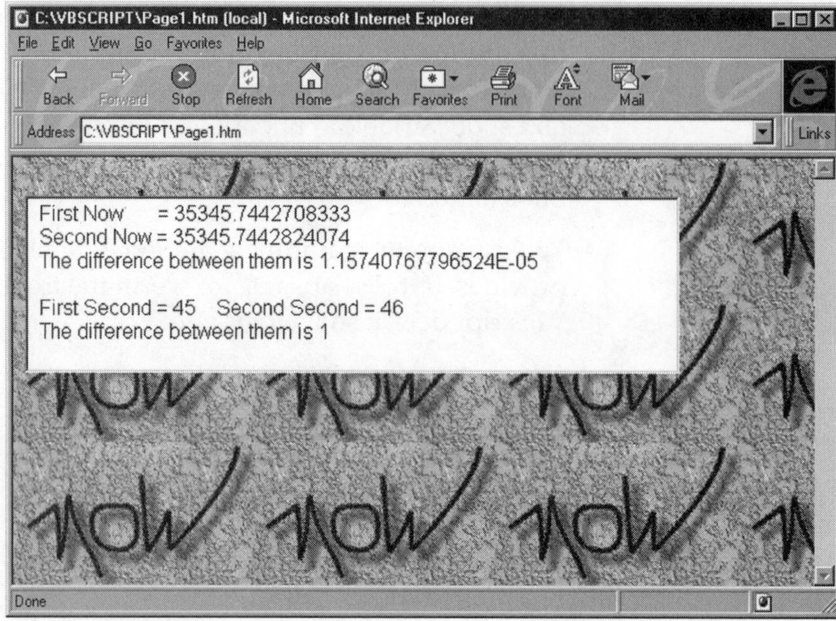

Figure N-3: If you want to measure the passage of time with precision, use the Now Function.

If you want to measure elapsed time, the Now Function will provide considerable precision. This example will tell us how long the computer takes to count from 1 up to 300,000. We'll measure it two ways. Using the Second Function, we get the results rounded off to the nearest second. However, if we use the raw double-precision floating point serial number provided by the Now Function, we get as much precision as we could possibly want.

Start the Microsoft ActiveX Control Pad (see the Introduction) and click on Edit | Insert ActiveX Control. Select Microsoft Forms 2.0 TextBox from the list in the window that pops up. Using the Properties window, change the MultiLine Property to True. Change the font to whatever typeface and typesize you want. Then close the TextBox's design window and get back to the HTML source code. Type in the following script, using whatever .GIF or .JPG file you want for your background wallpaper.

```
<HTML>
<BODY BACKGROUND="now1.jpg">
<BR>

<OBJECT ID="TextBox1" WIDTH=515 HEIGHT=135
 CLASSID="CLSID:8BD21D10-EC42-11CE-9E0D-00AA006002F3">
  <PARAM NAME="VariousPropertyBits" VALUE="2894088219">
  <PARAM NAME="Size" VALUE="13617;3545">
  <PARAM NAME="FontName" VALUE="Arial">
  <PARAM NAME="FontHeight" VALUE="240">
  <PARAM NAME="FontCharSet" VALUE="0">
  <PARAM NAME="FontPitchAndFamily" VALUE="2">
</OBJECT>

<SCRIPT LANGUAGE="VBScript">
<!--
cr = chr(13) & chr(10)

N = cDbl(Now)
S = Second(Now)

For i = 1 to 300000
Next

N1 = cDbl(Now)
S1 = Second(Now)

TextBox1.Text = "First Now  = " & N & cr & "Second Now = " &
N1 & cr & "The difference between them is " & N1-N

TextBox1.Text = TextBox1.Text & cr & cr & "First Second = " &
S & "   Second Second = " & S1 & cr  & "The difference between
them is " & S1-S

-->
</SCRIPT>

</BODY>
</HTML>
```

N

First we define a carriage return/line feed character named *cr* so we can move down to new lines in the TextBox (see "Chr"). Then we put the value of Now into the variable *N* and the value provided by the Second Function into *S*. Then we use a loop to count up from 1 to 300,000.

Then we again store the time as represented by Now and by Second. Finally, we display the two values we got from Now, and the difference between them. The difference is the elapsed time. Similarly, we display the two values we got from the Second Function, and their difference.

See also Day, Hour, Minute, Month, Second, Year

Number

PROPERTY

Description Some programmers, when debugging their programs, like to simulate errors. Then they can see how their program reacts to a particular error. You can use the Number Property of the Err object to accomplish this (see the following example). You can also use the Number Property to get an error number and, thereby, find out what error occurred. See "Err."

The Number Property is the *default* Property of the Err object. Therefore, you need never type in the word *Number.* It's implicit when you use the Err object:

```
Err.Number = 144
```

is the same as

```
Err = 144
```

Used with The Err object

Variables To load in a specific error message:

```
Err = 1900
```

To read the error number:

```
X = Err
```

The error number is a Long Integer Variable subtype (see "Variables"). If you are merely reacting to an actual (as opposed to simulated) error generated by VBScript, the error number will either be a VBScript error code or an OLE error code. These error codes have not been released at the time of this writing.

Uses Use Err.Number (or just Err) to find out what error occurred if your script halts while running. See "Err" or the Introduction to this book for details on error-handling and debugging.

Example

```
<HTML>
<HEAD>
<TITLE>Err.Number</TITLE>
</HEAD>
<BODY>
<SCRIPT LANGUAGE="VBSCRIPT">

Err.Number = 1344
Msgbox Err

</SCRIPT>
</BODY>
</HTML>
```

See also Err, Description

O

Object

ACTIVEX

See Properties

Object

INTERNET EXPLORER

Description The word *object* can mean several things in the context of Internet programming. It can mean a built-in entity—something inherent to and contained within every HTML document, such as the inherent History Object (that contains the "history list" of previously visited Internet sites) and the inherent Document Object.

There are three Objects used in VBScript programming. The Tab Object of a TabStrip Control (see "TabStrip"); the Font Object (see Font under the "Properties" entry); and the Err Object built into VBScript (see "Err").

An Object can also be an external entity such as a button or TextBox that's been "inserted" into an HTML document using the <OBJECT> tag. It's this second sense of the word *object* that we'll deal with here.

Objects inserted into HTML with the <OBJECT> tag offer the Internet document creator a considerable set of useful, often dynamic, Controls. You can provide video, audio, attractive sculpted frames, ListBoxes, and, as time goes on, many additional Objects will become available. Microsoft estimates that there are currently over 2,000 ActiveX Controls.

HTML Version 2.0 included only one way—the <IMG> command—for you to add multimedia into a document. However, additional features and media are being added all the time to the

Internet. The IMG tag wasn't designed to embrace a wide variety of media or special effects and capabilities. It deals only with graphic files.

Microsoft's DYNSRC command and Netscape's EMBED command attempt, each in their own way, to expand the multimedia capabilities of Internet documents. However, to embrace *practically any kind of Control*, the Object command seems to be the best solution. Object has been designed to be highly open-ended or, to use the current buzzword, *extensible.*

Various words have been used to describe Objects—Controls, applets, plug-ins, components, media handlers—but we'll use the terms *Object* and *Control* in this book.

The behaviors (*Methods* the Object can *do* and *Events* that *happen to* an Object) and qualities (*Properties*) of an Object can be listed and described within the <OBJECT> and </OBJECT> tags. Also, there are some standard Properties, such as Height, that can be provided in a standardized way for most any Object.

ActiveX Objects can be sent over the Internet to the user's hard drive, if the Object isn't already available locally to the user. This is similar to the way that a .GIF or .JPG graphic image is sent to the user, but Objects are far more sophisticated than simple visual images. Objects often have dozens of qualities and behaviors and, in effect, are little computer programs in themselves.

The Good Part

If you had to type in all the specifications for an ActiveX Object like a Rich Text Box, you'd go mad. For one thing, there's a long and, to humans, meaningless string of characters for the CLASSID. For the Rich Text Box, it is:

```
CLASSID="CLSID:3B7C8860-D78F-101B-B9B5-04021C009402"
```

Luckily, you can avoid all the trouble of typing in the required parameters, and just insert an Object using Microsoft's ActiveX Control Pad. It's available for free from several of Microsoft's Internet sites, including http://www.microsoft.com/workshop/author/authoring-contents1.htm#products.

With this nifty program, you just click on the Edit menu and select "Insert ActiveX Control."

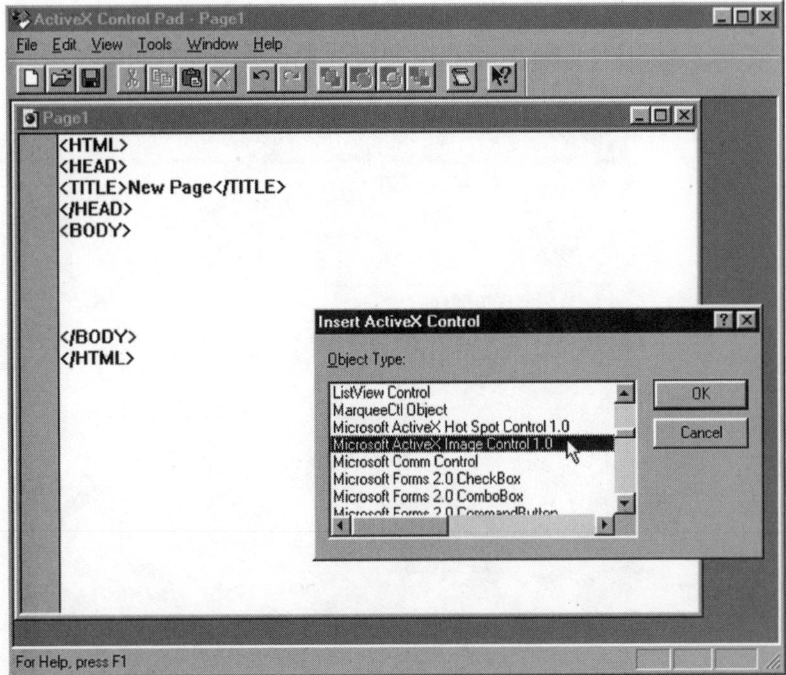

Figure O-1: The ActiveX Control Pad makes it a snap to insert Objects into your documents.

However, before we try some experiments with Objects in the examples below, let's first answer the question: "What is an ActiveX Control?"

What's ActiveX?

An ActiveX Control is an OLE Object that's designed to work on the Internet. (In truth, ActiveX is just the new name for what used to be called an OLE Control. The well-behaved OLE Controls should work without problems in an Internet Explorer browser.)

Some ActiveX Controls—like the Gradient Control that displays a smooth transition between two colors—are entirely original. Others—like the Rich Text Box—are improvements on Controls (the TextBox) that already exist in HTML. The HTML specification includes seven classic Controls that are invoked with the INPUT command: Command Button, CheckBox, Image, Radio Button, Reset Button, Submit Button, and TextBox.

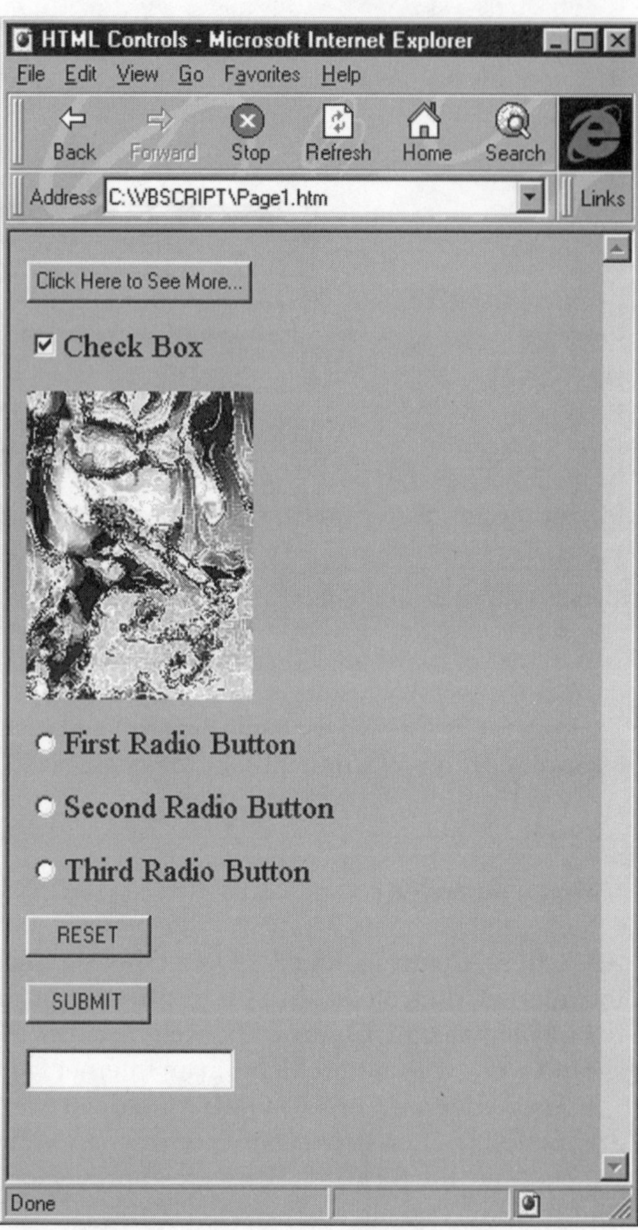

Figure O-2: The seven classic HTML Controls.

```
<HTML><HEAD>
<TITLE>HTML Controls</TITLE>
</HEAD><BODY>
<INPUT TYPE = Button VALUE = "Click Here to See More...">
<BR><BR>
<INPUT TYPE = Checkbox CHECKED=TRUE> Check Box
<BR><BR>
<INPUT TYPE = Image SRC="d2.gif"
<BR><BR><BR>
<INPUT TYPE = radio>First Radio Button
<BR><BR>
<INPUT TYPE = radio>Second Radio Button
<BR><BR>
<INPUT TYPE = radio>Third Radio Button
<BR><BR>
<INPUT TYPE = reset VALUE = "RESET">
<BR><BR>
<INPUT TYPE = submit VALUE = "SUBMIT">
<BR><BR>
<INPUT TYPE = text HEIGHT=250 WIDTH=90>
</BODY>
</HTML>
```

At the time of this writing, some ActiveX Controls written specifically for the Internet are working, others are not. However, we've gone ahead and included the most useful and interesting ActiveX Controls in this book—even the currently non-functioning ones—on the assumption that all will be working smoothly shortly.

Variables The easy way to insert an Object into your HTML source code is to use the ActiveX Control Pad (see the Introduction to this book). You click on its Edit | Insert ActiveX Control and choose the Control you want to insert from a ListBox. Alternatively, you click on the Edit | Insert HTML Layout option, then provide a name for your Layout Control, then click on the icon next to the Object definition and drag a Control from the Toolbox onto the HTML Layout. No matter which of these two approaches you take, you'll see a Properties window pop up for the Object you've just inserted.

Each Object has its own set of qualities (*Properties* or Parameters, such as Height) that you can adjust. Likewise, many Objects feature a set of actions they can take (*Methods*, such as Add, Clear, and Repaint) and reactions to outside triggers it is sensitive to (*Events*, such as Click or MouseMove). Properties, Methods, and Events unique to a Control are explored within the entry for each Control. Properties, Methods, and Events common to many Controls are described in the entries on "Properties," "Methods," and "Events."

Let's take a look at a typical Object, a ListBox, as it appears within HTML source code:

```
<OBJECT ID="ListBox1"
CLASSID="CLSID:8BD21D20-EC42-11CE-9E0D-00AA006002F3"
STYLE="TOP:146pt;LEFT:182pt;WIDTH:124pt;HEIGHT:128pt;→
TABINDEX:5;DISPLAY:NONEZINDEX:7;">
   <PARAM NAME="ScrollBars" VALUE="3">
   <PARAM NAME="DisplayStyle" VALUE="2">
   <PARAM NAME="Size" VALUE="4374;4506">
   <PARAM NAME="MatchEntry" VALUE="0">
   <PARAM NAME="FontName" VALUE="Comic Sans MS">
   <PARAM NAME="FontHeight" VALUE="280">
   <PARAM NAME="FontCharSet" VALUE="0">
   <PARAM NAME="FontPitchAndFamily" VALUE="2">
   <PARAM NAME="FontWeight" VALUE="0">
</OBJECT>
```

The **ID** is the unique name of this Control. It can be referenced elsewhere in your script, to adjust this ListBox's Properties, or to trigger its Events or Methods. For example, in the Click Event of a button, you might change the ListBox's BackColor Property:

```
Sub Button1_Click
ListBox1.BackColor = 16776960
End Sub
```

CLASSID identifies the ActiveX Control. Objects are registered (in, for example, the Windows 95 registry, a huge database). If the Control is already available on the user's computer, the browser will display the Control. If not, the Control can be automatically downloaded to the user, then registered. In other words, a Control needs to be downloaded to the user only once. After it's registered,

OLE-capable applications (such as Internet Explorer 3.0) can access the Control and use its features. To see what's registered on your machine running Windows 95, click Start, then Run. Type in RegEdit and press Enter. Press Ctrl+F to search for CLSID. Alternatively, you can see a list of Controls by clicking on the ActiveX Control Pad's Edit menu, then selecting "Insert ActiveX Control."

STYLE is an Internet Explorer parameter and describes the location (top and left coordinates, relative to the HTML Layout form); the size (width and height); the TabIndex Property (when the user cycles among the Controls by pressing the Tab key, this ListBox is the fifth to be Tabbed to); and the ZIndex (the Z coordinate, the *depth* coordinate, meaning that if the Controls overlapped each other, the ones that are on top of the other ones). A Z of 1 is the bottom (all other Controls would cover it if they overlapped it), and 7, among these Controls, is the top of the pile.

Additional parameters in the PARAM list include various Properties of the Object. You can find these same parameters in the Properties Window. Just click on the icon next to the <OBJECT> definition in the ActiveX Control Pad and the Properties Window will pop up. Any change you make within the Properties Window will appear in the PARAM list in the HTML source code. (To get to the source code for an HTML Layout Control, right-click on the Layout Control and choose View Source Code.)

O

Uses Add Java applets, ActiveX Controls, multimedia, and richness to your Web pages. With Objects, you can provide more sophisticated interactivity than was possible with traditional HTML user-interaction and multimedia features.

Cautions Internet programming in general, and ActiveX Controls in particular, are a work in progress. At the time this book was written, there were hundreds of ActiveX Controls either available, announced, or being worked on quietly in software labs around the world. Several dozen were chosen for inclusion in this book. The basis for this selection was, first, utility: TextBoxes, Images, and HotSpot Controls are highly useful general-purpose Controls. Thirteen of these most-often-used Controls are included with the HTML Layout Control built into the Microsoft ActiveX Control Pad. If you've got the ActiveX Control Pad, you've got these Controls.

The second set of ActiveX Controls we included in this book are those that Microsoft has included within the Internet Explorer 3.0 browser. These include Gradient, Marquee, and Chart Controls, among others. You'll find these Controls by clicking in the ActiveX Control Pad's Edit menu and selecting Insert ActiveX Control. Scroll within the window that pops up to locate the Controls whose names begin with "Microsoft IE 30."

Both the Internet Explorer browser and the ActiveX Control Pad can be found on Microsoft's Web site at http://www.microsoft.com. Additional ActiveX Controls can be found at http://www.microsoft.com/activex/controls.

Recall, however, that ActiveX Controls are a work in progress. To us, the Internet programmer, this means that sometimes things won't quite work as specified. For example, *most* of the features of the Marquee Control work just fine. However, the Array list of URLs isn't quite working yet, or if it is, the specifications and syntax for making it work haven't yet been published. In any case, when we couldn't get a feature to work, we tell you. You'll find any such warnings in the Cautions section of an entry.

Examples There are two ways to add Objects (Controls) to your HTML pages. (Actually, you could type the CLASSID and all the other parameters into your HTML source code yourself, but who's going to go to that much trouble?)

Let's say there are two *practical* ways to insert Objects into your HTML document: directly, by using the Edit | Insert ActiveX Control menu choice in the ActiveX Control Pad, or indirectly, by adding an HTML Layout Control to the HTML document, then adding other Controls to the Layout Control (you do this by clicking on the ActiveX Control Pad's Edit | Insert HTML Layout). We'll illustrate both approaches in this example.

There are two primary differences between adding Objects directly and indirectly. When you put a Control directly into HTML source code, the rest of your source code (the Object definitions and any associated VBScript) will appear within that HTML source code. However, if you go the indirect route, all the source code (except the Object definition of the HTML Layout Control itself) appears in a special .ALX file. Therefore, there are *two* source code files.

The second primary difference is that all Controls (Objects) registered on your computer are available for direct insertion into HTML source code. However, only a predetermined set of 13 Controls are initially available on the Layout Control's Toolbox. If you want to add any additional Controls that are available on your hard drive, right-click on the Layout Control's Toolbox and select Additional Controls.

First we'll put a Marquee Control directly into HTML source code. Start the ActiveX Control Pad and select Insert ActiveX Control from the Edit menu. Choose from among any Controls beginning with "Microsoft IE 30." We'll choose a Chart Control.

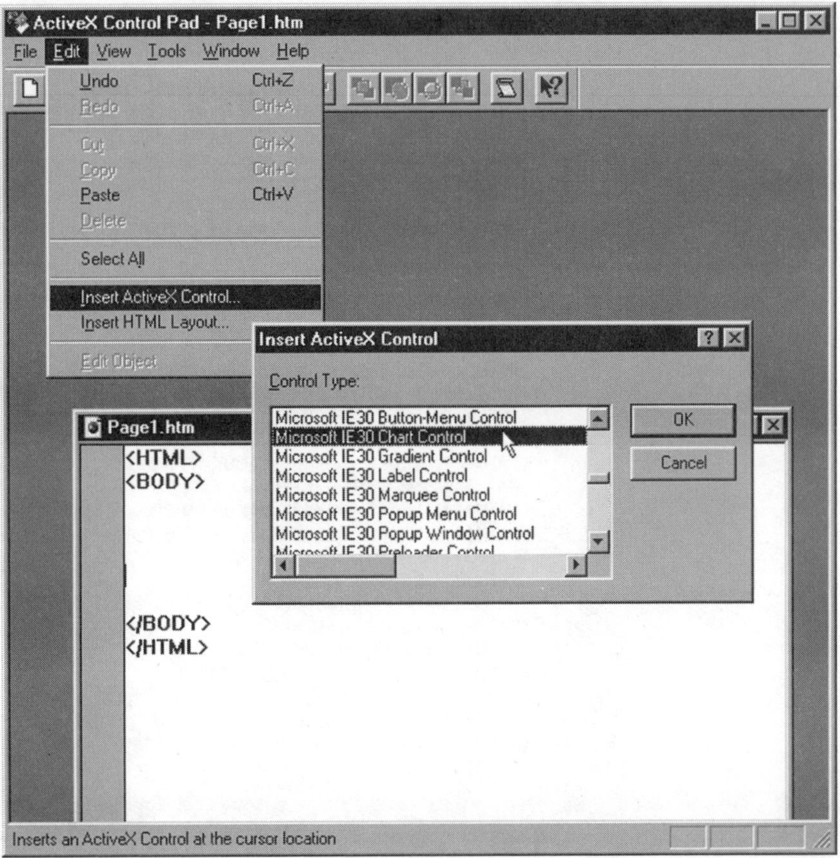

Figure O-3: When you insert an Object directly into HTML source code using the Microsoft ActiveX Control Pad, this list of all registered Objects appears.

When you click the OK button, an Editing window and a Properties window appear. The Control is visible within the Editing window and can be resized by dragging. Within the Properties window you can adjust any of the Properties of the new Object. When you're finished, close both the Editing and Properties windows by clicking on the X icon in their upper right corners. You'll then see the Object's definition and parameter list appear within your HTML source code, as shown in Figure O-4:

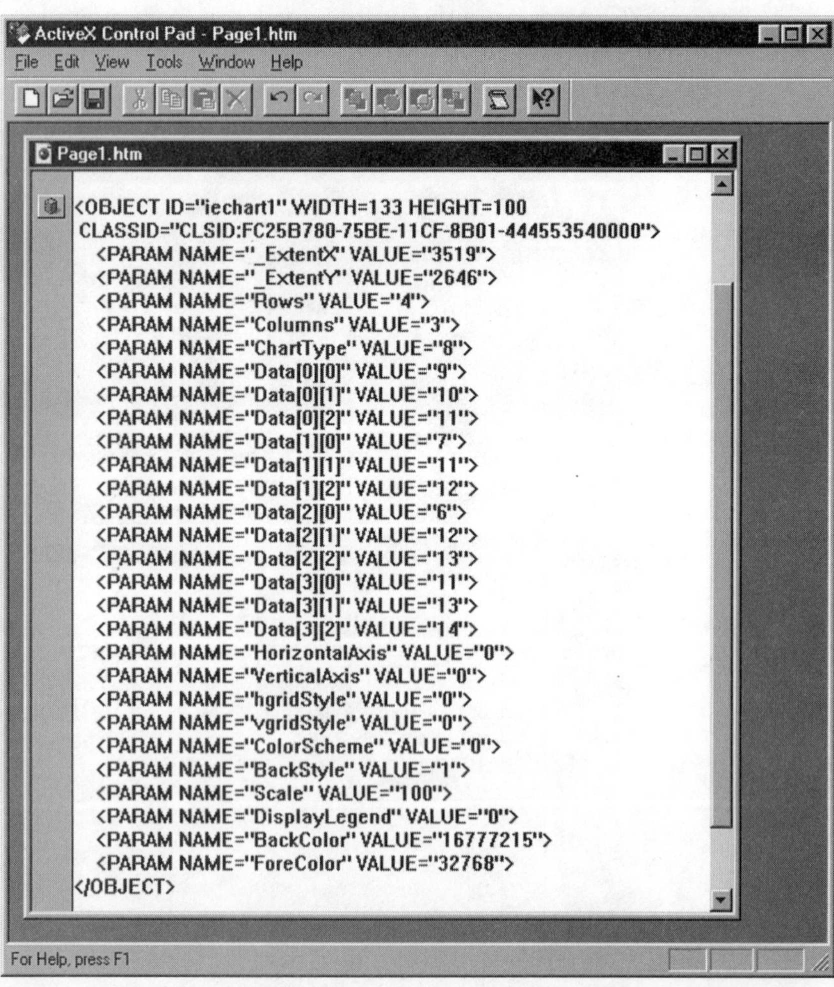

Figure O-4: This Object definition is inserted directly into your HTML source code. As far as the browser is concerned, this is just one more item to parse and display to the user.

Now let's add a Control to a Layout Control, the indirect way to put an Object into an HTML document. In the ActiveX Control Pad, click on Edit | Insert HTML Layout. Give it a name. A new Layout Control will be put into your HTML source code. Click on the small icon next to this new Object and a special Layout editing window will open up, as shown in Figure O-5.

Figure O-5: We've dragged an Image Control from the Standard Toolbox onto the Layout, and used the Properties window to fill it with a graphic.

For a more extensive discussion of using Objects with HTML and the various features of the Microsoft ActiveX Control Pad, see the Introduction to this book.

See also Entries throughout this book labeled "ActiveX Control," such as Label, Command Button, Option Button, Marquee, and many others. Also see the Introduction, a tutorial overview of Internet programming using VBScript, ActiveX Controls, and the Microsoft ActiveX Control Pad.

Oct

VBSCRIPT FUNCTION

Description The Oct command is rarely used. It gives you a text ("string") Variable that contains a translation of a decimal number into an *octal* number. Translating numbers into octal numbers has few real uses in contemporary programming.

The idea of a number is always the same: 7 Objects are always 7, regardless of how you describe them. The computer can manipulate the concept 7; we can, too.

But to manipulate numbers mathematically, the computer prefers to work with the powers of two: 2, 4, 8, 16, 32, and so on. This creates a conflict because we humans prefer to use a system that manipulates and expresses numbers in groups of ten: 10, 100, 1,000. Our *decimal* system is not terribly compatible with the computer's *binary* system. The numbers remain the same, but the approach to manipulating them differs.

The decimal system has 10 symbols, 10 "digits," 0 through 9, but the octal system has only eight, 0 through 7. In the decimal system, when you reach 9 and run out of symbols, you move over one place and use two columns, 10, and then start repeating the symbols. We are in effect saying: 1 of the "tens" and none of the "ones." In octal, "10" means eight items. It moves over to the next column every *eight* increments.

A Few Used Octal: A few early programming languages operated in octal. (Most early languages operated in hexadecimal (base 16), see "Hex.") The decision as to which numerical base to use seems to have been whimsical—the DEC PDP 11 series of early computers were based on octal, yet the successor to these machines, the VAX, was based on hexadecimal.

Fortunately, programming has become more human-oriented. You no longer have to deal with anything other than the decimal system for anything beyond a few oddball computing tasks. However, "low-level" computing—where you get right down into the innards and manipulate things directly—can still require that you calculate in number bases other than ten. The Windows API and Registry use hex values to reference Constants and other data. The use of binary (base two) counting systems is absolutely necessary when working at the hardware level with a program. One advantage of octal in this context is that it is relatively easy to see that 0x42 or octal 102 means that bits 1 and 6 are high. It's not so easy to see the same thing with the decimal number 66. Also, hex numbers are still used in many situations, including port addresses (2F8, 3F8, and so on). For more about hex numbers in HTML, see "Hex Numbers for the Color Command" in the entry on "BODY."

Used with Numbers translated to text for display onscreen or to a MsgBox and rare mathematical calculations.

Variables

```
X = Oct(19)
```

OR

```
Q = 8
X = Oct(Q)
```

Cautions Oct rounds off the number you ask it to translate to the nearest whole number. It does not express fractions, numbers involving decimal points.

Example

```
MsgBox Oct(8)
```

Results in

```
10
```

See also Hex

OL

HTML & NETSCAPE

Description The OL command tells a browser that the text between <OL> and </OL> is to be displayed in an "ordered list" format, like a shopping list. OL is similar to the other list format commands: <DIR> (a "filename-like" style), <MENU> (a list made up of short phrases), and <UL> (a bulleted list—bullets, small dots, are automatically added at the start of each item). However, with <OL>, numbers are automatically added at the start of each item, and the items are indented from the left margin.

Like all the list format commands, each item (each separate line) in the list must be preceded by the LI command. There is also a set of additional formatting codes that can be used with any LI command. See Variables below.

Used with ***Can be enclosed by***

<BANNER>, <BODY>, <BODYTEXT>, <DD>, <DIV>, <FIGTEXT>, <FN>, <FORM>, <LI>, <NOTE>, <TD>, <TH>

Can enclose

<LI>

O

Variables **CONTINUE:** This command specifies that any previous number sequence should be continued (don't restart with item 1).

```
<OL CONTINUE>
```

SEQNUM: Start the numbering of the list with a number other than the default 1:

```
<OL SEQNUM=11>
```

COMPACT: Some browsers will reduce the vertical space between the lines if you use the COMPACT command. This vertical space is called *leading* by typographers. Other browsers will reduce the font size.

Variables that can be used with LI: Note that the following TYPE commands currently work only with Netscape browsers.

`<LI TYPE=A>`	Uses large characters.
`<LI TYPE=a>`	Uses small characters.
`<LI TYPE=I>`	Start with large Roman numerals.
`<LI TYPE=i>`	Start with small Roman numerals.
`<LI TYPE=1>`	Start with numbers.

Uses Display a numbered list to the user.

Cautions LI is used alone (there is no </LI> command).

Example

This is normal body text.

1. This is item one
2. This is item two

Figure O-6: An ordered list format indents each item, and automatically adds sequential numbers.

```
<HTML>
<BODY BGCOLOR=WHITE>
<FONT SIZE=+1>
This is normal body text.<br>
<OL>
<LI>This is item one
<LI>This is item two
</OL>
</HTML>
```

See also LI, DIR, MENU, UL

OldHeight, OldWidth, OldTop & OldLeft

ACTIVEX

See Properties

OnClick

HTML

Description Some of the Controls built into HTML, such as the Button Control, will respond to user mouse-clicks. You can write a script that will react to such Events:

```
<HTML>
<INPUT TYPE=BUTTON VALUE="Click Here" NAME="Btn">
<BR><BR>
<INPUT NAME="Box" SIZE=45>
<SCRIPT LANGUAGE=VBS>
Sub Btn_OnClick
Box.Value = "Thank you for clicking."
End Sub

</SCRIPT>
</FONT>

</HTML>
```

ActiveX Controls include an Event that's identical to the HTML OnClick attribute, but with ActiveX Controls it's called the Click Event. See "Events."

See INPUT

On Error

VBSCRIPT STATEMENT

See Err

OnLoad

VBSCRIPT EVENT

Description If you want something to happen when the browser first loads your document, you can put it in the OnLoad Event of the Window Object:

```
Sub window_onLoad()
  msgbox "Welcome"
end sub
```

See Layout in the entry on "Events."

Operators

Description Any intelligent entity must make distinctions. You base decisions on your perception of the relation between two Objects. Is this piece of pie bigger than the other one? Does Jones come before Johnson alphabetically? Is there more profit selling balls or bats?

The computer uses *operators* to discover a relationship between two or more things. There are three main categories of operators. There are *relational* operators, which tell you whether one thing is greater than or equal to another thing. There are *arithmetic* operators, which perform all the usual math (addition, subtraction, multiplication, division) along with some special effects such as modulo arithmetic. And finally there are *logical* operators, which compare Objects based on tests such as "and" and "or."

Most of the time, you'll use the If…Then structure with an operator:

```
If N - T < 5 Then
MsgBox "Yes, it's true"
End If
```

The above example tests the contents of two Variables, *n* and *t*. If the contents of t subtracted from n are less than 5, the message box will be displayed.

Relational "Comparison" Operators

Operator	Meaning
<	Less than
<=	Less than or equal to
>	Greater than
>=	Greater than or equal to
<>	Not equal
=	Equal

Note: You can use the relational operators with text as well. When used with literal text (or text Variables), the operators refer to the *alphabetic* qualities of the text, with *Andy* being "less than" *Anne*. The relational operators are *comparisons*, and the result of that comparison is always True or False.

Arithmetic Operators

Operator	Meaning
^	Exponentiation (the number multiplied by itself: 5 ^ 2 is 25 and 5 ^ 3 is 125)
-	Negation (negative numbers, such as –25)
*	Multiplication
/	Division
\	Integer Division (Division with no remainder, no fraction, and no "floating-point" decimal point: 8 \ 6 is 1. Integer division is easier, and the computer performs it faster than regular division.)
`Mod`	Modulo arithmetic (See "Special Note on Mod," later in this section.)
+	Addition
-	Subtraction
&	String Concatenation ("Tom" & " Jones" results in: Tom Jones)

Variant Variables can be combined in a similar way to the traditional text Variable concatenation:

```
A = "This":B = "That":MsgBox A + B
```

Results in

```
ThisThat
```

However, you are urged to use the + operator only with arithmetic operations (to add numbers). In this book, you may have noticed that we frequently resort to the + operator for text concatenation. Why? Until late in the process of writing this book, the & operator was not functional. However, it now works, so to concatenate text, use the & operator:

```
MsgBox A & B
```

When you use *Variants* (recall that unless you specify otherwise with one of the coercing commands such as cInt or cDbl, VBScript always defaults to Variants):

```
x = 5:a = "This":MsgBox x & a
```

Results in

```
5This
```

Logical Operators

`Not`	Logical Negation
`And`	And
`Or`	Inclusive OR
`XOR`	(Either but not Both)
`Eqv`	(Equivalent)
`Imp`	(Implication—first item False or second item True)

In practice, you'll likely need to use only *Not*, *And*, *XOR*, and *Or* from among the logical operators. And you're likely to need to use them only rarely, if at all. The four most significant operators work pretty much the way they do in English:

```
If 5 + 2 = 4 Or 6 + 6 = 12 Then MsgBox "One of them is true."
```

(One of these expressions is True, so the comment will be printed. Only one OR the other needs to be True.)

```
If 5 + 2 = 4 And 6 + 6 = 12 Then MsgBox "Both of them are
true."
```

(This is False, so nothing is displayed. Both expressions, the first AND the second, must be True for the message box to pop up.)

Getting & Setting Bits: AND and XOR

Sometimes an individual bit will be used to represent something. For example, Windows disk file attributes are stored this way. A file might have more than one quality—hidden, archive, read-only—so those respective bits in the file attribute byte would all be "on." To read these individual bits, to find out which ones are "on" and which "off," you use the And operator. In this example, we used the command GetAttr, which is part of Visual Basic, but *not part of VBScript.* We're just providing an illustration here of how you can read and write to individual bits. Let's assume that we've put a particular disk file's attribute into the Variable *fa.* To read these bits, then:

```
If fa And 0 Then f = "Normal"
If fa And 1 Then f = f + cr + "Read-Only"
If fa And 2 Then f = f + cr + "Hidden"
If fa And 4 Then f = f + cr + "System"
If fa And 8 Then f = f + cr + "Volume Label"
If fa And 16 Then f = f + cr + "Directory"
If fa And 32 Then f = f + cr + "Archive--file has changed"
```

If you want to change ("flip") a bit, use the XOR operator. The XOR operator will "flip" an individual bit without disturbing the other bits in the number. More than one attribute can be "on," but they are all stored in a single number so you don't want to change more than the bit representing the attribute you are interested in. In this example, we want to reset the archive attribute that is coded as the number 32. Here's how we flip it on and off each time the user presses a Button:

```
Sub Button1_Click ()
  fa = fa Xor 32
End Sub
```

Testing for Intervals: Mod

Special Note on Mod: The Modulo (Mod) operator gives you any remainder after a division—but not the results of the division itself. This operation is useful when you want to know if some number divides evenly into another number. That way, you could do things at intervals. If you wanted to print the page number in bold on every fifth page, for example, you could enter the following:

```
If PageNumber Mod 5 = 0 Then
  FontBold = -1
Else
  FontBold = 0
End IF
```

15 Mod 5 results in 0.
16 Mod 5 results in 1.
17 Mod 5 results in 2.
20 Mod 5 results in 0 again.

The Text Operator
The + operator adds pieces of text together (though you are encouraged to use the & operator instead).

```
N = "Lois "
N1 = "Lane"
J = N + " " + N1
MsgBox J
```

Results in

```
Lois Lane
```

(You can also use the "relational operators" to compare the alphabetical relationship between two pieces of text.)

Operator Precedence: When you use more than one operator in an expression, which operator should be evaluated first?

```
MsgBox 3 * 10 + 5
```

Does this mean first multiply 3 times 10, getting 30? And then add 5 to the result? Should VBScript display 35?

O

Or does this mean add 10 to 5, getting 15? And then multiply the result by 3? *This* would result in 45.

Expressions are not necessarily evaluated by the computer from left to right. (A left-to-right evaluation would result in 35 because 3 would be multiplied by 10 before the 5 was added to that result.)

Instead there is an "order of precedence," a hierarchy of operators. Some operators are executed before others. For instance, multiplication is carried out before addition. To make sure that you get the results you intend when using more than one operator in an expression, use parentheses to enclose the items you want evaluated first. If you intended to say 3 * 10 and then add 5:

```
MsgBox (3 * 10) + 5
```

By enclosing something in parentheses, you tell VBScript that you want the enclosed items to be considered a single value and to be evaluated before anything else happens.

If you intended to say 10 + 5 and then multiply by 3:

```
MsgBox 3 * (10 + 5)
```

In complicated expressions, you can even *nest* parentheses to make clear which items are to be calculated in which order:

```
MsgBox 3 * ((9 + 1) + 5)
```

If you work with numbers a great deal, you might want to memorize the following table. Although most people just use parentheses and forget about this precedence problem, it may be helpful to know the order in which VBScript will evaluate an expression, from first-evaluated to last:

Arithmetic Operators in Order of Precedence

^	Exponents (6 ^ 2 is 36. The number is multiplied by itself X number of times.)
-	Negation (Negative numbers like –33)
* /	Multiplication and Division
\	Integer Division (Division with no remainder, no fraction, and no "floating-point" decimal point. 8 \ 6 is 1.)

`Mod`	Modulo Arithmetic (Any remainder after division. 23 Mod 12 is 11. See "Mod.")
`+ -`	Addition and Subtraction

The Relational Operators

The Logical Operators

Given that multiplication has precedence over addition, our ambiguous example would be evaluated in the following way:

```
MsgBox 3 * 10 + 5
```

Results in

```
35
```

OPTION

HTML

Description Indicates an item in a ListBox. OPTION is used within the <SELECT> and </NOSELECT> structure. OPTION is to the SELECT command what LI is to the DIR or MENU command.

See Select

Option Button

ACTIVEX CONTROL

Description Option Buttons offer the user a set of possible choices, but the user can choose only one of them. Option Buttons are mutually exclusive—click on any Option Button and all the other buttons in its group are deselected (like the buttons on a car radio). An alternative, but similar, mode of selection, CheckBoxes, allow the user to choose one, none, or as many of the boxes as needed. A third possibility is the new ToggleButton ActiveX Control. ToggleButtons act like CheckBoxes (individual discrete choices). See the entry for "ToggleButton."

Therefore, you use Option Buttons when the user can select only a *single* option among several (boldface versus normal text). Use CheckBoxes when the user can select more than one option (boldface and italic text; the user could choose boldface, italic, or both boldface and italic).

A third technique when offering the user a set of choices is the ListBox. It's valuable when you offer more than a few choices.

The user can trigger an Option button by clicking anywhere within the frame of the button (on the button graphic, the picture, if any, on the caption, or even outside the caption if the frame is larger than the caption). The button that has the focus is indicated visually by a dotted-line box around the caption. In other words, if a particular Option Button—among all the Controls on a document—has the focus, it will have that faint gray line around it.

Variables

VALUE: The Value Property of Option Buttons determines whether a given box is undotted, dotted, or contains a grayed dot—meaning neither checked nor unchecked (nothing has happened yet to any of the buttons in the group). The Value Property can be read:

```
X = OptionButton1.VALUE
```


OR changed:

```
OptionButton1.VALUE = 0
```

Because Value is the default Property, you can also omit the VALUE if you wish:

```
X = OptionButton1
OptionButton1 = 0
```

VALUE = NULL: The item is neither selected nor cleared (a gray dot appears within it, and the entire button is lighter than normal). For this NULL value to be possible, the TripleState Property must also be set to True. TripleState defaults to False.

–1 True. The item is checked.

0 False. The item is blank, unselected.

GROUPNAME: This Property is unique to the Option Button. It allows you to define sets, groups of buttons that act together (click on one, all others are deselected). This way, you can have more than a single group of Option Buttons on a single document or page.

By default, the GroupName Property is blank (an empty text Variable ""). In effect, this means that all Option Buttons that you create on a given document share the same GroupName and thus will toggle each other. It doesn't matter if they're proximate: one could be at the top of the page and the rest could be at the bottom of the page—but as long as they share the same GroupName, they're interactive.

If, however, you change the GroupName Property of one or more of the buttons to some other name, then those buttons leave the default "" blank GroupName and become members of the new group. See the example for an illustration.

OR (to change an Option Button's caption while the program is running):

```
OptionButton1.Caption = "Last Month's Bills"
```

OR (to change the type size of an Option Button's caption):

```
OptionButton1.FontSize = 12
```

OR (to make one button the same size vertically as another):

```
OptionButton1.Height = OptionButton2.Height
```

Properties

Accelerator, Alignment, AutoSize, BackColor, BackStyle, Caption, CodeBase, Enabled, Font, ForeColor, GroupName, Height, Left, Locked, MouseIcon, MousePointer, Picture, PicturePosition, SpecialEffect, TabIndex, TabStop, Top, TripleState, Value, Visible, Width, WordWrap

Methods

Move, SetFocus, ZOrder

Events

AfterUpdate, BeforeDragOver, BeforeDropOrPaste, BeforeUpdate, Change, Click, DblClick, Enter, Error, Exit, KeyDown, KeyPress, KeyUp, MouseDown, MouseMove, MouseUp

For details about these Properties, Events, and Methods, see the entries for "Properties," "Events," and "Methods."

Uses

- Use Option Buttons when you want the user to be able to customize or otherwise control the way your document looks or behaves—but among the choices, the user can select only one option. If the user should be able to select more than a single choice from among a group of choices, use a CheckBox Control instead.
- Option Buttons are not the most visually attractive Controls. If you need them, you might want to make them visible in a special frame of their own (selected, say, when the user clicks on a Command Button with the caption "OPTIONS"). Then hide that frame when it's no longer needed.

  Alternatively, you can fiddle with the way Option Buttons appear: make their borders overlap to bring the text lines closer together; offset the lines, staggering them; put them on a frame or an Image Control; or use icons in the Picture Property of the Option Buttons themselves to provide more dramatic visual symbols.

Cautions When you load a graphic with the Picture Property, the Option Button's caption will become invisible. This differs from the current behavior of the CheckBox, which permits the caption to be seen on top of any graphic. Perhaps soon this fault of the Option Button will be remedied.

Example We'll create two groups of Option Buttons by using the GroupName Property. Groups are not interactive: clicks on buttons in the first group will have no effect on the buttons in the second group. This way, you can create independent sets of "radio buttons."

Start the ActiveX Control Pad and select Edit | Insert HTML Layout. (See the Introduction for details about using the Control Pad.) Put six Option Buttons on the Layout. Change the GroupName Property of the bottom three buttons to: *SecondGroup* or whatever name you want to use. You can do this to all three buttons simultaneously by holding down the Shift key while clicking on each of the bottom three buttons in turn. Then right-click on one of them and choose Properties. Now you can change the GroupName of all three at once.

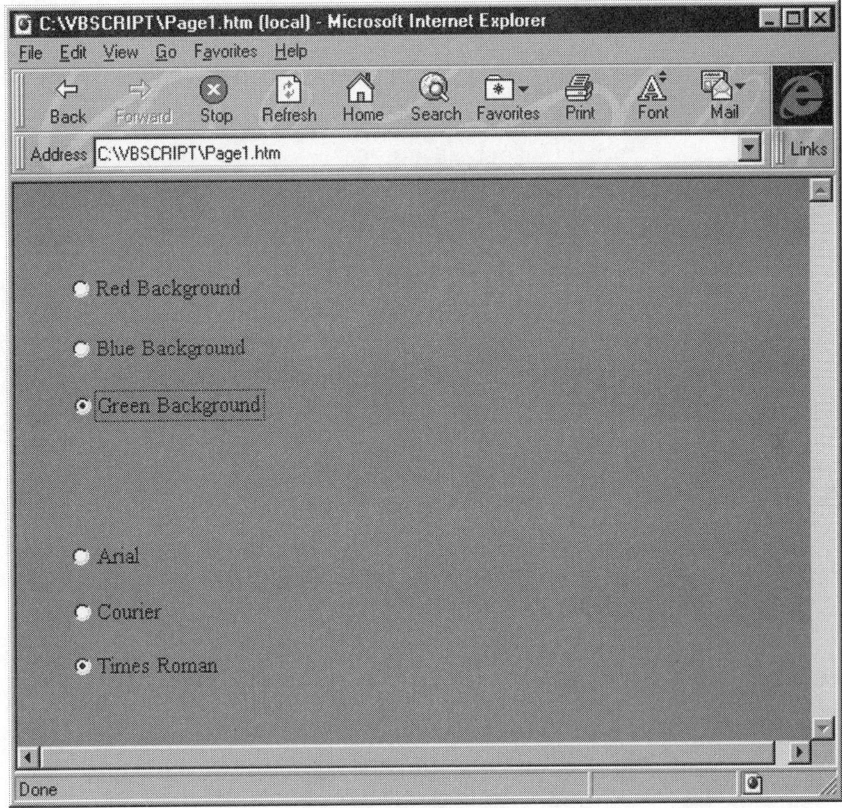

Figure O-7: Use the GroupName Property to create independent sets of Option Buttons on the same document.

With the first three buttons in one set and the second group of three in another set, we can now expect that clicking on a button within one set won't have any effect on the other set. Name the Caption Properties as shown in Figure O-7. Since we have to change the BackColor Property of the Layout itself, as well as the BackColor of each button, we decided to create a separate Subroutine to do this. That way, we don't have to repeat the whole process within each of the buttons' Click Events:

```
Sub ChangeColor (c)
OptionButton1.BackColor = c
OptionButton2.BackColor = c
OptionButton3.BackColor = c
OptionButton4.BackColor = c
OptionButton5.BackColor = c
OptionButton6.BackColor = c
n.BackColor = c
End Sub
```

Similarly, we created another Subroutine to handle the Font.Name changes:

```
Sub ChangeFont (n)
OptionButton1.Font.Name = n
OptionButton2.Font.Name = n
OptionButton3.Font.Name = n
OptionButton4.Font.Name = n
OptionButton5.Font.Name = n
OptionButton6.Font.Name = n
End Sub
```

Now, within each button's Click Event we put the appropriate Subroutine call. Here's the entire HTML Layout source code. If you're going to test this, save the section below between <DIV> and </DIV> under the filename N.ALX and customize the path to represent its location on your hard drive. In other words, change this path within the <OBJECT> definition: REF VALUE= "file:C:\Program Files\ActiveX Control Pad\n.alx."

```
<SCRIPT LANGUAGE="VBScript">
<!--
Sub OptionButton4_DblClick(Cancel)
OptionButton1.Font.Name = "arial"
end sub

Sub OptionButton1_Click()
ChangeColor "&H0000FF"
end sub

Sub OptionButton2_Click()
ChangeColor "&HFF0000"
end sub

Sub OptionButton3_Click()
ChangeColor "&H00FF00"
end sub

Sub OptionButton4_Click()
ChangeFont "Arial"
end sub

Sub OptionButton5_Click()
ChangeFont "Courier"
end sub

Sub OptionButton6_Click()
ChangeFont "Times New Roman"
end sub

Sub ChangeFont (n)
OptionButton1.Font.Name = n
OptionButton2.Font.Name = n
OptionButton3.Font.Name = n
OptionButton4.Font.Name = n
OptionButton5.Font.Name = n
OptionButton6.Font.Name = n
End Sub
```

```
Sub ChangeColor (c)
OptionButton1.BackColor = c
OptionButton2.BackColor = c
OptionButton3.BackColor = c
OptionButton4.BackColor = c
OptionButton5.BackColor = c
OptionButton6.BackColor = c
n.BackColor = c
End Sub
-->
</SCRIPT>

<DIV BACKGROUND="#c0c0c0" ID="n"
STYLE="LAYOUT:FIXED;WIDTH:409pt;HEIGHT:271pt;">
<OBJECT ID="OptionButton1"
CLASSID="CLSID:8BD21D50-EC42-11CE-9E0D-00AA006002F3"
STYLE="TOP:31pt;LEFT:20pt;WIDTH:110pt;HEIGHT:20pt;TABINDEX:0;ZINDEX:0;">
  <PARAM NAME="BackColor" VALUE="2147483663">
  <PARAM NAME="ForeColor" VALUE="2147483666">
  <PARAM NAME="DisplayStyle" VALUE="5">
  <PARAM NAME="Size" VALUE="3881;706">
  <PARAM NAME="Caption" VALUE="Red Background">
  <PARAM NAME="FontName" VALUE="Arial">
  <PARAM NAME="FontHeight" VALUE="220">
  <PARAM NAME="FontCharSet" VALUE="0">
  <PARAM NAME="FontPitchAndFamily" VALUE="2">
  <PARAM NAME="FontWeight" VALUE="0">
</OBJECT>
<OBJECT ID="OptionButton2"
CLASSID="CLSID:8BD21D50-EC42-11CE-9E0D-00AA006002F3"
STYLE="TOP:56pt;LEFT:20pt;WIDTH:100pt;HEIGHT:30pt;TABINDEX:1;ZINDEX:1;">
  <PARAM NAME="BackColor" VALUE="2147483663">
  <PARAM NAME="ForeColor" VALUE="64">
  <PARAM NAME="DisplayStyle" VALUE="5">
  <PARAM NAME="Size" VALUE="3528;1058">
  <PARAM NAME="Caption" VALUE="Blue Background">
  <PARAM NAME="FontName" VALUE="Arial">
  <PARAM NAME="FontHeight" VALUE="220">
  <PARAM NAME="FontCharSet" VALUE="0">
  <PARAM NAME="FontPitchAndFamily" VALUE="2">
```

```
  <PARAM NAME="FontWeight" VALUE="0">
</OBJECT>
<OBJECT ID="OptionButton3"
CLASSID="CLSID:8BD21D50-EC42-11CE-9E0D-00AA006002F3"
STYLE="TOP:82pt;LEFT:21pt;WIDTH:118pt;HEIGHT:35pt;TABINDEX:2;ZINDEX:2;">
  <PARAM NAME="BackColor" VALUE="2147483663">
  <PARAM NAME="ForeColor" VALUE="2147483666">
  <PARAM NAME="DisplayStyle" VALUE="5">
  <PARAM NAME="Size" VALUE="4163;1235">
  <PARAM NAME="Caption" VALUE="Green Background">
  <PARAM NAME="FontName" VALUE="Arial">
  <PARAM NAME="FontHeight" VALUE="220">
  <PARAM NAME="FontCharSet" VALUE="0">
  <PARAM NAME="FontPitchAndFamily" VALUE="2">
  <PARAM NAME="FontWeight" VALUE="0">
</OBJECT>
<OBJECT ID="OptionButton4"
CLASSID="CLSID:8BD21D50-EC42-11CE-9E0D-00AA006002F3"
STYLE="TOP:164pt;LEFT:20pt;WIDTH:93pt;HEIGHT:20pt;TABINDEX:3;ZINDEX:3;">
  <PARAM NAME="BackColor" VALUE="2147483663">
  <PARAM NAME="ForeColor" VALUE="2147483666">
  <PARAM NAME="DisplayStyle" VALUE="5">
  <PARAM NAME="Size" VALUE="3281;706">
  <PARAM NAME="Caption" VALUE="Arial">
  <PARAM NAME="GroupName" VALUE="SecondGroup">
  <PARAM NAME="FontName" VALUE="Arial">
  <PARAM NAME="FontHeight" VALUE="220">
  <PARAM NAME="FontCharSet" VALUE="0">
  <PARAM NAME="FontPitchAndFamily" VALUE="2">
  <PARAM NAME="FontWeight" VALUE="0">
</OBJECT>
<OBJECT ID="OptionButton5"
CLASSID="CLSID:8BD21D50-EC42-11CE-9E0D-00AA006002F3"
STYLE="TOP:193pt;LEFT:20pt;WIDTH:90pt;HEIGHT:19pt;TABINDEX:4;ZINDEX:4;">
  <PARAM NAME="BackColor" VALUE="2147483663">
  <PARAM NAME="ForeColor" VALUE="2147483666">
  <PARAM NAME="DisplayStyle" VALUE="5">
  <PARAM NAME="Size" VALUE="3175;670">
  <PARAM NAME="Caption" VALUE="Courier">
  <PARAM NAME="GroupName" VALUE="SecondGroup">
```

O

```
  <PARAM NAME="FontName" VALUE="Arial">
  <PARAM NAME="FontHeight" VALUE="220">
  <PARAM NAME="FontCharSet" VALUE="0">
  <PARAM NAME="FontPitchAndFamily" VALUE="2">
  <PARAM NAME="FontWeight" VALUE="0">
</OBJECT>
<OBJECT ID="OptionButton6"
CLASSID="CLSID:8BD21D50-EC42-11CE-9E0D-00AA006002F3"
STYLE="TOP:220pt;LEFT:20pt;WIDTH:93pt;HEIGHT:19pt;TABINDEX:5;ZINDEX:5;">
  <PARAM NAME="BackColor" VALUE="2147483663">
  <PARAM NAME="ForeColor" VALUE="2147483666">
  <PARAM NAME="DisplayStyle" VALUE="5">
  <PARAM NAME="Size" VALUE="3281;670">
  <PARAM NAME="Caption" VALUE="Times Roman">
  <PARAM NAME="GroupName" VALUE="SecondGroup">
  <PARAM NAME="FontName" VALUE="Arial">
  <PARAM NAME="FontHeight" VALUE="220">
  <PARAM NAME="FontCharSet" VALUE="0">
  <PARAM NAME="FontPitchAndFamily" VALUE="2">
  <PARAM NAME="FontWeight" VALUE="0">
</OBJECT>
</DIV>
```

O

In the separate HTML window of the Microsoft ActiveX Control Pad, here's the source code for the Layout Control Object itself and the HTML source code that surrounds it:

```
<HTML>
<BODY>

<OBJECT CLASSID="CLSID:812AE312-8B8E-11CF-93C8-00AA00C08FDF"
ID="n_alx" STYLE="LEFT:0;TOP:0">
<PARAM NAME="ALXPATH" REF VALUE="file:C:\Program
Files\ActiveX Control Pad\n.alx">
 </OBJECT>

</BODY>
</HTML>
```

See also ToggleButton, CheckBox, ListBox

Option Explicit

Description If you put the Option Explicit command at the top of your VBScript, you'll be forced to Dim (declare) each Variable you use. Trying to get away with an *implicit* Variable (one that you create by merely using it) will result in an error message from the Internet Explorer browser. Here we're just going to put a value into the Variable *N* and thereby create it implicitly:

```
<HTML>
<BODY>

<SCRIPT LANGUAGE="VBSCRIPT">

Option Explicit

Sub Window_OnLoad
  N = 12
  MsgBox N
End Sub

</SCRIPT>

</BODY>
</HTML>
```

When you load this into Internet Explorer, it puts up the following error message:

```
Microsoft VBScript runtime error
[Line: 9] Variable is undefined
```

You won't get this message if you omit the Option Explicit from this script. You can also avoid this error if you explicitly declare *N* like this:

```
<SCRIPT LANGUAGE="VBSCRIPT">

Option Explicit
Dim N
```

```
Sub Window_OnLoad
  N = 12
  MsgBox N
End Sub

</SCRIPT>
```

Some programmers believe that all Variables should be declared explicitly. They feel that this prevents some bugs. Indeed, some languages require explicit declaration for this exact reason. Basic, though, with its philosophy of giving programmers freedom of choice, allows implicit Variable usage. However, if you want to enforce Variable declaration on yourself, put Option Explicit into all your scripts.

See Dim

OR

VBSCRIPT OPERATOR

See Operators

Orientation

ACTIVEX

See Properties

P

P

HTML

Description <P> stands for *paragraph*. The precise way that a browser displays text when the P command is used will vary—how much space between lines, any indentation at the start of the paragraph, and so on. See the proceeding example for the format used by Internet Explorer.

Used with

Can be enclosed by

<ADDRESS>, <BANNER>, <BODY>, <BODYTEXT>, <DD>, <DIV>, <FIGTEXT>, <FN>, <FORM>, <LI>, <NOTE>, <TD>, <TH>

Can enclose

<A>, <ABBREV>, <ACRONYM>, <AU>, <B>, <BIG>, <BR>, <CITE>, <CODE>, <DEL>, <DFN>, <EM>, <I>, <IMG>, <INS>, <KBD>, <LANG>, <MATH>, <PERSON>, <Q>, <S>, <SAMP>, <SMALL>, <STRONG>, <SUB>, <SUP>, <TAB>, <TT>, <U>, <VAR>

Uses Format text into paragraph-style blocks.

Cautions

- The </P> closing command is not required.
- You can get the same general effect by using

 to insert a line break and a blank line, though some browsers do more than merely insert a blank line.

Example

It stands for paragraph. The precise way that a browser displays text when the P command is used will vary--how much space between lines, any indentation at the start of the paragraph, and so on. See the Example below for the format used by Internet Explorer.

It stands for paragraph. The precise way that a browser displays text when the P command is used will vary--how much space between lines, any indentation at the start of the paragraph, and so on. See the Example below for the format used by Internet Explorer.

It stands for paragraph. The precise way that a browser displays text when the P command is used will vary--how much space between lines, any indentation at the start of the paragraph, and so on. See the Example below for the format used by Internet Explorer. It stands for paragraph. The precise way that a browser displays text when the P command is used will vary--how much space between lines, any indentation at the start of the paragraph, and so on. See the Example below for the format used by Internet Explorer.

Figure P-1: The top half of this figure uses the PRE command to create paragraphs; the bottom half is the same text, but without PRE.

```
<HTML>
<BODY BGCOLOR=WHITE>
<FONT SIZE=+1>
  It stands for paragraph. The precise way that a browser
displays text when the P command is used will vary-how much
space between lines, any indentation at the start of the
paragraph, and so on. See the Example below for the format
used by Internet Explorer.
<P>
  It stands for paragraph. The precise way that a browser
displays text when the P command is used will vary-how much
space between lines, any indentation at the start of the
paragraph, and so on. See the Example below for the format
used by Internet Explorer.
</P>
<Compu</HTML>
```

See also
, <TAB>

PARAM

ACTIVEX

Description The <PARAM> tag appears within an <OBJECT> </OBJECT> definition. A PARAM is a *Property* (or *quality*) of an object. If you run the Microsoft ActiveX Control Pad and select Insert ActiveX Control from its Edit menu, you'll see a list of qualities within the OBJECT definition in your HTML source code. For example, if you insert a Label ActiveX Object, you'll see something like this:

```
<OBJECT ID="Label1" WIDTH=96 HEIGHT=24
 CLASSID="CLSID:978C9E23-D4B0-11CE-BF2D-00AA003F40D0">
  <PARAM NAME="Size" VALUE="2540;635">
  <PARAM NAME="FontCharSet" VALUE="0">
  <PARAM NAME="FontPitchAndFamily" VALUE="2">
  <PARAM NAME="FontWeight" VALUE="0">
</OBJECT>
```

Each PARAM describes a Property of the Label. Each PARAM has a NAME and a VALUE. If you click on the icon next to the <OBJECT> definition in the ActiveX Control Pad's source code, you'll see a Properties Window pop up. You'll find equivalent Properties (NAMEs) and equivalent VALUEs—though there might be some variance.

You can directly edit the PARAM list, or make changes from within the Properties Window. Any changes you make in the Properties Window will automatically be updated in the PARAM list. For example, if you change the TextAlign Property in the Properties Window to "Right," then close the Properties Window and the Label positioning Window, you'll see that the following PARAM has been added to your source code:

```
<PARAM NAME="ParagraphAlign" VALUE="3">
```

For more on OBJECTS and their parameters, see "Properties," "Objects" or each ActiveX Control by name, such as "Label."

See Objects

P

Parent

ACTIVEX

See Properties

PasswordChar

ACTIVEX

See Properties

Paste

ACTIVEX

See Methods

Picture

ACTIVEX

See Properties

PictureAlignment, PicturePath, PicturePosition

ACTIVEX

See Properties

PictureSizeMode, PictureTiling

ACTIVEX

See Properties

PopUp Menu

ACTIVEX CONTROL

Description The PopUp Menu is similar to what happens in Windows or NT when you right-click: a menu appears at the location where you clicked. However, with the PopUp Menu, you can optionally specify an alternative location for the menu.

Note that at the time of this writing, you have to add menu items by editing parameters within your HTML source code (as we'll demonstrate in the example that follows). There is no provision for adding items via the Properties window. (Alternatively, if you prefer, you can dynamically add menu items from within a script, using the AddItem Method. See Variables below.)

Variables Start the Microsoft ActiveX Control Pad and click on Edit | Insert ActiveX Control. Scroll until you locate "PopUp Menu Object." When you first add a PopUp menu to your HTML source code, it will look something like this:

```
<OBJECT ID="IEPOP1" WIDTH=95 HEIGHT=56
 CLASSID="CLSID:7823A620-9DD9-11CF-A662-00AA00C066D2">
  <PARAM NAME="_ExtentX" VALUE="0">
  <PARAM NAME="_ExtentY" VALUE="0">
</OBJECT>
```

Edit the parameter list to add menu items, like this:

```
<OBJECT ID="IEPOP1" WIDTH=95 HEIGHT=56
 CLASSID="CLSID:7823A620-9DD9-11CF-A662-00AA00C066D2">
   <PARAM NAME="_ExtentX" VALUE="0">
   <PARAM NAME="_ExtentY" VALUE="0">
   <PARAM NAME="Menuitem[0]" VALUE="Red Letters">
   <PARAM NAME="Menuitem[1]" VALUE="Yellow Letters">
   <PARAM NAME="Menuitem[2]" VALUE="Black Letters">
</OBJECT>
```

Adding & Removing Menu Items

If you want to add menu items from within a script, here's how to do it when your document first loads into the user's browser:

P

```
<SCRIPT LANGUAGE="VBScript">
Sub window_onLoad()
IEPOP1.AddItem("Red Letters")
IEPOP1.AddItem("Yellow Letters")
IEPOP1.AddItem("Black Letters")
end sub
</SCRIPT>
```

Note that we've provided no index number for each AddItem, so they are simply added to the end of the list of whatever other menu items exist already. If you want to specify the insertion location for a new item, use this format:

```
IEPOP1.AddItem("New One", 3)
```

This 3 specifies that a new item named "New One" will be inserted in the *fourth* position. The list begins with zero, so 3 is really the fourth item. At this time, this indexed add or removal is not yet working.

To remove the second item, do this:

```
IEPOP1.RemoveItem(1)
```

And to remove all items:

```
IEPOP1.Clear
```

P

Clicking on Menu Items

To react to user clicks on your PopUp menu, create a Sub that reacts. Provide the name of your PopUp Control (in this case the name or ID is "Iepop1") and attach the word Click. Also type in (x) because the x will tell you which menu item has been clicked:

```
<SCRIPT LANGUAGE="VBScript">
Sub Iepopl_Click (x)
Select Case x
Case 1
CommandButton1.ForeColor = 255
Case 2
CommandButton1.ForeColor = 65535
Case 3
CommandButton1.ForeColor = 0
End Select
```

```
End Sub
</SCRIPT>
```

Note that the first item in your menu list is represented by 1, not 0.

Uses Offer the user a set of options. Unlike traditional menus that are always visible to the user, the PopUp style appears only briefly and disappears as soon as the user makes a selection or clicks somewhere outside the menu.

Cautions At the time of this writing, the indexed AddItem Method was not yet working, though the simple (add to end of list) AddItem Method was working. The indexed RemoveItem Method and the Clear Method are also working.

Example Here's the complete source code for a PopUp menu that allows the user to adjust the color of the caption on a CommandButton:

Figure P-2: Clicking on this menu changes the text color of the Command Button.

```
<HTML>
<BODY BGCOLOR=WHITE>
<BR><BR>

<SCRIPT LANGUAGE="VBScript">
<!--
Sub CommandButton1_Click()
IEPOP1.PopUp
end sub
-->
</SCRIPT>

<SCRIPT LANGUAGE="VBScript">
```

```
Sub Iepop1_Click (x)

Select Case x
Case 1
CommandButton1.ForeColor = 255
Case 2
CommandButton1.ForeColor = 65535
Case 3
CommandButton1.ForeColor = 0
End Select

n = cint(x)

IEPOP1.RemoveItem(2)
End Sub

</SCRIPT>

<OBJECT ID="CommandButton1" WIDTH=145 HEIGHT=32
 CLASSID="CLSID:D7053240-CE69-11CD-A777-00DD01143C57">
  <PARAM NAME="Caption" VALUE="Show Letter Color Menu">
  <PARAM NAME="Size" VALUE="3837;846">
  <PARAM NAME="FontCharSet" VALUE="0">
  <PARAM NAME="FontPitchAndFamily" VALUE="2">
  <PARAM NAME="ParagraphAlign" VALUE="3">
  <PARAM NAME="FontWeight" VALUE="0">
 </OBJECT>
<OBJECT ID="IEPOP1" WIDTH=95 HEIGHT=56
 CLASSID="CLSID:7823A620-9DD9-11CF-A662-00AA00C066D2">
  <PARAM NAME="_ExtentX" VALUE="0">
  <PARAM NAME="_ExtentY" VALUE="0">
  <PARAM NAME="Menuitem[0]" VALUE="Red Letters">
  <PARAM NAME="Menuitem[1]" VALUE="Yellow Letters">
  <PARAM NAME="Menuitem[2]" VALUE="Black Letters">
</OBJECT>

</BODY>
</HTML>
```

See also ListBox, CheckBox

PopUp Window

ACTIVEX CONTROL

Description You can show a URL to the user within a PopUp Window. The user can't do anything with it—can't click on links or type anything. In fact, as soon as the user clicks or presses a key, the PopUp Window disappears. It's purely to provide the user with a visual preview of an Internet site or document.

Variables The PopUp Window is quite similar in behavior to the PopUp Menu. Both are designed to be evanescent—brief visitors to a document—not permanently visible features of the page.

The object definition looks like this:

```
<OBJECT ID="PreVul" WIDTH=400 HEIGHT=100
 CLASSID="CLSID:A23D7C20-CABA-11CF-A5D4-00AA00A47DD2">
  <PARAM NAME="_ExtentX" VALUE="5054">
  <PARAM NAME="_ExtentY" VALUE="3519">
</OBJECT>
```

The primary way you program the Window is with the PopUp Method. You provide the target URL, followed by a comma and the word True or False. *True* means stretch or shrink the URL's contents to fit into the Window. *False* means size the window to fit the URL's contents. The default, should you leave off True or False, is False.

In this example, we're showing a CommandButton to the user. When the user clicks on the CommandButton, the PopUp Window's PopUp Method is invoked, showing a preview of Microsoft's home page:

```
<SCRIPT Language="VBSCRIPT">

Sub CommandButton1_Click
PreVul.Popup "http://www.microsoft.com", True
End Sub

</SCRIPT>
```

There is also a Dismiss Method that you could use, for example, within a Timer Control to programmatically close the PopUp Window:

```
PreVul.Dismiss
```

Uses

- Let the user see how a Web site looks, without actually *going* there.
- Provide previews of various Internet documents or sites, so the user can choose where to go.

Example

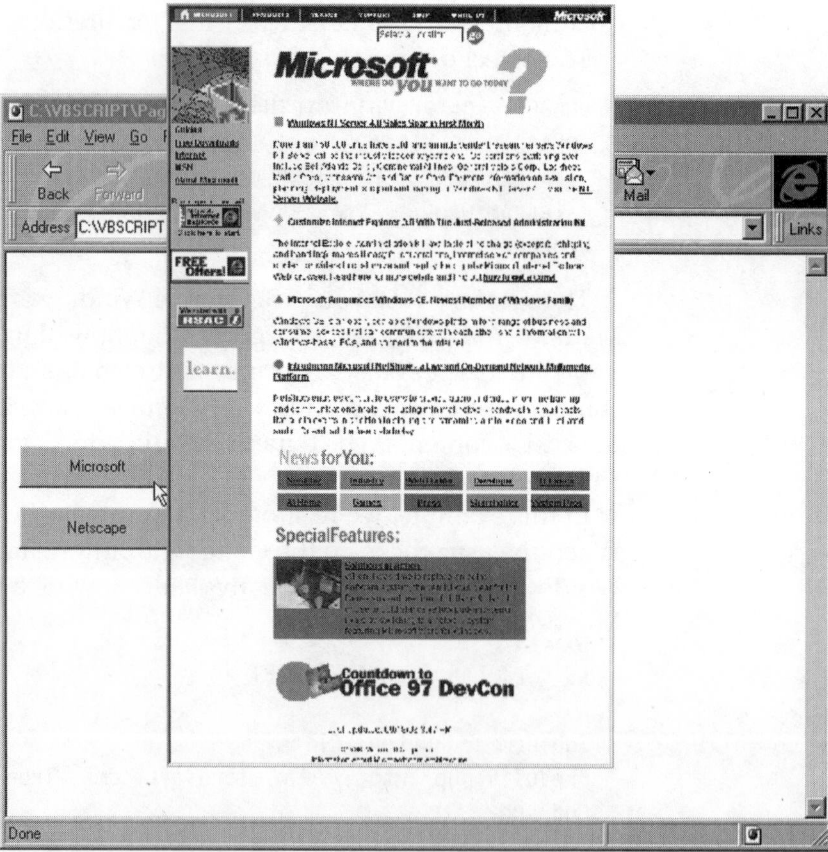

Figure P-3: Click on the upper CommandButton and you get a pop-up preview window of the Microsoft home page.

Start the Microsoft ActiveX Control Pad running (see the Introduction to this book). Using the Edit | Insert ActiveX Control, put two CommandButtons on the HTML source code, then add a PopUp Window Object (not the "Microsoft IE 30 PopUp Window Control" which is not working at the time of this writing). In the CommandButton's Click Events, type in the URLs that you want to display. Here's the complete HTML source code:

```
<HTML>
<BODY BGCOLOR=WHITE>
<BR><BR>

<SCRIPT Language="VBSCRIPT">
Sub CommandButton1_Click
PreVu1.Popup "http://www.microsoft.com"
End Sub

Sub CommandButton2_Click
PreVu1.Popup "http://www.netscape.com", True
End Sub
</SCRIPT>

<OBJECT ID="PreVu1" WIDTH=400 HEIGHT=100
 CLASSID="CLSID:A23D7C20-CABA-11CF-A5D4-00AA00A47DD2">
  <PARAM NAME="_ExtentX" VALUE="5054">
  <PARAM NAME="_ExtentY" VALUE="3519">
</OBJECT>

<BR>
<OBJECT ID="CommandButton1" WIDTH=123 HEIGHT=32
 CLASSID="CLSID:D7053240-CE69-11CD-A777-00DD01143C57">
  <PARAM NAME="Caption" VALUE="Microsoft">
  <PARAM NAME="Size" VALUE="3254;846">
  <PARAM NAME="FontCharSet" VALUE="0">
  <PARAM NAME="FontPitchAndFamily" VALUE="2">
  <PARAM NAME="ParagraphAlign" VALUE="3">
  <PARAM NAME="FontWeight" VALUE="0">
</OBJECT>
<BR><BR>
```

```
<OBJECT ID="CommandButton2" WIDTH=123 HEIGHT=32
 CLASSID="CLSID:D7053240-CE69-11CD-A777-00DD01143C57">
  <PARAM NAME="Caption" VALUE="Netscape">
  <PARAM NAME="Size" VALUE="3254;846">
  <PARAM NAME="FontCharSet" VALUE="0">
  <PARAM NAME="FontPitchAndFamily" VALUE="2">
  <PARAM NAME="ParagraphAlign" VALUE="3">
  <PARAM NAME="FontWeight" VALUE="0">
</OBJECT>

</BODY>
</HTML>
```

See also Image, Frame

PRE

HTML

Description PRE is a way of setting up tables, columns, vertically aligned lists, or other text that you want formatted in a precise way. However, the TAB command—and especially the TABLE command—are superior to PRE when you want to display a stable layout.

This command tells a browser that the text enclosed between <PRE> and </PRE> is *pre*formatted. In other words, it should be displayed using a non-proportional typeface (such as Courier). Such fonts are also called *fixed-width*. Fixed-width is a typewriter-style typeface where each character is the same width (*i* is as wide as *w*). (The opposite typeface style—Variable-width type—is typified by Times Roman, where the characters vary in width. Variable-width is the default HTML font for body text. The PRE command does essentially the same thing as the CODE, LISTING, and TT commands.

PRE also preserves any repeated blank (a blank is inserted into your text each time you press the spacebar) characters:

```
This blank space is preserved
```

Ordinary body text in HTML will ignore embedded blanks, treating a series of blanks as a single-space character.

P

Likewise, PRE preserves your line breaks (instead of automatically breaking lines at the right margin and wrapping the text down to the next line). Even if a line is long enough to go off the right side of the browser, it will not break—the user must resort to the browser's horizontal scrollbar to read this extra long line.

Used with ***Can be enclosed by***

<BANNER>, <BODY>, <BODYTEXT>, <DD>, <DIV>, <FIGTEXT>, <FN>, <FORM>, <LI>, <NOTE>, <TD>, <TH>

Can enclose

<A>, <ABBREV>, <ACRONYM>, <AU>, <B>, <BIG>, <BR>, <CITE>, <CODE>, <DEL>, <DFN>, <EM>, <I>, <IMG>, <INS>, <KBD>, <LANG>, <MATH>, <PERSON>, <Q>, <S>, <SAMP>, <SMALL>, <STRONG>, <SUB>, <SUP>, <TAB>, <TT>, <U>, <VAR>

Uses Preserve spacing and line breaks, thereby permitting you to create vertically aligned columns. However, the TABLE command is more flexible and reliable for these purposes.

Example

```
This is normal body text. The blank spaces are collapsed into a single blank.

This          has been rendered with the PRE command, blanks preserved.
You      can     create      simple      tables      this      way.
You      can     create      simple      tables      this      way.
You      can     create      simple      tables      this      way.
```

Figure P-4: You can use the PRE command to vertically align columns of text, but the TABLE command is superior.

```
<HTML>
<BODY BGCOLOR=WHITE>
<FONT SIZE=+1>
This is normal   body text. The blank spaces are collapsed
into a single blank.<br>
<PRE WIDTH=45>
This  has been rendered with the PRE command, blanks →
preserved.
You can create simple tables this way.
```

P

```
You can create simple tables this way.
You can create simple tables this way.
</PRE>
</HTML>
```

See also TABLE, TAB, CODE, LISTING, TT, XMP

Precedence Operators

Description 3 * 10 + 5

Does this mean first multiply 3 by 10, getting 30? And then add 5 to the result?

Or does it mean add 10 to 5, getting 15? And then multiply the result by 3? *This* would result in 45.

VBScript has a set of rules that describe which operations are performed first. The answer to the above problem is 35 because multiplication is performed before addition. You can, however, avoid trying to remember all the precedence rules by using parentheses. Anything within parentheses is considered a single idea—it's evaluated first. For example, if you intend to add 10 to 5, then multiply the result by 3, use a set of parentheses:

```
3 * (10 + 5)
```

See Operator Precedence, at the end of the entry on Operators

PreLoader

ACTIVEX CONTROL

Description You tell the PreLoader which URL (Web site document) you want downloaded to the user's cache (on the user's hard drive). Then, when the PreLoader's Enabled Property is set to True, the URL is sent. If the download is successful, the PreLoader's Complete Event is triggered; if not, its Error Event is triggered.

Variables The PreLoader has five Properties:

- To define the URL you want loaded:

```
PreLoader1.URL = "http://www.usatoday.com/"
```

- To cause the URL to be loaded:

```
PreLoader1.Enable = 1
```

OR, to prevent loading:

```
PreLoader1.Enable = 0
```

- To find out where the user's cache file is located:

```
X = PreLoader1.CacheFile
```

- To find out how many bytes have been loaded:

```
X = PreLoader1.Bytes
```

- To find out what percent of the total bytes have been loaded:

```
X = PreLoader1.Percentage
```

The PreLoader has two Events that it triggers. When it has finished loading a URL, the Complete Event is triggered:

```
Sub PreLoader1_Complete
  Alert "They've finished loading!"
End Sub
```

* If there is an error, the Error Event is triggered:

```
Sub PreLoader1_Error
  Alert "There was a problem!"
End Sub
```

* AboutBox is the only Method of a PreLoader.

Uses Anticipate what the user might want to see next, and save some time. For example, if page two of your document contains complex graphics that require a long time to download, you can have the PreLoader send page 2 into the user's cache while the user is reading the text on page 1.

P

Cautions The PreLoader, unique among Controls, has an *Enable* Property. For all other Controls with this feature, it's called the *Enabled* Property (Timer1.Enabled = True, for example).

Example

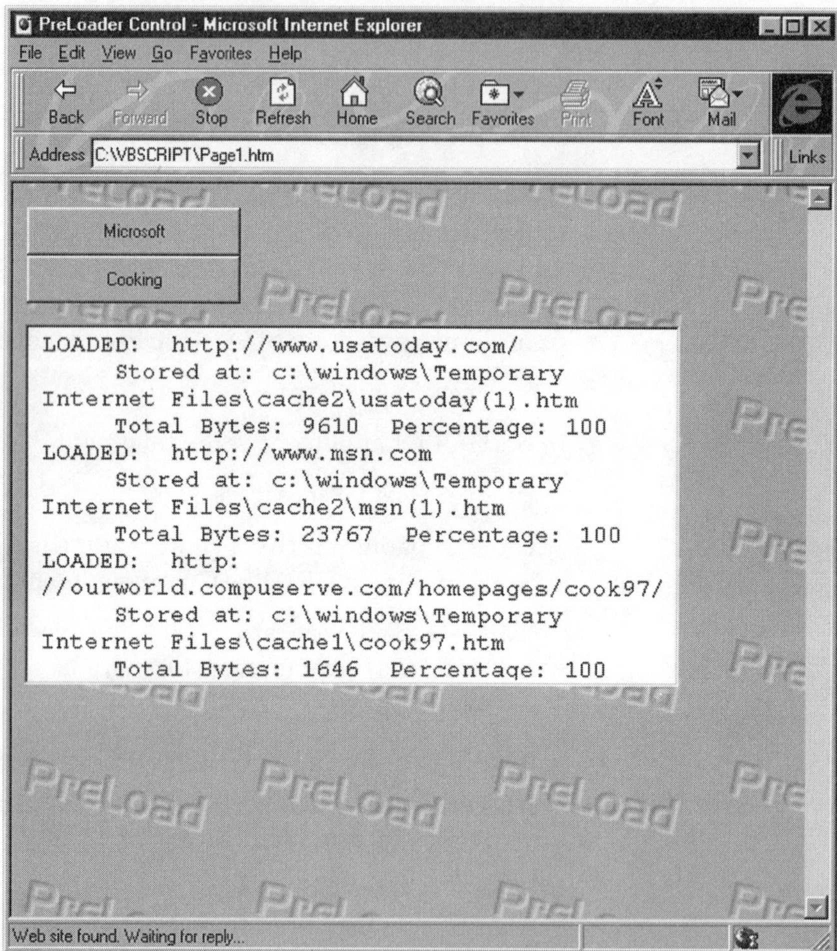

Figure P-5: This page automatically preloads three Web sites, then switches the browser to the first one.

Let's construct a useful tool that you might want to use yourself. Assume that every time you log on to the Internet you first go to the *New York Times* home page. Well, all you have to do is make this the default start page by editing your browser's View | Options |

Navigation menu. So far, so good. But, being a creature of habit, you then always go to the *USA Today* home page, followed by a COOK97 site, then, finally, the MSN site. Why not load the following .HTM file as your second move when logging on (put this .HTM file in your Favorites list). As soon as this .HTM file is loaded, it immediately (using the Sub window_onLoad( ) Event) *preloads* all three of your favorite sites and then switches to your *USA Today* site. You should notice that switching to these sites is quicker than before. The site still has to be contacted, but most of the visuals are already on your hard drive and, once the site is reached, the visuals appear immediately (unless a graphic requires an update).

Start the Microsoft ActiveX Control Pad running (see the Introduction). Then from the Edit | Insert ActiveX Control menu, add two CommandButtons and a TextBox to your HTML document. Put captions on the Buttons representing your second and third favorite sites. Then in a script, Dim a counter Variable and an Addr( ) Array (see "Dim" and "Array").

In the window's OnLoad Event, define two of the Array Variables as URLs that you're interested in, and then turn on the PreLoader by setting its Enable Property to 1. In the PreLoader_Complete Event, define a carriage return character, then fill the TextBox with the notice that we've loaded a URL, where it was put, how many bytes were stored, and the fact that it is 100 percent loaded. Raise the counter Variable. If this is the first time we're in this Event, switch the browser to our *USA Today* site. If this is the third time, just quit. If it's the first or second time, define the PreLoader URL as the next site in our list (the *Addr* Array).

In the two Button Click Events, allow the user to send the browser to those other two sites. The user will first go to the default primary location automatically (to *USA Today* in this example). But after that, the user has to click on the Back button to return to our .HTM page here and click on one of those two Buttons.

```
<HTML>
<HEAD>
<TITLE>PreLoader Control</TITLE>
</HEAD>
<BODY BACKGROUND="PREL.GIF">
<SCRIPT LANGUAGE="VBScript">
```

P

```
<!--
dim counter
dim Addr(4)

Sub window_onLoad()
Addr(1) = "http://www.msn.com"
Addr(2) ="http://ourworld.compuserve.com/homepages/cook97/"
PreLoader.Enable = 1
end sub

Sub PreLoader_Complete
cr = chr(13) & chr(10)
TextBox1.Value = TextBox1.Value & cr & "LOADED: " &
PreLoader.URL
TextBox1.Value = TextBox1.Value & cr & "   Stored at: " &
PreLoader.CacheFile
TextBox1.Value = TextBox1.Value & cr & "   Total Bytes: " &
PreLoader.Bytes & " Percentage: " & PreLoader.Percentage
counter = counter + 1
If counter = 1 then
location.href="http://www.usatoday.com/"
End if
If counter = 3 then exit sub
PreLoader.URL = Addr(counter)
End Sub

Sub PreLoader_Error
  alert "Error"
End Sub

Sub CommandButton1_Click
location.href=Addr(1)
End sub

Sub CommandButton2_Click
location.href=Addr(2)
End sub
-->

</SCRIPT>
```

```
<OBJECT ID="CommandButton1" WIDTH=149 HEIGHT=32
 CLASSID="CLSID:D7053240-CE69-11CD-A777-00DD01143C57">
  <PARAM NAME="Caption" VALUE="Microsoft">
  <PARAM NAME="Size" VALUE="3890;846">
  <PARAM NAME="FontCharSet" VALUE="0">
  <PARAM NAME="FontPitchAndFamily" VALUE="2">
  <PARAM NAME="ParagraphAlign" VALUE="3">
  <PARAM NAME="FontWeight" VALUE="0">
</OBJECT>
<BR>

<OBJECT ID="CommandButton2" WIDTH=149 HEIGHT=32
 CLASSID="CLSID:D7053240-CE69-11CD-A777-00DD01143C57">
  <PARAM NAME="Size" VALUE="3943;846">
  <PARAM NAME="Caption" VALUE="Cooking">
  <PARAM NAME="FontCharSet" VALUE="0">
  <PARAM NAME="FontPitchAndFamily" VALUE="2">
  <PARAM NAME="ParagraphAlign" VALUE="3">
  <PARAM NAME="FontWeight" VALUE="0">
</OBJECT>
<BR><BR>

<OBJECT ID="TextBox1" WIDTH=400 HEIGHT=100
 CLASSID="CLSID:8BD21D10-EC42-11CE-9E0D-00AA006002F3">
  <PARAM NAME="VariousPropertyBits" VALUE="2894088219">
  <PARAM NAME="Size" VALUE="10583;2646">
  <PARAM NAME="FontName" VALUE="Arial">
  <PARAM NAME="FontHeight" VALUE="220">
  <PARAM NAME="FontCharSet" VALUE="0">
  <PARAM NAME="FontPitchAndFamily" VALUE="2">
  <PARAM NAME="FontWeight" VALUE="0">
</OBJECT>

<OBJECT
  ID="PreLoader"
  CLASSID="CLSID:16E349E0-702C-11CF-A3A9-00A0C9034920"

CODEBASE="http://activex.microsoft.com/controls/iexplorer/
iepreld.ocx#Version=4,70,0,1161"
```

```
  TYPE="application/x-oleobject"
  WIDTH=1
  HEIGHT=1
  <PARAM NAME="URL" VALUE="http://www.usatoday.com/">
  <PARAM NAME="Enable" VALUE="0">
</OBJECT>

</BODY>
</HTML>
```

Procedures

VBSCRIPT

See Sub or Function

Properties

ACTIVEX

Each ActiveX Control has its own set of *Properties*—qualities like its color, width, and so on. Some Properties, such as height, are available to nearly all Controls. Others, like the MatchFound Property of a ComboBox, are unique to a single Control. For the Controls so far released by Microsoft, there are 134 Properties.

Some Properties, like the ListCount Property of a ListBox, can only be *read* (queried) to find out information—in this case, the number of entries in the list displayed to the user. Other Properties, like width, can be read but can also be *written to* (changed). If you change the Width Property of a Control, the Control becomes wider or narrower.

You can specify Properties for a Control four different ways. We'll illustrate this by changing the BackColor Property of a TextBox in each of the four ways.

Run the ActiveX Control Pad (see the Introduction to this book for details on using the Pad). Select Insert ActiveX Control from the Edit menu:

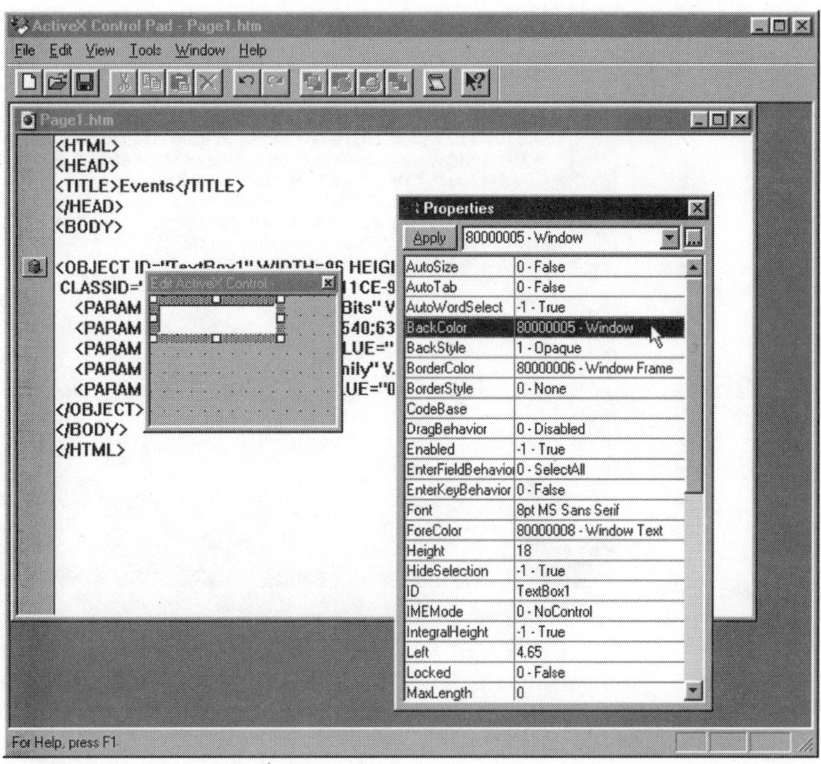

Figure P-6: A new TextBox Control, ready to get a new BackColor.

As you can see in the figure above, the Properties Window for this TextBox includes a BackColor Property. By default, the BackColor is white, but double-click on the word BackColor, or click on the dotted button at the top. A color-selection window pops up. Now you can select a different BackColor.

The second way to adjust the BackColor is by looking at the source code and changing the PARAM for this TextBox Object.

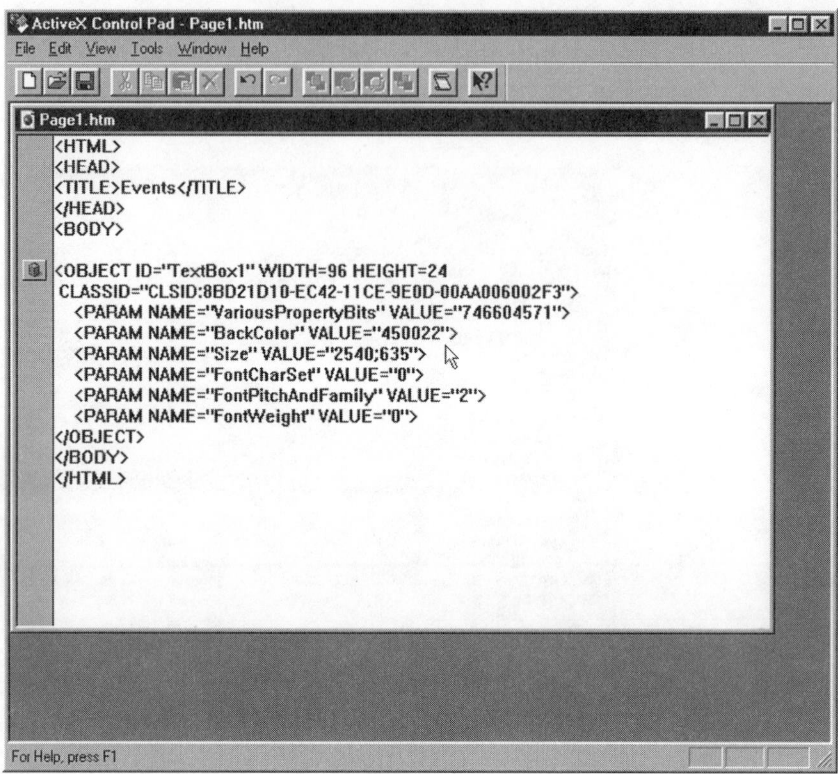

Figure P-7: A second way to change a Property: edit the Control's PARAM list in the source code.

In the figure above, we've typed in a new value, "450022," a light yellow, as the BackColor.

The third way to adjust a Property like a BackColor is to do it dynamically using VBScript to make the change when the user's browser loads in the document:

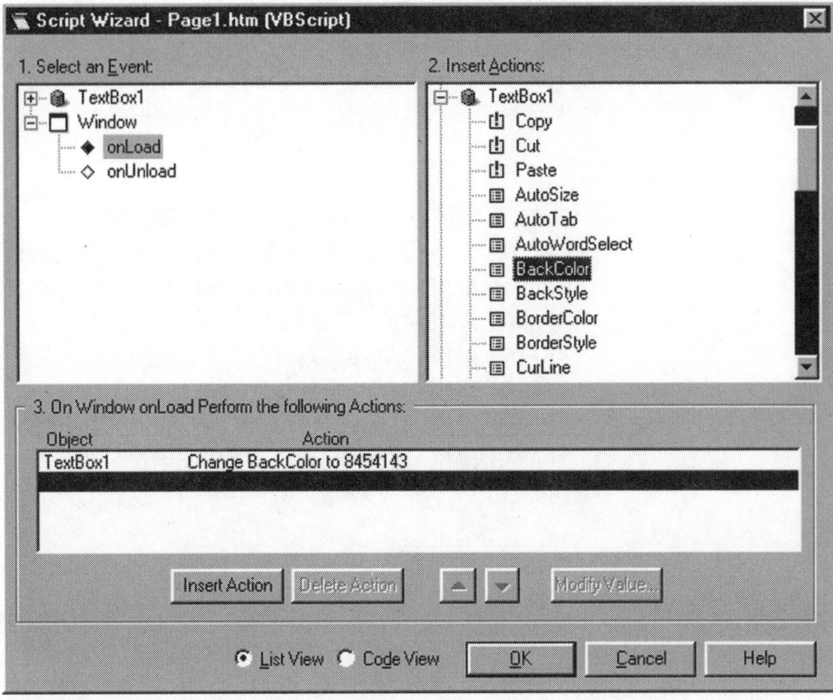

Figure P-8: You can use the Script Wizard to create a VBScript that changes a Property.

Move your cursor to a location outside the <OBJECT> structure, but within the <BODY>…</BODY> commands. This will be the location within your HTML script where the VBScript will be inserted. From the ActiveX Control Pad's Tools menu, select Script Wizard and click on the Window object; choose its OnLoad Event. Then in the right pane, double-click on BackColor to bring up the color selector and choose a color. Click OK to insert the action.

The fourth way to adjust a Property is similar to the third except that you don't use the Wizard. Just type in the source code between <SCRIPT> and </SCRIPT>, like this:

```
<HTML>
<HEAD>
<TITLE>Properties</TITLE>
</HEAD>
<BODY>
```

```
<SCRIPT LANGUAGE="VBScript">
Sub Window_onLoad()
  TextBox1.BackColor = 8454143
end sub
</SCRIPT>

 <OBJECT ID="TextBox1" WIDTH=96 HEIGHT=24
 CLASSID="CLSID:8BD21D10-EC42-11CE-9E0D-00AA006002F3">
   <PARAM NAME="VariousPropertyBits" VALUE="746604571">
   <PARAM NAME="BackColor" VALUE="450022">
   <PARAM NAME="Size" VALUE="2540;635">
   <PARAM NAME="FontCharSet" VALUE="0">
   <PARAM NAME="FontPitchAndFamily" VALUE="2">
   <PARAM NAME="FontWeight" VALUE="0">
 </OBJECT>

</BODY>
</HTML>
```

How to Change a Property

As with most Properties of most ActiveX Controls, you can change a Property in a VBScript script. You separate the Property name from the name of the Control with a period:

P

```
<SCRIPT LANGUAGE="VBScript">
CheckBox1.backcolor = 1233442
CheckBox1.Caption = " Tried & True"
</SCRIPT>
```

Note that numeric values like 1233442 aren't quoted, but text values like "Tried & True" must be enclosed by quotes.

You can also change most Properties within the Object's definition, by using the PARAM, NAME, and VALUE commands. In this case, *all* values must be enclosed in quotes:

```
<OBJECT ID="CheckBox1" WIDTH=144 HEIGHT=24
 CLASSID="CLSID:8BD21D40-EC42-11CE-9E0D-00AA006002F3">
  <PARAM NAME="VariousPropertyBits" VALUE="746588179">
  <PARAM NAME="BackColor" VALUE="1233442">
  <PARAM NAME="ForeColor" VALUE="-2147483630">
  <PARAM NAME="DisplayStyle" VALUE="4">
```

```
    <PARAM NAME="Size" VALUE="3810;635">
    <PARAM NAME="Caption" VALUE=" Tried & True">
    <PARAM NAME="GroupName" VALUE="Views">
    <PARAM NAME="FontName" VALUE="Arial">
    <PARAM NAME="FontHeight" VALUE="220">
    <PARAM NAME="FontCharSet" VALUE="0">
    <PARAM NAME="FontPitchAndFamily" VALUE="2">
    <PARAM NAME="FontWeight" VALUE="0">
</OBJECT>
```

Note also that CheckBox and Option Button captions look better if you first insert a space before the text: " Tried & True" rather than "Tried & True."

Figure P-9: Always insert a space as the first character of a caption for CheckBoxes and Option Buttons.

Tip

The name that you use to identify a Control when adjusting its Properties in VBScript is the ID in the OBJECT definition in your HTML source code. (ID="CheckBox1" for example.) The ID Property is also found in the Properties Window of the ActiveX Control Pad (when you double-click on an Object in the layout view, or right-click and choose Properties).

P

Names, IDs & Automatic Naming

By default, when you create a new Object in the ActiveX Control Pad (by choosing Insert ActiveX Control from the Edit menu), the Control Pad will provide a name (ID) for the new Object that ends with a number. The first CheckBox that you create will be given the ID Property "CheckBox1," and the second that you create will be given the ID "CheckBox2," and so on. TextBoxes start with TextBox1, then TextBox2, and so on.

Feel free to change the ID Property (in the Properties Window) if you feel that a more descriptive name, like BoldCheckBox, would be helpful to you. The user, of course, will never see these IDs. They're merely for the convenience of the programmer, as a way of pointing to a particular object so you can create an Event for it (Sub CheckBox1_Click); invoke one of its Methods (CheckBox1.Move); or adjust one of its Properties.

Accelerator

For the Accelerator Property, you provide a letter of the alphabet. If your option's Caption Property is "BoldFace," allowing the user to switch on boldface for some text, you might use the letter B as the Accelerator key. Then VBScript will underline that letter in the caption of the CheckBox: Boldface. The user can press Alt+the Accelerator key to trigger the CheckBox (to check or uncheck it). This is an alternative to using the mouse to adjust the CheckBox.

ActiveControl

This is a Property of the Layout Control, and it tells you which, of the Controls on a given layout, currently has the focus. See "All About Focus" under "TabIndex" later in this section.

P

ActiveControl is the way to find out (while your script is running) which Command Button, ListBox, or other Control has the *focus*—in other words, which Control was used last or was most recently tabbed to or clicked on with the mouse.

You can use ActiveControl to find out about or change the Properties of the Control with the focus. In other words, you don't need to specify the Control's ID Property:

```
Command1.Width = 140
```

Instead, you can say, "Whichever Control has the focus" like this:

```
Mylayout.ActiveControl.Width = 140
```

For example, to find out the caption of the currently active Control:

```
X = MyLayout.ActiveControl.Caption
```

OR, to change the caption of the currently active Control:

```
MyLayout.ActiveControl.Caption = "New Name"
```

This kind of thing can be risky, though. What if the Control with the focus has no Caption Property? An error occurs if you request information that's unavailable or make a change that's impossible. For instance, asking for the Caption Property of a TextBox generates an error, since a TextBox has no Caption Property.

Alignment

The Alignment Property determines whether the caption appears to the right (the default) or the left of a CheckBox or other Control that has a Caption Property.

AutoSize

AutoSize, when true, automatically adjusts the Height and Width Properties to fit contents of a CheckBox, Label, Image, or other Control.

For example, caption text in a Label may be chopped off or appear asymmetrical and ragged. To solve the problems of truncated or unsightly Label text, you can adjust the size of the Label or edit the caption text while designing your program. But what if text will be assigned to the caption while the program is running? What if the user is allowed to load a graphic into an Image Control? You, the script writer, may not know the amount of text for that caption or the size of the graphic image.

One solution is to use the AutoSize Property. If you set AutoSize to True, the Label will stretch or shrink to accommodate the amount of text (the Caption Property). Likewise, the Image box will stretch or shrink. However, with AutoSize set to False (the default), a Label Box's text may not fit the size of the box, or a graphic image might be *clipped.* Using the AutoSize Property can solve this problem, but then the Alignment Property's effect will be nullified.

If you turn on AutoSize while a program is running, the upper left corner of the Control won't move, but the Control will widen and/or lengthen as necessary to display the complete contents. In other words, the *position* of the Control remains the same—its Top and Left Properties are not changed.

AutoTab

This is a Property of a TextBox or a ComboBox (ComboBoxes have a "TextBox zone" within which the user can type). You can restrict the number of characters a user can type into a box by setting the MaxLength Property. AutoTab, if set to True, automatically moves the focus to the next Control in the Tab order once the user has typed in the MaxLength number of characters. AutoTab defaults to False (off).

For example, say that you've got a set of TextBoxes that the user must fill in. One of them is for the state abbreviation, like CA or NC or NY. You can make things more convenient for the user by setting that TextBox's MaxLength to 2, then turn on the AutoTab feature. When the users type in their state abbreviation, the cursor is automatically moved to the TextBox for the ZIP Code (which is set to 5 MaxLength) and so on. This avoids the necessity for users to click (or Tab) on each TextBox in turn to give it focus so they can type in the next item of data.

AutoWordSelect

This is a Property of a TextBox or a ComboBox (ComboBoxes have a "TextBox zone" within which the user can type). This same feature is found in Word for Windows (from the Tools menu, click on Options, then Edit). With AutoWordSelect on, when the user positions the "insertion point" (the typing cursor) within a word, then drags the mouse to select some characters within that word (or additional words), the selection will jump from word to word. Put another way, selection is accomplished by chunks—by whole words, rather than by individual characters. AutoWordSelect defaults to True (On).

BackColor

BackColor is the background color for an object or layout; it's like colored paper on which text or graphics appear. For a layout, it's the color between the outer border of any Controls and the inner border of the layout background (the space on the layout not covered by objects). The printed text is in the *ForeColor*.

To adjust the BackColor while designing your script, you can use the Properties Window and the Color Palette of the ActiveX Control Pad.

Or to change the color while your program is running, using the full available range of colors, use the RGB specification. The range of possible colors in VBScript is large. All the colors and hues are there, but the color code is not a continuum like a rainbow or a color wheel; they're not sequentially arranged from 0 to 17 million. VBScript and Windows use a scheme that puts *some* shades of orange around 75,000 and other oranges around 33,000. For example, 33,023 is a pumpkin orange and 75,050 is an olive drab (for more on RGB, see "Hex Numbers for the COLOR command" under Body):

```
BackColor = 8 '(This can be a number between 0 and
16,777,215.)
```

OR, in theory, you can use one of the built-in color definitions: black, silver, gray, white, maroon, red, purple, fuchsia, green, lime, olive, yellow, navy, blue, teal, or aqua. We say in theory because at the time of this writing, this will not work:

```
Label1.BackColor = lime
```

Tip

You can define colors with either hexadecimal numbers or, as we've done in the example above, ordinary English words like green *or* lime. *For a complete list of all 140 English word colors you can use—including rare and sometimes alarming colors such as mintcream, mistyrose, and moccasin—see "Many New Colors" in the entry on BGCOLOR. For an explanation of hexadecimal, see "Hex Numbers for the Color Command" in the entry on BODY.*

Note: According to the help documents, you're supposed to be able to define a BackColor using three values (one each for red, green, and blue). However, this too is not working at the time of this writing:

```
Label1.BackColor = 128, 12, 0
```

BackStyle

BackStyle can be opaque (the default) or transparent. When you change it to transparent, whatever color or wallpaper graphic (using the HTML command: <BODY BACKGROUND = "ROUGH.GIF">) you've used for the document will show through. In other words, the text of your caption will look good, as if it were printed on the background rather than applied, like a gray Band-Aid, on top of the background. However, if you're not using the standard, gunmetal gray background, you'll lose the 3D effect that shades the CheckBox Control itself.

Bold

P

See Font

BorderColor

This Property adjusts the color of the frame around a Label, ComboBox, ListBox, Image, or TextBox. The Control's BorderStyle Property must be set to True (On). Additional border effects can be achieved with the SpecialEffect Property.

BorderStyle

This Property determines whether or not a line (or a thicker border, depending on the SpecialEffect Property) is drawn around a Label, ComboBox, ListBox, Image, or TextBox. This creates a framing effect. BorderStyle defaults to False (Off) for all Controls except the Image. If you specify any SpecialEffect other than none, BorderStyle is set to False automatically. Also see BorderColor.

BoundColumn

This Property applies only to the ComboBox and ListBox Controls. In a multi-column ListBox or ComboBox, the user can click on a row. The BoundColumn Property specifies which item from that row to save, which item is the Value.

These Properties are useful if you're showing the user one list of information but actually storing something else as the true data. You might, for instance, have a special code that you use for each country of the world. You would display the ordinary names of countries to the user, but when the user selects a country, you save the *code* rather than that country's name. To accomplish this trick, you assign the column containing the visible country names as the TextColumn Property, and assign the column containing your codes to the BoundColumn Property.

Cancel

Only the Command Button Control has a Cancel Property. The Cancel Property can be used to make one of the Command Buttons on a layout double as the Esc key. In other words, pressing the Esc key on the keyboard will trigger the Command Button's Click Event, just as if the user had mouse-clicked on the Button.

The Esc key could be used to move back a level, to the previous state. For instance, say that the user has selected a Button labeled Save, so your script shows a data-saving window with various options. One of those options would be Cancel. You could set the Cancel Property of the Command Button that you've labeled "Cancel." Then the user can either click on your Cancel Button or press the Esc key to achieve the same result—return to the previous window, thus aborting the data-saving.

Over the years, people have gotten used to using the Esc key to go back one level in a series of menus, undo the previous action, or even exit a script. It may be a good idea to allow them that alternative.

Only one button on a given layout can be the Cancel Button, but VBScript handles this for you. Whenever you set one of the buttons to Cancel, any other button that has that Property loses it. The Cancel Property defaults to False.

If you have other Controls on a layout that contain a Cancel Button, pressing the Esc key does not trigger their KeyPress, KeyDown, or KeyUp Events, as it normally would. This has the effect of reserving the Esc key for special actions governed only by whatever commands you have put within your designated Cancel Button's Click Event.

There is a similar Property of Command Buttons called Default. This Property causes the Enter key to trigger a Command Button if its Default Property is set to True (On).

CanPaste

This is a Property of a TextBox or a ComboBox (ComboBoxes have a "TextBox zone" within which the user can type). You cannot *set* (change) this Property; it can only be read (queried). VBScript automatically maintains the CanPaste Property, switching it between True and False as appropriate.

If True, this means that there is text in the user's clipboard that can be successfully pasted into the TextBox or ComboBox. If CanPaste is False, the clipboard contains graphics or some other data that cannot be pasted. You could query the CanPaste Property and, if it's False, explain to the user why a paste attempt failed:

```
If TextBox1.CanPaste = False Then MsgBox "The current →
clipboard contents cannot be pasted here."
```

P

CanRedo

CanRedo can be either True or False and tells you whether or not the most recent Undo can be reversed. (ReDo is the opposite of UnDo. For example, if the user deletes a word from a TextBox, then clicks on an Undo button, the word is restored. But if the user clicks on a Redo button, the word is deleted again.)

Sometimes an Undo cannot be reversed. The CanRedo Property will tell you if it's impossible to reverse it.

CanUndo

CanUndo can be either True or False and tells you whether or not the most recent action taken by the user can be reversed. (ReDo is the opposite of UnDo. For example, if the user deletes a word from a TextBox, then clicks on an Undo button, the word is restored. But if the user clicks on a Redo button, the word is deleted again.)

Sometimes an action cannot be undone. The CanRedo Property will tell you if it's impossible to reverse it.

Caption

Caption determines the text that will appear within or near a Control. Captions are not required; you can delete them in the Properties Window, or delete or change them while a script is running.

You usually set a caption while designing a script, using the Properties Window. Or to change a caption while a script is running:

```
Label1.Caption = "ON"
```

OR to find out the caption of a Command Button while a script is running:

```
X = Command1.Caption
```

See also AutoSize

ClientHeight, -Left, -Top, -Width

These are Properties of the TabStrip Control only. They specify size and position of the display area of a TabStrip. If, for example, you want to display a graphic image within the "client area" (the available blank space on the TabStrip), you can find out where to position the image (ClientTop and ClientLeft) and also how large to make the image (ClientHeight and ClientWidth).

In other words, these Properties tell you how to avoid going off the edge of a TabStrip or covering up its tabs. To place an Image Control neatly within a TabStrip Control:

```
Image1.ZOrder = 0 'make it visible on top
Image1.Left = TabStrip1.ClientLeft
Image1.Top = TabStrip1.ClientTop
Image1.Width = TabStrip1.ClientWidth
Image1.Height = TabStrip1.ClientHeight
```

CodeBase

CodeBase is the URL from which an ActiveX Control can be downloaded to the user's computer, if the user doesn't already have this ActiveX Control registered on his or her local computer. ActiveX Controls, once registered, are thereafter available for use by the user's browser without requiring any further downloading. But if, when the user first loads in your document, the document contains a Control the user doesn't have, CodeBase tells the browser where that Control can be located for immediate downloading. For more on ActiveX Controls, see "Objects."

P

Column

This Property points to one or a group of items in a ListBox or ComboBox. It is not currently working in VBScript. When it is working, it's supposed to provide a quick way of reading, or filling, a List or ComboBox. Instead of using the AddItem command within a loop to fill a ListBox, you can assign an entire Array directly to a ListBox—for example:

```
ListBox5.Column() = MyArray
```

Likewise, to transfer the contents of a ComboBox or ListBox to an Array, you could avoid looping and using the List and ListCount Properties. Instead, just assign an entire column to your Array all at once.

ColumnCount

This Property of a ListBox or ComboBox determines the number of columns that the box will contain. You can set the widths of these Columns with the ColumnWidths Property. The ColumnCount can range from 0 to 9, with 9 being the upper limit:

```
ComboBox2.ColumnCount = 2
```

ColumnHeads

This Property allows you to specify that the first row within a ListBox or ComboBox are labels describing the columns within the box. When this is the case, the user cannot click on or select any of the items in this first row:

```
ListBox2.ColumnHeads = True
```

ColumnHeads defaults to False. When you set it to True, thin frames appear at the top of each column.

ColumnWidths

Interestingly, this Property expresses a dimension (the width of the columns in a multi-column ListBox or ComboBox). However, the value is a *text* Variable subtype:

```
ListBox1.ColumnWidths = "88;72;88"
```

Note that you separate the width specifications with semicolons and the default unit of measurement is the point (72 per inch).

P

If you leave the setting blank (or use -1), the width will be calculated for you automatically by VBScript. Any of the column measurements can be left blank. Here, the middle column will be calculated by VBScript by subtracting the 144 points from the width of the ListBox:

```
ListBox1.ColumnWidths = "72;;72"
```

If the size of the columns exceeds the width of the box, the user can scroll to see the hidden columns. You can also specify measurements in centimeters (12 cm) or inches (2.3 in).

ControlTipText

ControlTipText allows you to create one of those little boxes that briefly describe the purpose of an object. The little box will pop out if the user holds his mouse pointer on top of the CheckBox but doesn't click:

```
CheckBox1.ControlTipText = "Makes boldface the default."
```

At the time of this writing, the CheckBox Control doesn't support this Property during run time, though it is listed among the CheckBox Properties.

Count

Count applies only to the Layout Control or the TabStrip Control. With the Layout Control, Count tells you the number of other Controls currently on the layout (the count of the "collection" of Control objects). For the TabStrip Control, it tells you how many tabs there are (in the Tabs Collection).

Example If a TabStrip has two tabs, you can find this out:

```
X = TabStrip1.Tabs.Count
MsgBox X
```

Results in

```
2
```

CurLine

CurLine tells you the current line in a TextBox. It identifies the location of the "insertion cursor," that I-beam cursor that shows where any typing will be displayed when the user starts pressing keys on the keyboard. If you want to show the user the current line number, here's how. Put a TextBox and a Label on a layout. Then type in this script:

```
<SCRIPT LANGUAGE="VBScript">
Sub TextBox1_Change()
Label1.Caption = TextBox1.CurLine
end sub
</SCRIPT>
```

You can also use CurLine with the LineCount, SelLength, SelStart, and SelText Properties, described later in this section.

Default

Default allows you to temporarily make one of the Command Buttons on a layout double as the Enter key. In other words, if the user presses the Enter key on the keyboard, that triggers the Default Command Button's Click Event, just as if the user had mouse-clicked on the Button.

The Default command determines which Command Button of several on a layout will respond to the Enter key (as well as to a mouse click). Only one Command Button at a time can be the "Default" Button. However, the "Default" condition only applies if the user doesn't shift the focus to another Control by clicking on a second Command Button.

In many scripts, pressing the Enter key tells the computer that the user has finished typing in some text, a number (in a calculator application), or some other data. Just as the Carriage Return key on an old-fashioned typewriter signified the end of a line, the Enter key on a computer often represents the completion of some task.

Say that you label one of your Command Buttons DONE or CALCULATE or something like that, so that it will respond the same way your script responds when the user presses the Enter key. In this hypothetical example, the response might be to accept a number in a "calculator." Then you make that Command Button the "Default" Button. Now the user can either click on your Default "Enter" Command Button or alternatively just press the Enter key to achieve the same result—accept the user's number. This avoids requiring that the user move his hands off the keyboard to click on the Button.

Default is False (Off) by default. Also see "Cancel" above.

Delay

Delay specifies the amount of time that will pass between when the user first clicks a SpinButton or ScrollBar and the triggering of Change Events (for a ScrollBar) or SpinUp or SpinDown Events (for a SpinButton). It works both when the user holds down the mouse button or repeatedly clicks it.

The Event is immediately triggered on the first mouse click. However, how long it takes before the Event is triggered again depends on the setting of this Delay Property. The real delay will be the Delay setting multiplied by five. Delay is specified in milliseconds and defaults to 50 (1/20th of a second). Therefore, the default Delay is 250 milliseconds (1/4th of a second).

After the first click, the interval between triggered Events is the actual delay (not multiplied by five). The default interval, then, is 50 milliseconds. You can adjust the Delay if you want to put some programming into a Change, SpinUp, or SpinDown Event but don't want a continuous rapid retriggering of the Event.

DragBehavior

Turns on or off the drag-and-drop capability of a TextBox or ComboBox.

```
TextBox2.DragBehavior = 0 'Not allowed
TextBox2.DragBehavior = 1 'drag & drop permitted
```

DragBehavior defaults to False (Off), but if you turn it on, the user can select some text within a TextBox or the TextBox portion of a ComboBox, then drag it. A ComboBox with its Style Property set to DropDownList cannot permit dragging.

DropButtonStyle

A ComboBox can display three symbols on its drop button, or it can be blank.

```
ComboBox4.DropButtonStyle = 0 'blank
ComboBox4.DropButtonStyle = 1 'the default Arrow
ComboBox4.DropButtonStyle = 0 'ellipsis
ComboBox4.DropButtonStyle = 0 'reduce
```

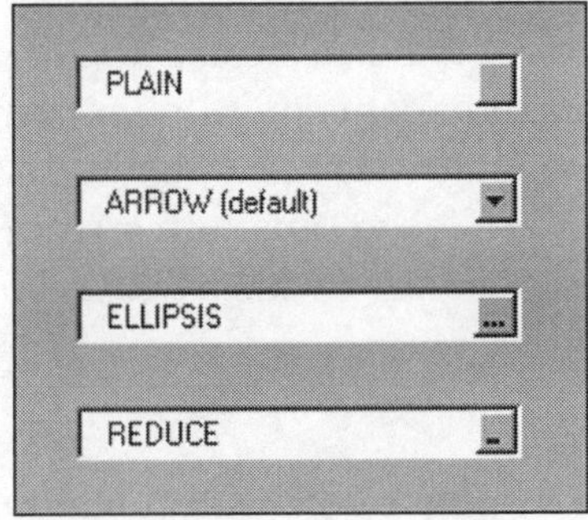

Figure P-10: The four drop button styles for a ComboBox.

Since the default down arrow symbol is nearly universally understood (and universally used) to let the user drop a hidden list, you might as well leave this Property alone so it displays the default.

However, if you're going to display a dialog box (like InputBox or a color selector window), you should switch to the ellipsis style. Then, you can intercept the usual dropping behavior of a clicked ComboBox drop button by putting your own programming in the ComboBox's DropButtonClick Event.

Enabled

Enabled defaults to True, meaning the CheckBox can be clicked on to toggle its check mark, and can also receive the focus (can be the one Control on the document that is currently active—if the user presses the spacebar, its check will toggle). If you set Enabled to False, the CheckBox check cannot be toggled. Also, the box, caption, and any picture you've provided to the CheckBox all appear faded, "grayed," as a visual signal to the user that they are inert. Also see "Locked" and "TripleState."

The Enabled Property allows you to *freeze* a Control. While it is frozen (disabled), the user cannot click on it or otherwise interact with it. The Control is *visible*, in pale gray (just enough to show that it's asleep), but not accessible to the user. Disabled Controls are often described as *grayed*.

Why would a Control be put onto a document and displayed to the user, only to be disabled and made unusable? In essence, you disable a Control to prevent the user from activating it—the Control is inappropriate in the current context or under current conditions. For example, a CheckBox that enlarges a map to 1024 x 768 might be disabled if the user has clicked on another CheckBox indicating that his or her current screen size is 800 x 600. Also see the TripleState Property.

Common Uses

You can use Enabled to display Controls and features that are part of your program but which, for one reason or another, are currently unavailable. For example, if the user has not typed anything into your program yet, there is no reason to have a Command Button labeled "Print" working; therefore, it can be disabled, grayed out. When the user starts typing (detected by a TextBox's Change Event), turn the Button back on (Command1.Enabled = True).

Some Controls, like TextBoxes, can be altered by the user. However, sometimes you want to use these Controls in other ways, and you don't want them altered. A TextBox may simply be used like a Label, showing the user information that's not to be tampered with. If its MultiLine Property is set on (True), you can freeze the text inside the TextBox by setting its Enabled Property off (False). (If the MultiLine Property is off [False], the text will freeze but turn pale gray.)

EnterFieldBehavior

When the user presses the Tab key to move to a TextBox or the TextBox section of a ComboBox, EnterFieldBehavior determines how the contents are selected. The default is to *select* (reverse text to white on black) the entire contents. If you change this Property to 1, the previous selection status of the box remains in effect. In other words, if the user had left a particular paragraph selected when the TextBox lost the focus, tabbing back to restore focus would leave that same paragraph selected.

```
TextBox1.EnterFieldBehavior = 0 'the default
TextBox1.EnterFieldBehavior = 1 'selection unchanged.
```

This Property is ignored if you use the SetFocus Method to move the focus to a Control. In that case, the contents are not selected, and the insertion cursor is moved to the end of the text.

EnterKeyBehavior

This Property specifies what happens when the user presses the Enter key while working in a TextBox.

```
TextBox3.EnterKeyBehavior = True
TextBox3.EnterKeyBehavior = False 'the default
```

If you change this Property to True, when the user presses Enter the insertion point cursor moves down one line to start a new paragraph (just as it would in a word processor).

However, if you leave the Property False, pressing Enter causes the focus to move to the next Control in the tab order (just as if the user had pressed the Tab key).

Cautions

- These specifications sound backward and we cannot test them because this Property is not currently working. Be sure to test this behavior in a script before sending it out onto the Web.
- EnterKeyBehavior interacts with the MultiLine Property. If MultiLine is False, pressing Enter always moves the focus to the next Control (there's only one line in the TextBox anyway, so there's nowhere to move down to). Also, if the user presses Ctrl+Enter with MultiLine set to True (False is the default), the TextBox always moves down to a new line. Also see TabKeyBehavior in this entry.

Font

Clicking on Font in the Properties Window of the ActiveX Control Pad's editing window brings up a standard Font adjustment window. You can adjust the weight, size, typeface, and style. To adjust the color, use the ForeColor Property instead of Font.

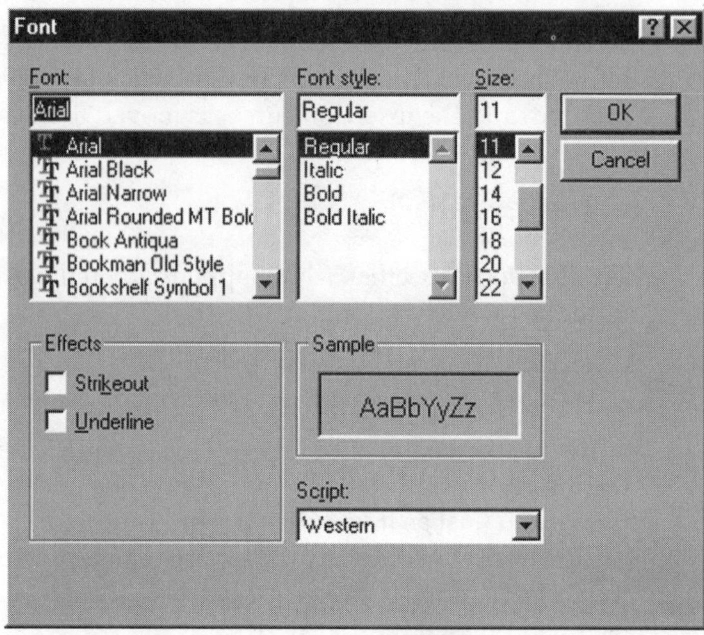

Figure P-11: Here's where you can adjust the qualities of the typeface used in the Caption Property.

Used with Any Object on which you can display text—CheckBoxes, TextBoxes, Labels, and so on.

Variables The Font Object has seven Properties: Bold, Italic, Name, Size, StrikeThrough, Underline, and Weight.

The Font Property can be used, with the normal syntax, in scripts, to change a Property while the user is viewing your document:

P

```
TextBox1.Font.Weight = 700 'this is boldface
Label1.Font.Italic = True
CommandButton1.Font.Size = 14
CommandButton4.Font.Name = "Times New Roman"
```

Cautions The default Weight is 400 (nonbold text). Bold and Bold Italic have a Weight of 700. These are your only choices at this time, though in the future there may be additional Weights. If you specify a Weight other than 400 or 700, it will be set to one of those numbers, whichever is closer.

ForeColor

ForeColor changes the color of the text in the caption. BackColor changes the background color (against which the text is placed).

Height

This Property reports or adjusts how high a Control or Object is. It is measured, like most measurements in VBScript, in Points (72 per inch).

See also Width

P

HideSelection

Determines whether any selected text (in a TextBox or ComboBox) remains highlighted (that is, remains selected at all) when the box loses the focus. If you drag the mouse to select some words in a TextBox and click on a CommandButton or some other Control, the focus moves off the TextBox and the text is deselected. Clicking back in the TextBox does not restore the selection. This is the default.

To preserve a selection when focus leaves a Control, do this:

```
TextBox1.HideSelection = False
```

Also see the EnterFieldBehavior Property described previously.

ID

ID is the unique identifier for each ActiveX Object. See "Names, IDs & Automatic Naming" under "How to Change a Property" above, and also see "Name" below.

Index

Index is a Property of the tabs on a TabStrip and specifies their order. If you want to adjust the order, so that the first tab switches places with the second tab, put a TabStrip Control and a CommandButton on a layout, then type this in:

```
Sub CommandButton1_Click()
tabstrip1.tabs(0).index = 1
end sub
```

Each time you click the Command Button, the tabs will switch places.

Note that the Tabs "collection" starts with 0. So to refer to the first tab we had to use Tabs(0). Likewise, to move the first tab to the second position, we use index = 1 (not, as you would think, index = 2). This is because both the Tabs collection and the index numbers start with a zeroth item.

InsideHeight, InsideWidth

These Properties tell you the measurements of a Layout Control (less any ScrollBar). In other words, if you want to fill an entire layout with an image, you can expand that image to the dimensions specified by these two Properties. This is similar to the ClientHeight and ClientWidth Properties of the TabStrip Control.

IntegralHeight

If the IntegralHeight Property of a TextBox or ListBox is set to True (the default) then the box will resize itself to display a full line or, for the ListBox, a full row. IntegralHeight is to the height what the

AutoSize Property is to width. In other words, IntegralHeight prevents text from being cut off vertically. See TextBox for a visual example.

Italic

See Font

KeepScrollBarsVisible

When the contents of a Layout Control exceed the dimensions of the Control (the user can't see everything), then a horizontal or vertical ScrollBar (or both) is automatically added to the Layout Control. (This is the same thing that happens to a TextBox when there's more text than can currently be viewed.)

However, if the contents of the Layout Control become entirely visible within the dimensions of the Control, then the ScrollBars automatically disappear.

If you wish, you can stipulate that the ScrollBars remain always available and visible, no matter what:

```
MyLayout.KeepScrollBarsVisible = 1 'default (automatic)
MyLayout.KeepScrollBarsVisible = 1 'Horizontal ScrollBar
MyLayout.KeepScrollBarsVisible = 2 'Vertical ScrollBar
MyLayout.KeepScrollBarsVisible = 3 'Both ScrollBars
```


LargeChange, SmallChange

It is a Windows convention that if the user clicks on one of the small arrows at either end of a ScrollBar, there is a *small* adjustment. Usually, clicking moves you to the next contiguous area of the contents. For instance, if you were viewing a text document, you would move down to the next line of text. This movement is governed by the SmallChange Property.

On the other hand, if the user clicks *within* a ScrollBar, there is a larger shift, a LargeChange. Depending on the size of the document, you might go to the beginning or end, fully to the right or left, or shift up or down by a single screenful or page of text. The shift, in this case, need not be contiguous although it usually is. This movement is governed by the LargeChange Property.

You, the programmer, determine the behavior of SmallChange and LargeChange by giving them values. You decide how much movement takes place.

The default LargeChange or SmallChange increment is 1. You can set the increment anywhere between -32,767 and 32,767. (You also establish the outer limits of the range that describes the shift, using the Max and Min Properties. You can restrict movement to a smaller area than the total size of the document under the window.)

Left

The Left Property describes the distance between the left edge of a Control and the left edge of the layout (or of another Control) that contains it.

As a Property of a layout, Left refers to the position of the left edge of the layout in relation to the left border of the screen.

Left, along with the Top Property, describes the *location* of an Object within another Object. (An Object's Height and Width Properties describe the *size* of the Object.) Using these four Properties you can both position and size the Object. And there are times when you will use all four Properties together (see the Move Method).

For example, there are no right or bottom Properties. If you want to position items all around an Object, you'll need to know the Object's right and bottom locations in addition to Top and Left. To find the right side of an Object, you add its Left and its Width Properties. To find the bottom of an Object, you add Top to Height.

For many additional positioning tips, see Top later in this entry.

LineCount

This Property tells you the total number of lines in a TextBox:

```
Z = TextBox1.LineCount
MsgBox cstr(Z)
```

List

List provides one way for your script to find out which item in a ListBox or ComboBox Control has been selected by the user. The List Property is used in conjunction with the ListIndex number; List is a variant Array containing all the items within a box. Each item has a particular row and column number that refers to it (it's a two-dimensional Array).

The ListIndex Property points to the currently selected item in a box. Therefore X = List(ListIndex) would provide your script with a text ("string") Variable subtype, *X*, which contained the currently selected item. You can also write to (change) the contents of a box:

```
ListBox1.List(3,0) = "Maurice"
```

To get item 6 from a ListBox, note that the first item in all box-type Controls has a 0 index. Asking for (5) gives us the sixth item in the box:

```
A = ComboBox1.List(5,0)
```

OR, to get the currently selected item:

```
A = ListBox1.List(ListBox1.ListIndex)
```

Combo and ListBoxes are empty when a script starts running. You can use the AddItem command to place items within these boxes (and RemoveItem to remove items, or Clear to wipe them out entirely). Normally, you would add items as part of your script's "initialization." You initialize your script when you Dim the Variables and other housekeeping preparations for your script (outside of any procedure—Sub or Function). You initialize right at the start. Initialization takes place during that pause when nothing seems to be happening after a script is first loaded in and is being parsed by the browser.

```
ListBox1.AddItem "Name"
ListBox1.AddItem "Birthday"
ListBox1.AddItem "Address"
```

The ListIndex number begins with the *zeroth* item in a list. If you attempt to identify the fifth item in a list, you should ask for List1.List(4). Another consequence is that ListCount is the total number of items. ListCount –1 is the number of the last item. This numbering system is an unhappy byproduct of the way computers currently handle Arrays and other indices—starting with a zeroth item. Note that there are two indices: row and column, separated by a comma.

To find out the name of the seventh item in a list:

```
X = ListBox1.List(6,0)
```

To find out how many items are in the list:

```
X = ListBox1.ListCount
```

ListCount

See List

ListIndex

See List

P

ListRows

This Property of a ComboBox allows you to adjust, from its default 8, the number of rows that will be displayed in a ComboBox before a ScrollBar is added.

```
ComboBox3.ListRows = 12
```

ListStyle

Combo and ListBoxes can now simulate OptionButton or CheckBox-style lists. The default is the familiar list style shown on the left in the following figure.

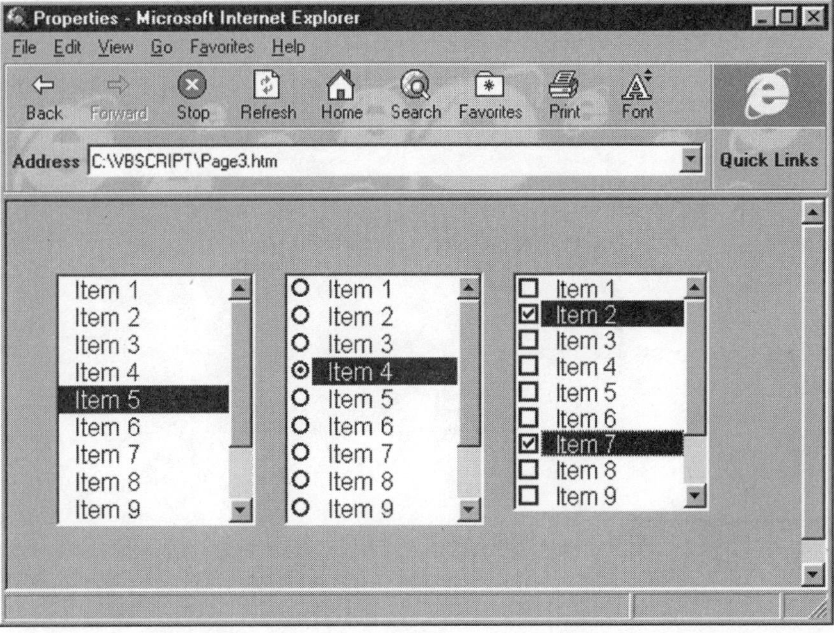

Figure P-12: The Three ListStyles: Plain, Option (MultiSelect single), Option (MultiSelect multi).

However, if you want, you can change to the Option style:

```
ListBox1.ListStyle = 1
```

That results in the middle box in the figure above. To achieve the CheckBox look shown on the right in the figure, change the MultiSelect Property to Multi (1).

ListWidth

ListWidth allows you to determine how wide the drop-down portion of the ComboBox will be. (The Width Property determines the width of the TextBox upper portion). ListWidth defaults to 0, which makes the drop-down portion match the Width of the upper portion. However, you can adjust this.

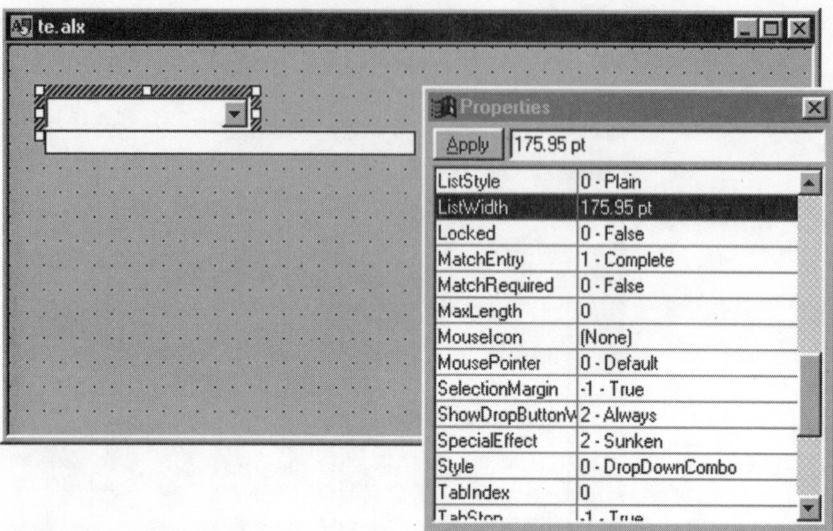

Figure P-13: We've made the lower, drop-down portion of this ComboBox wider than the upper portion. By default they would be the same width.

Locked

Locked=True has a similar effect to Enabled=False—the user cannot edit the contents or change the status of the Control. However, if Locked is True and Enabled is also True, the user can *copy* the contents of a Control (such as a TextBox) to the clipboard but cannot edit (change) those contents. If you really want to lock the user out, make Enabled False and Locked True. Now, not only are users prevented from editing the contents, they can't even copy them to the clipboard.

MatchEntry

This Property determines how a List or ComboBox reacts while the user types. By default (MatchEntry = 1), the box searches for an entry that matches all the characters the user has typed in so far. You can change this, though. To have the box cycle through all entries starting with a particular letter (if the user repeatedly presses that key):

```
ComboBox.MatchEntry = 0
```

OR, to have the box ignore the typing entirely:

```
ComboBox.MatchEntry = 2
```

Note that if the user types in an exact match to one of the items in the box, the box's Click Event is triggered so you can take some action with a script if you want.

MatchFound

The MatchFound Property cannot be changed by you, the programmer, but you can read it to find out if the user has typed in an exact match to one of the items in a ComboBox.

```
If MatchFound = True then
```

Note that if the user types in an exact match to one of the items in the box, the box's Click Event is triggered so you can take some action with a script immediately if you want.

MatchRequired

This Property defaults to False (Off), but if you set it to True, then the user must type in an exact match to one of the items in a ComboBox's list. The price paid by users is that they cannot "leave" the ComboBox until they have typed in a correct match. This isn't as bad as it sounds—the user can still escape by clicking outside the box, or even by pressing the Tab key.

Max

Max defines the position at the far right of a Horizontal ScrollBar Control or the position at the bottom of a Vertical ScrollBar Control. For a SpinButton, Max is the highest possible value.

You determine the measurement system of your ScrollBar and SpinButton Controls based usually on what information they slide the user through. For instance, if you are showing data about your family and there are five of you, set Max to 5. For a calendar, set Max to 12 if you want to allow the user to slide through pages for each month. For a cookbook with 150 recipes, set Max to 150.

Any change the user makes by moving the lozenge-shaped button (called the ScrollBox or "Tab") inside a ScrollBar will change that ScrollBar's *Value* Property. Your script can use the Value to take appropriate actions. Normally, these actions are taken by programming you write within the ScrollBar's Change Event. A ScrollBar's or SpinButton's Min and Max Properties set the limits that its Value Property can change.

Min defaults to 0 and Max defaults to 32767. Ordinarily you'll set these Properties while designing your document, using the Properties window in the ActiveX Control Pad.

MaxLength

Applying to ComboBoxes and TextBoxes, the MaxLength Property determines how many characters the user can type into the Control. If you leave it at the default 0, there is no limit imposed (other than the computer's memory of course).

MaxLength is also an Attribute of the HTML INPUT command (with TYPE=TEXT or TYPE=PASSWORD). You can assign a number to the MaxLength Attribute and thereby limit the number of characters that the user is permitted to type into the TEXT or PASSWORD Control.

Min

See Max

MouseIcon

MouseIcon allows you to cause the mouse icon (usually a simple arrow) to change when it passes over one of your Controls. Notice that in Windows 95, the mouse icon changes automatically from an arrow to an I=beam shape whenever the mouse pointer is located within a text-entry area such as a TextBox or Word Processor. This gives the user a cue about the purpose of the Control. The MouseIcon Property allows you to specify a *custom* graphics file of your own design that will be used when the pointer passes over a particular Control. (Note that the MousePointer Property must be set to 99 for this to work.)

```
<SCRIPT LANGUAGE="VBScript">
CheckBox1.MousePointer = 99
CheckBox1.MouseIcon = LoadPicture("msgbox03.ico")
</SCRIPT>
```

MousePointer

MousePointer—the ActiveX Controls include a set of 13 mouse pointers that you can specify will appear when users move their mouse over one of your Controls.

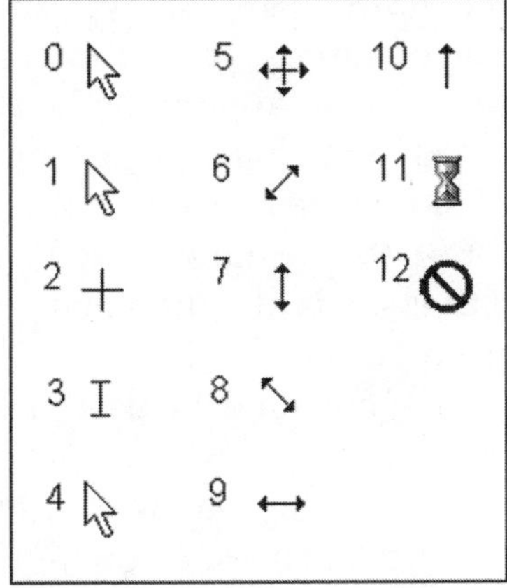

Figure P-14: You can select any of these MousePointers for most ActiveX Controls.

You can adjust the MousePointer within the OBJECT specifications in your HTML document:

```
<PARAM NAME="MousePointer" VALUE="3">
```

OR, adjust it within a VBScript:

```
<SCRIPT LANGUAGE="VBScript">
CheckBox1.MousePointer = 3
</SCRIPT>
```

MultiLine

The MultiLine Property determines whether a TextBox can accept or display more than a single line of text. You must explicitly set MultiLine to True to allow the user to type in (or permit your script to display) multiple lines in the TextBox. Oddly, MultiLine defaults to False (Off).

If you want more than one line to appear in a TextBox, you must specifically change this Property. The creators of Visual Basic explained this by pointing out that MultiLine makes your script run more slowly and should be avoided unless you need more than one line. But it doesn't, in fact, run noticeably more slowly. Just make a mental note that you nearly always have to change this Property when you add a TextBox Control to your document. Fortunately, the RichTextBox Control defaults to MultiLine = True.

Without MultiLine On, the more the user types, the more text disappears off the left side of the box. The text isn't *gone*; it's still in the TextBox's Text (also the Value) Property, and the user can still access it by going backward through the single long line by repeatedly pressing or holding down the Left arrow or Backspace keys, or using the Home key. But it's like the sign on Times Square that displays the news with thousands of light bulbs—it scrolls horizontally but never wraps onto another line.

P

If MultiLine is set to False, any time the user presses the Enter key, that keypress is ignored.

If a Horizontal ScrollBar is "attached" to the TextBox via the TextBox's ScrollBars Property, then the text will only move horizontally—regardless of MultiLine's setting. However, if you want the Enter key recognized by such a TextBox, you must set MultiLine = True.

Pressing Enter normally moves you down to the next line in a TextBox with MultiLine set on. However, if the layout has a Command Button with its Default Property set to –1, the user must press Ctrl+Enter to move down a line. Because pressing Ctrl+Enter is cumbersome for the user, you should avoid setting any Default Properties of Command Buttons to –1. Fortunately, the default (for the Default Property) is 0.

MultiRow

This Property defaults to False, meaning that a TabStrip Control will have only a single row of tabs. However, if you set MultiRow to True, there can be more than the one row. How many rows will appear depends on the size of the TabStrip itself as well as the number of tabs and their captions (the fontsize, font, and the text itself).

If you leave MultiRow False, some of the tabs might be cut off if they cannot all be displayed in that single row. However, a ScrollBar will automatically be added to the TabStrip to allow the user to see the missing tabs. So, no harm done.

MultiSelect

By default, the user can select (click on and thereby highlight) only one item at a time within a ListBox. However, if you change this Property, the user can select more than one item.

```
ListBox3.MultiSelect = 0 'this is the default
ListBox3.MultiSelect = 1 'toggle works
ListBox3.MultiSelect = 2 'various selection techniques
```

If you set the Property to 1, the user can turn the selection on and off by repeatedly clicking on it (or by pressing the spacebar). If you set it to 2, the user can hold down the Shift key and select a range of items, or, holding down the Ctrl key, individually select or deselect any items or any combination of items. At the time of this writing, value 1 also permits the same freedom as value 2.

P

Name

At the time of this writing, there is the possibility that there will be a Name Property for ActiveX Controls. If it is included in the final specifications for ActiveX, the Name Property will serve the same purpose as the ID Property (see ID earlier in this entry).

Object

VBScript includes a group of Properties and Methods. This could create a conflict if you're using a Control that features a Property or Method with the same name. VBScript will, by default, use *its own* Property or Method rather than the Control's.

To get around this, you can force VBScript to use the Property or Method in the Control by inserting the Object command between the Control's name and the Property or Method, separated by periods:

```
CControl.Object.BackColor = Green
```

OR:

```
CControl.Object.Clear
```

OldHeight, OldWidth, OldTop & OldLeft

OldHeight, OldWidth, OldTop, and OldLeft Properties are simply storage Variables, places where the previous size and position of a Control are stored after you use the Move Method or resize the Control. They work only with the Layout Event. These Properties are adjusted automatically any time you move or resize a Control. If you change the Height Property, the previous value of the Height Property is automatically stored in the OldHeight Property. For example:

```
Label1.Height = 400
```

This way you can go back to the previous size (or position) of a Control following any adjustments you might make.

Orientation

Applying to SpinButtons and ScrollBars, the Orientation Property allows you to override the default position of the Control: horizontal or vertical. By default, VBScript decides the orientation based on the height and width of the Control. If a SpinButton is taller than it is wide, VBScript displays it vertically.

If you want to ignore this default and take matters into your own hands, you can adjust the Orientation Property three ways:

```
ScrollBar2.Orientation = -1 'the default (automatic →
orientation)
ScrollBar2.Orientation = 0 'displayed vertical
ScrollBar2.Orientation = 1 'displayed horizontal
```

Parent

The Parent Property identifies the container that holds a Control (or collection or other object). For example, if you put a CommmandButton onto a Layout Control, the Layout Control is the parent of the CommandButton. Although it's not yet implemented, here's how you'll be able to use the Parent Property to access container Properties and Methods. If you have a Label Control on a layout, you can change both their BackColors by:

```
<SCRIPT LANGUAGE="VBScript">
Sub Label1_Click()
Label1.BackColor = 33023
Label1.Parent.BackColor = 33023
end sub
</SCRIPT>
```

When you are designing your script and you put a Label on it, you obviously know which layout you put that Label on. However, there is a specialized use for the Parent Property: it can come in handy when your script has several layouts and you want to use a single Subroutine that can affect all the layouts.

Say that you have three layouts and you want each of them to respond by turning blue when the user presses a button marked "CLOSE." You can write the same procedure in each of the three Command Button Click Events. Or, using Parent to identify which layout has been clicked, you can write a single, general-purpose Subroutine.

This Subroutine would service each layout the same way, and it would know *which* layout to manipulate based on the Parent Property of the Control that is "passed" to the Subroutine:

P

```
Sub TurnBlue (whichone As Control)
  whichone.Parent.BackColor = blue
End Sub
```

Recall that this technique is not currently implemented, but is expected to be included in VBScript.

Cautions: You cannot adjust Parent, either during script design or when the script runs. You cannot say "Command1.Parent = Layout2." Nor can you directly quiz Parent to get the Layout Name of the Parent like this:

```
X = Command1.Parent
```

You can, however, use

```
X = Command1.Parent.Width
```

to get the Width, or any other Property that can be "read" while a script is running.

Tip

A Collection is a group of objects that can be manipulated or accessed collectively, as if they were an Array. In VBScript there are, currently, three collections: all the Controls on a given layout are a collection, and all the tabs on a TabStrip Control are in the Tabs collection of that TabStrip. So, a TabStrip is a container *of the Tabs collection. (The links/anchors objects are collections too.) A Tabs collection is itself a* container *of the individual tabs. To change the Caption Property of the fourth tab (the tabs are numbered from 0 on up in the collection), type:*

```
TabStrip2.Tabs(3).Caption = "NewCap"
```

P

PasswordChar

This Property is used with TextBoxes only and it determines which character is displayed on the screen while a user types in a password. If you don't specify a PasswordChar, the normal characters are displayed. Most programmers use the asterisk * as the PasswordChar.

When you assign a character to a TextBox's PasswordChar Property, VBScript intercepts all characters typed into the TextBox and changes them into a special character before displaying them onscreen. It is common practice not to echo passwords to the screen, in case someone nearby is *watching*.

Even though the false PasswordChar is displayed onscreen, the TextBox's Value or Text Properties contain the true characters that the user typed in. Therefore you can store their secret password for future use.

```
TextBox1.PasswordChar = "*"
```

Picture

Picture allows you to add a graphic image (.BMP, .ICO, .WMF, .GIF, or .JPG graphic filetypes) to a Control. There are three ways to add a picture: while designing your script, while the script is running (using the LoadPicture command), or while the script is running (by assigning the Picture Property of one Control to another).

You can add a picture while designing a script by going into the edit view of the Microsoft ActiveX Control Pad, then double-clicking on the Control to bring up the Property Window. Click on Picture (or for some Controls, notably the Image Control, this Property is called the *PicturePath*), then click on the button labelled … at the top right to browse through your disk for the image file (or just type in the name and path of the file). Note that the Picture's image file will be embedded directly into your source code using the DATA command. Here's an icon (.ICO) graphic image embedded into this source code for a CheckBox:

```
<OBJECT ID="OptionButton1"
CLASSID="CLSID:8BD21D50-EC42-11CE-9E0D-00AA006002F3"
DATA="DATA:UB3SiOLszhGeDQCqAGAC8wACNABGAYCQAAAAAA8AAIASAACABQAAAAOAAID/
/wAA1R8AADQGAABPcHRpb25CdXR0b24xDQCqBFLjC5GPzhGd4wCqAEu4UWx0
sAAAAAC7u7u7AAAAALu7u7sAAAALu7u7u7AAAAu7u7u7sAAAC7u7u7uwAAAL
u7u7u7AAALu7u7u7u7ALu7u7u7u7AAC7u7u7u7u7u7u7u7u7uwAAu7u7u7sA
AAAAu7u7u7sAC7u7u7u7AAAAALu7u7u7sAu7u7u7uwAAAAC7u7u7u7ALu7u7
u7sAAAAAu7u7u7uwC7u7u7u7AAAAALu7u7u7sAu7u7u7uwAAAAC7u7u7u7AL
```

```
u7u7u7sAAAAAu7u7u7uwC7u7u7u7AAAAALu7u7u7sAu7u7u7uwAAAAC7u7u7
u7AAu7u7u7sAAAAAu7u7u7sAALu7u7u7AAAAALu7u7u7AAC7u7u7uwAAAAC7
u7u7uwAAC7u7u7sAAAAAu7u7u7AAAAu7u7u7AAAAALu7u7uwAAAAu7u7uwAA
AAC7u7u7AAAAAAu7u7sAAAAAu7u7sAAAAAAAu7u7AAAAALu7uwAAAAAAAAu7
uwAAAAC7u7AAAAAAAAAAC7u7u7u7AAAAAAAAAAAAAAu7u7uwAAAAAAAAAA
AAAAAAAAAAAAAAAAAD/8A///4AB//4AAH/8AAA/+AAAH/AAAA/gAAAHwAAA
A8AAAAOAAAABgAAAAYAAAAEAAAAAAAAAAAAAAAAAAAAAAAAAAAAAAAAAAAA
AAAAAIAAAAGAAAABgAAAAcAAAAPAAAAD4AAAB/AAAA/4AAAf/AAAP/4AAH//
gAH///AP/wACCACwAAAAAAIAAACg"
STYLE="TOP:90pt;LEFT:33pt;WIDTH:231pt;HEIGHT:45pt;TABINDEX:0;ZINDEX:0;">
  </OBJECT>
```

Alternatively, you can use the LoadPicture Function to dynamically bring in the graphic while the script is running:

```
<SCRIPT LANGUAGE="VBScript">
CheckBox1.Picture = LoadPicture("c:\gallery\dmage.bmp")
</SCRIPT>
```

Finally, you can dynamically assign the Picture Property of one Control to another:

```
<SCRIPT LANGUAGE="VBScript">
OptionButton2.Picture = OptionButton1.Picture
</SCRIPT>
```

P

Note that these two techniques are not yet working at the time of this writing.

PictureAlignment

This determines where within a container a graphic will be placed (top-left, top-right, center, bottom-left, or bottom-right) if the container (for example, an ActiveX Layout Control you're creating wallpaper for) is larger than the graphic.

```
Image1.PictureAlignment = 0 'top-left
Image1.PictureAlignment = 1 'top-right
Image1.PictureAlignment = 2 'center
Image1.PictureAlignment = 3 'bottom-left
Image1.PictureAlignment = 4 'bottom-right
```

If you set the PictureSizeMode to Stretch (1), the graphic will fill the Layout or other container Control that has a Picture Property. In that case, PictureAlignment will be ignored.

PicturePath

This specifies the URL of the location of a graphic that is to be displayed within an ActiveX Image Control (placed onto an HTML Layout Control, see the Introduction to this book). You can use a complete Internet site URL address, or merely the name of a "local" directory (on your own hard drive) or a default to the directory where the document originates.

Full URL required: http://www. tryn/images/country.gif. Or a path to the picture file on your hard drive: c:\picts\mypic.gif.

Or, if the picture file resides in the same subdirectory as does the .HTM file that describes the document you're using, you can leave off the path: mypic.gif.

PicturePosition

The PicturePosition Property describes how a graphic image in a Control (inserted using the Picture Property) is aligned within the Control relative to a caption. If there is no caption, PicturePosition describes the alignment relative to the center of the Control itself. There are 13 possible PicturePositions. You can specify the PicturePosition within VBScript source code:

```
<SCRIPT LANGUAGE="VBScript">
Label1.PicturePosition = 4
</SCRIPT>
```

This positions the caption in the center of the Control and puts the graphic to the right of the caption. Or you can use the edit view of the Microsoft ActiveX Control Pad and double-click on the Control to bring up the Property Window for that Control.

The PicturePosition Property works with the CheckBox, Command Button, Label, Option Button, and Toggle Button.

Here are the settings. Note that in each case, the caption and graphic, taken together, are *centered* within the Control:

0	The graphic is located at the **top left** of the caption.
1	The graphic is located at the **left center** of the caption.
2	The graphic is located at the **left bottom** of the caption.
3	The graphic is located at the **right top** of the caption.
4	The graphic is located at the **right center** of the caption.
5	The graphic is located at the **right bottom** of the caption.
6	The graphic is located **above** and to the **left** of the caption.
7	The graphic is located **above** and at the **center** of the caption.
8	The graphic is located **above** and to the **right** of the caption.
9	The graphic is located **below** and to the **left** of the caption.
10	The graphic is located **below** and at the **center** of the caption.
11	The graphic is located **below** and to the **right** of the caption.
12	The graphic is located in the **center** of the image, **overlapping** it.

P

PictureSizeMode

This describes how a graphic image will be displayed on any Control or background container that can display images (such as the Image Control).

The options are:

```
Image1.PictureSizeMode = 0 'crop, cut off any portion of the
graphic that doesn't fit within the container.

Image1.PictureSizeMode = 1 'stretch, make the image the same
size as the container. Unless the container is the same
aspect ratio as the original graphic, the graphic will appear
distorted, stretched.
```

```
Image1.PictureSizeMode = 3 'enlarge, make the image the same
size as the container, but don't permit any distortion. If
the aspect ratios of the container and graphic aren't identi-
cal, there will be blank strips along the sides (or the top
and bottom) to preserve the aspect ratio of the original
graphic and prevent distortion.
```

PictureTiling

If PictureTiling is set to True, a graphic smaller than the dimensions of the container Image Control will be repeated (tiled) within the Control so that the entire Control is filled. This is the equivalent of selecting Tile for Windows wallpaper.

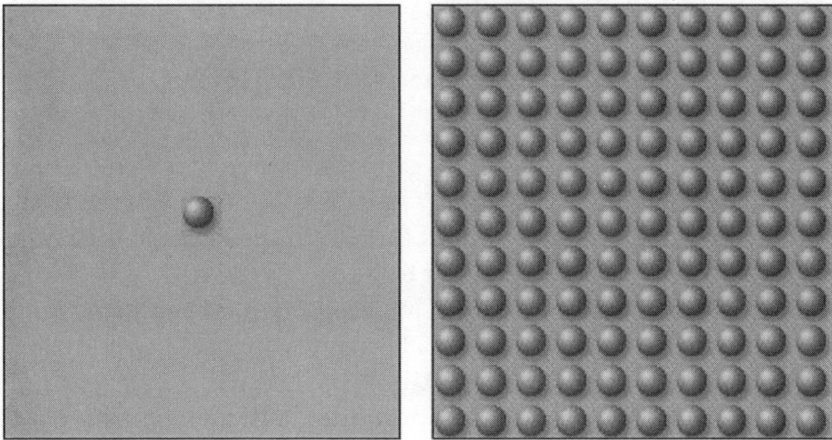

Figure P-15: PictureAlignment=Center (left), then PictureAlignment=TopLeft along with PictureTiling=True (right).

ProportionalThumb

The "thumb" is the sliding bar within a ScrollBar that the user can drag to move the contents into view within a container like a TextBox. With Windows 95, thumbs became indicators as well. They visually cued the user as to the amount of the contents that were currently hidden. For example, if a TextBox contained 100 lines of text, but you could see 50 lines displayed, the thumb would be 50 percent of the size of its ScrollBar. In VBScript, this proportional thumb is the default for ScrollBars. However, if you wish, you can turn this feature off by:

```
ScrollBar2.ProportionalThumb = False
```

ScrollBars

The ScrollBars Property of a TextBox allows you to add Vertical, Horizontal, or both types of ScrollBars to the Object. By default, the TextBox Control automatically adds either (or both) ScrollBars should the contents exceed the visible space of the TextBox. You can, however, specify otherwise:

```
0 'don't display any ScrollBars
1 'display a horizontal ScrollBar only
2 'display a vertical ScrollBar only
3 'display both ScrollBars (the default)
```

These settings cannot be made in a script; you must adjust them in the Properties window of a Control in the ActiveX Control Pad.

Even if you set the ScrollBars Property and attempt to add a vertical ScrollBar to a TextBox, it will not be added unless the TextBox's MultiLine Property has been turned on (set to True). If MultiLine is turned on but you have not added a horizontal ScrollBar to a TextBox, the text will automatically "wrap" (move to the next line as appropriate). It doesn't matter in this case whether or not you have the WordWrap Property turned on.

If your TextBox is not set to MultiLine, you can add a horizontal ScrollBar if the AutoSize Property is True.

When a horizontal ScrollBar is added to a TextBox, text the user types will keep moving off to the right unless the user presses the Enter key. Normally, a multiline TextBox automatically *wraps* the text—and moves down to the next line when the text reaches the right side of the TextBox.

Neither the MultiLine Property nor the ScrollBars Property of a TextBox can be set while a script is running. You must set them with the Properties Window while designing your script.

If the contents of an Object are entirely visible within the Object, ScrollBars will not appear on the Object—even if the ScrollBar's Property is on, set to True.

Selected

This Property applies to a ListBox Control. It should be used only to find out, in a multiple-selection-style ListBox (MultiSelect = True) which items are currently selected. Unlike the similar Value or ListIndex Properties, Selected is an *Array*. It is only of use when multiple selection is possible, and it only tells you true or false, whether or not each item in the ListBox is selected. To see how this works, put a CommandButton and a ListBox onto an ActiveX layout. Then type this script in:

```
</SCRIPT>
<SCRIPT LANGUAGE="VBScript">

ListBox1.MultiSelect = 2 'various selection techniques

for i = 1 to 10
  listbox1.additem "This " & cstr(i) & " is a large item and
long."
next

Sub CommandButton1_Click

for i = 0 to listbox1.listcount - 1
  If ListBox1.Selected(i) = True then
    msgbox "Selected " & cstr(i + 1)
  else
    msgbox "Not selected " & cstr(i + 1)
  end if
next

End Sub
</SCRIPT>
```

When you run this script, you'll see the For/Next loop go through all the items in the ListBox. For each one, it will tell you whether that item is selected or not.

If you're working with a default single-selection ListBox, use either the ListIndex or Value Properties instead of Selected. For example, if you want to find out the contents of the currently selected item, use Value. If the selected item in the list is currently Betty Rando then the message box will show her name:

```
MsgBox ListBox1.Value
```

If you want to find out the index number of the currently selected item, use the ListIndex Property. If the third item in this box is selected, the message box will display the number 2 (the list starts with the zeroth item, and counts up from there):

```
MsgBox ListBox1.ListIndex
```

Setting Items: Although the primary use of Selected is to tell you which items in the ListBox are selected, you can also use it to programmatically (in a script rather than by the user) select or deselect items:

```
ListBox1.Selected(4) = False
```

Note that when the MultiState Property is set to 2, so the user can select more than a single item within a ListBox, the *ListIndex* Property tells you the index of the item that currently has the focus. It's possible that the item with the focus isn't selected.

P

SelectionMargin

This Property of a TextBox (or the TextBox portion of a ComboBox) determines whether clicking in the left margin selects text (highlights it for copying, cutting, dragging, or other manipulations).

In Word for Windows you can click in the left margin to select a line. Hold down Shift to select multiple lines. Hold down Ctrl to select the entire text. This selection facility is also built into the TextBox Control. The default is to leave it on, but you can turn it off in a TextBox's Properties window, or like this:

```
TextBox1.SelectionMargin = False
```

SelLength, SelStart, SelText

The SelLength, SelStart, and SelText Properties together describe the current cursor position within a Text or ComboBox, as well as any text that the user has highlighted (selected). This is useful for cut, copy, drag, and paste operations, as well as searching or other kinds of editing. It defines a region within a larger piece of text.

SelLength describes how many characters are highlighted, if any.

SelStart points to the character position of the first highlighted character. If no characters are highlighted, SelStart points to the current cursor position within the text.

SelText contains whatever text has been highlighted. (It is like a text "string" Variable.)

To find out the current cursor position within the text in the TextBox. Or, if SelLength isn't 0 because some text has been selected, SelStart points to the first selected character:

```
X = TextBox1.SelStart
```

OR (X will be 0 if no characters have been selected. If some characters are selected, X holds the number of selected characters.):

```
X = TextBox1.SelLength
```

OR (A will now contain whatever characters the user has selected. If no characters have been selected, A will be an "empty string" ("").):

```
A = TextBox1.SelText
If A = " " Then MsgBox "Nothing Selected."
```

Alternatively, you can cause your script to *select* text, to move the position of the cursor or even to *insert* (to "paste") text.

To paste text, set SelStart to where you want the new piece of text inserted. Then put the replacement text into the SelText Property.

If the original text is "HOW ARE YOU?"

```
TextBox1.SelStart = 4
TextBox1.SelText = "NEW PIECE"
```

Results in

```
HOW NEW PIECE ARE YOU?
```

OR (to have the script highlight some text, set the SelStart and SelLength Properties):

```
SelStart = 6
SelLength = 12
```

ShowDropButtonWhen

This works only with a ComboBox. By default, a button appears on the right side of ComboBox, allowing the user to open the list portion of the box. However, you can make it invisible:

```
ComboBox1.ShowDropButtonWhen = 0 'don't show it at all.
```

OR, make it visible only when the ComboBox gets the focus:

```
ComboBox1.ShowDropButtonWhen = 1 'show it when the box has →
the focus.
```

You can also change the symbol on this DropButton. See DropButtonStyle earlier in this section.

P

Size

Size is a Property of the Font object, describing in points (there are 72 points per inch) how large some text is. It is one of several Properties used by the Font object to govern how text is displayed on an ActiveX Layout Control or on other Controls.

See Font

SmallChange

See LargeChange

SpecialEffect

The SpecialEffect Property determines what kind of frame or outline will be placed around a Control. You have a choice of five options: Flat (no framing), Raised (best for Command Buttons and other things that get clicked on), Sunken (best for TextBoxes and other Controls that you type something into), Etched (looks as if it were impressed or stamped into the background—a more subtle version of Sunken), and Bump (a rather odd one that looks as if the Control were framed by a very thin noodle).

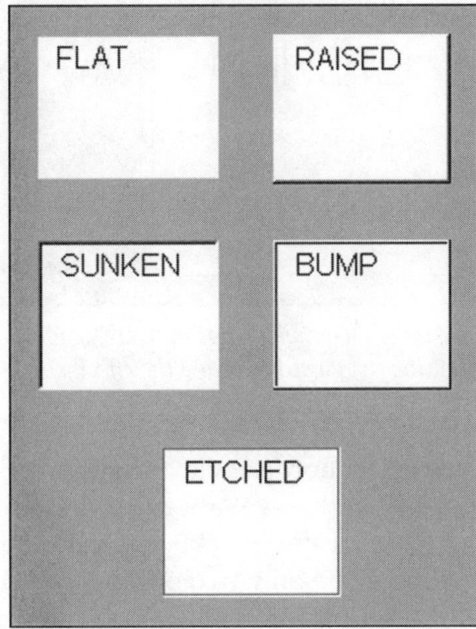

Figure P-16: The five framing options available for most Controls when you adjust the SpecialEffect Property.

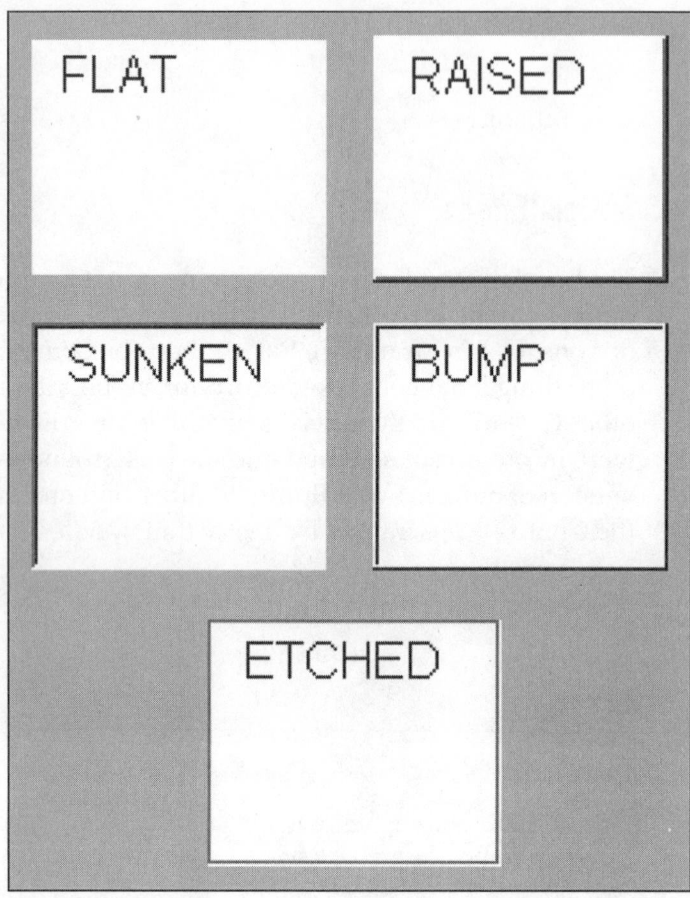

Figure P-17: A close-up of the previous figure. Here, you can see precisely what shading and highlighting were used to create the effects.

Note that if you select BorderStyle=Single, any SpecialEffect is cancelled. So you will probably want to leave BorderStyle to its default, "None." Also, for the CheckBox, OptionButton, and ToggleButton Controls, the only two options possible are Flat or Sunken.

You can adjust the SpecialEffect Property in the Properties Window of the ActiveX Control Pad (see the Introduction to this book). Or you can adjust it directly in the OBJECT definition:

```
<PARAM NAME="SpecialEffect" VALUE="1">
```

P

OR, you can adjust it in VBScript:

```
TextBox1.SpecialEffect = 2
```

The possible values are:

Value	Description	Notes
0	Flat	This is the default for the Image and Label Controls.
1	Raised	Best for TextBoxes and other Controls that get clicked on.
2	Sunken	The most commonly used and generally the best-looking of the SpecialEffect Settings. For many Controls, this is the default.
3	Etched	A Subtler variation on "Sunken."
6	Bump	Avoid this one—it would be attractive if the border were thicker, but at its fixed thickness, it merely looks curious and messy. See the last two figures.

StrikeThrough

See Font

Style

This Property has two different meanings, depending on whether it is the Style Property of a TabStrip Control or the Style Property of a ComboBox.

For the TabStrip, it determines whether tabs are displayed (the default):

```
TabStrip1.Style = 0
```

OR specifies that the tabs are displayed as buttons (rather than the default "index card" visual metaphor):

```
TabStrip1.Style = 1
```

OR no tabs are displayed:

```
TabStrip1.Style = 2
```

The Style Property of a ComboBox determines which of its two possible states the box will be in. The default state allows the user to click on the button ("DropButton") and what is, in effect, a ListBox drops down then below the text-input portion of the ComboBox:

```
ComboBox1.Style = 0 'the default
```

OR, if you set Style to 1 (or adjust it in the Properties Window within the ActiveX Control Pad), the ComboBox behaves exactly like a ListBox, requiring that the user choose from among the items in the list (the user cannot type in an alternative item):

```
ComboBox1.Style = 1 'no user-typed values allowed.
```

In effect, both ComboBox Styles look the same. However, with Style = 1, the user cannot type anything into the upper (TextBox) portion of the ComboBox.

TabFixedHeight, TabFixedWidth

These Properties allow you to query, or change, the height or width of the tabs in a TabStrip Control. The measurement is in points (72 per inch).

To change the height while a script is running:

```
TabStrip1.TabFixedHeight = 13
```

By default, the TabFixedHeight and TabFixedWidth Properties are 0, causing the widths and heights of the tabs to be automatically adjusted for you—based on the captions of the tabs. However, if you provide a TabFixedHeight and/or TabFixedWidth, those measurements will be used, and the size of the tabs will not be adjusted based on their captions.

Also, while automatic spacing is used, the tabs can be of varying widths and heights (again, based on whatever caption each tab has). However, if you set TabFixedHeight and/or TabFixedWidth, each tab will be of identical height and/or width.

TabIndex

TabIndex specifies the position of this Control in the document's *tab order.* If you have more than a single Control on a document, there is a tab order.

All About Focus

When the user presses the Tab key, the *focus* moves from Control to Control. This provides an alternative to using the mouse: the user can cycle through the "tab order" to eventually give the focus to a particular Control (just as if the user had clicked on that Control with the mouse). Then, when that Control has the focus, other keys can be used to trigger or manipulate that Control (the Enter key triggers a Command Button, arrow keys move within a ListBox, the spacebar toggles a CheckBox, and so on).

The tab order is established automatically when you add Controls to a document. The first Control you add has the tab order of zero, the next Control you place on the document gets the tab order of one, and so on. If you want to reorganize this tab order to make it more logical for the user, you can adjust this TabIndex Property. What do we mean by "more logical?" Perhaps you have a Command Button that copies some text into a TextBox. You might want to make the TextBox itself the next higher Control in the tab index. This way, users can trigger the Command Button. Then, since they will usually then want to immediately edit this text, they can just press Tab and move the focus to the TextBox, permitting editing.

You can adjust the TabIndex in a Control's Property Window while designing a script, or you can adjust it while the script is running (while the document is in a browser and is being parsed):

```
X = CommandButton1.TabIndex
TextBox4.TabIndex = X + 1
```

TabKeyBehavior

Ordinarily, when the user presses the Tab key while typing into a TextBox, the focus changes to the next Control in the tab order (see "All About Focus" under TabOrder). However, if you change the

TabKeyBehavior Property to True, then a normal tab indent occurs within the TextBox, just as it would in a word processor. The TabKeyBehavior Property, though, defaults to False.

Of course, if the TextBox's MultiLine Property is set to False (its default), pressing the Tab key will always move the focus to the next Control in the tab order. Also see "EnterKeyBehavior" in this entry.

TabOrientation

On a TabStrip Control, the row (or rows) of tabs can appear on the top, bottom, or the right or left side of the Control. By default, the tabs are along the top so the Control simulates a 3x5 card recipe box, its analogy in the real world. However, if you have a compelling reason to adjust the position of the tabs, you can change them:

```
TabStrip1.TabOrientation = 0 ' the default, along the top
TabStrip1.TabOrientation = 1 'along the bottom
TabStrip1.TabOrientation = 2 ' on the left
TabStrip1.TabOrientation = 3 ' on the right
```

TabStop

The TabStop Property determines whether, when the user repeatedly presses the Tab key, the focus ever shifts to a particular Control. (See TabIndex earlier in this entry.) This Property is either True or False:

```
TextBox2.TabStop = False
```

In this example, we set TabStop to False for this TextBox; therefore it will never get the focus. However, it nonetheless retains its position within the tab order.

Text

This Property allows you to find out (query, or put into a Variable) the contents of a TextBox or a ComboBox's text portion—the top cell. You can also *change* the Text Property of a TextBox but not of a ComboBox.

```
(TextBox1.Text = "Now this is the contents.")
```

The Text Property is the "default Property" of a TextBox, so you need not specify it if you want to streamline your programming a bit:

```
TextBox1.Text = "This is new."
```

is equivalent to:

```
TextBox1 = "This is new."
```

Note that there is also another Property that operates functionally identically to the Text Property—the Value Property of a TextBox.

There is also a Text Property for a ListBox. It allows you to query (or change) the currently selected item in the list.

You can clear (reduce to nothing) the contents by supplying an empty text Variable:

```
TextBox1.Text = ""
```

You'll generate an error if you attempt to assign a text Variable to the ListBox's Text Property that doesn't match any of the items in the list.

The Text Property can be used to change the contents of a TextBox but not of a ComboBox or ListBox. To do that, use either the Column or List Properties (listed earlier in this entry).

TextAlign

For a Label, ComboBox, or TextBox Control, the TextAlign Property determines whether the text is flush-left, centered, or right-aligned. The default is flush-left.

```
Label1.TextAlign = 1 'the default, left-aligned
Label1.TextAlign = 2 'centered
Label1.TextAlign = 3 'right aligned
```

With a ComboBox, this Property affects only the edit-box portion of the Control, not the drop-down list area.

TextColumn

See BoundColumn

TextLength

Tells you how many characters are in the text within a TextBox, or the edit region (the area the user can type into, not the list portion) of a ComboBox. For a TextBox with its MultiLine Property set to True, this character count includes the carriage-return and line-feed characters as well as the ordinary visible characters. In other words, there will be two extra characters for each line break in the text.

However, there's a simple way to get this same statistic, which makes you wonder why the TextLength Property was added to VBScript at all:

```
X = TextBox1.TextLength
```

is equivalent to:

```
X = Len(TextBox1.Text)
```

Top

P

Manipulations

Sometimes you want to position an Object smack against the sides or top of the user's browser window. Browsers generally add a bit of default spacing between their frames and the contents in the window. To get flush against the window border, use these commands within the BODY specification:

```
<BODY TOPMARGIN=0 LEFTMARGIN=0>
```

Is an Object Flush Against the Top of Its Container? If the Top Property is 0, the Object is flush against the top of its container, less any margin enforced by the container.

Is an Object Flush Against the Bottom of Its Container? An Object is butted up against the bottom of its container if its Top Property plus its Height Property equal the Height Property of the container:

```
X = CommandButton1.Top + CommandButton1.Height
If Layout1.Height = X Then
```

To Move an Object Flush Against the Bottom of Its Container:

```
CommandButton1.Top = Layout1.Height -- CommandButton1.Height
```

You'll sometimes need to adjust the Object's Top Property to take into account any borders, frames, or margins of the container.

To Center an Object Within Its Container:

```
Image1.Top = (Layout1.Height -- Image1.Height) / 2
Image1.Left = (Layout1.Width -- Image1.Width) / 2
```

TopIndex

You can query or change the TopIndex Property of a ListBox or ComboBox. This Property specifies which item (of all the items within the box) is currently in the topmost position of the box.

List or ComboBoxes can contain more items than are currently displayed within the box—the user can scroll the list. Therefore, which item appears at the top of the visible list can vary; TopIndex tells you the index number of that item.

Put a ListBox, CommandButton, and Label on an ActiveX layout or HTML document. Then type this in:

```
<SCRIPT LANGUAGE="VBScript">
<!--

For i = 1 to 23
listbox1.additem " This Item is " & i
next

Sub CommandButton1_Click
Label1 = "The TopIndex of the ListBox is: " & →
ListBox1.TopIndex
```

P

```
end sub
-->
</SCRIPT>
```

You'll note that the index numbers of a List or ComboBox begin with a zeroth item. Therefore, when the top item in the ListBox in this example says "This Item is 12" the Label will report "The TopIndex of the ListBox is: 11."

The TopIndex defaults to 0 because, when first displayed, the first (zeroth index) item is at the top. No scrolling has taken place. If the list is empty or not visible, TopIndex will be -1.

TripleState

The TripleState Property is either on or off, permitting or forbidding the Control from having three "conditions"—True, False, or Null. TripleState works only with a CheckBox, Option Button, or ToggleButton. The True condition means that, for example, a CheckBox is checked (has a check mark in it). False means unchecked. Null means that it is neither checked nor unchecked but instead is grayed.

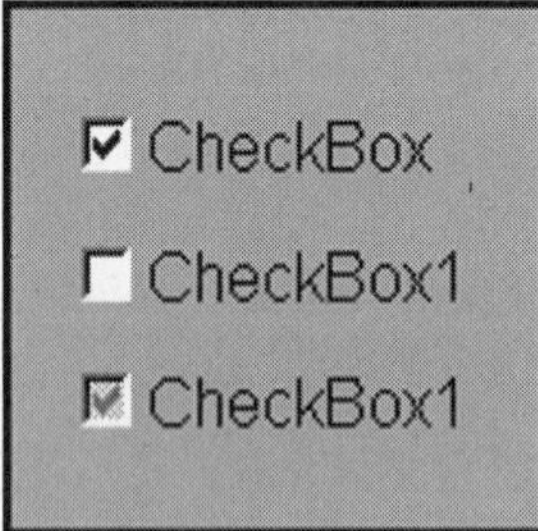

Figure P-18: A Control with a TripleState Property can be, as shown from top to bottom in this illustration, True, False, or Null.

These "states" are ordinarily user-controlled. TripleState is off (False) by default. You, the programmer, must explicitly turn it on by adjusting the Control's Property Window, or by doing it in a script:

```
<SCRIPT LANGUAGE="VBScript">
CheckBox1.TripleState = True
</SCRIPT>
```

When the user clicks, the Control goes from True to False to Null to True and so on. You, the programmer, however, can also assign Values to Controls:

```
<SCRIPT LANGUAGE="VBScript">
CheckBox1.Value = Null
</SCRIPT>
```

See also the Enabled Property, described earlier.

Underline

See Font

Value

Value is the Property that describes the status or contents of a Control. Precisely what the Value can be varies from Control to Control:

P

Control	Contents of Value Property
CheckBox, ToggleButton, or Option Button	Null, True, or False.
ComboBox or ListBox	The contents of the BoundColumn of the currently selected rows. To add or remove items from a List or ComboBox, use the AddItem or RemoveItem Methods. To read (find out) the contents of one of these boxes, use the ListCount, List, and ListIndex Properties.

Control	Contents of Value Property
SpinButton or ScrollBar	A number (Integer) representing the current "position" of the Control. This number must fall between the Max and Min Properties of the Control. If, for example, the Min Property of a ScrollBar was 1 and its Max Property was set to 24, then if the tab (the square sliding button) were in the middle of the ScrollBar, the Value Property would be 12. This Property changes as the user slides the tab in a ScrollBar or clicks on one of the arrows in a SpinButton.
TextBox	The text within the TextBox, a text Variable.

To read (find out) the Value:

```
<SCRIPT LANGUAGE="VBScript">
X = TextBox.Value
MsgBox X
</SCRIPT>
```

OR, to write (change) the Value:

```
<SCRIPT LANGUAGE="VBScript">
TextBox.Value = "This new text."
</SCRIPT>
```

Note that the Value Property of a TextBox is identical to the TextBox's Text Property.

Visible

Adjusting its Visible Property can make any Control appear or disappear on the screen. You can change this Property while designing your script or while the script is running, like this:

```
ToggleButton2.Visible = False
```

You can also quiz the Visible Property while the script is running to find out whether an object is currently visible.

P

Virtually every Control has a Visible Property. The only exceptions are those few, like the Timer, that are merely utilities for the programmer and never become visible to the user.

Having Controls appear or disappear in an intelligent way while a script is running makes an impression on the user. If the user clicks on a Command Button captioned "OPTIONS," perhaps a whole row of other Command Buttons could suddenly appear, with the following captions: Font Size, Type Style, Font Color, Bold, Italic. This approach is a pleasing alternative to menus. VBScript makes it easy to bring whole suites of Controls instantly into view and just as swiftly make them go away.

Invisibility is also a good technique to use when you want to conceal certain information from some users. If they don't know the correct password, or they're not on the list, the Control's Visible Property is never set to True.

If you are filling a Control with a lot of information by using a For...Next loop, the Control can flicker on the screen. If you notice this problem, just make the Control invisible prior to filling it. It will fill faster that way and won't flicker. You could even temporarily put a second, empty Control in its place, so the user won't know that you made the real Control temporarily invisible.

Weight

The Weight is the *darkness* of characters in some text. It can vary from 1 to 1,000, with the additional alternative of 0 that permits the user's computer to select the most appropriate weight. 1 is the lightest; 1,000 the darkest. If you set Bold=True, the Weight immediately goes up to 700. With Bold=False, the Weight is 400. Conversely, if you set the Weight=550 or lower, the Bold Property is turned off. If you set Weight to any number 551 or higher, Bold is automatically turned on.

See Font

Width

Using the Width Property you can find out the width of a layout or Control, or change it. Width, like most measurements in VBScript, is measured in points (72 per inch).

Usually, you establish the width of a Control while designing your script using the ActiveX Control Pad—by dragging a side of the object with the mouse:

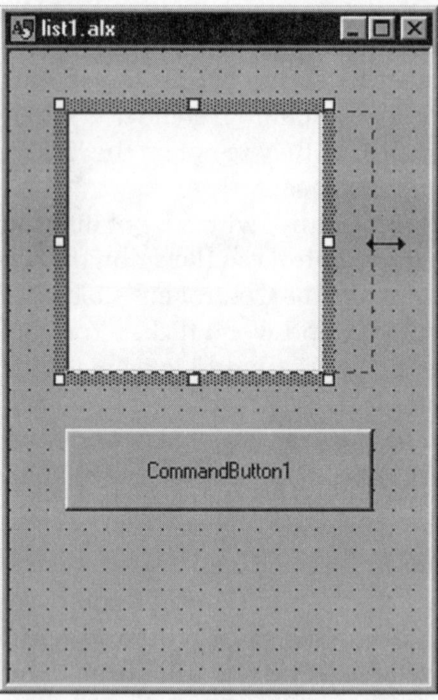

Figure P-19: We're dragging this TextBox so that its width matches the width of the CommandButton below it.

OR (to make one Control the same width as another while the script is running):

```
Image2.Width = Image1.Width
```

OR (to make a Control square):

```
Image2.Width = Image2.Height
```

OR (to change the width while the script is running):

```
TextBox1.Width = 400
```

OR (to use a Variable to set the width):

```
X = 400
Text1.Width = X
```

OR (to make a TextBox 80 percent of the size of its container Layout Control, and centered):

```
TextBox1.Width = .80 * Layout1.Width
TextBox1.Height = .80 * Layout1.Height
TextBox1.Left = (Layout1.Width - TextBox1.Width) / 2
TextBox1.Top = (Layout1.Height - TextBox1.Height) / 2
```

OR (to find where on the screen you should place an Object that you want to be flush against the right side of ListBox1):

```
RightBeside = ListBox1.Left + ListBox1.Width
```

WordWrap

The WordWrap Property determines whether the text or caption within a Control moves down a line if necessary, or just runs off the right side where it can't be read by the user. WordWrap defaults to True, and is a Property of the CheckBox, Command Button, Label, Option Button, TextBox, and ToggleButton Controls.

The TextBox Control also has a MultiLine Property. (It defaults to False, oddly enough. However, paradoxically, it defaults to True for the Rich TextBox Control.) If the MultiLine Property is set to False, it doesn't matter what you do with WordWrap—it is just ignored because there is only a single line for text and it cannot wrap.

P

ProportionalThumb

ACTIVEX

See Properties

Q

Q

HTML

Description <Q> is a rather frivolous formatting code. It is supposed to enclose any text between <Q> and </Q> in quotation marks. Because this is so easy to do via the computer keyboard, one wonders why it is included. Similarly cumbersome and perplexing would be an <EX>.</EX> command pair to insert an exclamation point. There is no <EX> command, so why is there a <Q> command?

It is not asserted that Q will change the typeface, spacing, or any other quality of the text—it just provides surrounding quotes. One problem with this (versus just typing the quotation marks in) is that punctuation rules require that you put a comma just before the close quotation mark but a semicolon just following it. Using Q makes this more awkward than simply typing the quotation marks.

The one advantage claimed for Q is that it will adjust the punctuation (single versus double quotation marks) according to the language in which the text is being written. However, if you're writing in Greek, you likely already know how Greek handles quotes.

In contrast, the <BLOCKQUOTE> command does have a use—it creates a special format for longer quotes.

Used with ***Can be enclosed by***

<A>, <ABBREV>, <ACRONYM>, <ADDRESS>, <AU>, <B>, <BANNER>, <BIG>, <BODY>, <BODYTEXT>, <CAPTION>, <CITE>, <CODE>, <CREDIT>, <DD>, <DEL>, <DFN>, <DIV>, <DT>, <EM>, <FIGTEXT>, <FN>, <FORM>, <H1>, <H2>, <H3>, <H4>, <H5>, <H6>, <I>, <INS>, <KBD>, <LANG>, <LH>, <LI>, <NOTE>, <P>, <PERSON>, <PRE>, <Q>, <S>, <SAMP>, <SMALL>, <STRONG>, <SUB>, <SUP>, <TD>, <TH>, <TT>, <U>, <VAR>

Can enclose
<A>, <ABBREV>, <ACRONYM>, <AU>, <B>, <BIG>, <BR>, <CITE>, <CODE>, <DEL>, <DFN>, <EM>, <I>, <IMG>, <INS>, <KBD>, <LANG>, <MATH>, <PERSON>, <Q>, <S>, <SAMP>, <SMALL>, <STRONG>, <SUB>, <SUP>, <TAB>, <TT>, <U>, <VAR>

Uses None

Cautions Internet Explorer doesn't, at this time, recognize the Q command.

Example

```
<Q>This is a quote.</Q>
```

See also <BLOCKQUOTE>

R

Raise

VBSCRIPT METHOD

Description The Raise command is used to simulate an error. Generally this is for the purpose of testing how well your script responds to an error. If you want it to seem that error number 44 has occurred, put the following within your script:

```
Err.Raise 44
```

See Err

Randomize

VBSCRIPT STATEMENT

Description Use Randomize as the first command in your script if you want to give your script the ability to produce truly random numbers each time it runs. Randomize makes your script produce a *different* series of random numbers each time the script runs—each time a document is loaded or refreshed (each time it is *parsed* by a browser).

The computer will provide a series of random numbers when you use the Rnd Function. However, each time you run a script, that same series repeats itself unless you use the Randomize Statement at the start of the script to provide a truly random "seed" for the Rnd Function.

Arbitrary and Erratic? The Rnd Function uses a complex series of calculations to create a random number out of another number. The original number that Rnd transforms is called the *seed*. Each time you use Rnd, it saves the result and uses that result as the seed the next time you use Rnd. Such a series of numbers will appear to be erratic and arbitrary, but because it is based on mathematical calculations designed to produce one random number from a previous number, it is not a truly random series *unless the first seed is itself randomly selected.* The Randomize Statement uses the computer's clock to provide just such an initial, chance seed. Without using the Randomize command, *the same seed is provided* when the Rnd command is first used in a program—therefore, all subsequent uses of Rnd produce a chain of random numbers that is identical to the chain produced any time the script runs.

Computers are relentlessly logical and orderly. Nonetheless, games, simulations, aspects of art, and other situations require a random element. The Rnd Function provides your program with numbers picked at random. You can then imitate the randomness of a shuffled deck of cards, of a cloud pattern, or of splattered paint.

Technical Note: Random numbers are created with a routine that imitates a shift register with feedback. Bits shifted out are fed back into the register at a certain bit position.

Used with The Rnd Function. Randomize ensures that Rnd will produce a unique series of random numbers each time a script runs.

Variables To make the Rnd Function behave in a completely random fashion (rather than creating a predictable chain of numbers), put Randomize as the first command in your script. Randomize will then create a truly random seed for the Rnd Function when it is used later in the program:

```
Randomize
```

OR, if you provide a particular number to Randomize, it saves that number as the seed for the next use of the Rnd Function. If N is always the same, the seed will always be the same. Subsequent use of the Rnd Function will produce a random series of numbers but each series started by the same seed will be the same *series,* the same chain.

```
Randomize N
```

In other words, if N = 12, the Rnd Function might generate .637310206890106 as its random number based on the seed of 12.

Rnd will always generate the same number from a seed of 12. The next time Rnd is used in a running program, it uses .637310206890106 as the seed to generate a new number. Then the result becomes the seed, and this process continues each time Rnd is used in a running program. However, if the series of random numbers starts from a seed derived from 12, the series, though internally random, will always be the same series.

You may want to allow the user to "save a simulation." In other words, you want the random famines, wars, and other events in an Egyptian Economy game to repeat in the same sequence in the next game. This would be a use for Randomize N.

A Unique Number: Most of the time you want non-repeating sequences of random numbers. That's why you would employ the Randomize command *with nothing after it* (no N in the previous example). As the first command in a running program, Randomize picks a seed from the unique serial number calculated from the computer's clock. This serial number will not repeat itself except once every 100 centuries—it combines the date and time into a unique number. Randomize thereby gets a unique seed that will differ every time a program is started. The seed will also be essentially unpredictable because it will depend on when the user invoked the script.

Uses Randomize allows a program to use the Rnd Function to produce different random series of numbers each time the program runs.

- Use Randomize if you want randomness that is entirely based on chance: drawing various spots on a document's background in chance locations; creating alien spaceships that appear at random times and in random places in a game; simulating the shuffling of cards or the rolling of dice; and so on.
- Use Randomize N—with some number after it—when you want repeatable series of random numbers.

R

Cautions

- Randomize should usually be the first command in a script using random numbers; this means that you will put it as the first command above the first procedure (Sub or Function).

- Sometimes you might want to create a drawing or a simulation that *is* always the same pattern—that repeats the random moves each time a program is run. In these cases, don't use Randomize alone, but follow it with a number (see Variables in this entry).

There May Be No Such Thing: The Rnd and Randomize commands do not produce *true* random numbers. In fact, number theorists say that there may be no such thing as a truly random series. The transcendental number *pi* has, so far, been calculated out a couple of million decimal places using high-speed computers and hasn't yet revealed any discernible pattern. Therefore pi would appear to be a good example of randomness. But no one can prove that pi is, in fact, random. Nobody has been able to demonstrate that God hasn't put a secret message within pi. Pi could start producing a letter-for-letter copy of the Bible when it's finally calculated beyond 23 million decimal places, for all we know. There has, as yet, been no mathematical proof that this cannot happen.

Mathematicians cannot even agree on a definition of *randomness.* For our purposes, though, for rolling dice—instead of something tougher like simulating global weather patterns—Rnd and Randomize suffice. These two commands produce results that are random enough for most programs.

R

Example Every time the following Subroutine is run, it produces the same sequence of numbers. This first example will not produce truly random sequences every time you load or refresh (reload) the document into Microsoft Internet Explorer. Some games, encryption schemes, and other programming depend on a repeatable sequence of numbers. This will do it.

```
<HTML>

<pre>
<SCRIPT LANGUAGE="VBSCRIPT">

For i = 1 To 5
x = Int(Rnd * 5000)
document.writeln cstr(x)
```

```
Next

</SCRIPT>
</pre

</HTML>
```

(To see how to control the range of random numbers using the Int command—and other programming tricks for use with random numbers—see "Rnd.")

Now, to produce a *different* series of random numbers each time the Subroutine runs, insert the Randomize Statement at the start:

```
<HTML>

<pre>
<SCRIPT LANGUAGE="VBSCRIPT">
Randomize

For i = 1 To 5
x = Int(Rnd * 5000)
document.writeln cstr(x)
Next

</SCRIPT>
</pre

</HTML>
```

Now the results will always differ. Not only are the lines random within each series, but also *the series themselves are random.*

See also Rnd

ReDim

VBSCRIPT STATEMENT

Description ReDim sets aside space in the computer's memory to temporarily hold an Array (see "Arrays").

R

ReDim works only within a Procedure (a Subroutine or Function). ReDim brings an Array into existence between the Sub...End Sub or the Function...End Function commands. ReDim temporarily cordons off some of the computer's memory to hold the Array, but when that particular Subroutine or Function is finished doing its work, the set-aside memory is released back to the computer for general use. ReDim cannot be used with ordinary Variables, only with Arrays.

Arrays that bloom and fade like this within a single procedure are called *dynamic* Arrays. The alternative to ReDim is the Dim command, which can also be used *outside* of a Sub…End Sub or Function…End Function. When used outside, the Array becomes available to the entire <SCRIPT> … </SCRIPT> structure and retains its contents *as long as the current document resides in the browser and hasn't been refreshed.*

In the following example, the first time you click this button, the message box displays nothing (there's no content within the Array *n*). However, each time you click the button thereafter, 44 will be displayed. If, however, you move the Dim command *within* the Sub…End Sub, or use the ReDim command (which must *always* be used within Sub…End Sub), the message box will never display anything.

```
<HTML>
<INPUT NAME="Button1" TYPE="Button" VALUE=" Click me ">
<SCRIPT LANGUAGE="VBSCRIPT">

Dim n(12)
Sub Button1_OnClick
msgbox n(1)
n(1) = 44
End Sub

</SCRIPT>
</HTML>
```

R

Used with Used within a procedure (a Sub or Function) to declare—to create—an Array. There are two ways to declare Arrays:

- You can declare (set aside memory for) an Array that *can be used by the entire script* if you use the Dim command outside a Sub…End Sub or Function…End Function structure. This Array's contents will be retained as long as a document resides in the user's browser (isn't reloaded or refreshed).
- If an Array is needed only within a single procedure, you can use the ReDim command. (Unlike other versions of Visual Basic, there are no Public, Global, Private, or Static commands in VBScript.) Once the browser has left the procedure (the Sub…End Sub or Function…End Function structure) within which the ReDim was used, the Array and its contents disappear.

Brief Lives Like Mayflies: If your Array is needed by only a single procedure and needed *only while that procedure is active*, declare it with ReDim. Such Arrays spring into life and die quickly, like mayflies.

ReDim can also *redeclare* an Array that has previously been declared using Dim with empty parentheses like this:

```
Dim n ( )
```

(Normally, you put the size of the Array—how many items it will contain—within the parentheses.) Such a Dim command alerts VBScript that this *n* will be an Array, but doesn't declare the size of the Array (how many elements it should be sized to hold). In such cases, however, you can ReDim no more than eight dimensions for the Array. If there is no previous Dim referring to this same Array (by using the same name, the *n* in this example, to declare it), you can use ReDim to create an Array with as many as 60 dimensions. (See "The Distinction Between Elements and Dimensions" later in this entry for information on *dimensions*.)

R

Variables In the following example, we are defining N as an Array holding 23 items. (See "Arrays" to find out why 22 really means 23.) You don't, of course, have to use all 23 items. You're saying "make room for no more than 23 items."

```
ReDim N(22)
```

OR, this next example also creates an Array, but with 701 individual elements.

```
ReDim F(700)
```

OR, (to declare a series of Arrays following a single ReDim Statement, to save yourself some typing):

```
ReDim datArray(12), Numbs(15), towns(3)
```

Uses Create temporary storage space for an Array that you need to use only while a particular procedure is active.

The virtue of temporary Arrays is that they don't use up the computer's memory by taking space that can be otherwise used while a program is running. Normally, space isn't much of an issue, but some programs are data-intensive and need to manipulate large amounts of information. In such cases, being able to create and then destroy dynamic Arrays can be valuable.

In other versions of Visual Basic you *can* preserve the data within a dynamic Array by using the Preserve or Static commands. These commands are unavailable in VBScript.

If you want to deliberately remove the contents of a static Array (one created with the Dim command outside a procedure), use the Erase command:

```
Erase N
```

This will destroy the contents of the Array and free up computer memory.

Cautions

- The range of elements defined for an Array—the index of the Array—can be negative. An index can range from –32,768 to 32,767.
- If the same Variable name was previously declared by using a Dim command, the maximum number of dimensions in a ReDimmed Array is eight. If this Array is being declared for the first time by ReDim (Dim isn't being used), however, there can be as many as 60 dimensions.

- ReDim resets (empties) all the elements of an Array to Empty each time the ReDim command is encountered.
- The number of elements in a ReDimmed Array can be changed at any time:

```
ReDim This(4)
This(3) = "Nadia C."
MsgBox This(3)
ReDim This(5)
This(4) = "Thomas R."
```

The preceding programming is perfectly legal. However, while you can change the number of elements, you *cannot* change the number of *dimensions* in the Array:

Wrong:

```
ReDim This(4)
This(3) = "Nadia C."
MsgBox This(3)
ReDim This(5, 2)
This(3,1) = "Thomas R."
```

This second ReDim attempted to create a two-dimensional Array out of an Array already declared as single-dimensional.

The Distinction Between Elements and Dimensions: The number of elements in an Array is the number of individual items of data it can contain—how many text or numeric Variables the Array can hold. Elements are defined as a *range:* ReDim F(44) is a range from 0 to 44, or 45 total elements. Each item in this Array will be identified by its unique *index number* such as F(12) or F(22).

An Array's *dimensions* are how many of these ranges it contains. Most Arrays have only a single dimension: Z(50) is a single-dimensional Array with 51 elements. But A(5,6,7) is a three-dimensional Array with 6, 7, and 8 elements in each respective dimension (a total of 336 elements). This Array could describe a cube—over 5, up 6, in 7 would be a cell position within that cube. For more on dimensions, see "Arrays."

Example This example fills a temporary (dynamic) Array with information, and then shows the information held within that Array. This illustrates how to create a temporary Array, and also helps you visualize how an Array stores pieces of data the same way mail is stored in the boxes in a post office. In this case, we're using a two-dimensional Array.

```
<HTML>
<INPUT NAME="Button1" TYPE="Button" VALUE=" Click me ">
<TEXTAREA NAME=RESULT ROWS=12 COLS = 55></TEXTAREA>
<SCRIPT LANGUAGE="VBSCRIPT">

Sub Button1_OnClick
cr = chr(13) + chr(10)

ReDim Nameaddr(3, 1)
Nameaddr(0, 0) = "Bobby Jones"
Nameaddr(1, 0) = "Marcia Delobia"
Nameaddr(2, 0) = "Sam Missile"
Nameaddr(3, 0) = "Bertha Vanation"
Nameaddr(0, 1) = "Arlington, VA"
Nameaddr(1, 1) = "Wilmington, DE"
Nameaddr(2, 1) = "Azuza, CA"
Nameaddr(3, 1) = "Bukon City, AL"

For i = 0 To 3
  For j = 0 To 1

Arr = Nameaddr(i,j)
RESULT.VALUE=RESULT.VALUE + Arr
Next
RESULT.VALUE=RESULT.VALUE + cr
Next
End Sub

</SCRIPT>
</pre>
</HTML>
```

We create a temporary Array, capable of holding a total of eight Variables. A multidimensional Array can help you maintain relationships between the Variables within its structure. In this example, we are providing two pieces of information (name and address) about four people. The first "dimension" of the Array (3) will contain the names of the four people. The second dimension (1) will contain each person's address.

We assign that information to the Array elements. Each element within an Array is uniquely identified by the index numbers (1,1) or (3,0) and so on. The point here is that we can manipulate such names *mathematically* within a pair of For...Next Loops. Once all the information is in this Array, we don't need to keep referring to each individual Array element by some text name.

The Inner, Nested Loop: Then, we display the name and the address (using the inner, "nested" Loop For j = 0 To 1: see "For...Next"). We want to display the contents of each element within the Array. Then, the second time through the *j* Loop, we pull each person's address out of the Array.

See also Dim, Set, Arrays, Variables

Rem

VBSCRIPT STATEMENT

R

Description Short for *rem*ark, Rem tells Visual Basic Script to ignore everything following the Rem command on the current line. Use the Rem command to attach comments to your program, without worrying that VBScript will try to interpret those comments as commands—and fail.

Rem is another holdover from earlier versions of Basic. The ' (single quotation mark) symbol is generally used instead and serves the same purpose. The ' is, of course, easier to type in, and ' has the added advantage of not requiring a colon to separate it from any previous commands on the same line, as does Rem (see the third item under the Cautions section of this entry).

Used with Any place in your script where you want to attach an explanatory note to the commands. Some people feel that such notes make it easier:

- To read a script, understanding the purpose of the nearby commands as you read through the script.
- To maintain a script, making adjustments and changes to improve the script or keep it current.
- To team-program, allowing others to read and maintain the script.
- To debug the script, tracking down and fixing errors.

Variables The HTML format for remarks is <!-- this is the comment, and the comment ends with the following symbol -->.

The traditional BASIC format is as follows:

```
If B = "Martha" Then ' If B is "Martha" print her an →
invitation to the ball.

PInvite "Martha Blivings"

End If
```

OR

```
' ........... PRINT A BALL INVITE FOR MARTHA.........
'
If B = "Martha" Then
  PInvite "Martha Blivings"
End If
'
'
'..................................................
```

Some programmers like to put ' at the beginning of lines and, as illustrated above, to create elaborate zones in their scripts, visually separating the various sections with dots or underline symbols. In this way, each part of the script is described and also framed into a quickly recognized functional unit. Such approaches are perhaps not as necessary as they once were—programs used to be just one long series of commands from start to finish, like a mystifying

R

insurance policy. VBScript, and Internet programming in general, however, naturally encapsulate commands into pages, documents, and Procedures of reasonable brevity, so there is less need to utilize drastic cryptographic Rem statements.

Uses If, or how much, *Rem*arking you do to your documents is essentially a matter of personal preference.

Just as some composers can read a score as easily as they read the daily paper, some programmers can read programs effortlessly. To them, commented programs are annoying, cluttered, and the comments are considered superfluous. These programmers understand computer language well and don't need the command purposes paraphrased for them in English.

Others find program syntax, and even the meaning of various commands obscure or hard to remember. This doesn't mean that these people are necessarily inferior programmers. Just because some people have a hard time remembering names doesn't mean they can't be a success at parties. It's often merely that a part of their brain doesn't work as well as, perhaps, other parts do. For these people, lots of commenting serves the same purpose as notes in a Latin textbook—a handy translation of the original.

Why We Don't Use Comments: In this book, we have rarely used comments. There are two reasons for this. First, most of the scripts are thoroughly paraphrased in a text explication immediately preceding or following the program. Second, if you are typing in programming from a book, comments are clutter.

If you frequently find yourself unable to understand the meaning or purpose of a program that you've written, comment as much as necessary. If you find it easy to read programs, perhaps you'll want to comment only when a particular section or command is especially obscure.

Cautions

- Once you have inserted a ' or a Rem, everything after that *on the same line* is ignored by VBScript. However, the following line will be parsed by the browser and assumed to be script programming rather than a comment.
- You can follow ' or Rem with spaces, symbols, anything that you wish.

- If you *do* choose to use the word *Rem* instead of the ' symbol, remember that Rem requires a colon to separate it from any previous commands on that line:

Right:

```
MSGBOX N: REM MsgBox Nancy's name and address
```

Wrong:

```
MSGBOX N REM MsgBox Nancy's name and address
```

When using the ' symbol, a colon is unnecessary—another reason for preferring ' over Rem:

Right:

```
MSGBOX N ' MsgBox Nancy's name and address
```

Example Some programmers like to tab over until all their comments line up on the page, creating a running commentary of the program:

```
ReDim Nameaddr(3, 1)                    'create a 4 x 2 array
Nameaddr(0, 0) = "Bobby Jones"          'enter the four names
Nameaddr(1, 0) = "Marcia Delobia"
Nameaddr(2, 0) = "Sam Missile"
Nameaddr(3, 0) = "Bertha Vanation"
Nameaddr(0, 1) = "Arlington, VA"        'enter the four addresses
Nameaddr(1, 1) = "Wilmington, DE"
Nameaddr(2, 1) = "Azuza, CA"
Nameaddr(3, 1) = "Bukon City, AL"

For i = 0 To 3                'in the outer loop we'll pick
                              'up each group
   For j = 0 To 1             'the inner loop provides each
                              'pair
   Arr = "Nameaddr(" + Str(i) + "," + Str(j) + ") "
      MsgBox Arr              'display the pair
   Next
Next
```

See also Comment

Remove

ACTIVEX

See Methods

RemoveItem

ACTIVEX

See Methods

Right

VBSCRIPT FUNCTION

Description Right extracts a piece of text from the right side of a larger piece of text. A variation of this command, the RightB function, allows you to specify the length in *bytes* rather than *characters*. (Characters in the 32-bit version of VBScript are 2-byte units.)

```
MsgBox Right("ABCDE", 2)
```

Results in

```
DE
```

Text Variables are called *strings* in computerese. When using Right, you specify how many characters you want extracted, and VBScript counts over that far from the right side of the larger text and provides you with the piece of text you requested.

Used with Text ("string") Variable subtypes, Constants, or expressions (see "Variables," or the Cautions below, for a definition of Constants and expressions).

Right can also be used with *text literals*. A "literal" means that you provide the actual text rather than a Variable:

```
X = "Pour the soup, Sam"
X (is a Variable)
"Pour the soup, Sam." (is a literal)
```

However, there is no real reason to use Right with a literal. If you want the rightmost three characters from the preceding literal, then just use X = "Sam" and you have no need to extract it by using the Right command.

Right is often used in conjunction with Left. Together, they enable you to divide a larger text into two smaller pieces. The Mid, InStr, and Len commands are often used with Right as well. See the descriptions under Uses.

Variables To put the rightmost five letters from A into Result:

```
Result = Right(A, 5)
```

OR (the Variable N determines how many text characters Result will get from the right side of X):

```
Result = Right(X, N)
```

OR

```
Result = Right("This message", 4)
```

Right is used here with a text literal—although you would more likely just enter Result = "sage" than go to the trouble of having your program calculate what you can plainly see in the "literal." (See "Variables.")

Uses *Parse* some text—pull out the various elements of the text.

Right is used along with several other Functions that manipulate text—Left, Mid, InStr, and Len—to isolate and extract a piece of text from within a larger group of characters.

Left pulls out a number of characters, counting from the start of the larger text:

```
X = "Montenegro is rising."
Y = Left(X,10)
MsgBox Y
```

Results in

```
Montenegro
```

Mid pulls out a piece of text anywhere from within a larger text using the format Y Mid (LargerText, StartingCharacter,

NumberOfCharacters). Use Mid when the target piece of text isn't flush against the left or right of the larger text:

```
X = "We Employ A Maid From Planet X."
Y = Mid(X,23,6)
MsgBox Y
```

Results in

```
Planet
```

Len tells you the length, in characters, of a text ("string") Variable:

```
X = "We employ a maid from Planet X."
MsgBox Len(X)
```

Results in

```
31
```

InStr finds the location of the first character of a piece of text within a larger group of characters:

```
X = "We employ a maid from Planet X."
L = InStr(X, "maid")
MsgBox L
```

Results in

```
13
```

InStr will give back a 0 if it cannot find the text you're searching for. InStr is case-sensitive—looking for "Maid" will give back a 0, meaning "not found."

Cautions

- Right usually extracts a smaller piece of text from a text ("string") Variable subtype. However, Right can also extract from a Constant (Const CALCAPITOL = "Sacramento"), or a string expression. (See "Variables.")
- The number of characters you are requesting Right to extract—the 15 in Right(X, 15)—can be a literal number like 15 or a numeric Variable like *N*.

- The number of characters you are requesting Right to extract from a larger piece of text can be large as 65,535. If you ask for more characters than are in the larger piece of text, you get back the whole larger text.

Example Right is often used together with Left and InStr to break a piece of text into pieces. For instance, you could pull in an .INI file from the disk and put each of its lines into a separate Array Variable (see "Arrays"). Then your program could examine the contents of the .INI file in detail.

Another way that Right can help is when you need to stuff information into an Array (or items into a List Box) but don't want to do it the normal VBScript way:

```
ReDim NolteMovies(1 To 9)
NolteMovies(1) = "Return To Macon County"
NolteMovies(2) = "The Deep"
NolteMovies(3) = "North Dallas Forty"
NolteMovies(4) = "Heart Beat"
NolteMovies(5) = "Cannery Row"
```

and so on until you've assigned all nine members of this Array.

This approach is (slightly) faster than the traditional approach, but it is certainly more trouble for the programmer. Traditionally, there were two commands in Basic—Data and Read—but they are unavailable in VBScript.

Using Data and Read, you could accomplish the same thing as the preceding example:

```
DATA "Return To Macon County", "The Deep", "North Dallas
Forty", "Heart Beat", "Cannery Row", "48 Hours", "Under
Fire", "Teachers", "Grace Quigley"

For I = 1 To 9
  Read NolteMovies(I)
Next I
```

We can use Left to provide an acceptable substitute for the Read command. Using Left, you can easily build an Array with data while the program is running.

R

Enter this declaration (using Dim outside of a Sub…End Sub or Function…End Function structure) to make the information available to the entire script:

```
Dim NolteMovies(8)
```

Then, in a Sub, add the following:

```
Sub Fillarray ()
D = "Return To Macon County, The Deep, North Dallas Forty,
Heart Beat, Cannery Row, 48 Hours, Under Fire, Teachers,
Grace Quigley"
L = InStr(D, ",")
Do While L
   c = c + 1
   NolteMovies(c) = Left(D, L - 1)
   D = Right(D, Len(D) - L - 1)
   L = InStr(D, ",")
Loop
c = c + 1
NolteMovies(c) = D
End Sub
```

This approach may seem like the long way around, but if you have a lot of data and you want it embedded within your program (as opposed to reading it in from a disk file), this little Subroutine can be very handy indeed. Instead of dozens of NolteMovies(18) = "Name of Movie," you can just use this Loop. Note that there is an Array Function that can solve this embedded-data problem handily; it's a good replacement for the Data…Read commands that have been purged from Basic.

The preceding routine first gets the location (L) of the first comma in the data (D). Then we enter a Loop that says: "Keep looping while L is not zero. If L is zero, we will not find any more commas."

Inside the Loop, we keep a counter (c), which will increase each time through the Loop and provide a unique index number for each item in the Array (NolteMovie). We pull the Left from D. Left will contain everything left of the comma—in other words, the name of the first movie. Then we use Right to strip off that first movie name. Now D will contain all the remaining movies, but not the first one. With each use of Left and Right, we subtract 1 from the location (L). That avoids including the comma in either the new small piece of text or in the remaining larger piece of text.

Then we keep repeating, splitting pieces of D off until we've reached a point where there are no commas left, and we exit the Loop and, one more time, insert the last movie name into the Array.

See also InStr, Left, Len, Mid

Rnd

VBSCRIPT FUNCTION

Description Rnd provides your program with random numbers. This Function is very useful in a variety of situations. With a random number, you can draw a card out of a deck, make aliens unpredictable in a space attack game, create "abstract" designs that never repeat, and accomplish many other tasks. Randomness is particularly important when you are creating simulations, games, and certain kinds of graphics.

Use the Randomize command as the first command in your procedure if you want Rnd to produce a truly random series of numbers. The computer can provide a series of random numbers when you use the Rnd Function. However, each time you run a program, *that same series will repeat itself* unless you use the Randomize Statement at the start of the procedure to provide a truly random "seed" for the Rnd Function. This repeatability of the series of numbers is used by games and cryptography; the repeatability has value. However, at this time, the RND series *does not repeat*. See the example later in this entry.

R

Used with The Randomize Function. Randomize ensures that Rnd will produce a unique series of random numbers every time a program is run. (See the example.)

Variables The following is the most common way to use Rnd. You decide what range of numbers you want and then multiply that number by Rnd. Adding 1 makes the result range between 1 and the upper limit. The Int Function rounds off any fractional part of the result. This example provides a random number between 1 and 50:

```
X = Int(Rnd * 50 + 1)
```

OR (to provide a range between 0 and an upper limit, supply as an upper limit a number higher than you actually want and don't add 1 inside the parentheses. This example provides a random number between 0 and 50):

```
X = Int(Rnd * 51)
```

OR (Rnd is *supposed* to be random, but you can make it behave predictably, non-randomly. There is no known use for this technique, but you *can* provide numbers or numeric Variables in parentheses following the Rnd Function. If you provide a number, Rnd will always produce the same result each time the program runs. However, subsequent uses of the Rnd (.2233) in this example, while the program runs, will produce varying numbers):

```
X = Rnd (.2233)
```

OR (if you provide 0 in parentheses following Rnd, you will get the *previous* random number that was generated by Rnd in the program):

```
X = Rnd(0)
```

Uses Use Rnd whenever you want things to happen by chance—for games, simulations, statistical analysis, or art—anytime you want to introduce unpredictable results into the relentlessly ordered world of the computer.

If you are doing an economic simulation, you might want to crash the stock market every 60 or 90 years, causing hardship for nine years thereafter. But exactly *when* the crash occurs should be unpredictable and should be different every time the program runs (see "Randomize"). Each time a "year" passes in the economic simulation, you use:

```
X = Int(Rnd * 60 + 1)
If X = 42 Then
...CRASH.
End If
```

You can have any of the numbers between 1 and 60 trigger the crash because each number will randomly occur with a probability of 1 in 60 each "year." For card games, shuffle an Array of cards with Rnd, and so forth.

Cautions In most situations you won't have to worry, but Rnd is capable of generating a huge range of random numbers. Most of the time you'll use it to toss a coin (range 0 to 1); or to determine which direction a dangerous asteroid will wander across the screen, threatening your space ship (range probably 1 to 8); or to roll dice (range 1 to 6). In these cases, don't worry about Variable types.

Rnd creates a fraction between 0 and 1. That's why you multiply and round off Rnd to get a whole number that you can use for things like tossing a coin.

Rnd Gives Good Fractions: The fraction produced by Rnd has an enormous range of possibilities, as you can see by this example:

```
<HTML>
<SCRIPT LANGUAGE=VBS>

For i = 1 To 20
N = cDbl(Rnd)
MsgBox N
Next

</SCRIPT>
</HTML>
```

Results in

```
.705547511577606
.533424019813538
.579518616199493
.289562463760376
.301948010921478
.774740099906921
.014017641544342
.76072359085083
.814490020275116
.709037899971008
4.53527569770813D-02
.414032697677612
```

```
.862619340419769
.790480017662048
.373536169528961
.961953163146973
.871445834636688
5.62368631362915D-02
.949556648731232
.364018678665161
```

Notice that if you run this example, *you'll get the same sequence that we've printed above—the same sequence that we got*. How "random" is it if you can always get the same sequence? To avoid this, see "Randomize."

Notice also that we had to use cDbl to force the result into a double-precision floating-point Variable subtype (see "Variables"). If we leave out cDbl, the result is truncated to a single-precision floating-point type and there are fewer digits, or fewer "decimal places." (If D-02 follows a number, you should move the decimal point over two spaces to the left, adding zeros if necessary. Therefore, 4.53527569770813D-02 means .0453527569770813.)

With this much variability in the series of digits that Rnd can supply, you can generate random numbers over an enormous range, should you ever need to. Just multiply the number provided by RND by the upper limit of the range you're after.

You should generally use Randomize as the first command in a procedure, to prevent repeated series of numbers.

R

Example

```
x = RND
Randomize
y = RND
Msgbox x + " " + y
```

The first call to Rnd always produces the same random number. The second one—following the Randomize command—always produces a different random number.

See also Randomize, Int

Rounding

Description The formula for rounding any number is:

```
X = Int(N + .5)
```

N can be any number and X holds the result. For example, to round off the number 12.633:

```
N = 12.633
X = Int(N + .5)
MsgBox X
```

Results In

```
13
```

See Int

Rows

HTML

Description Rows is a command used with the TEXTAREA to define how high the TEXTAREA will be. In other words, Rows determines the number of text lines that will appear within the TEXTAREA Object. COLS defines the number of characters per line within a TEXTAREA and, therefore, describes the width of the TEXTAREA object.

See TEXTAREA

RTrim

VBSCRIPT FUNCTION

See LTrim

S

S

HTML

Description Draws a line through text. S stands for "strikeout."

Used with ***Can be enclosed by***

<A>, <ABBREV>, <ACRONYM>, <ADDRESS>, <AU>, <B>, <BANNER>, <BIG>, <BODY>, <BODYTEXT>, <CAPTION>, <CITE>, <CODE>, <CREDIT>, <DD>, <DEL>, <DFN>, <DIV>, <DT>, <EM>, <FIGTEXT>, <FN>, <FORM>, <H>, <I>, <INS>,<KBD>, <LANG>, <LH>, <LI>, <NOTE>, <P>, <PERSON>, <PRE>, <Q>, <S>, <SAMP>, <SMALL>, <STRONG>, <SUB>, <SUP>, <TD>,<TH>, <TT>, <U>, <VAR>

Can enclose

<A>, <ABBREV>, <ACRONYM>, <AU>, <B>, <BIG>, <BR>, <CITE>, <CODE>, <DEL>, <DFN>, <EM>, <I>, <IMG>, <INS>, <KBD>,<LANG>, <MATH>, <PERSON>, <Q>, <S>, <SAMP>, <SMALL>, <STRONG>, <SUB>, <SUP>, <TAB>, <TT>, <U>, <VAR>

Uses Indicate that some text has been deleted.

Cautions There aren't many uses for strikethrough. It's generally only seen in word processor applications to indicate that some text has been deleted.

Example

```
<S>Don't pay attention to this.</S>
```

Samp

HTML

Description Yet another typeface specification that indicates to the browser to display non-proportional text. Essentially identical to the CODE command.

Used to display programming ("code") such as HTML source code. The font used is fixed-width. Fixed-width means a font such as Courier, a typewriter-style typeface where each character is the same width (*i* is as wide as *w*). (The opposite variety—Variable-width type—is typified by Times Roman. Characters vary in width.) Variable-width is the default HTML font for body text; fixed-width is the default for headlines and "code." However, most browsers permit users to define their preferences in these matters.

Used with ***Can be enclosed by***

<A>, <ABBREV>, <ACRONYM>, <ADDRESS>, <AU>, <B>, <BANNER>, <BIG>, <BODY>, <BODYTEXT>, <CAPTION>, <CITE>, <CODE>, <CREDIT>, <DD>, <DEL>, <DFN>, <DIV>, <DT>, <EM>, <FIGTEXT>, <FN>, <FORM>, <H>, <I>, <INS>,<KBD>, <LANG>, <LH>, <LI>, <NOTE>, <P>, <PERSON>, <PRE>, <Q>, <S>, <SAMP>, <SMALL>, <STRONG>, <SUB>, <SUP>, <TD>,<TH>, <TT>, <U>, <VAR>

Can enclose

<A>, <ABBREV>, <ACRONYM>, <AU>, <B>, <BIG>, <BR>, <CITE>, <CODE>, <DEL>, <DFN>, <EM>, <I>, <IMG>, <INS>, <KBD>, <LANG>, <MATH>, <PERSON>, <Q>, <S>, <SAMP>, <SMALL>, <STRONG>, <SUB>, <SUP>, <TAB>, <TT>, <U>, <VAR>

Variables

```
<SAMP> SOME HTML PROGRAMMING </ SAMP >
```

Uses Indicate that you are displaying non-standard text, something that should be set off from ordinary body text. Many computer books, this one included, switch to a different font to indicate computer programming—lines that the user can type in to cause something to happen in a computer language such as HTML.

S

Example

```
<FONT SIZE=+1>
Use the following for an Input Button:
<BR><BR>

<SAMP>

INPUT TYPE=BUTTON VALUE="Click me" NAME="Btn"

</SAMP>
 <BR><BR>
```

(Also, the cStr command transforms the numeric variable subtype.)

Use the following for an Input Button:

`INPUT TYPE=BUTTON VALUE="Click me" NAME="Btn"`

(Also, the cStr command transforms the numeric variable subtype)

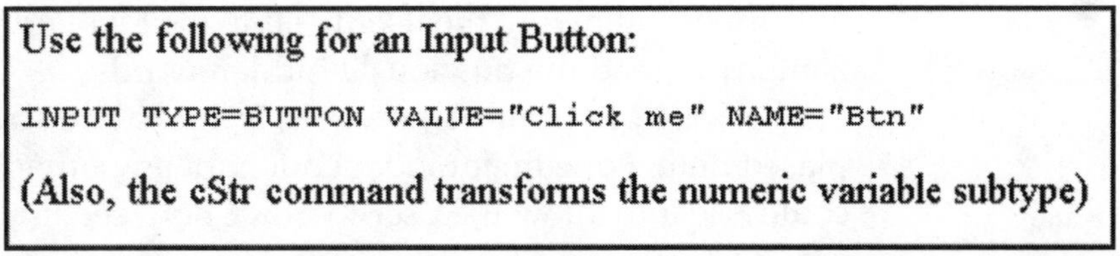

Figure S-1: SAMP causes non-proportional text to be displayed by the browser.

See also CODE

Scope

Description The scope (sometimes called the "lifetime") of a Variable or Array determines how widely within a document the Variable or Array can be accessed. Is it available only within a single Subroutine or Function, or is it available to the entire document? See "Dim" for a complete discussion of scope in VBScript.

See Dim

Scroll

ACTIVEX

See Events

ScrollBar

ACTIVEX CONTROL

Description ScrollBars are associated with, you guessed it, scrolling. They are automatically attached to certain Controls when the contents of the Control are not completely visible. For example, if there's more text within a TextBox than can be displayed all at once, a ScrollBar will appear, allowing the user to slide the text vertically or horizontally to read the previously hidden words.

The ScrollBar Control, however, is a separate object and can be placed onto a document independent of any other Control. You could use it to allow the user to move between, for instance, various frames in your document. However, users are likely to find an unattached ScrollBar eccentric. Instead of using the ScrollBar Control, you might consider the *Slider* object. Sliders are used to move or change other objects, and users grasp their purpose (an ActiveX Slider Control should be available shortly). Or, consider using a SpinButton.

Variables The Delay Property specifies the amount of time that will pass between when the user first clicks a ScrollBar and the triggering of the ScrollBar's Change Event. It works both when the user holds down the mouse button (such as during dragging) and when the user repeatedly clicks the button.

The Change Event is immediately triggered on the first mouse click. However, how long it takes before the Event is triggered a second time depends on the setting of this Delay Property. The real delay will be the Delay setting multiplied by five. Delay is specified in milliseconds and defaults to 50 (one-twentieth of a second). Therefore, the default Delay is 250 milliseconds (one-fourth of a second). After the first click, the interval between triggered Events is the actual delay (not multiplied by five). The default interval, then, is 50 milliseconds. You can adjust the delay if you want to put some programming into a Change Event but don't want a continuous rapid retriggering of the Event.

The LargeChange and SmallChange Properties specify the *granularity* of the ScrollBar. It is a Windows convention that if the user clicks on one of the small arrows at either end of a ScrollBar, there is a *small* adjustment. Usually, clicking moves you to the next contiguous area of the contents. For instance, if you were viewing a text document, you would move down to the next line of text. The amount of movement is governed by the SmallChange Property. On the other hand, if the user clicks *within* a ScrollBar, there is a larger shift, a LargeChange. Depending on the size of the document, you might go to the beginning or end, fully to the right or left, or shift up or down by a single screenful or page of text. The shift, in this case, need not be contiguous—although it usually is. This movement is governed by the LargeChange Property. You, the programmer, determine the behavior of SmallChange and LargeChange by giving them values. You decide how much movement takes place.

The default LargeChange or SmallChange increment is 1. You can set the increment anywhere between -32,767 and 32,767. (You also establish the outer limits of the range that describes the shift, using the Max and Min Properties. You can restrict movement to a smaller area than the total size of the document under the window.)

Max is the value of the Control at the position at the far right of a horizontal ScrollBar Control or the position at the bottom of a vertical ScrollBar Control. You determine the measurement system of your ScrollBar Control based usually on what information it slides the user through. For instance, if you are showing data about your family and there are five of you, set Max to 5. For a calendar, set Max to 12 if you want to allow the user to slide through pages for each month. For a cookbook with 150 recipes, set Max to 150.

Any change the user makes by moving the lozenge-shaped button (called the Scroll Box or Tab) inside a ScrollBar will change that ScrollBar's Value Property. Your script can use the Value to take appropriate actions. Normally, these actions are taken by programming you write within the ScrollBar's Change Event. A ScrollBar's

Min and Max Properties set the limits that its Value Property can change. Min defaults to 0 and Max defaults to 32767. Ordinarily, you'll set these Properties while designing your document, using the Properties window in the ActiveX Control Pad.

The Orientation Property allows you to override the current shape of the Control: horizontal or vertical. By default, VBScript decides the orientation based on the height and width of the Control. If a ScrollBar is taller than it is wide, VBScript displays it vertically. And vice versa. If you want to ignore this default and take matters into your own hands, you can adjust the Orientation Property three ways:

```
ScrollBar2.Orientation = -1 'the default (automatic →
orientation)
ScrollBar2.Orientation = 0 'displayed vertically
ScrollBar2.Orientation = 1 'displayed horizontally
```

The ProportionalThumb Property allows you to refuse to display a Windows 95 convention. The "thumb" is the sliding bar within a ScrollBar that the user can drag to move the contents into view within a container like a TextBox. With Windows 95, thumbs became indicators as well. They visually cue the user as to the amount of the contents that are currently hidden. For example, if a TextBox contains 100 lines of text, but you can see 50 lines displayed, the thumb would be 50 percent of the size of its ScrollBar. In VBScript, this proportional thumb is the default for ScrollBars. However, if you wish, you can turn this feature off with:

```
ScrollBar2.ProportionalThumb = False
```

S

Properties

BackColor, CodeBase, Delay, Enabled, ForeColor, Height, ID, LargeChange, Left, Max, Min, MouseIcon, MousePointer, Orientation, ProportionalThumb, SmallChange, TabIndex, TabStop, Top, Value (the default Property), Visible, Width

Events

AfterUpdate, BeforeDragOver, BeforeDropOrPaste, BeforeUpdate, Change, Enter, Error, Exit, KeyDown, KeyPress, KeyUp Scroll

Methods
Move, SetFocus, ZOrder

For details about these Properties, Events, and Methods, see the entries for Properties, Events, and Methods.

Uses Scrolling. ScrollBars can also be used to adjust properties. For example, you can create a ScrollBar that, when adjusted, changes the BackColor of another Control.

Cautions By default, you get a vertical ScrollBar when you insert the ScrollBar ActiveX Control into an HTML document or layout. However, to make it horizontal, just drag one of the sides until the ScrollBar is wider than it is tall. It will change into a horizontal version.

The ScrollBars that appear within TextBoxes and ListBoxes are part of those Controls, and the scrolling is handled automatically. However, the stand-alone ScrollBar Control that we're discussing here causes no intrinsic behaviors in other Controls. You must use the ScrollBar's Change or Scroll Events to cause things to happen in other Controls when the user drags the ScrollBar thumb or clicks within the ScrollBar. The programming is up to you. See the example below.

The ScrollBar's Change Event provides the same functionality as the Scroll Event, but with an important difference. The Change Event is only triggered when the user releases the mouse button—thereby stopping a drag, stopping the tab from moving within the ScrollBar. The Scroll Event is triggered *continuously* while the tab is being moved (it's similar to the MouseMove Event in this respect). Therefore, use the Scroll Event when you want a continuously changing effect. See the example below for an illustration of the difference.

Example We'll put a ScrollBar on an HTML Layout Control and allow the user to move the ScrollBar, thereby widening or narrowing a TextBox. Start the Microsoft ActiveX Control Pad and click on Edit | Insert HTML Layout. Give it a new name and then click on the icon next to the <OBJECT> definition. Now, from the toolbox, put a horizontal ScrollBar on the bottom of the Layout Control, and put a TextBox above it. Right-click on the ScrollBar and select Properties. Set the Min Property to, say, 135, and its Max Property to whatever ultimate width you're willing to allow the user to stretch your TextBox to, perhaps 500.

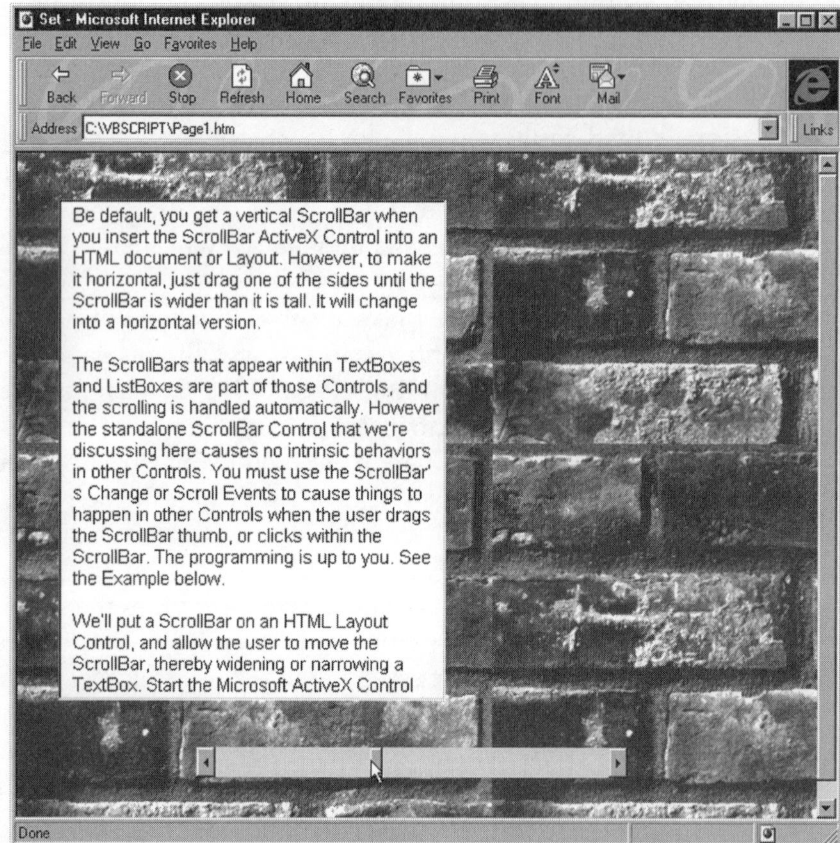

Figure S-2: When the user adjusts this ScrollBar, the TextBox widens or narrows.

Then right-click on the HTML Layout Control and choose "View Source Code." Type in the following:

```
<SCRIPT LANGUAGE="VBScript">
<!--
Sub ScrollBar1_Scroll()
```

```
TextBox1.Width = ScrollBar1.Value
end sub

Sub ScrollBar1_Change()
TextBox1.Width = ScrollBar1.Value
end sub

-->
</SCRIPT>
```

Note that if you leave out the Change Event, the TextBox will only move if the user is dragging the ScrollBar Tab. If you leave out the Scroll Event, clicking will move the TextBox but dragging won't.

See also SpinButton

ScrollBars

ACTIVEX PROPERTY

See Properties

Second

VBSCRIPT FUNCTION

Description The Second Function tells you the second of the minute. It gives you a number between 0 and 59.

You can locate any minute between January 1, 100, and December 31, 9999, using VBScript's built-in "serial number" representation of date+time. VBScript can provide or manipulate individual serial numbers for *every second* between those two dates. These serial numbers also include coded representations of all the minutes, hours, days, months, and years between those dates.

Used with

- Second is often used with the Now Function to tell you the current second as registered by your computer's clock:

```
<HTML>
<SCRIPT LANGUAGE="VBScript">
MsgBox Second(Now)
</SCRIPT>
</HTML>
```

- The Now Function provides the serial number for the current date and time. Second extracts the second portion of the serial number.
- You can use Second with any of the commands in VBScript that produce a serial number for date+time (see "DateSerial").

Variables

```
X = Second(Now)
```

Uses

- Create "digital" clocks.
- Create timers, using Second with the Timer Control.
- Time-stamp data or files.

Example

```
<HTML>
<HEAD>
<TITLE>Second</TITLE>
</HEAD><BODY>

<INPUT TYPE=Button Name="Btn" Value=" Time Since Page Loaded
">

<TEXTAREA NAME=RESULT ROWS=12 COLS = 45></TEXTAREA>

<SCRIPT LANGUAGE="VBScript">
Dim S, M

S = Second(Now) 'established on document loading
M = Minute(Now)
```

```
Sub Btn_OnClick
RESULT.VALUE="" 'Clear out display
cr = chr(13) + chr(10)

SN = Second(Now)
MN = Minute(Now)

TS = SN - S
TM = MN - M

If TS < 0 then
 TM = TM - 1 ' subtract to adjust for fewer seconds than 60
 TS = 60 + TS
End If

RESULT.VALUE=RESULT.VALUE & "Seconds Elapsed: " & cstr(TS) →
& cr & cr
RESULT.VALUE=RESULT.VALUE & "Minutes Elapsed: " & cstr(TM) →
& cr

End Sub

</SCRIPT>
</BODY>
</HTML>
```

We put a button on the document, so the user can click it and get a report of the elapsed time. The TextArea Control will show the results. The Dim S, M is necessary to establish a pair of Variables to hold the minute and second when the document is first loaded into the browser (see "ReDim" or "Dim").

When the user clicks on the button, we put a blank text value into the TextArea, to clear it out. We define a line-down value (cr), so the results will appear on separate lines in the TextArea. Then we find out, again, the current second and minute, but this time it's when the user clicks. To get the elapsed minutes and seconds, we subtract the original S and M from the current Variables.

If elapsed seconds is less than zero, this means that we have to make an adjustment. It might be, for example, that the original minutes/seconds were 3 minutes 56 seconds when the document was loaded. Then, when the user clicked on the button, we got 4 minutes 10 seconds. When subtracting the original from the current we get 1 minute -46 seconds. In this situation, we must subtract the total minutes by one, then add 60 seconds to the (less than zero) elapsed seconds, making things right. Finally, the results are displayed in the TextArea.

See also Day, Hour, Minute, Month, Now, Weekday, Year

Select

HTML

Description Displays a ListBox from which the user can make a selection.

Variables **ALIGN:** Used to position text relative to the ListBox. You can specify ALIGN as TOP, MIDDLE, or BOTTOM. ALIGN=LEFT, for example, forces the ListBox to the left margin and causes any text (that follows the ALIGN command) to wrap around to the right of the box.

DISABLED: If you use the DISABLED command, the ListBox cannot be accessed by the user. It's visible but doesn't respond to clicking or keypresses. Ordinarily, a browser will indicate disabled controls by graying them or making them lighter than an active control.

HEIGHT: specifies the height of the ListBox in pixels or in em spaces. It is pixels by default, unless you change it with the UNITS command (see UNITS in this entry).

MULTIPLE: If you include the MULTIPLE command, the ListBox can display more than a single item at one time. When you leave out the MULTIPLE command, you create a *drop-down list box* which displays only the first item; to see the rest, the user must click on a tab to drop the list down. This type of ListBox is useful if you need to conserve space on a page, but it can be inconvenient for the user who can't see the entire list. Also see SIZE below.

NAME: Identifies the ListBox. Can be used to trigger Subroutines and to refer to the Control elsewhere in the script. NAME is a text Variable that is associated with a particular Control (such as NAME="ListBox4"). It doesn't matter whether or not any capitalization is used; NAME is not case-sensitive. More often, though, the ID parameter is used to provide a unique name for a Control (ID="ListBox4").

SIZE: You can determine how many of the items in your list will be displayed to the user (without the user having to scroll to see the rest of them). Enclose the SIZE specification in quotes. See the example later in this entry.

SELECTED: Allows you to provide the user with a default selection. The selected item will appear different from the rest of the list (usually reversed, with light text on a dark background). You use the SELECTED command with the OPTION command, as illustrated in the example.

UNITS: Allows you to change the default width and height measurement units. If you use UNITS=EM, the default isn't used. Instead, the unit of measurement is the width of the letter m in the current typeface.

WIDTH: Specifies the width of the ListBox in pixels or in em spaces. It is pixels by default, unless you change it with the UNITS command (see above).

Uses The primary alternative to a ListBox is a set of Option Buttons. SELECT displays a list of items which the user can click on.

Example

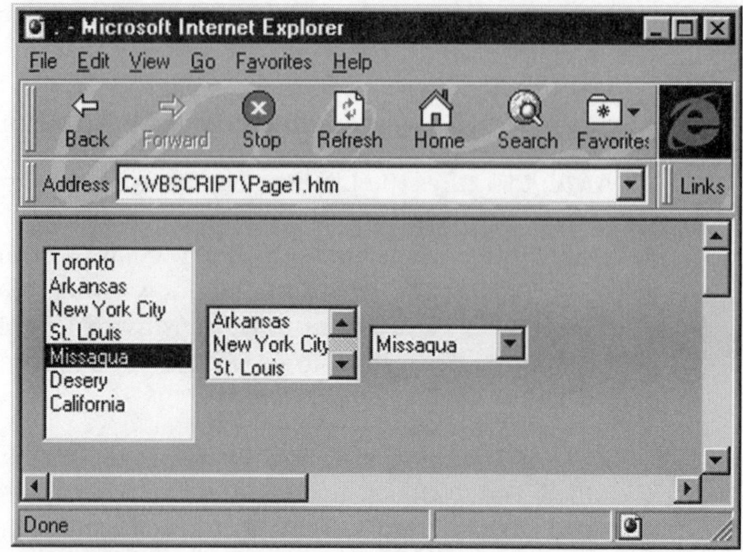

Figure S-3: Three ListBox Styles: nonscrolled, scrolled, and drop-down.

```
<HTML>

<SELECT NAME="Destinations" MULTIPLE SIZE="9" >
<OPTION VALUE="1">Toronto
<OPTION VALUE="2">Arkansas
<OPTION VALUE="3" >New York City
<OPTION VALUE="4">St. Louis
<OPTION VALUE="5" SELECTED>Missaqua
<OPTION VALUE="6">Desery
<OPTION VALUE="7">California
</SELECT>

<SELECT NAME="Destinations" MULTIPLE SIZE="4">
<OPTION VALUE="1">Toronto
<OPTION VALUE="2">Arkansas
<OPTION VALUE="3" >New York City
<OPTION VALUE="4">St. Louis
<OPTION VALUE="5" SELECTED>Missaqua
<OPTION VALUE="6">Desery
<OPTION VALUE="7">California
</SELECT>
```

S

```
<SELECT NAME="Destinations">
<OPTION VALUE="1">Toronto
<OPTION VALUE="2">Arkansas
<OPTION VALUE="3" >New York City
<OPTION VALUE="4">St. Louis
<OPTION VALUE="5" SELECTED>Missaqua
<OPTION VALUE="6">Desery
<OPTION VALUE="7">California
</SELECT>

</HTML>
```

See also FORM, INPUT

Select Case

VBSCRIPT STATEMENT

Description Select Case is similar to the If...Then structure, but Select Case is generally used for multiple-choice situations. If...Then is primarily designed for True-False situations (but If...Then can be used for multiple choices as well).

Often, Select Case and If...Then structures can be used interchangeably, but Select Case is somewhat easier to read and understand for those times when there are more than one or two possible "cases."

The general distinction between If...Then and Select Case goes something like this:

```
If it's raining, Then take your umbrella.

Select Case Weather
   Case Raining
      Take your umbrella.
   Case Sunny
      Wear light clothing.
   Case Snowing
      Wear snowshoes.
   Case Hot
      Wear cotton.
End Select
```

S

(You can set up a similar structure for If...Then using repeated ElseIf commands. See "If...Then.")

Select Case works from a list of possible "answers." Your script can respond to each of these answers differently.

If you use Select Case, you can make your scripts look something like ordinary English. For that reason, Select Case is often better in multiple-choice situations than the If...Then structure. There is one drawback, though, to Select Case. In VBScript, you can't test logical, relational, or range expressions. In other languages, such as Visual Basic, you *can* test a range like this:

```
Case 5 To 5000
```

OR, you can test using relational operators. In this example, you are testing to see if the item is greater than 1600:

```
Case Is > 1600
```

These complex kinds of tests *cannot be performed in VBScript* using Select...Case. If you need to do this kind of testing in VBScript, you'll have to use If...Then.

Used with Situations where the If...Then structure is too restrictive or becomes obscure because there are so many possible choices.

Select Case is useful if you have several possible conditions you must respond to, so you want to list a variety of causes along with a variety of responses.

Variables Note that unlike the If...Then structure, Select...Case (in VBScript) can only test for *literals* like 5 or "hornet." No Case can be a Variable (like MyVar) or an expression (like Z > N). You *can* use Variables and expressions with If...Then, but not with Select...Case.

To test against numeric literals:

```
Select Case X

Case 4
     (put one or more commands here)
Case 8
     (put one or more commands here)
End Select
```

OR (to test against text ("string") literals):

```
Select Case X
Case "blue"
     (put one or more commands here)
Case "green"
     (put one or more commands here)
Case "money"
     (put one or more commands here)
End Select
```

Uses Use Select Case when you think that multiple If...Then structures (or If...Then with interior If...Else commands) are more confusing than Select Case.

Select Case tests something against a whole list of possible matches. Each element in the list is followed by one or more commands that are carried out in the event of a match. In this way, a script can respond in multiple ways to the current state of a numeric or string Variable, or an *expression.* (See "Variables" for a definition of *expression.*)

The Select Case structure acts the same as a series of If...Then structures, but Select Case simplifies the process:

```
If X = 4 Then MsgBox "Four"
If X = 5 Then MsgBox "Five"
If X = 6 Then MsgBox "Six"
```

OR (the same script expressed differently by using the ElseIf command):

```
Sub CommandButton1_Click ()
x = InputBox("number please?")
If x = 4 Then
  MsgBox "Four"
ElseIf x = 5 Then
  MsgBox "Five"
ElseIf x = 6 Then
  MsgBox "Six"
End If
End Sub
```

Both of the preceding examples are the same as the following:

```
Select Case X
  Case 4
    MsgBox "Four"
  Case 5
    MsgBox "Five"
  Case 6
    MsgBox "Six"
End Select
```

Cautions What if you want to use one of the comparative (relational) operators (see "Operators") such as greater than (>)? In ordinary Visual Basic, you can do this:

```
Select Case Z
Case Is > 1200
    Msgbox "It's greater than 1200"
Case Is >= 1600
    Msgbox "It's greater than, or equal to, 1600"
Case Is <> 55
    Msgbox "It's certainly not 55"
End Select
```

However, at the time of this writing, the special Case Is command is not working and results in an error message in VBScript.

The match can include several items, separated by commas. The following will display "Odd" for any odd number between 1 and 10:

```
  Case 1,3,5,7,9
    MsgBox "Odd"
```

It's often a good idea to force a text Variable into all-lowercase and then write out all the possible matches in lowercase, too. The LCase Function forces all letters in Name here to be tested as lowercase letters:

```
Select Case LCase(Name)
  Case nancy
  Case donald
  Case roy
```

Case Else: You can use a Case Else command at the end of a Case Structure. Case Else will be triggered if no match is found in the list of cases above it. The following will trigger the Case Else:

```
X = 5
Select Case X
  Case 4
    MsgBox "Match"
  Case 6
    MsgBox "Match"
  Case Else
    MsgBox "No Match"
End Select
```

If you don't use a Case Else and no match is found, the script moves to the line following End Select and resumes carrying out the instructions found there. In other words, none of the commands inside any of the cases will be carried out, and nothing will happen at all in the entire Case Structure.

Case Else is equivalent to the Else command within an If...Then structure:

```
X = 5
If X = 4 OR X = 6 Then
    MsgBox "Match"
  Else
    MsgBox "No Match"
End If
```

Results in

```
No Match
```


You can, if you wish, *nest* Select Case structures, but nesting will get rather confusing quickly. Nesting means putting one thing inside of another, as in the following:

```
Select Case Name1
  Case "A" To "C"
    Select Case Name2
      Case "Rose"
        MsgBox "This could be Audrey Rose..."
    End Select
End Select
```

Example In this example we ask the user to describe in words how big a character font he or she wants to use for a set of Command Buttons. Then the Select...Case structure searches among a variety of possible text answers and translates them into numbers that can be used with the Font object. This is a simple example of artificial intelligence.

Start the Microsoft ActiveX Control Pad and use Edit | Insert ActiveX Control (see the Introduction to this book). Put a CommandButton and a TextBox onto your HTML source code. Then create the following script. When the user types in a font size, then clicks on the button, our Select...Case command searches through a list of words and associated font sizes. If it finds a match, it invokes our ChangeSize subroutine to adjust the caption and text to match the user's preference.

Note that you might consider using the TextBox's KeyDown Event to trigger the Select...Case (if KeyCode = 13 then Select...Case would wait until the user pressed Enter, then start the Select...Case analysis).

```
<HTML>
<HEAD>
<TITLE>Select Case</TITLE>
</HEAD>
<BODY>
 <SCRIPT LANGUAGE="VBScript">
<!--

Sub CommandButton1_Click()

Select Case LCase(TextBox1.Text)
Case "tiny", "really small", "mousetype"
 ChangeSize (7)
Case "small"
 ChangeSize (9)
Case "medium", "average"
 ChangeSize (18)
Case "large", "big"
 ChangeSize (36)
Case "really big", "huge", "immense"
 ChangeSize (76)
```

S

```
Case "beyond belief"
 ChangeSize (126)
Case Else
 MsgBox "We didn't understand your requested fontsize"
End Select

End Sub

Sub ChangeSize (n)
TextBox1.Font.Size = n
CommandButton1.Font.Size = n
End Sub

-->
 </SCRIPT>

<OBJECT ID="CommandButton1" WIDTH=267 HEIGHT=32
 CLASSID="CLSID:D7053240-CE69-11CD-A777-00DD01143C57">
  <PARAM NAME="Caption" VALUE="Click when finished">
  <PARAM NAME="Size" VALUE="7064;846">
  <PARAM NAME="FontCharSet" VALUE="0">
  <PARAM NAME="FontPitchAndFamily" VALUE="2">
  <PARAM NAME="ParagraphAlign" VALUE="3">
  <PARAM NAME="FontWeight" VALUE="0">
</OBJECT>
<BR>
<BR>

 <OBJECT ID="TextBox1" WIDTH=335 HEIGHT=177
 CLASSID="CLSID:8BD21D10-EC42-11CE-9E0D-00AA006002F3">
  <PARAM NAME="VariousPropertyBits" VALUE="2894088219">
  <PARAM NAME="Size" VALUE="8837;4683">
  <PARAM NAME="FontCharSet" VALUE="0">
  <PARAM NAME="FontPitchAndFamily" VALUE="2">
  <PARAM NAME="FontWeight" VALUE="0">
 </OBJECT>

</BODY>
</HTML>
```

See also If...Then

Selected

ACTIVEX

See Properties

SelectionMargin

ACTIVEX

See Properties

SelLength, SelStart, SelText

ACTIVEX

See Properties

Set

VBSCRIPT STATEMENT

S

Description VBScript allows you to assign Variable names to objects. This can come in handy if, for example, your script often refers to an object that has a long, complicated name. You can replace that complex name with a simple Variable name.

Using Set you can assign an object, such as an ActiveX Control, to an *Object Variable Subtype.* Before using Set, you first declare a Variable. We'll call this one *O*:

```
Dim O
```

Then, after the Variable has been declared, you can use the Set command to attach a particular Control to the Object Variable:

```
Set O = TextBox1
```

Note that the Set command alerts VBScript that you're assigning an object to a Variable. The Variable changes, at this point, from a Variant to a Variant of the Object subtype (see "Variants").

Now you can use O to query or change Properties of TextBox1. This will move the TextBox down to 123 pixels from the top of the browser:

```
O.Top = 123
```

And if you have another Variable name Dimmed, you can assign the object of one Variable to the other:

```
<HTML>
<HEAD>
 <SCRIPT LANGUAGE="VBScript">
<!--
Sub window_onLoad()
Dim R
Dim O
Set O = TextBox1
Set R = O
Z = R.Font.Size
Msgbox Z
end sub
-->
 </SCRIPT>

 <OBJECT ID="TextBox1" WIDTH=335 HEIGHT=177
 CLASSID="CLSID:8BD21D10-EC42-11CE-9E0D-00AA006002F3">
  <PARAM NAME="VariousPropertyBits" VALUE="2894088219">
  <PARAM NAME="Size" VALUE="8837;4683">
  <PARAM NAME="FontCharSet" VALUE="0">
  <PARAM NAME="FontPitchAndFamily" VALUE="2">
  <PARAM NAME="FontWeight" VALUE="0">
 </OBJECT>
</BODY>
</HTML>
```

Controls already have their ID Property, so what's the point of giving them a Variable name? You can create names that are easier to use. For example, TextBox1 has a Font object. Therefore, you can assign the entire phrase: TextBox1.Font to a simpler Variable name, like *F*.

Note that when you use Set to declare a Variable of the "Object" type, you are creating an *Object Variable*. You can use an Object Variable much the way you would use a normal Variable, but Object Variables "point to" or "refer to" a single entity (their object, such as CommandButton1). Object Variables do not *contain* data the way a normal text or numeric Variable does. (For more on this, see "Objects.")

However, merely declaring an Object Variable does not create a new "instance" of an object. It's possible that in the future, Set will also be used with the New command to create new "instances" of objects (a collection, for example, of dynamically created Command Buttons). However, at this time, the New command is not implemented in VBScript. For a complete discussion of how objects are used in VBScript (and several examples), see "Objects."

Variables First, you must declare an Object Variable with the Dim command. If you use the Dim command outside of a procedure (outside of a Sub...End Sub or Function...End Function), the Variable will be available to all procedures within your script (see "Dim").

When you Dim a Variable name, you are merely announcing a new Variant Variable's existence. Then, when you use the Set command *within a procedure*, the Variant becomes, at that point, an Object Variable subtype (see "Variants").

Note that ActiveX Controls aren't the only objects in Internet programming. HTML Controls created with the INPUT command are also objects and therefore can be referenced by Object Variables:

```
<HTML>
<TITLE>Set</TITLE>
<FORM NAME="ThisForm">
<INPUT TYPE="TEXT" NAME="TextHTMLType" SIZE="40">
</FORM>

<SCRIPT language="VBScript">

Dim O
```

```
Sub Window_OnLoad
Set O=ThisForm.TextHTMLType
O.Value="We're using O now, not ThisForm.TextHTMLType"
End Sub

</SCRIPT>
```

Uses Object Variables are used to assign references to particular objects. In this way, Set is similar to the Let command (assignment of value to a Variable: A = 12).

Set can also be used to copy references from one Object Variable to another. In this way, Set works similarly to the equals (=) symbol used with regular text or numeric Variables (A = B).

Cautions If you have an Object Variable that your script no longer needs, you can use the Nothing command to release the computer's resources that were used by the Variable:

```
Set MyObjVar = Nothing
```

You can use the IsObject command to see if a particular Variable refers to an object:

```
If IsObject(ObjVar) Then
```

To find out if two Object Variables are referencing the same object, use the Is command (not the equals sign):

```
<HTML>
<TITLE>Set</TITLE>
<FORM NAME="ThisForm">
<INPUT TYPE="TEXT" NAME="TextHTMLType" SIZE="40">
</FORM>

<SCRIPT language="VBScript">

Dim O
Dim R

Sub Window_OnLoad
```

```
Set O=ThisForm.TextHTMLType
Set R = O
If R Is O Then MsgBox "They're pointing to the same object"

End Sub
</SCRIPT>

</HTML>
```

OR, similarly to see if an Object Variable is pointing to a particular object:

```
If R Is ThisForm.TextHTMLType Then MsgBox "R is this object."
```

Example One interesting use of Object Variables is to provide parameters to procedures. Say you had several TextBoxes on a document and the user has to fill them in with personal information. You want to see if the word *Ohio* appears in any of the boxes.

Start the Microsoft ActiveX Control Pad running (see the Introduction). Click on Edit | Insert HTML Layout and give the .ALX file a new name. Click on the small icon next to the Layout Control Object definition to open the Control. Add three TextBoxes, three Labels, and one Command Button, as shown in Figure S-4.

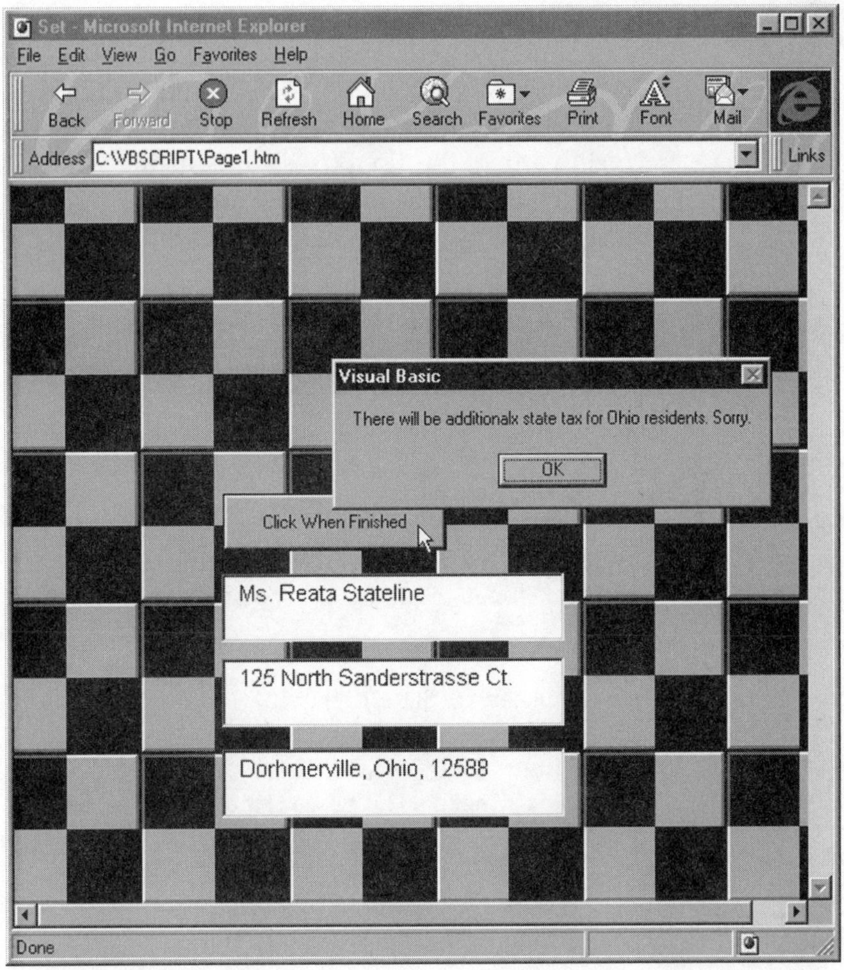

Figure S-4: We'll pass the TextBoxes as objects to a procedure to check them for the word Ohio.

Then add the following script. First we declare the Variable O. When the user clicks on the CommandButton, we send each of the TextBoxes, as objects, to be tested for the word *Ohio*. In the CheckOhio Subroutine, we used the InStr command to see if the text in any of the TextBoxes contains the word Ohio. If so, we display a message about state tax.

```
<SCRIPT LANGUAGE="VBScript">

Dim O

Sub CommandButton1_Click ()
Set O = TextBox1
CheckOhio O
Set O = TextBox2
CheckOhio O
Set O = TextBox3
CheckOhio O
End Sub

<Computer  . Sub CheckOhio (L)

If Instr (1,L.Text,"Ohio",1) then
MsgBox "There will be additional state tax for Ohio →
residents. Sorry."
end If

End Sub

</SCRIPT>
```

However, you can even pass objects directly, without first creating an Object Variable, if you wish:

```
<SCRIPT LANGUAGE="VBScript">

Sub CommandButton1_Click ()
CheckOhio TextBox1
CheckOhio TextBox2
CheckOhio TextBox3
End Sub
```

S

```
Sub CheckOhio (O)

If Instr (1,O.Text,"Ohio",1) then
MsgBox "There will be additional state tax for Ohio →
residents. Sorry."
end If

End Sub

</SCRIPT>
```

See also Dim, ReDim, Objects

SetFocus

ACTIVEX

See Methods

Sgn

VBSCRIPT FUNCTION

Description The Sgn Function tells you whether a numeric Variable is positive, negative, or zero.

Used with Numeric Variables (as opposed to text "string" Variable subtypes). See "Variables."

Variables Sgn returns 1 if the number is positive, 0 if the number is zero, and –1 if the number is negative.

```
Z = 55
X = Sgn(Z)
MsgBox X
```

Results in

```
1
```

S

Uses Sgn is a semi-useful shortcut. You can find the sign of a number this way as well:

```
X = -2

If X < 0 then MsgBox "It's negative"
```

To learn the sign status of a number, you can use Sgn to do it in an abbreviated, slightly more efficient way, but some would say that is hardly a reason to add a word to the Basic language:

```
If Sgn(X) = 0 Then Print "It's Zero"
```

You could just as easily enter the following:

```
If X = 0
```

Example

```
Z = 45
MsgBox Sgn(Z)
```

Results in

```
1
```

See also Abs

ShowDropButtonWhen

ACTIVEX

See Properties

Sin

VBSCRIPT FUNCTION

Description Sin gives you the sine of an angle expressed in radians.

You can use a number, a numeric Variable, a numeric Constant, or a numeric "expression."

You can get the sine of any subtype of Variable—integer, floating-point, and so on. (See "Variables" for more on Variable types and expressions.)

Variables

```
MsgBox Sin(x)
```

OR

```
F = Sin(.3)
```

Uses Trigonometry

Cautions If the Variable or Constant you use with Sin is an integer or single-precision number, the result will be single-precision. All other data types are calculated in double-precision. (See "Variables.")

Example

```
z = Sin(.3)
MsgBox z
```

See also Atn, Cos, Tan

Size

ACTIVEX

See Properties

SIZE

HTML

Description The SIZE attribute is used with the HTML TEXT Object. SIZE defines how many characters wide the TextBox will be:

```
<INPUT TYPE="TEXT" SIZE="45">
```

This example specifies that the TextBox will be 45 characters wide. Just how wide this is depends on the font size used within the TextBox.

See INPUT

SMALL

HTML

Description Displays text in a smaller typeface than the surrounding text.

Used with ***Can be enclosed by***

<A>, <ABBREV>, <ACRONYM>, <ADDRESS>, <AU>, <B>, <BANNER>, <BIG>, <BODY>, <BODYTEXT>, <CAPTION>, <CITE>, <CODE>, <CREDIT>, <DD>, <DEL>, <DFN>, <DIV>, <DT>, <EM>, <FIGTEXT>, <FN>, <FORM>, <H>, <I>, <INS>,<KBD>, <LANG>, <LH>, <LI>, <NOTE>, <P>, <PERSON>, <Q>, <S>, <SAMP>, <SMALL>, <STRONG>, <SUB>, <SUP>, <TD>, <TH>,<TT>, <U>, <VAR>

Can enclose

<A>, <ABBREV>, <ACRONYM>, <AU>, <B>, <BIG>, <BR>, <CITE>, <CODE>, <DEL>, <DFN>, <EM>, <I>, <IMG>, <INS>, <KBD>, <LANG>, <MATH>, <PERSON>, <Q>, <S>, <SAMP>, <SMALL>, <STRONG>, <SUB>, <SUP>, <TAB>, <TT>, <U>, <VAR>

Uses De-emphasize some text, or conserve space.

Cautions The SMALL command, like other relativistic text formatting commands such as STRONG, are interpreted differently by different browsers. Therefore, you can't really know how your formatting will look to any given user. If you want greater control over the formatting, use this:

```
<FONT SIZE=4>
```

where the specification can range from 1 to 7. See FONT.

S

Example

```
<HTML>
<BODY BGCOLOR=WHITE>
<FONT SIZE=+2>
This isn't small
<SMALL>This is</SMALL>
</HTML>
```

See also Font

SmallChange

ACTIVEX

See Properties

Source

VBSCRIPT PROPERTY

See Err

Source Code

Description This is the term given to computer programming. In some ways, it's an unhappy term because *code* suggests that something has been made obscure. Fortunately, the Basic language and its off-spring like VBScript are, to the extent possible, English-like in their diction and syntax.

Source code means those lines of HTML and VBScript commands that you write and that instruct the browser how to behave when your document (the .HTM file and any associated files) is loaded into the browser.

Interestingly, until Internet programming, source code was hidden from the user. Programmers could read their lines of source code, but the final application was compiled into a format (an .EXE file) unreadable to everyone except the computer itself. As a programmer, you might notice some cool effect or clever trick, but you couldn't look at the source code to see how that effect was accomplished.

Now, though, if you like something you see in an Internet document, you can quickly see the source code that produced it. In Internet Explorer, just click on the View | Source menu option. Windows's Notepad will open up, filled with all the programming that went into the creation of the page you're viewing.

Tip

If you are looking at a document in Internet Explorer that has frames—individually scrollable zones that subdivide the page—clicking on the View | Source option will only reveal the programming for the outermost, host frame. You can still see the source code for any other frame in the document, though. Just right-click on the frame you're interested in, then from the menu that pops out, choose View Source. You'll then see the source code for that frame.

What if you want to calculate something for the user in your Web page, but you don't want anyone seeing your top-secret formula? What, in other words, if you want to hide your source code from prying eyes? VBScript and HTML source code are there, exposed to the entire world as soon as you put your document up onto the Internet.

You could write an ActiveX Control. They're secure—people can't see what's going on inside a Control. But ActiveX Controls are difficult to create (you have to use the C language, or write it in Java).

Probably the best solution at this time, if you're trying to hide your source code, is to move sensitive data onto an HTML Layout Control (see the Introduction to this book). This way, when the user tries to view your source code from his browser, he'll see the Object definition of the Layout Control, but not the source code used with the Layout Control itself. Layout Control source code, including any VBScript code, is kept in an .ALX file, not loaded into the browser as is an .HTM file.

Special Characters

HTML

Description How do you enter special text characters, symbols like the copyright symbol or that n-tilde used in Spanish words like *mañana*? There are two ways. You can use a special code name, such as *°*, which displays a small o for degrees of temperature. Or you can use the numeric code for the same symbol, °.

However, whereas most browsers will have no trouble recognizing some of the common word codes (such as © for the copyright symbol), they can fail to recognize other word codes, like °. Therefore, you're safer if you use the numeric codes. Here, for example, is how Internet Explorer 3.0 translates the following, and stumbles on °:

This message is copyrighted ©
And so is this message ©
Today the high temperature will be 75°
Yesterday the high temperature was 68°

```
<HTML>
<BR>
This message is copyrighted&copy
<BR>
And so is this message&#169
<BR>
Today the high temperature will be 75&deg
<BR>
Yesterday the high temperature was 68&#176
</HTML>
```

Used with Can be placed anywhere within text.

Variables

Description	Character	Numeric Code	Code Word
quotation mark	"	"	"
ampersand	&	&	&
less-than sign	<	<	<
greater-than sign	>	>	>
non-breaking space			
inverted exclamation	¡	¡	¡
cent sign	¢	¢	¢
pound sterling	£	£	£
general currency sign	¤	¤	¤
yen sign	¥	¥	¥

➡

S

Description	Character	Numeric Code	Code Word
broken vertical bar	¦	¦	¦
section sign	§	§	§
umlaut (dieresis)	¨	¨	¨
copyright	©	©	©
feminine ordinal	ª	ª	ª
left angle quote, guillemotleft	«	«	«
not sign	¬	¬	¬
soft hyphen	–		
registered trademark	®	®	®
macron accent	¯	¯	¯
degree sign	°	°	°
plus or minus	±	±	±
superscript two	²	²	²
superscript three	³	³	³
acute accent	´	´	´
micro sign	µ	µ	µ
paragraph sign	¶	¶	¶
middle dot	·	·	·
cedilla	¸	¸	¸
superscript one	¹	¹	¹
masculine ordinal	º	º	º
right angle quote, guillemotright	»	»	»
fraction one-fourth	¼	¼	¼
fraction one-half	½	½	½
fraction three-fourths	¾	¾	¾
inverted question mark	¿	¿	¿
capital A, grave accent	À	À	À
capital A, acute accent	Á	Á	Á
capital A, circumflex accent	Â	Â	Â

Description	Character	Numeric Code	Code Word
capital A, tilde	Ã	Ã	Ã
capital A, dieresis or umlaut mark	Ä	Ä	Ä
capital A, ring	Å	Å	Å
capital AE diphthong (ligature)	Æ	Æ	Æ
capital C, cedilla	Ç	Ç	Ç
capital E, grave accent	È	È	È
capital E, acute accent	É	É	É
capital E, circumflex accent	Ê	Ê	Ê
capital E, dieresis or umlaut mark	Ë	Ë	Ë
capital I, grave accent	Ì	Ì	Ì
capital I, acute accent	Í	Í	Í
capital I, circumflex accent	Î	Î	Î
capital I, dieresis or umlaut mark	Ï	Ï	Ï
capital Eth, Icelandic	Đ	Ð	Ð
capital N, tilde	Ñ	Ñ	Ñ
capital O, grave accent	Ò	Ò	Ò
capital O, acute accent	Ó	Ó	Ó
capital O, circumflex accent	Ô	Ô	Ô
capital O, tilde	Õ	Õ	Õ
capital O, dieresis or umlaut mark	Ö	Ö	Ö
multiply sign	x	×	×
capital O, slash	Ø	Ø	Ø
capital U, grave accent	Ù	Ù	Ù
capital U, acute accent	Ú	Ú	Ú
capital U, circumflex accent	Û	Û	Û
capital U, dieresis or umlaut mark	Ü	Ü	Ü
capital Y, acute accent	Y	Ý	Ý
capital THORN, Icelandic	Þ	Þ	Þ
small sharp s, German (sz ligature)	ß	ß	ß

Description	Character	Numeric Code	Code Word
small a, grave accent	à	à	à
small a, acute accent	á	á	á
small a, circumflex accent	â	â	â
small a, tilde	ã	ã	ã
small a, dieresis or umlaut mark	ä	ä	ä
small a, ring	å	å	å
small ae diphthong (ligature)	æ	æ	æ
small c, cedilla	ç	ç	ç
small e, grave accent	è	è	è
small e, acute accent	é	é	é
small e, circumflex accent	ê	ê	ê
small e, dieresis or umlaut mark	ë	ë	ë
small i, grave accent	ì	ì	ì
small i, acute accent	í	í	í
small i, circumflex accent	î	î	î
small i, dieresis or umlaut mark	ï	ï	ï
small eth, Icelandic	ð	ð	ð
small n, tilde	ñ	ñ	ñ
small o, grave accent	ò	ò	ò
small o, acute accent	ó	ó	ó
small o, circumflex accent	ô	ô	ô
small o, tilde	õ	õ	õ
small o, dieresis or umlaut mark	ö	ö	ö
division sign	÷	÷	÷
small o, slash	ø	ø	ø
small u, grave accent	ù	ù	ù
small u, acute accent	ú	ú	ú
small u, circumflex accent	û	û	û
small u, dieresis or umlaut mark	ü	ü	ü

Description	Character	Numeric Code	Code Word
small y, acute accent	ý	ý	ý
small thorn, Icelandic	þ	þ	þ
small y, dieresis or umlaut mark	ÿ	ÿ	ÿ

Table S-1: The text and numeric codes you can use to insert symbols or special characters.

Cautions

- Use the numeric codes rather than the text codes. More browsers will recognize the codes.
- Precede all numeric codes with the &# symbols. Precede text codes with &.

Example

```
In the ongoing effort to simplify English, some of its beauty
is being destroyed. A perfect example is the replacement of
the word formulas for the original formul&#230.
```

Results in

In the ongoing effort to simplify English, some of its beauty is being destroyed. A perfect example is the replacement of the word *formulas* for the original *formulæ*.

SpecialEffect

ACTIVEX

See Properties

SpinButton

ACTIVEX CONTROL

Description A SpinButton is similar to a Slider (an ActiveX Control not yet available) and is also similar to a ScrollBar. However, the primary use of a SpinButton is to adjust numbers or dates or some other serial data. For example, you could allow users to specify how many days they're willing to wait for a backordered item from your catalog (see the example).

To make your SpinButton horizontal, just drag one of the sides until the SpinButton is wider than it is tall. It will change into a horizontal version. And vice versa.

The Value Property is the default Property for a SpinButton.

Variables For a discussion of the Delay, Max, Min, Orientation, and SmallChange Properties, see the entry for "ScrollBar."

It's within the SpinUp and SpinDown Events that you'll likely want to write the script that adjusts something in response to user clicks (see the example).

These SpinUp and SpinDown Events are available only for the SpinButton Control. They are functionally identical to the Scroll Event for the ScrollBar Control—they are triggered continuously if the user holds down the left mouse button while positioned on one of the SpinButton arrows. Therefore, the SpinDown and SpinUp Events are useful when you want to display some continuously changing data or quality in response to the user pressing the SpinButton.

The SpinButton has a Change Event that provides the same functionality as the SpinDown and SpinUp Events, but with an important difference. The Change Event is only triggered when the user releases the mouse button, so you can react only once per mouse click. However, the SpinDown and SpinUp Events are triggered *continuously* while the user depresses the mouse button (similar to the MouseMove Event in this respect).

Properties
BackColor, CodeBase, Delay, Enabled, ForeColor, Height, ID, Left, Max, Min, MouseIcon, MousePointer, Orientation, SmallChange, TabIndex, TabStop, Top, Value (the default Property), Visible, Width

Events
AfterUpdate, BeforeDragOver, BeforeDropOrPaste, BeforeUpdate, Change, Enter, Error, Exit, KeyDown, KeyPress, KeyUp, SpinDown, SpinUp

Methods
Move, SetFocus, ZOrder

For details about these Properties, Events, and Methods, see the entries for "Properties," "Events," and "Methods."

Uses Change items in a series, such as the time or a date. A SpinButton is similar to the sets of buttons used to adjust the time on a digital clock.

Example We'll allow users to specify, by clicking a SpinButton, how many days they're willing to wait for an item that's back-ordered from our catalog.

We'll put a SpinButton and a Label on an HTML Layout Control. Start the Microsoft ActiveX Control Pad (see the Introduction) and click on Edit | Insert HTML Layout. Give the layout a new name and then click on the icon next to the <OBJECT> definition. Now from the toolbox, put a SpinButton and a Label on the layout. Right-click on the SpinButton and choose Properties. Set its Min Property to 3 and its Max to 90. That will be the range of days the user can specify.

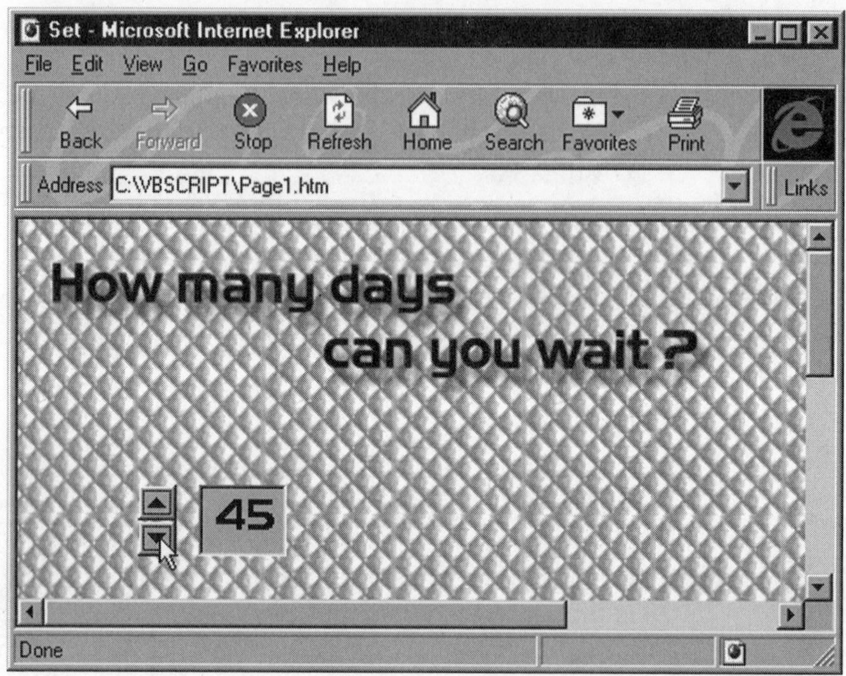

Figure S-5: As the user clicks (or holds down) the mouse button, the numbers scroll up or down.

The programming that makes this work is, of course, typed into a VBScript. So, right-click on the HTML Layout Control and choose "View Source Code." Type in the following:

```
<SCRIPT LANGUAGE="VBScript">
<!--

Sub SpinButton1_SpinDown()
Label1 = " " & SpinButton1
end sub

Sub SpinButton1_SpinUp()
Label1 = " " & SpinButton1
end sub

-->
</SCRIPT>
```

Note that we didn't specify any Properties because the Caption Property of the Label Control and the Value Property of the SpinButton Control are their defaults. However, we could have written it this way and gotten the same effect:

```
Label1.Caption = " " & SpinButton1.Value
```

Also note that we added a blank space to the displayed number, just so it would look better and wouldn't appear butted up against the left side of the Label.

See also ScrollBar

SpinDown & SpinUp

ACTIVEX

See Events

Sqr

VBSCRIPT FUNCTION

Description Sqr provides the square root of a positive number. (The number cannot be negative.)

Used with Any positive *numeric expression* (see "Variables" for a definition of "expression").

Variables To use a literal number:

```
X = Sqr(144)
```

OR (to use a Variable):

```
Z = 144
X = Sqr(Z)
```

Uses Mathematical calculations.

S

Example

```
MsgBox Sqr(144)
```

The opposite of the square root is raising a number to the power of two:

```
MsgBox 12 ^ 2
```

See also Abs, Sgn (the other two arithmetic Functions in Basic)

Str

VBSCRIPT FUNCTION

Description The Str and Val commands are supposed to change numbers into text (Str) and text into a real, computable number, a number that the computer can use in arithmetic (Val). However, at the time of this writing, neither Val nor its sister command, Str, are operative. These two commands are listed in the VBScript specifications, but it's possible that they will both be dropped from the language. With the new Variant Variable type, you can let VBScript make translations back and forth between string and numeric Variable types (see "Variant"). You can also force conversions with the cStr and cDbl commands (see "cBool"). The example below demonstrates the cStr command.

Traditionally, Str provides you with a text version of a number. Another way of putting this is that Str is supposed to transform a numeric Variable subtype into a text subtype, temporarily. (Temporarily because the actual Variable hasn't changed its subtype. You merely use Str to display the Variable's value. If you want to change the Variable's actual subtype, use the cStr command.)

Str translates a pure number into a character (or series of characters); these characters are *digits* that can be displayed but cannot be manipulated mathematically. This next example will not work:

```
<HTML>
<SCRIPT LANGUAGE="VBScript">
A = "This is text"
A = A + 5
msgbox A
</SCRIPT>
</HTML>
```

The actual *number* 5 is not a text character to VBScript. The digit "5" is a character. Even the Variant Variable type (see "Variant")—ordinarily so versatile and accommodating—cannot handle the problem when you try to "add" the *number* 5 to the text characters *This is text.*

There are two fundamental kinds of Variable subtypes:

- Text Variables (often called "string" Variables) can be printed to a printer and displayed on screen. They are made up of the *symbols* that we call the English, or some other, language. You cannot divide or use text Variables to calculate the amount of linoleum that you would need to redo your kitchen floor. Text is for *communication,* not calculation.

- Numeric Variables are used to calculate things; they are really numbers, rather than symbols. The digits 12 printed on top of a carton of eggs is *text* and the actual number of eggs in that carton is *numeric,* a real number.

Str mediates between the two kinds of numbers. It translates a real number into a text digit that can be displayed. Can you translate a text Variable like "5" back into a real number that you could multiply? Yes, you use the Val Function for that. It can turn "1992" into 1992 for you.

(Val cannot translate *words* like "Nineteen hundred and ninety-three." You have to do a lot of programming to change words into real numbers. But Val can translate digits—characters that stand for numbers.)

VBScript is wonderfully inventive: it features a special Variable type called *Variant,* which often allows you to forget about Variable "types." A Variant *embraces* text and numeric as well as date/time and all other Variable types into a single "Variant" type. VBScript then handles things for you; VBScript decides how to manipulate the Variable based on the context. Are you multiplying? VBScript will treat the Variant as a numeric Variable. Are you putting it into a caption? VBScript changes it to text. The Variant is VBScript's *default* Variable type. For more on this, see "Variant."

Used with TextBoxes, MsgBoxes, and other entities that display information. Str changes real numbers into displayable text. In theory, the Variant Variable should morph into a text Variable subtype all by itself, without your having to coerce it. However, at the time of this writing, you have to use cStr to change a numeric Variable into a text Variable.

Variables To turn a real number into a text Variable subtype:

```
N = Str(15)
```

OR (to use Str within an "expression"):

```
Msgbox Str(x)
```

(This currently doesn't work in VBScript.)

OR (to translate a numeric Variable into text):

```
X = 12
A = Str(X)
```

Str can translate any *numeric expression* into text (see "Variables" for a definition of *expression*).

Uses Display numbers

Cautions When you are using Str, you usually intend to display the results. VBScript adds a space character to the left of the text it creates out of a number "to leave room for a minus sign." (See the example and the "LTrim" entry.)

If you do not want this extra space, use Str in combination with LTrim. LTrim removes any "leading spaces" from text:

```
N = 122
MsgBox Str(N)
MsgBox LTrim(Str(N))
```

Results in

```
 122
122
```

Example This example prints a mixed batch of positive and negative numbers. In the two lists of numbers, some will have a minus sign. Because VBScript adds a space character to the left of positive numbers, the lists will line up neatly in a vertical column:

```
<HTML>
<HEAD>
<TITLE>ForNext</TITLE>
</HEAD>
<BODY>
<TEXTAREA NAME=RESULT ROWS=12 COLS = 45></TEXTAREA>

<SCRIPT LANGUAGE="VBSCRIPT">
cr = chr(13) + chr(10)

For i = 1 To 20
  x = Int(10 * Rnd + 1)
y = i - x
z = x - i
RESULT.VALUE = RESULT.VALUE + CR + cstr(y) + "   " + cstr(z)
Next
</SCRIPT>

</BODY>
</HTML>
```

We are printing two columns of 20 numbers each. The Rnd Function provides us with a random number between 1 and 10. We then create one list by subtracting the loop counter Variable *i* from the random number, and the other list by reversing the subtraction. All the numbers, though, line up in two clean columns.

See also LTrim, Val, Variant

S

StrComp

VBSCRIPT FUNCTION

Description StrComp is a slight variation on the normal way of comparing text ("string") Variables. Ordinarily, you would use the < operator for less than (meaning alphabetically lower: *cat* is less than *dog*), > for greater than, and = for equal.

StrComp does the same thing but produces a *Variant* Variable type (see "Variables"), which tells you how the text Variables compare. Aside from this, the only virtue of StrComp is that it includes an option that eliminates the need to use the LCase or UCase commands to force VBScript to ignore capitalization (case-sensitivity) during a text comparison.

Used with Text ("string") Variables

Variables To find out how a compares to b:

```
X = StrComp(a,b)
```

If X is:

–1	then a is less than b
0	then a equals b
1	then a is greater than b
NULL	then one of the two pieces of text is a Null (the variable has never been used in this program—you probably misspelled the variable name)

OR (to specify that the comparison should *not* be case-sensitive, should not pay attention to how or if the words are capitalized):

```
X = StrComp(a,b,1)
```

OR (to specify that the comparison *should* be case-sensitive):

```
X = StrComp(a,b,0)
```

If you leave out the "case-sensitivity" Variable (the 1 or 0 in the examples above), then StrComp defaults to case-sensitive.

S

Uses StrComp, because of its optional control over case-sensitivity, allows you to compare items of text without resorting to the UCase or LCase command. String comparisons are done when alphabetizing lists, testing for a match to passwords, and so forth. Although VBScript defaults to case-sensitive comparisons, you most often want them insensitive.

Example

```
<HTML>
<HEAD>
<TITLE>ForNext</TITLE>
</HEAD>
<BODY>
<TEXTAREA NAME=RESULT ROWS=12 COLS = 45></TEXTAREA>

<SCRIPT LANGUAGE="VBSCRIPT">
cr = chr(13) + chr(10)

a = "Terry"
b = "Dean"
x = StrComp(a, b)

Select Case x
 Case -1
 Result.Value = a + " is less than " + b
 Case 0
 Result.Value = a + " is equal to " + b
 Case 1
 Result.Value = a + " is greater than " + b
End Select

</SCRIPT>

</BODY>
</HTML>
```

See also InStr, Variables, LCase

S

StrikeThrough

ACTIVEX

See Properties

String

VBSCRIPT FUNCTION

Description String provides you with a piece of text that is filled with a particular character. You specify the character and how many of them you want:

```
<SCRIPT LANGUAGE="VBSCRIPT">
N = String(20, "*")
MsgBox N
</SCRIPT>
```

Results in

```
********************
```

Used with Text Variables and text expressions (see "Variables" for a definition of *expression*).

Variables First, you tell String how many characters you want and then which character. You can use a *text literal,* an actual character enclosed within quotation marks:

```
A = String(15, "-")
MsgBox A
```

Results in

```
---------------
```

OR (you can use a text Variable):

```
A = "#"
MsgBox String(25, A)
```

Results in

```
#########################
```

OR (you can provide the ANSI code for the desired character—see "Chr" about this code—instead of a text Variable or text literal):

```
x = String(30, 47)
msgbox x
```

Results in

(The number 47 is the ANSI character code for the / (slash) character.)

Uses

- Create simple design elements when displaying text by printing a line of periods, hyphens, underline characters, etc.
- "Pad" text ("string") Variables so they are all the same length for use with user-defined Variables (see "Type"). When you need a "fixed-length" text Variable, create one by using A = String(20," "), which causes A to have 20 space characters (instead of 20, you can specify whatever fixed length you're after).

Cautions If you provide a text Variable that has more than one character, String will use the first character:

```
A = "ABCD"
MsgBox String(9,A)
```

Results in

```
AAAAAAAAA
```

The number of characters that you request can be between 0 and 65,535.

If you provide a character code instead of a literal character, the code number you provide can be any numeric expression but must be between 0 and 255, the limits of the ANSI code. (See "Chr.")

Example

```
Design = String(150, ".")
MsgBox Design
```

Strong

HTML

Description Tells the browser to display text in a more noticeable typestyle than the surrounding text. Browsers usually just change the text to boldface.

Used with ***Can be enclosed by***

<A>, <ABBREV>, <ACRONYM>, <ADDRESS>, <AU>, <B>, <BANNER>, <BIG>, <BODY>, <BODYTEXT>, <CAPTION>, <CITE>, <CODE>, <CREDIT>, <DD>, <DEL>, <DFN>, <DIV>, <DT>, <EM>, <FIGTEXT>, <FN>, <FORM>, <H>, <I>, <INS>,<KBD>, <LANG>, <LH>, <LI>, <NOTE>, <P>, <PERSON>, <PRE>, <Q>, <S>, <SAMP>, <SMALL>, <STRONG>, <SUB>, <SUP>, <TD>,<TH>, <TT>, <U>, <VAR>

Can enclose

<A>, <ABBREV>, <ACRONYM>, <AU>, <B>, <BIG>, <BR>, <CITE>, <CODE>, <DEL>, <DFN>, <EM>, <I>, <IMG>, <INS>, <KBD>, <LANG>, <MATH>, <PERSON>, <Q>, <S>, <SAMP>, <SMALL>, <SUB>, <SUP>, <TAB>, <TT>, <U>, <VAR>

Uses Emphasize a word or series of words. In practice, boldface is generally avoided in favor of the more attractive, less crude look of italics. See I.

Example

```
<HTML>
<BODY BGCOLOR=WHITE>
<FONT SIZE=+2>
This isn't "strong"
<STRONG>This is</STRONG>
</HTML>
```

See also ITAL, BOLD

S

Style

ACTIVEX

See Properties

Style Sheets

INTERNET EXPLORER 3.0

Description Style sheets offer three primary advantages over traditional HTML commands when you're designing Web pages:

- They allow you to specify colors under text, indents, leading, margins, and point sizes—none of which is possible using simple HTML commands.
- Simplify revisions: you can change the format of dozens of headlines in all your Web pages without editing any of those pages. Just make a single change to your style sheet.
- Simplify your pages—eliminate many HTML tags.

When you want to do something elementary like create margins, you don't have to resort to clumsy HTML half-solutions like the BLOCKQUOTE command. Instead, do this:

```
<P STYLE="margin-left: 0.8in; margin-right: 0.8in">
We wanted this line to be indented.
<P>
This line isn't indented
```

You may have noticed that HTML specifications often leave things up to the user's browser. Spyglass, Internet Explorer, and Netscape interpret some HTML commands in three different ways. Throughout this book you'll see HTML formatting commands like H, which is supposed to result in a headline-style typeface and typesize, or LISTING, which is supposed to display a fixed-width typeface.

But what if you want to be more specific about the appearance of your pages? What if you don't want to leave things up to the browser? What if you want to stipulate exactly the look you're after in an exact typeface point size? And what if you want to specify formatting features like leading (spacing between lines of text) that aren't even available in HTML?

Beyond the greater formatting control they provide, style sheets also make it easier to revise your pages. You can put all your highly specific formatting instructions into a single style block. Then, if you want to make a global change to a document (or many documents), you don't have to go through each one finding all the specific codes. Instead, you can just make a simple change to your master style sheet and all the documents using that style will automatically follow suit.

How does it work? On the simplest level, you just redefine the HTML formatting "tags" to specify what you want. Then the browser will follow your instructions rather than using its default format. You can put brief and simple styles directly into your HTML source code, as if they were ordinary HTML tags. Or you can provide a link, a URL address where a large, complete style sheet can be found, so it will be referenced when a document is loaded into a browser. Or you can embed the entire large style sheet into a document.

Who Uses It?

At the current time, only Internet Explorer 3.0 interprets style sheets. However, Netscape and Spyglass have indicated that they, too, will support style sheets in future versions.

How Do You Create a Style Sheet?

Simple Inline Styles

The most elementary style is just embedded within your HTML source code. This way you can just make a simple change to a single line or block of text. If you're only interested in specifying some formatting for one or a few zones within a document, try inline styles. These styles are inserted into ordinary HTML tags, like the <P> command:

```
<P STYLE="line-height: 18pt">

   The most elementary style is just embedded within your HTML
source code. This way you can just make a simple change to a
single line or block of text. If you're only interested in
specifying some formatting for one or a few zones within a
document, try inline styles.

</P>
```

Conveniently, in one location, you can specify a variety of formatting and page-design attributes: alignment, background colors, colors, graphic images, grouped font specifications, indentation, leading (spacing between lines of text), margins, point size, special effects, and style.

The Style="line-height:" command allows you to change the leading, the space between lines of text. You can be highly specific—the pt measurement means *points.* There are 72 points per inch. So what we're saying in the example is: for this paragraph (between the <P> and </P> tags), space the lines 1/4 inch apart instead of the narrower default spacing.

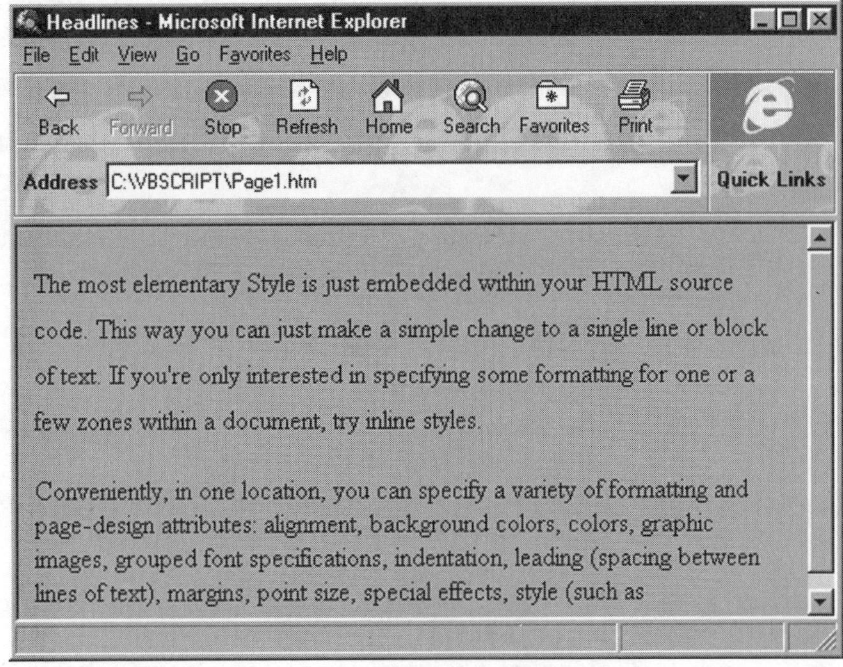

Figure S-6: Spacing between lines is only one formatting element you can adjust with Styles.

Cascading Styles

The new style sheet specifications sometimes refer to them as *cascading style sheets.* In essence this means that you could use multiple styles and style sheets in a given document (in the future, users can even have a style sheet of their preferences). Obviously these various styles might sometimes compete with each other. If there is more than one definition for a particular style, the browser is supposed to resolve the conflict according to a "cascading order." For example, inline styles (like the one illustrated in the previous example) take precedence over linked or embedded style sheets.

The order of precedence for the various kinds of style definitions is:

1. Document author style definitions override reader definitions (when, in the future, readers have the ability to create personalized style sheets).
2. Reader style sheets override browser styles (standard browser default values for the HTML tags like H2, and so on).
3. Inline styles override embedded style sheets.
4. Embedded style sheets override linked style sheets.

Spans

If you want to use an inline style but have it affect a whole region or block of a document, use the SPAN command.

```
<HTML>
<HEAD>
<TITLE>Styles</TITLE>
</HEAD>
<BODY><FONT SIZE=+1 FACE="Arial">

<SPAN STYLE="font-weight: bold; color: blue">
<BIG>Conveniently</BIG>
<I>in one location, you can specify a variety of formatting
and page-design attributes:</I>
alignment, background colors, colors, graphic images, grouped
font specifications, indentation, leading (spacing between
lines of text), margins, point size, special effects, style
(such as italic), typeface, weight (such as boldface).
</SPAN>

<BR><BR>

  Update or revise your documents easily--you need make only a
single change to a style sheet to cause dozens of adjustments
to an attribute within a document or documents using the
style sheet.

</FONT></BODY>
</HTML>
```

S

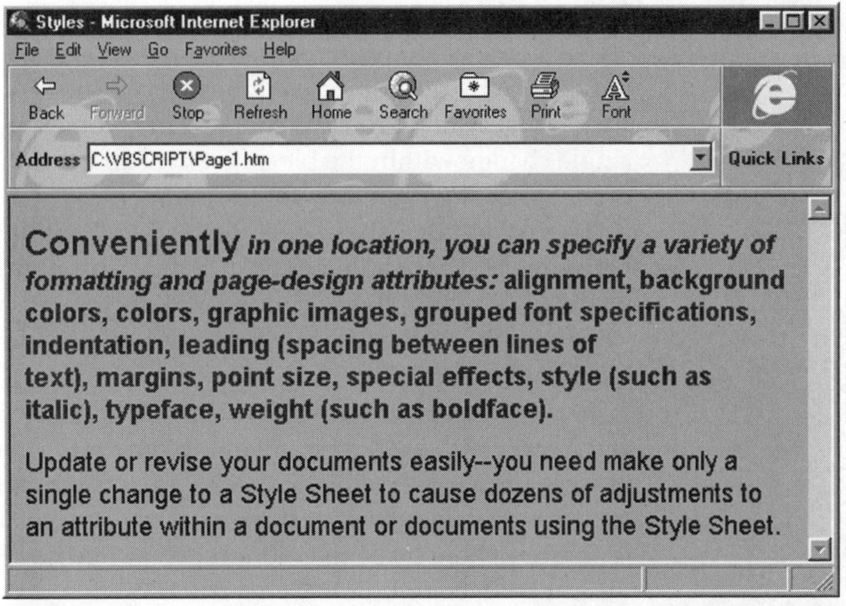

Figure S-7: Use the SPAN command to change the style of a whole region within a document.

In the example above, we first adjust the font size and typeface in the traditional HTML fashion. However, we also define a style that will span a portion of this document, ending with the </SPAN> tag. The style changes the text color to blue and the weight to boldface.

You can interrupt a SPAN with a different style, if you wish. Change the above example by inserting a new line that overrides the blue style with a temporary red style. Only the line between <P> and </P> will be red. That's because we redefined the meaning of the <P> tag, if only briefly. (You could just as well redefine other tags.) Here's an override style:

```
<SPAN STYLE="font-weight: bold; color: blue">
<BIG>Conveniently</BIG>
<P STYLE="color:red"> We want this red, not blue.</P>
<I>in one location, you can specify a variety of formatting
and page-design attributes:</I>
```

Embedded Style Blocks

Inline style adjustments are fine for a line or two, but if you use them extensively, you're going to find that a principal advantage of styles is lost. If you go to revise a document with many inline styles, you have to hunt them all down and revise each one individually. Why not coalesce all these styles into a single block? That way, if you want to make a change later, you only have to make a single change within the block to affect all the individual instances of that format within the whole document.

It's easy to put a style sheet into a document. Just enclose it between <STYLE> and </STYLE> tags. The style block is supposed to appear at the beginning of a document, prior to the <BODY> tag. Any style specifications you list within the style block will affect the entire document.

To define a new style, start with an HTML tag (like LI, H1, P) or *any other HTML tag* that you want to redefine. Then, enclosed in braces {}, type in a property:specification (such as font:11pt). You can include a whole list of these property:specification pairs, separating them by semi-colons (such as font:48pt "Arial"; font-weight:bold; color:blue).

In the following example of an embedded style block, we define three typefaces. The default BODY will be 11 point Courier, any <P> paragraphs will be 14 point Arial and rendered in red. Any <H1> headlines will be bold, blue, and 48 points large.

```
<HTML>
<HEAD>
<TITLE>Styles</TITLE>
</HEAD>

<STYLE TYPE="text/css">
<!--
 BODY {font: 11pt "Courier"};
 P {font: 14pt "Arial"; color: red}
 H1 {font: 48pt "Arial";
     font-weight: bold;
     color: blue}
 -->
</STYLE>

<BODY>
This is ordinary
<P> This is paragraph style </P>
```

S

```
and this is a
<H1>HEADLINE</H>

</BODY>
</HTML>
```

Note the punctuation for each style definition: HTML tag, left brace, general parameter, colon, specification, semicolon, any additional parameters, right brace.

```
P {font: 14pt "Arial"; color: red}
```

Avoiding Print-Through

The example above attempts, in two ways, to prevent a browser that cannot handle styles from displaying the style specifications themselves. First, the command *TYPE="text/css"* is supposed to alert a browser to ignore the following lines (don't display them). Second, by putting the specifications between the "comment" commands <!— and —>, browsers will ignore the style codes. Those HTML comment tags tell a browser to ignore everything between the <!— and the —> tags. Note that many people use this same technique with VBScript programming as well:

```
<HTML>
<HEAD>
 <SCRIPT LANGUAGE="VBScript">
<!--
MsgBox "Don't Display this source code"
MsgBox "If you can't handle scripts, ignore all this
-->
 </SCRIPT>
<TITLE>New Page</TITLE>
</HEAD>
<BODY>
</BODY>
</HTML>
```

What if you *want* to add some comments within your Style definition? The usual <!— —> HTML tags for comments don't work inside <STYLE> </STYLE>. Instead, use /* and */ like this:

```
P {font: 12pt; color=blue} /* blue for paragraphs */
```

S

Linked Style Sheets

If you don't want to embed a style sheet within each of your documents, you can put a style sheet on the hard drive of a server, and merely put that URL into your documents. When the browser comes upon this link, it will open your style file and take appropriate action—just as if you'd embedded the style sheet in the documents' source code.

Create a style sheet (as described earlier under "Embedded Style Blocks"). But, instead of putting it into a document, save it as a file to disk instead. Give it a file extension .CSS.

Let's try it. Here's our style sheet:

```
BODY {font: 11pt "Courier"};
P {font: 14pt "Arial"; color: red}
H1 {font: 48pt "Arial";
     font-weight: bold;
     color: blue}
```

Save this in an ordinary text file (you could use Windows Notepad) as STY.CSS *in the same directory as your documents* for testing purposes. That way, you don't have to provide a complete URL and path, just the filename will do. (See the Introduction for more on links, or see the entry on "A.")

Briefly, there are two ways to reference a linked style sheet (or a linked graphic or linked document, for that matter):

To link to another site entirely, provide its complete URL address:

```
"http://altavista.digital.com"
```

S

But to link to another document file in the same directory as the document itself, just provide the filename:

```
"mypict.htm"
```

OR, for a style sheet:

```
"STY.CSS"
```

So, assuming that we've saved our STY.CSS file in the same directory as our source code (our .HTM file), here's how to provide a link to that style sheet. As with an embedded style sheet, you put a link to a style sheet *within the* <HEAD> … </HEAD> *area of your document* (before the <BODY> tag):

```
<HEAD>
<TITLE>Style Sheets</TITLE>
<LINK REL=STYLESHEET HREF="STY.CSS" TYPE="text/css">
</HEAD>
<BODY>
This is ordinary
<P> This is paragraph style </P>
and this is a
<H1>HEADLINE</H>

</BODY>
</HTML>
```

Note that linked style sheets, such as STY.CSS described above, are not interpreted by the current beta version of Internet Explorer. This will soon be fixed. At the time of this writing, you are limited to inline or embedded styles.

Grouped Styles

You can simplify style definitions in various ways. For example, if you want to create an identical style for several HTML tags, you can just list all these tags prior to the definition:

These two definitions are identical:

```
BODY {font-size: 12pt;
 font-style: normal;
     font-family: "Arial";
     color: blue}
P {font-size: 12pt;
 font-style: normal;
     font-family: "Arial";
     color: blue}
```

So, you can just collapse them into a single definition, like this:

```
BODY P {font-size: 12pt;
   font-style: normal;
        font-family: "Arial";
        color: blue}
```

Similarly, you can omit the -style and -family commands, just providing a whole string of specifications for font, with spaces instead of punctuation separating them:

```
H1 {font: 12pt normal "Arial" blue}
```

Note: this is not currently working in the Internet Explorer beta.

Classes for Variations

If you want to create several different styles for, say, the P (paragraph) or H (headline) or some other HTML tag, you can create *classes*.

Let's assume that you want three different paragraph styles, one that's red, one green, and one blue. Define them this way, using whatever .class name you want. We'll use .red, .green, and .blue, but you can use whatever identifier you choose:

```
<HEAD>
<TITLE>Style Sheets</TITLE>
<STYLE TYPE="text/css">
<!--
P.red {font: 14; color: red}
P.green {font: 14; color: green}
P.blue {font: 14; color: blue}
-->
</STYLE>

</HEAD>
<BODY>

This is ordinary body text

<P CLASS=red> This is our red paragraph style </P>
<P CLASS=green> This is our green paragraph style </P>
<P CLASS=blue> This is our blue paragraph style </P>

</BODY>
</HTML>
```


Variables Here is a complete list of the style attributes you can specify, the values you can assign to those attributes, and examples of the syntax and punctuation.

Color

You can specify the color of text two ways: provide one of the 16 built-in color definitions: black, silver, gray, white, maroon, red, purple, fuchsia, green, lime, olive, yellow, navy, blue, teal, aqua. Or you can use RGB color values:

```
{color: #FFAA00}
{color: teal}
```

For more on RGB, see "Hex Numbers for the COLOR command" in the entry on "Body").

Font-family (typeface)

You can either specify a particular typeface:

```
{font-family: "Arial"}
```

OR a set of choices, aliases, in order of your preference, in case the user doesn't have your first choice(s):

```
{font-family: "Arial," "Sans-Serif," "Helvetica"}
```

Font-size

The size of the text. The size can be expressed in points, inches, centimeters, or pixels.

```
{font-size: 14pt}
{font-size: 1in}
{font-size: 4cm}
{font-size: 28px}
```


Indentation

To supplement margins, you can specify indentations as well (that will be added to any margins). This is like a tab stop. If you want all H1 headlines to be indented 1/2 inch from the left margin:

```
H1 {text-indent: 0.5in}
```

Indentation can be specified in points, inches, centimeters, or pixels.

Justification

You can left-justify, center, or right-justify text with the text-align attribute:

```
{text-align: left}
{text-align: center}
{text-align: right}
```

Leading (space between lines of text)

Technically, leading is the amount of space between the baselines of two lines of text. Baseline means the line on which most of the characters (except p, q, and others with descenders) rest. As with font size, leading can be expressed in points, inches, centimeters, or pixels:

```
{line-height: 14pt}
{line-height: 1in}
{line-height: 4cm}
{line-height: 28px}
```

Margins

Use the margin-left and margin-right attributes to establish page margins. Margins can be specified in points, inches, centimeters, or pixels:


```
BODY {margin-left: 35pt; margin-right: .5in}
```

OR

```
BODY {margin-left: 12cm; margin-right: 18px}
```

Also see "Indentation" on the previous page.

Style (italic)

You can specify italics this way:

```
{font-style: italic}
```

Underline & StrikeThrough

For these effects, you can use the text-decoration attributes: line-through, underline, italic, or none.

```
{text-decoration: line-through}
{text-decoration: underline}
```

Wallpaper & BackColor

If you want a colored background or a graphic image, use the background attribute. You can specify a color for the background two ways: provide one of the 16 built-in color definitions: black, silver, gray, white, maroon, red, purple, fuchsia, green, lime, olive, yellow, navy, blue, teal, or aqua. Or you can use RGB color values:

```
BODY {background: #FF00}
BODY {background: olive}
```

(For more on RGB, see "Hex Numbers for the COLOR command" in the entry on "Body.")

OR you can display an image in the background, by specifying its URL address, like this:

```
BODY {background: URL(http://www.myserver.com/slides.gif)}
```

Weight (boldface)

You can specify two character thicknesses:

```
{font-weight: normal}
{font-weight: bold}
```

Uses Conveniently, in one location, you can specify a variety of formatting and page-design attributes: alignment, background colors, colors, graphic images, grouped font specifications, indentation, leading (spacing between lines of text), margins, point size, special effects, style (such as italic), typeface, weight (such as boldface).

Update or revise your documents easily—you need make only a single change to a style sheet to cause dozens of adjustments to an attribute within a document or documents using the style sheet.

Cautions At this time, only Internet Explorer recognizes and reacts to style sheets. The other browsers will in future versions, but for now you'll want to take steps to prevent Netscape from *displaying your Style commands* as if they were ordinary text. To learn of the two techniques that accomplish this suppression, see "Avoiding Print-through" earlier in this entry.

BODY is a special HTML tag. It provides the default specifications for much of the formatting. For example, if you define a color text style for BODY, *all the other styles* (and HTML tags like <P>, too) *will use this same color*, unless you specifically mention a different color in the other styles. So, assign a style to BODY if you want to set a default background color; forecolor (text color); font family, typesize, style, weight or decoration; page margins; or background colors or graphics. See the example below.

Example

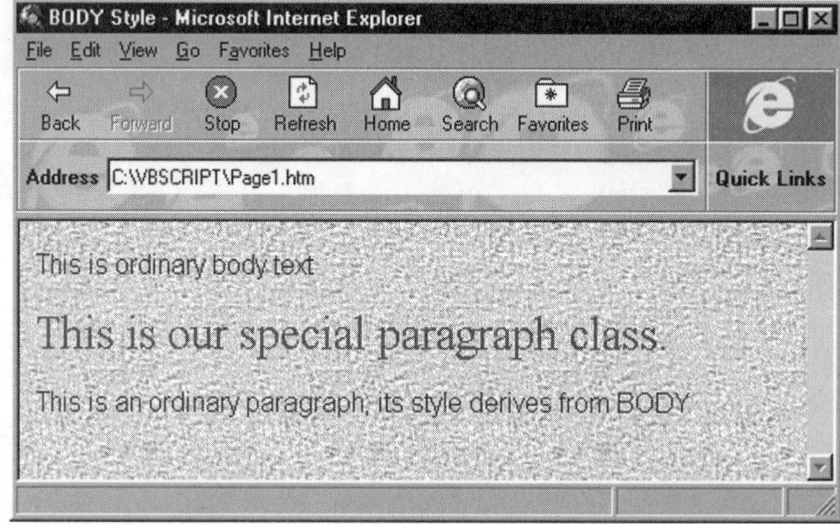

Figure S-8: We override the usual <P> typeface, typesize, and color by redefining the meaning of the HTML tag BODY.

```
<HEAD>
<TITLE>BODY Style</TITLE>
<STYLE TYPE="text/css">
<!--
BODY {background: URL(rough1.gif)
```

```
    font-family: "Arial";
    color: blue}

P.Special {font: 28; family: "Times New Roman"; color: red}
-->
</STYLE>

</HEAD>
<BODY>

This is ordinary body text

<P CLASS=Special> This is our special paragraph class.</P>

<P> This is an ordinary paragraph; its style derives from
BODY</P>

</BODY>
</HTML>
```

Here we've defined BODY as the Arial typeface in blue. Therefore, all text in the document will default to that font and color. The only way to adjust any of these qualities is to provide an additional style definition, as we did with the P.Special class. We said that a P.Special would be Times font at 28 points in red. Note that the other <P> in the document follows the defaults established by our definition of BODY.

S

Sub & Sup

HTML

Description Display text in subscript or superscript. The text is also generally switched to a smaller type size than the surrounding text.

Used with ***Can be enclosed by***
<A>, <ABBREV>, <ABOVE>, <ACRONYM>, <ADDRESS>, <AU>, <B>, <BANNER>, <BAR>, <BELOW>, <BIG>, <BODY>, <BODYTEXT>, <BOX>, <BT>, <CAPTION>, <CITE>, <CODE>, <CREDIT>, <DD>, <DDOT>, <DEL>, <DFN>, <DIV>, <DOT>, <DT>, <EM>, <FIGTEXT>, <FN>, <FORM>, <H>, <HAT>, <I>,

<INS>, <ITEM>, <KBD>, <LANG>, <LH>, <LI>, <MATH>, <NOTE>,<OF>, <P>, <PERSON>, <Q>, <ROOT>, <S>, <SAMP>, <SMALL>, <SQRT>, <STRONG>, <T>, <TD>, <TH>, <TILDE>,<TT>, <U>, <VAR>, <VEC>

Can enclose

<A>, <ABBREV>, <ACRONYM>, <AU>, <B>, <BIG>, <BR>, <CITE>, <CODE>, <DEL>, <DFN>, <EM>, <I>, <IMG>, <INS>, <KBD>, <LANG>, <MATH>, <PERSON>, <Q>, <S>, <SAMP>, <SMALL>, <STRONG>, <SUB>, <SUP>, <TAB>, <TT>, <U>, <VAR>

Uses Specialized text formatting to indicate degrees of temperature, footnotes, molecular composition (like H_2O), and so on.

Example

The temperature in Moose Jaw today is 15° below zero.

Figure S-9: Note that the o between the SUP commands is not only superscripted but also rendered in a smaller type size than the o in the words today, below, *and* zero.

```
<HTML>
<BODY BGCOLOR=WHITE>
<FONT SIZE=+2>

The temperature in Moose Jaw today is 15<SUP>o</SUP> below
zero.

</BODY>
</HTML>
```

S

Sub

VBSCRIPT STATEMENT

Description The Sub command announces that you are creating a Subroutine, a structure that, in many ways, is like adding a new command to VBScript. Subs are often called *procedures* (and Functions, which are quite similar to Subroutines, can also be called procedures). Most often, a Sub in VBScript is associated with a particular Control. For example, the commands within this Sub will be carried out whenever the Control named Button1 is clicked:

```
Sub Button1_Click
Button1.width = Button1.width + 20
End Sub
```

The other primary use for Sub is to create a specialized behavior that you want to repeatedly use from different locations in your script.

A Subroutine is like a little program within your larger program—performing some limited task and available to be called upon to execute that task from anywhere in the program.

Subroutines are available anytime, part of a larger structure (your entire VBScript), and limited but useful.

HTML is a "markup" language—its essential purpose is to describe how a computer screen should look. HTML specifies to the user's browser what text, pictures, borders, typefaces, colors, and formatting should appear onscreen. In this way, HTML is essentially equivalent to a word processor except that word processors describe how a page should look when printed on paper.

But we can assume that the inherent limitations of a *page description language* (or "markup" language) will be rapidly overcome as the Internet marches on. We can already see the increasing emphasis on the *behavior* of Web pages, including interaction with the user, multimedia, data processing such as database searches, encryption, and other *actions*.

VBScript, like any other traditional computer language, is designed to do things to data. However, given the modular nature of Internet programming—links and pages rather than a single monolithic application—VBScript relies much less on *classic* Subroutines than do older computer languages.

Subroutines are, of course, an inherent part of programming and will always exist as long as people need to communicate with computers. Subroutines are fundamentally efficient because they extend the language in much the same way that abbreviations and acronyms extend human language. We use *U.S.A.* for the same reason Romans used *SPQR*—they're shortcuts that save time and also express a complete idea.

Just how Subroutines work in any particular computer language, though, can differ considerably. VBScript's design essentially eliminates the need for traditional Subroutines to which you would GoSub and then Return. There are, in fact, no GoSub…Return commands in VBScript.

Traditional Subroutines: GoSub...Return: A typical traditional program was structured as follows:

```
(Main Program)
10 GoSub Reset
20 ? "HELLO"
30 GoSub Ask
40 If A = "Y" Then End
50 GoSub Reset
(Subroutine #1)
400 Reset:
410 CLS
420 A = " "
430 Return
(Subroutine #2)
500 Ask:
510 Input "Do you want to quit now? (Y/N) "; A
520 Return
```

S

The GoSub command temporarily transfers control of your program to a Subroutine. The preceding example of a traditional program structure started by going to a Subroutine in line 400, which cleared the screen and cleared a Variable. Then, that Subroutine having finished its job, the Return command caused the program to go back to the line following the GoSub, line 20. Notice that lines 10 through 50 are not within a Subroutine.

VBScript Subroutines: Typically, you write Subroutines to save yourself from having to repeat the same instructions over and over in various locations in your program. A second primary reason for Subroutines is that you can use them to assign behavior to an object. For example, if you create a Command Button that the user can click:

```
<INPUT TYPE=Button Name="Btn" Value=" Click me to see 2 + 2 ">
```

This button is an *object,* and the user is invited to click the button with his mouse to see something happen as a result of the click. Note that objects permit the user to determine when some event takes place. For this reason, more than any other, the programmer's control over what happens in the program is seriously limited. You—as the programmer—can't specify the sequence of events in your entire program (or document). You can display a page, but the user might never choose to go to your second page. You can display a button, but the user might never choose to click on that button.

The object, the button in our example above, is given a name ("Btn" in this case). It doesn't matter what name you give it, but that name allows you to attach behavior to the button. You just use the same name in an On_Click Subroutine:

```
Sub Btn_OnClick
  Msgbox "The result of 2 + 2 is 4."
End Sub
```

Subroutines are useful if you want to give an object some behavior, or, secondarily, if there is some task that you'll need to have done repeatedly from different places in your program (such as alphabetizing several Arrays of names).

Variables

```
Sub MySubsName (Variables passed to the Sub)
```

Scope: You can create a simple Subroutine by simply naming it and entering commands into it. Subroutines can be called (accessed or triggered by using their name in your script) from anywhere within a particular script. This is called the *scope,* and it means the range of influence, the locations that can access the Sub.

S

```
<HTML>
<HEAD>
<TITLE>Scope</TITLE>
</HEAD>
<BODY>

<SCRIPT LANGUAGE="VBSCRIPT">
Show5
Show6
```

```
Sub Show5
Msgbox "5"
End Sub
</SCRIPT>

<SCRIPT LANGUAGE="VBSCRIPT">
Sub Show6
Msgbox "6"
End Sub
</SCRIPT>

</BODY>
</HTML>
```

The first "call" (to the Sub named Show5) works fine. The second call, to Show6, fails and generates an error message. This is because you can only trigger Subs (or Functions) from within the same <SCRIPT LANGUAGE="VBSCRIPT">...</SCRIPT> structure. *You can't call on a Sub or Function outside a particular SCRIPT, even though they're in the same document.*

OR (to allow a Subroutine to accept Variables, to "pass" Variables to a Sub):

Often you will want to "pass" information to a Sub. Unless you use the special ByVal command (see the first Caution), any Variables that you "pass" to a Subroutine can be changed by that Subroutine.

You can pass a number, for example, to a Subroutine that multiplies by 5:

```
<HTML>
<SCRIPT LANGUAGE="VBScript">

Sub Byfive (n)
  Msgbox n * 5
End Sub

</SCRIPT>
</HTML>
```

We said that it doesn't matter what names you use with Subs, but that's not strictly true. You must follow the same rules for naming these "passed" items as you would for creating new

Variable names: you cannot use names already in use by VBScript commands (such as Second or MsgBox). We used *n* above, and that's not a command in VBScript, so *n* is fine.

Notice that this example above *does nothing* because no button is attached (named the same, with an On_Click). The Subroutine is never "called." Any commands you put inside the <SCRIPT> </SCRIPT> will be triggered when the page is loaded into a browser *except commands enclosed within Sub...End Sub or Function...End Function.* Those "procedures" as they are called must be specifically triggered either by the user (clicking, for example, on a button) or by your programming, as we'll now illustrate.

From elsewhere in your <SCRIPT> program, you can "call" this Sub to do its job, and at the same time pass the number that you want to multiply:

```
<HTML>
<HEAD>
<TITLE>Scope</TITLE>
</HEAD>
<BODY>

<SCRIPT LANGUAGE="VBSCRIPT" >

Byfive (4)

Sub Byfive (n)
  Msgbox n * 5
End Sub

</SCRIPT>

</BODY>
</HTML>
```

OR, to pass a Variable instead of a literal number:

```
X = 4
Byfive X
```

OR (to pass more than one Variable to a Sub):

```
<HTML>
<SCRIPT LANGUAGE="VBScript">
```

S

```
Anymultiply 3, 12

Sub Anymultiply (a, b)
  Msgbox a * b
End Sub

</SCRIPT>
</HTML>
```

You can add as many "arguments," the Variables that can be passed to a Sub, as you wish. But when *calling* on this Sub, you must provide all the Variables that Sub expects to receive. Note that you enclose the "arguments" in parentheses when defining a Sub, but you do not use parentheses when *calling* on that Sub to do its job. In both cases, though, you must separate the items by commas.

OR (to pass an Array, add empty parentheses to identify the Variable as an Array):

```
Sub Sort (Appointments())
```

OR (to leave the Sub prematurely, to refuse to carry out the rest of the commands in it for some reason, use the Exit Sub command):

```
Sub StretchPicture (ThePic, HowMuch)
TargetSize = ThePic.Width * HowMuch
If TargetSize > 2000 Then
 Exit Sub
End If
ThePic.Width = TargetSize
End Sub
```

Here, the amount to stretch a picture is passed to this Sub. If the amount to stretch it (the Variable HowMuch multiplied by the Width Property of the picture) causes the picture to get wider than 2000, we abort with Exit Sub.

Uses Use a Subroutine (or Function) whenever you want a task performed in several places in your program. If the task isn't trivial, like simply changing a font size, but involves a series of actions, such as manipulating seven different Properties of a Control or alphabetizing a list of names, a Subroutine is the ideal solution.

How Functions Differ From Subroutines: A Function is the same thing as a Subroutine, with a single exception—a Function directly returns a result (a value) to the caller. The *name* of the function becomes a kind of Variable:

```
<HTML>
<SCRIPT LANGUAGE="VBScript">

msgbox mult

Function mult
  mult = 444
End Function

</SCRIPT>
</HTML>
```

Results in
A message box that displays 444.

You must use a Function inside an expression, but you cannot use a Subroutine inside an expression. A Subroutine must be a separate command, whereas a Function is part of one or more additional commands that "evaluate" to something simpler (see *expression* under "Variables"). In the above example, the MsgBox function contained the mult function. Here's another way to use a function inside an expression:

```
z = mult + 3
msgbox z

Function mult
  mult = 444
End Function
```

Results in
A message box that displays 447.

You "call" a Function by making it part of an "expression," even if you don't pay any attention to the results of that expression. Here we don't care what's in A, but we nevertheless must create an expression. Also note that, unlike a Subroutine, you must enclose the Variable or Variables that you are "passing" to a Function in parentheses:

```
a = mult (3)

Function mult (n)
  msgbox 444 + n
End Function
```

Admittedly, this isn't a good example of a Function. It could just as easily be written as a Subroutine. The essence and value of a Function is that it does allow you to return a value.

The *a* is entirely ignored by our program (nothing happens to *mult* so no value gets passed back to *a*). However, a Function cannot be constructed without putting it into that expression structure with the return variable (a =). But remember that if you do want to pass back a value from a Function to the place that calls it—the Function's *name* must be given the result, the thing you want passed back. Then the Variable used in the expression gets this value. In the following example, *a* gets the value that is given to *mult* inside the Function:

```
a = mult (6)
msgbox a

Function mult (n)
  mult = 444 + n
End Function
```


Results in

A message box that displays 450.

Notice also that you can pass as many Variables as you want *to* a Function (or Sub), but you can pass only one value *back to a Function*. And you can't pass *any* Variables back to a Sub. So, what if you want to change one or more Variables with a Sub? The answer is to create a Variable or Variables that exist outside of the procedure (the Sub or Function), Variables that have wider *scope*. In VBScript, you would define (DIM) the Variable outside of any Sub or Function.

This:

```
Dim x
Sub Tryint
End Sub
```

Not this:

```
Sub Tryint
Dim X
End Sub
```

In the second case, the X can only be used *within* the Tryint Sub, because it was Dimmed within the Sub…End Sub structure.

(For more examples of how you can use Functions, see "Function.")

Use Subroutines in more than one program. If you spend some time writing a useful Subroutine, you should save it in a disk file. Then you can import it into other programs that you write in the future.

Cautions

- There is no ByVal command in VBScript (allowing you to prevent a Sub or Function from changing the value of a passed Variable).
- Subroutines can be "recursive," can call themselves. This advanced technique, though, can lead to an endless loop, an echo chamber effect, an infinite regression, or worse. If you understand and use recursion, you don't need it explained here. If you don't, avoid using Subroutines in this fashion. The following is a recursive Subroutine:

  ```
  Sub Endless ()
   MsgBox "One more time around."
   Endless
  End Sub
  ```

  This Sub includes its own name and thus calls itself, again and again.
- You cannot put one Subroutine inside another; Subroutines cannot be "nested."

Wrong:

```
Sub FirstSub
 Sub SecondSub
 End Sub
End Sub
```

- All Variables inside a Subroutine are "local"; they are created when the Sub is called and die when the program reaches the End Sub (or Exit Sub) command. The exceptions are Variables declared with the Dim command, outside of a Sub…End Sub.

Example

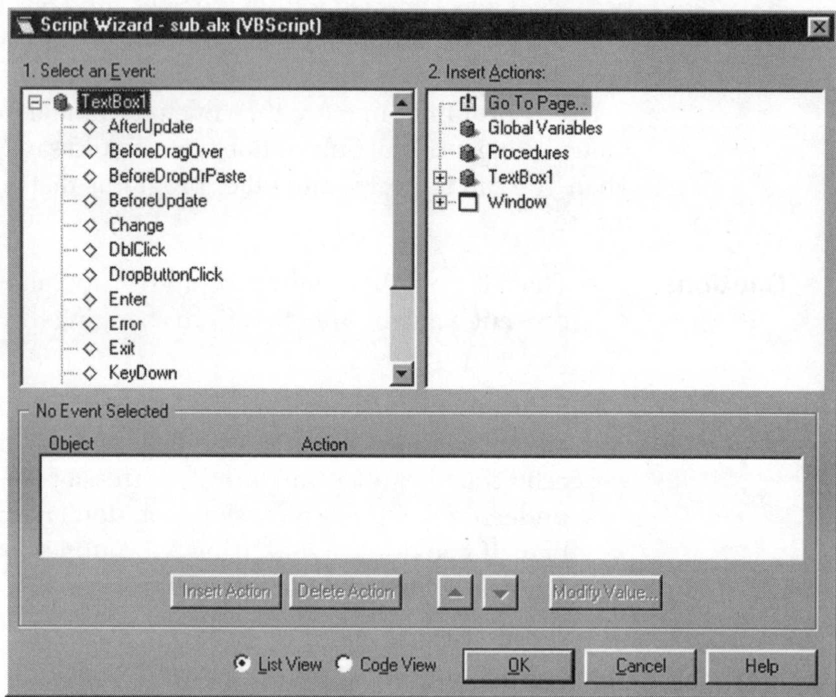

Figure S-10: There are 16 Events (Subs) that you can use with a TextBox.

After you've put a Control onto a document in the ActiveX Control Pad, select Script Wizard from the Tools menu, then click on the small + next to the name of the Control. A list of all its "Events" will drop down. These are the Subs that the Control will respond to—when outside Events (like a double-click) occur, these Subs are triggered.

You might well think the Label Control would be inert, merely displaying a message to the user. However, it has eight Events to which it can react: BeforeDragOver, BeforeDropOrPaste, Click, DblClick, Error, MouseDown, MouseMove, MouseUp. In this example, we'll use the MouseMove to detect, and react to, the user moving the mouse pointer onto and around the Label's surface:

```
<HTML>
<TEXTAREA ROWS=2 COLS=55 NAME="RESULT">
</TEXTAREA>
<SCRIPT LANGUAGE="VBScript">
Dim Toggle
cr = chr(13) & chr(10)

Sub Label1_MouseMove(ByVal Button, ByVal Shift, ByVal X,
ByVal Y)
RESULT.VALUE = ""
Toggle = Not Toggle
If Toggle Then
  Label1.Caption = "GET OFF!!"
Else
  Label1.Caption = "I'm Sensitive."
End If
RESULT.VALUE="X = " + cstr(X) + " Y = " + cstr(Y)
end sub
</SCRIPT>
<BR><BR>
<OBJECT ID="Label1" WIDTH=291 HEIGHT=60
 CLASSID="CLSID:978C9E23-D4B0-11CE-BF2D-00AA003F40D0">
  <PARAM NAME="Caption" VALUE="A Sensitive Label">
  <PARAM NAME="PicturePosition" VALUE="524290">
  <PARAM NAME="Size" VALUE="7694;1588">
  <PARAM NAME="SpecialEffect" VALUE="1">
  <PARAM NAME="FontName" VALUE="Arial">
  <PARAM NAME="FontHeight" VALUE="240">
  <PARAM NAME="FontCharSet" VALUE="0">
  <PARAM NAME="FontPitchAndFamily" VALUE="2">
  <PARAM NAME="ParagraphAlign" VALUE="3">
  <PARAM NAME="FontWeight" VALUE="0">
</OBJECT>
</HTML>
```

S

We've added a TextArea and Label Object to this document. (Add the Label Object by clicking on the Edit Menu, then selecting "Insert ActiveX Control" in Microsoft's ActiveX Control Pad.) We created a Variable called *Toggle* that will switch back and forth (Toggle=Not Toggle) each time the mouse moves. It will keep changing the Label's caption while the user moves the mouse on the Label.

Then we created a Sub that responds whenever the user's mouse is moved over the Label. Every time our Sub is triggered (or "fired," as it's currently called), the Caption Property is adjusted and the TextArea is cleared of its previous contents (RESULT.VALUE="") by putting an empty text Variable into it.

Finally, we display the current coordinates of the mouse pointer within the Label: the X (horizontal) and Y (vertical) values.

See also Function, Variables

T

TAB

HTML

Description Specifies an indentation in text, as if you'd pressed the Tab key on a keyboard. Allows highly precise control over horizontal spacing. The distance over from the left margin (but see ALIGN below) of a page that TAB moves is specified in terms of en-space. An *en* is the width of the letter *n* in the current typeface. (En is one-half the point size. If you are displaying a 12-point typeface, the en measurement will be 6 points.) A point is a typographical measurement equal to 1/72nd of an inch. So, given that a typical type size used in Internet body text is 12 points, you can specify horizontal distance with TAB in .08 inch increments. At the time of this writing, the TAB command is not supported by the Internet Explorer browser.

Used with ***Can be enclosed by***

<A>, <ABBREV>, <ACRONYM>, <ADDRESS>, <AU>, <B>, <BANNER>, <BIG>, <BODY>, <BODYTEXT>, <CAPTION>, <CITE>, <CODE>, <CREDIT>, <DD>,<DEL>, <DFN>, <DIV>, <DT>, <EM>, <FIGTEXT>, <FN>, <FORM>, <H1>, <H2>, <H3>, <H4>, <H5>, <H6>, <I>, <INS>, <KBD>, <LANG>, <LH>, <LI>, <NOTE>,<P>, <PERSON>, <Q>, <S>, <SAMP>, <SMALL>, <STRONG>, <SUB>, <SUP>, <TD>, <TH>, <TT>, <U>, <VAR>

Can enclose

Nothing

Variables **ALIGN:** ALIGN can be LEFT, RIGHT, CENTER, or DECIMAL. ALIGN=LEFT is the default; it means that the text will be displayed immediately following the distance specified by the TAB command. RIGHT means to right-justify the text, minus the TAB distance specified. If the TO command is not used, the text will be flush against the right margin. CENTER centers the text, *on the specified TAB stop* (this will be centered within the margins of the page, if you have not used the TO command). DECIMAL searches the text (following the ALIGN command) for a decimal point, then aligns to it. Note: Any ALIGN command will be canceled as soon as a line break <BR> command or new TAB command is encountered further down in the text.

DP: The DP command specifies the character that is being used as a decimal point for the ALIGN=DECIMAL command. A period is the default, but you could change the default with DP="," or some other symbol.

INDENT: INDENT specifies how many en units over from the left margin text displays. (*En* is defined above under "Description.") <TAB INDENT=6> will indent 6 en units.

TO: The TO command says to use a TAB that has been previously defined with the ID command.

Uses

- Indent the start of each paragraph.
- Create columns and tables (though the TABLE command is preferred because it is more flexible, permitting frames and other optional formatting).

Example At the time of this writing, the TAB command is not supported by Internet Explorer.

```
<HTML>
This line is not indented.
<BR>
<TAB ALIGN=10>This line is indented by 10 en units.
</HTML>
```

See also TABLE

TabFixedHeight, TabFixedWidth

ACTIVEX

See Properties

TabIndex

ACTIVEX

See Properties

TabKeyBehavior, TabOrientation, TabStop

ACTIVEX

See Properties

TabStrip

ACTIVEX CONTROL

Description As a way of organizing user options, the TabStrip (called a "Property Sheet" in Windows 95 parlance) is a considerable improvement over anything offered for this purpose before—namely menus or simple dialog boxes.

Variables Depending on your point of view, the TabStrip's approach to Variables and Events represents a useful new programming technique or a nightmare of unnecessary and bug-inducing syntactic complication.

No matter what your view of the current rage for "object-oriented programming," there's no getting away from it these days. The TabStrip, for example, is described this way in the Microsoft ActiveX Control Pad Help: "The TabStrip is implemented as a container of a Tabs collection, which in turn contains a group of Tab objects."

What does this statement mean for us, the programmers? It means long names, mainly, plus some strange inverted syntax. The following example adds five new tabs. What the fifth line literally says is: "to the Tabs Collection of TabStrip1, use TabStrip1's Add Method to add a new Tab object." Got that? Unhappily, some of this new object-oriented syntax is pulling Basic away from one of its earliest and most valuable goals: that it sound as much as possible like plain English.

Here's how you add new tabs to the TabStrip:

```
<SCRIPT LANGUAGE="VBScript">
<!--
Sub Window_OnLoad
for i = 1 to 5
  Set TabStrip1.Tabs = TabStrip1.Add
next
End Sub
-->
</SCRIPT>
```

To change the caption on the *third* tab:

```
TabStrip1.Tabs(2).Caption = "Hold"
```

Note that (2) changes the third tab because you're supposed to start counting from zero. The first tab is really the zeroth tab.

You'll have to remember several eccentricities when trying to write scripts involving a TabStrip. One of them is that you've got a set of nested objects here: "The TabStrip is implemented as a container of a Tabs collection, which in turn contains a group of Tab objects." Among other consequences, you've got a set of Properties for the TabStrip Control, and *a separate set of Properties for the Tabs collection.*

Each Tab object has five Properties: Caption, Enabled, ID, Index, and Visible. The TabStrip has many more Properties (see the list below). The Tab object has no Events or Methods. You use the TabStrip's Events *to make things happen for an individual tab.* Let's say that our "Fonts" tab, when clicked, should cause five OptionButtons to become visible. It's the tab with an Index number of *two* (but, visually, it's the *third* tab because they're numbered 0, 1, 2):

```
Sub TabStrip1_Click(Index)
If Index = 2 Then
OptionButton1.Visible = True
OptionButton2.Visible = True
OptionButton3.Visible = True
OptionButton4.Visible = True
OptionButton5.Visible = True
Else
OptionButton1.Visible = False
OptionButton2.Visible = False
OptionButton3.Visible = False
OptionButton4.Visible = False
OptionButton5.Visible = False
End If
end sub
```

As you can see in the above example, you can tell which tab was clicked by using the built-in Index Variable in the TabStrip's Click Event. If, however, you need to adjust one of the five Properties of the currently selected tab at some other, later time:

```
TabStrip1.SelectedItem.Caption = "This One is Selected"
```

So, when you're talking about a TabStrip, you're also talking about a separate interior ("contained") collection of Tab objects *that have different Properties from their container* (the TabStrip Control itself). However, even though the TabStrip "contains" the tabs, those tabs themselves cannot contain anything else—such as CheckBoxes. This presents a problem. You'll perhaps want to have the user click on a tab labelled "Fonts" and then see a ListBox with all the possible typefaces that the user's system can display. Well, how do you get that ListBox to suddenly appear when the user clicks on the Fonts tab?

What about the practical problem of displaying other Controls on a Tab page (a set of Option Buttons, a TextBox, or whatever other Controls will aid the user)? Unlike Visual Basic (where you place a "container object" such as a Frame Control onto the TabStrip), in VBScript you must use the HTML Layout Control as the container for any Controls that will appear to be on each tab.

And you pile the Controls for each tab up there underneath—then toggle their Visible Properties depending on which tab the user clicks. To see how this is done, see the example.

You can refer to a particular tab either by its Index Property (as we've done in the examples above), or by its Name Property. Note that there is no Name Property listed in the Help specifications for tabs. They don't even have a Caption Property listed. But these Properties will produce results if you use them in a script. And they seem to be the same Property. This next example demonstrates the interaction of Caption and Name. Click on, say, Tab 1 and you'll see that this Tab's name is "Tab1," just as displayed:

```
Sub TabStrip1_Click(Index)

N = TabStrip1.Tabs(Index).Name
MsgBox N

TabStrip1.Tabs(Index).Name = "NEW"
end sub
```

The first half of the above example works: you see in the message box the Name of the tab. However, attempting to change the Name fails. To change the tab's Name (and Caption) you must use the Caption Property instead:

```
TabStrip1.Tabs(Index).Caption = "NEW"
```

Each tab has a unique name and index value within the collection. You can reference a tab by either its name or its index value. The index of the first tab is 0; the index of the second tab is 1; and so on. When two Tab objects have the same name, you must reference each tab by its *index* value. References to the name in code will access only the first tab that uses the name.

The MultiRow Property defaults to False, meaning that a TabStrip Control will have only a single row of tabs. However, if you set MultiRow to True, there can be more than the one row. How many rows will appear depends on the width of the TabStrip itself as well as the number of tabs and their captions (the font size, font, and the text itself).

If you leave MultiRow False, some of the tabs might be cut off if they cannot all be displayed in that single row. However, a ScrollBar will automatically be added to the TabStrip to allow the user to see the missing tabs. So, no harm done. (See Figure T-1.)

According to the VBScript specifications, when you want your script (as opposed to user clicks) to determine which tab is currently selected, use the SelectedItem Property. However, at this time, you cannot accomplish this. The following script will generate an error:

```
<SCRIPT LANGUAGE="VBScript">
<!--

Sub Window_OnLoad
for i = 1 to 5
Set TabStrip1.Tabs = TabStrip1.Add
next
TabStrip1.SelectedItem = 3
End Sub

-->
</SCRIPT>
```

However, you can use SelectedItem to change a Property of the currently selected tab:

```
TabStrip1.SelectedItem.Caption = "Click"
```

The Style Property determines whether tabs are displayed (the default):

```
TabStrip1.Style = 0
```

OR specifies that the tabs are displayed as *buttons* (rather than the default "index card" visual metaphor):

```
TabStrip1.Style = 1
```

OR no tabs are displayed whatsoever:

```
TabStrip1.Style = 2
```

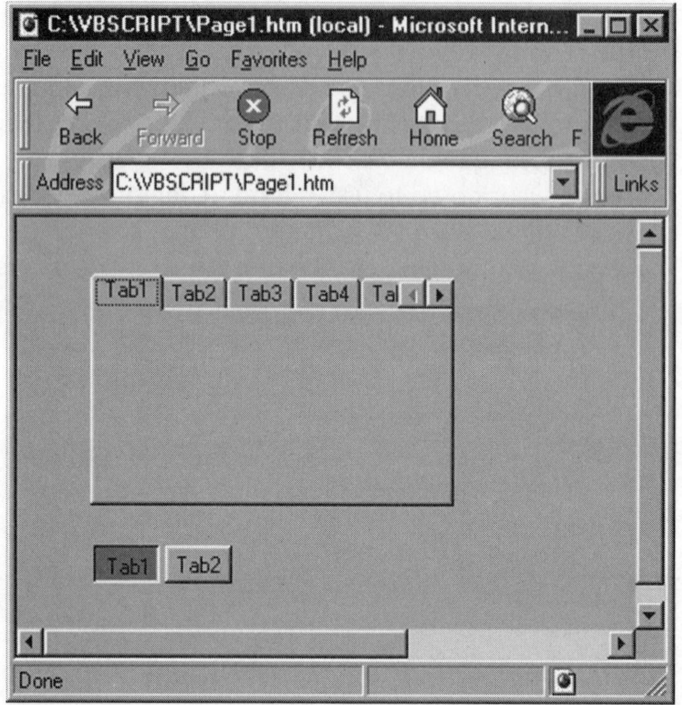

Figure T-1: The default Style (above) and the "button" Style (below). If you set the Style to 2 ("None"), the tabs and the TabStrip Control both disappear.

The TabFixedHeight and TabFixedWidth Properties allow you to query, or change, the height or width of the tabs in a TabStrip Control. The measurement is in points (72 per inch).

To change the height while a script is running:

```
TabStrip1.TabFixedHeight = 13
```

By default, the TabFixedHeight and TabFixedWidth Properties are 0, causing the widths and heights of the tabs to be automatically adjusted for you—based on the size of the caption in each tab. However, if you provide a TabFixedHeight and/or TabFixedWidth, those measurements will be used, and the size of the tabs will not be adjusted based on their captions.

Also, while automatic spacing is used, the tabs can be of varying widths and heights (again, based on whatever caption each tab has). However, if you set TabFixedHeight and/or TabFixedWidth, each tab will be of identical height and/or width.

On a TabStrip Control, the row (or rows) of tabs can appear on the top, bottom, or the right or left side of the Control. By default, the tabs are along the top so the Control simulates a 3x5 card recipe box, its analogy in the real world. However, if you have a compelling reason to adjust the position of the tabs, you can change them by adjusting the TabOrientation Property:

```
TabStrip1.TabOrientation = 0 ' the default, along the top
TabStrip1.TabOrientation = 1 'along the bottom
TabStrip1.TabOrientation = 2 ' on the left
TabStrip1.TabOrientation = 3 ' on the right
```

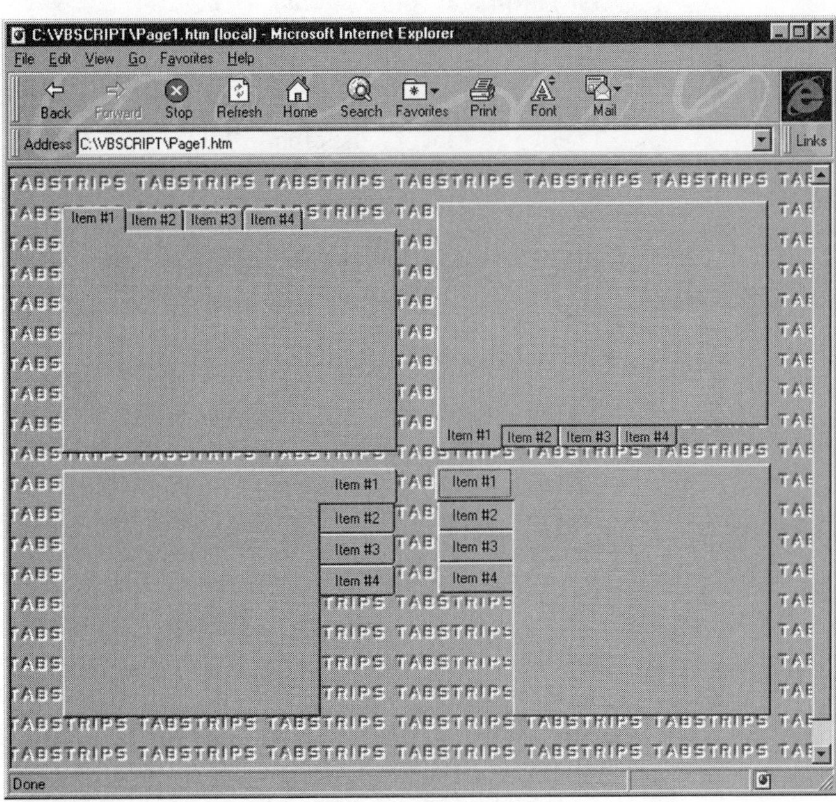

Figure T-2: The four possible TabStrip Orientations.

T

To create the TabStrips shown in Figure T-2, we used the following script to add two new tabs to the default two tabs that each TabStrip always has. Then we adjusted the Caption Properties of the various tabs:

```
<SCRIPT LANGUAGE="VBScript">
<!--
Sub Window_OnLoad

for i = 0 to 1

Set TabStrip1.Tabs = TabStrip1.Add
TabStrip1.Tabs(i).Caption = "Item #" & i + 1
Set TabStrip2.Tabs = TabStrip2.Add
TabStrip2.Tabs(i).Caption = "Item #" & i + 1
Set TabStrip3.Tabs = TabStrip3.Add
TabStrip3.Tabs(i).Caption = "Item #" & i + 1
Set TabStrip4.Tabs = TabStrip4.Add
TabStrip4.Tabs(i).Caption = "Item #" & i + 1

next

TabStrip1.Tabs(2).Caption = "Item #3"
TabStrip1.Tabs(3).Caption = "Item #4"
TabStrip2.Tabs(2).Caption = "Item #3"
TabStrip2.Tabs(3).Caption = "Item #4"
TabStrip3.Tabs(2).Caption = "Item #3"
TabStrip3.Tabs(3).Caption = "Item #4"
TabStrip4.Tabs(2).Caption = "Item #3"
TabStrip4.Tabs(3).Caption = "Item #4"

End Sub
-->
</SCRIPT>
```

Properties
Accelerator, BackColor, CodeBase, Enabled, Font, ForeColor, Height, ID, Left, MouseIcon, MousePointer, MultiRow, SelectedItem, Style, TabFixedHeight, TabFixedWidth, TabIndex, TabOrientation, TabStop, Top, Value, Visible, Width

Events
BeforeDragOver, BeforeDropOrPaste, Change, Click, DblClick, Enter, Error, Exit, KeyDown, KeyPress, KeyUp, MouseDown, MouseMove, MouseUp

Methods
Move, SetFocus, ZOrder

For details about these Properties, Events, and Methods, see the entries for "Properties," "Events," and "Methods."

Uses Whenever you want to display a fairly extensive set of options, and segregate them into logical groups, or you've got a database that lends itself to 3x5-card-style visualization, allow the user to interface with the collection of information through a TabStrip.

Cautions Two or more tabs can have the same Name Property. If you use the Name to reference a tab, VBScript will take you to the first one that has that Name. The index numbers, though, are always unique.

Example A TabStrip Control is a visual rather than physical or logical organizer. In other words, you must put other Controls onto the HTML Layout Control—you cannot add Controls to a TabStrip Control. It's not built to be a container.

To illustrate how to create the illusion that the user is clicking on a tab and revealing a separate "page," we'll construct a TabStrip that's designed to allow the user to choose between a set of songs (via Option Buttons) and also play as many movies as they wish (via CheckBoxes).

To create this example, start the Microsoft ActiveX Control Pad (see the Introduction) and click on Edit | Insert HTML Layout. Give the layout a new name and then click on the icon next to the <OBJECT> definition. Now from the toolbox, put one TabStrip, four OptionButtons, and three CheckBoxes onto the layout. Right-click on each OptionButton and each CheckBox and choose Properties. Give each a different caption. Arrange the CheckBoxes and OptionButtons so they appear to be "on" the TabStrip. It doesn't matter if CheckBoxes interfere with OptionButtons—only one set will be visible at any give time.

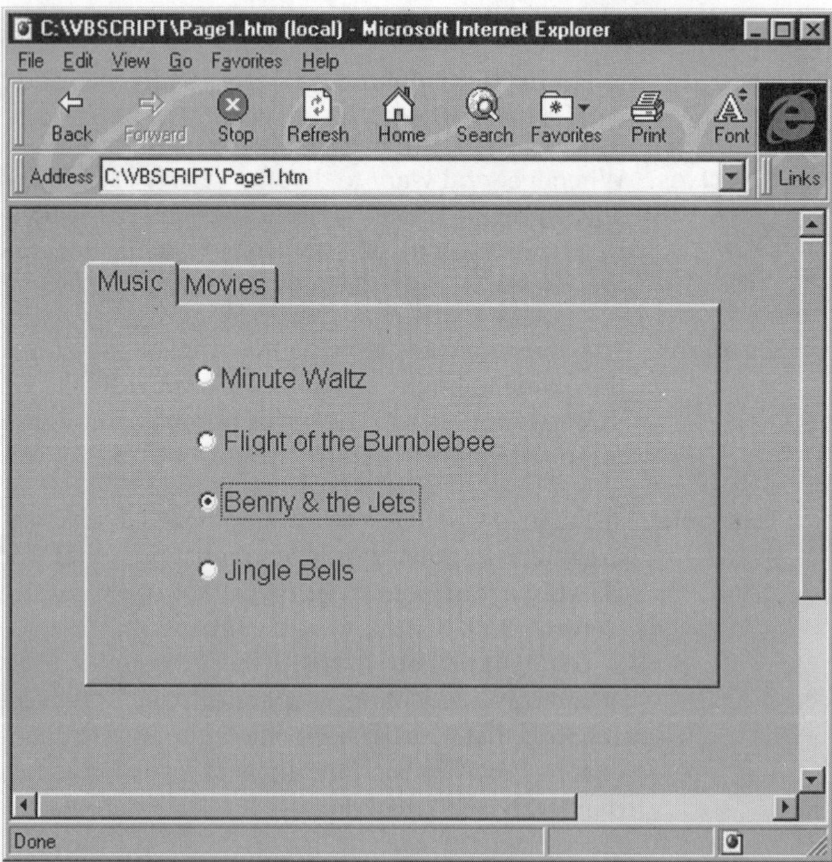

Figure T-3: When this TabStrip is first displayed, it shows only the OptionButtons. But when the user clicks on the second tab, the OptionButtons disappear.

T

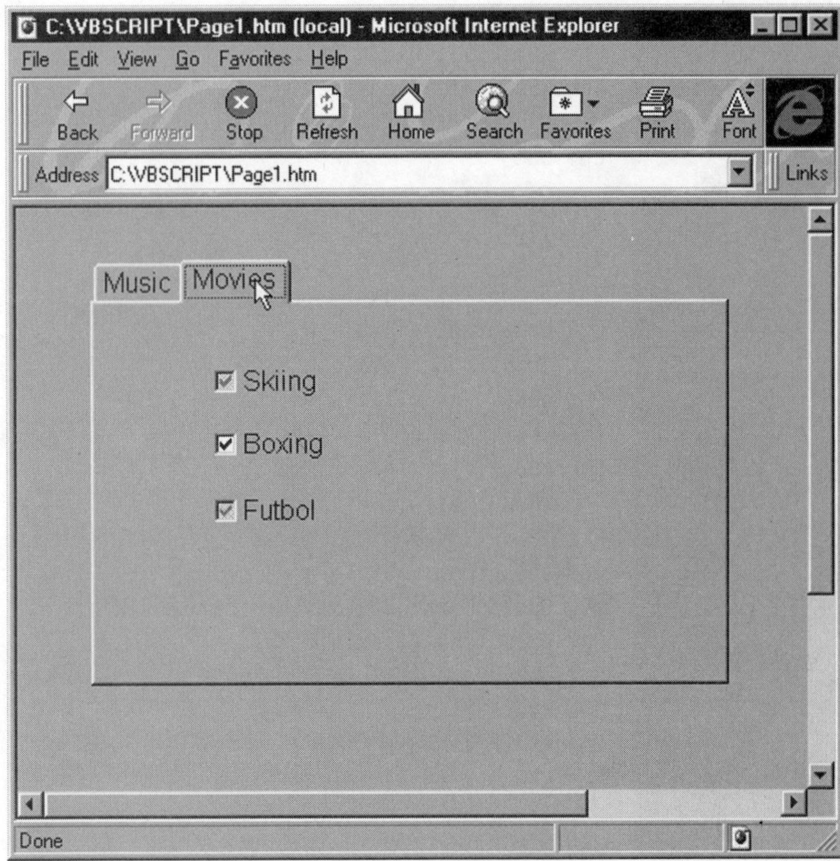

Figure T-4: The user has clicked on the MOVIES tab, so we set the group of CheckBoxes' Visible Properties to True and set the group of OptionButtons' Visible Properties to False.

Then right-click on the layout and choose View Source Code. Type in the following script, or cut it from this book's CD and paste it into the source code:

```
<SCRIPT LANGUAGE="VBScript">
<!--
Sub Window_OnLoad

TabStrip1.Tabs(0).Caption = "Music"
TabStrip1.Tabs(1).Caption = "Movies"
```

```
CheckBox1.Visible = False
CheckBox2.Visible = False
CheckBox3.Visible = False

End Sub

Sub TabStrip1_Click(Index)
If Index = 0 Then
OptionButton1.Visible = True
OptionButton2.Visible = True
OptionButton3.Visible = True
OptionButton4.Visible = True
CheckBox1.Visible = False
CheckBox2.Visible = False
CheckBox3.Visible = False
Else
OptionButton1.Visible = False
<C. OptionButton2.Visible = False
OptionButton3.Visible = False
OptionButton4.Visible = False
CheckBox1.Visible = True
CheckBox2.Visible = True
CheckBox3.Visible = True
End If
end sub

-->
</SCRIPT>
<DIV ID="as" STYLE="LAYOUT:FIXED;WIDTH:480pt;HEIGHT:350pt;">
 <OBJECT ID="TabStrip1"
  CLASSID="CLSID:EAE50EB0-4A62-11CE-BED6-00AA00611080"
STYLE="TOP:11pt;LEFT:26pt;WIDTH:290pt;HEIGHT:188pt;TABINDEX:0;ZINDEX:0;">
   <PARAM NAME="ListIndex" VALUE="0">
   <PARAM NAME="Size" VALUE="10231;6632">
   <PARAM NAME="Items" VALUE="Tab1;Tab2;">
   <PARAM NAME="TipStrings" VALUE=";;">
   <PARAM NAME="Names" VALUE="Tab1;Tab2;">
   <PARAM NAME="NewVersion" VALUE="-1">
   <PARAM NAME="TabsAllocated" VALUE="2">
   <PARAM NAME="Tags" VALUE=";;">
```

T

```
  <PARAM NAME="TabData" VALUE="2">
  <PARAM NAME="Accelerator" VALUE=";;">
  <PARAM NAME="FontName" VALUE="Arial">
  <PARAM NAME="FontHeight" VALUE="240">
  <PARAM NAME="FontCharSet" VALUE="0">
  <PARAM NAME="FontPitchAndFamily" VALUE="2">
  <PARAM NAME="FontWeight" VALUE="0">
  <PARAM NAME="TabState" VALUE="3;3">
 </OBJECT>
 <OBJECT ID="OptionButton1"
 CLASSID="CLSID:8BD21D50-EC42-11CE-9E0D-00AA006002F3"
STYLE="TOP:53pt;LEFT:76pt;WIDTH:149pt;HEIGHT:18pt;TABINDEX:1;ZINDEX:1;">
  <PARAM NAME="BackColor" VALUE="2147483663">
  <PARAM NAME="ForeColor" VALUE="2147483666">
  <PARAM NAME="DisplayStyle" VALUE="5">
  <PARAM NAME="Size" VALUE="5256;635">
  <PARAM NAME="Caption" VALUE="Minute Waltz">
  <PARAM NAME="FontName" VALUE="Arial">
  <PARAM NAME="FontHeight" VALUE="240">
  <PARAM NAME="FontCharSet" VALUE="0">
  <PARAM NAME="FontPitchAndFamily" VALUE="2">
  <PARAM NAME="FontWeight" VALUE="0">
 </OBJECT>
 <OBJECT ID="OptionButton2"
 CLASSID="CLSID:8BD21D50-EC42-11CE-9E0D-00AA006002F3"
STYLE="TOP:80pt;LEFT:77pt;WIDTH:157pt;HEIGHT:20pt;TABINDEX:2;ZINDEX:2;">
  <PARAM NAME="BackColor" VALUE="2147483663">
  <PARAM NAME="ForeColor" VALUE="2147483666">
  <PARAM NAME="DisplayStyle" VALUE="5">
  <PARAM NAME="Size" VALUE="5539;706">
  <PARAM NAME="Caption" VALUE="Flight of the Bumblebee">
  <PARAM NAME="FontName" VALUE="Arial">
  <PARAM NAME="FontHeight" VALUE="240">
  <PARAM NAME="FontCharSet" VALUE="0">
  <PARAM NAME="FontPitchAndFamily" VALUE="2">
  <PARAM NAME="FontWeight" VALUE="0">
 </OBJECT>
 <OBJECT ID="OptionButton3"
 CLASSID="CLSID:8BD21D50-EC42-11CE-9E0D-00AA006002F3"
STYLE="TOP:106pt;LEFT:77pt;WIDTH:125pt;HEIGHT:23pt;TABINDEX:3;ZINDEX:3;">
```

```
    <PARAM NAME="BackColor" VALUE="2147483663">
    <PARAM NAME="ForeColor" VALUE="2147483666">
    <PARAM NAME="DisplayStyle" VALUE="5">
    <PARAM NAME="Size" VALUE="4410;811">
    <PARAM NAME="Caption" VALUE="Benny &amp; the Jets">
    <PARAM NAME="FontName" VALUE="Arial">
    <PARAM NAME="FontHeight" VALUE="240">
    <PARAM NAME="FontCharSet" VALUE="0">
    <PARAM NAME="FontPitchAndFamily" VALUE="2">
    <PARAM NAME="FontWeight" VALUE="0">
  </OBJECT>
  <OBJECT ID="OptionButton4"
  CLASSID="CLSID:8BD21D50-EC42-11CE-9E0D-00AA006002F3"
 STYLE="TOP:136pt;LEFT:77pt;WIDTH:105pt;HEIGHT:23pt;TABINDEX:4;ZINDEX:4;">
    <PARAM NAME="BackColor" VALUE="2147483663">
    <PARAM NAME="ForeColor" VALUE="2147483666">
    <PARAM NAME="DisplayStyle" VALUE="5">
    <PARAM NAME="Size" VALUE="3704;811">
    <PARAM NAME="Caption" VALUE="Jingle Bells">
    <PARAM NAME="FontName" VALUE="Arial">
    <PARAM NAME="FontHeight" VALUE="240">
    <PARAM NAME="FontCharSet" VALUE="0">
    <PARAM NAME="FontPitchAndFamily" VALUE="2">
    <PARAM NAME="FontWeight" VALUE="0">
  </OBJECT>
  <OBJECT ID="CheckBox1"
  CLASSID="CLSID:8BD21D40-EC42-11CE-9E0D-00AA006002F3"
 STYLE="TOP:54pt;LEFT:75pt;WIDTH:116pt;HEIGHT:22pt;TABINDEX:5;ZINDEX:5;">
    <PARAM NAME="BackColor" VALUE="2147483663">
    <PARAM NAME="ForeColor" VALUE="2147483666">
    <PARAM NAME="DisplayStyle" VALUE="4">
    <PARAM NAME="Size" VALUE="4092;776">
    <PARAM NAME="Caption" VALUE="Skiing">
    <PARAM NAME="FontName" VALUE="Arial">
    <PARAM NAME="FontHeight" VALUE="240">
    <PARAM NAME="FontCharSet" VALUE="0">
    <PARAM NAME="FontPitchAndFamily" VALUE="2">
    <PARAM NAME="FontWeight" VALUE="0">
  </OBJECT>
  <OBJECT ID="CheckBox2"
```

```
 CLASSID="CLSID:8BD21D40-EC42-11CE-9E0D-00AA006002F3"
STYLE="TOP:78pt;LEFT:75pt;WIDTH:125pt;HEIGHT:29pt;TABINDEX:6;ZINDEX:6;">
  <PARAM NAME="BackColor" VALUE="2147483663">
  <PARAM NAME="ForeColor" VALUE="2147483666">
  <PARAM NAME="DisplayStyle" VALUE="4">
  <PARAM NAME="Size" VALUE="4410;1023">
  <PARAM NAME="Caption" VALUE="Boxing">
  <PARAM NAME="FontName" VALUE="Arial">
  <PARAM NAME="FontHeight" VALUE="240">
  <PARAM NAME="FontCharSet" VALUE="0">
  <PARAM NAME="FontPitchAndFamily" VALUE="2">
  <PARAM NAME="FontWeight" VALUE="0">
 </OBJECT>
 <OBJECT ID="CheckBox3"
 CLASSID="CLSID:8BD21D40-EC42-11CE-9E0D-00AA006002F3"
STYLE="TOP:106pt;LEFT:75pt;WIDTH:127pt;HEIGHT:32pt;TABINDEX:7;ZINDEX:7;">
  <PARAM NAME="BackColor" VALUE="2147483663">
  <PARAM NAME="ForeColor" VALUE="2147483666">
  <PARAM NAME="DisplayStyle" VALUE="4">
  <PARAM NAME="Size" VALUE="4480;1129">
  <PARAM NAME="Caption" VALUE="Futbol">
  <PARAM NAME="FontName" VALUE="Arial">
  <PARAM NAME="FontHeight" VALUE="240">
  <PARAM NAME="FontCharSet" VALUE="0">
  <PARAM NAME="FontPitchAndFamily" VALUE="2">
  <PARAM NAME="FontWeight" VALUE="0">
 </OBJECT>
</DIV>
```

See also OptionButton, CheckBox, ListBox

T

TABLE

NETSCAPE & INTERNET EXPLORER

Description The TABLE command includes a sophisticated, highly flexible set of commands for displaying and formatting tabular data—information intended to be vertically aligned in columns.

Alas, like other elements of HTML, there are many browsers that can at this time display only the most simple, unadorned tables. Therefore, to be safe, you might want to limit yourself to the essential commands only: TABLE, CAPTION, TR, TH, and TD.

Nonetheless, the TABLE command includes additional, optional specifications for frames; rules; alignment on such characters as the period (decimal point) and colon (:); scrollable tables with fixed headers; large tables extending across pages; varying line styles (dotted, thick, and so on); controlling the size, color, border, and background graphic of individual cells; and much more.

However, the goal of the TABLE command is to permit you to display data in columnar format flexibly, reliably, and, if you wish, easily and simply. If you want to display your tables to the majority of users at this time, stick with the basic TABLE commands.

A table is automatically formatted based on the contents you specify for your various cells, and also on the size of the user's current browser window. You can use the WIDTH and other commands to specify precise (or relative) table (or individual cell) dimensions. However, this formatting is customarily left up to the user's browser because there is so much variability, from user to user, in monitor size and window size. And, as we've been stressing, many browsers currently in use simply don't recognize TABLE commands beyond the fundamental five described above.

Tables can contain lists, paragraphs, preformatted text, other tables, and even forms. Yet tables can be easy to design. The following table is straightforward:

Figure T-5: A simple, easily constructed table.

```
<HTML>

<TABLE BORDER>
 <CAPTION>OUR FIRST TABLE</CAPTION>
 <TR><TH>Car<TH>MPG<TH>Color
 <TR><TH>Dorice<TD> 28 Highway <TD> Blue
 <TR><TH>Caprix<TD> 26 Highway <TD> Black
</TABLE>

</HTML>
```

The CAPTION command centers a caption that describes the contents of the table. TR means Table Row. TH means Table Header (rendered in bold, a descriptive label for a row or column). TD means Table Data, the informational contents of the table (as distinguished from the header labels).

Creating a Table Step-by-Step: The easiest approach to building a table is to follow these steps first, then add more specialized options (such as a background texture) later.

Announce the table, and add a border:

```
<TABLE BORDER>
```

Enter a caption (optional):

```
<CAPTION>Train Schedule</CAPTION>
```

Now enter as many rows (horizontal lines of cells) as you wish (using the TR command), including any headers (labels for rows or columns), using the TH command. If you want column labels, the first row will be made up of a series of TH commands:

```
<TR><TH>Hamburg<TH>Essen<TH>Berlin<TH>Tubingen
```

Then add the rest of the rows, filling in the data, or waiting until later to fill it in:

```
<TR><TH>9:00AM<TD> <TD> <TD> <TD>
<TR><TH>10:00AM<TD> <TD> <TD> <TD>
<TR><TH>11:00AM<TD> <TD> <TD> <TD>
<TR><TH>12:00AM<TD> <TD> <TD> <TD>
```

End the table with: </TABLE>
The whole thing, ready for viewing, looks like this:

```
<HTML>
<TABLE BORDER>
<CAPTION>Train Schedule</CAPTION>
<TR><TH><TH>Hamburg<TH>Essen<TH>Berlin<TH>Tubingin
<TR><TH>9:00AM<TD> On Time <TD> 10 Minute Delay <TD> On Time
<TD> On Time
<TR><TH>10:00AM<TD> On Time <TD> On Time <TD> On Time <TD> On
Time
<TR><TH>11:00AM<TD> 4 Minute Delay <TD> On Time <TD> On Time
<TD> On Time
<TR><TH>12:00 Noon<TD> On Time <TD> On Time <TD> On Time <TD>
On Time
</TABLE>
</HTML>
```

T

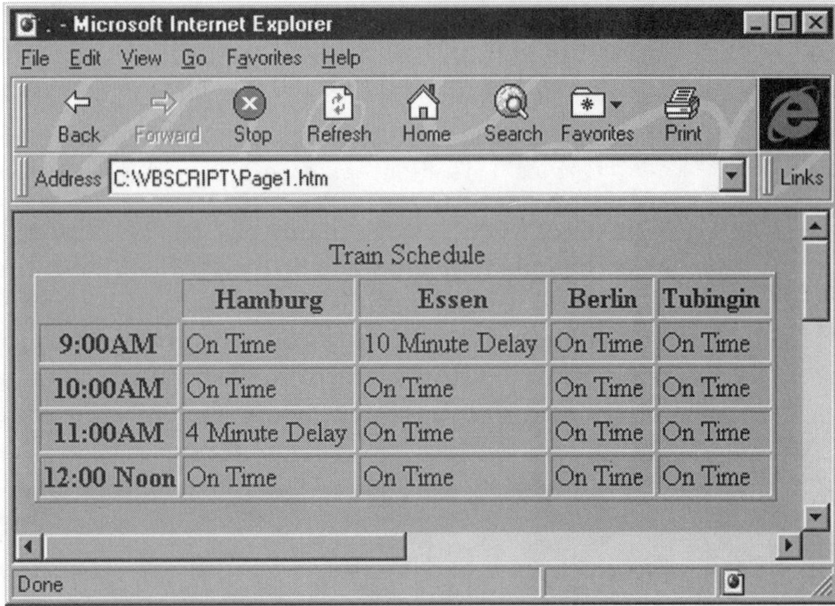

Figure T-6: The only commands you really need in order to create a complete table are TABLE, BORDER, TR, TH, and TD.

Variables There are now nearly 100 commands and modifiers associated with the TABLE command. However, many Internet browsers currently in use will not recognize these commands. Therefore, we've limited the following descriptions to those TABLE-associated modifiers that we feel are the most useful to the Web page designer, and also the most likely to be available to the majority of users.

ALIGN=LEFT, or RIGHT: Specifies that the entire table (or the text in a particular cell within the table) is to be left- or right-aligned. The default is left for TABLE, TR (row), and TD (data), but centered for headers (TH). Note that you can specify the alignment of an entire row by including the ALIGN command within the TR command: <TR ALIGN=RIGHT>, for example.

```
<TABLE BORDER=1 ALIGN=RIGHT> <TR><TD>We wanted this table
right-aligned.</TD></TR></TABLE>
```

Here we'll use the WIDTH command to make the table 50 percent of the screen width, thereby illustrating the right alignment within this cell (the cell will be larger than the text within it):

```
<TABLE BORDER=1 WIDTH=50%> <TR><TD ALIGN=RIGHT>The data in
this cell is right-aligned</TD></TR></TABLE>
```

BACKGROUND="filename or URL": Describes a graphic (.GIF or .JPG file type) that will be tiled behind the entire table, or behind the head or individual cell.

In the same directory as our document, we've got a small .GIF image called BACK1. Here we'll specify that this table should be rendered with this image texture behind it:

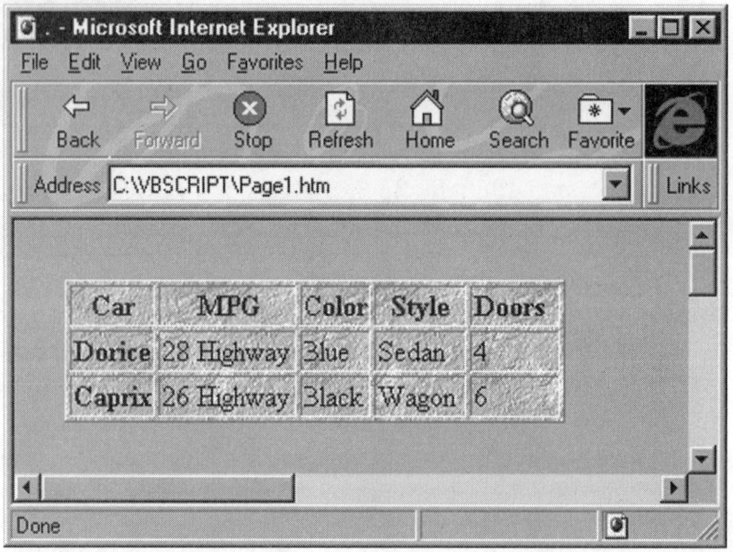

Figure T-7: You can specify a texture (or other graphic) background for your tables.

```
<HTML>
<TABLE BACKGROUND="BACK1.GIF" BORDER>
 <TR><TH>Car<TH>MPG<TH>Color<TH>Style<TH>Doors
 <TR><TH>Dorice<TD> 28 Highway <TD> Blue<TD> Sedan <TD
```

```
ALIGN=CENTER> 4
 <TR><TH>Caprix<TD> 26 Highway <TD> Black<TD> Wagon <TD
ALIGN=CENTER> 6
</TABLE>
</HTML>
```

Note that we also included <TD ALIGN=CENTER> to make the Doors column look better.

You can also specify backgrounds for individual cells:

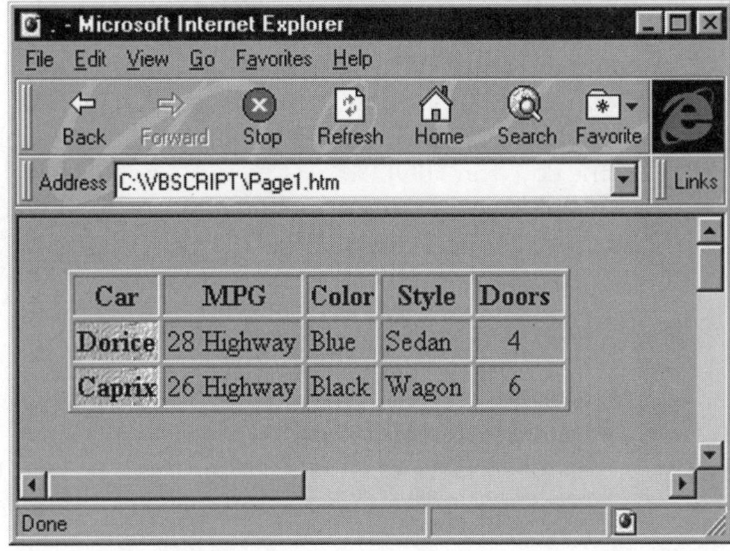

Figure T-8: You can put whatever graphic you want behind individual cells.

```
<HTML>
<TABLE BORDER>
 <TR><TH>Car<TH>MPG<TH>Color<TH>Style<TH>Doors
 <TR><TH BACKGROUND="BACK1.GIF">Dorice<TD> 28 Highway <TD>
Blue<TD> Sedan <TD ALIGN=CENTER> 4
 <TR><TH BACKGROUND="BACK1.GIF">Caprix<TD> 26 Highway <TD>
Black<TD> Wagon <TD ALIGN=CENTER> 6
</TABLE>
</HTML>
```

T

BGCOLOR=FF0000 (or RED): This specifies the background color of the table or cell. You can specify the background color, using hexadecimal numbers (see "Hex"). Essentially, the paired numbers specify the red, green, and blue content of the color. For example, if you wanted pure red, you would use FF0000; green is 00FF00; blue is 0000FF.

You can also use a set of ordinary English words, like red, instead of the hex number. The following 16 words are recognized by most browsers: black, white, green, maroon, olive, navy, purple, gray, red, yellow, blue, teal, lime, aqua, fuchsia, silver.

Internet Explorer 3.0 adds another 124 colors to this list. For a complete list of all 140 English word colors you can use, see "Many New Colors" in the entry on "BGCOLOR." For an explanation of hexadecimal, see "Hex Numbers for the Color Command" in the entry on "BODY."

Here's how to color the entire table, or, in the second example, how to color an individual cell:

```
<HTML>
<TABLE BORDER BGCOLOR=BLUE width=70%>
<TR><TD>Our table is blue</TD></TR>
</TABLE>
<TABLE BORDER width=70%>
<TR><TD>This is a default-background for a cell</TD></TR>
<TR><TD BGCOLOR=BLUE>Only this one cell is blue.</TD></TR>
</TABLE>
</HTML>
```

BORDER: Specifies whether or not there is a set of lines around the table and each cell. Border defaults to a thickness of 1 but can be made larger: BORDER=5, for example, displays very thick frames. If you leave out the BORDER command, the table will have no lines around it, or around the individual cells within it.

BORDERCOLOR=FF0000 (or RED): Describes the color (see BGCOLOR above) of the lines that enclose the table or the cells. If you put the BORDERCOLOR command within a TD or TH command (<TD BORDERCOLOR=GREEN</TD), only that cell will feature that colored border. These commands will be ignored if the BORDER command isn't also used.

BORDERCOLORLIGHT or BORDERCOLORDARK=FF0000 (or RED): Describes the color (see BGCOLOR above) of the highlights or shadows on the lines that enclose the table or the cells. If you put the BORDERCOLORLIGHT command within a TD or TH command (<TD BORDERCOLORLIGHT=GREEN</TD), only that cell will feature that colored border highlight. Likewise with BORDERCOLORDARK. These commands will be ignored if the BORDER command isn't also used.

CAPTION: Displays text, centered by default, that describes the table. CAPTION ALIGN=LEFT or RIGHT will counteract the default centered. You can use the VALIGN=BOTTOM command to position the caption at the bottom of the table (it will default to the top). Likewise, you can use the ALIGN command.

COLSPAN: (See ROWSPAN.)

HEIGHT: (See WIDTH.)

NOWRAP: This command, used within individual cells (within the TH or TD commands) prevents the contents of the cell from *wrapping*—moving down to the next line to preserve the width of the cell. Be aware that this can force the browser to display extravagantly wide cells.

In the following code we allow the browser to wrap the lengthy text in one of the cells (preserving, to some degree, a similarity between the width of all cells).

T

```
<HTML>
<TABLE WIDTH=40% HEIGHT=75% BORDER>
<TR><TH><TH>Hamburg<TH>Essen-on-the-Rhine (Some delays are
inevitable due to snow)
<TR><TH>9:00AM<TD> On Time <TD> 10 Minute Delay
<TR><TH>10:00AM<TD> On Time <TD> On Time
<TR><TH>11:00AM<TD> 4 Minute Delay <TD> On Time
<TR><TH>12:00 Noon<TD> On Time <TD> On Time
</TABLE>
</HTML>
```

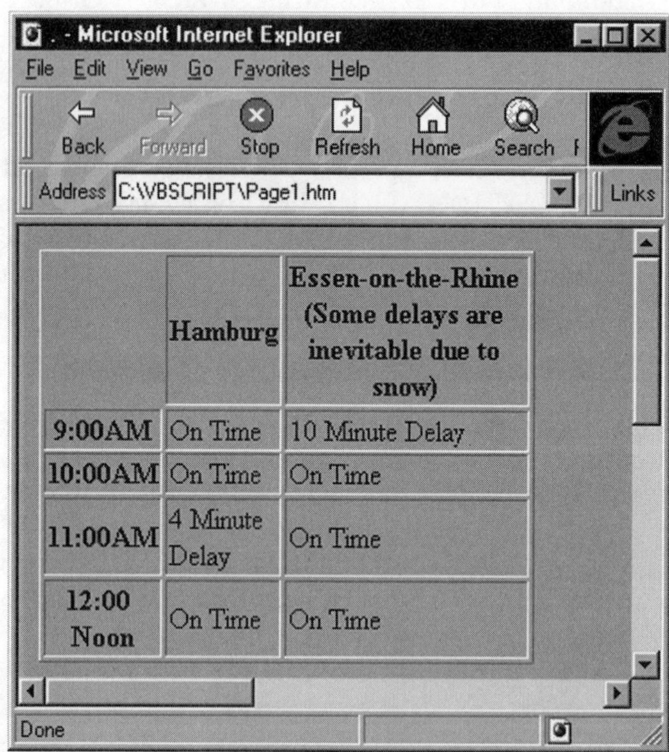

Figure T-9: Without the NOWRAP command, the browser breaks a long line into several smaller lines.

However, if we add NOWRAP, the browser is forced to display the entire line by widening the cell (and ignoring our WIDTH command in the process as well):

```
<TR><TH><TH>Hamburg<TH NOWRAP>Essen-on-the-Rhine (Some delays
are inevitable due to snow)
```

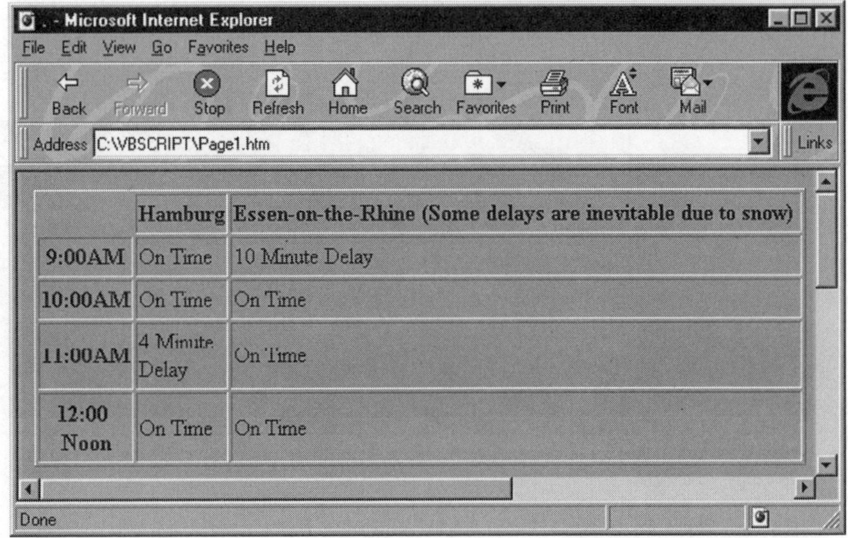

Figure T-10: With NOWRAP, the browser must size the cell to fit its contents.

However, using the <BR> command, you can specify precisely where a line break will occur, even though NOWRAP is active:

```
<TR><TH><TH>Hamburg<TH NOWRAP>Essen-on-the-Rhine<BR>(Some
delays are inevitable due to snow)
```

T

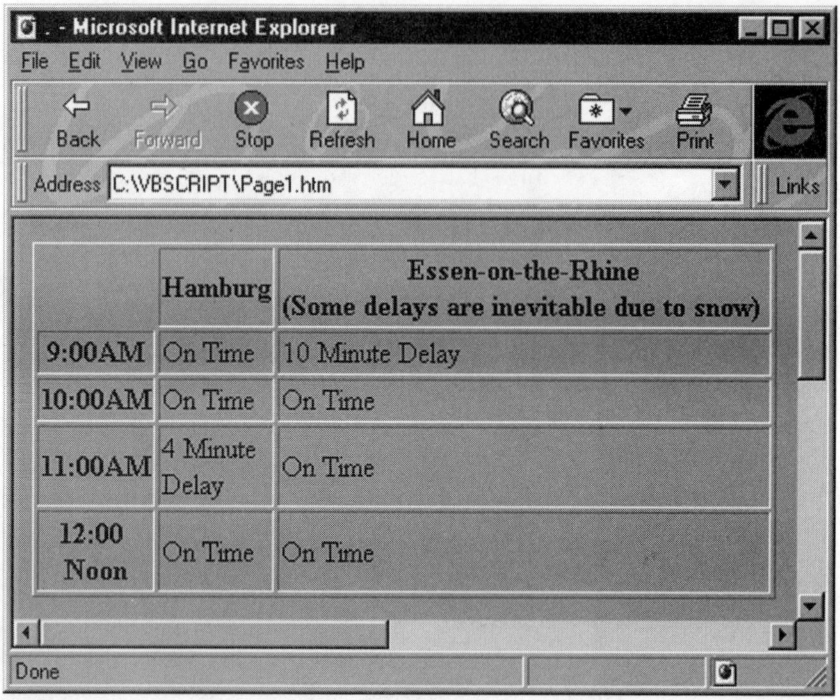

	Hamburg	Essen-on-the-Rhine (Some delays are inevitable due to snow)
9:00AM	On Time	10 Minute Delay
10:00AM	On Time	On Time
11:00AM	4 Minute Delay	On Time
12:00 Noon	On Time	On Time

Figure T-11: You have the most precise control over cell configuration when you use both the NOWRAP and BR commands.

ROWSPAN: Allows you to create large cells, cells that span more than a single row. For example, <TD ROWSPAN=5> would cause this data cell to be five rows high—no borders would be drawn within this space. See the examples later in this section. Similarly, the COLSPAN command creates unusually wide cells—spanning more than a single column. ROWSPAN and COLSPAN are used within the TH and TR commands.

VALIGN=TOP or BOTTOM: This describes how the text is aligned. Specifies that the text can be top- or bottom-aligned. The default is center-aligned.

```
<HTML>

<TABLE BORDER width=60% height=15% VALIGN=TOP>
<TR><TD>This table is top-aligned.</TD></TR></TABLE>

<TABLE BORDER width=60% height=15%>
<TR><TD VALIGN=BOTTOM>Just the text in this cell is bottom-
aligned.</TD></TR>
</TABLE>

<TABLE BORDER width=60% height=15%>
<TR><TD>This is the default center-aligned text</TD></TR>
</TABLE>

</HTML>
```

WIDTH: *Can* be specified in absolute units (pixels or en spaces), but as usual you should respect the fact that the size of users' monitors (and browser windows) varies considerably. Therefore, it's best to specify the WIDTH of your tables in *relative* terms (%, as a percent of the browser window width).

This example will cause the table to stretch (or shrink) itself to fill horizontally 100 percent of the browser window (minus margins) and 75 percent of the height of the window. Also notice the thick border:

```
<HTML>
<TABLE WIDTH=100% HEIGHT=75% BORDER=8>

<TR><TH><TH>Hamburg<TH>Essen
<TR><TH>9:00AM<TD> On Time <TD> 10 Minute Delay
<TR><TH>10:00AM<TD> On Time <TD> On Time
<TR><TH>11:00AM<TD> 4 Minute Delay <TD> On Time
<TR><TH>12:00 Noon<TD> On Time <TD> On Time
</TABLE>
</HTML>
```

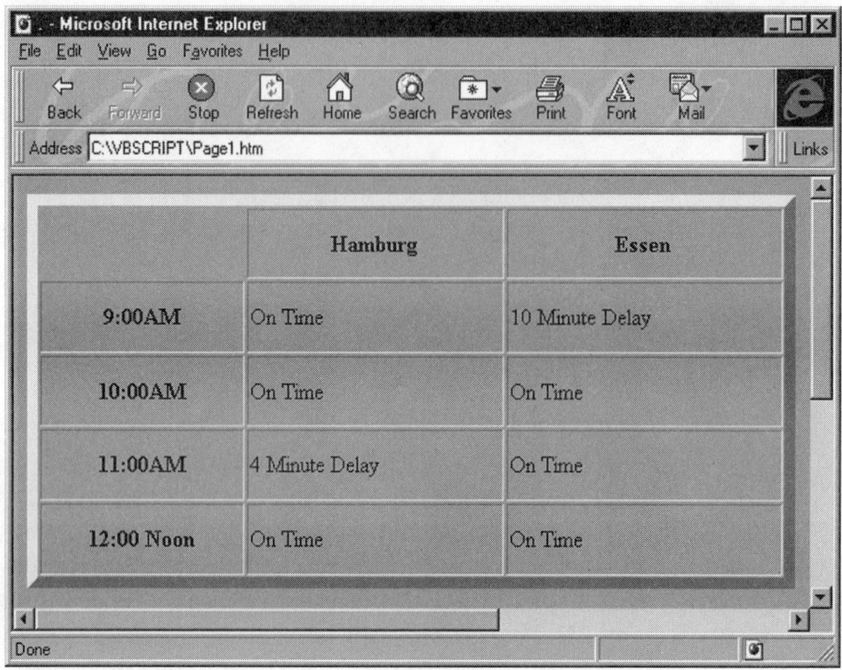

Figure T-12: Here we've specified that the table should be as wide as the browser window, and 75 percent as high. Note the thick border, too.

Uses

- Display tables.
- Organize information into a grid format. Useful for everything from product comparisons to TV listings.
- Display spreadsheet or database-type information.

Used with

Can be enclosed by

<BANNER>, <BODY>, <BODYTEXT>, <DD>, <DIV>, <FIGTEXT>, <FN>, <FORM>, <LI>, <NOTE>, <TD>, <TH>

Can enclose

<CAPTION>, <TR>

Cautions

- Many people are currently using browsers such as Netscape 2.0 and Internet Explorer 3.0, which do not fully support tables. Such commands as BACKGROUND might well distort your intended formatting or fail to display the table entirely. Therefore, at this time, you should create conservative tables. For many users, the only table commands recognized are TABLE, CAPTION, TR, TH, and TD.

- There is a precedence order to some TABLE commands. Commands within <TH></TH> or <TD></TD> pairs take precedence (override) commands enclosed within <TR> and <TABLE>. For example, <TABLE BGCOLOR=BLUE><TH BGCOLOR=RED></TH></TABLE> would render the background of the table in blue but change the background of that particular header to red.
- Cells need not be filled with data. They can remain empty (see the upper left cell in Figure T-12). To create an empty cell, just leave out any data or header information following a TD or TH command. Here the first cell is blank:

```
<TR><TH><TH> First Heading<TH> Second Heading
<TR><TD><TD> First Data<TD> Second Data
```

The blank cells are created by using <TH><TH> or <TD><TD>.

- Text within header cells <TH> are centered by default, but all data cells <TD> are displayed flush-left by default. You can override these defaults by using the ALIGN command.
- Leave the document's background color alone. Tables look best when displayed against the gray used by default by Netscape and Internet Explorer. Against a white background, for example, the default highlight will disappear—making the frames and borders look peculiar.
- If you do change the document's background to some other color, you'll want to adjust the BORDERCOLOR, BORDERCOLORLIGHT, and BORDERCOLORDARK to work well with your new color.

Example #1

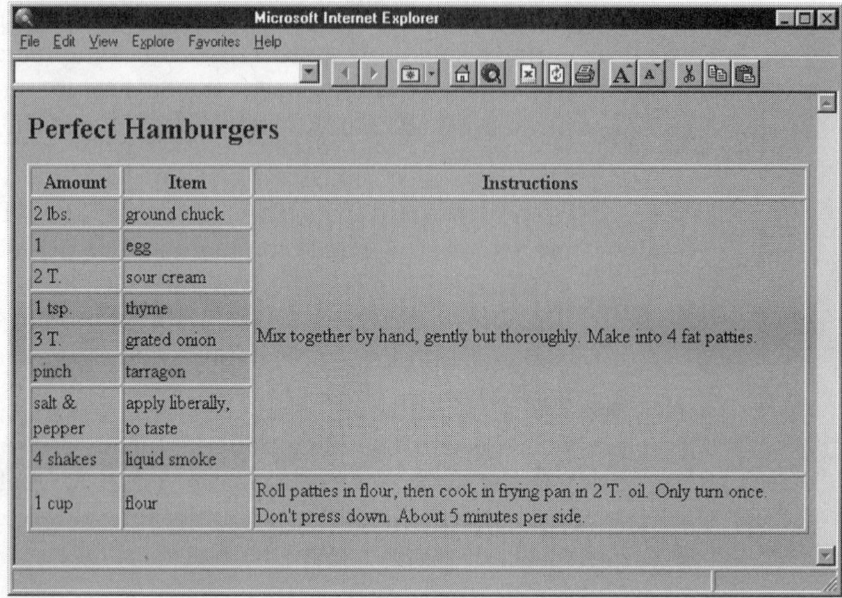

Amount	Item	Instructions
2 lbs.	ground chuck	Mix together by hand, gently but thoroughly. Make into 4 fat patties.
1	egg	
2 T.	sour cream	
1 tsp.	thyme	
3 T.	grated onion	
pinch	tarragon	
salt & pepper	apply liberally, to taste	
4 shakes	liquid smoke	
1 cup	flour	Roll patties in flour, then cook in frying pan in 2 T. oil. Only turn once. Don't press down. About 5 minutes per side.

Figure T-13: This illustrates a variety of table options and features.

```
<HTML>
<H2>Perfect Hamburgers</H2>

<TABLE BORDER>

<TR ALIGN=CENTER><TH>Amount</TH><TH>Item</
TH><TH>Instructions</TH></TR>

<TR> <TD>2 lbs.</TD> <TD>ground chuck</TD>
<TD ROWSPAN=8>
 Mix together by hand, gently but thoroughly. Make into 4 fat
patties.</TD> </TR>

<TR BGCOLOR=AQUA><TD>1</TD> <TD> egg </TD></TR>
<TR><TD>2 T.</TD> <TD> sour cream</TD></TR>
<TR BGCOLOR=AQUA> <TD>1 tsp.</TD> <TD> thyme</TD></TR>
<TR><TD>3 T.</TD> <TD> grated onion</TD> </TR>
<TR BGCOLOR=AQUA> <TD>pinch</TD> <TD> tarragon</TD></TR>
<TR><TD>salt & pepper</TD> <TD> apply liberally, to taste</TD>
```

```
</TR>
<TR BGCOLOR=AQUA> <TD>4 shakes</TD> <TD> liquid smoke</TD>
</TR>
<TR> <TD> 1 cup</TD> <TD> flour </TD>
<TD> Roll patties in flour, then cook in frying pan in 2 T.
oil.
 Only turn once. Don't press down. About 5 minutes per side.
</TD></TR>

</TABLE>
</HTML>
```

There are several features to note in this example. First, we avoided using a caption, which often looks feebly small, particularly when used with a large table. Instead, we used a level-2 headline. Then, for the labels (the TH header fields), we centered them. That just looks better, and, along with their boldface text, serves to set them off from the data fields below.

Then comes the body of our table—eight rows. It's often helpful to the reader to alternate colors in rows, especially if the rows are wide. This assists the eye in staying on the row. That kind of color coding is frequently seen in, for instance, television listings. This coloring is accomplished by inserting the BGCOLOR=AQUA command within every other row command <TR>.

Finally, to make the instructions span several rows (indicating that those instructions apply to that many ingredients), we use the ROWSPAN command. This tells the browser not to insert borders until, in our example, eight rows have been displayed.

Example #2 ***Border Adjustments***

Here we'll illustrate several recent (HTML 3) additions to the TABLE command.

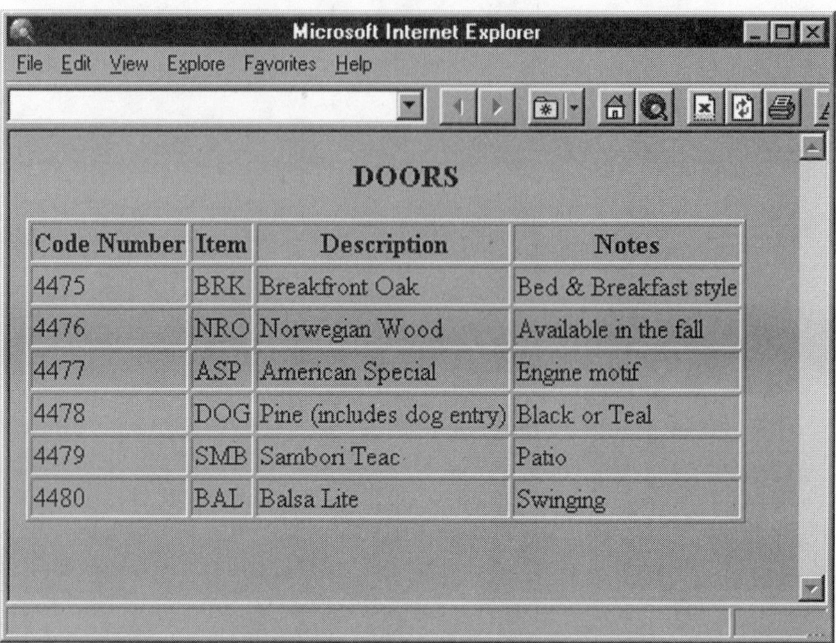

Code Number	Item	Description	Notes
4475	BRK	Breakfront Oak	Bed & Breakfast style
4476	NRO	Norwegian Wood	Available in the fall
4477	ASP	American Special	Engine motif
4478	DOG	Pine (includes dog entry)	Black or Teal
4479	SMB	Sambori Teac	Patio
4480	BAL	Balsa Lite	Swinging

Figure T-14: This table is typical. Note that the text in each cell is uncomfortably flush against the cell borders.

```
<HTML>
<H1 ALIGN=CENTER>DOORS</H1>
<TABLE BORDER>
<TR ALIGN=CENTER><TH>Code Number</TH><TH>Item</TH>
<TH>Description</TH><TH>Notes</TH></TR>
<TR><TD>4475</TD><TD>BRK</TD><TD>Breakfront Oak</TD>
<TD>Bed & Breakfast style</TD>
<TR><TD>4476</TD><TD>NRO</TD><TD>Norwegian Wood</TD>
<TD>Available in the fall</TD>
<TR><TD>4477</TD> <TD>ASP</TD><TD>American Special</TD>
<TD>Engine motif</TD>
<TR><TD>4478</TD><TD>DOG</TD><TD>Pine (includes dog entry)
</TD><TD>Black or Teal</TD>
<TR> <TD>4479</TD> <TD>SMB</TD><TD>Sambori Teac</TD>
```

```
<TD>Patio</TD>
<TR> <TD>4480</TD> <TD>BAL</TD><TD>Balsa Lite</TD>
<TD>Swinging</TD>
</TABLE>
</HTML>
```

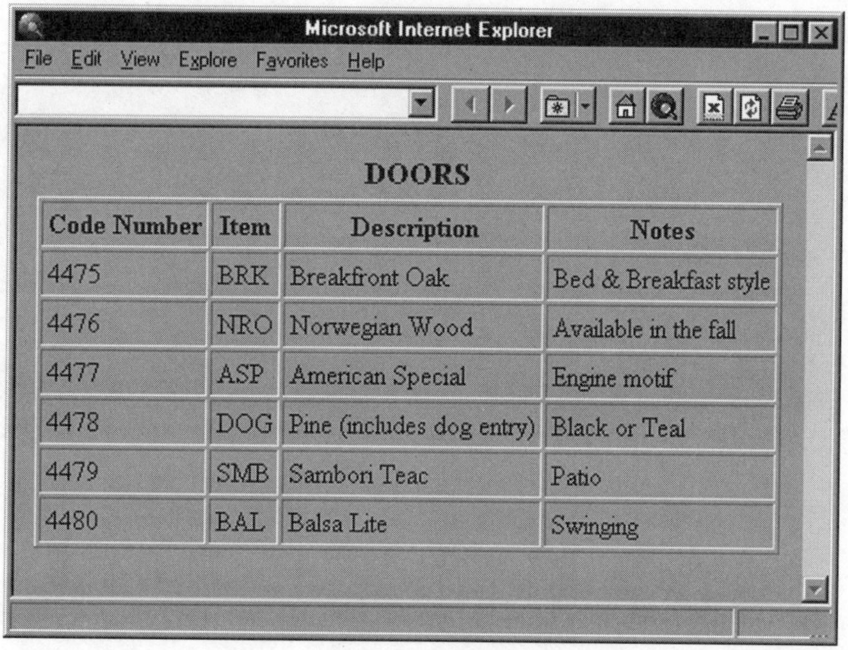

Microsoft Internet Explorer

File Edit View Explore Favorites Help

DOORS

Code Number	Item	Description	Notes
4475	BRK	Breakfront Oak	Bed & Breakfast style
4476	NRO	Norwegian Wood	Available in the fall
4477	ASP	American Special	Engine motif
4478	DOG	Pine (includes dog entry)	Black or Teal
4479	SMB	Sambori Teac	Patio
4480	BAL	Balsa Lite	Swinging

Figure T-15: Now that we've added a CELLPADDING command, the frame of each cell is slightly separated from the text.

As you can see in Figure T-15, we've made a slight adjustment to the spacing around the text in each cell. This improves the overall look of the table and also assists readability. Here's the command that added three pixels of space around each text item in the entire table.

We changed:

```
<TABLE BORDER>
```

To:

```
<TABLE BORDER CELLPADDING=3>
```

The CELLPADDING command provides fine control over the interior spacing of each cell. Similarly, you can adjust the thickness of the borders of your table by using the CELLSPACING command:

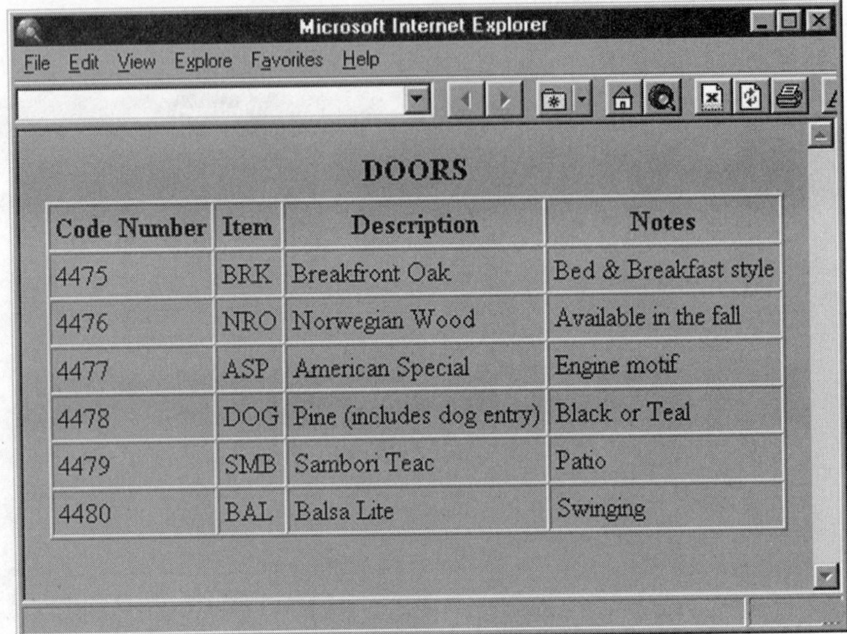

Code Number	Item	Description	Notes
4475	BRK	Breakfront Oak	Bed & Breakfast style
4476	NRO	Norwegian Wood	Available in the fall
4477	ASP	American Special	Engine motif
4478	DOG	Pine (includes dog entry)	Black or Teal
4479	SMB	Sambori Teac	Patio
4480	BAL	Balsa Lite	Swinging

Figure T-16: We've reduced the borders to the near-minimum size (1 pixel, plus a pixel for a line of shading and another pixel for a line of highlighting).

In Figure T-16, you see borders that are one pixel less than the default two pixels (plus one pixel each for shading and highlighting). You use the CELLSPACING command like this:

```
<TABLE BORDER CELLPADDING=3 CELLSPACING=1>
```

If you set CELLSPACING to 0, you remove the border, leaving only the naked shadow and highlight lines as a frame around each cell. This actually looks quite good, if a bit delicate.

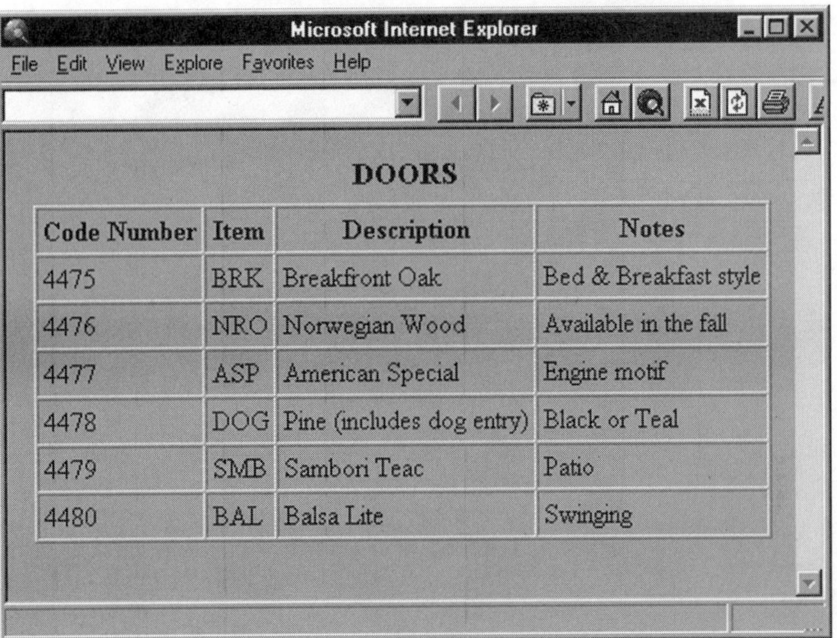
Microsoft Internet Explorer
File Edit View Explore Favorites Help

DOORS

Code Number	Item	Description	Notes
4475	BRK	Breakfront Oak	Bed & Breakfast style
4476	NRO	Norwegian Wood	Available in the fall
4477	ASP	American Special	Engine motif
4478	DOG	Pine (includes dog entry)	Black or Teal
4479	SMB	Sambori Teac	Patio
4480	BAL	Balsa Lite	Swinging

Figure T-17: With CELLSPACING set to zero, you get this subtle effect.

Of course you can set CELLSPACING to create fat borders with a value of 5 or 8 or something. This has the same effect as changing the BORDER element, but BORDER adjusts the highlight and shadow lines (and only on the frame around the entire table, not within individual cells). CELLSPACING leaves the highlight and shadow lines at their original one-pixel width, no matter how fat you make the border proper.

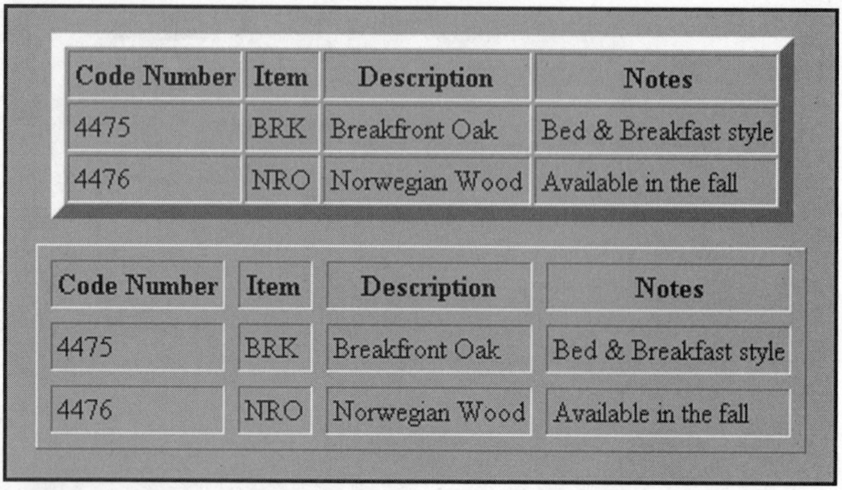

Code Number	Item	Description	Notes
4475	BRK	Breakfront Oak	Bed & Breakfast style
4476	NRO	Norwegian Wood	Available in the fall

Code Number	Item	Description	Notes
4475	BRK	Breakfront Oak	Bed & Breakfast style
4476	NRO	Norwegian Wood	Available in the fall

Figure T-18: Two table styles. Fattening a table frame with the BORDER command thickens only the shadow and highlight elements (above). With the CELLSPACING command (below), only the frames are thickened.

Example #3 ***Frame & Rule Adjustments***

You can also selectively remove individual frame elements (the top and bottom, for example) with the FRAME command. This doesn't affect the interior cells, only the frame around the entire table. To alter interior cell borders, see the RULES command below. Here's how FRAME is used:

```
<HTML>
<H4>FRAME=LHS </H4>
<TABLE BORDER FRAME=LHS CELLSPACING=1 CELLPADDING=3>
<TR ALIGN=CENTER><TH>Code</TH><TH>Item</TH><TH>Desc</
TH><TH>Notes</TH></TR>
<TR> <TD>4475</TD> <TD>BRK</TD><TD>Oak</TD><TD>Bedstyle</TD>
<TR> <TD>4476</TD> <TD>NRO</TD><TD>Wood</TD><TD>Available</TD>
</TABLE>
</HTML>
```

The FRAME=LHS command displays only the left-hand side of the table's outer frame. Your other options, illustrated in Figure T-19, are: VOID (no frame), ABOVE (no bottom frame), BELOW (no top frame), HSIDES (no left or right side), VSIDES (no top or bottom), and RHS (no left side).

FRAME=VOID

Code	Item	Desc	Notes
4475	BRK	Oak	Bedstyle
4476	NRO	Wood	Available

FRAME=ABOVE

Code	Item	Desc	Notes
4475	BRK	Oak	Bedstyle
4476	NRO	Wood	Available

FRAME=LHS

Code	Item	Desc	Notes
4475	BRK	Oak	Bedstyle
4476	NRO	Wood	Available

FRAME=BELOW

Code	Item	Desc	Notes
4475	BRK	Oak	Bedstyle
4476	NRO	Wood	Available

FRAME=RHS

Code	Item	Desc	Notes
4475	BRK	Oak	Bedstyle
4476	NRO	Wood	Available

FRAME=HSIDES

Code	Item	Desc	Notes
4475	BRK	Oak	Bedstyle
4476	NRO	Wood	Available

FRAME=VSIDES

Code	Item	Desc	Notes
4475	BRK	Oak	Bedstyle
4476	NRO	Wood	Available

Figure T-19: The FRAME command allows you to selectively eliminate portions of a table's outer frame.

The RULES command allows control over the interior cell borders.

```
<H4>RULES="NONE"</H4>
<TABLE BORDER RULES="NONE" CELLSPACING=1 CELLPADDING=3>
<TR ALIGN=CENTER><TH>Code</TH><TH>Item</TH><TH>Desc</
TH><TH>Notes</TH></TR>
<TR> <TD>4475</TD> <TD>BRK</TD><TD>Oak</TD><TD>Bedstyle</TD>
<TR> <TD>4476</TD> <TD>NRO</TD><TD>Wood</TD><TD>Available</TD>
</TABLE>
```

Your options with the RULES command are NONE (no interior cell borders), ALL and BASIC (the default, all cell borders displayed), ROWS (horizontal cell borders only), and COLS (vertical cell borders only).

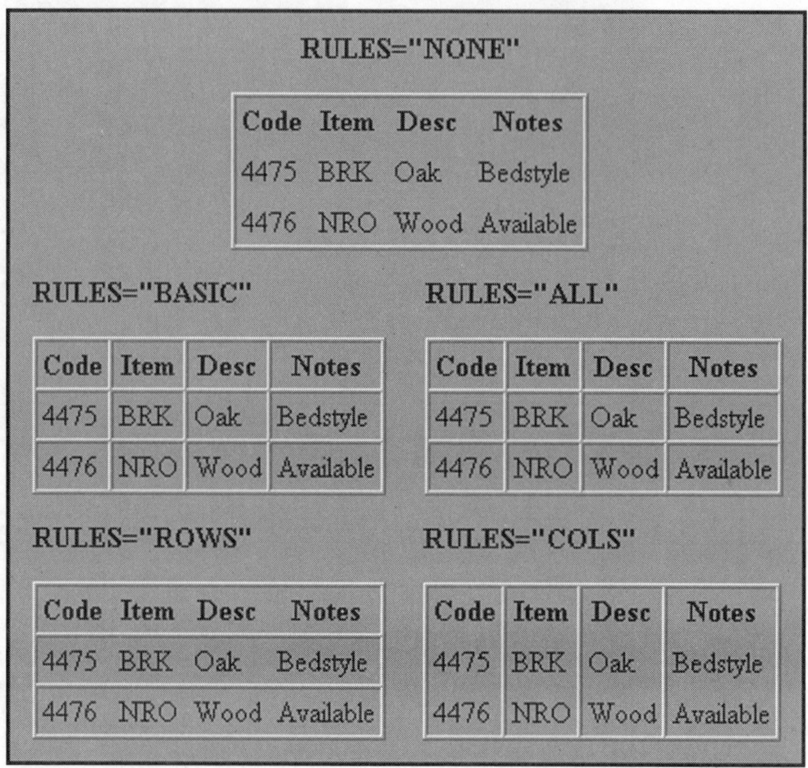

RULES="NONE"

Code	Item	Desc	Notes
4475	BRK	Oak	Bedstyle
4476	NRO	Wood	Available

RULES="BASIC"

Code	Item	Desc	Notes
4475	BRK	Oak	Bedstyle
4476	NRO	Wood	Available

RULES="ALL"

Code	Item	Desc	Notes
4475	BRK	Oak	Bedstyle
4476	NRO	Wood	Available

RULES="ROWS"

Code	Item	Desc	Notes
4475	BRK	Oak	Bedstyle
4476	NRO	Wood	Available

RULES="COLS"

Code	Item	Desc	Notes
4475	BRK	Oak	Bedstyle
4476	NRO	Wood	Available

Figure T-20: The RULES command gives you control over the cell borders within a table.

Example #4 ***Empty Cells***

Cells containing no data or header information (empty <TD></TD> or <TR></TR> pairs) are, by default, drawn without any borders, as shown in Figure T-21.

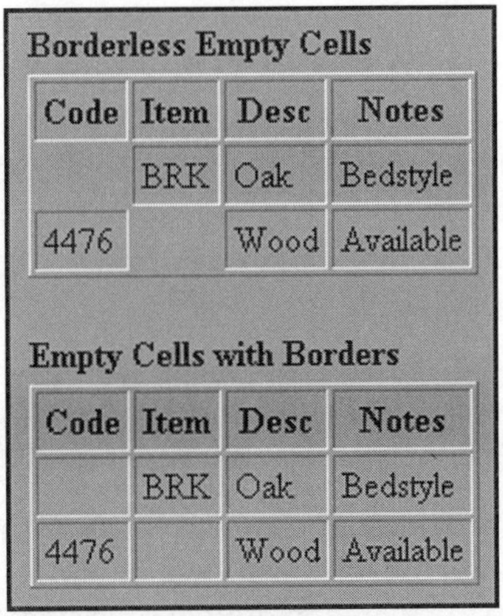

Borderless Empty Cells

Code	Item	Desc	Notes
	BRK	Oak	Bedstyle
4476		Wood	Available

Empty Cells with Borders

Code	Item	Desc	Notes
	BRK	Oak	Bedstyle
4476		Wood	Available

Figure T-21: By default, an empty cell is displayed with no border (above). This often looks crude, a strange protrusion in the context of all the other normal, concave cells. It can even be mistaken for a Command Button the user could click on. To cure this, put a non-breaking space code into empty cells.

```
<H4>Empty Cells with Borders</H4>
<TABLE BORDER CELLPADDING=3>
<TR ALIGN=CENTER><TH>Code</TH><TH>Item</TH><TH>Desc</TH>
<TH>Notes</TH></TR>
<TR><TD> </TD><TD>BRK</TD><TD>Oak</TD><TD>Bedstyle</TD>
<TR><TD>4476</TD><TD> </TD><TD>Wood</TD><TD>Available</TD>
</TABLE>
```

Some browsers provide a border around an empty cell if you merely press the spacebar, inserting a blank character or two within the cell. However, Internet Explorer ignores these blank characters. To be certain that a blank cell will be given a border, use the special code for a non-breaking space: . For more on these character codes, see "Special Characters."

See also TAB

Tan

VBSCRIPT FUNCTION

Description You use Tan to give you the tangent of an angle expressed in radians. The argument can be a number or a numeric Variable or a numeric Constant.

Variables

```
MsgBox Tan(x)
F = Tan(.3)
```

Uses Trigonometry

Cautions If the Variable or Constant you use with Tan is an integer or single-precision Variable subtype, the result will be single-precision. All other data types are calculated in double-precision. (See Variables.)

Example

```
MsgBox Tan(.01745)
```

See also Atn, Cos, Sin

TD

HTML

Description A Table Data command indicates a cell within a table that's filled with text or numeric data (as opposed to a cell filled with a label—a header, designated by TH).

See Table, HTML

Text

ACTIVEX

See Properties

TextAlign, TextColumn, TextLength

ACTIVEX

See Properties

TEXTAREA

HTML

Description This command creates a mini word processor on your page, a text area, into which you can put multiline text, or from which you can gather the user's typed-in multiline text.

TEXTAREA is similar to the TextBox (see TEXT under "FORM"), but instead of being limited to a single line, TEXTAREA permits multiple lines of text to be entered by the user or displayed to the user. Horizontal and Vertical ScrollBars are available on the TEXTAREA text box, so the user can scroll in either direction if the text overflows the visible area of the box.

Normally, in HTML, you just type in what you want the user to see—adding various formatting commands such as <H> or <SMALL> and so on. However, what if you want to display text that can change? What if you want to display an immediate *reaction* to something the user types or selects? There are two ways to do this: load it in from your URL, or create it dynamically by programming it and then assigning the VALUE to the NAME of your TEXTAREA.

You can provide contents for TEXTAREA by just typing things in, when designing your page, between the <TEXTAREA> and </TEXTAREA> commands. Or you can use the VALUE command to assign text dynamically when the page is displayed.

T

Variables ***Options Used With TEXTAREA:***

COLS: The number of columns (how many characters appear in a single line). This determines the width of the TEXTAREA.

DISABLED: Prevents the user from making any changes to the TEXTAREA contents. Use this when you merely want to display text to the user, rather than gather input from the user.

NAME: The TEXTAREA's Variable name. In other words, the contents of the TEXTAREA are identified by the value Property of the NAME Variable. This allows you to send the information—whatever the user typed into the text area—back to your home site or wherever you're going to process the information. You can also use *NAME*.VALUE to *assign* the text that will be displayed in the TEXTAREA. This is a way of displaying information to the user dynamically—while the page is being viewed. You can also use it to provide default text (so the user need not type something in, if what you display is the common response). In programming terminology, you can *set* or *read* this NAME Variable.

ROWS: The number of rows (lines of text) that will appear within the TEXTAREA. This determines the height of the TEXTAREA.

Uses

- Accept multiline text from the user, or display multiline text to the user.
- Acts as a simple mini word processor.

Cautions The TEXTAREA command is used within the FORM command.

Example

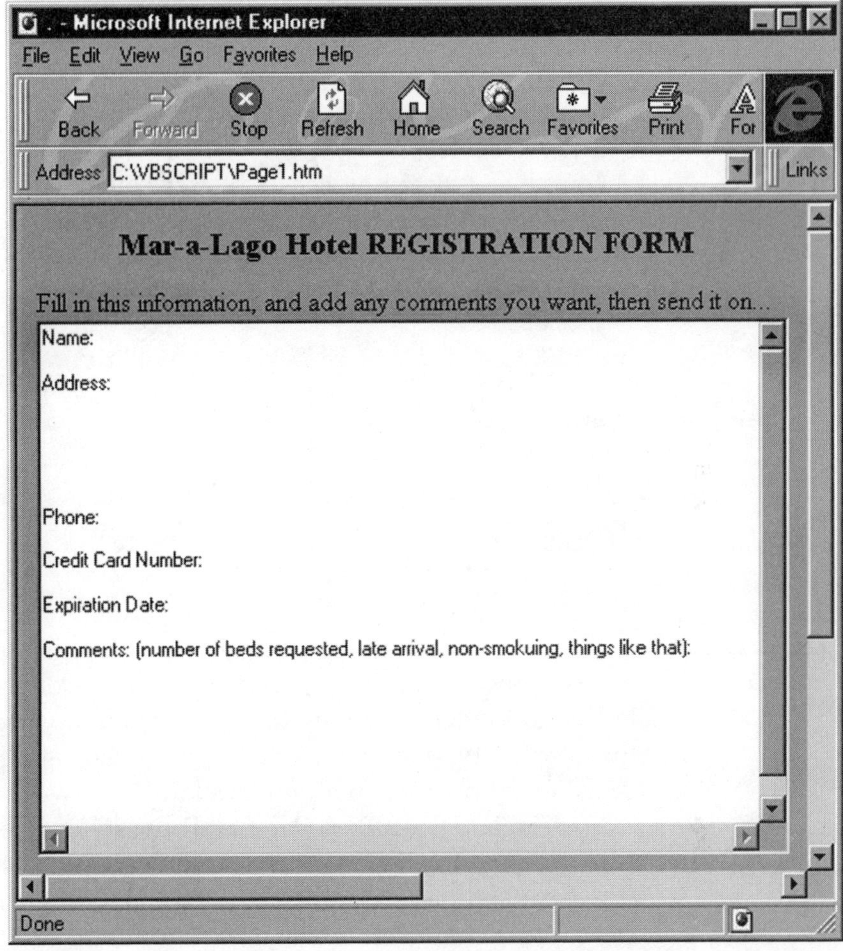

Figure T-22: An alternative to the usual fixed-field data-entry format, this free-form TEXTAREA allows users the liberty to fill in the information as they wish.

```
<HTML>
<H3 ALIGN=CENTER>Mar-a-Lago Hotel REGISTRATION FORM</H3>
Fill in this information, and add any comments you want, then
send it on...
<BR>
<FORM METHOD="POST" ACTION="/cgi/res">
<TEXTAREA NAME="thestory" ROWS="22" COLS="90">
Name:
```

```
Address:

Phone:
Credit Card Number:
Expiration Date:
Comments: (number of beds requested, late arrival, non-
smoking, things like that):

</TEXTAREA>
</FORM>
</HTML>
```

See also FORM

TextBox

ACTIVEX CONTROL

Description TextBox is a simple, though surprisingly functional, word processor.

It responds to all the usual editing keys—Del, Ins, Backspace, PgUp, and PgDn. It automatically "word wraps" (detects when the user has typed to the right side of the box and moves the word down to the next line without breaking it in two).

You can add ScrollBars (via that Property of a TextBox). By manipulating the SelText and related Properties, you can create a cut, copy, and paste feature. By using the KeyDown Event, you can capture characters as the user types them and thus add special, additional features triggered by Ctrl or Alt or Function keys.

You cannot add a selective boldface or italics feature, however, or include varying typefaces or font sizes. These Properties are set for the entire TextBox at once, so you cannot mix and match them in the text inside the box.

There is, however, a more advanced TextBox (TB) Control—the RichTextBox (RTB). The RTB Control does permit individualized formatting: italics, boldface, various typefaces and typesizes, bulleted lists, even color. You can import and export .RTF files, thereby retaining the formatting (most word processors recognize the RTF codes). In Windows, the user can drag an .RTF file from Explorer or a folder right into the RTB. And last but not least, the RTB has a useful built-in find utility.

However, the RTB isn't yet offered as an authenticated, safe ActiveX Control. So we'll confine ourselves here to a description of the classic TextBox Control.

Variables Because a TextBox is a Control, you can adjust its Variables, its qualities, in the Properties Window while designing your script.

OR (to make changes to its Properties while the script is running):

```
TextBox1.Text = "Please enter your name..."
```

OR (to make changes by using a Variable while the script is running):

```
N = "Howard Slow"
TextBox1.Text = N
```

OR

```
N = 700
TextBox1.Width = N
```

OR (to set a limit on the number of characters the user can type into a TextBox):

```
TextBox1.MaxLength = 30
```

(You must adjust some of the Properties of a TextBox, such as MultiLine, from the Properties Window. They cannot be changed while the script is running.)

The TextBox has more Properties than any other ActiveX Control at this time: 44. Many of them are the same as the Properties of other Controls, such as Width. For details about these common Properties, Events, and Methods, see the entries for "Properties," "Events," and "Methods."

However, here we'll examine some of the Properties that are unique to the TextBox (or to the TextBox and the TextBox portion of a ComboBox).

AutoTab is a Property of a TextBox or a ComboBox (ComboBoxes have a "TextBox zone" within which the user can type). You can restrict the number of characters a user can type into a box by setting the MaxLength Property. AutoTab, if set to True, automatically moves the focus to the next Control in the tab order once the user has typed in the MaxLength number of characters. AutoTab defaults to False (off). For example, say that you've got a set of TextBoxes that the user must fill in. One of them is for the state abbreviation, like CA or NC or NY. You can make things more convenient for the user by setting that TextBox's MaxLength to 2, then turn on the AutoTab feature. When users type in their state abbreviation, the cursor is automatically moved to the TextBox for the ZIP Code (which is set to 5 MaxLength), and so on. This avoids the necessity for users to click (or tab) on each TextBox in turn to give it focus so they can type in the next item of data.

AutoWordSelect is a Property of a TextBox or a ComboBox. This same feature is found in Word for Windows (from the Tools menu, click on Options, then Edit). With AutoWordSelect on, when the user positions the "insertion point" (the typing cursor) within a word, then drags the mouse to select some characters within that word (or additional words), the selection will jump from word to word. Put another way, selection is accomplished by chunks, by whole words, rather than by individual characters. AutoWordSelect defaults to True (on).

When the user presses the Tab key to move to a TextBox or the TextBox section of a ComboBox, the EnterFieldBehavior Property determines how the contents are selected. The default is to *select* (reverse text to white on black) the entire contents. If you change this Property to 1, the previous selection status of the box remains in effect. In other words, if the user had left a particular paragraph selected when the TextBox lost the focus, tabbing back to restore focus would leave that same paragraph selected.


```
TextBox1.EnterFieldBehavior = 0 'the default
TextBox1.EnterFieldBehavior = 1 'selection unchanged.
```

This Property is ignored if you use the SetFocus Method to move the focus to a Control. In that case, the contents are not selected, and the insertion cursor is moved to the end of the text.

The EnterKeyBehavior Property specifies what happens when the user presses the Enter key while typing in a TextBox.

```
TextBox3.EnterKeyBehavior = True
TextBox3.EnterKeyBehavior = False 'the default
```

If you change this Property to True, when the user presses Enter, the insertion point cursor moves down one line to start a new paragraph (just as it would in a word processor). However, if you leave the Property False, pressing Enter causes the focus to move to the next Control in the tab order (just as if the user had pressed the Tab key).

Warning

These specifications sound backward, and we cannot test them because this Property is not currently working. Be sure to test this behavior in a script before sending it out onto the Web.

EnterKeyBehavior interacts with the MultiLine Property. If MultiLine is False, pressing Enter always moves the focus to the next Control (there's only one line in the TextBox anyway, so there's nowhere to move down to). Also, if the user presses Ctrl+Enter with MultiLine set to True (False is the default), the TextBox always moves down to a new line. Also see the TabKeyBehavior and AutoTab Properties.

The HideSelection Property determines whether any selected text (in a TextBox or ComboBox) remains highlighted (that is, remains selected at all) when the box loses the focus. If you drag the mouse to select some words in a TextBox, then click on a CommandButton or some other Control, the focus moves off the TextBox and the text is deselected. Clicking back in the TextBox does not restore the selection. This is the default.

To preserve a selection when focus leaves a Control, do this:

```
TextBox1.HideSelection = False
```

Also see the EnterFieldBehavior Property described above.

If the IntegralHeight Property of a TextBox or ListBox is set to True (the default) then the box will resize itself to display a full line or, for the ListBox, a full row. IntegralHeight is to the height what the AutoSize Property is to width. In other words, IntegralHeight prevents text from being cut off vertically.

Figure T-23: The TextBox on the top is permitted to cut off the characters because its IntegralHeight Property is set to False.

Applying to ComboBoxes and TextBoxes, the MaxLength Property determines how many characters the user can type into the Control. If you leave it at the default 0, there is no limit imposed (other than the computer's memory, of course).

The SelectionMargin Property of a TextBox (or the TextBox portion of a ComboBox) determines whether clicking in the left margin selects text (highlights it for copying, cutting, dragging, or other manipulations). In Word for Windows you can click in the left margin to select a line. Hold down Shift to select multiple lines. Hold down Ctrl to select the entire text. This selection facility is also built into the TextBox control. The default is to leave it on, but you can turn it off in a TextBox's Properties window, or like this:

```
TextBox1.SelectionMargin = False
```

The SelLength, SelStart, and SelText Properties together describe the current cursor position within a Text (or Combo) Box, as well as any text that the user has highlighted (selected). This is useful for cut, copy, drag, and paste operations, as well as searching or other kinds of editing. It defines a region within a larger piece of text.

SelLength describes how many characters are highlighted, if any.

SelStart points to the character position of the first highlighted character. If no characters are highlighted, SelStart points to the current cursor position within the text.

SelText contains whatever text has been highlighted. (It is like a text "string" Variable.)

You can find out the current cursor position within the text in the TextBox. Or, if SelLength isn't 0 because some text has been selected, SelStart points to the first selected character:

```
X = TextBox1.SelStart
```

OR (X will be 0 if no characters have been selected. If some characters are selected, X holds the number of selected characters):

```
X = TextBox1.SelLength
```

OR (A will now contain whatever characters the user has selected. If no characters have been selected, A will be an "empty string" ("")):

```
A = TextBox1.SelText
If A = " " Then MsgBox "Nothing Selected."
```

Alternatively, you can *cause your script to select text*, to move the position of the cursor or even to *insert* (to "paste") text.

To paste text, set SelStart to where you want the new piece of text inserted. Then put the replacement text into the SelText Property.

If the original text is "HOW ARE YOU?"

```
TextBox1.SelStart = 4
TextBox1.SelText = "NEW PIECE"
```

Results in

```
HOW NEW PIECE ARE YOU?
```

OR (to have the script highlight some text, set the SelStart and SelLength Properties):

```
SelStart = 6
SelLength = 12
TextBox1.SelectionMargin = False
```

Ordinarily, when the user presses the Tab key while typing into a TextBox, the focus changes to the next Control in the Tab order. However, if you change the TabKeyBehavior Property to True, then a normal tab indent occurs within the TextBox, just as it would in a word processor. The TabKeyBehavior Property, though, defaults to False. Of course, if the TextBox's MultiLine Property is set to False (its default), pressing the Tab key will always move the focus to the next Control in the Tab order. Also see "EnterKeyBehavior" above.

For a Label, ComboBox, or TextBox Control, the TextAlign Property determines whether the text is flush-left, centered, or right-aligned. The default is flush-left.

```
TextBox1.TextAlign = 1 'the default, left-aligned
TextBox1.TextAlign = 2 'centered
TextBox1.TextAlign = 3 'right-aligned
```

Properties

AutoSize, AutoTab, AutoWordSelect, BackColor, BackStyle, BorderColor, BorderStyle, CodeBase, CurLine, DragBehavior, EnterFieldBehavior, EnterKeyBehavior, Enabled, Font, ForeColor, Height, HideSelection, ID, IMEMode, IntegralHeight, Left, LineCount, Locked, MaxLength, MouseIcon, MousePointer, MultiLine, PassWordChar, ScrollBars, SelectionMargin, SelLength, SelStart, SelText, SpecialEffect, TabIndex, TabKeyBehavior, TabStop, Text, TextAlign, Top, Value, Visible, Width, WordWrap

Events

Note that a TextBox has no Click Event.

AfterUpdate, BeforeDragOver, BeforeDropOrPaste, BeforeUpdate, Change, DblClick, Enter, Error, Exit, KeyDown, KeyPress, KeyUp, MouseDown, MouseMove, MouseUp

Methods

Copy, Cut, Move, Paste, SetFocus, ZOrder

Uses

- A TextBox is like the Notepad program that comes with Windows—a simple but usable word processor.
- You can use TextBoxes for data entry, or any situation where the user needs a convenient way to type something in that is to be made available to your script.

- If you want to limit the number of characters the user is permitted to enter into a TextBox, use the MaxLength Property. It can be set in the Properties Window or while the script is running. When not 0 (the default), a TextBox will refuse to accept—will not display onscreen or add to the Text Property—any further characters typed by the user.
- You can also use TextBoxes to display information, such as a large document that the user may want to view or edit.

Cautions

- The Value Property is the same as the Text Property. Both describe the contents of a TextBox.
- The MultiLine Property—which allows a TextBox to display more than one line—is off by default. You need to set it to On (True) by using the Properties Window.
- Also, if you add a Horizontal ScrollBar with the ScrollBars Property, all text will be on a single line. This single line can contain up to 255 characters. Any additional characters that the user attempts to type in—or your script attempts to add to the Text Property—will be ignored. It's therefore usually practical to use only a Vertical ScrollBar, both Horizontal and Vertical Bars, or none. A Horizontal Bar by itself is restrictive. If there is only a Horizontal Bar, there will be no way to move down through multiple lines if Carriage Return/LineFeeds (cr = Chr(13) & Chr(10)) are used to attempt to display additional lines.
- If the MultiLine Property of a TextBox is True, the maximum amount of text (the maximum size of the Text or Value Property) becomes limited only by the user's available memory.
- A TextBox's Text Property (Text1.Text, for instance) behaves just like a text Variable (see "Variables").

  (Also see "Asc" and "Chr" for text Variable manipulations involving the ANSI code that is used in Windows to handle text characters.)

- You can use the KeyDown Event of a TextBox to intercept characters as they're typed in, which allows you to control user input—refusing to accept letters, for example, if the user is supposed to be entering a phone number. You can also add shortcut commands with this technique, such as Ctrl+Q for Quit. The KeyDown Event is useful for detecting when users press Enter and, thereby, indicate that they are through filling in a single-line TextBox:

  ```
  Sub TextBox1_KeyDown(KeyCode, Shift)
  If KeyCode = 13 then
  ' Start Searching, or whatever...the user has finished
  typing.
  End If
  end sub
  ```

  To add a cut, copy, and paste feature, see "SelText."

- Windows uses the Tab key as a way of moving between the items, the Controls, on a window. Pressing Tab cycles you through the various Option Buttons, Command Buttons, or whatever Controls are on a layout (see "TabIndex"). In a TextBox (unless it is the only Control on the layout that can respond to tabbing), the user cannot use the Tab key to move the cursor over, as would be possible in most word processors (and typewriters). Ctrl+I, however, will tab in a TextBox.

- However, if you wish to permit the user to just press Tab and get a normal tabbing response (move over about five blank spaces)—change the TabKeyBehavior Property from its default False to True. A normal tab indent will then occur within the TextBox, just as it would in a word processor.

Example

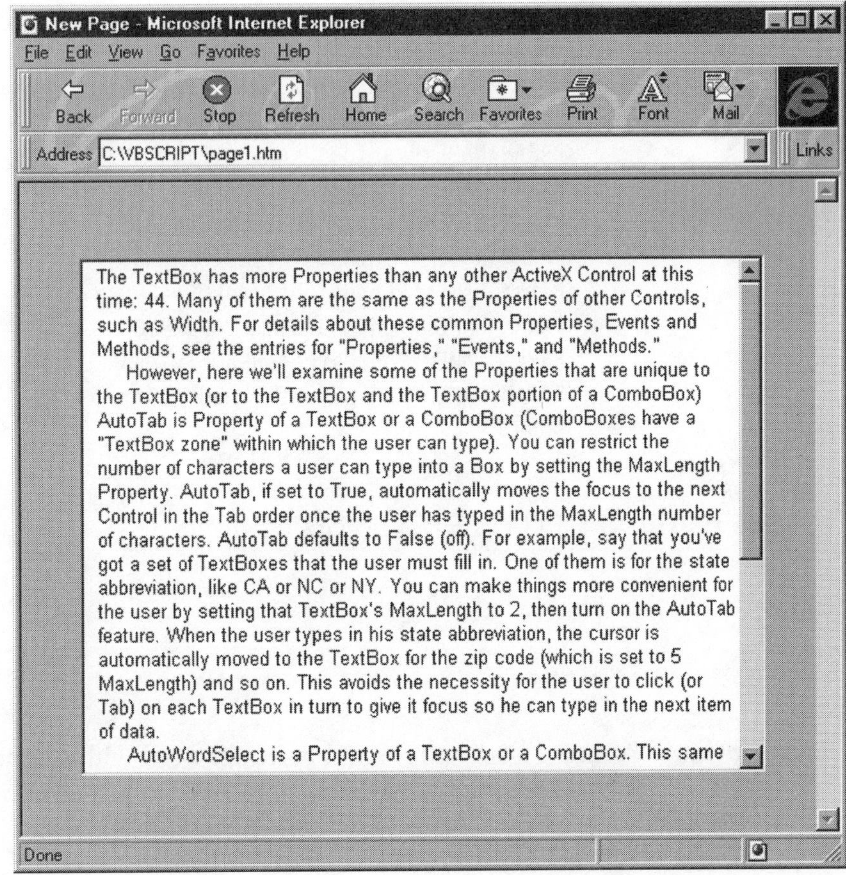

Figure T-24: With its ScrollBar Property set to Vertical, a ScrollBar is automatically added to a TextBox if the text is greater than the visible surface of the TextBox.

Start the Microsoft ActiveX Control Pad (see the Introduction) and click on Edit | Insert HTML Layout. Give the layout a new name and then click on the icon next to the <OBJECT> definition. Now from the toolbox, put a TextBox on the layout. Right-click on the TextBox and choose Properties. Change the MultiLine Property from its default False to True so we can type in more than one line. Also, set the ScrollBars Property to Vertical. Then right-click on the layout and choose View Source Code. You'll see the following Object definition:

```
<DIV ID="TB" STYLE="LAYOUT:FIXED;WIDTH:400pt;HEIGHT:300pt;">
 <OBJECT ID="TextBox1"
 CLASSID="CLSID:8BD21D10-EC42-11CE-9E0D-00AA006002F3"
STYLE="TOP:26pt;LEFT:23pt;WIDTH:356pt;HEIGHT:260pt;TABINDEX:0;ZINDEX:0;">
   <PARAM NAME="VariousPropertyBits" VALUE="2894088219">
   <PARAM NAME="ScrollBars" VALUE="2">
   <PARAM NAME="Size" VALUE="12559;9172">
   <PARAM NAME="FontName" VALUE="Arial">
   <PARAM NAME="FontHeight" VALUE="200">
   <PARAM NAME="FontCharSet" VALUE="0">
   <PARAM NAME="FontPitchAndFamily" VALUE="2">
   <PARAM NAME="FontWeight" VALUE="0">
  </OBJECT>
 </DIV>
```

See also INPUT (TYPE=TEXT), TEXTAREA

TH

HTML

Description A Table Header command indicates a cell within a table that's a label (a header), as opposed to a cell filled with text or numeric data.

See Table, HTML

Time

VBSCRIPT FUNCTION

Description Several Functions in VBScript give you information about the current computer (such as Date, which tells you the current date).

Time tells you what time the computer thinks it is, based on the battery-driven clock inside the machine. Time is similar to typing in DOS: C:> TIME.

A Better Alternative to Time: Time functions as a text Variable that contains the hours, minutes, and seconds in an HH:MM:SS format. For example, 2:12:22 PM.

In addition, the components of time are easily available by using the Hour, Minute, and Second Functions, along with the Now Function.

Variables To put Time into a Variable:

```
X = Time
```

OR (to use Time itself as if it were a normal text Variable):

```
MsgBox Time
```

Results in

```
1:55:38 PM
```

(meaning 1:55 PM and 38 seconds)

Uses

- Stamp the time on documents or files.
- Use for calendar or datebook-like features within databases, word processors, or other applications.

Cautions Time as a Function is a text Variable used to display the time.

Because Time contains three pieces of information, you may want to extract just the hour, minute, or second. To do this, you could use the InStr Function. However, the Now Function, along with the Hour, Minute, and Second Functions are easier to use for this purpose. (See the example below.)

Example This example illustrates the difference between Time and Now Functions:

```
<HTML>
<SCRIPT LANGUAGE=VBS>
msgbox time
msgbox now
</SCRIPT>
</HTML>
```

Results in

```
2:59:56 PM
5/11/96 2:59:56 PM
```

See also Date, Hour, Minute, Now, Second

Timer

ACTIVEX CONTROL

Description A Timer is a powerful and sophisticated clock. It is accurate to a millisecond—1/1,000th of a second. To specify a delay of two seconds, you would set the Timer's Interval to 2,000:

```
Timer1.Interval = 2000.
```

Once started, a Timer works independently and constantly. No matter what else might be happening in your Visual Basic script or in Windows, your Timer keeps ticking away.

The Interval Property of a Timer is a *duration*. The Interval determines how long the Timer must wait before it can carry out any instructions you've put into the Timer's Event. In other words, nothing happens until the Interval passes, then whatever programming you've put into the Timer's Event will be carried out.

This Timer Event is quite different from the other Events in VBScript. The commands within most Events are carried out as soon as the Event is triggered. CommandButton1_Click is triggered the very moment the user clicks on that Command Button, for example.

A Timer is different. When its Event is triggered, it looks at its Interval Property. It then *waits until that interval of time has passed before it carries out any instructions you've put into its Event.*

Why Timers Are Confusing at First: Timers are a little confusing if you haven't yet worked with them. They *are* called Controls, but they are unlike any other VBScript Control:

- Most Controls have more than a dozen Properties. A TextBox has 44; Timers have only nine.
- Most Controls have at least 10 Events they can respond to; Timers have only one Event. It's confusingly called the Timer Event, so the Sub is awkwardly expressed: Sub Timer1_Timer ().
- Most Controls are accessed and triggered by the user of the script; Timers work in the background, independent of the user. They are always invisible to the user.

- Most Controls' Events are triggered instantly; Timers don't carry out the instructions you've put into their Events until their Interval (duration) passes.

How to Visualize a Timer's Purpose: It's best to think of a Timer as one of those kitchen timers that you wind to, say, 20 and then the Timer starts ticking. Twenty minutes later it goes BING! The BING is whatever instructions you have put into the Sub Timer1_Timer()Event. The Interval Property is the number of minutes (or *milliseconds*) that you set the Timer to.

There's just one kink to remember: unlike a kitchen timer, a VBScript Timer *resets itself after going BING.* And then it starts counting down from 20 again. After 20 more minutes pass—BING! Reset. Count down. BING! It keeps repeating its countdown, and then repeating whatever instructions you've put inside the Event.

This resetting will continue forever unless you deliberately turn off the Timer by setting the Timer1.Enabled Property to False while your script is running. (You can also stop it by setting the Interval Property to 0.) If you need the Timer again, turn it on again with Timer1.Enabled = True (or put something other than 0 into the Interval Property).

Timers Are Superior to Loops for Measuring Duration: If you create a loop structure in one of your scripts, the amount of time the loop takes to finish will *depend on the speed of the user's computer*:

```
For I = 1 to 20000
Next I
```

A few years ago, programmers inserted a delay like the one above into their programs so that the user could, for instance, view a message onscreen. After the loop was completed, the message was made invisible or another message replaced it. But the delay caused by a loop is so computer-dependent that this approach is basically useless these days. IBM computers using Windows can have speeds that range from 15 to over 200 MHz.

A Timer is far superior to a loop because the Timer will delay the same amount of time on any machine. It uses the computer's vibrating crystal clock, so the time it measures is absolute. Well, pretty near absolute.

What Timers Do: When you put a Timer onto one of your HTML documents, it can keep interrupting whatever else might be going on—even if the user is doing something that's not in your script.

By itself, a Timer won't go off when your document is first loaded. By default, its Enabled Property is True, but its Interval Property is 0. For the Timer to trigger, it must have a True Enabled Property and some Interval other than zero.

When you set a Timer's Interval Property to anything greater than 0, which is the default, the Timer operates independently of anything else that's happening in the computer at the time. The Timer will repeatedly do what you tell it to do, carrying out any commands you put inside the Timer1_Timer Event until your script turns off the Timer:

```
Timer1.Enabled = False
```

OR

```
Timer1.Interval = 0
```

Timers are relentless in their effects. Remember that the commands you place inside a Timer Event are carried out *after* the Interval Property elapses. And they are carried out *every time* the Interval Property elapses. You can make a Timer do pretty much anything you want that involves duration, delay, and repetition by using the Interval and Enabled Properties in various ways.

The Job You Give to a Timer: A Timer, once turned on, becomes an alien robot agent loose in Windows. It has its instructions, and it knows how often you want the job done. Its instructions are the commands you have given it in its Timer Event.

T

```
Sub Timer1_Timer ()
```

and . . .

```
End Sub
```

Doing a Job on Schedule: Of a Timer's nine Properties, Enabled and Interval are the most important. (Indeed, its Width, Height, Left, and Top Properties are nonsensical—the Timer is never visible and never occupies any position or size in space for the user. In ordinary Visual Basic, it has a Left and Top Property—who knows why—but has no Height or Width Property.)

When you want the Timer's job done is determined by the time between when your script turns on the Timer (Timer1.Enabled = True) and the Timer's Interval Property (Timer1.Interval = 6000). If you use the Properties Window of a Timer to change its Interval Property while writing your script, the Timer will start counting when your document is first loaded into a browser (unless you specify otherwise by setting its Enabled Property to False).

For the Timer to do its job only once, include Timer1.Enabled = False (or Timer1.Interval = 0) within the Timer Event to turn it off after one Event trigger:

```
Sub Timer1_Timer ()
MsgBox ("This Timer has done its job for you.")
Timer1.Enabled = False
End Sub
```

A Timer is by default activated (Enabled) when your document is loaded into a browser; its Enabled Property defaults to On. If you've given it an Interval and you don't want the Timer to start counting until you tell it to, put Timer1.Enabled = False into the Window_OnLoad Event. That way, it will remain dormant until you turn it on somewhere else in the script. Or set the Enabled Property to False using the Properties Window while designing your script.

A Timer's Interval Property, the amount of time it can measure, ranges between 0 and 64,767 *milliseconds* (there are 1,000 milliseconds in every second). This means that the longest time an unassisted Timer can regulate is 1.079 minutes. You can, however, magnify the amount of time that a Timer will delay. You can make it wait until next Wednesday if that's what you want.

To measure time in longer intervals than the one-minute limit of a Timer's Interval Property, Dim a Variable outside of any Sub...End Sub or Function End Sub, then raise it by one each time the Timer's Event is triggered. Recall that a Timer *keeps going off, triggering its Timer Event,* until it's turned off (Timer1.Enabled = False). To wait two hours, set the Interval Property to 60000 (one minute) and then enter the following:

```
<SCRIPT LANGUAGE="VBScript">
<!--
Dim Counter
```

T

```
Sub Timer1_Timer
Counter = Counter + 1
If Counter >= 120 Then
   MsgBox "TIME'S UP!"
   Timer1.Enabled = 0
End If
End Sub
-->
</SCRIPT>
```

Timers have another capability, too, aside from their wonderful capacity to float within Windows and touch down from time to time, intervening and doing what you want them to do in spite of whatever else might be happening. They can *delay* things as well. When you set a Timer's Enabled Property to On (True), it waits until its Interval Property passes and *then carries out the instructions* you have placed between:

```
Sub Timer1_Timer ()
```

and . . .

```
End Sub
```

Variables Because the Timer is a Control, you can set its Properties from the Properties Window while you are creating your script: in the HTML window of Microsoft ActiveX Control Pad, click on the Timer's icon on the left of the <OBJECT> definition within the HTML document source code, then right-click on the Timer Control and choose Properties. A Timer has the following Properties: CodeBase, Enabled, Height, ID, Interval, Left, Top, Visible, Width.

The only commonly used Timer Properties are the *Interval*, which determines how long the Timer waits until doing something, and *Enabled*, which simply turns a Timer on or off. Each time Enabled is turned on, the Interval starts over again from 0. If you turn off a Timer before it has finished counting and then turn it back on, the Interval will restart from the beginning.

T

OR (to adjust a Timer while the script is running, in this case, setting it to two seconds duration):

```
Timer1.Interval = 2000
```

OR (to start a Timer ticking while the script is running):

```
Timer1.Enabled = True
```

Properties

These are the nine Properties listed in the Timer's Properties Window: CodeBase, Enabled, Height, ID, Interval, Left, Top, Visible, and Width.

Clearly, though, the Height, Left, Visible, Top, and Width Properties are meaningless. A Timer is never visible to the user.

The Enabled Property can be either True (the default) or False. If False, the Timer will be inactivated until you change the Enabled Property back to True. Note that Enabled must be True *and* the Interval Property must be some positive number—*or the Timer is disabled*.

The interval is expressed in milliseconds, thousandths of a second. Three seconds would be 3,000. If you set the interval to 0 (the default) or a negative number, the Timer will be inactivated (until you change the Interval Property back to some positive number).

Events

Timer

Methods

AboutBox

For details about these Properties, Events, and Methods, see the entries for "Properties," "Events," and "Methods."

Uses A Timer can perform a variety of jobs in your scripts:

- It can act like *a traditional kitchen timer*—counting down from a preset time and then ringing a bell (or doing whatever you want) after the preset interval has elapsed.
- It can *cause a delay*, so a window with a message appears onscreen for four seconds and then disappears, for example.
- It can cause events to *repeat at prescribed intervals*, like a digital clock changing its readout every second.

- It can look at the computer's built-in battery-powered clock to *see if it is time to do something*. In this way, you can build reminder scripts, to-do schedulers, that will display a message or take some other action based on the current time. In this application the Timer looks at the computer's clock at regular intervals, independent of what the user might be doing or what is going on in Windows.
- It can show the user the time at regular intervals, and thus you can *make a clock*.
- It can *measure the passage of time,* acting like a stopwatch and reporting the amount of time that something took to complete its behavior.

Cautions You can place a Timer anywhere on an HTML document. Unlike other Controls, it is never visible when the script runs.

By default, a Timer's Enabled Property is *on* when a script starts running. Therefore, a Timer will start its countdown when a script starts, unless one of three things has happened: 1) You have not set its Interval Property yet. The interval defaults to 0, and a Timer will not become active until the interval is greater than 0. 2) You turn off the Timer's Enabled Property from the Properties Window while designing your script. 3) Your script turns off the Timer's Enabled Property (Timer1.Enabled = False) while the script is running.

Unless turned off, Timers continue to run, even after their interval has finished. When the interval is over, a Timer resets itself and starts counting the Interval again, then again carries out whatever commands are in its Timer Event. When the interval is finished, the Timer again resets itself, then carries out the commands. This cycle—countdown, reset, carry out commands—continues until you turn the Timer off from somewhere within the script by using the commands Timer1.Enabled = False (or Timer1.Interval = 0).

If you set a Timer to do something every second (interval = 1,000), it may occasionally fail to go off *precisely on the second.* The computer may have been tied up doing something that briefly took complete control of the machine (so the Timer couldn't react when its interval was over). Even though it might be temporarily prevented from carrying out the commands in its Timer Event, however, the Timer *will keep counting.*

A related issue is the frequency with which the Timer counts. If you need extremely fine control over timing, set the Interval Property very small, perhaps 100 (one-tenth of a second). The tradeoff here is that setting a small interval will slow down the computer somewhat because it must service your Timer so often. If you want the Timer's Event to happen every second, yet you have set the Timer's interval to 100, use a Variable to count up to 10:

```
Dim Counter

Sub Timer1_Timer
Counter = Counter + 1
If Counter >= 10 Then
  MsgBox "TIME'S UP!"
End If
End Sub
```

Inaccuracies Can Occur at Extremely Small Intervals: The computer itself must do a few things each time it activates a Timer (or any other) Event. As a result, if you set the Timer's Interval Property to a very small value (attempting to time something precisely), the accuracy is not certain.

Because of the potential for slight inaccuracies, always use *greater than or equal,* rather than equal, when checking against a Variable. This way, on the odd chance that the computer was otherwise occupied when your Variable reached its target, your Timer will still respond as soon as it can. In the preceding example, the Counter could get up to 9; at that point the computer was otherwise engaged. When the Timer Event next gets an opportunity to check the Variable, the Counter is up to 11 or greater. Therefore, the Timer would never see Counter = 10. Using the comparison operator "greater than or equal" (Counter >=10) solves this problem.

A Timer has only one Event, also named, unfortunately, *Timer:*

```
Sub Timer1_Timer ()
```

And its name isn't the only thing that is a little perplexing about this Event. Most VBScript Events, such as a Click Event, trigger an immediate response—performing at once those actions that you have listed as instructions within the Click_Event Procedure:

```
Command1_Click
  MsgBox "OUCH!"
  MsgBox "Press me again!"
End Sub
```

Here, the instant the user clicks on Command1, the word *OUCH!* is displayed, and any other instructions in the Event are carried out.

When you enable a Timer (Timer1.Enabled = True), you are triggering the Timer Event (technically, you're triggering a counter that counts down to zero, then triggers the Event). The Timer's *countdown* starts, but the instructions within the Timer1_Timer Event *will not be carried out until the countdown has finished.* No bell will ring, no message will be displayed, no commands within the Event will be carried out—until the Timer has counted down from the number of milliseconds you put in its Interval Property, to zero.

Example We'll create an animation. The word *Zoom* will wiggle back and forth between normal text and italic. The Interval Property will time these Events.

Figure T-25: The word Zoom is animated. More than twice a second it wiggles between normal and italic.

Start the Microsoft ActiveX Control Pad (see the Introduction) and click on Edit | Insert ActiveX Control. Add a Microsoft IE 30 Label Control and go to the Edit menu again and insert a Microsoft IE 30 Timer Control. Then click on the icon next to the

<OBJECT> definition for the Label and in its Properties Window, change the Caption, the Font, and the FontSize to whatever you wish. Then close the Properties Window and the sizing Window and, in the HTML source code, type in the following script.

We set the Timer's Interval to 200 (one-fifth of a second) when the document first loads (OnLoad). Also, we define a scriptwide Variable, *Toggle*. In the Timer Event, we flip Toggle between two states using the Not operator (see "Operators"). If Toggle is in a True state (If Toggle), we change the Label to italics. If not, we change it back to normal text.

```
<HTML>
<HEAD>
<TITLE>New Page</TITLE>
</HEAD>
<BODY>

<SCRIPT LANGUAGE="VBScript">

<!--
Dim Toggle

Sub Window_OnLoad()
<Compu. IeTimer1.Interval = 200
End Sub

Sub IeTimer1_Timer()
Toggle = Not Toggle
If Toggle then
IeLabel1.FontItalic = True
else
IeLabel1.FontItalic = False
end If
end sub
-->
 </SCRIPT>

<OBJECT ID="IeLabel1" WIDTH=257 HEIGHT=55
CLASSID="CLSID:99B42120-6EC7-11CF-A6C7-00AA00A47DD2">
   <PARAM NAME="_ExtentX" VALUE="6800">
   <PARAM NAME="_ExtentY" VALUE="1455">
```

```
    <PARAM NAME="Caption" VALUE="-Zoom-">
    <PARAM NAME="Angle" VALUE="0">
    <PARAM NAME="Alignment" VALUE="4">
    <PARAM NAME="Mode" VALUE="1">
    <PARAM NAME="FillStyle" VALUE="0">
    <PARAM NAME="FillStyle" VALUE="0">
    <PARAM NAME="ForeColor" VALUE="#000000">
    <PARAM NAME="BackColor" VALUE="#C0C0C0">
    <PARAM NAME="FontName" VALUE="Aero">
    <PARAM NAME="FontSize" VALUE="56">
    <PARAM NAME="FontItalic" VALUE="0">
    <PARAM NAME="FontBold" VALUE="0">
    <PARAM NAME="FontUnderline" VALUE="0">
    <PARAM NAME="FontStrikeout" VALUE="0">
    <PARAM NAME="TopPoints" VALUE="0">
    <PARAM NAME="BotPoints" VALUE="0">
  </OBJECT>

  <OBJECT ID="IeTimer1" WIDTH=39 HEIGHT=40
  CLASSID="CLSID:59CCB4A0-727D-11CF-AC36-00AA00A47DD2">
    <PARAM NAME="_ExtentX" VALUE="1032">
    <PARAM NAME="_ExtentY" VALUE="1058">
  </OBJECT>
  </BODY>
  </HTML>
```

TimeSerial

VBSCRIPT FUNCTION

T

Description You provide the TimeSerial command with an hour, minute, and second, and it provides you with a unique VBScript "serial number" that represents the described time. A serial number is a number within a series of numbers, like a number from a roll of movie tickets. Each number is unique, and each points to a particular position in the roll. The TimeSerial number is a unique number from among the 86,400 seconds in a day.

TimeSerial is the close relative of the DateSerial command. DateSerial does the same thing but reports a unique serial number for any date between January 1, 100 A.D. and December 31, 9999.

TimeSerial is also a close relative of the TimeValue Function. TimeValue does the same thing as TimeSerial. But where TimeValue translates a *text* expression of the time (like 1 PM), TimeSerial translates a *numeric* expression of the time (like 13,0,0) into three numbers—hour, minute, and second.

TimeSerial provides a fractional number.

DateSerial provides a whole number between –657,434 and 2,958,465.

Put the two together and you get a range of unique serial numbers for every second between the years 100 A.D. and 9999.

The Now command also provides a serial number with this combination of date and time; however, Now gets its data from the computer's built-in clock.

These various "date+time serial numbers" can be the basis for calendar programs and other applications. VBScript takes the intelligent approach to time and dates by creating a huge range of unique numbers in a series to represent each second, minute, hour, day, month, and year over a span of 98 centuries.

Because this range is a series of numbers, you can perform arithmetic with them. You can't subtract "12 Feb." from "18 Jan." But if you have their serial numbers, you *can* find out how many days there are between these two dates.

Variables **Variable type:** TimeSerial returns a "Variant" and stores the data as a double-precision floating-point subtype. To translate literal numbers representing the hour, minute, and second into a serial number:

```
X = TimeSerial(9,22,0)
```

OR (to use Variables instead of literal numbers):

```
hr = 9:mn = 22: se = 0
X = TimeSerial(hr,mn,se)
```

OR (to use an *expression*; see "Variables"):

```
X = TimeSerial(hr-1,mn + 10, se)
```

Note that the hour number must be in 24-hour format, a range between 0 (midnight) and 23 (11 PM). The minute and second numbers must range between 0 and 59.

T

Uses

- Create to-do programs, calendars, and other applications involving manipulation of time and dates as if they were numbers in a series.
- Use TimeSerial or DateSerial to generate a "registration number" or as part of an encryption scheme.

See also DateSerial, Hour, Minute, Now, Second, TimeValue

TimeValue

VBSCRIPT FUNCTION

Description You provide TimeValue with time expressed as *text* (either literal text, 2 PM, or a text Variable, ZA). Then TimeValue provides you with a unique VBScript "serial number" that represents the described time. A serial number is a number within a series of numbers, like a number from a roll of movie tickets. Each number is unique, and each points to a particular position in the roll. In this instance, TimeValue will give you a unique number from among the 86,400 seconds in a day.

TimeValue is the close relative of the DateValue Function. DateValue does the same thing but reports a unique serial number for any date between January 1, 100 A.D. and December 31, 9999.

TimeValue is also a close relative of the TimeSerial Function. TimeValue does the same thing as TimeSerial, but TimeValue translates a *text* expression of the time (like 1 PM). TimeSerial translates a *numeric* expression of the time (like 1, 0, 0) into three numbers—hour, minute, and second.

TimeValue provides a fractional number.

DateValue provides a whole number.

Put the two together and you get a range that is capable of assigning a unique serial number to *every second* between the years 100 A.D. and 9999.

The Now command also provides a serial number with this combination of date and time; however, Now gets its data from the computer's built-in clock. These various "date+time serial numbers" can be the basis for calendar programs and other applications. VBScript creates a huge range of unique numbers in a series to represent each second, minute, hour, day, month, and year over a span of 98 centuries.

Because this range is a series of numbers, you can perform arithmetic. You can't subtract "12 Feb." from "18 Jan." But if you get their serial numbers, you *can* find out how many days there are between these two dates.

Variables **Variable type:** TimeValue returns a "Variant" and stores the data as a double-precision floating-point subtype.

TimeValue is surprisingly forgiving in the variety of formats it will accept. It will see 5 as 05:00:00, 5.25 as 05:25:00. It will accept nothing (an empty text Variable "") as 00:00:00 (midnight). It will accept uppercase or lowercase AM and PM.

TimeValue also ignores extraneous information. It will translate 2 PM Tuesday into the correct serial number for 2 PM and pay no attention to *Tuesday.* TimeValue also ignores extra spaces.

To provide a literal text expression of a particular time:

```
X = TimeValue("1:00")
```

OR (to use AM or PM):

```
X = TimeValue("1 PM")
```

OR (to use a Variable):

```
T = "05:23:15"
X = TimeValue(T)
```

OR (to use an *expression*; see "Variables"):

```
T = "5":V = "pm"
X = TimeValue(T + V)
```

Uses

- Create to-do programs, calendars, and other applications involving manipulation of time and dates as if they were numbers in a series.
- Use TimeValue or DateValue to generate a "registration number" or for encryption schemes.

Cautions

- TimeValue accepts text Variables in either military format (24-hour time like 17:05:15) or normal AM/PM style (5:05:15 PM).
- TimeValue can accept a range between 00:00:00 and 23:59:59, or 12 AM and 11:59:59 PM.

Example

```
<HTML>

<SCRIPT LANGUAGE="VBScript">
cr = chr(13) & chr(10)

info = "The current time is "
n = time()
info = info + cstr(n)

info = info + cr + " Please enter the adjusted time."

t = InputBox(info)
x = TimeValue(t)
msgbox cstr(x)

</SCRIPT>
</HTML>
```

You can use the Time command to adjust the computer's built-in clock. Time, though, requires military-style (24-hour) time in an awkward HH:MM:SS format.

This example lets your program take a detailed look at how the user entered the time—and compensate for a variety of user errors by translating their input into HH:MM:SS format. TimeValue allows the user to enter time in the more common 5:24 PM format.

First we build a text Variable that will be displayed in an Input Box. Building text Variables by repeatedly adding text is a common approach if you are dealing with relatively small messages.

T

See also DateValue, Hour, Minute, Now, Second, TimeSerial

TITLE

HTML

Description This command is supposed to be included in every HTML document. It is the text that will appear in the title bar of the user's browser's window as the description in a bookmark file, and stored in a "history" list. In other words, TITLE is a plain-language description of your document (as opposed to the often hard-to-remember URL).

The TITLE must be placed within the HEAD, and the TITLE isn't displayed on the page to the user.

```
<HEAD>
<TITLE>Newspaper Selections</TITLE>
</HEAD>
<BODY>
</BODY>
```

Used with ***Can be enclosed by***

<HEAD>

Can enclose

Nothing

Uses Identifies the contents of your document in a clearer, more descriptive way than does its URL.

Cautions There isn't a limit on the length your title can be, but it's a good idea to remember that it will appear as an identifier in the user's browser, and thus should be fairly short. It should also be descriptive of the contents of your document.

No formatting (such as <H>) is permitted for a TITLE.

Example

```
<HEAD><TITLE>Raising Vegetables</TITLE></HEAD>
```

See also HEAD, BODY

ToggleButton

ACTIVEX CONTROL

Description A ToggleButton can be used like a CheckBox to provide a set of discrete, individual choices. (With a little programming, you can also make a group of ToggleButtons act like grouped Option Buttons—only one can be selected at a time. See the example.)

A ToggleButton is also similar to a CommandButton, but when you click on a CommandButton, it bounces right back out. When you click on a ToggleButton, it remains depressed until you click on it again to pop it out.

Like CheckBoxes, the user can easily see the status of a ToggleButton—it's either extruded and, by default, a dark gray, or it's depressed and colored a light gray.

Figure T-26: The two states of a ToggleButton—extruded and depressed.

Variables The Value Property of ToggleButtons determines or reveals whether a given button is depressed or not. When depressed, its Value is True and when extruded the Value is False. The Value Property can be read:

```
X = ToggleButton1.VALUE
```

OR changed:

```
ToggleButton1.VALUE = False
```

Because Value is the default Property, you can also omit the VALUE if you wish:

```
X = ToggleButton1
ToggleButton1 = 0
```

VALUE = NULL: The item is neither selected nor cleared (the caption is gray, and the entire button is lighter than normal when in its extruded state. For this NULL value to be possible, the TripleState Property must also be set to True. TripleState defaults to False.) The NULL condition is the default startup condition: when the browser first loads a ToggleButton, it appears in its third state—nether selected nor unselected. All this changes as soon as the user depresses it the first time.

True. The item is selected.

False. The item is blank, unselected.

OR (to change an ToggleButton's caption while the program is running):

```
ToggleButton1.Caption = "Last Month's Bills"
```

OR (to change the type size of an ToggleButton's caption):

```
ToggleButton1.FontSize = 12
```

OR (to make one button the same size vertically as another):

```
ToggleButton1.Height = ToggleButton2.Height
```

T

Properties

Accelerator, AutoSize, BackColor, BackStyle, Caption, CodeBase, Enabled, Font, ForeColor, Height, ID, Left, Locked, MouseIcon, MousePointer, Picture, PicturePosition, TabIndex, TabStop, Top, TripleState, Value, Visible, Width, WordWrap

Events

AfterUpdate, BeforeDragOver, BeforeDropOrPaste, BeforeUpdate, Change, Click, DblClick, Enter, Error, Exit, KeyDown, KeyPress, KeyUp, MouseDown, MouseMove, MouseUp

Methods
Move, SetFocus, ZOrder

For details about these Properties, Events, and Methods, see the entries for "Properties," "Events," and "Methods."

Uses

- Use ToggleButtons whenever you'd consider using CheckBoxes—for example, when you want the user to be able to customize or otherwise control the way your document looks or behaves—but among the choices the user can select more than one option. If the user should select only a single choice from among a group of choices, use an OptionButton Control instead.
- Using the technique described in the example below, you can also use a group of ToggleButtons instead of grouped OptionButtons.
- CheckBoxes and OptionButtons are not the most visually attractive Controls. ToggleButtons are *animated* like Command Buttons and are simply better looking.

Cautions Although the TripleState Property is supposed to default to False (off)—and indeed it appears as False in a ToggleButton's Properties window—in fact, the TripleState Property is True and on by default.

Example For a car rental Web site, we wanted to allow the user to select from among four autos to rent. Because the user can only choose one auto, we wanted the buttons to behave like radio buttons. When one button is clicked in, the others should be popped out. In other words, these four ToggleButtons should behave like OptionButtons.

To do this, we first define a Variable named *Dn* that is Dimmed outside of any procedure and thus is available to all five procedures in our script. Then, when a ToggleButton is clicked, the CheckStatus Sub looks at what's in the Dn Variable and deselects it. A new number (1 to 4) is placed into Dn in case the user clicks on a different button and we have to deselect again.

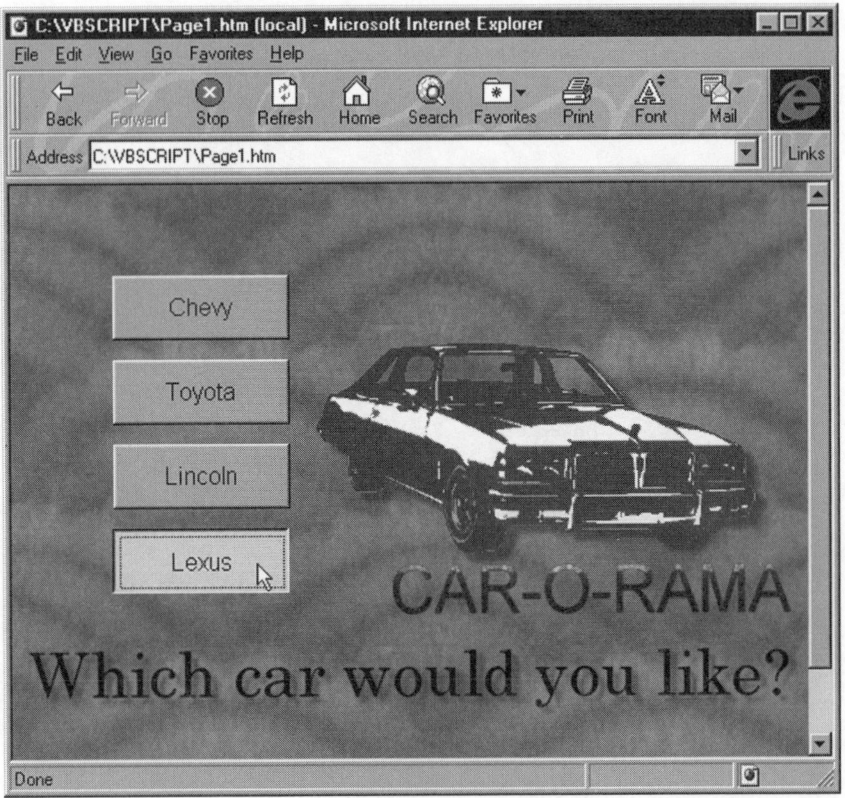

Figure T-27: These ToggleButtons will behave like OptionButtons—click on one and all others are deselected.

To create this example, we'll first put four ToggleButtons on an HTML Layout Control. Start the Microsoft ActiveX Control Pad (see the Introduction) and click on Edit | Insert HTML Layout. Give the layout a new name and then click on the icon next to the <OBJECT> definition. Now from the toolbox, put four ToggleButtons on the layout. Right-click on each ToggleButton and choose Properties. Give each a different caption. Then right-click on the layout and choose View Source Code. Type in the following script:

```
<SCRIPT LANGUAGE="VBScript">
<!--
Dim Dn
```

T

```
Sub ToggleButton1_Click()
CheckStatus
Dn = 1
end sub

Sub ToggleButton2_Click()
CheckStatus
Dn = 2
end sub

Sub ToggleButton3_Click()
CheckStatus
Dn = 3

end sub

Sub ToggleButton4_Click()
CheckStatus
Dn = 4

end sub

Sub CheckStatus ()
Select Case Dn
  Case 1
ToggleButton1 = False
  Case 2
ToggleButton2 = False
  Case 3
ToggleButton3 = False
  Case 4
ToggleButton4 = False
End Select
End Sub

-->
</SCRIPT>
<DIV ID="as" STYLE="LAYOUT:FIXED;WIDTH:400pt;HEIGHT:300pt;">
<OBJECT ID="ToggleButton1"
```

```
CLASSID="CLSID:8BD21D60-EC42-11CE-9E0D-00AA006002F3"
STYLE="TOP:33pt;LEFT:45pt;WIDTH:90pt;HEIGHT:32pt;TABINDEX:0;ZINDEX:0;">
  <PARAM NAME="BackColor" VALUE="2147483663">
  <PARAM NAME="ForeColor" VALUE="4194368">
  <PARAM NAME="DisplayStyle" VALUE="6">
  <PARAM NAME="Size" VALUE="3175;1129">
  <PARAM NAME="Caption" VALUE="Chevy">
  <PARAM NAME="FontName" VALUE="Arial">
  <PARAM NAME="FontHeight" VALUE="240">
  <PARAM NAME="FontCharSet" VALUE="0">
  <PARAM NAME="FontPitchAndFamily" VALUE="2">
  <PARAM NAME="ParagraphAlign" VALUE="3">
  <PARAM NAME="FontWeight" VALUE="0">
</OBJECT>
<OBJECT ID="ToggleButton2"
CLASSID="CLSID:8BD21D60-EC42-11CE-9E0D-00AA006002F3"
STYLE="TOP:75pt;LEFT:45pt;WIDTH:90pt;HEIGHT:32pt;TABINDEX:1;ZINDEX:1;">
  <PARAM NAME="BackColor" VALUE="2147483663">
  <PARAM NAME="ForeColor" VALUE="2147483666">
  <PARAM NAME="DisplayStyle" VALUE="6">
  <PARAM NAME="Size" VALUE="3175;1129">
  <PARAM NAME="Caption" VALUE="Toyota">
  <PARAM NAME="FontName" VALUE="Arial">
  <PARAM NAME="FontHeight" VALUE="240">
  <PARAM NAME="FontCharSet" VALUE="0">
  <PARAM NAME="FontPitchAndFamily" VALUE="2">
  <PARAM NAME="ParagraphAlign" VALUE="3">
  <PARAM NAME="FontWeight" VALUE="0">
</OBJECT>
<OBJECT ID="ToggleButton3"
CLASSID="CLSID:8BD21D60-EC42-11CE-9E0D-00AA006002F3"
STYLE="TOP:117pt;LEFT:45pt;WIDTH:90pt;HEIGHT:32pt;TABINDEX:2;ZINDEX:2;">
  <PARAM NAME="BackColor" VALUE="2147483663">
  <PARAM NAME="ForeColor" VALUE="2147483666">
  <PARAM NAME="DisplayStyle" VALUE="6">
  <PARAM NAME="Size" VALUE="3175;1129">
  <PARAM NAME="Caption" VALUE="Lincoln">
  <PARAM NAME="FontName" VALUE="Arial">
  <PARAM NAME="FontHeight" VALUE="240">
```

```
    <PARAM NAME="FontCharSet" VALUE="0">
    <PARAM NAME="FontPitchAndFamily" VALUE="2">
    <PARAM NAME="ParagraphAlign" VALUE="3">
    <PARAM NAME="FontWeight" VALUE="0">
</OBJECT>
<OBJECT ID="ToggleButton4"
CLASSID="CLSID:8BD21D60-EC42-11CE-9E0D-00AA006002F3"
STYLE="TOP:159pt;LEFT:44pt;WIDTH:90pt;HEIGHT:32pt;TABINDEX:3;ZINDEX:3;">
    <PARAM NAME="BackColor" VALUE="2147483663">
    <PARAM NAME="ForeColor" VALUE="2147483666">
    <PARAM NAME="DisplayStyle" VALUE="6">
    <PARAM NAME="Size" VALUE="3175;1129">
    <PARAM NAME="Caption" VALUE="Lexus">
    <PARAM NAME="FontName" VALUE="Arial">
    <PARAM NAME="FontHeight" VALUE="240">
    <PARAM NAME="FontCharSet" VALUE="0">
    <PARAM NAME="FontPitchAndFamily" VALUE="2">
    <PARAM NAME="ParagraphAlign" VALUE="3">
    <PARAM NAME="FontWeight" VALUE="0">
</OBJECT>
</DIV>
```

See also CheckBox, ListBox, OptionButton

Top

ACTIVEX

See Properties

TopIndex

ACTIVEX

See Properties

T

TR

HTML

Description Establishes a new row within a table.

See Table, HTML

Trim

VBSCRIPT FUNCTION

Description Trim removes any blank spaces from the left and right sides of a piece of text. A blank space (caused by pressing the spacebar) has a character code like the other, visible characters. This code is 32. Trim looks in a text Variable for any leading or trailing blanks and removes them from the Variable. There are two associated commands. LTrim removes leading spaces only; RTrim removes trailing spaces only.

Used with The text ("string") Variable subtype.

Variables

```
N = Trim(" Hello")
```

Uses

- Clean up user input. You can never tell what the user might do. When typing in a lot of data, the user might accidentally hit the Tab key or enter some extra spaces. If your script is going to alphabetize a list, and one of the items has a space as its first character, that item will appear before the *A*'s as the first item in the list. To prevent this kind of confusion, you want to clean up any items that you are about to alphabetize (or are going to compare, such as If A < B).
- Use Trim to make sure that you are comparing apples to apples and not dealing with some accidental leading spaces. And, while you're at it, you might as well eliminate random capitalization with the LCase Function, too. (For an alternative to LCase, see "StrComp.")

Example We'll add two blank spaces to the start and end of the characters ABCD, to demonstrate the effects of LTrim, Trim, and RTrim. Then, we'll add some pipe symbols to illustrate the effects of the various trims:

```
A = "  ABCD  "
MsgBox "|" & LTrim(A) & "|"
MsgBox "|" & Trim(A) & "|"
MsgBox "|" & RTrim(A) & "|"
```

Results In

```
|ABCD  |
|ABCD|
|  ABCD|
```

TripleState

ACTIVEX

See Properties

TT

HTML

Description Displays text in a non-proportional font, usually Courier. TT stands for *teletype*, an early printing device that acted as a typewriter automatically rendering the results of a telegram.

TT changes the typeface. TT can be used to display programming ("code") such as HTML source code. The font used is fixed-width. Fixed-width (non-proportional) means a font-style typeface where each character is the same width (*i* is as wide as *w*). The opposite variety—Variable-width type—is typified by Times Roman. Characters vary in width. Variable-width is the default HTML font for body text. The CODE, LISTING, PRE, and HTML commands do essentially the same thing as TT.

Used with ***Can be enclosed by***

<A>, <ABBREV>, <ACRONYM>, <ADDRESS>, <AU>, <B>, <BANNER>, <BIG>, <BODY>, <BODYTEXT>, <CAPTION>, <CITE>, <CODE>, <CREDIT>, <DD>, <DEL>, <DFN>, <DIV>, <DT>, <EM>, <FIGTEXT>, <FN>, <FORM>, <H>, <I>, <INS>, <KBD>, <LANG>, <LH>, <LI>, <NOTE>,<P>, <PERSON>, <PRE>, <Q>, <S>, <SAMP>, <SMALL>, <STRONG>, <SUB>, <SUP>, <TD>, <TH>, <TT>, <U>, <VAR>

Can enclose

<A>, <ABBREV>, <ACRONYM>, <AU>, <B>, <BIG>, <BR>, <CITE>, <CODE>, <DEL>, <DFN>, <EM>, <I>, <IMG>, <INS>, <KBD>, <LANG>, <MATH>, <PERSON>, <Q>, <S>, <SAMP>, <SMALL>, <STRONG>, <SUB>, <SUP>, <TAB>, <TT>, <U>, <VAR>

Uses

- When you want to display something that suggests machine-origin (the time of day, for instance).
- Create simple tables using a non-proportional font (thus a predictable width—so words will line up vertically). Use in combination with the TAB command.

Example

```
<TT>April 12, 1997</TT>
```

See also CODE, LISTING, PRE, HTML

TYPE

HTML

See INPUT

U

U

HTML

Description Causes text to be underlined when displayed.

Used with ***Can be enclosed by***

<A>, <ABBREV>, <ABOVE>, <ACRONYM>, <ADDRESS>, <AU>, <B>, <BANNER>, <BAR>, <BELOW>, <BIG>, <BODY>, <BODYTEXT>, <BOX>, <BT>, <CAPTION>, <CITE>, <CODE>, <CREDIT>, <DD>, <DDOT>, <DEL>, <DFN>, <DIV>, <DOT>, <DT>, <EM>, <FIGTEXT>, <FN>, <FORM>, <H1>, <H2>, <H3>, <H4>, <H5>, <H6>, <HAT>, <I>, <INS>, <ITEM>, <KBD>, <LANG>, <LH>, <LI>, <MATH>, <NOTE>, <OF>, <P>, <PERSON>, <PRE>, <Q>, <ROOT>, <S>, <SAMP>, <SMALL>, <SQRT>, <STRONG>, <SUB>, <SUP>, <T>, <TD>, <TH>, <TILDE>, <TT>, <U>, <VAR>

Can enclose

<A>, <ABBREV>, <ACRONYM>, <AU>, <B>, <BIG>, <BR>, <CITE>, <CODE>, <DEL>, <DFN>, <EM>, <I>, <IMG>, <INS>, <KBD>, <LANG>, <MATH>, <PERSON>, <Q>, <S>, <SAMP>, <SMALL>, <STRONG>, <SUB>, <SUP>, <TAB>, <TT>, <U>, <V>

Uses Can be used to emphasize text. It's more attractive than using boldface, but less attractive than italics. Many browsers use underlining to indicate a hot link (see the "A" command), a jump to another location, page, document, or URL. Therefore, using underlining might be confusing. If you want to emphasize a word or phrase, try italics instead. See "I."

Cautions Since browsers often indicate hypertext links by underlining them, you should avoid underlining your text.

Example

```
<U>This is underlined</U>
```

See also B, I

UBound

VBSCRIPT FUNCTION

Description UBound tells you the upper limit of an Array's index (see "Arrays").

You will probably use this command rarely because you *know* when you are writing your program how big your Arrays are—you have to define Arrays, including their range. And if you should ReDim an Array based on some Variable affected by the user while the program was running (or a Variable loaded from disk or some other outside source), you could nonetheless just check that Variable to know the size of the Array.

Here is how UBound works:

```
<HTML>

<SCRIPT LANGUAGE="VBScript">

Dim A (50)
X = UBound(A)
MsgBox X

</SCRIPT>
</HTML>
```

Results in

```
50
```

But there is always that specialized situation where you have allowed the user to specify the size of an Array or have a Subroutine or Function that accepts various Arrays—to search for something in them, for instance. Knowing an Array's size would be useful to a Sub that sorted several different Arrays. If you are working with dynamic Arrays, which could be of varying sizes, UBound would allow you a simple, direct way of finding out how big one of these Arrays is. You might use this approach:

```
For I = LBound(ArrayName) To UBound(ArrayName)
```

Used with Arrays

Variables **Variable type:** Integer
The complete syntax of UBound is:

```
X = UBound(Arrayname [,Dimension])
```

The dimension is optional and defaults to 1.

Assume that you've defined an Array like this: Dim Names (16,12). It now has two dimensions, so:

```
X = UBound(Names, 1): MsgBox X
```

Results in

```
16
```

OR (to get the upper limit of the second "dimension" of this Array):

```
X = UBound(Names, 2): MsgBox X
```

Results in

```
12
```

Uses When you cannot know, while designing your program, the size of an Array. Perhaps you allow the user to define the size, or perhaps you are using a multipurpose Subroutine that performs a job for several Arrays of different sizes that are passed to the Sub. The Sub can then query the Array for its size.

Cautions

- An equivalent Function, LBound, provides the lower limit of an Array's index.
- You can omit the "dimension number"—the 2 in UBound(A,2)—if there is only one dimension. Dim Z As String has only one dimension; Dim A (5, 7, 4) has three

dimensions. In the second case, the Array A has more than one dimension so you must specify which dimension you are interested in. To find out the upper limit of Array A, third dimension:

```
N = UBound(A,3)
```

Example

```
Dim A(44)
X = UBound(A)
MsgBox X
```

Results in

```
44
```

See also Arrays, Dim, LBound, ReDim

UCase

VBSCRIPT FUNCTION

Description UCase forces all the characters in a piece of text to become uppercase letters. For example, it changes "homer" to "HOMER."

Used with Text Variable subtypes, text Constants, literal text, or text expressions (see "Variables" for an explanation of these terms).

Variables To turn a text Variable into all-uppercase letters:

```
<HTML>

<pre>
<SCRIPT LANGUAGE="VBScript">

A = "Monetary Policy Debated By Monkey Boys"

document.writeln A

B = UCase(A)

document.writeln B
```

```
</SCRIPT>
</pre>
</HTML>
```

Results in

```
Monetary Policy Debated By Monkey Boys
MONETARY POLICY DEBATED BY MONKEY BOYS
```

OR (because UCase is a Function, you can use it as part of an *expression*; see "Variables"):

```
A = "\\ Donkeys Found Alive In Grand Canyon \\"
MsgBox UCase(A)
```

Results in

```
\\ DONKEYS FOUND ALIVE IN GRAND CANYON \\
```

Notice that the \\ symbols, not being characters, remain unaffected by UCase; they are not shifted to pipe (|) symbols.

Uses Some commands in VBScript and other elements of programming are *case-sensitive.* They make a distinction between *This* and *this.* Sometimes when the user is providing input, you cannot know how he or she might capitalize the input. If your program needs to analyze the user's input, capitalization differences can cause errors. For instance, the InStr command will fail to find a match between *This* and *this.*

To avoid a problem, you can force the user's response to all-uppercase letters and then not worry about unwanted mismatches. Using UCase in general-purpose Subroutines and Functions that you write is a good idea. That way, you don't need to worry about capitalization when providing Variables to them.

U

Cautions Only alphabetic letters are affected by UCase—not digits, nor symbols like & (the ampersand) or the backslash.

A companion command, LCase, forces all characters into lowercase.

VBScript has a string-comparison (compares one piece of text to another) command called StrComp that can optionally be made case-insensitive. In some situations, you can use StrComp as an alternative to using UCase or LCase.

Example InStr is a useful command when you need to search for something within a text Variable. In this example, the user answers a question posed by our program, and our program checks to see if the answer contains any detectable impatience on the user's part. Because we can't know whether the user might capitalize some letters—particularly if the user is irate—we will force all letters to uppercase. InStr would not report a match if the capitalization doesn't match. InStr is thus said to be *case-sensitive*. *Heck* doesn't match *heck*, and neither matches *HECK*.

```
<HTML>

<SCRIPT LANGUAGE="VBScript">

reply = InputBox("Shall we proceed?")
reply = UCase(reply)
If InStr(reply, "HECK") Then
  MsgBox ("Tch. Tch. Tch.")
End If

</SCRIPT>
</HTML>
```

Our message box will become visible if the word *heck* is found *anywhere* within the text Variable reply. The value of the UCase command in this example is that it doesn't matter how the user might capitalize *heck*—all possible variations will match *HECK* once all the characters have been made uppercase within the reply.

See also LCase, StrComp

UL

HTML & NETSCAPE

Description Creates an "unordered" list. Used with the LI command, the UL command generally renders an indented, bulleted list. However, the actual format is browser-dependent. The companion command, OL (ordered list) automatically provides numbers, in sequence. UL provides bullets.

Like all the list format commands, each item (each separate line) in the list must be preceded by the LI command. There is also a set of additional formatting codes that can be used with any LI command. See Variables below.

Used with ***Can be enclosed by***

<BANNER>, <BODY>, <BODYTEXT>, <DD>, <DIV>, <FIGTEXT>, <FN>, <FORM>, <LI>, <NOTE>, <TD>, <TH>

Can enclose

<LI>

Variables **COMPACT:** Some browsers reduce the vertical space between the lines if you use the COMPACT command. This vertical space is called *leading* by typographers. Other browsers will reduce the font size.

Variables that can be used with LI: Note that the following TYPE commands currently work only with Netscape browsers.

`<LI TYPE=A>`	Uses large characters.
`<LI TYPE=a>`	Uses small characters.
`<LI TYPE=I>`	Start with large Roman numerals.
`<LI TYPE=i>`	Start with small Roman numerals.
`<LI TYPE=1>`	Start with numbers.

Uses Display a bulleted list to the user.

Cautions LI is used alone (there is no </LI> command).

Example

```
<UL>
<LI>First item
<LI>Second item
<LI>Third item
</UL>
```

See also LI, DIR, MENU, OL

U

Underline

ACTIVEX

See Properties

URL

HTML

Description The URL (Uniform Resource Locator) is, most often, an address on the Internet. For instance, if you type this URL into your Internet Explorer browser's address field, you'll go to the Microsoft home page: http://www.microsoft.com/.

However, a URL address can also be *local* (on a hard drive), such as an .HTM file that you load into the browser without going onto the Internet at all. Frequently, when you're writing scripts and creating Web pages, you work with local .HTM files to test them before actually storing them on an Internet server for all the world to see and access.

Yet another kind of URL is a pointer to a different location within the same document. Sometimes you'll see an index or table of contents for a lengthy document. It might be a series of 26 buttons, each with a letter of the alphabet on it. When users click on one of those buttons, they're sent to the appropriate location within the current document.

This example, taken from the entry on the "A" (hypertext linking) command, illustrates all three kinds of URLs. Each HREF command points to a URL: "http://www.weather.com/indexwx2.html" is a Web site URL; keypress.htm is a browser file on the current hard drive (in the same subdirectory as the host document, or there would be a more complete path to this file); and "#First" is a URL that refers to a location within this same document (identified by NAME="FIRST").

```
<HTML>

<A HREF="http://www.weather.com/indexwx2.html"> Click here to
activate Weather Channel site link.</A>
```

```
<BR>
<A HREF="keypress.htm"> Click here to go to an alternative →
page.</A>
<BR>
<A HREF = "#First">First Things</A><BR>
<A HREF = "#Second">Second Things</A><BR>
<BR>
<CENTER><IMG SRC="FRUIT.JPG"></CENTER>
<BR>
<A NAME="First">This is where we explain first things.</A>
<BR>
First things first.
<BR>
<A NAME="Second">This is about second things.</A>
<BR>
Second things go here.

</HTML>
```

URL

ACTIVEX PROPERTY

Description URL is a Property (parameter) of the PreLoader Control. You tell the PreLoader which URL (Internet Web site document) you want downloaded to the user's cache (on the user's hard drive). Then, in the background, that document is copied from the Internet onto the user's hard drive for quick access. For example, if page two of your document contains complex graphics that require a long time to download, you could have the PreLoader send page two into the user's cache while the user was still reading the text on page one.

See PreLoader

V

Val

VBSCRIPT FUNCTION

Description The Val command is supposed to change text into a real, computable number, a number that the computer can use in arithmetic. However, at the time of this writing, neither Val nor its sister command, Str, are operative. These two commands are listed in the VBScript specifications, but it's possible that they will both be dropped from the language. With the new Variant Variable type, you can let VBScript make translations back and forth between string and numeric Variable types (see "Variant"). You can also force conversions with the cStr and cDbl commands (see "cBool").

You cannot multiply "5" times "5" because data inside text Variables or literal text inside quotation marks are only *text—only digits, not true numbers.*

In theory, to transform "5" into a real number, you use Val:

```
X = Val("5")
```

After that, X can be used in calculations by the computer:

```
MsgBox X * X
```

Results in

```
25
```

```
MsgBox Val("5") * Val("5")
```

Results in

```
25
```

The Val command is the opposite of the Str command. Str changes a true number into a text digit:

```
X = 5: MsgBox Str(X).
```

Value

ACTIVEX

See Properties

VAR

HTML

Description Changes the typeface to indicate a computer Variable name. In this book, we sometimes use italics when referring to a Variable name:

```
Sub Btn_OnClick
```

Btn is the Variable name above. Netscape renders text enclosed by the VAR command in italics. Microsoft's Internet Explorer, however, renders it in a smaller type size and in a fixed-width font, like Courier.

Used with ***Can be enclosed by***

<A>, <ABBREV>, <ACRONYM>, <ADDRESS>, <AU>, <B>, <BANNER>, <BIG>, <BODY>, <BODYTEXT>, <CAPTION>, <CITE>, <CODE>, <CREDIT>, <DD>, <DEL>, <DFN>, <DIV>, <DT>, <EM>, <FIGTEXT>, <FN>, <FORM>, <H>, <I>, <INS>, <KBD>, <LANG>, <LH>, <LI>, <NOTE>,<P>, <PERSON>, <PRE>, <Q>, <S>, <SAMP>, <SMALL>, <STRONG>, <SUB>, <SUP>, <TD>, <TH>, <TT>, <U>, <VAR>

Can enclose

<A>, <ABBREV>, <ACRONYM>, <AU>, <B>, <BIG>, <BR>, <CITE>, <CODE>, <DEL>, <DFN>, <EM>, <I>, <IMG>, <INS>, <KBD>, <LANG>, <MATH>, <PERSON>,<Q>, <S>, <SAMP>, <SMALL>, <STRONG>, <SUB>, <SUP>, <TAB>, <TT>, <U>, <VAR>

Uses

- Distinguish a Variable name from the surrounding text.
- Used in documents that discuss or describe computer programming, such as VBScript or HTML programming.

Example The Variable <VAR>texorg</VAR> is used twice in our document. It contains the current character count of the text box.

See also CODE, LISTING, HTML

Variables

Description Important tools in computer programming, you create Variables for the same reason that you might write *VISA* on a manila envelope and put your most recent Visa statement inside. Each time you get a new bill, you throw out last month's bill and put the new bill into the envelope.

The amount you owe *varies* from month to month, but this particular envelope, called *VISA*, always "contains" the value (the amount) of the current bill. If someone asks to know your current balance, you could just hand them the envelope. In a computer program, you can use the *Variable's name* in place of the number or piece of text that it contains:

```
MsgBox 704.12
```

is the same as:

```
CurrentBill = 704.12
MsgBox CurrentBill
```

You put the current Visa total into your envelope each month. You can always go to your stack of envelopes and look for the one labeled VISA to find out how much you owe. Similarly, once you create a Variable in a running VBScript script, a location in the computer's memory always contains the Variable's name and its "contents" (the information that this label "holds") until the contents are changed by the running program or until a new document is loaded. (An exception: a Variable declared *within* a procedure, a Sub...End Sub or Function...End Function, only exists—and its contents are only preserved—*while that procedure is being executed*. Other procedures or other programming within the script cannot change the contents of that Variable, nor can they "read" the Variable, using it to access the contents.)

How to Create a Variable: You can create a Variable by assigning some value to a Variable name, anywhere in your script. This act simultaneously creates the Variable's name (the label you give it) and assigns some value to it:

```
Donkeys = 15
```

Here you have provided a label (a Variable name)—Donkeys—and said that there are 15 of these entities. Your document's user won't ever see this label, *Donkeys*. You use it when you are programming, and you give it a name that means something to you. Most programmers give Variables names that help them to remember the meaning of the contents. A Variable named X is less useful than one named *MasterCard* when you later want to read, test, or modify your script. However, when the meaning of a Variable is obvious, you can use labels like *X* or *Y* or *N*.

You can use any label you want when creating a Variable, but the label cannot be the name of a word that VBScript uses, like *MsgBox* or *Show* or *End*. VBScript will tell you if you make this error; it won't allow you to assign a value to one of these "reserved words."

Formal Declarations

Alternatively, you can create a Variable by formally "declaring" it with the *only* command in VBScript that declares Variables—Dim. (In other versions of Visual Basic, there are several additional Variable-declaring commands: Public, Private, ReDim, ReDim Preserve, and Static. All these commands are missing in VBScript, except for ReDim. However, ReDim can only be used for declaring Arrays. It cannot declare a Variable.)

There are, however, two different ways to use Dim to declare a Variable. This is because Variables can have different levels of impact, different ranges of influence in a script. Sometimes called "scope," this range of influence determines whether a Variable can be used or recognized *everywhere* in the program (Dim used outside of a procedure) or only within a particular procedure, in other words, within a Subroutine or Function (Dim used *within* a procedure).

Public Variables: Everything in your script can access a Variable if you declare the Variable with the Dim Statement outside a procedure, like this:

```
<SCRIPT LANGUAGE="VBScript">
Dim Z

Sub ShowZ ( )
MsgBox Z
End Sub

Sub Button_OnClick
Z = Z + 1
ShowZ
End Sub

</SCRIPT>
```

Because we used Dim outside the Sub…End Sub structure, the Variable Z is *global* to this script. That is, it can be accessed or changed anywhere within the script. Also, its contents will be preserved as long as the user doesn't load a new document into the browser or refresh (reload) the current document. This is important because you might, for example, present the user with a button that, when clicked, adds 1 to the contents of Z. You want Z to remember, between clicks, its contents (in other words, Z should retain its value even when your script isn't actively executing and the user is just staring at the document in the browser, not clicking anything to reactivate your script). Also, note that because we used Dim outside the Sub…End Sub structure, the Variable Z can be given a different value (increased by 1, in this example) from *anywhere* in the script. And we can "read" the contents of Z from anywhere in the script (within the ShowZ Sub, in this example).

Private Variables: Nothing except a single procedure in your script can access a Variable if you declare the Variable with the Dim Statement inside that procedure, like this:

```
<SCRIPT LANGUAGE="VBScript">

Sub ShowZ ( )
Dim Z
MsgBox Z
End Sub

Sub Button_OnClick
Z = Z + 1
ShowZ
End Sub

</SCRIPT>
```

In this example, we've Dimmed Z inside the procedure ShowZ, so the Z = Z + 1 within the OnClick procedure is *working with a different Variable*. They have the same name, but these are different Variables to VBScript. Changes made to the Z in the OnClick Sub will not show up when the Z in the ShowZ procedure is executed.

Procedure-Only Variables—For Use Within a Single Sub or Function: At the lowest level—within Subroutines or Functions (collectively called "procedures")—Variables are like insects that live only briefly, do their duty, and then die. Variables created inside procedures pop into existence only when the script is running *within that procedure,* and disappear again as soon as the script goes on to some other procedure or to programming that's not enclosed within any procedure. The next time the Subroutine or Function containing that Variable is triggered, the Variable comes back to life—but any value you assigned to it while writing commands within that Event (A = "Norman") will be *reassigned*. Any value it contained previously will have been lost (the procedure might have changed the value).

Three Advantages of Locally Restricted Variables

If their contents are local and temporary, why would you ever use a local Variable? Why not Dim all Variables outside procedures, so that all Variables will be global to the script and also retain their contents? Often you will want to Dim all your Variables. However, there are three reasons you might sometimes want to use local, temporary Variables. For one thing, you can use the same Variable name over and over should you wish (in different procedures), without any negative effects. Each instance of this Variable label will be considered a unique Variable, specific to its procedure.

The use of local Variables also makes for an efficient use of memory. You could create a large Array of information, for instance, and then manipulate it within a procedure. When you're done, the Array collapses, returning the memory space it used to the computer for other uses. (See "ReDim" for the method to use for declaring temporary Arrays.)

Local Variables also eliminate one of the most frequent—and hardest to track down—errors in traditional programming: two Variables with the same name that are interacting and messing each other up as a program runs. Recall that you need not declare (Dim) local Variables at the procedure level; you can just *use them* and they will come into existence. Y = 2346 creates a numeric Variable and puts the number 2,346 into that Variable. Dim Y is not necessary unless you are using Dim outside a procedure to create a global, persistent Variable.

Interaction

Variables Interact: Variables can interact, as follows:

```
Donkeys = 15
Monkeys = 3
TotalAnimals = Donkeys + Monkeys
```

In other words, you can use the *Variables' labels* ("Variable names") as if they were the same as the contents of the Variables. If you say Monkeys = 3, then you have made the word Monkeys stand for the number 3. You can thereafter use Monkeys just as you would use the number 3:

```
TotalAnimals = Donkeys + Monkeys
```

The preceding line is the same as the following:

```
TotalAnimals = Donkeys + 3
```

V

Expressions

What is an *expression*? If someone tells you she has *a coupon for $1 off a $15 Mozart CD*, you immediately think *$14*. In the same way, VBScript reduces any items linked into an "expression" into its simplest form.

The phrase "numeric expression" means anything that represents or results in a single number. Computer programming terminology says that the expression "evaluates" into a single number. When an intelligent entity hears an expression, the entity collapses that expression into its simplest form.

In plain English, if you type 15 – 1 into one of your programs, VBScript reduces that group of symbols to 14. VBScript simply evaluates what you've said and uses it in the program as the essence of what you are trying to say. (The process of evaluating your entire script is called "parsing" the script. This happens when your document is loaded into a browser capable of handling VBScript, such as Microsoft's Internet Explorer.)

We humans tend to reduce things, too. Sometimes we call it *intuition*; sometimes we call it *putting two and two together*. But the result is the essence of a more complicated expression or idea.

5 * 3 is a numeric expression and, as far as Basic is concerned, 5 * 3 is just another way of expressing 15 (a single number). 5 * 3 collapses into 15 inside the program and is essentially that single number.

There are many kinds of numeric entities you can combine into expressions:

- a numeric Variable
- a numeric Variable in an Array
- a Function that returns a number
- a literal number (12 is a literal number, as opposed to a Variable):

```
Z = Sqr(12) 'literal number
N = 12: Z = Sqr(N) 'variable
```

- a combination of literal and Variable numbers:

```
Z = X + 14
```

- a combination of several Variables and/or literals:

```
Z = X + 14 + 3 / 44 - X
```

Any combination of the preceding examples that can evaluate to a single numeric value is an *expression*. An expression is made up of two or more of the preceding items connected by *one or more* "operators." The plus symbol in 2 + 2 is an operator. Altogether there are 23 operators. (See the entry for "Operators.")

Variable Expressions: When you combine Variables with other Variables, you create a *Variable expression*. An expression is a collection of items, which—seen as a unit—has a single value. This value can be either numeric or text ("string"). If the Variable *Days* has the value 7 and the Variable *Hours* has the value 24, this expression has the value 168:

```
Days * Hours
```

You can assign the preceding expression to another Variable:

```
HoursInAWeek = Days * Hours
```

You can also use the expression within a structure, such as If...Then, to test its "truth."

Expressions True and False: An expression can be evaluated by VBScript as either 0 (False) or not 0 (True). Let's see how this works:

```
BobsAge = 33
BettysAge = 27
If BobsAge > BettysAge Then MsgBox "He's Older"
```

BobsAge > BettysAge is an expression making the assertion that BobsAge is "greater than" BettysAge. The "greater than" (>) symbol is one of several "relational operators" (see the entry for "Operators"). VBScript looks at the Variable BobsAge and at BettysAge and at the relational operator that combines them into the expression. VBScript then determines whether or not your expression is True. The If...Then structure bases its actions on the truth or falsity of the expression. With text, the idea of "greater than" or "less than" refers to the alphabetical order of the items of text.

Variants

Variants are the default Variable type in VBScript. (For a detailed discussion of Variants, see the entry on "Variant.") Variant Variables are in an indeterminate state, like Schroedinger's Cat, until they are used. When a Variant Variable is assigned a value, it turns into the "subtype" appropriate to the number. In the following, both Variants *x* and *y* become Integer subtypes:

```
<SCRIPT LANGUAGE="VBScript">

Dim x, y
x = 32760
msgbox vartype(x)
y = 22
x = x + y
msgbox vartype(x)

</SCRIPT>
```

Results in

```
2
3
```

The VarType command can tell you what "subtype" a Variant currently is (2 means Integer; 3 means Long Integer). Notice in the example above how the Variant Variable *x* changes from an Integer type into a Long Integer type. An Integer type uses less memory in the computer but is only capable of holding numbers up to 32,768. To accommodate the addition of 22, which boosts the contents of X beyond the capacity of the Integer type, VBScript automatically changes X into a Long Integer type.

Compound Expressions

Expressions Combined Into Larger Expressions: You can put expressions together, building a larger entity that, itself, is an expression:

```
Z = "Tom"
R = Right(Z,2)
L = "om"
N = 3
M = 4
O = 5
P = 6
If N + M + O + P = 18 AND Z = "Tom" OR R = L Then MsgBox
"Yes."
```

Expressions Can Contain Literals and Constants, as Well as Variables: You can include literals as well as Variables when creating an expression. Z is a Variable, but "Tom" is a literal. *M* is a Variable in the preceding example, and *4* would be a literal. You can mix and match. You could also create the preceding example with some literal numbers mixed in:

```
If 3 + M + 5 + P = 18 And Z = "Tom" Then MsgBox "Yes."
```

Expressions can also include *Functions*:

```
A = "44 Rue Madeline"
If Val(A) <> 55 Then MsgBox "The text Variable doesn't begin
with 55"
```

Variables Versus Constants

V

A Variable's label, its name, remains the same. But the contents of a Variable can *vary*, which is how a Variable differs from a Constant. The content (the "value") of a Constant does not change while a program runs; Constants are a known quantity, like the number of doughnuts in a dozen:

```
Const MONTHSINYEAR = 12
```

Variables vary:

```
MyVisaBillAtThisPoint = 1200.44
```

(but a month later...)

```
MyVisaBillAtThisPoint = 1530.78
```

In practice, some programmers love Constants, while others avoid them. If you read some people's programs, you can see they are making their programs more *readable*, more English-like, by including several Constants:

```
Const MEDIUM = 23
Margin = MEDIUM
```

The preceding line is preferred by many people to the following line:

```
Margin = 23
```

VBScript and Netscape include some built-in, predefined Constants, such as the colors you can provide to such Properties as BackColor. With these Constants, you can program

```
BackColor = GREEN
```

instead of

```
BackColor = 4227072
```

and so forth.

The Case Against Constants: Some programmers feel that because Constants are known and stable numbers, you can just use the number itself. To calculate your average monthly bank interest, for example, you would use two Variables and the number 12:

```
MyAverageMonthlyInterest = MyTotalInterestThisYear / 12
```

rather than:

```
Const MONTHSINYEAR = 12
MyAverageMonthlyInterest = MyTotalInterestThisYear /
MONTHSINYEAR
```

Constants can certainly make programs more readable and can make odd things like *&HFF00* (green) more easily understood. Nevertheless, a contingent of the programming community finds that there's rarely any compelling reason to use Constants.

The Case for Constants: Many other programmers, though, like to use Constants. They argue that in the interest of program maintainability (being able to go back and easily change the program later) it is always better to use Constants to define a number that would otherwise not be obvious. This is especially true for programmer-defined values (e.g., CONST NUMBEROFSTATES = 50). That way, if you need to alter the value, you need to change it only in one place in the program (the place where you define the Constant), rather than track down every occurrence where 50 refers to the number of states. Memory or disk storage is cheaper than the hours a programmer would spend trying to decipher somebody else's code that had numbers or text Variables "hard-coded" (used literally, like the digits *50* instead of the Constant NUMBEROFSTATES).

The general convention is to capitalize the first letter of a Variable name, but to capitalize the *entire* name of a Constant.

Arrays—Cluster Variables

Arrays, unlike Constants, are universally regarded as extremely useful. Arrays are Variables that have been clustered together into a structure, and they enable you to manipulate the items in the cluster by using loops.

By giving a group of Variables all the same name, distinguished only *by an index number*, you can manipulate the group by referring to the index number. This approach might look like a small savings of effort, but imagine a script that has to use these Variables in many situations. (See "Arrays" for ways to utilize this important programming tool.)

Text and Numeric—The Two Basic Kinds of Variables

Following are two fundamental subtypes of Variables:

- Text Variables (often called "string" Variables) can be used in captions, TextBoxes, and so on. Text Variables are made up of the individual character *symbols* that we call the letters of the English alphabet. They cannot be divided or used to calculate the amount of linoleum that you would need to redo your kitchen floor. Text is for *communication*, not calculation. Text is for user input or output, for display, not for computation.
- Numeric Variables cannot be displayed as captions or in message boxes or TextBoxes. (Technically, with the new Variant Variable, you actually now can assign numeric subtypes to text objects.) Numeric Variables are used to calculate things; they are actual numbers rather than symbols. The 12 stamped on top of a carton of eggs is *text*, and the real number of eggs in that carton is *numeric*.

(The MsgBox command, TextBoxes, and other text-only devices, however, may in the future accept numeric Variable subtypes. At this time, though, when you provide a numeric Variable subtype to a MsgBox, you sometimes get an error. To fix this, you are required to use the cStr command to change it into a text subtype. You'll notice this use of cStr frequently in this book. However, we expect that when VBScript is finished and is no longer a Beta test, cStr will no longer be necessary in this context.)

How do you change a text Variable into a numeric Variable and vice versa? The Str and Val commands mediate between the two kinds of numbers, as do the cStr and cInt (or other c- commands that coerce one subtype into another). Str translates a true number into a text digit, or series of digits, that can be displayed. Val does the opposite: it turns a text digit like "5" into a real number that you could multiply. Val can turn "1992" into 1,992 for you.

There is only one kind of text Variable, but there are several "types" of numeric Variables because there are several ways of expressing numbers to a computer.

Variant—A Special New Variable Type: The "Variant" Variable type is relatively new to the Basic language, and it has been made the *default* Variable type in VBScript. Default means that unless you deliberately coerce a Variable's type (see "cBool"), all Variables will be of the *Variant* type. (For a complete discussion of the Variant type and its advantages and disadvantages, see "Variant.")

Variants Allow You to Be Ambiguous About the Nature of Variables: Are the following Variables text or numeric types? If these Variables are *Variants*, then the *context defines the type*. If your program tries to manipulate them mathematically, they will behave like numbers (and VBScript will automatically adjust the subtype so that they are numeric inside the computer). If your program tries to use them with a MsgBox, they will act like text (and in fact be changed into a text Variable subtype):

```
<HTML>
<TEXTAREA ROWS=25 COLS=55 NAME="L">
</TEXTAREA>

<SCRIPT LANGUAGE="VBScript">
cr = chr(13) & chr(10)

A = 12
B = 3
L.VALUE = L.VALUE & cr & A
L.VALUE = L.VALUE & cr & A & B
L.VALUE = L.VALUE & cr & A + B
L.VALUE = L.VALUE & cr & A / B

</SCRIPT>
</HTML>
```

Results in

```
12
123
15
4
```

Notice that the first two times we display a result, we are printing text *digits* (characters), not actual numbers. Then the Variables are used as *actual numbers* to arrive at arithmetic results: 15 and 4.

What's more, Variants can tell when different numeric subtypes (Integer where there is no decimal point, floating-point where a decimal point is required, and so on) are necessary. In other words, when you assign 15/40 to a Variant, the Variant "understands" that an Integer Variable type can't be used because Integers can't hold decimals. The Variant turns itself into a "single" floating-point Variable type to accommodate the fractional number.

The arithmetic operations—addition, subtraction, multiplication, and division—are not symmetrical: multiplication is pretty easy to get once you understand the idea of *addition*. And anyone who has written a list for Santa or made a stack of cookies understands addition. Subtraction, too, is clear enough—older brother steals some cookies from the stack.

But division is in a class by itself. Division can cause something to go below unity, below one, into the problematic world of fractions. Suddenly, two simple digits like 3 and 1 can expand into a list of digits bigger than the universe, .3333333333333333333, infinitely long, if you try to divide 1 by 3. And there are those *remainders*, unsettling things left over after the arithmetic is supposedly finished.

Computers have exactly the same problems working with division—there's more to consider and more to manipulate. Just like us, the computer calculates more slowly when you use numeric Variable types that can have fractions.

Here is a list of the numeric Variable subtypes that you can use in VBScript—along with the range of numbers they can "hold" and the amount of space each requires in the computer to store a number of that type:

Name	Range	Storage Required
Boolean	True or False	2 bytes
Byte	0 to 255	1 byte
Integer	–32,768 to 32,767	2 bytes
Long Integer (or "Long")	–2,147,483,648 to 2,147,483,647	4 bytes
Single (single-precision floating-point)	–3.402823E38 to –1.401298E-45 (negative numbers)	4 bytes
Double(double-precision floating-point)	–1.79769313486232E308 to –4.94065645841247E-324 (negative numbers)	8 bytes
Date	January 1, 100 to December 31, 9999	8 bytes

Table V-1: Numeric Variable subtypes, the range of numbers they can hold, and the amount of space each requires.

Fixed-Length Versus Dynamic Text Variables

A text ("string") Variable subtype can be either a specific, predefined size, or it can change its size to accommodate the different pieces of text you might assign to it. Each type has its advantages and uses.

You create a *fixed-length string* by describing its length and its contents. Here we've filled a string with 30 a's:

```
A = String(30,"a")
```

If you don't assign a length, a string Variable will be *dynamic* and will expand and contract as necessary, depending on what data you assign or reassign to it while the program is running. The following string Variable is not given a specific length, so it becomes a *dynamic*, Variable-length string:

```
Dim String
```

If you are just going to use a text Variable within a single procedure (Subroutine or Function) and you want it to be dynamic, an expandable length to fit the size of whatever text is assigned to it, you don't need to define, to Dim, the Variable. Just assign some text to it and it's a string Variable subtype automatically:

```
A = "Noisome"
```

See also Arrays, Dim, ReDim, Variant, VarType

Variant

Description The Variant Variable type was first added to the Basic language with Visual Basic Version 3 in 1994. And it has been made the *default* Variable type in VBScript. Default means that unless you deliberately *coerce* a Variable's type (see "cBool"), all Variables will be of the *Variant* type.

In fact, where there used to be several data types in Basic—text, numbers without any fraction (Integers and "Long Integers"), numbers with fractions (floating-point)—there is now, with VBScript, only the one Variable type, the *Variant*. All the rest are now called *subtypes* of the Variant type.

But the really important thing to realize is that you can't directly create a Variable subtype. You can't, for example, do this:

```
Dim MyText As String
```

OR

```
Dim MyText$
```

Neither of these traditional ways of creating Variables of a particular type are permitted. Everything starts out as a Variant. There are, in VBScript, no Variable type symbols (the $ above), nor is the "As String" or "As Integer" format permitted. Just Dim MyText and that's it. A Variant comes into being.

You can *coerce* a Variable into a particular subtype. To do that, you use one of a set of nine commands that begin with the letter *c*: cBool, cByte, cDate, cDbl, cInt, cLng, cSng, cStr, cVerr. Each of these commands transforms a Variant Variable of a particular "subtype" into a different subtype: respectively, boolean, byte, date, double, integer, long, single, string, and error.

Originally the reason for having Variable types was that it makes things easier for the computer. If you specifically tell the computer that something is supposed to be treated as text, the computer won't get confused and try to add it together or perform some other impossible calculation.

Traditionally, there have been two main types of Variables, numeric and text ("string"). Text Variables cannot be arithmetically *divided* by each other, for instance, because they are *characters*—letters of the alphabet or character-digits like "123." Clearly, it is meaningless to divide *Cadillac* by *marble.*

Text characters are just *graphic symbols* to the computer—important containers of information to humans; impossible to manipulate for arithmetic purposes to the computer. The cStr and cInt (and other "c-" commands, see "cBool") in the VBScript language translate numeric-to-text and text-to-numeric Variables, respectively. This translation, prior to the Variant, was sometimes necessary. For example, if you use the InputBox Function to get users to type in their age, the InputBox provides you with a *text* Variable: "35" rather than the number 35. If you wanted to use this data mathematically, to find out how much older the user is than someone else, you had to use the cInt command to change the text into a numeric Variable. However, in theory, a Variant should be able to recognize a "display this" context and shift the Variable from a numeric to a text subtype.

Variants Allow You to Be Ambiguous About the Nature of Variables: Let's try an experiment. Are the Variables A and B text or numeric subtypes? These Variables are *Variants*, so the context defines the type. If your program tries to manipulate them mathematically, they will behave like numbers. If your program tries to concatenate them as text (with the & operator), they will act like text:

```
<HTML>
<TEXTAREA ROWS=25 COLS=55 NAME="L">
</TEXTAREA>
```

```
<SCRIPT LANGUAGE="VBScript">
cr = chr(13) & chr(10)

A = 12
B = 3
L.VALUE = L.VALUE & cr & A
L.VALUE = L.VALUE & cr & A & B
L.VALUE = L.VALUE & cr & A + B
L.VALUE = L.VALUE & cr & A / B

</SCRIPT>
</HTML>
```

Results in

```
12
123
15
4
```

Notice that the first two times we display the result, we are printing *text* digits (characters), not actual numbers. Then the Variables are used *as actual numbers* to arrive at arithmetic results: 15 and 4.

Variant Variables shift some of the burden of worrying about Variable types from the programmer to VBScript. Variants automatically *change type* depending on the context in which they are used. They are sensitive to the way you are using them at any given time (though there are exceptions—see Cautions). For example, if you use the & command, Variants will know you intend to combine "text" Variables as if you placed two pieces of text next to each other (123123), but if you use the + command, the *same Variables* behave as if they are numeric, and addition takes place:

```
a = 123
MsgBox a & a
MsgBox a + a
```

Results in

```
123123
246
```

Sensitive to Numeric Types, Too: This chameleon behavior is interesting and valuable (it makes the computer do more of the work). As we've seen, Variants can, at least in a limited way, cross the traditional border separating text from numeric data.

There is only one style of text Variable, but there are many kinds of numeric Variables. And a Variant can also sense which of the five *numeric Variable subtypes* in VBScript you want to use, based on which kind of number you give it. For instance, an Integer type can only hold whole numbers up to 32,767. We'll test this by assigning a number that will be an Integer and another number that must be a Long Integer type (this Variable type can hold numbers up to 2,147,438,647). Then we'll use the VarType command that reports to us how VBScript is handling these Variables—which type VBScript thinks each Variable is:

```
<HTML>
<SCRIPT LANGUAGE="VBScript">

  a = 15
  b = 123456
  MsgBox VarType(a)
  MsgBox VarType(b)

</SCRIPT>
</HTML>
```

The number 15 is an integer, but 123456 is too large to fit into an Integer subtype, so VBScript automatically makes *b* a Long Integer type.

Results in

```
2
3
```

The VarTypes

The VarType Function tells you what kind of Variable is involved:

0 Empty

1 Null

2 Integer

3 Long Integer

4 Single

5 Double

6 Currency

7 Date

8 Text (String)

9 OLE Automation Object

10 Error

11 Boolean

12 Variant (Variant Array only)

13 Object (Not an OLE Automation Object)

17 Byte

8192 Array

Note, though, that in VBScript, there is no Currency data subtype.

Before the Variant type was available, you would have had to explicitly Dim a Long Integer or add a Long Integer symbol to the Variable name. The important point here is that you need not specify that the number 123456 be of a Long Integer type (it's too big to fit into a regular Integer type, so it must be a Long Integer). VBScript's new Variant data type has the brains to understand this distinction, and it makes the adjustment by itself.

IsEmpty, IsNumeric, IsNull: These commands can also tell you the status of a Variant Variable. To see if you can use a Variant type in a mathematical calculation:

```
A = "N123"
B = "456"
If IsNumeric(A) Then MsgBox A + 1
If IsNumeric(B) Then MsgBox B + 1
```

Results in

```
457
```

Here the *N* in N123 prevents it from being seen as a number, and the IsNumeric Function reveals this fact. For more on this, see the entry on "IsQueries."

Used with Variables

Uses The most obvious use for this novel addition to computer languages is to relax and let Variants manipulate the various Variable types, more or less without you, the programmer, worrying much about types at all. However, see Cautions.

Arrays also default now to the Variant type. You can therefore *mix* text, numbers, and date/time data within the same Array. This, too, is new to computer programming and, let's admit, is pretty useful.

Cautions The Variant can get mixed up about the + operator. In this example, the first + is correctly interpreted as an *arithmetic* plus. If the user enters 45 as his age, VBScript will print 50. However, if the user types in 45 to the second InputBox, VBScript prints 4545. In this case VBScript thinks that we're trying to concatenate (push together) two pieces of text.

```
x = InputBox("How old are you?")
MsgBox "In five years, you'll be " & x + 5
x = InputBox("How old are you?")
MsgBox "When twice as old, you'll be " & x + x
```

The solution to this would be to reserve the + operator to *only* arithmetic activity and reserve the new & operator to only text concatenation. But VBScript doesn't yet do this. It can interpret + in two ways and thus sometimes gets things wrong.

A Variant's main job when handling a number is to use a Variable type large enough to hold the number. Variants can *promote* themselves to larger numeric types as necessary. If you first put an Integer-sized number, like 143, into a Variant, subsequent operations treat the Variant as if it were an Integer. But if later you do some math with this Variable and the result of that math is a value larger than an Integer subtype can hold, the Variable is "promoted" to the next larger data type. A Byte is promoted to an Integer, an Integer is promoted to a Long, and a Long and a Single are promoted to a Double. All this works as expected at the time of this writing. (For definitions and examples of these subtypes, see the entry "Variables.")

Variants are an exciting new capability—let the language handle the Variable type details. VBScript can generally figure out a Variant Variable type on the fly based on the context and how you, the programmer, are using the Variable. If you are putting a number into a TextBox VALUE (A = 33:MyBox.Value = A), VBScript will sense this and transform it to a text "string" Variable type for that operation (so you can forget the cStr command). But if you then use the same Variable to calculate some arithmetic result, the Variable is treated as a pure numeric Variable.

Variants introduce some new Variable data subtypes that didn't exist in earlier programming languages. The Null type is different from the Empty type (you'll see this when using VarType to quiz a Variable about what type it is). Null means that the Variable has deliberately been made empty because zero or an empty text string ("") has been assigned to the Variable.


```
X = 0
```

OR

```
X = ""
```

These commands create a zero number or a text Variable with nothing in it.

However, an "Empty" Variable, by contrast, *has not yet been used* in the program in *any* fashion (even to fill it with emptiness). An Empty Variable has not been declared either implicitly, by giving it a value (V = 12) or by explicitly declaring it with the Dim command (Dim V).

Null Is Special: The Null type has another unique quality you need to remember—it always makes an expression *False.* For example, this might fool you:

```
z = Null
If z = Null Then MsgBox "Yes."
```

This will not result in Yes. Null more or less *infects* ("propagates") an otherwise True expression, turning it False.

To find out if a Variable is of the Null type, use the following:

```
If IsNull(z) Then MsgBox "Yes."
```

Note that the other predefined VBScript Constants *True* (–1) and *False* (0) do not "propagate" and can be freely used as if they were normal numbers:

```
z = True
If z = True Then MsgBox "Yes"
If z = -1 Then MsgBox "Yes"
If z Then MsgBox "Yes"
```

Results in

```
Yes Yes Yes
```

Nulls are useful in some kinds of programming (where ""—now-empty text Variables or zero numeric Variables don't mean the same thing as Null—never used). For example, in database programming, there can be an important difference between a currently empty Variable, and one that has never been used at all.

In general, with the exceptions noted above, you can let VBScript worry about the Variants. However, if you try to perform math with Variants that hold text (such as "Word"), or at least text that cannot be translated by VBScript into a numeric Variable ("z12" cannot be translated; "12" can), then you'll generate an error. If you are unsure whether a Variant holds text, add this line:

```
If IsNumeric(A) And IsNumeric(B) Then X = A + B
```

Example This example program shows the first eight Variant VarTypes, with one exception.

Note that each of these Variant Variables will configure itself according to the data that we assign to it, with a single exception. (The exception is type 4, single-precision floating-point, which defaults to double. To make it work in the example below, we had to *coerce* the Variant into a single subtype by using the cSng command. For more about coercion, see "cBool.")

Note also that we didn't define, or even *use*, the Variable *a*. Nothing was assigned to *a* so it's in the cleanest possible state—it is of the "Empty" VarType, meaning it's never been used in the program prior to our querying it with VarType.

```
<HTML>
<TEXTAREA NAME=R ROWS=12 COLS = 55></TEXTAREA>

<SCRIPT LANGUAGE="VBScript">
cr = chr(13) + chr(10)

b = Null
c = 55
d = 123456
e = cSng(.2)
f = .222222222
h = Now
i = "hello"
R.VALUE = R.VALUE & cr & VarType(a)
R.VALUE = R.VALUE & cr & VarType(b)
R.VALUE = R.VALUE & cr & VarType(c)
R.VALUE = R.VALUE & cr & VarType(d)
```

V

```
R.VALUE = R.VALUE & cr & VarType(e)
R.VALUE = R.VALUE & cr & VarType(f)
R.VALUE = R.VALUE & cr & VarType(h)
R.VALUE = R.VALUE & cr & VarType(i)

</SCRIPT>
</HTML>
```

See also Variables, cBool

VarType

VBSCRIPT FUNCTION

Description Tells you which Variable subtype a particular Variable is.

See Variant

ViewTracker

ACTIVEX CONTROL

Description You put a graphic image into the ViewTracker Control. Then ViewTracker triggers an Event (OnHide) when the user scrolls that image so it disappears from view in the browser. (The user could slide a ScrollBar, press one of the arrow keys, or PgUp/PgDown—the point is that the ViewTracker is no longer visible to the user.) Similarly, another Event (OnShow) is triggered when the ViewTracker is scrolled back into view.

If you want, you can make the ViewTracker Control invisible by loading it with an image that is merely the same color as the BackColor of your HTML document. Currently, the Visible Property is not working (you can't make the ViewTracker invisible by setting Visible=False).

Variables While designing your HTML document, you can put a graphic image into the Image Property (see the example).

The OnHide Event is triggered when the ViewTracker disappears—via scrolling—from the browser view window. The OnShow Event is triggered when the ViewTracker reappears. OnShow is not triggered when the document is first loaded into the browser; use the Window_OnLoad Event for that.

Properties

CodeBase, Height, ID, Image, Left, Top, Visible, Width

Events

OnHide, OnShow

Methods

AboutBox

For details about these Properties, Events, and Methods, see the entries for "Properties," "Events," and "Methods."

Uses When the browser first loads your document, you can react if you wish by putting some VBScript commands within the OnLoad Event. If you want the user to see today's date and the current time when your document is loaded:

```
Sub Window_OnLoad
  Label1.Caption = Now
End Sub
```

However, what if you want to respond when the user scrolls your document? That's where the ViewTracker comes in. You could create special effects with it—for example, set up three or four ViewTrackers and as each one triggers its OnHide Event, you could slightly darken the backcolor. OnShow Events could reverse the process. You could make the effect even smoother by using a Timer Control to make the gradation between two colors happen during ten or so intervals.

Other effects could include updating information following a scroll (see the example); displaying a message to the user describing the contents of each visible "page" in your document; updating the Title, icon, or other contents of a *static* frame as the user scrolls through another frame.

Cautions The ViewTracker's Visible Property doesn't currently have any effect.

If you try to use the Microsoft ActiveX Control Pad's Edit | Insert ActiveX Control menu option, you'll crash the Control Pad. At the time of this writing, the only way to add a ViewTracker to your HTML document is to cut the following source code from this book's CD (or type it in), then paste it into your Control Pad source code:

```
<OBJECT
    classid="clsid:1A771020-A28E-11CF-8510-00AA003B6C7E"
    id=Track1
    width=400
    height=2
    align=left
  >
   <PARAM NAME="Image" VALUE="c:\vbscript\button.bmp">
</OBJECT>
```

Change the VALUE of the Image parameter to point to some .BMP file on your hard drive to test this.

If you try to put a MsgBox within the OnShow Event, you'll cause an infinite loop that will crash Internet Explorer. Oddly, the Alert command—so similar to MsgBox—does not crash IE.

Note that the ViewTracker's Events are not triggered merely because the ViewTracker isn't visible to the user (because the browser was minimized or some other window covered up the browser, for example). The ViewTracker's Events only react when the user *scrolls* or *pages* (PgUp or PgDn) or uses the arrow keys to make the ViewTracker *disappear from view within the browser window itself.*

At the time of this writing, you can display a .BMP image file type by naming it in the Image Property. However, .JPG or .GIF file types fail to display any graphic in the Internet Explorer browser.

Example

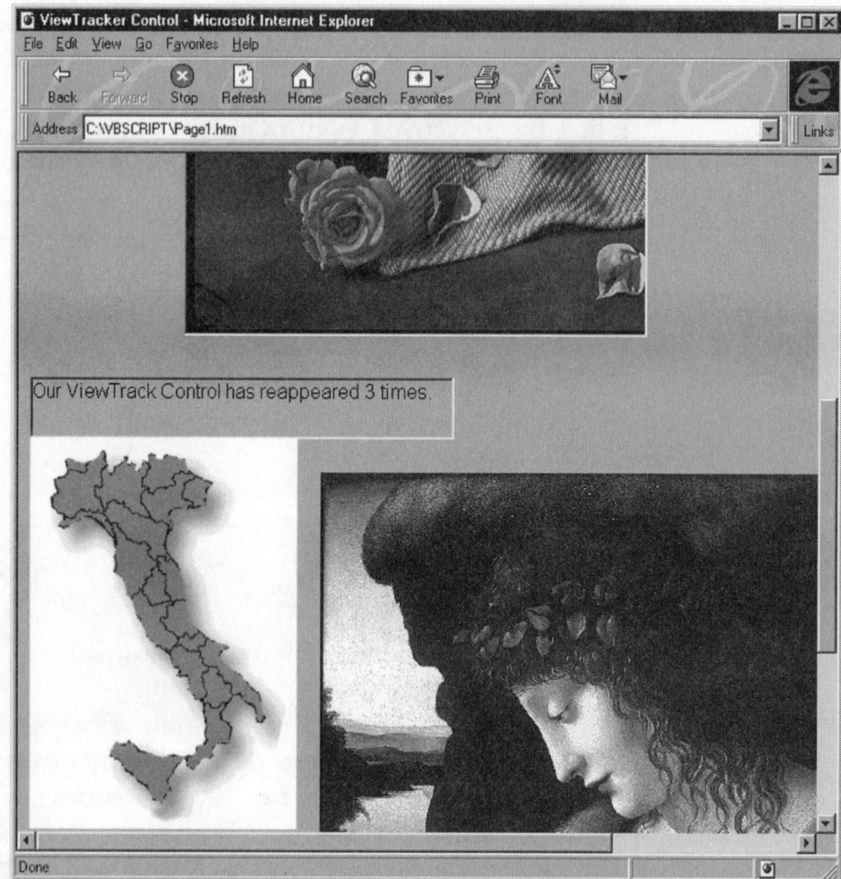

Figure V-1: Each time the user scrolls the browser window enough to make this map of Italy disappear, an OnHide Event is triggered.

We'll fill a couple of virtual "pages" in a document with images. This will take up enough space so there's room for the user to scroll ViewTracker Control in and out of sight. Each time it comes back into view, we'll increment our counter and display the result. We'll also use a Label Control to display the number of times the user has caused the ViewTracker to reappear.

To create this example, start the Microsoft ActiveX Control Pad (see the Introduction) and click on Edit | Insert HTML Layout.

Give the layout a new name and then click on the icon next to the <OBJECT> definition. Now, from the toolbox, put one or two Image Controls onto the layout and set their PicturePath Property to a graphic file on your hard drive. Then go back to the HTML source code window (you can close the HTML Layout window) and copy and paste the following source code, just below the HTML Layout Control:

```
<OBJECT
   classid="clsid:1A771020-A28E-11CF-8510-00AA003B6C7E"
   id=Track1
   width=400
   height=2
   align=left
  >
  <PARAM NAME="Image" VALUE="italy.bmp">
 </OBJECT>
```

We're copying and pasting because that's the only way, at this time, to insert the ViewTracker (see Cautions). Change the VALUE= to the path of a .BMP graphic file on your hard drive. Remember to provide a complete path, not just the filename, unless that file is located in the same subdirectory as your .HTM source code file.

Now, use Edit | Insert ActiveX Control and add a "Microsoft Forms 20 Label." Finally, repeat the process of adding a couple of Images to a second HTML Layout Control. Click on Edit | Insert HTML Layout. Give the layout a new name and then click on the icon next to the <OBJECT> definition. From the toolbox, put one or two Image Controls onto the layout and set their PicturePath Property to a graphics file on your hard drive. Then go back to the HTML source code window (you can close the HTML layout window).

Now, into the HTML source code, type or paste in the following script below. First, in the OnLoad Event for the Window object, we've used the Now command to display the date and time to the user—just so something will be in the label when the document first loads. Then, in the OnShow Event of our ViewTracker Control, we increment our counter Variable *C* and display in the label the total number of times the user has scrolled.

```
<HTML>
<HEAD>
<TITLE>ViewTracker Control</TITLE>
</HEAD>
<BODY>

<OBJECT CLASSID="CLSID:812AE312-8B8E-11CF-93C8-00AA00C08FDF"
ID="vie_alx" STYLE="LEFT:0;TOP:0">
<PARAM NAME="ALXPATH" REF VALUE="file:C:\Program
Files\ActiveX Control Pad\vie.alx">
 </OBJECT>

<OBJECT ID="Label1" WIDTH=351 HEIGHT=49
 CLASSID="CLSID:978C9E23-D4B0-11CE-BF2D-00AA003F40D0">
  <PARAM NAME="Size" VALUE="9268;1288">
  <PARAM NAME="SpecialEffect" VALUE="2">
  <PARAM NAME="FontName" VALUE="Arial">
  <PARAM NAME="FontHeight" VALUE="240">
  <PARAM NAME="FontCharSet" VALUE="0">
  <PARAM NAME="FontPitchAndFamily" VALUE="2">
  <PARAM NAME="FontWeight" VALUE="0">
</OBJECT>

  <OBJECT
   classid="clsid:1A771020-A28E-11CF-8510-00AA003B6C7E"
   id=Track1
   width=400
   height=2
   align=left
  >
  <PARAM NAME="Image" VALUE="italy.bmp">
  </OBJECT>

<SCRIPT LANGUAGE="VBScript">

<!--
Dim C

Sub Window_OnLoad
Label1.Caption = Now
End Sub
```

```
Sub Track1_OnShow
C = C + 1
  Label1.Caption = "Our ViewTrack Control has reappeared " →
& C & " times."
End Sub

-->
  </SCRIPT>

<OBJECT CLASSID="CLSID:812AE312-8B8E-11CF-93C8-00AA00C08FDF"
ID="viewt_alx" STYLE="LEFT:0;TOP:0">
<PARAM NAME="ALXPATH" REF VALUE="viewt.alx">
 </OBJECT>

</BODY>
</HTML>
```

Visible

ACTIVEX

See Properties

WBR

NETSCAPE

Description WBR forces a line break (the text moves down and starts on the next lower line). This is sometimes called a carriage return. WBR works within the NOBR command. NOBR *prevents* any line breaks, even if the text runs off the right side of the window. However, WBR forces exceptions within a block of text enclosed between <NOBR> and </NOBR>.

See NOBR

Weekday

VBSCRIPT FUNCTION

Description The Weekday command tells you the day of the week by giving you a number between 1 (Sunday) and 7 (Saturday).

Which week? Any week between January 1, 100, and December 31, 9999, using VBScript's built-in "serial number" representation of date+time. VBScript can provide or manipulate individual serial numbers for *every second* between those two dates. These serial numbers also include coded representations of all the minutes, hours, days, weekdays, months, and years between 100 A.D. and 9999.

Used with You can use Weekday with the Now Function to tell you the current weekday as registered by your computer's clock. You would set up an Array and then fill it with the names of the weekdays. To find which item in the Array to use, get the day-of-the-week number from Now by using the Weekday Function. However, as this example illustrates, this is more easily accomplished with the powerful Format Function, which can directly provide a day name if you use the Format dddd option:

```
<HTML>
<SCRIPT LANGUAGE="VBScript">

Dim Daynames(8)
Daynames(1) = "Sunday"
Daynames(2) = "Monday"
Daynames(3) = "Tuesday"
Daynames(4) = "Wednesday"
Daynames(5) = "Thursday"
Daynames(6) = "Friday"
Daynames(7) = "Saturday"
x = Weekday(Now)
n = Daynames(x)
z = "Today is " + n
MsgBox z

</SCRIPT>
</HTML>
```

Results in

```
Today is Friday
```

The Now Function provides the serial number for the current date and time. Weekday extracts a number between 1 and 7, which represents the day of the week.

Variables To find the number representing the current day of the week as reported by the user's computer's built-in clock:

```
X = WeekDay(Now)
```

Results in

```
July 1, 1996 falls on the 2nd day of the week.
```

Uses

- Display the day of the week.
- Create calendar or scheduler programs where you need to *physically* show the days of the week on a grid. When you are creating a calendar, you need to know *on which "numerical" weekday (1-7) the first of the month falls.* Weekday can give you that information.

Example Here's how to find the day of the week from a text representation of some past or future date:

```
<HTML>
<SCRIPT LANGUAGE="VBScript">

T = "September 30, 1992"
x = Weekday(DateValue(T))
MsgBox T + " falls on the " & cstr(x) & "th day of the week."

</SCRIPT>
</HTML>
```

See also Date, Day, Hour, Minute, Month, Now, Time, Year

Weight

ACTIVEX

See Properties

While...Wend

VBSCRIPT STATEMENT

Description While...Wend is like the For...Next structure, except that it doesn't use a counter to decide how many times to *loop*, how many times to perform the commands within it. Instead, While...Wend keeps looping as long as a "condition" you give it remains true. In other

words, you don't specify a number of times the loop should execute (as with For…Next loops). Instead, you specify a trigger condition that will terminate the loop and move on to the programming below the loop.

This While...Wend will loop seven times because we are saying: While X does not equal 7, do the commands inside:

```
While X <> 7
  X = X + 1
  MsgBox X
Wend
```

Results in

```
1 2 3 4 5 6 7
```

While...Wend isn't used by most programmers. The similar Do...Loop structure offers you more options and is easier to use.

Why Is Do...Loop Usually Superior to While...Wend? With Do...Loop you can easily set up various interior tests and quit the loop with Exit Do. In other words, you can create several conditions that will cause the computer to quit the loop. Do...Loop is more flexible and more readable.

Also, you can place the condition to be tested at the beginning or end of the loop; this allows you to determine whether the loop will stop immediately or repeat one more time after the condition has been satisfied.

Do...Loop also permits two kinds of conditional tests: *While* or *Until.* The distinction is often merely semantic—sweep *until* the porch is clean versus sweep *while* the porch is dirty. Nonetheless, putting the condition one way or the other can clarify the meaning of the condition.

While...Wend is a less powerful version of Do...Loop.

- While...Wend merely continues looping while a condition is true.

  ```
  WHILE X < 3: X = X + 1: MsgBox X: WEND.
  ```

- While...Wend has no built-in Exit feature similar to Exit Do in a Do...Loop.
- While...Wend is limited to a test at the start of the loop.
- While...Wend does not permit you to clarify things with a distinction between *while* and *until*.

Used with Infrequently used, but can be employed for some of the simpler tasks performed by the more powerful Do...Loop structure.

Variables You provide the *condition* that must become true for the computer to leave the loop, to stop repeatedly executing the commands between the While and the Wend. The condition can be any "expression" that the computer can evaluate as being True (–1) or False (0):

```
While S = 5
```

OR (B doesn't = 4):

```
While B <> 4
```

OR (as long as the text Variable N still contains the text *Frank*):

```
While N = "Frank"
```

OR (expressions can be complex. The following says "Loop as long as the Variable A holds a larger number than the Variable C, and the Variable G is less than 3):

```
While A > C And G < 3
```

(See "Variables" for more about expressions, and see "Operators" for more about those symbols such as >, <, and such commands as And and Or which, collectively, are called *operators*.)

Uses Use While...Wend when you want something done repeatedly but don't know the *number* of times you want it done. You know a *condition* that must be satisfied rather than the precise number of times the task should be performed. (For instance, continue to show a flashing arrow until the user clicks on a choice.)

However, the Do...Loop structure is superior for any situation in which you might be tempted to use While...Wend.

Cautions

- While...Wend can cause peculiar errors that are difficult to track down if you ever use GoSub or GoTo to move to a Label within the While...Wend.
- While...Wend, like If...Then and Do...Loop, takes control of the computer until the condition of the While...Wend is satisfied. In other words, using this Statement it would run until the browser stopped it. After about 30 seconds of an endless loop, Internet Explorer gracefully puts up a message to the user, saying "This page contains a script which is taking an unusually long time to finish. To end this script now, click Cancel."

```
X = 12

While X = 12

Wend
```

Because X will always = 12 (nothing inside the loop would ever allow X to become anything other than 12), the preceding lines become an "endless loop" and lock up the browser until the browser informs the user of the problem.

- The *condition* that will end a While...Wend loop must happen before the computer can leave the loop or move past the Wend. The condition is the *A <> "ABCDE"* in the following:

```
<HTML>
<TEXTAREA ROWS=14 COLS=55 NAME="ShowIt">
</TEXTAREA>
<SCRIPT LANGUAGE="VBScript">

cr = chr(13) & chr(10)

n = 64

While A <> "ABCDE"
   n = n + 1
   A = A + Chr(n)
   ShowIt.Value = ShowIt.Value & A & cr
Wend
```

```
ShowIt.Value = cr & ShowIt.Value & "DONE"
</SCRIPT>
</HTML>
```

Results in

```
A
AB
ABC
ABCD
ABCDE
DONE
```

Here we said: As long as A does not equal "ABCDE," keep looping. (See "Chr" for the way that this command translates a number from built-in ANSI code into a text character.)

- While...Wend, like If...Then, can be *nested,* one structure placed inside another:

```
<HTML>
<TEXTAREA ROWS=24 COLS=55 NAME="ShowIt">
</TEXTAREA>
<SCRIPT LANGUAGE="VBScript">

cr = chr(13) & chr(10)

F = 11
While F > 2
  While X < 15
  ShowIt.Value = ShowIt.Value & cr & cstr(x)
    X = X + 1
  Wend
  F = F - 1
  ShowIt.Value = ShowIt.Value & cr & cstr(f)

  Wend

</SCRIPT>
</HTML>
```

Results in

```
1 2 3 4 5 6 7 8 9 10 11 12 13 14 10 9 8 7 6 5 4 3 2
```

You can nest as many While...Wends as you are capable of understanding. But the more you nest them, the harder it becomes to visualize what's going on.

Example

```
While z < 14
z = z + 1
Wend
```

See also Do...Loop, For...Next

Width

ACTIVEX

See Properties

WordWrap

ACTIVEX

See Properties

Write or Writeln

Description These commands allow you to write onto an HTML document directly, but from within VBScript. The primary advantage of this is that you can place variable information—such as the current date—in with ordinary HTML text.

See Document

XMP

HTML

Description Causes text to be displayed in a fixed-width (non-proportional) typeface such as Courier. XMP is similar to PRE, except a line break isn't inserted at the end of the text with </XMP> as it is with </PRE>, nor can you use any other commands within <XMP>, as you can with PRE.

However, XMP is evidently being abandoned as an HTML command. It is not included in the most recent HTML specifications. XMP means *example* and was apparently intended as a format for displaying examples.

See Code

Xor

VBSCRIPT OPERATOR

Description Xor is one of the more interesting Operators, if you find encryption interesting. The Xor command is used in many schemes designed to disguise information. Xor has a pleasant feature: it *toggles* things. Xor a text character (actually, you Xor the character's numeric code, derived with the Asc command) and you get a different number (with no obvious relationship to the original number). Then Xor that *second* number and you get back the first number. Thus, Xor is a little black box that you can feed characters into and get a garbled result. But when you then feed that garbled result back through Xor, you get your original message. You are encrypting, then decrypting, with the same black box.

Caution This technique seems fairly secure, but it does have a fatal flaw. If you Xor with a zero, *no change takes place in the original*. If you Xor the password against a series of zeros, the password is revealed (it will be repeated over and over as long as the series of zeros continues). Alas, many contemporary computer documents contain just such strings of zeros.

Example

```
<HTML>
<SCRIPT LANGUAGE="VBScript">

Original = "r"
Original1 = "m"

Key = "I"
Key1 = "T"

X = Asc(original) Xor Asc(key)

X1 = Asc(original1) Xor Asc(key1)

X = chr(X)
X1 = chr(X1)

Msgbox X & X1

</SCRIPT>
</HTML>
```

Results in

```
;9
```

The message we want to encrypt is *rm*. The key (password) that we'll use is *IT*. First we Xor the r against the I, then the m against the I. The results are put into the Variables X and X1, which are then transformed from the character codes back into actual displayable character symbols with the Asc command.

Now if you run this same script again, but this time substitute the encrypted version, you'll get the original *rm* back:

```
Original = ";"
Original1 = "9"
```

Most Xor encryption schemes follow this example—Xoring each letter of the original message against some key known only to the sender and recipient. (If the key is shorter than the message, the key is repeated as many times as necessary.)

See Operators

Year

VBSCRIPT FUNCTION

Description The Year command tells you the year, any year between 100 A.D. and 9999, using VBScript's built-in "serial number" representation of date+time. For more on the Day, Month, and Year commands, see "Day."

Example Here's a trick you can use to find out if a date exists within a particular month. In this case, we want to let the user know which years in the current century are leap years. We test each year to see if it has a February 29. If it does, we announce that it is a leap year:

```
<HTML>
<TEXTAREA ROWS=25 COLS=55 NAME="L">
</TEXTAREA>

<SCRIPT LANGUAGE="VBScript">

cr = chr(13) & chr(10)

L.Value = L.Value & "LEAP YEARS IN THIS CENTURY"

For y = 1900 To 2000
   z = DateSerial(y, 2, 29)
   If Month(z) = 2 Then L.Value = L.Value & cr & Year(z)
Next

</SCRIPT>
</HTML>
```

We set up a loop that will let the Variable *y* count up from 1900 to 2000 so that we can check each year. Then we create a date+time serial number for February 29 of each year and put the serial number into the Variable *z*. This serial number will actually contain a code *for the month of March* if the year in question has no February 29. This way, we can check to see if the Month command gets a 2 for February out of the serial number. If it does, we print the year because this must be a leap year.

See also Day, Month, Now, Hour, Minute, Second, Weekday

Z

Zoom

ACTIVEX

See Events

ZOrder

ACTIVEX

See Methods

Z

Appendix

About the Companion CD-ROM

The CD-ROM included with your copy of *The Comprehensive Guide to VBScript* contains valuable software programs and an online version of the text.

Navigating the CD-ROM

Your choices for navigating the CD-ROM appear on the opening screen. You can quit the CD, view the software, browse the Hot Picks, or learn more about Ventana.

The software is listed in the Install folder on the CD.

To View the CD-ROM

Double-click on the LAUNCHME.EXE file from your Windows Explorer or File Manager.

You'll see a menu screen offering several choices. See "Navigating the CD-ROM" for your option choices.

If the viewer does not run properly on your machine, follow the instructions below for optimum performance.

1. Copy the LAUNCHME.EXE and LAUNCHME.INI files to the same directory on your hard drive.
2. Open the LAUNCHME.INI file in a text editor such as Notepad.
3. Find the section in the INI file that reads:

```
[Memory]
;ExtraMemory=400
;Amount of kBytes over and above physical memory for →
  use by a projector.
```

4. If your computer has enough memory to do so, delete the semicolon from the ExtraMemory line, and change the ExtraMemory setting to a higher number.
5. Save the changes to the LAUNCHME.INI file, and close the text editor.
6. With the CD-ROM still inserted, launch the viewer from the hard drive.

If the viewer still does not run properly on your machine, you can access the material on the CD-ROM directly through Windows Explorer.

Contents of the CD-ROM

Software	Description
HTML Assistant Pro-Freeware	HTML Assistant Pro-Freeware Edition is a "point-and-click" editor for making World Wide Web pages. For more information on HTML Assistant, please visit http://www.brooknorth.com.
HTML Reference Library	The HTML Reference Library is a single-source guide to current HTML syntax. With numerous screenshots and examples, it details how to create HTML documents to be used on the World Wide Web.
InContext Spider 1.2 Trialware	InContext Spider is a Web page authoring software program for Windows. The trial period is 30 days. For more information visit http://www.incontext.com on the World Wide Web.
Web Edit	Editor for Web pages.
Web Media Publisher Pro R11	This multi-functional Web publishing kit supports all tags and all browsers with many features, including a Web timer, unlimited file size, extended character list, and much more. For more details and up-to-date downloads, visit http://www.wbmedia.com.
ONLINE BOOK	In this folder you will find the entire text of the book in HTML.

Technical Support

Technical support is available for installation-related problems only. The technical support office is open from 8:00 A.M. to 6:00 P.M. Monday through Friday and can be reached via the following methods:

Phone: (919) 544-9404 extension 81

Faxback Answer System: (919) 544-9404 extension 85

E-mail: help@vmedia.com

FAX: (919) 544-9472

World Wide Web: http://www.vmedia.com/support

America Online: keyword Ventana

Limits of Liability & Disclaimer of Warranty

The authors and publisher of this book have used their best efforts in preparing the CD-ROM and the programs contained in it. These efforts include the development, research, and testing of the theories and programs to determine their effectiveness. The authors and publisher make no warranty of any kind, expressed or implied, with regard to these programs or the documentation contained in this book.

The authors and publisher shall not be liable in the event of incidental or consequential damages in connection with, or arising out of, the furnishing, performance, or use of the programs, associated instructions, and/or claims of productivity gains.

Some of the software on this CD-ROM is shareware; there may be additional charges (owed to the software authors/makers) incurred for their registration and continued use. See individual programs' README or VREADME.TXT files for more information.

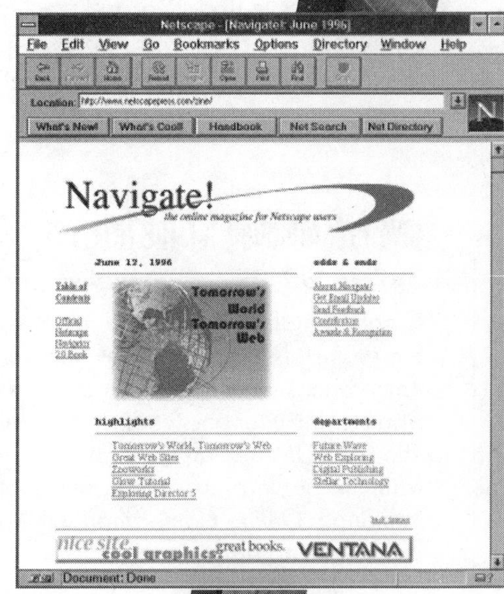

Netscape - [Navigate! June 1996]
File Edit View Go Bookmarks Options Directory Window Help
What's New! What's Cool! Handbook Net Search Net Directory
Navigate!
the online magazine for Netscape users
June 12, 1996
odds & ends
Tomorrow's World Tomorrow's Web
highlights
departments
nice site. cool graphics. great books. VENTANA
Document: Done

http://www.netscapepress.com/zine

Add Power to Web Pages

Official Netscape JavaScript Book

$29.99, 520 pages, illustrated, part #: 465-0

Add life to Web pages—animated logos, text-in-motion sequences, live updating and calculations—quickly and easily. Sample code and step-by-step instructions show how to put JavaScript to real-world, practical use.

Java Programming for the Internet

$49.95, 806 pages, illustrated, part #: 355-7

Create dynamic, interactive Internet applications. Expand the scope of your online development with this comprehensive, step-by-step guide to creating Java applets. Includes four real-world, start-to-finish tutorials. The CD-ROM has all the programs, samples and applets from the book, plus shareware. Continual updates on Ventana's *Online Companion* will keep this information on the cutting edge.

The Comprehensive Guide to VBScript

$39.99, 800 pages, illustrated, part #: 470-7

The only encyclopedic reference to VBScript and HTML commands and features. Complete with practical examples for plugging directly into programs. The companion CD-ROM features a hypertext version of the book, along with shareware, templates, utilities and more.

Books marked with this logo include a free Internet *Online Companion*™, featuring archives of free utilities plus a software archive and links to other Internet resources.

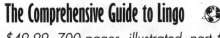